Disability Rights Handbook

34th Edition
April 2009 - April 2010

by Ian Greaves

Address list compiled by
Michèle Holland

Acknowledgements

We would like to acknowledge the valuable contribution of all the contributors and checkers of this edition of the Handbook.

Thanks also to colleagues at Disability Alliance for their work on Handbook sales administration and distribution, in particular: Isabel Cravinho, Peta Leith and Jim Lenton.

Thanks also to Paula McDiarmid for her patience and efficiency in co-ordinating the writing and checking of the Handbook and for her copy-editing skill.

Design and print production management is by Deborah Kamofsky, Anderson Fraser Partnership. Typesetting is by Humphrey Weightman. I am most grateful to them for their professional support and high-quality work.

Special acknowledgements go to Judith Paterson who wrote the Disability Rights Handbook from the 19th through to the 26th edition and to her predecessor Sally Robertson.

We do our best to ensure the information in the Handbook is correct. However, changes in the law after April 2009 might affect the accuracy of some of the information. Where this could be important to you, you should check the details with a local advice centre or your local Jobcentre Plus office.

If you think anything in the Handbook is incorrect, please write and tell us. Thanks to all those who wrote to us this year with comments and suggestions on the Handbook. Your contributions are always very welcome.

To the memory of Paul Bradley, John Hargreaves and Michelle Jacob.

Contributors
Miranda Bayliss
Philippa Bromley
Douglas Campbell
Paddy Cullen
Andrew Dutton
Caroline Ellis
Mike Ellison
Kate Fincham
Sarah Goldberg
Lindsay Goward
Daphne Hall
Susan Hubbard
Sandie Lock
Alan Markey
Cleo Nixon
Judith Paterson
Derek Sinclair
Kate Smith
Rebecca Walker
Sally West
Helen Winfield
Debbie Witton

and
Kelly Hayworth
Victoria Todd and
Robin Williamson
(Low Incomes Tax Reform Group)

Checkers
Michael Beacroft
(Independent Living Funds)
Sara Cochrane
(National Assembly for Wales)
Pamela Fitzpatrick
Ann Flint
Joan Greening
(RNIB)
Janet Lambe
(Department for Work and Pensions)
David Malcolm
(National Union of Students)
Clive Martin and David Allsop
(Ferret Information Systems)
Chris Parsons
(Tower Hamlets Law Centre)
Nikola Plunkett
(Criminal Injuries Compensation Authority)
Jim Rawlings
(Mobilise)
Liz Woskett-Burton
(RNIB)
Martin Inch, Vanessa Stanislas and Paul Treloar
(Disability Alliance)

and staff at
Communities and Local Government
Compensation Recovery Unit
Department for Children, Schools and Families
Department for Work and Pensions
Department of Health
Service Personnel and Veterans Agency

Disability Rights Handbook
34th Edition
April 2009 - April 2010
ISBN: 978-1-903335-47-5

Published by

Contents

Benefits checklist

This is a quick guide to help you see which benefits you might be entitled to. It is not a guide to the benefits themselves – you will need to read the relevant chapters. More than one of the circumstances below may apply to you and you may qualify for more than one benefit, especially if you have low savings and income. Box A.1 in Chapter 1 tells you which benefits depend on your national insurance (NI) record and which are affected by other income.

Circumstance	Benefit	Chapter
Problems with walking		
■ aged under 65 when you claim	**disability living allowance mobility component**	**3**
■ hire or buy a car using the mobility component	**Motability**	**5**
■ if you get higher rate mobility component	**road tax exemption**	**5**
■ parking concessions	**Blue Badge scheme**	**5**
Need help with personal care		
■ aged under 65 when you claim	**disability living allowance care component**	**3**
■ aged 65 or over when you claim	**attendance allowance**	**4**
■ severely disabled and need help with personal care or household assistance and aged under 66	**Independent Living Funds**	**29**
Caring		
■ you care for a disabled person for at least 35 hours a week	**carer's allowance**	**6**
■ you or your partner get carer's allowance or would do but for an overlapping benefit	**carer premium with means-tested benefits**	**24**
Limited capability for work		
■ employed	**statutory sick pay (SSP)**	**8**
■ not employed or after 28 weeks SSP	**employment and support allowance (ESA)**	**9**
Unemployed or working less than 16 hours a week		
■ payable for 26 weeks if you've paid enough NI contributions	**contribution-based jobseeker's allowance (JSA)**	**15**
■ if you've not paid enough NI contributions, or your contribution-based JSA has run out or is not enough to live on	**income-based jobseeker's allowance**	**15**
■ if you don't have to sign on for work (eg you are a carer or a lone parent with a young child) and any income or savings are low	**income support**	**14**
Working at least 16 hours a week		
■ you are 50 or over and returning to work, or you have a child, or you have a disability and get a qualifying disability benefit or recently got a qualifying incapacity benefit, or you are 25 or over and are working at least 30 hours a week	**working tax credit**	**18**
Housing problems		
■ repairs, adaptations, improvements	**housing grants**	**31**
■ help with the mortgage	**income support**	**14**
	income-based jobseeker's allowance	**15**
	income-related employment and support allowance	**12**
	pension credit (guarantee credit)	**42**
■ help with the rent	**housing benefit**	**20**
■ help with the council tax	**council tax benefit**	**20**
	disability reduction or discount schemes	**21**
If you do not have enough to live on		
■ limited capability for work	**income-related employment and support allowance**	**12**
■ not working, or working less than 16 hours a week, and you do not have to sign on for work (eg you are a carer)	**income support**	**14**
■ if you have to sign on for work	**income-based jobseeker's allowance**	**15**
■ from age 60	**pension credit**	**42**
■ working at least 16 hours a week (see above)	**working tax credit**	**18**
■ responsible for a child (see below)	**child tax credit**	**18**
■ paying rent for your home	**housing benefit**	**20**
■ paying council tax	**council tax benefit**	**20**

Circumstance	Benefit	Chapter
If you have needs difficult to meet out of regular income		
■ if you get income-related ESA, income support, income-based JSA or pension credit	**social fund community care grant**	23
■ if you've had income-related ESA, income support, income-based JSA or pension credit for at least 26 weeks	**social fund budgeting loan**	23
■ following emergency or disaster	**social fund crisis loan**	23
Practical help at home		
■ practical help if you are disabled	**care services, eg home care, Meals on Wheels**	28
■ equipment and adaptations	**help from social services or the NHS**	30
Pregnancy		
■ all pregnant women	**health in pregnancy grant**	36
■ employed	**statutory maternity pay (SMP)**	36
■ recently employed or self-employed, but not entitled to SMP	**maternity allowance**	36
■ limited capability for work	**employment and support allowance**	9
■ if income and savings are low	**income support**	14
■ help with maternity expenses	**Sure Start maternity grant**	22
■ vouchers for milk and fresh fruit and vegetables	**health benefits**	55
Responsibility for children		
■ employed	**statutory paternity pay**	36
■ employed (responsible for adopted child)	**statutory adoption pay**	36
■ responsible for a child under 16, or 16-19 in full-time, non-advanced education or approved unwaged training	**child benefit**	38
	child tax credit	18
■ responsible for an orphan	**guardian's allowance**	38
■ disabled child	**disability living allowance**	37
	Family Fund	37
■ vouchers for milk and fresh fruit and vegetables	**health benefits**	55
Retirement		
■ from age 60 for women or 65 for men	**state pension**	43
■ from age 60 and income or savings are low	**pension credit**	42
■ from age 80 and little or no state pension before	**non-contributory state pension**	43
Injured or contracted disease in work		
■ disabled through an industrial accident or prescribed disease	**industrial injuries disablement benefit**	45
■ the industrial accident or disease occurred before 1.10.90 and your earnings capacity is reduced	**reduced earnings allowance**	45
■ replaces reduced earnings allowance when you give up regular employment after state pension age	**retirement allowance**	45
War disablement		
■ injured because of service in the Armed Forces (prior to 6.4.05), or a civilian disabled due to the 1939-45 war	**war disablement pension**	46
■ your spouse or civil partner died because of the war, or because of service in the Armed Forces	**war widow(er)'s pension**	46
■ injured because of service in the Armed Forces on or after 6.4.05	**Armed Forces Compensation scheme**	46
Disabled due to vaccine damage	**vaccine damage payment**	48
Injured due to violent crime	**criminal injuries compensation**	47
Need help with NHS costs, glasses, hospital fares	**health benefits**	55
Death		
■ widow, widower or surviving civil partner under state pension age, or whose husband, wife or civil partner did not get state pension	**bereavement payment**	54
■ widow, widower or surviving civil partner with a dependent child	**widowed parent's allowance**	54
■ paid for 52 weeks to a widow, widower or surviving civil partner aged 45 or over but under state pension age when spouse or civil partner dies	**bereavement allowance**	54
■ help with the cost of a funeral	**social fund funeral payment**	22

Legal references

The footnotes in this Handbook are references to Acts and Regulations, case law and official guidance. Each footnote applies to the block of text above it. If there are several paragraphs in a block, with just one footnote at the bottom, the footnote applies to all text within the block. If text contains several footnotes, each one refers to the text directly above it, up to the previous footnote. Text that provides tactical advice or discussion on specific points is not generally footnoted.

Acts and Regulations

Acts of Parliament (also knows as statutes) contain the basic rules for social security benefits, tax credits and community care administration.

Regulations flesh out the law and provide the detail that determines procedure for the rules as laid down in the Acts. These are also known as statutory instruments (SIs) and can be amended at any time using other SIs.

Finding Acts and Regulations – You can buy Acts and Regulations from The Stationery Office, PO Box 29, Norwich NR3 1GN (0870 600 5522) or look them up on the Office of Public Sector Information website (www.opsi.gov.uk). Most have been amended. Consolidated and updated legislation is set out in:

- *The Law Relating to Social Security* (The Blue Volumes), distributed by Corporate Document Services (0113 399 4040) or available on our website (www.disabilityalliance.org/links2.htm).

Reference books – Consolidated and updated legislation is also available in:

- *Social Security: Legislation 2008 Volumes I, II, III* and *IV* (Sweet & Maxwell). These books have detailed footnotes explaining the legislation and highlighting relevant case law. They are used by members of appeal tribunals (see Chapter 60).

Case law

Case law is created through decisions or judgments made on points of law by the Upper Tribunal, the Court of Appeal or the House of Lords.

These decisions clarify any doubt about the meaning of the law or its application to individual cases. When case law sets up a general principal, it also creates a precedent to be followed in similar cases.

The Upper Tribunal (previously the Social Security Commissioners) hears appeals against appeal tribunal decisions (see Box T.7 in Chapter 60), the Court of Appeal against decisions of the Commissioners/Upper Tribunal, and the House of Lords against Court of Appeal judgments.

Finding case law – All Commissioners/Upper Tribunal decisions are available from their office individually on request at a small charge (see inside back cover for their address). Decisions are also available on their website (www.administrativeappeals.tribunals.gov.uk), where reported decisions from 1991 and selected unreported decisions deemed to be of interest from 2002 are published.

Case law summaries – Brief outlines of the main reported decisions can be found in:

- *Neligan's Digest,* available from Corporate Document Services and on our website (www.disabilityalliance.org/links2.htm).

Disability Alliance has produced case law summaries covering disability living allowance, attendance allowance, incapacity benefit and adjudication generally. Our factsheet *Finding the Law* (F.19) helps you find the law relevant to disability benefits. These are all available from our website (www.disabilityalliance.org/digest.htm) or by sending us a stamped addressed envelope (see back cover for our address) stating which packs you want.

Official guidance

See www.disabilityalliance.org/links2.htm for the following:

- *Decision Makers Guide* – Covering all benefits administered by the Department for Work and Pensions (DWP)
- *Social Fund Guide* – National guidance on the social fund (see Chapter 23)
- *Disability Handbook* and *A-Z of medical conditions* – To help decide disability living allowance and attendance allowance (see Chapter 3(24))

See also the boxes entitled 'For more information' in various chapters of the Handbook (including Box L.1 in Chapter 32 for Sections K and L).

Acts

CCH(S)A	Community Care and Health (Scotland) Act 2002
CSA	Care Standards Act 2000
CSDPA	Chronically Sick and Disabled Persons Act 1970
DDA	Disability Discrimination Act 1995
HASSASSA	Health and Social Services and Social Security Adjudication Act 1983
HGCRA	Housing Grants, Construction and Regeneration Act 1996
HSA	Housing (Scotland) Act 2006
HSCA	Health and Social Care Act 2001
JSA	Jobseekers Act 1995
LGFA	Local Government Finance Act 1992
NAA	The National Assistance Act 1948
PA	Pensions Act 2007
RC(S)A	Regulation of Care (Scotland) Act 2001
SPCA	State Pension Credit Act 2002
SSA	Social Security Act 1998
SSAA	Social Security Administration Act 1992
SSCBA	Social Security Contributions and Benefits Act 1992
TCA	Tax Credits Act 2002
TCEA	Tribunals, Courts and Enforcement Act 2007
VDPA	Vaccine Damage Payments Act 1979
WRA	Welfare Reform Act 2007

Regulations

AA Regs	Social Security (Attendance Allowance) Regulations 1991 (SI 1991/2740)
AOR Regs	National Assistance (Assessment of Resources) Regulations 1992 (SI 1992/2977)
CB Regs	Child Benefit (General) Regulations 2006 (SI 2006/223)
CE Regs	Social Security Benefit (Computation of Earnings) Regulations 1996 (SI 1996/2745)
Cont. Regs	Social Security (Contributions) Regulations 2001 (SI 2001/1004)

C&P Regs	Social Security (Claims and Payments) Regulations 1987 (SI 1987/1968)
Credit Regs	Social Security (Credits) Regulations 1975 (SI 1975/556)
CTB Regs	Council Tax Benefit Regulations 2006 (SI 2006/215)
CTB(SPC) Regs	Council Tax Benefit (Persons who have Attained the Qualifying Age for State Pension Credit) Regulations 2006 (SI 2006/216)
CTC Regs	Child Tax Credit Regulations 2002 (SI 2002/2007)
D&A Regs	Social Security and Child Support (Decisions and Appeals) Regulations 1999 (SI 1999/991)
DLA Regs	Social Security (Disability Living Allowance) Regulations 1991 (SI 1991/2890)
DP(BMV) Regs	Disabled Persons (Badges for Motor Vehicles) (England) Regulations 2000 (SI 2000/682)
EEEIIP Regs	Social Security (Employed Earners' Employment for Industrial Injuries Purposes) Regulations 1975 (SI 1975/467)
ESA Regs	Employment and Support Allowance Regulations 2008 (SI 2008/794)
GB Regs	Social Security (General Benefit) Regulations 1982 (SI 1982/1408)
HB Regs	Housing Benefit Regulations 2006 (SI 2006/213)
HB(SPC) Regs	Housing Benefit (Persons who have Attained the Qualifying Age for State Pension Credit) Regulations 2006 (SI 2006/214)
HB Amdt Regs	Housing Benefit (General) Amendment Regulations 1995 (SI 1995/1644)
HB&CTB Amdt Regs	Housing Benefit and Council Tax Benefit (General) Amendment Regulations 1997 (SI 1997/852)
HB&CTB (D&A) Regs	Housing Benefit and Council Tax Benefit (Decisions and Appeals) Regulations 2001 (SI 2001/1002)
HB&CTB (SPC) Regs	Housing Benefit and Council Tax Benefit (State Pension Credit) Regulations 2003 (SI 2003/325)
HIP Regs	Social Security (Hospital In-Patients) Regulations 2005 (SI 2005/3360)
HR Regs	Social Security Pensions (Home Responsibilities) Regulations 1994 (SI 1994/704)
HRG Regs	Housing Renewal Grants Regulations 1996 (SI 1996/2890)
(IA)CA Regs	Social Security (Immigration and Asylum) Consequential Amendments Regulations 2000 (SI 2000/636)
ICA Regs	Social Security (Invalid Care Allowance) Regulations 1976 (SI 1976/409))
II&D(MP) Regs	Social Security (Industrial Injuries and Diseases) Miscellaneous Provisions Regulations 1986 (SI 1986/1561)
IIPD Regs	Social Security (Industrial Injuries)(Prescribed Diseases) Regulations 1985 (SI 1985/967)
IS Regs	Income Support (General) Regulations 1987 (SI 1987/1967)
IW Regs	Social Security (Incapacity for Work)(General) Regulations 1995 (SI 1995/311)
JPI Regs	Social Security (Jobcentre Plus Interviews) Regulations 2002 (SI 2002/1703)
JPIP Regs	Social Security (Jobcentre Plus Interviews for Partners) Regulations 2003 (SI 2003/1886)
JSA Regs	Jobseeker's Allowance Regulations 1996 (SI 1996/207)
LATO(EDP) Regs	Local Authorities' Traffic Orders (Exemptions for Disabled Persons)(England) Regulations 2000 (SI 2000/683)
MPL Regs	Maternity and Parental Leave etc Regulations 1999 (SI 1999/3312)
NHS(CDA) Regs	National Health Service (Charges for Drugs and Appliances) Regulations 2000 (SI 2000/620)
NHS(TERC) Regs	National Health Service (Travel Expenses and Remission of Charges) Regulations 2003 (SI 2003/2382)
NMAF(DD) SP Order	Naval, Military and Air Forces Etc. (Disablement & Death) Service Pensions Order 2006 (SI 2006/606)
OB Regs	Social Security (Overlapping Benefits) Regulations 1979 (SI 1979/597)
PA Regs	Social Security Benefit (Persons Abroad) Regulations 1975 (SI 1975/563)
PAOR Regs	Social Security (Payments on account, Overpayments and Recovery) Regulations 1988 (SI 1988/664)
RR(HA)E&W Order	Regulatory Reform (Housing Assistance) (England and Wales) Order 2002 (SI 2002/1860)
SDA Regs	Social Security (Severe Disablement Allowance) Regulations 1984 (SI 1984/1303)
SFM&FE Regs	Social Fund Maternity and Funeral Expenses (General) Regulations 2005 (SI 2005/3061)
SMP Regs	Statutory Maternity Pay (General) Regulations 1986 (SI 1986/1960)
SPC Regs	State Pension Credit Regulations 2002 (SI 2002/1792)
SSP Regs	Statutory Sick Pay (General) Regulations 1982 (SI 1982/894)
TC(A) Regs	Tax Credits (Appeals) (No.2) Regulations 2002 (SI 2002/3196)
TC(C&N) Regs	Tax Credits (Claims and Notifications) Regulations 2002 (SI 2002/2014)
TC(DCI) Regs	Tax Credits (Definition and Calculation of Income) Regulations 2002 (SI 2002/2006)
TC(I) Regs	Tax Credits (Immigration) Regulations 2003 (SI 2003/653)
TC(IT&DR) Regs	Tax Credits (Income Thresholds and Determination of Rates) Regulations 2002 (SI 2002/2008)
TC(R) Regs	Tax Credits (Residence) Regulations 2003 (SI 2003/654)
TP(FTT)SEC Rules	Tribunal Procedure (First-tier Tribunal)(Social Entitlement Chamber) Rules 2008 (SI 2008/2685)
TP(UT) Rules	Tribunal Procedure (Upper Tribunal) Rules 2008 (SI 2008/2698)
VDP Regs	Vaccine Damage Payments Regulations 1979 (SI 1979/432)
WBRP Regs	Social Security (Widow's Benefit and Retirement Pensions) Regulations 1979 (SI 1979/642)
WTC(E&MR) Regs	Working Tax Credit (Entitlement and Maximum Rate) Regulations 2002 (SI 2002/2005)

Abbreviations

Most abbreviations used in the Handbook are explained here. If you come across one that isn't listed, you will usually find it explained towards the beginning of the chapter, towards the beginning of the section in a chapter, or in a box headed 'For more information'.

AA attendance allowance
AIP assessed income period
art article
BEL Benefit Enquiry Line
CA carer's allowance
CAA constant attendance allowance
CB child benefit
CBEP child benefit extension period
CCG community care grant
CCLR Community Care Law Reports
CESA(Y) contributory employment and support allowance in youth
CLA Community Legal Advice
CoA Court of Appeal
CRAG Charging for Residential Accommodation Guide
CTB council tax benefit
CTC child tax credit
DBC Disability Benefits Centre
DCSF Department for Children, Schools and Families
DDA Disability Discrimination Act
DEA disability employment adviser
DHP discretionary housing payment
DIAL Disability Information and Advice Line
DLA disability living allowance
DMG Decision Makers' Guide
DSA disabled students' allowance
DWP Department for Work and Pensions
EC European Community
ECJ European Court of Justice
EEA European Economic Area
EMP examining medical practitioner
ESA employment and support allowance
GB Great Britain (England, Scotland and Wales)
GP general practitioner
HB housing benefit
HMRC HM Revenue & Customs
HoL House of Lords
HRP home responsibilities protection
HRT habitual residence test
IB incapacity benefit
IIDB industrial injuries disablement benefit
ILF Independent Living Fund
IS income support
JSA jobseeker's allowance
LHA local housing allowance
LHB local health board
MA maternity allowance
NASS National Asylum Support Service
NDDP New Deal for Disabled People
NHS National Health Service
NI national insurance
NIHE Northern Ireland Housing Executive
p./para paragraph in a schedule to an Act or set of Regulations, or in a Guidance Manual
PAYE pay as you earn
PC pension credit
PCA personal capability assessment
PCT primary care trust
PDCS Pension, Disability & Carers Service
PPF Pension Protection Fund
RA retirement allowance
REA reduced earnings allowance
Reg regulation in a set of Regulations
s. section of an Act of Parliament
S2P state second pension
SAAS Student Awards Agency for Scotland
SAP statutory adoption pay
Sch schedule, at the end of an Act or a set of Regulations
SDA severe disablement allowance
SDP severe disability premium
SERPS state earnings-related pension scheme
SHA statutory health authority
SI statutory instrument
SMP statutory maternity pay
SPP statutory paternity pay
SPVA Service Personnel and Veterans Agency
SSP statutory sick pay
UK United Kingdom (England, Northern Ireland, Scotland, Wales)
WCA work capability assessment
WFHRA work-focused health-related assessment
WPA widowed parent's allowance
WTC working tax credit

Overview A

This section of the Handbook looks at:

1 Introduction

1. What does the Handbook include?

This Handbook is a comprehensive guide to social security and related benefits for disabled people, their families and their carers and the many professionals who work with them. It is aimed at disabled people, whether their impairment is physical, mental or sensory.

You may find it helpful to start by looking at the benefits checklist (pages 4-5). In addition to social security benefits and tax credits, the Handbook covers practical help and services and other essential matters such as community care, income tax, council tax and housing grants, as well as disability rights legislation.

A list of the abbreviations used in the Handbook is on page 8, opposite.

2. What's new in this edition?

The most significant change this year has been the introduction of employment and support allowance. This new benefit replaced incapacity benefit and income support paid on the grounds of incapacity from 27 October 2008.

The introduction of employment and support allowance has affected many different benefits and this is reflected throughout this edition of Handbook. As much of the content of this edition is new, we have taken the opportunity to completely reorganise the structure to make it easier to use.

The new structure – The first benefits we describe in this edition are the principle benefits paid to disabled people and their carers. These are disability living allowance and attendance allowance (covered in Section B) and carer's allowance (covered in Section C).

We describe employment and support allowance in detail in Chapters 9 to 12 (in Section D). In Chapter 13 we describe what will happen to existing incapacity benefit and income support claimants.

We have a new section (Section E) covering the two benefits you may receive when you are out of work: income support and jobseeker's allowance.

A further new section (Section J) describes the common rules that cover means-tested (or income-related) benefits, such as income support, housing benefit and the new income-related employment and support allowance. This section includes a chapter on the premiums that are included in these benefits, a chapter on the housing costs they can cover (explaining the recent changes) and chapters dealing with the way your income or savings affect these benefits.

Another new section (Section R) combines chapters on income tax and VAT relief.

Other changes – Other changes explained in this Handbook include:

- the radical restructuring of the Tribunals Service, with appeal tribunals and Social Security Commissioners being replaced by First-tier Tribunals and Upper Tribunals. See Chapter 60;
- the effects of the coming equalisation of state pension age for men and women. See Chapter 43.

3. Updates

We produce Handbook updates six times a year for members. Organisations can become members of Disability Alliance and receive a free copy of each update. See back cover for contact details.

The 35th edition of the Handbook will be published in May 2010.

REMEMBER TO ORDER THE 35TH EDITION OF THIS HANDBOOK BEFORE APRIL 2010.

4. Disability and benefits

What is disability?

Few of your rights depend on what your condition is called. In most cases, your right to a benefit or service depends on the effect of the disability on your life.

Benefits and tax credits – Within the benefits and tax credits systems there are six main tests of disability:

- **limited capability for work** – used for the new employment and support allowance;
- **incapacity for work** – used for statutory sick pay, incapacity benefit, severe disablement allowance, income support and the unemployability supplement under the Industrial Injuries and War Disablement schemes. There are different tests of incapacity depending on the benefit you claim;
- **needing care, supervision or watching over by another person** – used for disability living allowance care component and attendance allowance. A similar test is used for constant attendance allowance under the Industrial Injuries and War Disablement schemes;
- **unable or virtually unable to walk** – used for disability living allowance mobility component and war pensioners' mobility supplement;
- **degree of disablement** – used for industrial injuries disablement benefit, war disablement pension and vaccine damage payments;
- **at a disadvantage in getting a job** – used for the disability element of working tax credit.

Further definitions – There are two further definitions in use:

- **substantially and permanently disabled** – used for registering as disabled with a local authority social services department and for getting a disability reduction in your council tax;
- **physical or mental impairment that has a substantial and long-term adverse effect on your ability to carry out normal day-to-day activities** – used to define those people covered by the Disability Discrimination Act 1995.

Besides these main tests of disability, there may be other criteria you must satisfy to get a particular benefit or service. The individual chapters give details of these.

The different types of benefits

Benefits can be divided into three broad categories:

- those that are intended to replace earnings;
- those that compensate for extra costs;
- those that help alleviate poverty.

The first category includes benefits that compensate you if you are unable to work because of sickness, disability, unemployment, pregnancy, retirement or caring responsibilities. In general, these benefits are not subject to a means test, but some will depend on your national insurance contribution record (see Box A.1).

Benefits intended to contribute towards the extra costs of disability or the extra cost of children are not means tested and do not depend on national insurance contributions.

Benefits intended to alleviate poverty by providing a basic income or topping up a low income are subject to a means test.

A.1 Benefits affected by other income or NI contributions

Means-tested benefits

The following means-tested or income-related benefits are affected by most other types of income and by the amount of savings you have. However, child tax credit and working tax credit are affected only by the income from your savings, not by the actual level of savings. Your national insurance (NI) contribution record does not matter.

- Child tax credit
- Council tax benefit
- Housing benefit
- Income-related employment and support allowance
- Income-based jobseeker's allowance
- Income support
- Pension credit
- Social fund
- Working tax credit

Non-means-tested benefits

The following non-means-tested benefits are not usually affected by other money that you have, although those marked (*) can be affected by your earnings or your occupational or private pension. See the relevant chapter for details.

For some of these benefits, your NI record does not matter and they are listed here as non-contributory benefits. However, for the other benefits you (or in some cases your partner, if you have one) must have made sufficient NI contributions, and those benefits are listed here as contributory benefits.

Non-contributory benefits

- Attendance allowance
- Carer's allowance*
- Child benefit
- Disability living allowance
- Guardian's allowance
- Industrial injuries benefits
- State pension: Category D
- Statutory adoption pay
- Statutory maternity pay
- Statutory paternity pay
- Statutory sick pay
- War disablement pensions

Contributory benefits

- Bereavement allowance
- Bereavement payment
- Contribution-based jobseeker's allowance*
- Contributory employment and support allowance*
- Maternity allowance (depends on earnings)*
- State pension: Categories A and B
- Widowed parent's allowance

2 The benefits system

In this chapter we look at: page

1. Department for Work and Pensions

The Department for Work and Pensions (DWP) is responsible for most of the help available for disabled people. Responsibility for policy making lies with the DWP, while services are delivered to the public by three service delivery organisations (see 2 below).

While most benefits are administered by the DWP, tax credits, child benefit and guardian's allowance are administered by HM Revenue & Customs (see 5 below).

The DWP contracts out some of its functions to private companies; for example, Atos Healthcare is contracted to provide medical advice and examinations.

In this Handbook we refer to the system as a DWP system – eg 'write to the DWP', 'DWP doctor', etc. This reflects the legal reality. However, when we talk about the local office that you need to deal with, we usually refer to 'your local Jobcentre Plus office'.

2. The structure of the DWP

The day-to-day running of the benefits system is undertaken by three service delivery organisations: Jobcentre Plus, the Pension, Disability & Carers Service and Debt Management.

Jobcentre Plus

Jobcentre Plus provides services to people of working age, administering most of the benefits they can claim through a network of local Jobcentre Plus offices. Jobcentre Plus aims to provide 'a work focus' to the benefits system. The benefits it administers include employment and support allowance, income support and jobseeker's allowance.

Pension, Disability & Carers Service

This provides services for pensioners and people planning for retirement, as well as administering important benefits for disabled people and their carers. It was created in April 2008 by merging The Pension Service with the Disability & Carers Service, both of which remain independent organisations within the new agency for the time being.

The Pension Service – this administers the state pension, pension credit and winter fuel payments, through largely telephone-based pension centres. These centres are supported by a local service network that provides appointment-based meetings in such places as libraries and community centres and home visits.

The Disability & Carers Service – this administers disability living allowance, attendance allowance, carer's allowance and vaccine damage payments through a network of regional Disability Benefits Centres, as well as three central units: the Disability Contact & Processing Unit in Blackpool and the Carer's Allowance Unit and Vaccine Damage Payments Unit in Preston. The initial contact for these benefits will usually be through the Benefit Enquiry Line (see Box A.2).

Debt Management

Debt management is responsible for the recovery of debts from claimants.

3. Northern Ireland

In Northern Ireland, the Department for Social Development is responsible for social security matters, and benefits are administered by the Social Security Agency.

Northern Ireland has its own legislation, and the structure and organisation of the system are different from that of Great Britain (GB). However, the legislation tends to mirror GB legislation and, consequently, the rates of benefits and their qualifying conditions are similar. An important difference, however, is that in Northern Ireland there are rate rebates instead of council tax benefit (see Chapter 20(28)).

4. Who's who in the benefits system

The services are organised in slightly different ways. What follows is an outline – you will find further details in the chapters on the individual benefits. The rules about claims, payments, decision making and appeals are in Chapters 59 and 60.

In all cases, you have the right to expect a good standard of service. Jobcentre Plus and the Pension, Disability & Carers Service both have customer charters that explain the standards; you can get a copy from the local office of each organisation. If you want to complain about something or have suggestions about how services could be improved, see Chapter 62.

Administrative staff

The people you talk to when you visit or phone a local office are not always legally responsible for making a decision on your claim. They will do the support and maintenance work for claims, and may handle many routine claims, particularly for means-tested benefits, but decisions must, in law, be made by a decision maker authorised by the Secretary of State.

The Secretary of State

The Secretary of State for Work and Pensions is responsible for decisions on your social security benefit entitlement. In practice, this responsibility is delegated to decision makers who are officers acting under the Secretary of State's authority. In a few cases, the Secretary of State delegates decision-making responsibility to officers of HM Revenue & Customs (eg for some national insurance credits decisions).

Decision makers

Decision makers are officers acting under the authority of the Secretary of State. They make decisions on your entitlement to benefits but will not always be based in your local office. If you are not satisfied with a decision, you can ask for an explanation of the decision, ask for a revision of the decision, or appeal to an independent tribunal. The letter giving you the decision must always explain what you can do next. See Chapter 60 for further information on decisions, revisions and appeals.

Social fund decision makers – Access to the social fund is through the Jobcentre Plus network (ie your local Jobcentre Plus office). For the discretionary social fund there is a different decision-making system. Initial decisions are taken by a decision maker authorised to do so by the Secretary of State. There is an ultimate right of review by a social fund inspector (see Chapter 23(7)).

5. HM Revenue & Customs

HM Revenue & Customs (HMRC) is responsible for decisions on tax credits, child benefit and guardian's allowance, and these are made by officers based in the Tax Credit Office in Preston or the Child Benefit Office in Newcastle upon Tyne. HMRC is also responsible for decisions on national insurance contributions and employer-paid benefits (statutory sick, maternity, paternity and adoption pay). Appeals on HMRC decisions are heard by First-tier Tribunals (see 6 below).

6. Ministry of Justice

The Ministry of Justice has responsibility for running the appeals system. It does this through the Tribunals Service, which provides common administrative support to the main central government tribunals. The Tribunals Service has recently undergone a radical reform, with the introduction of 'First-tier Tribunals' and 'Upper Tribunals'.

First-tier Tribunals – First-tier Tribunals have replaced the social security appeals tribunals. In addition to hearing appeals on decisions made by the Secretary of State for Work and Pensions (on benefits such as employment and support allowance, income support and disability living allowance), First-tier Tribunals also hear appeals against local authority decisions on housing benefit and council tax benefit and HMRC decisions on tax credits, national insurance contributions and employer-paid benefits. As well as hearing appeals on disputes related to social security benefits, First-tier Tribunals cover a range of other areas, including mental health reviews, care standards, criminal injuries compensation and special educational needs. The role and powers of the First-tier Tribunals are explained in Chapter 60.

Upper Tribunals – Upper Tribunals have replaced the Social Security Commissioners. They hear appeals against decisions of the First-tier Tribunals. Their decisions set precedents and form case law. Chapter 60(18) explains more about appealing to the Upper Tribunal.

A.2 Contacting the DWP

Details of local Jobcentre Plus offices can be obtained from their website (www.jobcentreplus.gov.uk). Claims for benefits administered by Jobcentre Plus can be made by contacting their claim-line (0800 055 6688; textphone 0800 023 4888). Details of pension centres can be obtained from The Pension Service (0845 606 0265; textphone 0845 606 0285 or www.thepensionservice.gov.uk). The addresses of DWP central units are listed on the inside back cover of this Handbook.

Northern Ireland – To find your local social security office, look in the phone book under 'Social Security' or on the website (www.dsdni.gov.uk).

Benefit Enquiry Line (BEL)

This is a confidential telephone advice and information line for people with disabilities, carers and representatives. It covers England, Scotland and Wales. BEL can provide general benefits advice and information, but staff do not have access to any claimant records and are therefore unable to give information on the progress of a claim or benefits you are already receiving. It is a confidential service and nothing you ask or say will go on your file.

For certain disability-related benefit claims, staff can arrange to fill in your form over the phone and send it to you to check and sign. The form can be in Braille or large print. The service covers carer's allowance, disability living allowance, attendance allowance and industrial injuries disablement benefit.

Ring the enquiry line on 0800 882200 or textphone 0800 243355. Lines are open 8.30am-6.30pm Monday to Friday and 9am-1pm Saturday. From a landline your call is free.

Northern Ireland Benefit Enquiry Line (BEL)

Ring 0800 220674 or textphone 0800 243787. Staff give general advice on benefits for disabled people and offer a forms-completion service. Lines are open 9am-5pm Monday, Tuesday, Wednesday, Friday and 10am-5pm Thursday.

B Care and mobility

This section of the Handbook looks at:

3 Disability living allowance

A. GENERAL POINTS

1. What is disability living allowance?

Disability living allowance (DLA) is a benefit for adults and children with disabilities. It is for people who need help looking after themselves and those who find it difficult to walk or get around. You don't need to have someone looking after you to qualify.

DLA is tax free, not means tested and you don't need to have paid any national insurance contributions. It is paid on top of any earnings or other income you may have. It is almost always paid in full on top of social security benefits or tax credits. DLA is divided into two parts:

- **a care component** – for help with personal care needs, paid at three different levels;
- **a mobility component** – for help with walking difficulties, paid at two levels.

You can be paid either the care component or the mobility component on its own, or both components at the same time. DLA is for you, not for a carer or parent. You can qualify for DLA whether or not you have someone helping you; what matters is the effects of your disability and the help you need, not whether you already get that help. You can spend your DLA on anything you like.

Although DLA can be paid indefinitely, there is an upper age limit for making your first claim. You can only get DLA if you claim before your 65th birthday. Otherwise you claim attendance allowance (AA; see Chapter 4). AA has no mobility component, but the disability tests are the same as for DLA middle and highest rate care components.

You can start your claim with a phone call to the Benefit Enquiry Line (BEL – 0800 882200). They will send you a claim-form and your claim can be backdated to the date of your call. You can also claim online or print a claim-form from www.direct.gov.uk/disability-dla.

2. Do you qualify for DLA?

To qualify for DLA you must pass a series of non-disability tests and satisfy at least one of the disability tests. Most of the non-disability tests have exceptions to the standard rules, so off-the-cuff advice may not always be correct.

To qualify for DLA, you must:

- pass at least one of the disability tests (see 9 and 18 below); *and*
- claim DLA (see 23 below); *and*
- pass the age test (see 3 below); *and*
- pass both the backwards and forwards qualifying period tests (see 4 below); *and*
- pass the residence and presence tests, and not be subject to immigration control (see Chapter 50(2) and (3)).

The DWP must also be satisfied there is nothing to prevent payment (see 6 below). If you pass all these tests, you will be entitled to DLA. You keep your underlying entitlement to DLA even if other rules mean you are not actually paid it.

Box B.1 gives a summary of the non-disability tests.

3. Age limits

Lower age limit – There is no lower age limit for DLA care component. But there is an extra disability test for children under 16 (see 9 below) and you cannot use the cooking test until you reach age 16.

Children can get the higher rate mobility component from age 3 and the lower rate from age 5. The rules for the higher rate are the same as for adults but lower rate mobility has an extra disability test if you are under 16 (see 18 below).

Upper age limit – DLA can be paid indefinitely, but you must establish your entitlement by making a successful claim no later than the day before your 65th birthday. You don't need to pass the qualifying period but you must satisfy all the other conditions of entitlement, including one of the disability tests, no later than the day before your 65th birthday. If you are 65 or over, you cannot claim DLA for the first time unless you count as having made a claim before reaching 65.

DLA Regs, reg 3 & Sch 1; C&P Regs, reg 4(1)

B.1 The non-disability tests

Qualifying criteria	Care component	Mobility component
Age limits		
■ To make your first claim	From birth to the day before your 65th birthday.	Higher rate from 2 years 9 months to the day before your 65th birthday. Lower rate from 4 years 9 months to the day before your 65th birthday.
■ To be paid	From 3 months old (birth if terminally ill). No upper limit.	From 3 years for higher rate and 5 years for lower rate. No upper limit.
■ Extra tests for children	From birth to the day before your 16th birthday.	For lower rate only, from 4 years 9 months to the day before your 16th birthday.
■ Shorter 'presence in the country' test for babies	Must claim and serve the 3-month qualifying period no later than the day before 6 months old.	Not payable to children under 3.
■ Cooking test	From 16 years to the day before your 65th birthday.	Doesn't apply.
■ Lowest/lower rate	The day before your 65th birthday. From 65 you can keep or renew your lowest rate component or make a repeat claim within one year.	Same as care component.
Qualifying periods		
■ Backwards test	If you're under 65 on the first day of entitlement, you must satisfy the disability tests throughout the 3 months before the award would start. If you're 65 or over – 6 months. No qualifying period if you're terminally ill.	If you're under 65 on the first day of entitlement, you must satisfy the disability tests throughout the 3 months before an award would start. If you're 65 or over and renewing a claim – also 3 months. No qualifying period if you're terminally ill.
■ Forwards test	6 months following first day of entitlement. No forwards test for renewal claims, revisions or supersessions if you're 65 or over, or for attendance allowance.	6 months following first day of entitlement.
Residence and presence		
■ Standard	Present for 26 out of the last 52 weeks. Present and ordinarily resident, not subject to immigration control.	Same as care component.
■ Babies	Present for 13 out of the last 52 weeks before award if less than 6 months old when claim made and qualifying period served. Present and ordinarily resident, not subject to immigration control.	Not payable to children under 3.
■ Terminal illness	Present and ordinarily resident, not subject to immigration control.	Same as care component.
Other rules		
■ Hospital and care homes	Payment may be stopped while in hospital or a care home.	Payment may be stopped while in hospital but is not affected in a care home.
■ Prison	Payment suspended while on remand, but arrears paid if you don't get a custodial or suspended sentence.	Same as care component.

B.2 Disability living allowance and other help

DLA acts as a gateway to other types of help. This table lists the rates and components of DLA that entitle you to further help (if you pass any other tests there are for that help).

If you get DLA middle or highest rate care component, you are also eligible for the help available to people receiving only the lowest rate. Similarly, if you get higher rate mobility component, you are also eligible for the help available to people receiving only the lower rate.

'Premiums' are those included in the assessments of income support (IS), income-based jobseeker's allowance (JSA), income-related employment and support allowance (ESA), housing benefit (HB), council tax benefit (CTB) and health benefits. 'Elements' are those included in child tax credit and working tax credit (WTC).

Note: The disabled child premium and enhanced disability premium for children are not included in income-related ESA or new claims for IS and income-based JSA, and are being phased out of existing claims. Income-related ESA does not include a disability premium.

Care component

❑ **Lowest rate**

- Disability premium and element
- Disabled child premium
- Qualifying benefit for WTC
- Childcare disregard in HB/CTB
- Childcare element in WTC
- Christmas bonus
- No non-dependant deductions (HB/CTB, ESA/IS/JSA housing costs)
- Student eligibility for income-related ESA
- Energy efficiency grant
- Parental leave from work (child up to age 17)

❑ **Middle or highest rate**

- Carer's allowance carer test
- Home responsibilities protection
- IS – carer's eligibility
- Carer premium test
- Severe disability premium
- Additional amount for severe disability – guarantee credit of pension credit

❑ **Highest rate**

- Enhanced disability premium
- Severe disability element
- Independent Living Fund
- Personal capability assessment exemption

Mobility component

❑ **Lower rate**

- Disability premium and element
- Disabled child premium
- Qualifying benefit for WTC
- Childcare disregard in HB/CTB
- Childcare element in WTC
- Christmas bonus
- Student eligibility for income-related ESA
- Energy efficiency grant
- Parental leave from work (child up to age 17)

❑ **Higher rate**

- Exemption from road tax
- Blue Badge
- Motability
- Driving licence at age 16

Renewal and top-up claims from age 65

If a DLA award ends after you reach 65, you can make a renewal claim within one year of your previous award ending. If you leave it longer than a year, you have to claim attendance allowance (AA), which has no mobility or lower rate care equivalents. You can only re-claim your former rate of mobility component under this concession – you cannot switch rates after 65.

Care component – You can maintain or renew the lowest rate if you qualified for it before reaching 65. If your care needs lessen after 65, you cannot drop to the lowest rate – you will lose the care component altogether. You can, however, regain the lowest rate if you re-claim within 12 months of your previous award for it ending. If your care needs change after reaching 65, you can switch between the middle and highest rates or move up from the lowest rate, but you must satisfy a 6-month qualifying period.

DLA Regs, Sch 1, para 3(2)&(3)

There is an exception that allows the DWP to drop you to the lowest rate even if you pass the disability test after age 65. This applies if the DWP decides you were not entitled to the rate you were getting before reaching 65 because the original decision maker did not know about, or made a mistake about, a fact in your case (rather than because your circumstances have changed).

CDLA/301/2005

If you have the mobility component, a change in your care needs after you reach 65 enables your DLA award to be 'superseded'. This means you can claim the care component (at the middle or highest rate), rather than AA, even if you are aged, say, 70. You can still claim the lowest rate of the care component after 65 if you met the qualifying conditions before 65 and have a current mobility award made before 65.

DLA Regs, Sch 1, para 7; CSDLA/388/00

Mobility component – Once you reach 65 you can only stay on the rate you got before you were 65. You cannot move up or down a rate. But there is an exception to this rule. You can switch to the higher rate after age 65 if you can show that you met the higher rate conditions before age 65.

If you have a current award of the care component, made before you were 65, you can claim the mobility component after your 65th birthday if your mobility difficulties began before you were 65. If your mobility problems are such that you can only satisfy the disability test after your 65th birthday, you cannot get the mobility component.

DLA Regs, Sch 1, paras 1, 5 & 6; CSDLA/388/00

4. Qualifying periods

Backwards test

Under 65 – To qualify for DLA you must pass the disability test(s) throughout the three months before your claim. You can, however, claim (or ask for the award to be superseded) before the three months are up. If your condition starts to get worse before you are 65, you can move up a rate from three months afterwards (even if you are over 65 at the end of this qualifying period).

SSCBA, Ss.72(2)(a) & 73(9)(a); DLA Regs, reg 3 & Sch 1

Over 65 – If your care needs change on or after your 65th birthday, the qualifying period is six months, the same as for attendance allowance. If your mobility gets worse on or after your 65th birthday, you cannot get mobility component for the first time or switch rates.

Terminal illness – Whatever your age, there is no qualifying period if you are awarded DLA because you are terminally ill (see Box B.4). You will automatically get the highest rate care component, but to get mobility component you have to pass one of the disability tests (see 18 below) from your date of claim.

SSCBA, Ss.72(5) & 73(12)

Renal dialysis – If you've passed the dialysis test (see 17 below) during the three months before your claim, you have served the qualifying period. Spells dialysing at least twice a week in hospital or as an outpatient getting help from hospital staff always count for the purposes of this qualifying period.

DLA Regs, reg 7(3)

Linked claims – If you re-claim DLA within two years of the end of your previous award, the claims are linked. This means if you have a relapse you don't have to re-serve the qualifying period. You can get DLA as soon as you re-claim, but only at the previous rate and component. If you qualify for a different amount, you will have to serve the qualifying period before it is paid.

If you are over 65, the 6-month qualifying period may apply and you can only have up to one year off DLA (see 3 below).

DLA Regs, Regs 6 & 11

Forwards test

You have to show you are likely to satisfy the disability test(s) throughout the six months after your claim.

SSCBA, Ss.72(2)(b) & 73(9)(b)

5. How much do you get?

You can get one of the three rates of care component and one of the two rates of mobility component. You'll always get the highest rate to which you are entitled. Each person in your family who qualifies for DLA may claim it. Payment of DLA is affected by some situations (see 6 below).

DLA acts as a 'passport' for other types of help (see Box B.2).

Care component	per week
Highest rate	£70.35
Middle rate	£47.10
Lowest rate	£18.65

Mobility component	per week
Higher rate	£49.10
Lower rate	£18.65

The disability tests for the care component are explained in 9 to 17 below. The disability tests for the mobility component are explained in 18 to 22.

6. Does anything affect what you get?

Earnings – DLA is not affected by earnings. It is payable whether you work or not, and no matter how much you earn. However, starting work may suggest your care needs or mobility problems have lessened, or you have found a way to cut back on the help you need from another person. Your DLA can be superseded because of this, but not just because you have started work. You should tell the DWP if you start work, but if your care needs or mobility problems are unchanged, you should have little to worry about. You may even have more care needs to enable you to do your job.

Other benefits or help – DLA is usually payable in full on top of any other social security benefit or tax credit. The only exceptions are outlined below.

Constant attendance allowance as part of industrial injuries disablement benefit or war pension overlaps with the care component. You'll be paid the higher of the two. War pensioners' mobility supplement overlaps with mobility component – so you'll get the supplement instead.

OB Regs, Sch 1, para 5

DLA is ignored as income for means-tested benefits and tax credits. However, if you are claiming income support (IS) on an 'urgent needs' basis, DLA is taken into account. In all other cases, however, DLA may trigger extra benefit or tax credit. If you are awarded DLA, check to see if you then qualify for IS, income-based jobseeker's allowance, income-related employment and support allowance, pension credit, housing benefit, council tax benefit, working tax credit or child tax credit, or higher amounts of any of these benefits. See Box B.2 for how getting DLA may help you qualify for other types of help in cash or kind.

The care component may be taken into account in non-social security means tests, such as in charging for local authority services (discretionary rules) and care in a care home (national rules) – see Chapter 28(6) and Box L.2 in Chapter 34. However, the mobility component has specific protection against means testing – it can only ever be taken into account if the law (not policy or practice) governing such a test of means specifically states that the mobility component should count. Always ask for a reference to the exact legal provision under which mobility component is said to count as income.

SSCBA, S.73(14)

If you go abroad – See Chapter 51(7) for details.

Refusing medicals – When you claim DLA, the decision maker can send a DWP-approved healthcare professional to visit you to carry out a medical examination. If you refuse to undergo the medical, the claim will be decided against you unless you have 'good cause' for your refusal.

SSA, S.19

You may also be asked to undergo a medical examination if you want your DLA award to be revised or superseded, or if the decision maker considers it necessary to check it is correct (eg as part of the Right Payment Programme – see 25 below). In these circumstances, two consecutive failures to undergo a medical examination can result in payment of some or all of your DLA being suspended – but not if you have good cause for your actions. You'll be repaid if the decision maker decides you no longer need to undergo a medical examination, eg if you have been able to supply acceptable alternative evidence. But if payment continues to be suspended for one month or more, your entitlement may end.

SSA, S.24; D&A Regs, regs 19 & 20

If you go into prison – Payment of DLA is suspended if you go into prison on remand to await trial. If you do not receive a custodial sentence, including a suspended sentence, you'll be paid arrears of DLA for the time you spent on remand.

SSCBA, S.113(1)(b)

If you go into hospital or a care home – Payment of the care component is affected by a period in hospital or a care home. Payment of the mobility component is affected only by a period in hospital; it is paid as normal in a care home. See 7 and 8 below.

7. If you go into hospital

Generally, payment of both the care component and the mobility component stops after you've been in hospital for 28 days (for adults) or 84 days (for children under 16).

Payment of benefit starts again from the first benefit pay day (usually a Wednesday) after you leave hospital. If you leave hospital temporarily and expect to return within 28 days, you can be paid DLA for each day out of hospital (see Chapter 35(6)).

The mobility component can continue to be paid in hospital while you have a Motability agreement in force. Long-stay patients in hospital since before 31.7.95 may be able to keep the mobility component, cut to the lower rate.

If you first claim DLA when you are already in hospital, you cannot be paid until you leave. But you can then be paid for the full 28 (or 84) days if you return to hospital, even if you do so within 28 days.

For more details of how DLA is affected by stays in hospital, see Chapter 35.

A B C D E F G H I J K L M N O P Q R S T U

Back to hospital within 28 days? – If you are readmitted to hospital, having been at home for 28 days or less since you were last in hospital, the number of days during each hospital stay are added together and payment of DLA stops after a total of 28 (or 84) days.

You count days in hospital from the day after you are admitted to the day before you go home. Neither the day you go in nor the day you leave count as days in hospital. Box B.3 shows how you can plan a pattern of respite care that enables you to keep your DLA.

Linked spells in a care home – For the care component, if you go into hospital straight from a care home, or after having been home for 28 days or less, the two periods are added together, and the care component stops after 28 (or 84) days in total (see 8 below).

DLA Regs, regs 8 & 10, 12A-12C

8. If you go into a care home

Normally, you cannot be paid the care component if you live in a care home, but you should apply for it anyway. Once you establish that you pass the disability tests, you can be paid the care component for any day you are not in a care home – eg you are in your own home or staying with relatives.

This chapter gives the main points about being paid the care component in a care home. Chapter 33(2) gives further details. If you are entitled to DLA care component but are

B.3 Respite care

This box explains how DLA is affected if you go in and out of hospital or a care home more than once and how you could keep your benefit if you plan a pattern of respite care. You should also read Chapter 3(7) and (8), Chapter 33 for the effect on benefits of a stay in a care home, and Chapter 35 for hospital stays.

The linking rule

Payment of both care and mobility components stops after you've been in hospital for 28 days (84 days for children under 16). If you go back into hospital after being at home for 28 days or less, the two (or more) hospital stays are linked. Adding together the number of days in hospital in each linked stay, DLA stops after a total of 28 (or 84) days. You are still paid for days at home.

Similarly, payment of care component stops after you've been in a care home for a total of 28 days (adults and children) in one stay, or in linked stays where the gaps at home are 28 days or less. The mobility component is not affected by stays in a care home.

If you go into hospital then into a care home, or the other way round, payment of care component stops after 28 days, adding together days spent in hospital and in the care home. Stays in hospital and a care home are linked if they follow on from each other or if you spend 28 days or less at home in between. If a child under 16 has linked spells in hospital and a care home, see 8.

You count a stay in hospital or a care home from the day after you enter to the day before you leave.

Careful counting

If you keep a careful count of the days you (or your disabled child) are in hospital or a care home, you can establish a pattern of respite care that will allow you to keep the mobility component and/or care component. But even if you can't keep your DLA for all the days in respite care, you can be paid for days at home.

Example: If you have two full days of respite care every weekend you can continue like this for 14 weeks (2 x 14 = 28 days). For 14 weekends, you can go into respite care on a Friday and return home on a Monday. Only Saturday and Sunday count as days in hospital or a care home – the day you enter and the day you leave count as days at home.

If your respite care is provided in a care home, the care component will not be paid for days of respite care (Saturday and Sunday) after the 14 weeks unless you break the link (see below) – although you can be paid for days at home (Monday to Friday). Your mobility component is not affected by a stay in a care home so continues to be paid as usual.

If your respite care is provided in hospital, neither the mobility component (unless you have a Motability agreement in force) nor care component will be paid for respite days after the 14 weeks unless you break the link. You will continue to be paid DLA for days at home.

If a child under 16 is in hospital, you could continue this pattern for 42 weeks (2 x 42 = 84 days), before losing payment of DLA for further days in hospital until you break the link.

Break the link

If you spend 29 days in your own home, you will break the link between respite care stays. The next time you go into respite care in a care home, your care component can be paid for another 28 days, in one stay or in linked stays. Similarly, the next time you go into respite care in hospital, your care and mobility component can be paid for another 28 days (84 days for children).

A pattern of respite care interrupted by spells of at least 29 days in your own home will allow you to keep the care and mobility component. Direct payments of DLA into a bank or other account will continue, but you must give the Disability Contact & Processing Unit details of all dates you enter or leave respite care.

In the example above, you can break the link and at the same time continue to have some respite care. For the next four weekends, instead of going into respite care on a Friday and leaving on a Monday, you go in on the Saturday morning and return home on the Sunday evening. Because the day you enter and the day you leave hospital or a care home count as days at home, you'll have spent more than 28 days in a row at home and so you'll have broken the link. For the next 14 weekends, you can return to your main Friday to Monday pattern of respite care.

Informing the Disability Contact & Processing Unit

When you first go into respite care, always write to the Disability Contact & Processing Unit (see inside back cover), giving the name and address of the home or hospital you are going to, the date you will be entering it and the date you will be leaving to return to your own home. If you have planned a specific pattern of respite care in advance, let the Unit have details. Keep a copy of your letter. If there are any changes from your planned pattern of care, write and let the Unit know.

Arranging or keeping to a pattern of respite care that allows you to keep your DLA (by breaking the link every 28 days) will not always be possible. Until that link is broken, you will not be entitled to the care component (or mobility component in the case of hospital stays) for any further days spent in respite care from the 29th day onwards. However, you will be entitled for the days spent in your own home. When you tell the Unit the dates you'll be entering and leaving care, the Unit adjusts each payment to your bank or other account as necessary. You are unlikely to wait longer than your next pay day for what you are owed.

told you will not be paid, or if your DLA stops because of the care home rules, it is worth seeking expert advice. If you receive a form asking about your accommodation and how it is funded, seek advice, as it is often not easy to know how your accommodation should be described.

The mobility component is not affected by stays in a care home. The rules below apply only to the care component.

What is a care home?
A care home is defined as an *'establishment that provides accommodation together with nursing or personal care'*. Payment of DLA care component may be affected if any of the costs of your accommodation, board or personal care are met out of public or local funds under any of the following legislation:

- Part III of the National Assistance Act 1948;
- Part IV of the Social Work (Scotland) Act 1968;
- the Mental Health (Care and Treatment) (Scotland) Act 2003;
- the Community Care and Health (Scotland) Act 2002;
- the Mental Health Act 1983; *or*
- any other legislation *'relating to persons under disability or to young persons or to education or training'*.

SSCBA, s.72(9)&(10); DLA Regs, reg 9(1)&(2)

People who are entitled to DLA care component in care homes
See Chapter 33(2) for more detail, but, in brief, you can receive DLA care component even if you are in a care home if:

- you are terminally ill and residing in a hospice, defined as *'a hospital or other institution whose primary function is to provide palliative care for persons... suffering from a progressive disease in its final stages'* (but not an NHS hospital);

DLA Regs, reg 10(6)&(7)

- the local authority has accommodated you with someone in a private dwelling and you are under age 18 and accommodated because of your disability or are under age 16 and being looked after by the local authority;

DLA Regs, reg 9(4)&(5)

- you are a child living outside the UK and being funded under the Education Act (such as at the Peto Institute Hungary);

DLA Regs, reg 9(4)(c)

- your accommodation is funded by a student grant or loan;

DLA Regs, reg 9(3)

- you are living in a care home and paying the fees for accommodation, board and personal care in full with or without the help of benefits such as income support or pension credit. In Scotland, if you are 65 or over and get free personal care payments from the local authority, you are not paid DLA care component in a care home even if you are otherwise self-funding. If you are self-funding except for nursing care payments, you can be paid DLA care component;

DLA Regs, reg 10(8)

- the local authority is paying your fees only until you are able to repay them in full (eg once you sell your house) – see Chapter 33(2).

The 4-week concession
If you claim the care component before you are in a care home, this can continue for up to 28 days (for adults and children), even if you are not normally entitled to it, as described in the rules above. Payment may stop sooner if you have been in a care home within the previous 28 days. In this case, the different periods are added together and treated as one stay, and your care component will stop after a total of 28 days. You count a stay in a care home from the day after you enter to the day before you leave. Box B.3 shows how you can plan a pattern of respite care that allows you to keep your care component.

If you are not normally entitled to the care component, as described in the rules above, and do not claim it before you go into a care home, it is not payable until you leave. Once you leave, you can be paid for the first 28 days after you return to the care home, even if you do so within 28 days. This only applies to your first period of payment. After that, any periods with less than 28 days between are added together.

DLA Regs, reg 10(5)

Temporary absences
Once you are entitled to DLA, it can be paid for days you spend away from a care home, including the day you leave and the day you return. For example, if you spend a weekend at home with relatives, going home on Friday and returning on Sunday, you will be paid the care component for those three days.

Linked spells in hospital and a care home
For the care component, spells in hospital and a care home are linked if the gap between them is no more than 28 days. There is no link for the mobility component because payment is not affected when you are in a care home.

For adults, the care component stops being paid after a total of 28 days in hospital or a care home, or both if you've moved from one to the other with a gap of 28 days or less in between.

The position for children under 16 is more complicated if they have linked spells in both a care home and hospital. Payment of the care component for children continues for the first 84 days (12 weeks) in hospital but in a care home it stops after 28 days. The following three examples show how the linking rule works for children.

- ❑ If you have been in a care home (eg residential school) for, say, six weeks, return home for a week, and then go into hospital, the care component is payable for your week at home and the first six weeks in hospital. This is because you have not yet had a linked spell in hospital or a care home of longer than 84 days – so you can be paid for the remainder of the 84 days you spend in hospital.
- ❑ If you had been in a care home for 12 or more weeks and then went into hospital, the two spells are linked and you will not be paid the care component. You cannot be paid for the 12-week hospital concession because you have already been in either type of accommodation for over 84 days.
- ❑ If you have spent 29 days in your own home, you have broken the link with any earlier spells in hospital or a care home (see Box B.3). If you go into hospital, you can then be paid for the first 84 days. If you go back to a care home you can then be paid for the first 28 days.

B. THE CARE COMPONENT

9. The disability tests
To qualify for DLA care component your care needs must ultimately stem from disability; both physical and mental disabilities may help you qualify. You must need care, supervision or watching over from another person because of your disabilities. You must be *'so severely disabled physically or mentally that ... you require [from another person]'*:

during the day
No. 1 *'frequent attention throughout the day in connection with [your] bodily functions' or*
No. 2 *'continual supervision throughout the day in order to avoid substantial danger to [yourself] or others' or*

at night

No. 3 *'prolonged or repeated attention in connection with [your] bodily functions' or*

No. 4 *'in order to avoid substantial danger to [yourself] or others [you require] another person to be awake for a prolonged period or at frequent intervals for the purpose of watching over [you]' or*

part-time day care

No. 5 *'[you require] in connection with [your] bodily functions attention from another person for a significant portion of the day (whether during a single period or a number of periods)' or*

cooking test

No. 6 *'[you] cannot prepare a cooked main meal for [yourself] if [you have] the ingredients'.*

SSCBA, S.72(1)

Highest rate care component – You'll pass the disability test for the £70.35 highest rate if you satisfy:

- either (or both) No. 1 or No. 2 daytime tests; *and*
- either (or both) No. 3 or No. 4 night-time tests.

Basically, your care or supervision needs are spread throughout both the day and the night. If you are terminally ill, you qualify automatically for the highest rate even if you need no care at all when you claim (see Box B.4 for details).

Middle rate care component – You'll pass the disability test for the £47.10 middle rate if you satisfy:

- either (or both) No. 1 or No. 2 daytime tests; *or*
- either (or both) No. 3 or No. 4 night-time tests.

Basically, your care or supervision needs are spread throughout just the day or just the night.

If you are undergoing dialysis two or more times a week and normally require some help with the dialysis, you may qualify automatically for the middle rate (see 17 below for details).

Lowest rate care component – You'll pass the disability test for the £18.65 lowest rate if you satisfy either (or both) the No. 5 or No. 6 part-time day care or cooking tests. There is an upper age limit for this rate: you must be under 65 when you first start to satisfy either the No. 5 or No. 6 lowest rate disability tests. There is also a lower age limit: if you are under 16 you cannot use the No. 6 cooking test, but you can use the No. 5 part-time day care test.

Children

As well as satisfying any of the No. 1 to No. 5 disability tests, a child or young person under 16 must show that *either:*

- their needs are *'substantially in excess of the normal requirements of persons [their] age'*; *or*
- they have *'substantial'* care, supervision or watching-over needs *'which younger persons in normal physical or mental health may also have but which persons of [their] age and in normal physical and mental health would not have'*.

SSCBA, S.72(1A)

Chapter 37(2) explains how the disability tests apply to children. To get payment from birth, a baby must be terminally ill, in which case the qualifying period, 26-week presence and extra children's tests do not apply. In all other cases, a baby must have needed substantially more help than a healthy baby throughout the qualifying period. For example, if your baby

B.4 Terminal illness

Automatic DLA

If you are considered terminally ill, you don't have to serve the qualifying period to get DLA. Claims from terminally ill people are given high priority under the 'Special Rules', in which case the DWP aims to send a decision within eight working days.

You will qualify automatically for DLA highest rate care component if your death *'can reasonably be expected'* within the next six months. If you pass the 'terminal illness' test, you are treated as satisfying the conditions for the highest rate – even if at the time of the claim you don't need nursing-type help from another person. However, to get the mobility component you must pass one of the disability tests (see 18).

Living with a terminal illness, particularly with the shock on first diagnosis, is distressing. Claiming benefits and sorting out any financial problems may be the last thing on your mind. In part, claiming DLA is an acknowledgement, if not acceptance, of what is happening to you: and you may not be ready to face up to that. Unfortunately, DLA cannot be backdated to before the day you actually claimed it, and there is no extension of the time limit for claiming. All we can advise is to claim as soon as you feel able.

Note that even if you have a terminal illness, you will fail the test if at the time you claim, your death cannot reasonably be expected within the next six months. Talk to your doctor to ensure a claim is submitted quickly. If you are turned down, check with your doctor and ask for a revision or lodge an appeal against that decision (see below), or make a fresh claim when your situation changes.

How do you claim?

Claim in the normal way (see 23). If you are claiming under the Special Rules, you are asked to send a factual statement (a DS1500 report) from your doctor or consultant to the DWP along with your claim-form. Your doctor should have a supply of DS1500 forms.

The person who is terminally ill does not have to sign the claim-form. Another person, including their doctor, can claim benefit on their behalf, for example if the terminally ill person is not up to completing the form, or has not yet been told the full nature of their condition. In this box we refer to the terminally ill person as the 'claimant' even though they may not physically make the claim, or even know about the claim. However, payment will be made direct to the claimant.

Hospital – If you are in hospital when you first claim DLA, it cannot be paid until you leave hospital. If you are in a care home, you can claim and be paid the mobility component as normal, and in some circumstances you may get the care component. See 7 and 8 for more details.

What happens once you claim?

Once you have claimed, a decision maker decides if you satisfy the test of terminal illness. Decisions are based on the evidence about your clinical condition, diagnosis and treatment, which your doctor or consultant gives in the factual statement. The DS1500 report does not ask about prognosis (ie about your life expectancy). However, the decision maker will refer your case to a doctor for expert advice. That doctor may phone your doctor to clarify matters.

If you satisfy the terminal illness test at this first stage, you will be awarded the highest rate care component. Awards are usually made for three years so they can be looked at again if you live longer than originally expected.

If the decision maker considers that you don't satisfy the terminal illness test, based on the information from you and your doctor, a medical examination may be arranged. A DWP healthcare professional will examine you and complete a report. If you still don't satisfy the test, the decision maker will go on to consider your claim under the ordinary disability tests. If the decision on part or all of your claim is negative, you can ask for a revision or you can appeal (see below).

has severe feeding problems from birth, the qualifying period means that payment can only start from the first pay day on or after the day they reach 3 months old – see 7 if your baby is still in hospital. A shorter (13-week) presence test applies if you are claiming for a baby who is under 6 months old. For a young person, the extra tests do not apply during the qualifying period if they will have reached their 16th birthday by the time the award starts.

The starting point

The starting point for your attention, care, supervision and/ or watching-over needs must be that you are *'so severely disabled physically or mentally that [you require]...'*. In most cases this poses no problem.

If you do not have a specific diagnosis of your condition, your needs can still be taken into account. What matters is that you have a disability (ie some impairment in your ability to perform activities) and it affects the way you can care for yourself. For example, a child with behavioural problems who is genuinely unable to control their behaviour can qualify without a medical diagnosis.

R(DLA)3/06

If you have a mental or physical disability (eg depression or cirrhosis) because of alcohol or drug misuse, your care needs should be taken into account even if you could control your habit. If you *choose* to drink alcohol, the short-term effects of intoxication (eg incontinence) should not be taken into account. If, however, you are dependent on alcohol, these effects can count, although you may need to provide evidence that rehabilitation programmes do not cure your dependence or are not suitable for you.

R(DLA)6/06

There is no extra test of the severity of your disability.

10. What is the cooking test?

The cooking test is the No. 6 disability test for the lowest rate care component. You must be aged 16 or over to qualify for the lowest rate on this basis. The upper age limit for starting to qualify for the first time is the day before your 65th birthday. But if you claim before your 65th birthday, the lowest rate can be maintained and renewed.

You have to show that you are *'so severely disabled physically or mentally that... [you] cannot prepare a cooked main meal for [yourself] if [you have] the ingredients'*.

SSCBA, S.72(1)(a)(ii)

The cooking test is intended to be a hypothetical test. It is intended to gauge the level of disability rather than examine your ability to cook. The test looks at whether you can carry out all the activities necessary to prepare a cooked main meal without help from another person.

The cooking test covers people whose disabilities mean they cannot cook at all, even if they had help. It also applies to people who don't normally cook, and to those who do cook but cannot prepare the type of cooked main meal at issue or who need some help to carry out the tasks they are capable of.

What does the cooking test involve?

There are a number of different issues involved in the cooking test. The nature of the *'cooked main meal'* which you have to show you *'cannot prepare'* for yourself is crucial. It should

What if you already get DLA?

If you are already getting the lowest or middle rate care component or the mobility component, you don't have to make a separate claim under the terminal illness provisions. Instead, write to ask for the award to be superseded on the basis that you are now terminally ill. You don't have to send a factual statement from your doctor with your letter, but it will speed up the decision if you do.

If you are successful, the highest rate care component should be backdated to the date you first counted as terminally ill if you told the DWP within one month. If it has been longer than one month, the highest rate can still be fully backdated if special circumstances caused the delay, so explain in your letter why it has taken you longer (eg you were too ill or distressed to cope).

The legal definition of terminal illness

S.66(2)(a) of the SSCBA provides that you count as being terminally ill at any time *'if at that time [you have] a progressive disease and [your] death in consequence of that disease can reasonably be expected within 6 months'*.

The diagnosis question should be straightforward. Are you suffering from a progressive disease? Is the disease one which, by its nature, develops and gets worse, perhaps in identifiable stages? AIDS, for example, counts as a progressive disease because it involves a progressive breakdown of the body's immune system.

What is crucial for qualifying for DLA automatically is the question of prognosis – that your *'death in consequence of that disease can reasonably be expected within 6 months'*. The prognosis test looks forwards, not backwards. It may be that, given your progressive disease alone, your death could not reasonably be expected within six months: but your age or general physical condition may, for example, make respiratory infections more likely. You may be more prone to complications associated with, but not part of, your progressive disease. As long as the progressive disease plays the key role in whether your death can reasonably be expected within six months, you should succeed in your claim for automatic DLA. With diseases such as AIDS or motor neurone disease, the progress and nature of the disease makes you more vulnerable to other conditions: the connection between the disease and those other conditions is clear.

This test does not put an upper limit on life expectancy: it is not a matter of what is the longest period you can reasonably be expected to live. Clearly, no one can predict death six months ahead to the day, nor even to the month. It is quite possible that your death could reasonably be expected at any time within a period of five to ten months ahead. In this case, the upper limit of your reasonable life expectancy would be ten months ahead, with death at that stage fairly certain; while five months ahead would be the start of the period during which your death could reasonably be expected, rather than just being a possibility.

Appeals

Decisions on whether or not you satisfy the terminal illness test can be revised or appealed in the normal way (see Chapter 60). An existing award can also be superseded if your prognosis changes so that you no longer count as terminally ill. If your DLA has been paid under the Special Rules for over three years, you may be sent an enquiry form asking for up-to-date information on your condition.

Harmful medical information – On appeal, if the claimant has not been told about specific medical evidence or advice about their condition or prognosis, and the tribunal considers that disclosure of that advice or evidence *'would be likely to cause [her or him] serious harm'*, it won't be included in any papers sent to the claimant. If you consider that such evidence should be kept from the claimant, you should say in your appeal letter why you think it would be harmful.

TP(FTT)SEC Rules, rule 14

be a labour intensive, reasonable, main daily meal, freshly cooked on a traditional cooker. The main daily meal is intended to be a standard meal for just one person, not for the rest of the household.

R(DLA)2/95

The use of the word 'prepare' in the law puts the emphasis on your ability to prepare all the ingredients ready for cooking. The meal is not intended to be a main meal made up of convenience foods, such as pies and frozen vegetables that involve no real preparation.

You *'cannot prepare a cooked main meal for [yourself]'* if you can only do so with some help. The need for any type of help counts – it doesn't have to involve any effort or be at all substantial. But it must be crucial in enabling you to start or carry on with the tasks you are capable of doing by yourself.

What kind of meal is reasonable (eg vegetarian) depends on the community to which you belong. Because this is a hypothetical test, it is irrelevant that you may never wish to cook such a meal or you cannot afford to do so. Nor is it relevant that you prepare, cook and freeze a number of main meals on the days you actually have the help you need (and then defrost and heat them up in the microwave on the other days). The test depends on what you cannot do, without help, if you tried to do it on each day.

If you would be limited to cooking a very narrow range of main meals you should pass the test (CDLA/17329/96).

Intermittent disability – You don't have to show you were unable to cook on every day of the three months before your claim and are likely to be unable to cook on every day of the next six months. The test is rather about what can be seen as normal for you over a period of time. Taking the ordinary English language meaning of the words, and applying the test to the effects of your disabilities, is it true to say that (over the 9-month period) you *'cannot prepare a cooked main meal...'*?

R(A)2/74; R(DLA)7/03 (HoL: 'Moyna')

The ability to cook a main meal on four out of seven days each week does not mean, in law, that you must fail the test. All depends on the pattern of what you cannot do over the whole of the qualifying period. If you still have difficulties on your good days, that can tip the balance your way, so explain fully what you cannot do on both your good and bad days. In practice, if you say on the DLA claim-form that you need help on one to three days only, your chances of success are much lower.

Reasonableness – The test is one of whether you cannot reasonably be expected to prepare a cooked main meal for yourself. Things like safety, tiredness, pain, nausea, breathing difficulties in a hot, steamy kitchen or the time it would take you to do everything may mean that although you can, in fact, prepare a cooked main meal, it is not reasonable to expect you to do so (see R(DLA)1/97). If you cannot stand for long enough, it may be suggested that you could use a stool. This might be reasonable if all you had to do was wait for a pan to boil, but you might not reasonably be able to peel or chop (eg you might only have the strength and leverage to cut vegetables from a standing position), stir or check food or move pans about on the cooker (see R(DLA)8/02 and CDLA/1714/2005).

Special equipment – The cooking test does not depend on the type of facilities or equipment you have available. The test is satisfied if you cannot perform the tasks necessary to prepare a main meal using normal reasonable facilities and devices (R(DLA)2/95). Whether you could manage by specially adapting the kitchen or making other arrangements is irrelevant. Being able to heat convenience food in a microwave is not relevant. However, if you know how to and do use a microwave to cook main meals with ingredients you prepare yourself, you might not pass the test. If you use a microwave in this way explain any drawbacks, eg can you only cook a narrow range of meals or do ingredients cooked first need to be kept warm and, if so, are you able to use a low oven?

Practice and process

To produce an edible cooked main meal calls for the ability to carry out, by yourself, all the physical and mental actions, tasks and stages involved in the process. If there is any part of the process you are (or would be) unable to carry out by yourself, you'll pass this test – even if you cope (or would cope) well with the rest. See R(S)11/81 for support.

If you have a severe mental disability and therefore cannot plan ahead or complete complex tasks, you will pass the cooking test. If lack of motivation is caused by, or is a symptom of, a mental disability, so that you cannot begin to prepare a meal or complete the preparations, you could pass the test (CSDLA/80/96).

The process of preparing a cooked main meal includes:

- planning what to prepare for the cooked main meal – eg each type of food and seasoning, and the quantities required. The law says you already have the ingredients for the main meal, so it's debatable whether or not preparation also includes getting them from their usual storage places;
- carrying out all the stages in the correct order and to the required timings;
- washing, peeling and chopping fresh vegetables, meat, etc;
- using taps – eg to fill a saucepan;
- using a cooker – eg lighting the gas, adjusting the heat, opening and closing an oven door;
- putting the food into pans, stirring, tasting, checking whether it's properly cooked;
- lifting and moving full pans on or off a cooker (you are usually expected to use a slotted spoon to drain vegetables, but explain any difficulties moving pans despite this);
- bending to lift pans into or out of the oven (explain why it is reasonable for you to want to use the oven – eg to prepare a reasonable variety of suitable meals – or to use a low-level grill); *and*
- dishing up your meal.

11. What is 'attention'?

'Attention' means active help from another person to do the personal things you cannot do for yourself. It does not matter whether you actually get the help; what counts is the help you need. It must also be help that would need to be given in your presence, not, for example, over the telephone.

To count as 'attention', the help you need because of your disability must be in connection with your 'bodily functions' and it must be 'reasonably required'.

Help with bodily functions

Bodily functions are personal things such as breathing, hearing, seeing, eating, drinking, walking, sitting, sleeping, getting in or out of bed, dressing and undressing, going to the toilet, getting in or out of the bath, washing, shaving, communicating, speech practice, help with medication or treatment, etc. Anything to do with your body and how it works can count.

R(A)2/80

Indirect or ancillary attention counts but is often forgotten. Think about the beginnings and ends of particular activities. If there are other tasks involved during the course of attending to a bodily function, these can count if they are done on the spot. For example, if you need help to change bedding because of incontinence, then rinsing out the bedclothes if done straight away also counts, as can soothing you back to sleep. If you need help with eating, then cleaning up spills may also count.

R(A)2/98 (HoL: 'Cockburn'); R(A)2/74; R(DLA)2/03 (CoA: 'Ramsden')

If there is part of an activity you need help with (and

could not carry on without it) that also counts. For example, you may be able to dress yourself, but you cannot get your clothes, or you need to be prompted to dress. It is irrelevant that you can manage most of the activity by yourself. If it takes you a long time to do something, eg getting dressed, you may reasonably require help even though you persevere and eventually manage by yourself.

If you are deaf, the help of an interpreter to communicate counts, as does assistance in developing communication skills. Extra effort attracting your attention may count (R(DLA)1/02). The extra effort involved in two-way communication if one of you is not adequately skilled in sign language may also be included as 'attention' (R(DLA)3/02).

Help to overcome problems communicating or interacting with others may count if, for example, you have a learning disability. This is because brain function also counts as a bodily function. This help can include someone prompting you or keeping you motivated if your concentration is impaired (R(DLA)1/07). If you have dyslexia, help to develop reading and writing skills may count (CDLA/1983/06).

Domestic duties and other kinds of help

You might need help with things that can't easily be seen as bodily functions, such as reading, guiding, shopping, cooking, housework, etc. But if your disability is such that there is one bodily function that is 'primarily impaired', then whatever activities you need help with in connection with that impaired bodily function can count (as long as it is *'reasonably required'*). For example, in the case of a blind person, the 'primarily impaired' function is seeing. So help reading correspondence or labels, or with guiding – anything you would do for yourself if your sight were not impaired – can count. In this example, the help would be attention in connection with the bodily function of seeing, not reading, which is not a bodily function, or walking, which is not itself impaired by loss of sight. Similarly, if you are deaf or paralysed, the primarily impaired function is hearing or movement. Once you have identified the impaired bodily function, think of all the help you need from other people to do things you could do for yourself if you did not have that disability. You don't actually have to be getting help, it is enough that the help is *'reasonably required'* (see below).

R(A)3/94 (HoL: 'Mallinson')

In each case, the help you need must be carried out in your presence and involve some personal contact with you – this can be physical contact or talking or signing. Generally, this rules out domestic tasks such as cooking, shopping and cleaning – they are not themselves bodily functions nor would they normally need to be carried out in your presence. However, while it would not count if someone does the cooking for you, if someone helps you to do the cooking *for yourself*, eg reading labels and recipes, checking cooker settings, this could count if it is reasonably required (see below). You might argue it is reasonable for you to develop or maintain a level of independence. In practice, the DWP has not accepted that help to do domestic tasks counts. But if you need to include such help to meet the required frequency of attention, give details of all the help you need. Try to link the help you need to the bodily function that is impaired – and be prepared to appeal.

There is conflicting case law. To start with, see CDLA/12045/96 about help for a blind person to carry out domestic tasks themself, in which the Commissioner approved CDLA/8167/95 as reflecting the weight of authority. See also CDLA/3376/05.

Disabled parents

Help to care for your child can count as attention. The help must be given to you to enable you to look after the child. For example, lifting a baby so a mother with arthritis can breastfeed counts as attention but undressing a child because the mother cannot manage buttons does not. Waking a deaf parent at night to feed or attend to a child can count. For any help you need to wash, dress, toilet, feed or play with your child, explain how the help is given to you rather than to the child. The help must be of a close and intimate nature involving you physically or involving talking or signing with you present. You must show that you reasonably need this help to look after your child yourself rather than having someone else do it for you. You could argue, for example, that you need to bond with a baby or that it is reasonable for you to have help to take part in your child's outdoor activities. Parents cannot always persuade the DWP that such help counts for DLA but you are likely to have more success for babies and younger children or for a sick child (see CDLA/5216/98, CDLA/4352/99 and CDLA/16129/96).

'Reasonably required'

The attention you need must be *'reasonably required'* rather than medically required (R(A)3/86). You may reasonably require more attention than you actually get. For example, if the only help you get is over the telephone, perhaps to encourage you to dress or eat or to check on you, you may well argue that your needs would be more reasonably met by direct help in your presence, or more direct help than is actually available to you. If you are deaf, communication might be easier if you had an interpreter (see R(DLA)3/02). Think about activities you manage only with difficulty or in an unsafe way, even if you don't actually get help from another person.

The test is whether *'the attention is reasonably required to enable [you] as far as reasonably possible to live a normal life'*. This includes social, recreational and cultural activities – what is reasonable depends on your age, interests and other circumstances.

R(A)2/98 (HoL: 'Fairey')

The DLA claim-form asks about the help you need with hobbies, interests and social or religious activities at home and when you go out. Include things you don't do now but would do if you had the help, perhaps things you used to enjoy or things you would like help to do. For each activity explain the help you need from another person with respect to your bodily functions (see above) – eg help getting into outdoor clothes, getting into a car, getting in or out of a chair.

Refusing medical treatment

If you refuse medical treatment that would reduce the help you need from others, you may find this help is consequently not taken into account. You should explain why your refusal is reasonable. You cannot be expected to undergo invasive surgery nor should it count against you if treatment would have unwanted side effects or if a psychiatric condition leads you to avoid treatment (R(DLA)10/02).

During the day

Frequent attention – To pass the No. 1 disability test (see 9 above), you must show that during the daytime you need this help frequently and throughout the day – during the middle of the day, as well as in the morning and evening. The fact that you can manage most of your bodily functions without help does not mean you fail this test; it depends on the pattern of your accepted care needs.

'Frequent' means *'several times – not once or twice'* (R(A)2/80), and the pattern of help must be such that, looking at all the facts about your accepted care needs as a whole, it is true to say you need *'frequent attention throughout the day'*. It is difficult to give a clear dividing line between passing the test and not, so give as full a picture of your care needs as you can. Describe the help you need, why you need it and when it is provided. Are your care needs spread throughout the day or in two or three parts of the day? Is the care provided when you need it or when your carer is available? Would it be better for you if help was provided at other times or for longer?

If your care needs vary because your condition fluctuates, give an idea of the pattern of those needs over, say, a month or whatever period of time accurately reflects your circumstances; it may help to keep a diary (see 15 below). The decision maker must then focus on what care you need and the pattern of those needs, rather than the length of time it takes to meet your needs and the gaps between the attention.

See R(A)4/78, CA/140/85 and 10 above (under 'Intermittent disability')

Significant portion – To pass the No. 5 disability test for the lowest rate (see 9 above), you must show you need help from another person for a *'significant portion of the day'*. That help may be needed all at once, or over a number of occasions. You should pass this test if it would take an hour or so in total to give you the help you need (see CDLA/58/93).

This test for the lowest rate is intended to cover people who, for example, need help only getting up and going to bed but can manage on their own for the rest of the day. But it can also cover anyone whose care needs aren't sufficiently spread out over the whole day to fit the pattern for *'throughout the day'*.

Less than one hour's care may still count as a significant portion of the day. In deciding this, the position of the carer may be taken into account. If the carer's own life is disrupted by the need to give attention for short periods of time on a considerable number of occasions in the day, then those periods of providing attention taken together may be significant, even though individually they may be relatively insignificant. Periods of intense, concentrated activity may be more significant than more routine tasks.

CSDLA/29/94; R(DLA)2/03 (CoA: 'Ramsden')

Depending on the frequency and pattern of your accepted care needs, it may also be possible to pass the *'frequent attention'* test for the middle rate even though it would take less than an hour in all to give you the help you need. If you need an hour (or less) of help on and off several times over the course of the day, the pattern of your care needs should pass the frequent attention test. If the pattern of your needs isn't clear on your DLA claim-form, keep a diary for a short time to make sure you are not wrongly awarded the lowest rate (see 15 below).

During the night

During the night the help that you need must either be *'prolonged'* (normally at least 20 minutes) or *'repeated'* (needed two times or more).

R(A)2/80, R(DLA)5/05

There is no fixed time for the start of the night. It depends on when your household closes down for the night. It normally starts when your carer goes to bed and ends when they get up in the morning. Night-time for a disabled child is when the parent is in bed, so any attention a parent gives after their child has gone to bed but before the parent's own normal bedtime would be daytime attention. On the other hand, if a parent or carer stays up late or gets up early to attend to you, that should count as night-time attention. If you live alone and keep unusual hours, like getting up at 4.30am, your care needs may count as night-time care between the more usual bedtime hours of 11pm to 7am.

R(A)4/74, CDLA/2852/02, CDLA/997/03, R(A)1/04 & CDLA/3242/03

12. What is 'continual supervision'?

Supervision means you need someone around to prevent accidents to yourself or other people. The words used are *'continual supervision'*. This means frequent or regular, but not non-stop; you don't need supervision every single minute. The supervision doesn't have to prevent the danger completely, but it must be needed *'in order to effect a real reduction in the risk of harm to the claimant'* (R(A)3/92).

The supervision must be *'reasonably required'*, rather than medically required (R(A)3/86). For example, you may be mentally alert and know what you should not do without someone on hand to help. Medically speaking, you could supervise yourself. But the question is whether or not you reasonably require supervision from someone else. In practice, supervising yourself might mean that to avoid the risk of danger you would have to do nothing but stay in bed or an armchair. If you would have to restrict your lifestyle in order to supervise yourself without help from someone else, the question is whether or not those restrictions are reasonable. Do they allow you to carry on anything approaching a normal life? If the restrictions on your lifestyle are not reasonable, then you reasonably require help from another person to live a normal life (CA/40/1988).

The next question is whether you satisfy the rest of the continual supervision test, which has four parts.

- ❑ You must show that your medical condition is such that it may (not will) give rise to substantial danger to yourself or to others. The danger to you could arise from your own actions or from the actions of other people. The danger to others could be wholly unintended (eg if you aren't able to care for a young child safely).
- ❑ The substantial danger must not be too remote a possibility. But the fact that an incident may be isolated or infrequent does not rule this out. As well as looking at the chances of the incident happening, the decision maker must look at the likely consequences if it does. If the consequences could be dire, then the frequency with which it is likely to happen becomes less relevant. Explain why a particular risk is reasonably likely in your circumstances.
- ❑ You must need supervision from someone else to avoid the substantial danger.
- ❑ The supervision must be continual, but the person providing the supervision need not always be alert, awake and active. Standby supervision, and being ready to intervene and help, can also count.

R(A)1/83

If you have epilepsy and the onset of an attack is unpredictable, with not enough warning for help to arrive or for you to put yourself in a place of safety, you may qualify for DLA care component, certainly at the middle rate for your daytime supervision needs. This is because of the case of *Moran v Secretary of State for Social Services* (reported in R(A)1/88). The principles in *Moran* help other people whose needs for supervision and attention are unpredictable, and if the consequences of an unsupervised attack would be grave. It particularly helps those who are mentally alert and can supervise themselves between attacks but not during attacks.

Supervision and falls – If you are mentally alert and sensible, it is sometimes said you could supervise yourself and so avoid the risk of falling without help from another person. This approach has been ruled too simplistic by R(A)3/89 and R(A)5/90.

Decision makers must consider the evidence, properly evaluate the risk of falling in any case, and give sufficient reasons for their conclusions. In particular, it is not enough to say you are sensible. They must identify precautions you could take and/or activities you should not do to avoid the risk of falls without help from someone else. It is only if it is *'possible to isolate one or two activities which alone might give rise to a fall, and which could be avoided except for one or two occasions during the course of the day, and [you would] still be left to enjoy a more or less normal life, [that] it would be justifiable to say that continual supervision was not required. Everything will depend upon the facts of the case'* (CA/127/88, para 8). However, there is a close overlap between supervision and attention. Even if your need for help to avoid the risk of falls does not amount to continual supervision, it is possible that particular help could count as attention (see 16 below).

13. What is 'watching over'?

'Watching over' has its ordinary English language meaning, so it includes needing to have someone else being awake and listening, as well as getting up and checking how you are.

Decision Makers Guide, para 61161

Remember, the care component is based on the help or supervision you reasonably need from another person, not the help or supervision you actually get. Your care needs must stem from physical or mental disablement, but it need not be medically essential to have that help or supervision. Rather, you should show that, given all the circumstances, the help is reasonably required. Nor must you need that level of help every night in the week. It depends on the normal pattern of your needs – three or four nights a week may be sufficient, perhaps less if the dangers would be very grave.

A *'prolonged period'* is normally at least 20 minutes.

Decision Makers Guide, para 61165

'Frequent intervals' means at least three times. But it's worth trying if someone has to check on you twice a night.

Tackle the test in the following way.

- ❑ If you need any active help at night (eg soothing back to sleep, rearranging bedding), state that your night-time care needs are both attention and supervision – you might pass the attention test more easily than the watching-over test.
- ❑ Show how your disability or medical condition is such that it may give rise to substantial danger (as in 12 above).
- ❑ Outline the nature of the danger(s). Explain the basis for your fears of danger; refer to anything that supports your fears – eg the previous pattern and course of attacks, wandering at night, falls, etc.
- ❑ Think about simpler methods (see 14 below) that may bypass the need to have another person watching over you. Explain fully how and why they haven't worked, or don't or would not work. Are they reasonable in your circumstances?
- ❑ Explain why you cannot avoid the substantial danger without help from another person – eg because of a mental disorder or an inability to administer medication, oxygen, etc during an attack.
- ❑ Relate the danger(s) to the need to have another person awake and watching over you. Do the dangers warrant having another person watching over you for 20 minutes or longer, or to wake up to listen out for you or get up to check on you two, three, or more times in the night? On how many nights a week?

Remember, the test is based on what you reasonably require, not on what is actually done for you. If you've had a fair number of accidents or incidents at night (or even just one bad accident), that may well suggest you need more watching-over than you've been getting. If you've had few accidents, etc, the chances are that the watching-over you get is the watching-over you need.

14. Simpler methods

It is important to explain why you need particular types of attention or supervision. There may be simpler, more practical ways of meeting your needs. This could mean you don't reasonably (or medically) need as much attention or supervision from another person as you are currently getting, and the decision maker might disregard part of the help you are getting.

If you can show you have tried the simpler methods (whatever they may be) and can explain why they are not suitable for your circumstances, the decision maker should take the help you get into account. In R(A)1/87, the Commissioners said the decision maker should *'explain how his suggestion is practical and compatible with the evidence of [the disabled person's abilities and] agility and with anything resembling normal domestic arrangements...'*. It is clear that a simpler method must also be reasonable.

A typical simpler method is the use of a commode or portable urinal. If you could use one without help, it is often said you don't reasonably require help with trips to the toilet. Doctors often write that you can use a commode, but don't consider all the practical issues involved (eg privacy, hand washing, etc) and without thinking about the effect on your morale or general health if trips to the toilet are your only regular exercise. Decision makers must properly consider the practical issues arising from the suggested use of a commode (CA/3943/06). In any case, you might also need help using a commode. Emptying and cleaning out the commode counts as attention if it needs to be done right away (as it generally would be during the day if not necessarily at night) (CSDLA/44/02).

15. Keeping a diary

Some people won't need to keep a detailed diary of care needs or daily events to support their claims. But for others, it could mean the difference between success or failure, or between being awarded different rates.

If your need for attention is unpredictable or changes from day to day, a diary can show exactly how much help had to be given and why.

If your condition is getting slowly worse, a diary can help pinpoint the date you began to qualify for a higher rate. It can also help you remember things you would otherwise forget because they are so much a part of your everyday life.

If you don't actually get much help, you could note down any incidents or worrying moments when you would have benefited from the help of another person.

If you need continual supervision or watching-over to prevent substantial danger to yourself or others, a diary can show exactly what happened, or what could have happened if someone hadn't been there to stop it.

16. Attention or supervision?

Attention tends to be active help, while supervision is more passive. There is often a close overlap and it can be difficult to distinguish between them. Sometimes both can be given at the same time; for example, if you are deaf and don't have much traffic sense, someone walking beside you could be supervising you (ready to stop you walking) and giving attention in connection with hearing (telling you what you need to know to continue walking in safety).

Similarly, if you are unsteady on your feet and liable to fall, you might need both supervision and attention when walking. The supervision could be a matter of looking out for any unexpected obstacles or uneven surfacing, and being on hand to catch you if you fell. The attention might involve telling you what is in front of you, or it could be a hand on your arm to steady you.

There are many other possibilities where the help you need can amount to both attention and supervision. It is sensible not to divide the help you need into rigid attention and supervision compartments. Keeping a 24-hour diary, listing all your needs throughout a typical day, may help you think about the types of help that could count as both.

If the decision maker does not look at the same needs under both the attention and supervision conditions, you may fail both the day attention and supervision conditions. A long gap during the middle of the day might mean the pattern of help you need does not amount to *'frequent... throughout the day'*. Under the supervision condition, the risk of danger and the situations of potential danger may not be great or frequent enough to warrant continual supervision. Yet if some of the needs considered only under the supervision condition were also considered under the attention condition, the combination of needs could well amount to frequent attention throughout the day (and give you the middle rather than the lowest rate). This argument only works if some of the supervision also amounts to active attention in connection with any bodily functions.

Use the DLA claim-form to explain about all your care needs. If you are unsuccessful, or are awarded a lower rate than you think you should get, you can ask for a revision or you can appeal (see 25 below). In either case, ask that all your needs are considered under both conditions. If you can, list those needs that could count as both attention and supervision.

17. Renal dialysis

Special rules for some kidney patients undergoing renal dialysis help them qualify for the middle rate of care component. Depending on when and where you dialyse, you'll be treated as satisfying the disability tests for the day or for the night. You must show that:

- you undergo renal dialysis two or more times a week; *and*
- the dialysis is of a type which normally requires the attendance or supervision of another person during the period of the dialysis; *or*
- because of your particular circumstances (eg age, visual impairment or loss of manual dexterity) during the period of dialysis you require another person to supervise you in order to avoid substantial danger to yourself, or to give you some help with your bodily functions.

DLA regs, reg 7

Hospital – If you are dialysing as an outpatient and getting help from hospital staff, you won't automatically satisfy the disability tests, but it does help you pass both qualifying periods for DLA (three months backward test and six months forward test – see 4 above). This is helpful if you alternate between outpatient dialysis and dialysis at home. You'll be treated as satisfying the disability tests for the period you dialyse at home (if this is at least twice a week and you need assistance) even if it is only for a short period. If the help you get as an outpatient is from someone who doesn't work for the hospital, this passes the disability test. Inpatient dialysis counts for both the qualifying period and the disability test, but payment of the care component is affected by a spell in hospital (see 7 above).

Other types of dialysis – Continuous ambulatory peritoneal dialysis (CAPD) and automated peritoneal dialysis (APD) are designed to be carried out without help. You can only be covered by the above rules if your disabilities or frailty mean you need help during the dialysis. If you are fully independent in dialysing you are not covered. But if you need even a small amount of help (eg to change the bag) you should pass the day or night disability test. You don't need to show that attention needed is frequent or supervision required is continual.

C. THE MOBILITY COMPONENT

18. The disability tests

Higher rate

To qualify for the £49.10 higher rate mobility component you must be aged 3 or over. For tests 1, 2 or 3, you must be *'suffering from physical disablement'* (but if it is accepted that you have severe learning disabilities which have a physical cause, you may also qualify). Your *'physical condition as a whole'* must be such that:

No. 1 you are unable to walk (see below); *or*

No. 2 you are virtually unable to walk (see 20 below); *or*

No. 3 the *'exertion required to walk would constitute a danger to [your] life or would be likely to lead to a serious deterioration in [your] health'* (see below); *or*

SSCBA, S.73(1)(a); DLA Regs, reg 12(1)(a)

No. 4 you have no legs or feet (from birth or through amputation) (see 19 below); *or*

SSCBA, S.73(1)(a); DLA Regs, reg 12(1)(b)

No. 5 you are both deaf and blind (see below); *or*

SSCBA, Ss.73(1)(b)&(2)(a); DLA Regs, reg 12(2)&(3)

No. 6 you are entitled to the highest rate care component and are severely mentally impaired with extremely disruptive and dangerous behavioural problems (see 21 below).

SSCBA, S.73(1)(c)&(3); DLA Regs, reg 12(5)&(6)

Lower rate

To qualify for the £18.65 lower rate mobility component you must be aged 5 or over. It doesn't matter that you are able to walk but you must be *'so severely disabled physically or mentally that, disregarding any ability [you] may have to use routes which are familiar to [you] on [your] own, [you] cannot take advantage of the faculty out of doors without guidance or supervision from another person most of the time'* (see 22 below).

SSCBA, S.73(1)(d)

Children – There is an extra disability test for the lower rate for children under 16. They must show that either:

- they require *'substantially more guidance or supervision from another person than persons of [their] age in normal physical and mental health would require'; or*
- people of their age *'in normal physical and mental health would not require such guidance or supervision'*.

SSCBA, S.73(4A)

See Chapter 37(2) for more on DLA for children.

Unable to walk?

Being 'unable to walk' means you cannot take a step by putting one foot in front of the other. If you have one artificial leg, your walking ability is considered when using it; you are unlikely to count as being unable to walk but you may qualify on the basis that you are virtually unable to walk.

Effects of exertion

For the third disability test for the higher rate it is the exertion needed to walk that must cause the serious problem. How far you can walk, were you to do so, is not relevant. What is relevant is the effect of the act of walking on your life or health. People with serious lung, chest or heart conditions may qualify in this way; in one case, a man with diabetic ulcers on his feet qualified (CDLA/2973/1999), in another, a woman with arthritis whose need for an operation was hastened by walking qualified (CDLA/3941/2005), and someone with severe anorexia who needed to conserve energy was able to qualify (CDLA/1525/2008).

The *'danger'* or *'serious'* deterioration does not have to be immediate (CM/23/1985). Although any deterioration in your health would not have to be permanent, your recovery would need to take a significant length of time or else need some kind of medical intervention (eg, oxygen, drugs) (R(M)1/98). If you would get better without medical intervention after a few days rest you won't qualify. Danger from other causes besides the effort needed to walk (eg being run over) cannot be taken into account.

Deaf and blind

You may qualify for the higher rate if you are blind and also profoundly deaf. You must show that because of those conditions in combination with each other, you are *'unable, without the assistance of another person, to walk to any intended or required destination while out of doors'*. Blind is defined as 100% disablement resulting from loss of vision. This means loss of vision such that you are unable to do any work for which eyesight is essential. Deaf is defined as 80% disablement resulting from loss of hearing (where 100% is absolute deafness). An average hearing loss at 1, 2 and 3 kHz of at least 87dB in each ear counts as 80% disablement. You will be referred to a DWP healthcare professional to assess your hearing loss and loss of vision.

DLA Regs, reg 12(2); R(DLA)3/95; GB Regs, Sch 2; II(PD) Regs, Sch 3, Part II

19. Other factors

In a coma – If your condition is such that you cannot *'benefit from enhanced facilities for locomotion'*, you won't be entitled to the mobility component. This generally only excludes people who are in a coma or whose medical condition means it is not safe to move them. If you can get out from time to time, even if no one has ever taken you out, you are not excluded from mobility component.

SSCBA, S.73(8)

Personal circumstances – The first three disability tests for the higher rate ignore the effects of personal circumstances on your mobility. Where you live (eg on a steep hill or far from the nearest bus stop), your ability to use public transport and the nature of your employment, are all ignored.

DLA Regs, Reg 12(1)(a)

Artificial aids and medical treatment – You will automatically qualify under the fourth disability test if you have no legs or feet, regardless of your ability to manage with prostheses. However, the first three disability tests for the higher rate do take into account your walking abilities when using suitable artificial aids such as a walking stick, built-up shoe or a prosthesis. If there is an artificial aid or prosthesis that is *'suitable in [your] case'*, and you wouldn't be unable or virtually unable to walk if you used it, you'll fail the test. If you use crutches and can only swing through them, rather than use them to walk with each leg able to bear your weight, then you are unable to walk (R(M)2/89).

A guide dog does not count as an artificial aid, nor do painkillers. What counts is your walking ability under any painkillers or other medication you normally take, if it is reasonable to expect you to take it. For example, it may not be reasonable to expect you to carry a bulky nebuliser even though it helps when you get breathless (CDLA/3188/02). If you have refused treatment which might have improved your condition, that cannot be held against you: it is your ability to walk as you are that counts (R(M)1/95).

DLA Regs, reg 12(4)

Terminal illness – Although you are treated as passing the qualifying period for mobility component, you must actually pass one of the disability tests to be paid mobility component from the time you claim it.

20. 'Virtually unable to walk'

Regulation 12(l)(a)(ii) of the DLA Regulations spells out the factors to be taken into account in deciding whether you are *'virtually unable to walk'*. The test is whether your *'ability to walk out of doors is so limited, as regards:*

- *the distance over which, or*
- *the speed at which, or*
- *the length of time for which, or*
- *the manner in which [you] can make progress on foot without severe discomfort, that [you are] virtually unable to walk'.*

Physical cause

The test of being *'virtually unable to walk'* looks only at physical factors that limit your walking and only at factors that restrict the act of walking outdoors on a flat surface and level ground, rather than, for example, where or when you walk outdoors.

People with a severe learning disability who cannot meet the No. 6 test (see 21 below) may qualify for the higher rate as virtually unable to walk if the interruptions to their walking ability can be shown to be physical in origin (see Box B.5). If you can physically walk but are often unable or afraid to do so, for example, because of mental illness, you may qualify for the lower rate instead (see 22 below).

If your walking is limited by pain or dizziness or some other symptom but your doctors do not know what is causing it or say there is no physical reason for it, it may be difficult to get the higher rate. However, a medical diagnosis is not necessary. Nor should decision makers assume that your disability must be psychological because there is no physical cause identified. They should consider all the evidence. But to get the higher rate your pain, dizziness or other symptoms must have at least some existing physical cause. If it is entirely psychological, you do not qualify. On the other hand, the physical cause need only contribute a little (more than minimally) towards your walking difficulty. So you could qualify even if the pain is made much worse by, for example, depression.

R(DLA)4/06; R(DLA)3/06

CDLA/2822/99 clarifies that, unless there is specific evidence to the contrary, the mobility problems of people with ME are physical in origin and not psychological. Chronic regional pain syndrome should also be accepted as a physical disablement (CDLA/1898/03).

Severe discomfort

From the point you start to suffer severe discomfort walking outdoors, any extra distance you walk should be ignored (R(M)1/81 and CM/267/93). For example, you may be able to walk about 20 metres without too much pain or breathlessness, but this discomfort begins to get worse until eventually you are forced to stop. By the time you stop, you may be in agony. The first question is: at what point do you start to suffer what can be called *'severe discomfort'*? If it is at, say, 40 metres, then any extra walking should be discounted. The second question is whether or not the 40 metres you are capable of walking *'without severe discomfort'* is *'so limited... that [you are] virtually unable to walk'*.

'Severe discomfort' is subjective; different people have different pain thresholds and will show pain in different ways. Severe discomfort does not mean severe pain or distress: *'discomfort is a lesser concomitant [of pain]'*; severe discomfort is a lesser problem than severe pain and is far from being excruciating agony, which would cause the most stoic person to stop walking.

R(M)2/92 (CoA: 'Cassinelli'). This overrules the opposite view taken in R(M)1/91

The Commissioners (in R(M)1/83) have said severe discomfort includes *'pain'* or *'breathlessness'* – factors brought on by the act of walking. It does not include the screaming fits of an autistic child or other factors brought on by resistance to the idea of walking. Normally, severe discomfort has to be brought on by walking, not just by being outside (so that, for example, someone whose skin blistered badly on exposure to sunlight would not qualify), but this does not mean your pain must increase when you walk. If you are already in severe discomfort when you start walking, you can still qualify (R(DLA)4/04).

Distance, speed, time and manner

These four factors affect the ability to walk outdoors and will often be closely interrelated. There is no set walking distance to mark the difference between success and failure. The decision maker must look at the speed, time and manner of walking as well as the question of severe discomfort.

If you are not sure how limited your mobility is, it helps to do a time and motion study on your outdoor walking ability, looking at these four points in turn. Walk until you start to feel severe discomfort (if it is safe for you to do so). If you start to feel severe discomfort, record what happens and when in terms of distance and time. This might include factors like pain, dizziness, coughing, spasms, uncontrollable actions or reflexes, breathlessness, angina or asthma attacks.

These examples are not exhaustive – record whatever you feel to be severe discomfort. Note how long it takes you to recover before you feel able to walk again without severe discomfort.

If an occupational therapist or physiotherapist has assessed you for equipment and adaptations to your home, or you have been getting therapy from one, they may be willing to write a report on your outdoor walking ability – either for a tribunal on appeal or when you first claim. The easiest report may be if they confirm they have read your own time and motion study and agree your results are consistent with their own view of the effects of your physical disabilities. It is useless to get a

B.5 Learning disabilities

If you don't qualify for higher rate mobility component on the basis of 'severe mental impairment' (see 21), you are likely to pass the test for the lower rate (see 22). However, some people who are autistic or deaf/blind, or who have a learning disability, may qualify for higher rate mobility component on the basis of 'virtual inability to walk' (see also 20).

'Virtually unable to walk'?

The need for help to get from one point to another and the purpose of walking are totally irrelevant to the 'virtually unable to walk' test. Instead, this test is tied to physical limitations on a person's ability to put one foot in front of the other and continue to make progress on foot. These physical limitations can include behavioural problems if they are a reaction to or result of the person's physical disablement (eg genetic damage in the case of Down's Syndrome or brain damage).

The virtual inability to walk test looks at interruptions in the ability to make progress on foot. These interruptions have been referred to in R(M)3/86 as *'temporary paralysis (as far as walking is concerned)'*. The interruptions must be accepted as physical in origin and part of your accepted physical disablement rather than, for example, being under your direct and conscious control. Thus, being able to put one foot in front of the other does not stop you passing the virtual inability test. But you must be able to show that:

- your behavioural problems, which may sometimes include a failure to exercise your powers of walking, stem from a physical disability; *and*
- your walking difficulties, including interruptions in your ability to make progress on foot, happen often enough so that your walking is *'so limited... that [you are] virtually unable to walk'*.

Commissioner's decision R(M)3/86 establishes two parts to the 'virtually unable to walk' test:

- ❑ The decision maker should consider separately the distance, speed, length of time, and manner in which you can make progress on foot (see 20). Any walking achieved only with severe discomfort must be discounted.
- ❑ If the decision maker finds you *'virtually unable to walk'*, they must then decide whether that is attributable to some physical impairment such as brain damage, or to a *'physical disability which prevents the co-ordination of mind and body'*.

If you have had a history of behavioural problems since birth, the decision maker *'should provide very clear reasons for attributing the behavioural problems in question to something other than brain damage'* [or Down's Syndrome, etc] (CM/98/89).

What can you do?

- ❑ Provide evidence (from a GP, consultant, etc) to show that:
- the learning disabilities have a physical cause (eg brain damage);
- all the behavioural problems that interrupt outdoor walking stem directly from that physical cause.
- ❑ You can also provide evidence (from a GP, etc) to show it is not appropriate to talk of the person concerned as being able to exercise deliberate and self-conscious choices in the sense of making a *'deliberate election'* to walk or not to walk. The key thing is to get evidence to show that the interruptions in the ability to make progress on foot outdoors are reactions to various stimuli. Those reactions are the result of the brain damage or the genetic damage that caused the learning disabilities, and prevent or interfere with the normal co-ordination of mind and body.
- ❑ You need to be able to give the decision maker a clear picture of the person's normal walking difficulties and the frequency of interruptions in their ability to make independent progress on foot. The idea is to present an objective picture of how the person normally makes, or doesn't make, progress on foot outdoors without active help from another person.

Focus on walking difficulties

We suggest you do this by carrying out a short outdoor walking test. Choose a period of time that you consider long enough to get a good impression of the person's walking difficulties, be it one minute or ten minutes. Ask someone else to take notes if necessary.

For each test:

- ❑ Describe the place where you carry out the test. Mark the starting point. Note the time.
- ❑ Let the person loose. Don't actively intervene to help them walk. A gentle hand on the shoulder or words to help them go in the right direction is OK (to help overcome any fear because they cannot see where they are going). But don't give any physical support or restraint you wouldn't routinely expect to give to a non-disabled person of the same age (so you'll need to be sure the test place you choose is a safe one).
- ❑ Describe exactly what happens. Do they move at all? If yes, then how do they walk? Note what size steps they take; how they lift their legs; the speed of walking; changes in speed and in direction; their balance; and the effect of distractions. This all relates to the manner in which a person walks, and the speed at which a person walks.
- ❑ For each stop or interruption in their walking, note the time, mark the place and measure the distance from the starting point (or from the previous stop).
- ❑ Describe exactly what happened. Why do you think they stopped? Note the time they start to move on again. What made them move on? Or, why do you think they moved on? Give all your reasons.
- ❑ At the end of the period, mark the place they have reached and note the time. How far, in a straight line, is it from their starting point? If they didn't move in a straight line, also measure how far they walked or ran.

Note: If the person's walking ability is also limited by severe discomfort do not continue with the test. As soon as they start to suffer what they, or you, consider to be severe discomfort, note the time and mark the place. Describe the severe discomfort that made them stop. Are there any physical changes in their appearance from when they started walking? Any breathing problems? Any outward and visible signs of their discomfort?

letter simply saying you need mobility component. It gives no help in establishing the extent of your physical walking difficulties, in terms of the legal criteria.

Intermittent walking ability
If your walking ability varies from day to day, you may have difficulty showing that you are virtually unable to walk (including during the two qualifying periods).

It helps to keep an accurate diary. The fact that you can walk on some days might not disqualify you. The question is whether or not the evidence about your walking abilities would allow a decision maker to consider that, looking at your physical condition as a whole, it would be true to say you are virtually unable to walk (including for the duration of the two qualifying periods).

21. Severe mental impairment

This way of qualifying for the higher rate mobility component is aimed at people with severe learning disabilities. If you don't pass this test, you may pass the virtual inability to walk test. Box B.5 looks at how that test applies to people with learning disabilities. If you fail both tests, you will probably pass the disability test for the lower rate (see 22 below).

To be entitled to higher rate mobility component on the basis of severe mental impairment, you must pass the following tests:

- you must be entitled to highest rate care component (even if it cannot be paid because you live in hospital or a care home); *and*

SSCBA, S.73(3)(c)

- you suffer from *'a state of arrested development or incomplete physical development of the brain, which results in severe impairment of intelligence and social functioning'*; *and*
- you *'exhibit disruptive behaviour'* that *'is extreme'*; *and*
- you *'regularly require[s] another person to intervene and physically restrain [you] to prevent [you] causing physical injury to [yourself] or another, or damage to property'*; *and*
- your behaviour *'is so unpredictable that [you require] another person to be present and watching over [you] whenever [you are] awake'*.

DLA Regs, reg 12(5)&(6)

The DWP will normally obtain a specialist's opinion before awarding the higher rate on the basis of severe mental impairment.

'Arrested development or incomplete physical development' must take place before the brain is fully developed, which will be before the age of 30 (R(DLA)2/96). This rules out anyone whose severe behavioural problems start later in life (eg because of a later head injury or a disease such as Alzheimer's). Also ruled out are people whose behavioural problems pass the test in the daytime, but who only get the middle rate care component because they sleep soundly and safely all night. If you are in either of these situations, see Box B.5.

An IQ of 55 or less is generally taken to be *'severe impairment of intelligence'*. But an IQ test is not the only measure of impaired intelligence. Some people, such as those with autism, may do well in abstract intelligence tests but cannot apply their intelligence in a useful way in the real world. For them, an IQ test can give a misleading impression of useful intelligence. Therefore, if IQ is above 55 or there is no IQ test, the decision maker must consider other evidence, including evidence of impairment of social functioning if that has an effect on useful intelligence. For example, having no sense of danger may indicate a severe impairment of intelligence (CDLA/3215/01).

R(DLA)1/00 (CoA: 'M')

You may have to show that the *'physical restraint'* you need to prevent you causing injury or damage involves more than just physical contact, such as a hand on the arm, and that you are likely to need restraining on a significant number of the times you walk outdoors.

CDLA/2470/06 but CDLA/2054/98 says otherwise

You must need watching over whenever you are awake due to your disruptive behaviour being so unpredictable. Because of this, you might have trouble passing the test if your home or school is structured so that your behaviour is no longer disruptive or so that you can be safely left alone behind closed doors. Emphasise the way in which your behaviour is disruptive despite such a structured environment.

If you think you satisfy each part of this disability test and are turned down, consider asking for a revision or lodging an appeal (see Chapter 60).

22. The lower rate

The lower rate is for people who can walk but cannot generally make use of the ability to do so outside unless accompanied by someone to guide or supervise them. People who are visually impaired or have learning difficulties or mental health problems such as agoraphobia are most likely to qualify. You may qualify if you are deaf and cannot understand spoken or written words sufficiently to seek or follow directions alone. You might also qualify if you have falls, fits or attacks and need someone with you to deal with the consequences. There is an extra test if you are under the age of 16 (see 18 above).

Your mobility problems must be due to physical or mental disability. If fear or anxiety prevents you from walking on unfamiliar routes, it must be a symptom of a mental disability. If your anxiety is connected to your physical condition, but could nevertheless be described as a symptom of mental disability, you may still be able to qualify. For example, a deaf person needing the reassurance of a companion to overcome anxiety about being on unfamiliar routes may qualify if their anxiety is classed as a mental disability.

DLA Regs, reg 12(7)&(8)

'Guidance' means directing or leading. It can be physical (eg holding your elbow or putting a hand on your arm) or it can be verbal (eg telling you which turning to take or helping you avoid obstacles). It can also include persuasion or encouragement if you are feeling panicked and too afraid to continue (CDLA/42/94). If you are deaf and cannot read enough to follow road maps or signs and cannot easily understand by lip reading, you may need someone with you to ask for directions or tell you which turnings to take (R(DLA)4/01).

'Supervision' can be more difficult, and there have been conflicting Commissioners' decisions on what constitutes supervision for the lower rate mobility component. If you get the middle rate care component for continual supervision to avoid danger, you could get the lower rate mobility component because of the same problems, but this is by no means automatic: you need to explain what supervision you need outdoors and how this enables you to get about (R(DLA)4/01). You may need supervision when out walking to avoid danger but this need not be the reason for supervision or guidance. What is important is that guidance or supervision enables you to overcome your mobility problems, whatever they are, and to take advantage of your ability to walk, which you would not otherwise be able to do.

You may find it helpful to consider what purpose your companion serves when you are out walking. If they are simply walking with you, you are unlikely to qualify even if you feel better by them being there. Supervision means taking a more active role in enabling you to make that journey. They may be watching you for signs of distress, and can encourage or persuade you to continue, or help you return home if necessary. They can be supervising you by looking out for situations you would find upsetting, such as groups of people. If they are aware of why you have difficulties walking outdoors, on the lookout for those problems and ready to step in to deal with or distract your attention from them, you are more likely to pass the test.

Give examples of what happens when you walk outside in unfamiliar surroundings. Explain what someone else does to enable you to continue walking. If no one was with you, what would happen? Although walking you can do on familiar routes is not relevant, it might help to think of why you can manage these trips. What problems would you have in unfamiliar surroundings? If you cannot manage in familiar places either, this is relevant, so explain any difficulties you have in routes you know and routes you don't know. If you never go out on your own, what is likely to happen if you did? If you never go out at all, you might need to argue that the nature of your disability means supervision or guidance could help you get out (CDLA/42/94). You need not be able to go very far, but you will have problems satisfying the test if no amount of help would enable you to go out (CDLA/2142/2005 and CDLA/2364/95).

D. CLAIMS, PAYMENTS & APPEALS

23. How do you claim?

The DLA claim-form (DLA1, or for children, DLA1 Child) contains a self-assessment questionnaire for the DLA disability tests.

The questions themselves are straightforward but it is important to give as much information as you can and not underestimate the help you need. If you need extra space, use the spare page in the form or a separate sheet (add your name and national insurance number or date of birth). Think about things you can't do or have trouble with, rather than things you can do. If you don't fill in the form fully or your answers don't give a clear picture of the effects of your disabilities, the DWP may get a factual report from your GP or ask a DWP-approved healthcare professional to examine you.

Try to give accurate answers, rather than guesses. Where the form asks how long something takes, don't guess – time it. Where it asks how far you can walk, measure the distance – most people find it difficult to estimate distances with any accuracy. Where it asks about aids or adaptations you use to help you, remember it is your need for help from another person that counts. Explain any problems you have using the aids or adaptations and what help you need from another person to use them, or what help you need despite the aids or adaptations (eg getting out of bed to use a commode at night). It is crucial to explain the help you need from another person, as this is why DLA is paid – not simply because you have a particular condition or disability.

There is a page on the claim-form for someone who knows you to confirm your statements. Ideally, this should be your doctor or another professional, but it could also be done by a carer, relative or friend. Your chances of success will be improved if this person knows about your practical, day-to-day care needs and mobility difficulties so that they can reply to DWP requests for information with more than just a diagnosis of your condition. Tell them you are claiming DLA and explain your needs, and if you have kept a care diary (see 15 above) give them a copy.

Getting help – Many advice and disability organisations can help and some produce guides to DLA and checklists to help people complete the forms. Keep a copy of your completed form in case you are not happy with the outcome and want to challenge it.

To get help from the DWP, ring the Benefit Enquiry Line (BEL – 0800 882200). BEL staff can answer queries about the questions in the DLA1 – using Minicom if you are deaf or sending you the form in Braille or large print. They may arrange for someone to ring you back to go through the form. Bear in mind, however, that the advice you receive from BEL, though often helpful, is not independent of the DWP.

Starting your claim

You can get a DLA claim-form (form DLA1, or DLA1 Child for a child under 16) by ringing BEL (0800 882200), using the postage-paid coupon in the DLA leaflets *Disability Living Allowance* or *Disability Living Allowance for Children* or printing one from the Directgov website (www.direct.gov.uk/disability-dla) – you can also claim online from this website. When you request a claim-form, you may be asked a few questions just to confirm that you do have a potential entitlement to DLA.

If you cannot make the claim yourself, someone else can do it for you. If they sign the form for you, there is space for them to explain why (eg you are too ill to sign).

Renewal claims – If you have been awarded either of the DLA components for a fixed period, the Disability Contact & Processing Unit will write to you up to six months before the award ends to invite you to reapply for the fixed-period component(s). Make sure you return your renewal claim before your current award expires or you could lose benefit. Note, however, that the decision maker may decide to supersede your current award before the expiry date if your renewal claim shows that your circumstances have changed. Your current award could be stopped early, reduced or increased as a result.

Your date of claim

If you write to the DWP or send in the coupon from the information leaflet, DLA can be backdated to the date your letter or coupon reached the DWP. If you phone BEL, DLA can be backdated to the date of your call.

A DLA claim-form issued by the DWP is stamped with the date when you asked for it and with a second date six weeks later, by which time you should return the completed form. The DWP will also give you a postage-paid envelope addressed to the Disability Benefits Centre that will be handling your initial claim. If you claim online, you are given six weeks from the date you accessed the claim online to submit your completed form.

If you return the completed claim-form within six weeks, the date you asked for the form counts as your date of claim. If you take longer than six weeks to return the completed claim-form, explain why on the claim-form. If your delay is reasonable, the time limit can be extended. If not, your date of claim is the day your completed form reaches the DWP.

Advice agencies – If you claim on a DLA1(A) form given to you by a Citizens Advice Bureau or other advice agency, your date of claim is the day your completed form reaches the DWP.

Don't delay – DLA only starts to be paid from the first pay day on or after your date of claim, so you might lose a week or more of benefit if you delay. DLA pay day is normally a Wednesday. If you ask for the claim-form on a Wednesday, you can be paid from your date of claim. If you ask for it on a Thursday, payment cannot start until the next Wednesday. To avoid these delays, start your claim as soon as you can by ringing BEL (0800 882200).

Backdating

DLA cannot be backdated to a date earlier than your date of claim. There are only limited situations in which an earlier date can be treated as your date of claim. These are:

- ❑ If industrial action has caused postal disruption, the day your claim would have been delivered to a DWP office is treated as your date of claim.
- ❑ If a decision maker uses their discretion to treat anything

written as being sufficient in the circumstances to count as a valid claim, the date of that earlier document is treated as your date of claim.

There are plans to allow DLA to be backdated for two weeks, which, when introduced, will also mean you will have just two weeks, rather than six, to return a completed claim-form.

24. Who decides your claim?

Claims for DLA are handled first by one of the regional Disability Benefits Centres or, in parts of Scotland and south England, by the Disability Contact & Processing Unit based in Blackpool. Decisions are made by DWP decision makers, not by healthcare professionals. To help make decisions, the DWP produces online guidance called the *A-Z of Medical Conditions*. This is still being developed and is gradually replacing the previous guidance, the *Disability Handbook*. Both sets of guidance are available on our website (www.disabilityalliance.org/links2.htm). The *A-Z* guidance does not cover children, so the *Disability Handbook* remains the relevant guide for children.

The guidance outlines the main care and mobility needs likely to arise in a number of different illnesses and disabling conditions. If your situation doesn't fit neatly within the picture painted by the guidance or if it emphasises the need for medical evidence, the decision maker may ask your doctor, consultant or other medically qualified person treating you, to complete a factual report. If this does not provide a complete picture, the decision maker can arrange for a DWP-approved healthcare professional to visit you at your home and carry out a medical examination in order to prepare a medical report. Such a visit can also be arranged as an alternative to getting in touch with your doctor, consultant, etc.

Delays – The DWP aims to give you a decision within 38 working days (ie not including weekends or public holidays) of the day your DLA claim is received. If you are claiming under the 'Special Rules' (see Box B.4 under 'Automatic DLA') you should get a decision within eight working days. Compensation may be payable for long delays (see Chapter 62(2) for details).

In any case, if your claim is taking too long, complain to the Customer Services Manager at the Disability Benefits Centre dealing with your claim.

25. What happens after you claim?

Once your claim is decided, you'll be sent a notification of that decision.

Length of your award – Your DLA award could be for an indefinite period or for a fixed period. You can have one component for a fixed period and one for an indefinite period. If you get both components for a fixed period, these will always end on the same day. The DWP may check your award periodically (see below).

In the past, DLA awards could be given for life but awards are now made for an indefinite period. In either case, your award continues for as long as you continue to satisfy the disability tests and other conditions of entitlement. A change in your condition may lead to your DLA award changing (or ending).

If you are not happy with the decision on your claim

Chapter 60 looks at how to challenge a decision. Here we give a brief outline.

You have the right to ask for a revision within one month of the date the decision was sent to you. Or you can ask for an appeal instead – again within one month.

With a revision, a decision maker has another look at your case to see if the decision can be changed. The DWP may ask for more information (eg a factual report or a medical examination) but won't do this in all cases. If some aspects of your claim are not clear, the DWP is more likely to arrange for a short factual report (perhaps from your doctor) concentrating on just those aspects. If the decision maker does not revise the decision, or does but you are still not satisfied with the outcome, you have another month to appeal.

An appeal is to an independent tribunal – the First-tier Tribunal. Before your appeal goes ahead, a decision maker will check to see if the decision can be revised to your advantage. If a decision is revised, you have another month in which to appeal if you are not happy with the result.

Revision or appeal – You can choose whether to have a revision or an appeal. You should get a quicker decision if you ask for a revision, especially if you can get helpful medical evidence to support your claim. But if you simply ask for the decision to be looked at again, it is unlikely to be changed, particularly if you can't add anything to the information you have already provided.

The decision letter gives reasons why your claim has been refused, although in a claim for a child the reasons are not usually detailed. If you are unclear, you should ask for your case papers (see below), which may help you give better information for the revision, but you need to tell the DWP you don't want a decision made until you have had the opportunity to examine the case papers and provide further information. This can add to the time a revision takes but will probably be helpful in ensuring the decision maker has the most relevant information. If you ask for a revision but are not happy with the outcome, you can appeal to a tribunal within one month of that decision.

An appeal takes longer to be determined, and you may be put off by the idea of having to go to a hearing. An appeal can give you more time to examine your case papers and see why your claim was refused. This may help you obtain the most relevant supporting reports from your doctors and carers, and prepare what you want to tell the tribunal about your care and mobility needs. You may also be able to get help with an appeal from your local Citizens Advice Bureau, DIAL or other welfare rights services (see Chapter 61). It is more difficult to appeal against a First-tier Tribunal decision, which would be your next step if the appeal was unsuccessful, so if you are uncertain about an appeal at the start and feel there is more information you can provide, you should try a revision. You will still have the appeal option if the revision is not successful.

You can dispute any aspect of the decision (eg the rate or length of the award, the starting date, etc) and for any reason. You can ask for a revision by phone but it is best to put it in writing. (If you need to phone, perhaps to avoid missing the deadline, confirm your call in writing straight away.) The decision letter should make it clear which office to write to and how to phone them. If you want to appeal, ask for form GL24. Whether you are asking for a revision or an appeal, it is crucial to do so within the one-month time limit, although it is possible to make late applications for appeal or revision if there are special circumstances (see Chapter 60(3) and (7)). If you are successful with the revision or appeal, benefit can be fully backdated.

An 'Alternative Dispute Resolution' scheme has been tested in some areas and may be introduced across the country later in the year. Under this scheme, when you appeal you can opt to have your case examined by the Tribunals Service before they arrange a hearing. If they think the DWP will probably lose, they will tell them, so the DWP can consider revising in your favour – avoiding the need for a hearing. If they think you are likely to lose, they will tell you and give you a chance to get a supporting report from a doctor or carer or look for a representative to help you present your case.

If the decision was notified more than one month ago or there has been a change of circumstances – To challenge a decision notified more than one month ago, you need to show there are specific grounds, eg:

- there has been a change of circumstances since the decision was made – eg your condition has deteriorated and your need for care or your mobility problems have increased;

- the decision maker didn't know about some relevant fact – eg you missed out some aspect of your care needs or mobility difficulties when you filled in the claim-form.

See Chapter 60, Box T.5 for more details.

Warning: When you challenge a decision, the decision maker may reconsider the whole of your DLA award. Similarly, if you make a top-up claim for one component, you may risk what you already have. If you are happy with the decision on one of the two DLA components, say so in your letter; the decision maker need not consider anything you don't raise in your application. This will not, however, afford cast-iron protection to your existing award.

When can you see your case papers? – Your case papers consist of all the evidence used, including any medical reports, in making the decision. If you appeal, they are sent to you but you can ask for copies at any stage.

If you haven't kept a copy of your DLA claim-form, or haven't seen any of the other evidence used in your case, you may have missed some obvious mistakes or gaps in the evidence. Once you have identified them through reading the case papers, get evidence to correct the mistakes or plug the gaps and write a very clear letter to the DWP. Concentrate on explaining how you satisfy the conditions of entitlement rather than, for example, why the evidence from a visiting doctor is inaccurate. By all means point to inaccurate elements of a report, and get further evidence to show it is inaccurate if you can. But then explain the correct situation and what this says about your care or mobility needs.

If you are happy with the decision on one component, you may risk it by asking for the other component. In this situation, it is sensible, before you take action, to ask for a copy of your case papers on the basis that you need to be sure your current award is 'safe'. An experienced adviser may be able to reassure you after reading the case papers.

If you are challenging a recent decision, take care to stay within the one-month time limit for requesting a revision or an appeal, even if you are still waiting for the case papers to be sent to you.

Checking of awards

Whether you have been awarded DLA for a specific period, indefinitely or for life, you must continue to satisfy all the qualifying rules throughout the award. Although the DWP tells you the main changes in your circumstances that you must report, it is up to you to let the DWP know if *anything* changes which might affect your existing benefit, such as improvements or deterioration in your condition.

There is also a system called the Right Payment Programme to check that DLA awards remain correct throughout their term. Under this process, some people on DLA are asked to give up-to-date information about their circumstances.

If your award has been looked at for another reason in the last year, you are exempt from further checking under this process.

Some people claiming because they are terminally ill may have their awards checked under a separate process (see Box B.4).

No one else is exempt from checking but only a small proportion of awards are checked each year. If you are selected, you will be sent an enquiry form that is based on the claim-form and so will be familiar to you. You can ask the DWP for copies of the last DLA claim-forms you filled in, if you have not kept copies, to use as a guide. The enquiry form must be returned within three weeks, although you can ask for a little longer if necessary. It is important to contact the Disability Contact & Processing Unit if you need more time because your benefit can be suspended and eventually terminated if you don't return the form.

D&A Regs, regs 17, 18, 19 & 20

26. How are you paid?

DLA is usually paid once every four weeks in arrears into your bank, building society or Post Office card account. The normal pay day for DLA is a Wednesday. If you are terminally ill, DLA is payable once a week.

Appointees – If you cannot manage your own affairs, the DWP can appoint another person to act on your behalf (see Chapter 59(4)). But DLA is your benefit, not your appointee's benefit. If you are under 16, the appointee is usually your mother. If you don't want someone else formally appointed to act for you, but cannot collect your DLA yourself, you can arrange with the bank, building society or Post Office for someone to do this for you.

27. What if your condition changes?

If your condition gets worse – If you already receive DLA, give the Disability Contact & Processing Unit details of your change of circumstances (see inside back cover for contact details). Your existing award may be superseded to include a higher rate or a new component. A top-up claim for the component you don't already have doesn't count as a new claim, but rather as a change to your existing award. (See also 25 above under 'If the decision was notified more than one month ago...'.)

If your condition improves – If your need for care or your mobility difficulties lessen, this could mean your rate of DLA should drop. Write to the Disability Contact & Processing Unit to give them details. The decision maker will usually supersede your entitlement.

If your rate of DLA drops (or it ends), but you have a relapse within two years, you can regain your former rate of benefit in a linked claim without having to serve the qualifying period again. If you are over 65, you must make your linked claim within a year of your previous award dropping or ending (see 3 and 4 above).

4 Attendance allowance

1. What is attendance allowance?

Attendance allowance (AA) is a tax-free benefit for people aged 65 or over who are physically or mentally disabled and need help with personal care or supervision to remain safe. You do not actually have to be getting any help. It is the help you need that is relevant, not what you get. You can get AA even if you live alone; you do not need to have a carer. AA is not means tested, there are no national insurance contribution tests, and it is paid in addition to other money in most cases (see 3 below).

In this chapter we give only an outline of AA, because the rules are almost exactly the same as for disability living allowance (DLA – see Chapter 3) care component at the middle or highest rate. Below (see 6), we give the key differences between AA and DLA, and list the parts of Chapter 3 which are also relevant to AA.

2. Do you qualify?

You must meet the following conditions:

- you are aged 65 or over; *and*
- you pass the residence and presence tests, and are not subject to immigration control (see Chapter 50(2) and (3)); *and*
- you satisfy one of the disability tests and have done so for the last six months (see below); *or*
- you are terminally ill (see Box B.4, Chapter 3).

If you have not yet reached your 65th birthday you should claim disability living allowance instead.

The disability tests
To pass the disability tests, you must meet at least one of these four conditions. You must be *'so severely disabled physically or mentally that... [you require] from another person'*
during the day
- *'frequent attention throughout the day in connection with [your] bodily functions, or*
- *continual supervision throughout the day in order to avoid substantial danger to [yourself] or others' or*

during the night
- *'[you require] from another person prolonged or repeated attention in connection with [your] bodily functions, or*
- *in order to avoid substantial danger to [yourself] or others [you require] another person to be awake for a prolonged period or at frequent intervals for the purpose of watching over [you]'.*

SSCBA, S.64(2)&(3)

These disability tests are explained in detail in Chapter 3(9) to (16).

Lower or higher rate
The higher rate of £70.35 is for people who need help day and night. If you meet one of the day conditions and one of the night conditions, you will qualify for the higher rate allowance. The lower rate of £47.10 is for people who need help only during the day or only during the night. If you meet one of the day conditions or one of the night conditions, you will get the lower rate.

Kidney patients
There are special rules for some kidney patients to help them qualify for AA at the lower rate (see Chapter 3(17)).

6-month qualifying period
New claim – You must have been in need of care for six months before your award can begin, but you can make your claim before the six months have passed. It doesn't matter if during these six months you could not receive AA in any case – eg if you were in hospital. Make a claim to establish your entitlement, even if you cannot be paid at that time.
SSCBA, S.65(1)(b)&(6)

Terminal illness – If you are claiming under the terminal illness provisions, you can be paid from the date the decision maker accepts that you satisfy the legal test of terminal illness (see Box B.4). Payment usually starts from the Monday on or after the day your claim is received in a DWP office. You do not have to serve the 6-month qualifying period or pass the 26-week presence test if you count as terminally ill.
SSCBA, S.66 & AA Regs, reg 2(3)

Current award – If you already have lower rate AA, you can qualify for the higher rate after you have needed the greater level of attention or supervision for six months. You can put in your request before the six months have passed.
SSCBA, S.65(3)

Linked claim – If you previously received AA (or dropped to the lower rate) and have a relapse no more than two years from the end of that award, you don't have to re-serve the 6-month qualifying period to regain your former rate of benefit. You still need to claim (or ask for your current lower award to be superseded), but you do not have to have needed the help or extra help for six months to be paid. For example, you previously received higher rate AA but this was reduced to the lower rate because your condition improved. You have a relapse within two years and ask for your award to be superseded to include the higher rate. Your higher rate can be paid from the date you make your request, or from the date of your relapse if you tell the DWP within one month. See Chapter 60 for more details on how to ask for benefit to be changed.
SSCBA, S.65(1)(b) & AA Regs, reg 3

3. Does anything affect what you get?
AA can be paid in addition to almost any other benefit – eg state pension or pension credit.

AA is ignored as income for means-tested benefits, so does not reduce the amount of pension credit, housing benefit or council tax benefit. It may, however, be taken into account in the means test for charging for local authority services, and for local authority-arranged care in a care home (see Chapter 28(6) and Box L.2, Chapter 34).

You will not get AA if you are entitled to disability living allowance (DLA). If you get constant attendance allowance with industrial injuries disablement benefit or war pension, this overlaps with AA and you'll be paid whichever is higher.

Check your benefits – Getting AA can trigger extra help with means-tested benefits. You might qualify for a severe disability premium with your housing benefit or council tax benefit, or a severe disability addition with your pension credit guarantee credit. If you have not been able to get these benefits before because your income was too high, you might qualify now. Contact The Pension Service and your local authority to make sure they know you are getting AA. See Box B.2 in Chapter 3 for other help available (in this box the highest rate of DLA care component corresponds with the higher rate of AA, and the middle rate of DLA care component corresponds with the lower rate of AA).

Hospital and care homes – If you go into hospital or a care home, your AA stops after four weeks (see Chapter 3(7) and (8) and Chapter 33(2)).

4. How do you claim?
You can ring the Benefit Enquiry Line (BEL – 0800 882200) and ask for the AA claim-form (AA1). Your date of claim will usually be the day you ring (see Chapter 3(23)). They can also answer any queries. If you write to the DWP requesting AA, your date of claim will usually be the day your letter reaches the DWP. You can also use the online claim service (www.direct.gov.uk/disability-aa); your date of claim will usually be the date you first accessed the online claim. You can also get a claim-form from a Citizens Advice Bureau or other advice centre or download one from the DWP website, but, in this case, your date of claim is the date your completed form reaches the DWP.

If you need help to fill in the form, ring BEL (0800 882200). A DWP adviser can answer queries about the questions on the form. (Bear in mind, however, that their advice, while often helpful, is not independent.)

Backdating – AA cannot be backdated to earlier than the Monday pay day on or after your date of claim. In some limited circumstances, an earlier date can be treated as your date of claim (see Chapter 3(23)).

Medical evidence – The claim-form includes a section to be completed by someone who knows you well; this could be your own doctor or another professional involved in your care. Your completed form may give the decision maker enough information to make a decision. If not, the decision maker may request a short report from your doctor or another medical person you've named on the form. Try to ensure that this person is fully aware of your care and/or supervision needs; if you have kept a diary of your care needs (see Chapter 3(15)), give them a copy. Alternatively, the decision maker can arrange for a DWP-approved healthcare professional to visit you to carry out a medical examination.

Length of award – AA may be awarded for a fixed period or indefinitely. If your award is for a fixed period, the Disability Contact & Processing Unit will invite you to make a renewal claim about four months before the end of your current award.

How are you paid? – AA is paid to you, not to a carer, and you can spend it as you wish. It is usually payable on a

Monday. It is normally paid every four weeks in arrears into your bank, building society or Post Office card account.

5. Decisions and appeals

If you are claiming AA for the first time or after a break, a decision maker at one of the regional Disability Benefits Centres or, in some parts of Scotland and south England, at a unit in Blackpool, will make the initial decision on every aspect of your claim. If you are making a renewal claim, a decision maker at the Disability Contact & Processing Unit in Blackpool makes the decision on your claim.

If you are not happy with a decision, you can ask for a revision or lodge an appeal within one month of the date the DWP sends you the decision. The decision letter should make it clear who to write to. If you ask for a revision, a decision maker will reconsider your claim. They can confirm the initial decision, or increase or reduce the rate of your award, or the length of your award. You have a further month to appeal if you are still not happy. If you appeal first, the DWP will look at the decision again in any case and if they do not revise it to your advantage, your appeal will go to a First-tier Tribunal. Appeal on form GL24.

The one-month time limit to ask for a revision or lodge an appeal can be extended, but only if there are special circumstances for the delay. Otherwise, outside of one month you can ask for the decision to be 'superseded', but only for certain reasons. For example, a change of circumstances such as an increase or decrease in your care needs enables a decision to be superseded. If your care needs increase or you no longer need as much help from other people as before, you should write to the central Disability Contact & Processing Unit in Blackpool (see inside back cover). The DWP can also decide of their own accord to supersede your award. Chapter 60 gives more details about this, as well as fuller details on the procedures for challenging decisions.

6. DLA or attendance allowance?

You cannot claim disability living allowance (DLA) for the first time after you reach your 65th birthday. Once you are 65, you must claim AA instead. If you already get DLA mobility component, however, you can claim DLA care component (at the middle or highest rate) rather than AA, even if you are aged, say 70.

What are the differences?

The main differences between AA and DLA care component are that AA:

- has no £18.65 lower rate for part-time care needs or for the cooking test;
- has a backwards qualifying period of six months in all cases;
- has no forwards qualifying period.

What is the same?

The DLA care component, apart from its £18.65 lowest rate (which has no equivalent in AA), is almost exactly the same as AA. The disability tests for the lower and higher rate of AA and for the middle and highest rate of DLA care component are exactly the same, as is the amount payable. Chapter 3 gives full details of DLA and is therefore also relevant to AA. The relevant parts are:

- Chapter 3(6) to (8);
- Chapter 3(9) and (11) to (17) – The disability tests: but only the No. 1, No. 2, No. 3 and No. 4 disability tests apply to AA;
- Chapter 3(23) to (25) and (27);
- Box B.1;
- Box B.3;
- Box B.4.

If you already get DLA

For someone already on DLA whose care needs start to change when they are aged 65 or older, the DLA rules for the care component are, for all practical purposes, the same as for AA. The qualifying period for changing from the lowest rate to the middle rate or to the highest rate switches from three to six months. See Chapter 3(4).

If you already get the lowest rate care component you can stay on it after reaching 65 and can make renewal claims (including renewal claims made after a break in entitlement to the lowest rate of up to a year). You can also move to the middle or highest rate after a supersession if your care needs increase, but if your care needs decrease you cannot drop to the lowest rate from the middle or highest rate after your 65th birthday. See Chapter 3(3).

5 Help with mobility needs

1. Blue Badge scheme

The Blue Badge scheme of parking concessions is designed to help people with severe mobility problems, registered blind people and those with severe disabilities in both arms by allowing them to park close to places they wish to visit.

You should not be wheel-clamped or towed away if you are displaying a current badge, although your vehicle may be moved if it is causing an obstruction. The badge does not apply to parking on private roads and land but the Security Industry Authority prohibits licensed vehicle immobilisers from clamping, blocking or towing a vehicle displaying a Blue Badge. The badge does not automatically confer exemption from car park charges.

The whole of the side of the badge showing the wheelchair symbol must be visible from outside the vehicle; displaying the wrong (photo) side can result in a penalty.

DP(BMV) Regs, regs 11 & 12

It is an offence not to allow a police officer, traffic warden, parking attendant or civil enforcement officer to fully examine a badge.

Where can you park? – The scheme allows a vehicle displaying a valid badge in the correct place to park:

- without charge or time limit at on-street parking meters and in Pay and Display bays;
- without time limit in streets where otherwise waiting is allowed for only limited periods;
- for a maximum of three hours in England, Wales and Northern Ireland, or without any time limit in Scotland, on single or double yellow lines. In England and Wales a special parking disc must also be displayed showing the time of arrival if you are parked on yellow lines or in a reserved parking place for badge holders that has a time limit (if you are visiting England or Wales from Scotland or Northern Ireland, ask your local authority for a disc). The time limit only applies during the operating hours of the restriction.

This is provided that:

- the badge holder is in the vehicle when it arrives at or when it leaves the parking place;
- the vehicle is not parked in a bus or cycle lane during the lane's hours of operation;
- the vehicle is not parked where there is a ban on loading or unloading; *and*
- all other parking regulations are observed.

LATO(EDP) Regs, regs 7-9

Red routes are subject to special controls on stopping, but there are usually parking bays for badge holders.

Where does the scheme apply? – The scheme applies throughout England, Northern Ireland, Scotland and Wales but there are major differences in the operation of the scheme in certain London boroughs (the City of London, Westminster, Kensington and Chelsea, and part of Camden). See the Blue Badge Map at www.tinyurl.com/Blue-Badge-Map or contact the local authority for details. The scheme does not apply in security zones, such as at airports.

LATO(EDP) Regs, reg 5(2)

In some places you can get a special badge to access pedestrian areas, but the criteria for issue may be different.

Do you qualify? – You qualify automatically for a Blue Badge if you are aged two or over *and*:

- receive the higher rate mobility component of disability living allowance; *or*
- get war pensioners' mobility supplement; *or*
- are registered blind.

You may also qualify if you are aged two or over *and*:

- drive regularly, have a severe disability in both arms and are unable to operate, or have considerable difficulty in operating, all or some types of parking meter; *or*
- have a *'permanent and substantial disability which causes inability to walk or very considerable difficulty in walking'*.

Children under the age of 2 may qualify for a Blue Badge if they have a specific medical condition which means they:

- must always be accompanied by bulky medical equipment that cannot be carried around with the child without great difficulty; *and/or*
- need to be kept near a motor vehicle at all times so that they can, if necessary, be treated in the vehicle or quickly driven to a place where they can be treated.

'Bulky medical equipment' includes in particular any of the following:

- ventilators;
- suction machines;
- feed pumps;
- parenteral equipment;
- syringe drivers;
- oxygen administration equipment;
- continual oxygen saturation monitoring equipment; *and*
- casts and associated medical equipment for the correction of hip dysplasia.

DP(BMV) Regs, reg 4

Applications are handled by local authorities (or the Roads

B.6 Mobility checklist

Information on choosing a car

It is important to choose the car and adaptations that are best suited to you. Contact the Forum of Mobility Centres (see below) for practical advice.

Motability

Motability is an independent charity set up to help people with disabilities use their higher rate mobility component of disability living allowance (DLA) or war pensioner's mobility supplement to improve their mobility. It offers two schemes: contract hire and hire purchase. Both schemes offer cars (including cars adapted to carry a driver or passenger seated in their wheelchair), powered wheelchairs and mobility scooters. Under the hire purchase scheme, it is possible to buy a used car. Many car adaptation costs can be included.

People receiving DLA higher rate mobility component (and the parents of children who receive it) or war pensioners' mobility supplement who need adaptations to their car or help with the initial deposit can apply to Motability for additional discretionary help.

To use any of the schemes, your higher rate mobility component must usually have at least 12 months still to run. The Disability Contact & Processing Unit will make payment directly to Motability.

You cannot start or renew a Motability car agreement if you are in hospital. See Chapter 35(4).

Motability can sometimes help towards the cost of driving lessons if the applicant receives DLA higher rate mobility component and is aged under 25.

For enquiries about the Motability Car Scheme, contact Motability Operations, City Gate House, 22 Southwark Bridge Road, London SE1 9HB (0845 456 4566; www.motability.co.uk). For enquiries about the Motability Wheelchair and Scooter Scheme, contact Route2mobility, Montgomery House, Newbury Road, Enham Alamein, Andover SP11 6JS (0845 607 6260).

Concessions on cars and wheelchairs

Some car companies offer discounts to disabled people, but with increased competition in the retail car market these are less common than in the past. For more information contact Mobilise (see Address List).

The NHS supplies free wheelchairs, and may provide a voucher towards the cost of a more expensive wheelchair of your choice (see Chapter 30(5)).

If you are working, you may be able to get financial help towards a mobility solution through Access to Work (see Chapter 17(2)).

For details on VAT exemption on car purchase price or the cost of adaptations to the car, see Chapter 53. This must be claimed before you purchase the car.

Concessions on public transport

You can buy a Disabled Person's Railcard (£18 for one year), which entitles you and a companion to one-third off the cost of most train journeys. The scheme is for people with a wide range of disabilities; check the claim-form or website for a full list. You can get details from www.disabledpersons-railcard.co.uk or by ringing 0845 605 0525 (textphone 0845 601 0132).

In England, people aged 60 and over and eligible disabled people are entitled to free off-peak travel on all local buses anywhere in England. Application forms are available from local authorities. In Wales, there is a similar concession at any time of the day.

In Scotland, older and disabled people are entitled to free Scotland-wide bus travel on nearly all services. Application forms are available from local authorities or SPT Travel Centres.

For travel concessions in Northern Ireland, enquire at Translink bus and rail stations or ring 0845 600 0049.

Concessions are available on some ferry routes and Eurotunnel for disabled people travelling with a car. Some toll roads, tunnels and bridges offer limited exemption for disabled people. Contact Mobilise for more information (see Address List).

Help with travel to work – see Chapter 17(2).

Assessment services and sources of information

There is a network of accredited mobility centres, members of the Forum of Mobility Centres, which offer professional assessment, advice and recommendations for drivers and passengers with mobility needs. For further information regarding accredited centres ring 0800 559 3636. Advice, information and contact details for Mobility Centres can also be found on their website (www.mobility-centres.org.uk).

Service in Northern Ireland: 028 6634 3700) who may charge a statutory maximum of £2 (or up to £20 in Scotland) to issue a badge, which lasts up to three years. There are plans to change the fee. Some local authorities have attempted to charge increased fees without legal authority to do so.

DP(BMV) Regs, reg 6

Congestion charging exemption – Exemption from congestion charging in central London is available to Blue Badge holders for an initial £10 administration fee if they apply to the Congestion Charging Office (for an application form ring 0845 900 1234 or visit www.cclondon.com). This exemption can be used on any vehicle. Vehicles with an exempt 'Disabled' class tax disc are automatically exempt if they are registered at DVLA, Swansea. Durham operates a similar scheme and other authorities are considering doing the same. Exemptions for disabled people vary, as there is no national exemption scheme.

Appeals – If your local authority refuses to issue you with a Blue Badge you have no formal right of appeal. As many authorities have internal procedures for dealing with appeals, it is worth writing to request a review. Alternatively, your councillor or a disability group or advice agency might help change their mind. You only have a formal right of appeal (to the Secretary of State for Transport) if you have been denied a badge on grounds of misuse, although a review of the scheme has recommended that an appeal procedure be adopted.

DP(BMV) Regs, reg 10

European concessions – Blue Badge holders visiting European Union (EU) countries that provide disabled parking concessions can take advantage of those by displaying their badge. Concessions vary. Details are in the Department for Transport (DfT) booklet *The Blue Badge Scheme: rights and responsibilities in England* (reference T/INF/1214, available from DfT publications 0300 123 1102, or at www.tinyurl.com/Blue-Badge-Guide.) For non-EU countries, see www.tinyurl.com/Blue-Badge-Abroad.

For more information – Contact Mobilise (01508 489449) or The Blue Badge Network (01384 257001). For information on how the scheme operates in London there is the *Blue Badge London Parking Guide* (£5.99, PIE Enterprises, 0844 847 0875; www.thepieguide.com).

2. Exemption from road tax (VED)

Who can get exemption?

All vehicles on the road are liable to Vehicle Excise Duty (VED), better known as road tax. However, exemption from VED (including the £55 first registration fee) for one car is given to some disabled people.

Mobility component – If you get disability living allowance (DLA) higher rate mobility component or war pensioners' mobility supplement, you (or your appointee or someone you choose to nominate in your place) can apply for exemption from VED. Long-stay hospital patients with transitional protection can still get the exemption.

Vehicle Excise & Registration Act 1994, Sch 2, para 19

Technically, the vehicle is only exempt while it is being used solely by or for the purposes of the disabled person. What exactly this means has never been defined. The disabled person does not necessarily have to be in the car: instead, it could be being used to do their shopping or running errands. The use of an exempt car for purposes totally unconnected with the disabled person is technically illegal, although the Driver and Vehicle Licensing Agency (DVLA) has implied that if the car is used substantially for the purposes of the disabled person there is nothing to worry about.

Anyone receiving DLA higher rate mobility component or war pensioners' mobility supplement may automatically be sent an application form for a VED exemption certificate. You can then use the certificate as proof of exemption when applying for a 'tax exempt disc' from the DVLA. If you are getting DLA higher rate mobility component and have not been sent an application form, or want guidance on it, write to the Disability Contact & Processing Unit (see inside back cover). If you are getting war pensioners' mobility supplement and have not been sent an application form, write to the Veterans Agency (see Chapter 46(7) for the address).

Motability contract hire customers enjoy the same exemptions, but the process is handled by Motability and no VED application form is issued.

Allow plenty of time when applying for a renewal of the exemption certificate or you may need to buy a tax disc and re-claim unused whole months when the certificate finally arrives.

If there is a delay in your DLA claim, the exemption will not be backdated.

Passengers getting DLA care component or attendance allowance – Road tax exemption for passengers getting DLA care component or attendance allowance was abolished on 12.10.93. If you were exempt from road tax or applied for help before this date, transitional arrangements allow you to continue getting help under the old scheme.

Nominating another person's vehicle

Someone getting DLA higher rate mobility component can nominate another person's vehicle to be exempt from road tax. This may also apply to a company car registered in the name of the company – the person receiving mobility component should nominate the company for exemption. In order to qualify for exemption, the vehicle should be used *'by or for the purposes of'* the disabled person.

The named person who gets the exemption may be changed at any time. For example, if you have nominated someone else for exemption and then get your own car, the exemption can be returned to you.

If you are refused exemption

Even if you have an exemption certificate from the DWP, it is within the discretion of the DVLA to refuse to grant exemption from road tax if they think the vehicle will not be used *'solely by or for the purposes of'* the disabled person. They are unlikely to do this unless your intended use of the vehicle would blatantly breach this condition.

If you are refused exemption, there is no formal procedure for appealing. However, you can write, giving full details of why you think you qualify for exemption, the purposes for which the vehicle will be used, etc to: DVLA, Vehicle Enquiry Unit Centre, Longview Road, Swansea SA99 1BL (0870 240 0010).

Help for carers

A B C D E F G H I J K L M N O P Q R S T U

6 Carer's allowance

1. What is carer's allowance?

Carer's allowance (CA) is a benefit for people who regularly spend at least 35 hours a week caring for a severely disabled person. You don't have to be related to, or live with, the disabled person. You can get CA even if you've never worked. You are not prevented from getting CA if you are disabled yourself and also need care. If you are paid CA, a carer premium of £29.50 will be included in your applicable amount for means-tested benefits (see Chapter 24(6)). If you have claimed CA and would have been paid it but for the fact that it overlaps with state pension or another benefit (see 6 below), you still get the carer premium.

If you are paid CA, the person you are caring for cannot get the severe disability premium included in their applicable amount for means-tested benefits (or the equivalent amount used in pension credit). Because of this, it is not always advantageous to claim CA even if you are eligible. See Chapter 24(3). The person you care for will not lose the severe disability premium (or the pension credit equivalent) if you are entitled to CA but cannot be paid it because of the overlapping benefits rule.

CA is not means tested and does not depend on national insurance (NI) contributions. It is taxable and counts as income for tax credits. CA gives you Class 1 NI contribution credits (see Box D.7, Chapter 11) and helps you qualify for additional state pension (see Chapter 43(4)).

2. Do you qualify?

- ❑ You must regularly spend at least 35 hours a week (see below) caring for a person who receives either:
  - disability living allowance (DLA) care component (at the middle or highest rate only); *or*
  - attendance allowance at either rate; *or*
  - constant attendance allowance (of £57.50 or more) paid with the Industrial Injuries or War Pensions schemes.
- ❑ You must be aged 16 or over.
- ❑ You must not be in full-time education. You are treated as being in full-time education if you attend a course for 21 hours or more a week. The 21 hours is the time spent in supervised study. It does not include breaks but can include coursework or homework set by the tutor.
- ❑ If you work, you must not earn more than a specific amount (see 5 below).
- ❑ You must pass the UK residence and presence tests, and must not be subject to immigration control (see Chapter 50(2) and (3)).

SSCBA, S.70 & ICA Regs, regs 3, 5, 8 & 9

CA can continue for up to eight weeks after the person you look after dies. You must continue to satisfy all the rules other than those related to the care of a disabled person or that person's receipt of a qualifying benefit.

SSCBA, S.70(1A)

If someone else gets CA to look after the same person you look after, you cannot also get CA to look after them. You can get home responsibilities protection and you may get income support as a carer (but not the carer premium). You and the other carer can decide between you who should claim CA. You can only get one award of CA, even if you care for more than one person.

SSCBA, S.70(7)

If you were aged 65 or over and entitled to CA on 27.10.02 (or invalid care allowance, as it was then called), you can continue to get CA even if you stop caring for 35 hours a week or if the DLA or attendance allowance of the person you look after stops or if you start full-time work. You must, however, continue to meet the other CA rules.

Regulatory Reform (Carer's Allowance) Order 2002, art 4

Caring for 35 hours a week – If you are caring for more than one person, you can't add together the time you spend caring for each of them. You have to show that for at least 35 hours each week you are caring for one person. If you meet the 35-hours test during part of the year (eg in school holidays) you may qualify for CA during that period.

CA benefit weeks run from the start of Sunday to the end of the following Saturday. The hours of caring in any given week must total at least 35: you cannot average the hours over a number of weeks. If, for example, you provide care on alternate weekends, it may be difficult to show you provide care for 35 hours in any given benefit week, as the care you provide on Saturday will fall within one benefit week and Sunday's care will fall into the next. The time you spend caring includes preparing for the visit of the person you care for on the day they arrive, clearing up after they leave, and collecting them from or taking them back to the place where they usually live (CG/6/1990).

ICA Regs, reg 4

3. How much do you get?

Carer's allowance	per week
For yourself	£53.10
For an adult dependant	£31.70
Extra for dependent children*	
For the oldest child	£8.20
For each other child	£11.35

*available on claims made before 6.4.03 only

You can get the adult dependant's addition for your spouse or civil partner. To get the addition for another adult who lives with you, that adult must look after your child. You cannot get the addition if your partner earns above set limits or receives other specified benefits (see 5 and 6 below).

Social Security Benefit (Dependency) Regs 1977, Sch 2, para 7

If you are making a fresh claim for CA and want financial help for a dependent child, claim child tax credit (see Chapter 18).

4. How do you claim?

Claim on form DS700, or on DS700(SP) if you get a state pension. These forms are available from a Jobcentre Plus office or Pension Centre or from the free Benefit Enquiry Line (0800 882200; 0800 220674 in Northern Ireland). You can also claim online (www.dwp.gov.uk/carersallowance). The claim-form includes a statement to be signed by the cared-for person. This asks them to confirm that they know a claim for CA is being made, that the carer provides them with at least 35 hours' care a week and that they are aware their own benefits could be affected by the claim (ie if they receive the severe disability premium – see Chapter 24(3)). If the cared-for person is unable to sign (eg because of health problems or because they are under 16), this can be done by someone acting on their behalf.

Once you claim CA you may be offered the option of attending a voluntary interview to discuss work prospects. However, if you are also claiming certain other benefits, eg income support, you may be obliged to attend an interview as a condition of receiving that other benefit (see Box T.1, Chapter 59).

Backdating – If you were entitled to CA prior to claiming it, you can ask that it be backdated for up to three months. If you have been waiting for the person you are caring for to be awarded the appropriate rate of disability living allowance or attendance allowance, and you claim CA within three months of the date either of those benefits is awarded, your claim for CA can be treated as having been made on the first day of the benefit week in which they became payable. Thus CA can be fully backdated to that time if you satisfied the other conditions of entitlement throughout that period.

C&P Regs, reg 6(33)

If entitlement to CA means you can start receiving a benefit such as income support because of the award of a carer premium, you should claim the benefit at the same time that you claim CA to ensure it is also backdated.

What happens next? – You will be sent a written decision on your claim. If you disagree with that decision you have one month in which to dispute it, either by asking a decision maker in the Carer's Allowance Unit to revise the decision or by lodging an appeal (see Chapter 60).

C.1 Caring away from your home

Seek legal advice

If you have to leave your own home to care for a disabled or elderly relative or friend, seek advice before you go (see Chapter 61). Consider what you will do when the need for that care stops, if your relationship with the cared-for person deteriorates, or if they die, go into a care home or become mentally incapable of looking after their own affairs.

Housing costs

If you leave your main home temporarily, you remain liable for housing costs, including the rent or mortgage. If the absence is for 13 weeks or less you can claim help with rent from housing benefit (see Chapter 20(6)) or help with mortgage interest from income-related employment and support allowance, income support, jobseeker's allowance or pension credit (see Chapter 25(1)). This help continues for up to 52 weeks of a temporary absence if the care you provide is medically approved. If you think your absence might be for longer than 13 weeks, ask a doctor or other medical professional (eg a nurse) involved in the care of the disabled person to provide a letter approving the care you provide.

Housing benefit and help with mortgage interest stop after a continuous absence of 13 or 52 weeks. However, if you return home (perhaps with the disabled person) for even a very short stay, a new period of absence should then start. This can allow you to continue getting benefit beyond these initial limits. Tell the office dealing with your claim of each visit to your home and keep a record of the dates of these visits. If you leave your home permanently, help with housing costs will stop immediately.

Council tax

If you have left your home empty to live elsewhere to care for someone, your former home may be exempt from council tax. The person you care for must need that care because they are elderly, ill or disabled, or have a mental disorder or a drug or alcohol problem. The empty property must have ceased to be your sole or main residence for the exemption to apply.

If the disabled person's home becomes your sole or main residence, you may be counted as living there for council tax purposes. However, under the council tax discount scheme your presence in their home will be disregarded if:

- the person you are caring for is not your child under 18 or your partner;
- they are entitled to higher rate attendance allowance, or highest rate disability living allowance care component, or constant attendance allowance; *and*
- you spend at least 35 hours a week on average caring for them.

This means council tax for the home will be the same as if you were not resident there. See Chapter 21(9).

If you are temporarily absent from your home, the rules for claiming council tax benefit during that absence are the same as those for housing benefit (see above).

5. How do earnings affect CA?

You cannot get CA if your net earnings are more than £95 a week – the 'earnings limit'. See below for the way in which earnings are calculated.

ICA Regs, reg 8

Your partner's earnings do not affect your basic benefit but can affect any addition(s) for a dependent adult or children. If your partner earns more than £31.70, the adult dependant's addition will not be paid. If you are still entitled to any child dependant's addition(s) and your partner earns £195 or more in any week, you will lose an addition for one child in the next week. For each extra £26 earned, you lose another child dependant's addition.

Social Security Benefit (Dependency) Regs 1977, Sch 2, para 2B

Occupational and personal pensions count as earnings for adult and child dependants' additions, but not for the basic rate of CA.

If you earn over £95 a week and get a means-tested benefit, that benefit may continue even though entitlement to CA (and the carer premium) stops. Earnings of £95 a week or less do not affect CA, but any means-tested benefit you receive may be reduced (see Chapter 26(3)-(5)).

Calculating earnings

In working out how much of your earnings are taken into account, certain deductions and disregards can be made from gross earnings. Count any payment from your employer as earnings (eg bonus, commission, payments for childminding, retainer). If you stop work and claim CA, most payments made at the end of your job are ignored, eg pay in lieu of notice or holiday pay. If you are self-employed, the rules on working out net profit follow the rules for means-tested benefits (see Chapter 26(4)).

From your gross weekly earnings (or net profit) deduct:

- income tax and national insurance contributions (Class 1, 2 or 4);
- half of any contribution you make to an occupational or personal pension;
- expenses *'wholly, exclusively and necessarily incurred in the performance of the duties of the employment'*, eg

equipment, special clothing, travel between workplaces (but not travel between home and work);
- advance of earnings or a loan from your employer;
- fostering allowance;
- payments from a local authority, health authority or voluntary organisation for someone temporarily in your care;
- the first £20 rent paid to you by a subtenant(s);
- the first £20 a week plus half the rest of the income from a boarder;
- the whole of any contribution towards living and accommodation costs from someone living in your home (other than boarders and subtenants);
- earnings from employment payable abroad where transfer to the UK is prohibited;
- charges for currency conversion;
- annual bounty paid to part-time members of the fire brigade or lifeboat service, or to auxiliary coastguards or members of a territorial or reserve force.

CE Regs, regs 9 & 10 & Sch 1

If earnings paid in one week are over the limit, CA is lost the following week. Monthly earnings are worked out on a weekly basis and affect benefit for the month ahead. If earnings fluctuate, they may be averaged over a recognisable cycle of work or over five weeks, but this is discretionary. One-off payments that are not for any specific period are divided by the relevant weekly earnings limit to work out the number of weeks your benefit will be affected.

CE Regs, reg 8

Care costs – For basic CA, if because of your work you pay someone other than a 'close relative' to look after the person you care for or to look after a child aged under 16, these payments are deducted from your earnings. A maximum of half your net earnings can be ignored in this way. A 'close relative' is the parent, son, daughter, brother, sister or partner of either yourself or the disabled person you care for.

CE Regs, regs 10(3)(b) & 13(3)(b) and Sch 3

For dependant additions in CA, or for calculating earnings in other non-means-tested benefits, more restrictive rules apply. Childcare costs of up to £60 a week can be deducted from earnings for children under 11. You must be paying a registered childminder or other registered childcare provider (or paying for childcare provided on Crown premises or by schools, hospitals, etc where childcare is exempt from registration) or paying an out-of-school-hours scheme (run on school premises or provided by a local authority) to look after at least one child aged 8 or over but under 11. In addition, you can only have childcare costs counted if you are a lone parent, or one of a couple and either you are both working or one of you is working and the other is 'incapacitated'.

CE Regs, regs 10(2)(b) & 13(2)(b) and Sch 2

You are treated as incapacitated if you get disability living allowance or attendance allowance (or the equivalent for War Pensions or Industrial Injuries schemes), long-term incapacity benefit or severe disablement allowance, or you are getting housing benefit or council tax benefit and either childcare costs have been allowed under the rules for these benefits (see Chapter 26(5)) or a disability premium or higher disability premium has been awarded based on your (not your partner's) disability. These rules have not been amended to include someone on employment and support allowance within the definition of incapacitated.

CE Regs, Sch 2 para 8

6. How do other benefits affect CA?

You cannot be paid CA while you are receiving the same amount or more from:
- state pension;
- maternity allowance;
- incapacity benefit or unemployability supplement;
- contributory employment and support allowance;
- contribution-based jobseeker's allowance;
- widows' benefits and bereavement benefits;
- a state training allowance.

This is known as the overlapping benefits rule. If you get less than the basic rate of CA from one of the above benefits, that benefit is paid and topped up with CA to the amount you would get from CA alone. Only the basic rate of these benefits overlap with CA. CA can be paid in addition to any earnings-related or age-related addition to the other benefit.

If your partner receives a dependency addition for you with one of these benefits, the addition cannot be paid if you get the same amount or more from CA. If CA is less than the addition, you receive CA and your partner gets the difference between CA and the standard rate of the dependency addition. The addition to your CA for an adult dependant will not be paid if your dependant gets an overlapping benefit of £31.70 a week or more.

OB Regs, regs 4 & 9

You can get CA at the same time as disability living allowance or attendance allowance.

If the person you look after gets the severe disability premium included in the calculation of a means-tested benefit, this will stop once you get CA. If you cannot be paid CA because of the overlapping benefit rules, the person you care for will not lose the severe disability premium, even if you get a carer premium.

Severe disablement allowance (SDA) – SDA and CA also overlap. Normally, CA is paid in full, topped up with any balance of SDA. However, if your SDA is the same amount or more than CA, you can ask for your SDA to be paid in full. The person you care for is then not excluded from the severe disability premium and you can still claim a carer premium.

7. Carer's allowance and income support

You may be entitled to both CA and income support (IS – see Box E.1, Chapter 14). Because IS is means tested, it is reduced by the amount of your CA. The advantages of claiming CA are outlined in 9 below. If you are paid CA, the person you care for is excluded from the severe disability premium, but only once CA is actually paid; arrears of CA do not affect entitlement to the premium.

IS Regs, Sch 2, para 13(3ZA)

8. Carer's allowance and state pension

If you begin receiving a state pension that is more than CA (not including age- or earnings-related additions), payment of CA will stop due to the overlapping benefit rules (see 6 above). If your state pension is less than CA, state pension is paid and topped up with CA to the basic weekly rate of CA. If all that prevents payment of CA is your state pension, a carer addition (£29.50) is included in the calculation of your pension credit (see Chapter 42(3)), and a carer premium (£29.50) is included in the calculation of housing benefit and council tax benefit (see Chapter 24(6)).

9. Why claim CA?

Your household income may not be higher after claiming CA, as it overlaps with other benefits, but if you are entitled to CA, and it can't be paid because of other benefits, you may get:
- a carer premium included in your income-related employment and support allowance (ESA), income support, income-based jobseeker's allowance (JSA), housing benefit, council tax benefit or health benefits. The premium is included if you get CA or have an underlying entitlement to CA but receive an overlapping benefit instead (see 6 above). An addition equivalent to the carer premium can be included in the calculation of pension credit. See Chapter 24(6);

A B C D E F G H I J K L M N O P Q R S T U

- national insurance contribution credits (see Box D.7, Chapter 11) or help towards satisfying the national insurance contribution conditions for contributory ESA (see Chapter 11(6)) and JSA (see Chapter 15(12));
- help to qualify for additional state pension (see Chapter 43(4));
- a £10 Christmas bonus.

10. Time off from caring

CA rules allow breaks in care of up to 12 weeks in any 26-week period. CA is payable for 12 weeks if you or the person you look after goes into hospital (but see below). Up to four of the 12 weeks can be for other temporary breaks in care – eg a holiday or short-term stay in a care home for the person you look after. After this, you cannot be paid CA for any week in which you do not provide care for at least 35 hours.

ICA Regs, reg 4(2)

Going into hospital – If you are in hospital, your CA will stop after 12 weeks. It may stop sooner if you have been in hospital or had a break in care within the last 26 weeks.

If the person you look after goes into hospital, the 12-weeks-off rule still applies, but in practice your CA may stop sooner. Your CA depends on the disabled person receiving attendance allowance (AA) or disability living allowance (DLA) care component. If they go into hospital and the stay is arranged by the NHS, payment of AA and DLA stops after four weeks if they are aged 16 or over, or after 12 weeks for children under 16. Your CA will stop when their AA or DLA stops. If the person can arrange a pattern of respite care that allows them to keep their AA or DLA, CA may continue to be paid (see Box B.3, Chapter 3).

Arranging care breaks – A week off is a week in which you care for the disabled person for less than 35 hours, so odd days or weekends away are unlikely to affect your CA entitlement. A weekend straddles two CA weeks: a CA week runs from Sunday to Saturday. This means if you arrange respite care from midweek to midweek, you may still care for the required 35 hours both in the week the disabled person goes into respite care and the week they come home. These weeks won't count as weeks off and CA will be paid even though you've had a full week of respite care.

New carers – To get paid CA for breaks in care, new carers must have received benefit for an initial period of 22 weeks. You can include up to eight weeks of hospital stays in those 22 weeks if you would have cared for the disabled person had they (or you) not been in hospital.

Tell the DWP – Report any of these changes in writing to the Carer's Allowance Unit as soon as possible to avoid having to repay overpaid benefit.

Keep a diary – If all this seems confusing, keep a diary.

7 Other help for carers

1. Introduction

This chapter covers some of the financial and practical help available for carers. Parents of disabled children should also look at Chapter 37. Some of the help depends on you getting carer's allowance (see Chapter 6). See Chapter 21(9) for details of the council tax discount scheme as it affects carers caring in their own home. Other help depends on your circumstances: eg whether you have given up work, or your income is low, or you have a disability yourself. The benefits checklist at the front of this Handbook can help you see the benefits to which you might be entitled. Carer's allowance is the only benefit specifically aimed at carers, but others may provide extra money now or help you claim in the future.

2. Giving up work

You may be entitled to carer's allowance (CA) if you spend at least 35 hours a week caring for someone who gets a qualifying disability benefit (see Chapter 6(2)). You are eligible for CA even if you have a partner who is working (see Chapter 6(5) for how their earnings are treated).

If your household income and savings are low and you are aged under 60, claim income support. If you have other income or savings, you may be better off claiming contribution-based jobseeker's allowance (JSA) for the first six months (see below). If you have a limited capability for work, you may be able to claim employment and support allowance (see 4 below). If you are aged 60 or over, you may be able to claim pension credit (see 5 below). If you have dependent children, you may be able to claim child tax credit (Chapter 18). You may be eligible for housing benefit and/or council tax benefit (see Chapter 20) and help with NHS costs (Chapter 55).

Income support

Income support (IS) is a means-tested benefit for people under 60 who are not expected to sign on as available for work, and is intended to provide for basic living expenses for you and your partner. It can be paid on its own if you (and your partner) have no other income, or it can top up your CA or other income. You normally cannot get IS if you have capital over £16,000 or a partner who works for 24 hours a week or more. See Chapter 14 for details.

You are eligible for IS if you get CA. You can also get IS if you are *'regularly and substantially engaged in caring for a disabled person'* who gets attendance allowance (AA) or disability living allowance (DLA) care component at the middle or highest rate (see Box E.1, Chapter 14); it is possible to get IS under this rule even if you provide less than 35 hours care a week. You can claim IS as a carer for up to six months while you are waiting for the AA or DLA claim of the person you look after to be processed. If you stop being treated as a carer for IS, you continue to be eligible for IS for eight weeks if you satisfy all of the other IS rules. Otherwise, you may need to claim JSA instead.

Carer premium – If you or your partner get CA, a carer premium of £29.50 a week is included in the assessment for IS and other means-tested benefits (see Chapter 24(6)). You can get this premium included if all that prevents the payment of CA is the overlapping benefits rule (see Chapter 6(6)).

Mortgage interest – When you claim IS, there is normally a 13-week waiting period before mortgage interest is included in your assessment. If you are planning to claim IS, but at present your income or capital is too high, consider making your claim now. If your income or savings go down and you qualify for IS on another claim made within 13 weeks, the time limits for the mortgage interest assessment will run from the date of your first claim. See Chapter 25(6).

Jobseeker's allowance

Contribution-based JSA of up to £64.30 a week (less if you are under 25) is payable for up to six months if you have paid enough national insurance contributions. You are eligible even if you have a partner who is working. The amount you get may be reduced if you have earnings or an occupational pension. It is not affected by other income or savings. You might be better off claiming JSA instead of IS for the first six months if you have other household income or savings. CA overlaps with contribution-based JSA – if you claim both you'll be paid JSA, perhaps topped up with CA if that is higher (see Chapter 6(6)).

JSA is for people who are available for, and actively looking for, work. Usually, you are expected to look for a full-time job even if you have given up work to be a carer. However, if you care for a person who is a close relative or member of your household, you can restrict your availability for work to whatever hours your caring responsibilities allow, subject to a minimum of 16 hours a week. You must show you have a reasonable chance of finding work despite this restriction. Carers are allowed to ask for one week's notice before taking up a job offer from Jobcentre Plus and 48 hours' notice to attend other employment opportunities (eg an interview). See Chapter 15(4).

JSA is not payable for up to 26 weeks if you leave your job voluntarily without 'just cause'. You should not be sanctioned in this way if your caring responsibilities meant it was no longer reasonable for you to continue working, but you are expected to look for alternatives before giving up work (see Chapter 15(9)). If possible, talk to your employer about your difficulties to see if there is any alternative to leaving. If your JSA is sanctioned, you can appeal against the sanction itself or against the length of it.

3. Working part time or full time

If you are eligible for income support (IS) as a carer, you can work without limit on your weekly hours. However, you can only keep £20 a week of your net earnings (or of your joint earnings if your partner works); anything over that reduces your IS penny for penny (see Chapter 26(3)). You cannot get IS if your partner works for 24 hours or more a week.

Your carer's allowance will stop if your net earnings go over £95 a week (see Chapter 6(5)). If your net earnings are below this, the amount you are paid is unaffected.

4. Limited capability for work

If you have a limited capability for work due to disability or ill health and are under state pension age, you may be able to claim employment and support allowance (ESA – see Chapter 9). Payment of carer's allowance usually stops when you get contributory ESA because these benefits overlap, but you keep an underlying entitlement. This means the carer premium continues to be included in any income-related ESA assessment (see Chapter 24(6)). Because your carer's allowance is not paid, the person you care for may still get the severe disability premium (see Chapter 24(3)).

5. Over state pension age

If you don't have enough contributions for the full rate basic state pension, it can be topped up to £53.10 with carer's allowance (CA). If you were 65 or over and entitled to invalid care allowance on 27.10.02, you can continue to be entitled to CA even if you cease to care for at least 35 hours a week, or the person you care for stops getting a qualifying benefit (see Chapter 6(2)).

Pension credit is a means-tested benefit to provide for basic living expenses once you are 60 or over (see Chapter 42). If you claim CA and the only reason it cannot be paid is because your state pension is higher, a 'carer addition' is still included in your pension credit calculation.

If you are disabled, you may be eligible for disability living allowance (DLA) or attendance allowance (AA) even though you are caring for another person (see Chapters 3 and 4). If you and your partner get AA or middle or highest rate DLA care component, or you live alone and get one of these benefits, you may be eligible for an extra amount for severe disability to be included in the pension credit calculation.

6. National insurance (NI) credits

For each week that you get carer's allowance (CA), you get a Class 1 NI contribution credit (as long as you have lost, given up or never had the right to pay reduced-rate contributions). But if you already get unemployment or incapacity (or limited capability for work) credits for that week, you cannot get CA credits for that same period. CA Class 1 credits can give you a better deal than these other credits. For instance: if you had CA for the 2006/07 and 2007/08 tax years (or would have got CA but for the overlapping benefit rules), your Class 1 credits for those years may mean that if you fall sick in 2009 you'll pass the second contribution condition for employment and support allowance (ESA); at the same time, CA entitlement helps you pass the first contribution condition for ESA.

Each tax year in which you have 52 Class 1 credits is a qualifying year for state pension (see Box O.1, Chapter 43).

Home responsibilities protection – If you do not get CA, you might be eligible for 'home responsibilities protection' (HRP), which helps protect your right to a state pension. See Chapter 44 for details. There will be changes to the system of HRP and NI credits for carers from April 2010 – see Chapter 44(5).

Additional state pension (state second pension) – For each complete tax year in which you get CA or HRP as a carer, you are treated as though you have earned enough to have made full contributions towards the state second pension for that year. See Chapter 43(4) for details.

7. Practical help

The person you care for is entitled to an assessment from the social services department (social work department in Scotland) of their need for services. Social services must also assess your support needs as a carer and look at your continuing ability to provide care if you ask them to do so (see Chapter 28(3)). See Box K.2, Chapter 28 for a checklist of services that might be available in your area. Contact your social services department for information about short-term break options and other practical help.

There might be a local carers' support group where you can share information with other carers. Contact Carers UK for details (see Address List).

8. If the person you care for dies

Your benefit entitlement may depend on the benefits of the person you care for. This is the case if you receive carer's allowance (CA) or income support (IS) for caring for someone. CA can continue for up to eight weeks following the death of the person you cared for. Throughout those eight weeks you must continue to satisfy all of the conditions for CA not related to caring or payment of a qualifying benefit to the person you cared for (see Chapter 6(2)). If you were 65 or over and entitled to invalid care allowance (ICA) on 27.10.02, you can continue to be entitled to CA indefinitely after the person you cared for has died.

You continue to be eligible for IS with a carer premium and/or to claim IS as a carer for eight weeks following the death (see Chapter 24(6)). You continue to be eligible for the additional amount for carers in pension credit for eight weeks following the death, or indefinitely if you were 65 or over and entitled to ICA on 27.10.02.

If you are under 60 you may be expected to sign on as available for work and claim jobseeker's allowance (JSA) from eight weeks after the death. If you gave up work to be a carer, you may qualify for contribution-based JSA based on national insurance contributions paid when you were working (see Chapter 15(12)). Check first to see if you might be eligible for IS (see Box E.1, Chapter 14) or employment and support allowance (see Chapter 9). Even if you hadn't claimed IS before the death, you may be able to claim it now, either as a carer for up to eight weeks following the death, or on other grounds after the eight weeks has ended.

You may be eligible for bereavement benefits if your spouse or civil partner has died (see Chapter 54).

D Unable to work

This section of the Handbook looks at:

8 Statutory sick pay

1. What is statutory sick pay?

Statutory sick pay (SSP) is paid to employees by their employers for up to 28 weeks in any period of sickness lasting for four or more days. SSP does not depend on national insurance contributions. You can work full or part time but must earn at least the lower earnings limit (£95 from April 2009). SSP is taxable. There are no additions for dependants.

SSP is primarily the responsibility of employers. The scheme is operated by HMRC. Detailed information for employers is provided in *E14 Employer handbook for statutory sick pay* (available from HMRC, including their website: www.hmrc.gov.uk). Help is also available from the National Insurance Enquiry Line (0845 302 1479).

Restrictions for agency workers with a contract of three months or less were removed from 27.10.08. SSP is now payable in exactly the same way as it is to other employees, if you satisfy the qualifying conditions.

Unemployed and self-employed people cannot get SSP, but may be able to claim employment and support allowance (see Chapter 9).

If your SSP and any other income you get is below your income support (IS) 'applicable amount', you can claim IS to top it up (see Chapter 14). If you don't get IS, you may still get housing benefit because SSP is treated more generously under that scheme (see Chapter 26(6) and Chapter 20).

2. Do you qualify?

There are three key terms that describe the qualifying conditions for SSP:

- SSP period of incapacity for work (PIW);
- period of entitlement;
- qualifying days.

You can only be paid SSP if you are sick on a qualifying day and your days of sickness form part of an SSP PIW that comes within a period of entitlement. These three different qualifying conditions are explained in 3 to 5 below.

3. SSP period of incapacity for work

The first qualifying condition for SSP is that there must be an SSP 'period of incapacity for work' (PIW). This means you must be incapable of doing the job you are employed to do because of sickness or disability for at least four days in a row. Weekends and public holidays count – therefore, every day of the week can count towards an SSP PIW, including days when you wouldn't have worked even if you had been fit. SSP PIWs separated by eight weeks or less are 'linked' and count as one PIW. Further spells of sickness must be at least four or more days in a row to link with a previous SSP PIW.

SSCBA, S.152

There are some situations when you will qualify even if you are not actually sick on a particular day. You can be treated as incapable of work for days when you are under medical care in respect of some specific disease or bodily or mental disablement and a doctor has advised you not to work for precautionary or convalescent reasons, provided you do not work on those days. You are also treated as incapable of work if you are excluded, abstain from or are prevented from working (having received the due notice in writing) because you are a carrier of, or have been in contact with, an infectious disease (including certain types of food poisoning).

SSP Regs, reg 2

4. Period of entitlement

The second qualifying condition for SSP is that there must be a 'period of entitlement', meaning the actual period of time when you are entitled to SSP. It begins with the start of the SSP period of incapacity for work (PIW) and ends when your employer's liability to pay you SSP ends.

Your employer's liability to pay SSP ends if:

- you are no longer sick; *or*
- you have had 28 weeks of SSP, either in one time period or linked; *or*
- your contract of employment comes to an end (unless your employer has dismissed you solely or mainly to avoid paying you SSP); *or*
- for pregnant women, you are at the start of the 'disqualifying period', which is the 39 weeks during which you are entitled to statutory maternity pay or maternity allowance. If you are entitled to neither, there are two possibilities, depending on whether or not you are already getting SSP:
  - if you are getting SSP, it cannot be paid after the day your baby is born or, if earlier, after the first day you are off work sick with a pregnancy-related illness on or after the start of the 4th week before the expected week of confinement;
  - if you are not getting SSP, it cannot be paid for a period of 18 weeks, which starts from the earlier of either the start of the week your baby is born or the start of the week you are first off sick with a pregnancy-related illness if this is after the beginning of the 4th week before your expected week of confinement; *or*
- you are taken into legal custody; *or*
- your linked SSP PIW has spanned three years.

SSCBA, Ss.153 & 155 and SSP Regs, reg 3

SSP will also end if your employer no longer considers you to be incapable of work. In this case, you can appeal against the decision (see 10 below).

People who cannot get SSP – In some circumstances, you won't be entitled to SSP at all (so no period of entitlement can start). These circumstances are listed in Box D.1 – but they must apply on the first day of an SSP PIW for you to be excluded from SSP altogether.

5. Qualifying days

SSP is only paid for 'qualifying days'. These are normally the days you would have been required to work under the terms of your contract if you hadn't been sick – but they don't have to be.

If your working pattern varies from one week to another, you and your employer can come to some other arrangement as to which days will be qualifying days. If you and your employer reach agreement, you have a free choice of qualifying days – as long as they are not fixed by reference to the actual days you are off sick and there is at least one qualifying day in each week.

If you can't reach agreement with your employer, the qualifying days are the days your contract would have required you to work if you hadn't fallen sick. If it isn't clear which days would be working days in a particular week, the law says every day of that week except days you and your employer agree are rest days should be SSP qualifying days.

If you would not normally have worked in a particular week and do not have an agreement on qualifying days with your employer, the Wednesday of that week will be a qualifying day regardless.

If there are any doubts about qualifying days, it is important to sort this out with your employer.

SSCBA, S.154 & SSP Regs, reg 5

Waiting days – SSP is not paid for the first three qualifying days of an SSP period of incapacity for work (PIW) – the 'waiting days'. However, you do not need to wait another three days if you re-claim SSP and your second spell of sickness (which must last for at least four days) starts no more than eight weeks after the end of the first PIW. The different PIWs are linked together and count as one continuous PIW. If different PIWs are linked in this way, your right to SSP in the later linked PIWs depends on your circumstances at the start of the first one.

SSCBA, Ss.155(1) & 152(3)

6. How much do you get?

SSP is £79.15 a week. There are no additions for dependants. If you are due SSP for a part week, your employer will work out the daily rate by dividing the weekly rate by the number of qualifying days in that week. To qualify, your average weekly earnings must be at least the level of the lower earnings limit (£95 from 6.4.09). You can qualify even if you are on a short-term contract, provided your earnings are sufficient. To get an average weekly figure, gross earnings are averaged over the eight weeks ending with the last pay day before the start of the SSP period of incapacity for work.

SSCBA, Sch 11, para 2(c) & SSP Regs, reg 19

SSP is subject to deductions for income tax and national insurance (NI) contributions. However, no NI deductions are due if SSP is the only payment you receive when you are sick because SSP is below the primary threshold for NI contributions (but you can get credits – see Chapter 11(4)). Other normal deductions, eg union subs, can be made from SSP. It is important to make sure your payslip shows details of SSP payments you have received, together with deductions made by your employer, so you can check that it's all correct.

SSCBA, S.151(3)

Payment of SSP – You should normally be paid SSP at the same time and in the same way as you would have been paid wages for the same period. SSP cannot be paid in kind or as board and lodging or through a service.

If there has been some disagreement with your employer about your entitlement to SSP, and HMRC states you are entitled to it (provided you pass all the other tests), your employer must pay SSP within a certain time limit. In certain circumstances, if your employer defaults on payment of SSP or becomes insolvent, liability for any outstanding SSP transfers to HMRC (see 11 below).

SSP Regs, regs 8, 9 & 9A

Occupational sick pay – If your employer has an occupational sick pay scheme, any sick pay you get under that scheme will count towards your SSP entitlement for a particular day. Similarly, SSP paid to you by your employer will count towards any pay due to you for a particular day. But if the occupational scheme pays less than your full SSP, your employer must make up the balance so that you get all the SSP you are due. Employers are not obliged to operate the SSP scheme rules provided they pay remuneration or occupational sick pay at or above the SSP rate. Employees retain an underlying right to SSP. If your employer has their own sick pay scheme, they may have different rules, which you must keep to get payment.

SSCBA, Sch 12, para 2

D.1 Who cannot get SSP?

You are not entitled to SSP if, on the first day of your SSP period of incapacity for work (PIW), any of the following apply.

- ❑ You are not treated as an employee.
- ❑ Your average earnings are below £95 a week. But remember the PIW linking rule – the first day of the first linked PIW should be used when working out your average earnings. If a new tax year starts while you're receiving SSP, this makes no difference (but you will get any increase in payment).
- ❑ You were entitled to employment and support allowance (ESA) within the previous 85 days or incapacity benefit (IB) or severe disablement allowance (SDA) within the previous 57 days.
- ❑ You were previously entitled to ESA, IB or SDA and you are within the 104-week linking period during which your entitlement is protected (see Chapter 16(12)).
- ❑ There is a stoppage of work at your workplace due to a trade dispute, unless you can prove you have no direct interest in the dispute.
- ❑ You have already received SSP from your employer for 28 weeks in the same PIW.
- ❑ You are pregnant and already into the 'disqualifying period' (see 4).
- ❑ You are employed in another country; however, you may be entitled if your employer is liable for Class 1 contributions in the UK for you, or would be if your earnings were high enough (see Chapter 51(4)).
- ❑ You are in legal custody.
- ❑ You have not yet done any work for your employer.

Remember that PIWs with the same employer which are separated by eight weeks or less count as one continuous PIW (ie they are linked together).

Once you have been off sick for four days in a row and your employer decides you cannot get SSP, they must give you form SSP1 so that you can claim ESA (see 13).

SSCBA, S.153 & Sch 11 and SSP Regs, reg 3

A B C D E F G H I J K L M N O P Q R S T U

7. Does anything affect what you get?

Other benefits – You cannot get SSP while you are receiving employment and support allowance, incapacity benefit, severe disablement allowance, contribution-based jobseeker's allowance, statutory maternity pay, maternity allowance, statutory paternity pay or statutory adoption pay. Other benefits do not affect your entitlement to SSP. See Box D.1 for other circumstances in which you cannot get SSP.

Earnings from another job – If your employer accepts you are incapable of doing the work they employ you to do, you can earn money from a different type of work while receiving SSP. For example, if a milkman injures his leg and can't deliver milk, he may be fit enough to, say, call bingo. If so, he can do that and get SSP from his first employer. There is no limit on what you can earn from a different type of job while receiving SSP. However, doing other work may lead an employer to doubt you are genuinely incapable of doing your usual job.

Going into hospital – This will not affect entitlement to SSP.

8. How do you get SSP?

To obtain SSP, you must notify your employer that you are off sick; you may be asked to provide evidence that you are incapable of work. Your employer can decide what kind of evidence is needed, but cannot ask for a doctor's certificate for the first seven days. Your employer may have a special form, but if not you can get self-certificate form SC2 from a GP surgery or HMRC office.

Notification of sickness absence – This means letting your employer know you are sick and incapable of work. To get SSP, you must provide evidence that you are incapable of work if your employer requires you to do so (see 9 below).

These are the rules on notification of sickness laid down in the law and your employer's SSP procedures must conform to them. If you also get occupational sick pay, you will have to keep to the rules of that scheme to safeguard those payments.

- ❑ Your employer has to make the rules clear to all the workforce in advance.
- ❑ Your employer cannot demand notification before the end of the first qualifying day of a period of incapacity for work.
- ❑ Your employer cannot demand notification in the form of medical evidence. But if you use medical evidence to notify your employer, it should be accepted.
- ❑ Your employer cannot insist you use a special form.
- ❑ If you post your notification, your employer should treat it as having been given on the day it was posted.
- ❑ Your employer cannot demand notification more than once a week during a spell of sickness.
- ❑ Your employer must accept notification from someone else on your behalf.

D.2 Lengthy absences

If you are off work for a long time, your employer may ask HMRC for an opinion on your continuing incapacity for work, although employers are expected to try to resolve any problem themselves and make their own arrangements to get more medical advice. HMRC will only assist if you give your consent and if they agree that the absence seems unduly long.

The table below is the HMRC guide on the more common and less serious ailments (from booklet E14 supplement). This suggests the time by which your employer should have started some form of control action – although there is nothing in law to stop them taking action sooner.

If HMRC agrees to help, they will refer the case to their Medical Services, who will ask your doctor for a report on your incapacity to work. They may further arrange for you to attend an examination by one of their doctors, who will produce a similar report. The Medical Services will reach an opinion on whether or not you are incapable of work on the basis of these reports. The reports will not be sent to your employer, who will only be told whether or not you are considered to be capable of work. This is not a decision, it is only to help your employer decide whether payment of SSP should continue. If your employer stops SSP and you disagree, see 10.

Illness or diagnosis	Control (by weeks)
Addiction (drugs or alcohol)	10
Anaemia (other than in pregnancy)	4
Anorexia	10
Arthritis (unspecified)	10
Back and spinal disorders – PID (prolapsed intervertebral disc), sciatica, spondylitis	10
Concussion	4
Debility	
– cardiac, nervous, post-op, post-partum	10
– other	4
Fainting	4
Fractures of upper limbs	10
Fractures of lower limbs	10
Gastro-enteritis, gastritis, diarrhoea and vomiting	4
Giddiness	4
Haemorrhage	4
Headache, migraine	4
Hernia (strangulated)	10
Inflammation and swelling	4
Insomnia	10
Investigation	10
Joint disorders, other than arthritis and rheumatism	10
Kidney and bladder disorders, cystitis, UTI (urinary tract infection)	4
Menstrual disorders, menorrhagia, D&C (dilation and curettage)	10
Mouth and throat disorders	4
No abnormality detected	Immediate
Nervous illnesses	10
Not yet diagnosed	4
Obesity	Immediate
Observation	4
Post-natal conditions	10
Respiratory illness	
– asthma	10
– cold, coryza, influenza, URTI (upper respiratory tract infection)	4
– bronchitis	4
Skin conditions, dermatitis, eczema	10
Sprains, strains, bruises	4
Tachycardia	10
Ulcers	
– perforated	10
– peptic, gastric, duodenal	4
– varicose	10
– corneal	4
Wounds, cuts, lacerations, abrasions, burns, blisters, splinters, FB (foreign bodies)	4

❑ If your employer does not make any rules about notification of sickness absence or the rules do not conform with SSP law, your employer must nevertheless accept notification of sickness on a qualifying day, if it is given in writing no later than seven days after that day.

SSP Regs, reg 7

Late notification – If your notification of sickness is late according to your employer's rules (and these rules comply with SSP law) you could be disqualified from SSP for any day of incapacity notified late. But SSP can be paid if your employer accepts you have 'good cause' for late notification, provided it is given within one month of the normal time limit. This can be extended to 91 days from the day of incapacity if the employer accepts it was not reasonably practicable for you to contact them within the month. After that time, your employer need not pay SSP for that day even if you have good cause for late notification. If your employer withholds SSP because they do not accept there is good cause for late notification, you can ask HMRC for a decision (see 10 below).

SSP Regs, reg 7(2)

9. Supporting evidence

HMRC employer's handbook E14 says a doctor's certificate is *'strong evidence of incapacity and should usually be accepted as conclusive unless there is more compelling evidence to the contrary'*. A medical certificate may be accepted from someone who is not a registered medical practitioner – eg an osteopath, acupuncturist or herbalist.

It is up to your employer to decide whether to accept the evidence that you are incapable of work. If they do not accept it, SSP can be withheld. But you can write and ask HMRC for a formal decision (see 10 below).

Employers can either use their own self-certificates as evidence of incapacity or accept a written note from you as evidence for the first seven days of sickness. It is important that you agree what type of evidence will be acceptable.

For SSP purposes, your employer cannot require initial notice of your sickness in the form of medical evidence, private or otherwise. But after your first seven days of a spell off sick, they can ask for supporting medical evidence.

If your employer wants more medical evidence they must arrange and pay for it – unless HMRC agrees to help (see Box D.2). They can only do this with your consent.

Frequent short spells of sickness – If you are frequently off sick for periods of four to seven days, you may not have seen your doctor and all your absences will probably be self-certificated. If you've had at least four sickness absences over 12 months and your employer is not satisfied you have been incapable of work, they should discuss the matter with you and try to resolve any problem internally. This could involve sending you (with your consent) to a company doctor. If your employer still has doubts, they can refer your case to HMRC for help, but only with your consent. HMRC will then forward your case to their Medical Services, who will either ask for a report from your doctor or arrange for you to attend an examination by one of their doctors. In either case, an opinion will be sought as to whether there are reasonable grounds for your frequent absences. Your employer would take this opinion into account on the next occasion you were off sick.

See Box D.2 if, given the cause of your sickness, you have been off sick for a long time.

10. Fit for work?

If your employer does not accept you are incapable of work, you have the right to ask them for a written statement setting out the reasons for this and the dates you will not receive SSP. You also have the right to apply to HMRC for a decision.

Applying for a decision – Write to HMRC Statutory Payments Disputes Team, National Insurance Contributions Office, Room BP3202, Benton Park View, Newcastle upon Tyne NE98 1ZZ (0191 225 5221). They will expect you to have discussed the matter with your employer if it is reasonable to do so, and to have gone through the agreed grievance procedure, if one exists where you work.

Both you and your employer will be asked to send comments in writing to HMRC. You can provide other evidence – eg further medical statements. A copy of the decision will be sent to you and your employer. If the decision says you are incapable of work, your employer must pay you the correct amount of SSP within fixed time limits, providing that you pass the other tests for SSP.

Both you and your employer have the right to appeal against the decision to a First-tier Tribunal (Finance and Tax Chamber). If your employer appeals, they do not have to pay SSP until a final decision has been given.

11. Enforcing a decision

If HMRC has issued a formal written decision that you are entitled to SSP, and your employer doesn't pay it within the time laid down by law and has not appealed, inform HMRC Statutory Payments Disputes Team (see 10 above). In this situation, responsibility for paying SSP transfers to HMRC, who will pay any SSP to which you are entitled.

SSP Regs, reg 9A

12. What information will Jobcentre Plus give?

To decide if you are entitled to SSP, your employer can ask Jobcentre Plus for limited information about you. Before disclosing it, Jobcentre Plus should be satisfied that the enquiry comes from your employer and no one else. Employers are told that detailed personal information about employees will not be disclosed.

13. What happens when SSP ends?

If you are still sick at the start of the 23rd week of your period of entitlement to SSP and likely to remain sick beyond the 28th week, you will need to claim employment and support allowance (ESA) (see Chapter 9). Your employer must complete and send you form SSP1. On the form, your employer must state why SSP is ending and the last day it will be paid. You will need this form for your ESA claim, but if your employer delays issuing it, you should register your claim for ESA so you do not lose benefit.

The employer must issue the SSP1 if you are not entitled to SSP or whenever they stop paying it. The form should be issued within seven days of your request for it or, if payroll arrangements make this impracticable, by the first pay day in the following tax month.

If your employer is holding any of your doctor's certificates covering days beyond the last day of your SSP entitlement, these should be returned to you with form SSP1. Send them to your local Jobcentre Plus office with the completed form.

SSP Regs, reg 15(3) & (4)

14. What if your job ends?

If your job ends and you have had less than 28 weeks' SSP from your last employer and are still incapable of work, you can claim employment and support allowance (ESA) – see Chapter 9. You will need to send your SSP1. But if your employer is found to have dismissed you solely or mainly to avoid paying SSP, they remain liable to pay it until liability ends for some other reason. Whatever the reason for your dismissal, you should claim ESA. Seek advice if you have difficulties or would not qualify for ESA.

SSP Regs, reg 4

A B C D E F G H I J K L M N O P Q R S T U

9 Employment and support allowance

1. What is employment and support allowance?

Employment and support allowance (ESA) is the new benefit paid to people whose ability to work is limited by ill health or disability. From 27.10.08 it replaced both incapacity benefit and income support paid on the grounds of incapacity. ESA retains features of both these benefits, having two elements: contributory ESA (which is similar to incapacity benefit) and income-related ESA (which is similar to income support paid on the grounds of incapacity).

What is new about ESA? – ESA has some similarities to the benefits it replaces, but has some features that mark it out as very different.

First, it is a single benefit. This should make it simpler to claim and administer than the two separate benefits, income support and incapacity benefit, which often had a complex interrelationship.

Second, ESA is not paid simply because you are found to be incapable of work. The Government felt that the previous assessment system, based on dividing people into two groups, those capable of work and those incapable of work, was clumsy and did not reflect reality. The strict divide could act as a disincentive for people wanting to move from benefits into work. Consequently, ESA claimants are dealt with differently. ESA is paid when you are found to have a *'limited capability for work'*. ESA claimants are then divided into two separate groups: the 'support group' and the 'work-related activity group'. The group you are placed in will determine the amount of ESA you receive and the responsibilities you will need to meet in order to keep receiving the benefit.

2. Contributory ESA

Contributory ESA is linked to your national insurance contribution record. It replaces incapacity benefit, which was also a national insurance benefit. To be entitled to contributory ESA, you must have paid national insurance contributions over a number of years, although if you have had a limited capability for work from before the age of 20 (or 25 if you have been in education or training), it may not be necessary for you to satisfy these contribution conditions.

For more details on contributory ESA, see Chapter 11.

3. Income-related ESA

Income-related ESA is the means-tested element of ESA. It replaces income support paid on the grounds of incapacity. It provides for your basic living expenses (and those of your partner).

Like income support, income-related ESA can help with mortgage interest payments and certain other housing costs (see Chapter 25). It can be paid on its own, or as a top-up to contributory ESA. Certain premiums are also paid, but not the disability premium.

For more details on income-related ESA, see Chapter 12.

4. The assessment phase

When you claim ESA, you enter a 13-week 'assessment phase'. This applies to all new ESA claimants, with the exception of those listed below. During the assessment phase you are paid a basic allowance of ESA. If you are under 25, this allowance is paid at a lower rate.

During the assessment phase you undergo a 'work capability assessment'. This determines whether you are entitled to ESA, as well as whether you join the support group or the work-related activity group. You also have a work-focused interview after the 8th week of your claim.

The assessment phase does not apply if:

- you are terminally ill and claiming ESA for that reason;
- your claim links to an earlier ESA award (see 14 below) during which the assessment phase was completed; *or*
- you are a lone parent previously on income support with a disability premium and within the last 12 weeks you have been moved off income support because of the age of your youngest child.

ESA Regs, reg 7

5. The work capability assessment

The work capability assessment (WCA) is more complex than the personal capability assessment (used to determine entitlement to incapacity benefit) as it has three parts.

Limited capability for work assessment – The first part of the WCA looks at whether you have a *'limited capability for work'*. If you do, you are entitled to ESA.

Limited capability for work-related activity assessment – The second part of the WCA looks at whether you have a *'limited capability for work-related activity'*. It determines whether you are placed in the support group or the work-related activity group of claimants (see 6 and 7 below). It also determines the amount of ESA you receive and the responsibilities you must meet to retain the benefit.

Work-focused health-related assessment – This third part of the WCA applies only if you are in the work-related activity group. The assessment looks at barriers to work and what support you could receive to help you move towards and into work. If you fail to attend or participate in the assessment, your ESA may be reduced.

See Chapter 10 for details of the WCA.

6. The support group

If you have a limited capability for work-related activity under the WCA, you are placed in the support group. You do not have to undertake work-related activities, although you can volunteer to do so. You receive a higher rate of ESA (see 8 below) than if you are in the work-related activity group.

7. The work-related activity group

If you do not have a limited capability for work-related activity under the WCA, you are placed in the work-related activity group. In this group you must meet work-related conditions, including attending six work-focused interviews. If you fail to meet the conditions, your ESA payment may be reduced (see 15 below).

8. ESA rates

ESA is paid at different rates depending on your circumstances. You may be entitled to income-related ESA or contributory ESA, or a combination of the two. The levels of payment for these two elements are detailed in Chapters 11(9) and 12(5)-(8) respectively.

The level of ESA you receive (whether income-related or contributory) is also determined by whether you are in the 'assessment phase' or the 'main phase' of your claim.

Assessment phase – During the 13-week assessment phase, ESA is paid at a lower level, which is called the 'basic allowance'. If you are aged under 25 during the assessment phase, you are paid a lower rate of the basic allowance.

Main phase – Once you have completed the 13-week assessment phase, you receive an additional payment on top of the basic allowance. The level of this payment will depend on whether you are in the support group or the work-related activity group. If you are under 25, the lower rate of the basic allowance will no longer apply; you will be paid the same rate as someone aged 25 or over.

The different levels of payment during the two phases are illustrated in the diagram below.

9. Do you qualify?

The following rules apply to all ESA claims. To be entitled to ESA, you need to satisfy all the following basic conditions. You must:

- have a limited capability for work – see Chapter 10(2);
- not be in work – see below;
- be aged 16 or over;
- be under pensionable age (currently 60 for a woman and 65 for a man);
- be in Great Britain (GB) – see below;
- not be entitled to income support;
- not be entitled to jobseeker's allowance (and not a member of a couple entitled to joint-claim jobseeker's allowance); *and*
- not be within a period of entitlement to statutory sick pay.

WRA, Ss.1(3) & 20(1)

You must also meet one of the following conditions:

- you satisfy the national insurance contribution conditions – see Chapter 11(5); *or*
- your limited capability for work began before you were 20 (or 25 in some cases) – see Chapter 11(8); *or*
- you satisfy the conditions for income-related ESA – see Chapter 12(2).

WRA, S.1(2)

You can be entitled to both contributory ESA and income-related ESA at the same time (see Chapter 12(5)).

Work

You are not entitled to ESA in any week in which you work. This means any work you do, whether or not you expect to be paid for it.

ESA Regs, reg 40(1)

However, there are certain types of work that you can undertake and still be entitled to ESA. For details see Chapter 16(3).

Presence in Great Britain

To be entitled to ESA you must be in GB, which means England, Scotland and Wales. You can, however, continue to be entitled to ESA during a temporary absence from GB in the circumstances set out in Chapter 51(3).

10. Making a claim

You are usually expected to start your claim for ESA by ringing the Jobcentre Plus claim-line (0800 055 6688; textphone 0800 023 4888). The claim-line should put you through to your nearest Jobcentre Plus contact centre. The contact centre will confirm your identity, then ask if you want to claim under the 'special rules' that apply to terminally ill claimants (see below). The contact centre then takes the details of your claim over the telephone. Once they have finished, a 'customer statement' is sent to you confirming the details so you can check they are correct. The contact centre may ring you back for additional information if you do not have it to hand.

If you cannot use a telephone, online claims can be made at www.dwp.gov.uk/eservice. Alternatively, you can ask for a paper claim-form, ESA1, to make a written claim at Jobcentre Plus offices, or a local authority housing benefit office in some circumstances.

Who should claim? – If you are a member of a couple and both of you could claim income-related ESA, you must decide which of you will make the claim. If one of you would be more likely to be assessed as having a limited capability for work-related activity (and thus be placed in the support group, where a higher level of ESA will be payable – see Chapter 10(3)), they should be the claimant.

If you cannot decide who should be the claimant, a decision maker will decide.

C&P Regs, reg 4I

ESA: Levels of payment during the two phases

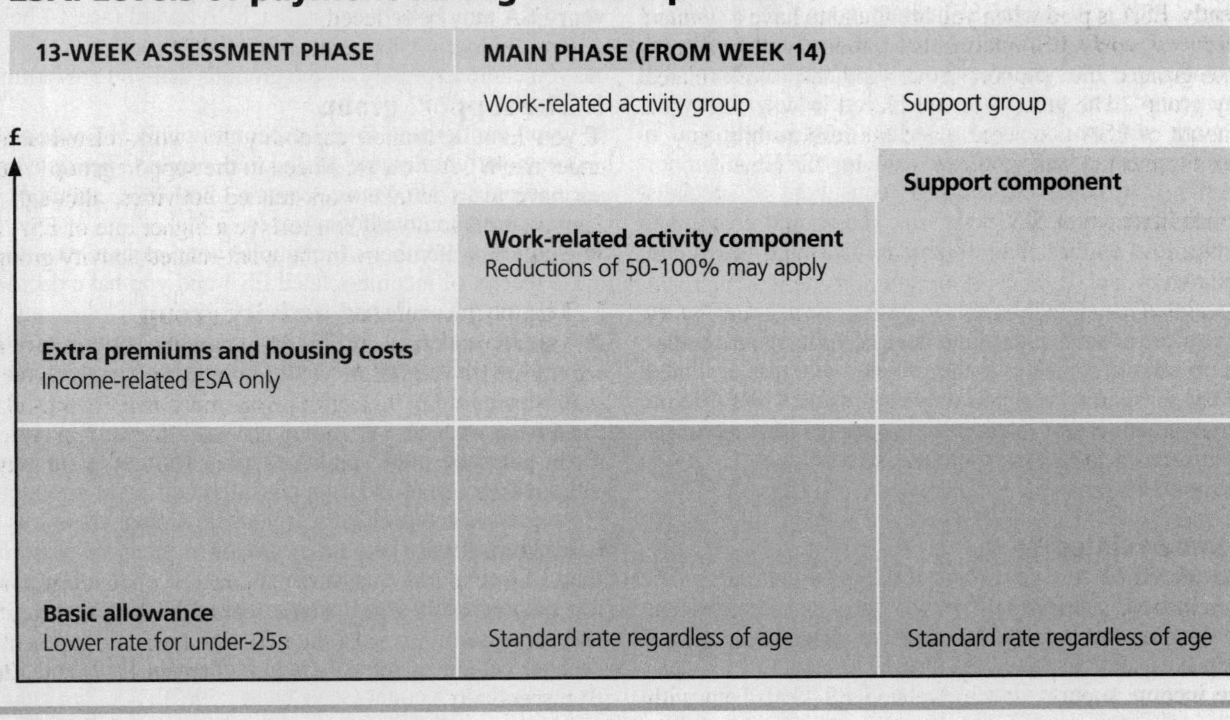

For anyone who cannot claim for themselves because of mental incapacity, Jobcentre Plus can appoint someone to act on their behalf (see Chapter 59(4)).

No claim necessary – If you are appealing against a decision that you do not have a limited capability for work, you do not need to submit a new claim in order to continue receiving ESA while your appeal is dealt with (although you should let Jobcentre Plus know that you want to continue receiving ESA while appealing).

C&P Regs, reg 3(j)

Medical evidence

For the first seven days of any period of limited capability for work, you do not need a medical certificate. Once you have had a limited capability for work for more than seven days, you must forward a medical certificate (form Med 3) from your doctor to the office dealing with your ESA claim (Jobcentre Plus should send you an envelope to do this when you first claim). If you are under 20 (or 25) and claiming contributory ESA without having to meet the contribution conditions (see Chapter 11(8)), you will also need a backdated medical certificate covering the 28 weeks before the date from which you are claiming.

Social Security (Medical Evidence) Regs 1976, regs 2 & 5

If you work for an employer and do not get statutory sick pay, you will also need to send in form SSP1, which you get from your employer, as well as a medical certificate from the first day of your claim.

C&P Regs, reg 10

It is important to keep your medical certificates up to date. Ask your doctor for a new certificate well before the old one runs out. If you are not covered by medical evidence for each day of your claim, benefit could be withheld. Until you have passed (or are treated as having passed) the limited capability for work test in the work capability assessment, you must carry on sending in certificates. Jobcentre Plus will let you know if this is no longer required. If you do not send in a certificate, Jobcentre Plus should suspend payment and apply the work capability assessment.

Special rules

If you are terminally ill, your claim can be dealt with under the 'special rules'. You count as terminally ill if you *'suffer from a progressive disease and [your] death can reasonably be expected within 6 months'*. Under the special rules, your ESA claim will be fast-tracked. Once you have made the claim, Jobcentre Plus will normally contact your GP, consultant or specialist nurse to confirm that you are terminally ill. Once Jobcentre Plus receives such confirmation, they will automatically treat you as having a limited capability for both work and work-related activity (thus putting you in the support group and entitling you to the ESA support component). If, however, your GP, consultant or specialist nurse has given you a DS1500 form, you should give this to Jobcentre Plus as they may be able to deal with your claim immediately.

Jobcentre Plus should be able to make a decision under the special rules within five working days of your initial claim.

When a claim is made on the grounds of terminal illness, you do not have to serve the 13-week assessment phase before being put in the support group and the support component can be paid from the beginning of your ESA award.

ESA Regs, regs 2 & 7(1)(a)

11. Date of claim

For telephone claims, your date of claim is the date of the initial telephone call to the Jobcentre Plus claim-line, as long as you provide the required information during that call and approve the customer statement (see 10 above).

For written claims, your date of claim is the date you inform Jobcentre Plus of your intention to claim, as long as that office receives a properly completed claim-form from you within a month of your first contact (this period can only be extended if the decision maker considers it reasonable to do so). The same time limit applies if you are making an ESA claim at a local authority housing benefit office.

C&P Regs, reg 6(1F)

Advance awards – If you are in one of the groups of people who are treated as having a limited capability for work (see Chapter 10(2)) and are not entitled to contributory ESA and have part-time earnings or other income, you may find you are not entitled to income-related ESA during the 13-week assessment phase if your income or earnings are greater than your ESA applicable amount (see Chapter 12(6)). This could change after the assessment phase, once the award of the support or work-related activity component increases your applicable amount (see Chapter 12(7)). In this case, you should make an advance claim for income-related ESA; the day after the end of the 13-week assessment phase is treated as your date of award of ESA and benefit will be paid from that point. You will still be subject to a work-focused interview after eight weeks (see 15 below) and the work capability assessment within 13 weeks (see Chapter 10).

ESA Regs, reg 146

Advance claims – If you are receiving statutory sick pay (SSP) you cannot claim ESA. However, if you know your SSP will be running out, you can make an advance claim for ESA up to three months before your SSP expires. This can help to ensure minimal delays in receiving any ESA to which you may be entitled.

12. Late claims

Your award of ESA can be backdated for up to three months prior to the date of your claim (see above) if you claim for that earlier period and meet all the entitlement conditions during it. You will need to ask your doctor for a backdated medical certificate (Med 5) to the date you want to claim from, or 28 weeks before this if you are under 20, or 25, and claiming contributory ESA without having to meet the contribution conditions – see Chapter 11(8).

C&P Regs, Sch 4, para 16

13. Payments

Waiting days – You are not normally entitled to ESA for the first three days of your claim (these are called 'waiting days'), unless:

- your claim links to an earlier ESA award (see 14 below); *or*
- you claim expressly on the grounds that you are terminally ill; *or*
- your entitlement to ESA begins within 12 weeks of a previous entitlement to income support, pension credit, jobseeker's allowance, carer's allowance, statutory sick pay or maternity allowance; *or*
- you are a member of a couple, your partner was already in receipt of income-related ESA and you have decided to become the claimant; *or*
- you are under 20 (or 25) and claiming contributory ESA without having to meet the contribution conditions (see Chapter 11(8)).

ESA Regs, reg 144

How you are paid – ESA is paid fortnightly in arrears, although Jobcentre Plus can consider a different arrangement if this causes you problems. If your ESA payment is less than £1 a week, it may be paid in arrears at intervals of no more than 13 weeks. The minimum payment of ESA is 10p a week; any entitlement of less than 10p a week is not payable.

C&P Regs, reg 26C

Your benefit is normally paid into a bank, building society or Post Office account (see Chapter 59(5)).

14. Linking rules

Any two periods of limited capability for work that are separated by no more than 12 weeks are treated as a single period. Therefore, if you have to reclaim ESA within 12 weeks of a previous award (eg if you started work but could not cope with it), you go back onto ESA on the same terms as before, without needing to undergo the 13-week assessment phase again.

ESA Regs, reg 145(1)

If you are covered by the extended linking rules for 'work or training beneficiaries', any two periods of limited capability for work separated by no more than 104 weeks are treated as one single period. Similar extended linking rules also apply to certain tax credit claimants and trainees. For details see Chapter 16(12).

15. Work-focused interviews

Most new ESA claimants are expected to take part in an initial work-focused interview during or shortly after the 8th week of their claim. If you are placed in the work-related activity group (see 7 above), you will be expected to take part in a series of five further work-focused interviews, the second at 14 weeks and then usually monthly. At each interview, you meet a personal adviser who helps you to explore barriers and identify support to assist you to move towards work. At the initial work-focused interview, the personal adviser will be an officer from Jobcentre Plus. At follow-up interviews, it is possible that the personal adviser will be from a private or voluntary sector organisation contracted to do this work.

A work-focused interview has the following functions:

- to assess your prospects and assist or encourage you to remain in or obtain work;
- to identify activities, training, education or rehabilitation you could undertake to improve your job prospects; *and*
- to identify current or future work opportunities (including self-employment) that are relevant to your needs and abilities.

ESA Regs, reg 55

If you do not attend or take part in a work-focused interview as required, your benefit can be reduced (see below).

Who is not required to take part

You are not required to take part in a work-focused interview if you:

- have been placed in the support group (see 6 above); *or*
- are aged under 18 (although you will have a learning-focused interview with Connexions); *or*
- are aged 60 or over; *or*
- are entitled to credits-only contributory ESA.

ESA Regs, reg 54

The requirement to take part can be waived altogether or deferred to a later date at the discretion of the personal adviser. If the adviser declines your request to defer or waive the interview, you cannot appeal against that decision (although you can appeal against any benefit reduction applied as a result).

D&A Regs, Sch 2, para 28

Attendance is waived – The personal adviser can waive the requirement to take part in an interview if they believe the interview would not be of assistance to you because you are likely to be starting or returning to work soon.

ESA Regs, reg 60

Attendance is deferred – The requirement to take part can be deferred if the personal adviser believes it would not be of assistance or appropriate in the circumstances at that particular time. A deferral can be made at any time after the requirement to take part in the work-focused interview is made, including after the time that the work-focused interview was due to take place. If the interview is deferred, the personal adviser will seek agreement with you for another appropriate date to hold the interview.

ESA Regs, reg 59

At the interview

Jobcentre Plus or the private or voluntary sector contractor must notify you of the requirement to attend the work-focused interview. They will usually phone you to arrange the date, time and place for the interview. If they are not able to do this, they will write to you with details of the appointment.

If they are persuaded that it would cause you undue inconvenience or endanger your health for you to attend a work-focused interview elsewhere, they can arrange for it to take place in your own home.

ESA Regs, reg 56

Taking part in the interview – To meet the interview requirement, you must not only attend the interview at the right time and place, but also must 'take part' in it. Taking part involves participating in discussions with the personal adviser on:

- any activity you are willing to undertake to improve your job prospects;
- any such activity that you may have done previously;
- any progress you may have made towards remaining in or obtaining work; *and*
- any work-focused health-related assessment you may have taken part in.

As a guide, the personal adviser may use a copy of the report that was obtained in the work-focused health-related assessment (see Chapter 10(4)).

ESA Regs, reg 57(3)

What are you asked at the interview? – When taking part in the interview, you are expected to answer questions about any of the following:

- your educational qualifications and vocational training;
- your work history;
- any paid or unpaid work you are doing;
- your aspirations for future work;
- your work-related skills and abilities;
- your opinion on the extent to which your condition restricts your ability to remain in or obtain work; *and*
- any caring or childcare responsibilities you may have.

You will also be asked to help the personal adviser complete an 'action plan'.

ESA Regs, 57(2)

What is an action plan? – An action plan is a record made by the personal adviser. It contains a written record of the work-focused interview and lists the steps you are willing to take to enhance your job prospects. You must be given a copy of the action plan.

ESA Regs, reg 58

What if you do not take part in the interview?

If you fail to take part in a work-focused interview, your ESA can be reduced. This reduction will not take place, however, if you can show 'good cause' for your failure to attend or participate. You will be notified that you have failed to take part. You then have five working days to show good cause. The five-day period is counted from the second day after the date on the notification letter.

ESA Regs, reg 61(1) & 65

Good cause – In deciding whether you had good cause for not taking part in an interview, Jobcentre Plus must consider whether any of the following apply:

- you misunderstood the requirement to take part because of learning disabilities, language or literacy difficulties, or because you were given misleading official information;
- you had transport difficulties and had no reasonable alternative;

A B C D E F G H I J K L M N O P Q R S T U

- you had a job interview or were pursuing self-employed work opportunities;
- you (or someone you care for) had a medical or dental appointment and it would have been unreasonable to rearrange it;
- you or a dependant or someone you care for became ill or had an accident;
- you were at the funeral of a close friend or relative that day;
- it was impossible for you to attend at the given time and place because of your physical or mental health;
- you could not attend on that day or time because of your religious custom and practice.

This list is not exhaustive and Jobcentre Plus can consider other reasons.

ESA Regs, reg 61(3)

Outside the five-day time limit – If you do not show good cause within five working days, you will receive a decision that you have failed to take part in the work-focused interview. If you subsequently obtain facts that show you did have good cause, you can ask Jobcentre Plus to revise their decision. You have one month from the date of the decision to do this. You need to be able to show that the facts could not reasonably have been brought to the attention of Jobcentre Plus within the 5-day time limit.

D&A Regs, reg 3(8C)

Reductions

When will the reduction take effect? – A reduction will only be made to your ESA once the assessment phase of your claim has passed. This is usually after you have been on ESA for 13 weeks. The reduction ceases to apply once you have taken part (or been treated as having taken part) in a work-focused interview. The reduction also ceases if you move into one of the groups of people who do not have to take part in a work-focused interview (see above), for example, if you are placed in the support group.

ESA Regs, reg 64(2)

How much is the reduction? – The reduction is made in two stages: for the first four weeks an amount equal to 50% of the work-related activity component is taken from your ESA. Thereafter, the reduction is equivalent to 100% of the work-related activity component. The reduction is only removed completely when it is decided you have taken part in a work-focused interview. The reduction applies regardless of the rate of payment of ESA that you actually receive.

ESA Regs, regs 63(2)

If you are entitled to both contributory and income-related ESA (see Chapter 12(5)), any reduction will first be applied to contributory ESA. A reduction is only applied to income-related ESA if the reduction has resulted in the complete removal of contributory ESA and there is still some reduction outstanding.

ESA Regs, reg 63(4)

A reduction will never result in the complete removal of ESA; you will always be left with at least 10p a week. This allows claimants receiving income-related ESA to retain their entitlement to ESA while the reduction is in place, thus preserving their rights to passported benefits such as free prescriptions and housing benefit.

ESA Regs, reg 63(3)(a)

Challenging decisions

You can appeal against a decision that you failed to take part in a work-focused interview. You can also appeal against a decision that you did not show good cause for failing to take part in a work-focused interview within five working days of the interview. You can appeal using form GL24, available from the Jobcentre Plus office. You have one month from the date of the decision to lodge the appeal.

Alternatively, you can ask Jobcentre Plus to reconsider and revise their decision. You have one month from the date of the decision in which to do this.

The process of challenging decisions is covered in Chapter 60.

16. Disqualification

You can be disqualified from receiving ESA for up to six weeks if you:

- have a limited capability for work through your own misconduct (but not if your limited capability is due to pregnancy or a sexually transmitted disease). Misconduct is a wilful act, eg recklessly and knowingly breaking accepted safety rules;
- do not accept medical or other treatment (not including vaccination, inoculation or major surgery) recommended by a doctor or hospital that is treating you – but only if the treatment would be likely to remove the limitation on your capability for work and you do not have good cause for your refusal;
- behave in a way calculated to slow down your recovery, without having good cause; *or*
- are absent from home without leaving word where you can be found, without having good cause.

A disqualification will not apply if you are considered to be a 'person in hardship'.

ESA Regs, reg 157

Hardship – You are considered to be a person in hardship if you:

- or a member of your family are pregnant;
- are under 18 (or if you have a partner, you are both under 18).

You will also be considered to be a person in hardship if you or your partner:

- are responsible for a child or young person who lives with you;
- have been awarded attendance allowance or disability living allowance care component (or have claimed one of these benefits within the last 26 weeks and the claim has not yet been determined);
- devote a considerable portion of each week to caring for another person who has been awarded attendance allowance or disability living allowance care component (or has claimed one of these benefits within the last 26 weeks and the claim has not yet been determined); *or*
- are aged 60 or over.

Even if one of the above grounds is not satisfied, you can still be considered a person in hardship if a decision maker is satisfied that unless ESA is paid, you or a member of your family will suffer hardship. The decision maker must take into account any resources likely to be available to you. They must also look at whether there is a substantial risk that you will have much-reduced amounts of, or lose altogether, essential items such as food, clothing and heating, and if so for how long.

If you have been disqualified from receiving ESA and you believe one of the above categories applies to you, you must tell Jobcentre Plus which one applies.

ESA Regs, reg 158

10 The work capability assessment

1. What is the work capability assessment?

The work capability assessment (WCA) is a key part of employment and support allowance (ESA). It has some similarities to the incapacity benefit personal capability assessment but it is more complex. This is because it is made up of three different parts.

The first part of the WCA determines whether or not you are entitled to ESA. The second determines whether you join the 'support group' or the 'work-related activity group' (see 3 below). The third provides a report for you and your personal adviser that can be used in any work-focused interviews you may be required to attend. The three parts of the assessment are explained below.

When will the WCA take place? – The first WCA takes place during the 13-week assessment phase that follows your initial claim (see Chapter 9(4)). Once this has taken place, and your entitlement to ESA has been established, you may be required to attend further WCAs at intervals in the future to determine whether you are still entitled to ESA and, if so, whether you should remain in the same group.

2. The limited capability for work assessment

The first part of the WCA looks at whether you have a limited capability for work and is used to decide whether you are entitled to ESA. If you are assessed as not having a limited capability for work, you need to consider claiming jobseeker's allowance instead (see Chapter 15) or appealing against the decision that you do not have a limited capability for work (see 9 below). If you appeal, you can continue to claim the basic allowance of ESA until a decision is made on your appeal by a tribunal.

This part of the WCA is a points-related assessment of your physical and mental health and cognitive functions considered within a range of activities. Points are awarded on the basis of any limitations with respect to each activity and added up. If the total reaches 15 points or more, you are assessed as having a limited capability for work and entitled to ESA.

ESA Regs, reg.19(3)

Some 'specific' disease or disablement – In assessing your capability or otherwise in performing each activity, it must be clear that an inability to do an activity arises:

- from a specific bodily disease or disablement;
- from a specific mental illness or disablement; *or*
- as a direct result of treatment provided by a registered medical practitioner for such a disease, illness or disablement.

ESA Regs, reg 19(5)

'Specific' is not the same as 'specified', so it may not be essential that the cause of the disease or disablement is identified (CS/7/82). For example, you may suffer pain, the cause of which has not yet been diagnosed. A normal pregnancy does not count as a disease or disablement, but conditions such as high blood pressure arising because of the pregnancy do count. Symptoms such as the pain experienced by those with 'chronic pain syndrome' or by those who are showing 'illness behaviour' are likely to be taken into account, as there is sufficient medical consensus that these are 'specific' conditions (CIB/5435/2002).

The physical descriptors

The physical descriptors in the limited capability for work assessment are grouped into 11 types of activity. These are:

- walking;
- standing and sitting;
- bending and kneeling;
- reaching;
- picking up and moving things;
- manual dexterity (using your hands);
- speech;
- hearing;
- seeing;
- controlling your bowels and bladder;
- remaining conscious.

Within each activity is a list of descriptors with scores ranging from 0 to 15 points. The descriptors explain related tasks of varying degrees of difficulty. You score points when you are not able to perform a task described. If more than one descriptor applies to you, you only include the score from the one with the highest points within each activity.

ESA Regs, reg 19(6)

If you score 15 points in any one activity, you are assessed as having a limited capability for work. Scores from any of the activities (in both the physical and the mental parts of the assessment) can be added together. If your total score reaches 15, you are assessed as having a limited capability for work.

ESA Regs, reg 19(3)

The descriptors and the points assigned to each one are listed in Box D.3.

Artificial aids – The test takes into account your abilities when using any aid or appliance that you would normally wear or use, eg glasses, a walking stick or a prosthesis.

ESA Regs, reg 19(4)

The mental, cognitive and intellectual function descriptors

The descriptors relating to mental, cognitive and intellectual functions in the limited capability for work assessment are grouped into ten types of activity. These are:

- learning or comprehension in the completion of tasks;
- awareness of hazard;
- memory and concentration;
- execution of tasks;
- initiating and sustaining personal action;
- coping with change;
- getting about;
- coping with social situations;
- propriety of behaviour with other people;
- dealing with other people.

As with the physical descriptors, there is a list of descriptors under each activity heading. The scoring follows the same pattern. You score points if you cannot perform the task described, with the highest points you score under each activity totalled up. If you score 15 points in any one activity, you are assessed as having a limited capability for work. Scores from any of the activities (in both the physical and the mental parts of the assessment) can be added together, and if your total score reaches 15 points you are assessed as having a limited capability for work.

ESA Regs, reg 19(3) & (6)

The descriptors and points assigned to each mental descriptor are listed in Box D.4.

Treated as having a limited capability for work

You can be automatically treated as having a limited capability for work, without having to undergo the assessment, in the following circumstances:

- you are suffering from a progressive disease and consequently your death can reasonably be expected within six months (ie you are terminally ill);
- you are receiving treatment by way of intravenous, intraperitoneal or intrathecal chemotherapy, or you are

D.3 Limited capability for work assessment – physical functions

Activities 1 to 11 cover physical functions. To be assessed as having a limited capability for work, you need to score 15 points or more. Add together the highest score from each activity that applies to you.

The scores from these activities can be added to those in the mental, cognitive and intellectual function activities (see Box D.4).

Activity	Points
1. Walking with a walking stick or other aid if such aid is normally used	
A Cannot walk at all	15
B Cannot walk more than 50 metres on level ground without repeatedly stopping or severe discomfort	15
C Cannot walk up or down two steps even with the support of a handrail	15
D Cannot walk more than 100 metres on level ground without stopping or severe discomfort	9
E Cannot walk more than 200 metres on level ground without stopping or severe discomfort	6
F None of the above apply	0
2. Standing and sitting	
A Cannot stand for more than 10 minutes, unassisted by another person, even if free to move around, before needing to sit down	15
B Cannot sit in a chair with a high back and no arms for more than 10 minutes before needing to move from the chair because the degree of discomfort experienced makes it impossible to continue sitting	15
C Cannot rise to standing from sitting in an upright chair without physical assistance from another person	15
D Cannot move between one seated position and another seated position located next to one another without receiving physical assistance from another person	15
E Cannot stand for more than 30 minutes, even if free to move around, before needing to sit down	6
F Cannot sit in a chair with a high back and no arms for more than 30 minutes without needing to move from the chair because the degree of discomfort experienced makes it impossible to continue sitting	6
G None of the above apply	0
3. Bending or kneeling	
A Cannot bend to touch knees and straighten up again	15
B Cannot bend, kneel or squat, as if to pick up a light object, such as a piece of paper, situated 15cm from the floor on a low shelf, and to move it and straighten up again without the help of another person	9
C Cannot bend, kneel or squat, as if to pick up a light object off the floor and straighten up again without the help of another person	6
D None of the above apply	0
4. Reaching	
A Cannot raise either arm as if to put something in the top pocket of a coat or jacket	15
B Cannot put either arm behind back as if to put on a coat or jacket	15
C Cannot raise either arm to top of head as if to put on a hat	9
D Cannot raise either arm above head height as if to reach for something	6
E None of the above apply	0
5. Picking up and moving or transferring by the use of the upper body and arms (excluding all other activities specified in Part 1 of this Schedule)	
A Cannot pick up and move a 0.5 litre carton full of liquid with either hand	15
B Cannot pick up and move a one litre carton full of liquid with either hand	9
C Cannot pick up and move a light but bulky object such as an empty cardboard box, requiring the use of both hands together	6
D None of the above apply	0
6. Manual dexterity	
A Cannot turn a 'star-headed' sink tap with either hand	15
B Cannot pick up a £1 coin or equivalent with either hand	15
C Cannot turn the pages of a book with either hand	15
D Cannot physically use a pen or pencil	9
E Cannot physically use a conventional keyboard or mouse	9
F Cannot do up/undo small buttons, such as shirt or blouse buttons	9
G Cannot turn a 'star-headed' sink tap with one hand but can with the other	6
H Cannot pick up a £1 coin or equivalent with one hand but can with the other	6
I Cannot pour from an open 0.5 litre carton full of liquid	6
J None of the above apply	0
7. Speech	
A Cannot speak at all	15
B Speech cannot be understood by strangers	15
C Strangers have great difficulty understanding speech	9
D Strangers have some difficulty understanding speech	6
E None of the above apply	0
8. Hearing with a hearing aid or other aid if normally worn	
A Cannot hear at all	15
B Cannot hear well enough to be able to hear someone talking in a loud voice in a quiet room, sufficiently clearly to distinguish the words being spoken	15
C Cannot hear someone talking in a normal voice in a quiet room, sufficiently clearly to distinguish the words being spoken	9

recovering from that treatment and Jobcentre Plus is satisfied that you should be treated as having a limited capability for work;

- you have been requested or given notice, under specific legislation, to refrain from work because you are a carrier of, or have been in contact with, an infectious disease;
- you are pregnant and there would be a serious risk to the health of you or your child if you did not refrain from work;
- you are pregnant or have recently given birth, are entitled to maternity allowance and are within the maternity allowance payment period;
- you are pregnant or have recently given birth but are not entitled to maternity allowance or statutory maternity pay from six weeks before the baby is due to two weeks after the birth.

ESA Regs, reg 20

D	Cannot hear someone talking in a loud voice in a busy street, sufficiently clearly to distinguish the words being spoken	6
E	None of the above apply	0

9. Vision including visual acuity and visual fields, in normal daylight or bright electric light, with glasses or other aid to vision if such aid is normally worn

A	Cannot see at all	15
B	Cannot see well enough to read 16 point print at a distance of greater than 20cm	15
C	Has 50% or greater reduction of visual fields	15
D	Cannot see well enough to recognise a friend at a distance of a least 5 metres	9
E	Has 25% or more but less than 50% reduction of visual fields	6
F	Cannot see well enough to recognise a friend at a distance of at least 15 metres	6
G	None of the above apply	0

10. Continence

A Continence other than enuresis (bed wetting) where the claimant does not have an artificial stoma or urinary collecting device

i	Has no voluntary control over the evacuation of the bowel	15
ii	Has no voluntary control over the voiding of the bladder	15
iii	At least once a month loses control of bowels so that the claimant cannot control the full evacuation of the bowel	15
iv	At least once a week, loses control of bladder so that the claimant cannot control the full voiding of the bladder	15
v	Occasionally loses control of bowels so that the claimant cannot control the full evacuation of the bowel	9
vi	At least once a month loses control of bladder so that the claimant cannot control the full voiding of the bladder	6
vii	Risks losing control of bowels or bladder so that the claimant cannot control the full evacuation of the bowel or the full voiding of the bladder if not able to reach a toilet quickly	6
viii	None of the above apply	0

B Continence where the claimant uses a urinary collecting device, worn for the majority of the time including an indwelling urethral or suprapubic catheter

i	Is unable to affix, remove or empty the catheter bag or other collecting device without receiving physical assistance from another person	15
ii	Is unable to affix, remove or empty the catheter bag or other collecting device without causing leakage of contents	15
iii	Has no voluntary control over the evacuation of the bowel	15
iv	At least once a month, loses control of bowels so that the claimant cannot control the full evacuation of the bowel	15
v	Occasionally loses control of bowels so that the claimant cannot control the full evacuation of the bowel	9
vi	Risks losing control of bowels so that the claimant cannot control the full evacuation of the bowel if not able to reach a toilet quickly	6
vii	None of the above apply	0

C Continence other than enuresis (bed wetting) where the claimant has an artificial stoma

i	Is unable to affix, remove or empty the stoma appliance without receiving physical assistance from another person	15
ii	Is unable to affix remove or empty the stoma appliance without causing leakage of contents	15
iii	Where the claimant's artificial stoma relates solely to the evacuation of the bowel, has no voluntary control over voiding of the bladder	15
iv	Where the claimant's artificial stoma relates solely to the evacuation of the bowel, at least once a week, loses control of bladder so that the claimant cannot control the full voiding of the bladder	15
v	Where the claimant's artificial stoma relates solely to the evacuation of the bowel, at least once a month, loses control of bladder so that the claimant cannot control the full voiding of the bladder	9
vi	Where the claimant's artificial stoma relates solely to the evacuation of the bowel, risks losing control of the bladder so that the claimant cannot control the full voiding of the bladder if not able to reach a toilet quickly	6
vii	None of the above apply	0

11. Remaining conscious during waking moments

A	At least once a week, has an involuntary episode of lost or altered consciousness, resulting in significantly disrupted awareness or concentration	15
B	At least once a month, has an involuntary episode of lost or altered consciousness, resulting in significantly disrupted awareness or concentration	9
C	At least twice in the six months immediately preceding the assessment, has had an involuntary episode of lost or altered consciousness, resulting in significantly disrupted awareness or concentration	6
D	None of the above apply	0

ESA Regs, Sch 2, part 1

Hospital inpatients – You are treated as having a limited capability for work on any day you are receiving medical or other treatment as an inpatient in a hospital or similar institution. You are also treated as having a limited capability for work on any day you are recovering from such treatment and Jobcentre Plus is satisfied that you should be treated as having a limited capability for work.

ESA Regs, reg 25

Renal failure and certain other regular treatments – You are treated as having a limited capability for work during any week in which you are receiving regular weekly treatment by way of haemodialysis for chronic renal failure, or treatment by way of plasmapheresis or radiotherapy, or regular weekly treatment by way of total parenteral nutrition for gross impairment of enteric function. You are also treated as having a limited capability for work during any week in which you

D.4 Limited capability for work assessment – mental, cognitive and intellectual functions

Activities 12 to 21 cover mental, cognitive and intellectual functions. To be assessed as having a limited capability for work, you need to score 15 points or more. Add together the highest score from each activity that applies to you.

The scores from these activities can be added to those in the physical function activities (see Box D.3).

Activity	Points
12. Learning or comprehension in the completion of tasks	
A Cannot learn or understand how to successfully complete a simple task, such as setting an alarm clock, at all	15
B Needs to witness a demonstration, given more than once on the same occasion, of how to carry out a simple task before the claimant is able to learn or understand how to complete the task successfully, but would be unable to successfully complete the task the following day without receiving a further demonstration of how to complete it	15
C Needs to witness a demonstration of how to carry out a simple task, before the claimant is able to learn or understand how to complete the task successfully, but would be unable to successfully complete the task the following day without receiving a verbal prompt from another person	9
D Needs to witness a demonstration of how to carry out a moderately complex task, such as the steps involved in operating a washing machine to correctly clean clothes, before the claimant is able to learn or understand how to complete the task successfully, but would be unable to successfully complete the task the following day without receiving a verbal prompt from another person	9
E Needs verbal instructions as to how to carry out a simple task before the claimant is able to learn or understand how to complete the task successfully, but would be unable, within a period of less than one week, to successfully complete the task without receiving a verbal prompt from another person	6
F None of the above apply	0
13. Awareness of hazard	
A Reduced awareness of the risks of everyday hazards (such as boiling water or sharp objects) would lead to daily instances of or to near-avoidance of: i) injury to self or others; *or* ii) significant damage to property or possessions, to such an extent that overall day-to-day life cannot successfully be managed	15
B Reduced awareness of the risks of everyday hazards would lead for the majority of the time to instances of or to near-avoidance of i) injury to self or others; *or* ii) significant damage to property or possessions, to such an extent that overall day-to-day life cannot successfully be managed without supervision from another person	9
C Reduced awareness of the risks of everyday hazards has led or would lead to frequent instances of or to near-avoidance of: i) injury to self or others; *or* ii) significant damage to property or possessions, but not to such an extent that overall day-to-day life cannot be managed when such incidents occur	6
D None of the above apply	0
14. Memory and concentration	
A On a daily basis, forgets or loses concentration to such an extent that overall day-to-day life cannot be successfully managed without receiving verbal prompting, given by someone else in the claimant's presence	15
B For the majority of the time, forgets or loses concentration to such an extent that overall day-to-day life cannot be successfully managed without receiving verbal prompting, given by someone else in the claimant's presence	9
C Frequently forgets or loses concentration to such an extent that overall day-to-day life can only be successfully managed with pre-planning, such as making a daily written list of all tasks forming part of daily life that are to be completed	6
D None of the above apply	0
15. Execution of tasks	
A Is unable to successfully complete any everyday task	15
B Takes more than twice the length of time it would take a person without any form of mental disablement to successfully complete an everyday task with which the claimant is familiar	15
C Takes more than one-and-a-half times but no more than twice the length of time it would take a person without any form of mental disablement to successfully complete an everyday task with which the claimant is familiar	9
D Takes one-and-a-half times the length of time it would take a person without any form of mental disablement to successfully complete an everyday task with which the claimant is familiar	6
E None of the above apply	0
16. Initiating and sustaining personal action	
A Cannot, due to cognitive impairment or a severe disorder of mood or behaviour, initiate or sustain any personal action (which means planning, organisation, problem solving, prioritising or switching tasks)	15
B Cannot, due to cognitive impairment or a severe disorder of mood or behaviour, initiate or sustain personal action without requiring daily verbal prompting given by another person in the claimant's presence	15
C Cannot, due to cognitive impairment or a severe	

have a day of recovery from such treatment and Jobcentre Plus is satisfied that you should be treated as having a limited capability for work.

However, you are only treated as having a limited capability for work from the first week in which at least two days of that week are days of treatment or recovery. The two days need not be consecutive.

ESA Regs, reg 26

3. The limited capability for work-related activity assessment

The second part of the WCA considers whether you have a limited capability for work-related activity. Although the wording is similar to that of the first part of the WCA, the second part has a different function. It determines whether you are placed in the support group or the work-related activity group (see below). The group you are placed in determines

disorder of mood or behaviour, initiate or sustain personal action without requiring verbal prompting given by another person in the claimant's presence for the majority of the time 9

D Cannot, due to cognitive impairment or a severe disorder of mood or behaviour, initiate or sustain personal action without requiring frequent verbal prompting given by another person in the claimant's presence 6

E None of the above apply 0

17. Coping with change

A Cannot cope with very minor, expected changes in routine, to the extent that overall day-to-day life cannot be managed 15

B Cannot cope with expected changes in routine (such as a pre-arranged permanent change to the routine time scheduled for a lunch break), to the extent that overall day-to-day life is made significantly more difficult 9

C Cannot cope with minor, unforeseen changes in routine (such as an unexpected change of the timing of an appointment on the day it is due to occur), to the extent that overall, day-to-day life is made significantly more difficult 6

D None of the above apply 0

18. Getting about

A Cannot get to any specified place with which the claimant is, or would be, familiar 15

B Is unable to get to a specified place with which the claimant is familiar, without being accompanied by another person on each occasion 15

C For the majority of the time is unable to get to a specified place with which the claimant is familiar without being accompanied by another person 9

D Is frequently unable to get to a specified place with which the claimant is familiar without being accompanied by another person 6

E None of the above apply 0

19. Coping with social situations

A Normal activities, for example, visiting new places or engaging in social contact, are precluded because of overwhelming fear or anxiety 15

B Normal activities, for example, visiting new places or engaging in social contact, are precluded for the majority of the time due to overwhelming fear or anxiety 9

C Normal activities, for example, visiting new places or engaging in social contact, are frequently precluded, due to overwhelming fear or anxiety 6

D None of the above apply 0

20. Propriety of behaviour with other people

A Has unpredictable outbursts of aggressive, disinhibited or bizarre behaviour, being either: 15
i) sufficient to cause disruption to others on a daily basis; *or*
ii) of such severity that, although occurring less frequently than on a daily basis, no reasonable person would be expected to tolerate them

B Has a completely disproportionate reaction to minor events or to criticism to the extent that the claimant has an extreme violent outburst leading to threatening behaviour or actual physical violence 15

C Has unpredictable outbursts of aggressive, disinhibited or bizarre behaviour, sufficient in severity and frequency to cause disruption for the majority of the time 9

D Has a strongly disproportionate reaction to minor events or to criticism, to the extent that the claimant cannot manage overall day-to-day life when such events or criticism occur 9

E Has unpredictable outbursts of aggressive, disinhibited or bizarre behaviour, sufficient to cause frequent disruption 6

F Frequently demonstrates a moderately disproportionate reaction to minor events or to criticism but not to such an extent that the claimant cannot manage overall day-to-day life when such events or criticism occur 6

G None of the above apply 0

21. Dealing with other people

A Is unaware of the impact of own behaviour to the extent that: 15
i) has difficulty relating to others even for brief periods, such as a few hours; *or*
ii) causes distress to others on a daily basis

B The claimant misinterprets verbal or non-verbal communication to the extent of causing himself or herself significant distress on a daily basis 15

C Is unaware of the impact of own behaviour to the extent that: 9
i) has difficulty relating to others for longer periods, such as a day or two; *or*
ii) causes distress to others for the majority of the time

D The claimant misinterprets verbal or non-verbal communication to the extent of causing himself or herself significant distress for the majority of the time 9

E Is unaware of impact of own behaviour to the extent that: 6
i) has difficulty relating to others for prolonged periods, such as a week; *or*
ii) frequently causes distress to others

F The claimant misinterprets verbal or non-verbal communication to the extent of causing himself or herself significant distress on a frequent basis 6

G None of the above apply 0

ESA Regs, Sch 2, part 2

A B C D E F G H I J K L M N O P Q R S T U

both the level of ESA you receive and the responsibilities you must meet to retain the benefit.

The assessment has a list of descriptors relating to both physical and mental/cognitive functions. If you meet at least one of these descriptors, you are placed in the support group of claimants. The descriptors are grouped together under the following 11 activity headings:

- walking;
- rising from sitting;
- picking up and moving things;
- reaching;
- manual dexterity;
- continence;
- maintaining personal hygiene;
- eating and drinking;
- learning or comprehension in the completion of tasks;
- personal action;
- communication.

The descriptors are listed in Box D.5 below.

Treated as having a limited capability for work-related activity

You can be automatically treated as having a limited capability for work-related activity if you are:

- suffering from a progressive disease and consequently your death can reasonably be expected within six months (ie you are terminally ill);
- receiving treatment by way of intravenous, intraperitoneal or intrathecal chemotherapy, or you are recovering from that treatment and Jobcentre Plus is satisfied that you have a limited capability for work-related activity;
- suffering from some specific disease or bodily or mental disablement and consequently there would be a substantial risk to the mental or physical health of any person if you were found not to have a limited capability for work-related activity; *or*

D.5 Limited capability for work-related activity assessment

If one or more of the following descriptors applies to you, you will be assessed as having a limited capability for work-related activity and will be placed in the support group of claimants.

1. Walking or moving on level ground

Cannot:

A walk (with a walking stick or other aid if such aid is normally used),

B move (with the aid of crutches if crutches are normally used), *or*

C manually propel the claimant's wheelchair,

more than 30 metres without repeatedly stopping, experiencing breathlessness or severe discomfort.

2. Rising from sitting and transferring from one seated position to another

Cannot complete both of the following:

A rise to standing from sitting in an upright chair without receiving physical assistance from someone else; *and*

B move between one seated position and another seated position located next to one another without receiving physical assistance from someone else.

3. Picking up and moving or transferring by the use of the upper body and arms (excluding standing, sitting, bending or kneeling and all other activities specified in this Schedule)

Cannot pick up and move 0.5 litre carton full of liquid with either hand.

4. Reaching

Cannot raise either arm as if to put something in the top pocket of a coat or jacket.

5. Manual dexterity

Cannot:

A turn a 'star-headed' sink tap with either hand; *or*

B pick up a £1 coin or equivalent with either hand.

6. Continence

A Continence other than enuresis (bed wetting) where the claimant does not have an artificial stoma or urinary collecting device:

a Has no voluntary control over the evacuation of the bowel;

b Has no voluntary control over the voiding of the bladder;

c At least once a week, loses control of bowels so that the claimant cannot control the full evacuation of the bowel;

d At least once a week, loses control of bladder so that the claimant cannot control the full voiding of the bladder;

e At least once a week, fails to control full evacuation of the bowel, owing to a severe disorder of mood or behaviour; *or*

f At least once a week, fails to control full voiding of the bladder, owing to a severe disorder of mood or behaviour.

B Continence where the claimant uses a urinary collecting device, worn for the majority of the time including an indwelling urethral or suprapubic catheter:

a Is unable to affix, remove or empty the catheter bag or other collecting device without receiving physical assistance from another person;

b Is unable to affix, remove or empty the catheter bag or other collecting device without causing leakage of contents;

c Has no voluntary control over the evacuation of the bowel;

d At least once a week loses control of bowels so that the claimant cannot control the full evacuation of the bowel; *or*

e At least once a week, fails to control full evacuation of the bowel, owing to a severe disorder of mood or behaviour.

C Continence other than enuresis (bed wetting) where the claimant has an artificial stoma appliance:

a Is unable to affix, remove or empty stoma appliance without receiving physical assistance from another person;

b Is unable to affix, remove or empty stoma without causing leakage of contents;

c Where the claimant's artificial stoma relates solely to the evacuation of the bowel, has no voluntary control over voiding of bladder;

d Where the claimant's artificial stoma relates solely to the evacuation of the bowel, at least once a week, loses control of the bladder so that the claimant cannot control the full voiding of the bladder; *or*

e Where the claimant's artificial stoma relates solely to the evacuation of the bowel, at least once a week, fails to control the full voiding of the bladder, owing to a severe disorder of mood or behaviour.

- pregnant and there would be a serious risk to the health of you or your child if you did not refrain from work-related activity.

ESA Regs, reg 35

The support group

If it is decided that you have a limited capability for work-related activity, you are placed in the support group. The work-related conditions do not apply to you. This means you do not have to attend work-focused interviews or undertake work-related activities (although you can volunteer to do so). Additionally, you receive a higher level of ESA than if you are placed in the work-related activity group.

The work-related activity group

If it is decided that you do not have a limited capability for work-related activity, you will be placed in the work-related activity group. You must meet certain work-related conditions to continue receiving ESA in full. These include attending a series of six work-focused interviews. If you fail to meet these conditions, your ESA payment can be reduced. If you are placed in the work-related activity group, you receive a lower level of ESA than if you are placed in the support group.

4. Work-focused health-related assessment

The third part of the WCA is the 'work-focused health-related assessment' (WFHRA). You only have to undergo this part of the assessment if you are in the work-related activity group, although you can volunteer to take part if you are in the support group. The WFHRA explores your views about returning to work, any barriers you face and what you could do to move back into work. It collects additional information about the things that you can do – your 'functional capacity' – despite your condition. The WFHRA collects information about any health-related or other interventions that could improve your functional capacity and support a move back into work. This

7. Maintaining personal hygiene

A Cannot clean own torso (excluding own back) without receiving physical assistance from someone else;

B Cannot clean own torso (excluding own back) without repeatedly stopping, experiencing breathlessness or severe discomfort;

C Cannot clean own torso (excluding own back) without receiving regular prompting given by someone else in the claimant's presence; *or*

D Owing to a severe disorder of mood or behaviour, fails to clean own torso (excluding own back) without receiving:
i) physical assistance from someone else; *or*
ii) regular prompting given by someone else in the claimant's presence.

8. Eating and drinking

A Conveying food or drink to the mouth:

a Cannot convey food or drink to the claimant's own mouth without receiving physical assistance from someone else;

b Cannot convey food or drink to the claimant's own mouth without repeatedly stopping, experiencing breathlessness or severe discomfort;

c Cannot convey food or drink to the claimant's own mouth without receiving regular prompting given by someone else in the claimant's physical presence; *or*

d Owing to a severe disorder of mood or behaviour, fails to convey food or drink to the claimant's own mouth without receiving:
i) physical assistance from someone else; *or*
ii) regular prompting given by someone else in the claimant's presence.

B Chewing or swallowing food or drink:

a Cannot chew or swallow food or drink;

b Cannot chew or swallow food or drink without repeatedly stopping, experiencing breathlessness or severe discomfort;

c Cannot chew or swallow food or drink without repeatedly receiving regular prompting given by someone else in the claimant's presence; *or*

d Owing to a severe disorder of mood or behaviour, fails to:
i) chew or swallow food or drink; *or*
ii) chew or swallow food or drink without regular prompting given by someone else in the claimant's presence.

9. Learning or comprehension in the completion of tasks

A Cannot learn or understand how to successfully complete a simple task, such as the preparation of a hot drink, at all;

B Needs to witness a demonstration, given more than once on the same occasion, of how to carry out a simple task before the claimant is able to learn or understand how to complete the task successfully, but would be unable to successfully complete the task the following day without receiving a further demonstration of how to complete it; *or*

C Fails to do any of the matters referred to in (A) or (B) owing to a severe disorder of mood or behaviour.

10. Personal action

A Cannot initiate or sustain any personal action (which means planning, organisation, problem solving, prioritising or switching tasks);

B Cannot initiate or sustain personal action without requiring daily verbal prompting given by someone else in the claimant's presence; *or*

C Fails to initiate or sustain basic personal action without requiring daily verbal prompting given by some else in the claimant's presence, owing to a severe disorder of mood or behaviour.

11. Communication

A None of the following forms of communication can be achieved by the claimant:
i) speaking (to a standard that may be understood by strangers);
ii) writing (to a standard that may be understood by strangers);
iii) typing (to a standard that may be understood by strangers);
iv) sign language to a standard equivalent to Level 3 British Sign Language;

B None of the forms of communication referred to in (A) are achieved by the claimant, owing to a severe disorder of mood or behaviour;

C Misinterprets verbal or non-verbal communication to the extent of causing distress to himself or herself on a daily basis; *or*

D Effectively cannot make himself or herself understood to others because of the claimant's disassociation from reality owing to a severe disorder of mood or behaviour.

ESA Regs, Sch 3

includes the use of appropriate aids and adaptations.

ESA Regs, reg 48

The information required for the WFHRA will be collected in a separate interview following the medical assessment for the first two parts of the WCA. This information is put into a report. The report will be sent to you and to a personal adviser, who can use it in any work-focused interviews you may be required to attend (see Chapter 9(15)). You will also be encouraged to share the report with your GP.

If the healthcare professional decides that, on the basis of the second part of the WCA, it is likely you have a limited capability for work-related activity, then the requirement to take part in the WFHRA can be deferred until Jobcentre Plus has made a decision on this issue.

ESA Regs, reg 52

You must take part in the WFHRA if required to do so, otherwise your ESA could be reduced (see 8 below).

5. How is the WCA applied?

A Jobcentre Plus decision maker looks at the information you have provided with your ESA claim to see if there is evidence that you have a limited capability for work and for work-related activity without having to make further enquiries. They should also see if there is evidence that you can be 'treated' as having a limited capability for work and for work-related activity (see 2 and 3 above). If the decision maker considers they do not have such evidence, they will send you the ESA50 questionnaire to complete.

6. Filling in the ESA50 questionnaire

The ESA50 questionnaire begins by asking for standard personal details (name, address, phone number, etc). It then asks about any help you may need to attend a medical, if one is arranged (see 7 below), and any times or dates that you would not be able to manage. You are asked to tell them about your illness or disability and the medication or treatment you are receiving for it (including side effects). You are asked to provide details of your GP and any other professionals who are giving you care, support or treatment (eg a physiotherapist, community psychiatric nurse, social worker, occupational therapist or support worker). There are also questions relating to any hospital or clinical treatment you may be receiving.

The rest of the form is an assessment of how your illness or disability affects your ability to work. It is divided into two parts: the first part asks about physical functions, the second about mental, cognitive and intellectual functions. Each part is divided into several headings, each of which relates to one of the activities listed in 2 above.

Part 1 – physical functions

This part is divided into 11 activity headings (see 2 above). In each case, you are first asked whether you can do that particular activity without any difficulty. Read the text under the heading before ticking the box, as you will find out more about what is meant by having a problem with that activity.

You are then usually asked about specific tasks related to each activity. For instance, with the activity 'bending and kneeling', you are asked about two such tasks: *'Can you bend to touch your knees and stand up straight again?'* and *'Can you bend, squat or kneel to pick up something very light off the floor without help from someone else?'*. In each case, you are usually offered one of three boxes to tick: *'yes'*, *'no'* or *'it varies'*, the last being helpful if your condition is variable. When deciding which box to tick, bear in mind that the question is whether you reasonably can or cannot do the particular task. Things like safety, tiredness, pain and discomfort may mean that, although you can actually perform the task, it is not reasonable to expect you to do so, or although you could perform it occasionally you could not repeat it with reasonable regularity.

There is a box in each section where you can give extra information on the difficulties you have with each task. Use the box to give details of how you are affected if you attempt to do a task. Are there any risks involved in attempting the task? Have you previously had any injuries or accidents attempting it? Say how often you would need to rest and whether you take pain killers, and explain the cumulative effects of exhaustion or pain on your ability to perform the tasks. If you take pain-killing medication, say whether it affects your ability to complete tasks. If your condition varies, try to give an idea of how many days each week you would be able to do the task and how many you would not.

This is a points-related test (see 2 above). To see how many points your answers in this part can potentially score, see Box D.3.

Risk – When a certain task would be a risk to your health, enough to put off any reasonable person from doing it, you should be treated as not able to do it. If you've been advised by a doctor, physiotherapist or other health professional to avoid an activity, be sure to note this in the box.

CSIB/12/96

Pain and fatigue – Pain, tiredness, stiffness, breathlessness, nausea, dizziness or balance problems might affect how difficult you find it to do things. If doing a particular task causes you too much pain or discomfort, you should be treated as not able to do it.

CIB/14587/96

Similarly, if you find it so tiring or painful to do a particular task that you could not repeat it within a reasonable time, or could only do it so slowly that you could not effectively complete the task, you should be treated as not able to do it.

Artificial aids – In each case, it is your abilities when using any aid or appliance that you would normally use, eg glasses, a walking stick or a prosthesis, that are taken into account.

ESA Regs, reg 19(4)

Part 2 – mental, cognitive and intellectual functions

This part of the form relates to a number of different types of condition, including mental illness, learning difficulties, the effects of head injuries and autistic spectrum disorders. You are asked broad questions about how your illness or disability affects your day-to-day life. The questions are grouped together into the ten headings (see 2 above).

In each case you are first asked whether you can manage that particular area of day-to-day life without any difficulty. Read the text under the heading before ticking the box. Each heading is usually broken down into two or three further questions. For instance, under 'Going out' you are asked, *'Do you feel confident enough to leave home on your own and go out to places you know?'* and *'Do you feel you cannot go out even if someone was there to look after you?'*. You are given a number of options in each case; such as *'usually'*, *'not very often'* and *'it varies'*.

There is a box within each heading where you can give extra information on the difficulties you have with each area of day-to-day life. Brief explanations are given next to the box as to the sort of things to write down.

To help you complete this part of the form, you might want to keep a diary for a couple of days listing all the day-to-day activities that you have difficulty doing or need assistance to do, including where you need reminding, prompting or encouraging to start or complete a task.

This is a points-related test (see 2 above). To see how many points your answers in this part can potentially score, see Box D.4.

Sending back the questionnaire

After completing the ESA50, sign and date the declaration at the end of the form. Before you send the form, photocopy it for future reference. You should return the form in the addressed envelope provided within four weeks from the day after it was sent. If you have not returned it within the time limit, you should be sent a further request asking you to complete the form. If you do not return the form within the next two weeks, you will be treated as not having a limited capability for work, and thus not entitled to ESA, unless you can show you had 'good cause' for failing to return it.

ESA Regs, reg 22

Good cause – When deciding whether you had good cause for failing to complete and send back the ESA50, Jobcentre Plus must take into account your health, your disability and whether you were outside Britain. However, other reasons could be valid. You have a right of appeal against a decision that you failed to send back a completed ESA50.

ESA Regs, reg 24

What happens next? – Your completed ESA50 is assessed by a DWP-approved healthcare professional. The healthcare professional considers all the evidence on your claim and may request further information from your own GP (or any other professional providing you with treatment) and/or ask that you be medically examined.

7. The medical assessment

Jobcentre Plus must give you at least seven days' notice of the time and place for the assessment, unless you agree to accept a shorter notice period. This may be arranged over the phone. If you cannot attend, you should inform the office that arranged the assessment as soon as possible.

ESA Regs, regs 23(3), 38(3) & 49(2)

The medical assessment is carried out by a healthcare professional working on behalf of the DWP. They should have read a copy of your completed ESA50 form. At the assessment, they will try to identify whether or not your account in that form of your functional limitations corresponds with their findings. You will be asked questions relating to your physical and mental capabilities, guided by what you wrote on the ESA50. Once this is finished, they may perform a physical examination of you if necessary.

The decisions as to whether or not you have a limited capability for work or a limited capability for work-related activity are not taken by the healthcare professional. They will send their medical report to a Jobcentre Plus decision maker, who will make the two decisions.

If you fail to attend – If you do not attend, you will be treated as not having a limited capability for work unless you can show you had 'good cause' for not attending (see 6 above). You will be contacted and asked to explain your reasons. If the decision maker refuses to accept that you had good cause, you can appeal. You should also make a new claim for benefit in case your appeal is unsuccessful.

ESA Regs, reg 23

At the assessment

When the healthcare professional is ready to see you, they will come to get you from the waiting area to take you into the examination room. Note that this gives them a chance to watch how you manage to rise from a chair and walk.

During the assessment, the healthcare professional will identify the descriptors that they consider apply to you with respect to both the limited capability for work test and the limited capability for work-related activity test. To do this, they will ask questions about your daily activities including hobbies or leisure activities. They will observe how you manage during the assessment itself and they may give you a clinical examination. They should provide a full explanation for their choice in the report to the decision maker, particularly where their opinion differs from yours.

Physical disabilities – Explain your abilities as fully as you can. You should not assume the healthcare professional knows you can only perform an activity with discomfort, that your ability varies, etc. You should tell the healthcare professional about any pain or tiredness you feel, or would feel, while carrying out these activities, both on the day of the examination and over time. Also consider how you would feel if you had to do the same activity repeatedly. Try not to overestimate your ability to do these tasks. Focus on the problems and difficulties you have, rather than on the ways you manage to deal with those difficulties.

The healthcare professional's opinion should not be based on a snapshot of your condition on the day of the examination. They should consider the effects of your condition over time.

Mental disabilities – The healthcare professional needs to consider a number of different disabilities and conditions that may apply to you, including mental health, learning disability and autistic spectrum disorders. To do this, they should ask how your condition affects your day-to-day abilities (eg going to the shops, cooking food and travelling on your own), whether you can understand and remember things, whether you can concentrate on tasks, how you cope with change and unexpected situations, and how you get on with other people. When you explain how your condition affects your day-to-day abilities, tell the healthcare professional how you are most of the time. If your condition varies over time or from day to day, tell them how often it varies and for how long at a time. Answer the questions as honestly and fully as you can. If you do not understand a question, ask the healthcare professional to explain what they mean or to repeat the question.

You may find it helpful to have someone with you at the assessment. This could be a relative, friend or care worker. They can help to fill in any gaps in what you tell the healthcare professional.

Exceptional circumstances

If the decision maker decides you do not meet the limited capability for work test, they can still treat you as having a limited capability for work if the healthcare professional has obtained evidence that exceptional circumstances apply. These are that you are suffering from either:

- a life-threatening disease, in relation to which there is medical evidence that the disease is uncontrollable or uncontrolled by a recognised therapeutic procedure, and in the case of a disease that is uncontrolled there is a reasonable cause for it not to be controlled by a recognised therapeutic procedure; *or*
- some specific disease or bodily or mental disablement that would be a serious risk to any person's mental or physical health if you were found not to have a limited capability for work.

ESA Regs, reg 29

Decisions on exceptional circumstances – The decision maker decides if any of the exceptional circumstances apply, based on the report from the healthcare professional who examined you. If there is medical evidence from your own doctor, they must consider this as well and decide on the basis of *'the most reliable evidence available'*. You can appeal against the decision made.

8. Taking part in the work-focused health-related assessment

The work-focused health-related assessment (WFRHA) usually takes place in a medical examination centre following the medical assessment relating to the first two parts of the WCA. In certain circumstances, however, it may be possible for it to take place in your home if attending elsewhere would cause you undue inconvenience or endanger your health. Wherever it takes place, you must *'take part'* in the WFHRA by attending and providing all the information required for the assessment and participating in discussions with the healthcare professional.

ESA Regs, regs 50 & 51

You should be notified in writing of the requirement to attend the WFHRA at least seven days in advance, although you can agree to a shorter notice period. The notification letter will be sent by the healthcare professional who is to carry out the assessment and must contain details of the date, time and place of the assessment.

ESA Regs, reg 49

Failure to take part

If you fail to attend, or participate, in the WFHRA, your ESA payment will be reduced, unless within five working days of being notified of your failure you can show *'good cause'* as to why you failed to attend or participate. In determining whether you have shown good cause, the decision maker should consider your disability and state of health at the time of the assessment, whether you were outside Great Britain and other appropriate reasons at their discretion. The reductions will be applied in the same way and at the same level as those that apply if you fail to take part in a work-focused interview (see Chapter 9(15)).

ESA Regs, reg 53

Outside the five-day time limit – If you do not show good cause within five working days, you will receive a decision that you failed to take part in the WFHRA. If you subsequently obtain facts that show you did have good cause, you can ask the decision maker to revise their decision. You have 30 days from the date of the decision to do this. You need to be able to show that the facts could not reasonably have been brought to the attention of Jobcentre Plus within the 5-day time limit.

D&A Regs, reg 3(8C)

9. Appeals

You can appeal against most decisions that are made during the work capability assessment. You can appeal against a decision:

- that you do not have a limited capability for work;
- that you do not have a limited capability for work-related activity;
- that you do not have good cause for failing to send back the ESA50 questionnaire or attending the medical assessment;
- that you failed to take part in a WFHRA;

D.6 Appeal tactics – limited capability for work assessment

If a decision maker finds that you do not have a limited capability for work you will be sent a decision notice. You have one calendar month from the date the decision was sent to you to lodge an appeal. Your appeal will be heard by a First-tier Tribunal, the members of which are independent of the DWP. Details of the appeal process are covered in Chapter 60. This box explains ways you can maximise your chances of success with appeals over the limited capability for work assessment.

Get the medical report – Attached to the decision will be a summary of the assessment, telling you the activities in which it was decided you had some limitation and the total number of points allocated. (For list of descriptors and points, see Boxes D.3 and D.4.) Unfortunately, this does not necessarily identify where there are areas of dispute. You should ask Jobcentre Plus to send you a copy of the DWP healthcare professional's medical report, form ESA85. This will allow you to see where you might need to dispute it, or point out misunderstandings.

Opt for a hearing – Your chances of success are much higher if you go in person to the appeal hearing. When you receive the 'pre-hearing enquiry form', make sure you opt for a hearing.

Prepare your case – Seek advice from a Citizens Advice Bureau, DIAL or other advice centre, if you haven't already done so. They can help you prepare your case and may be able to represent you at the tribunal.

Here are some general guidelines to start with:

- ❑ Use Box D.3 and/or Box D.4 to see which descriptors apply to you and add up the points. Remember to think about your ability to perform the task reliably, safely, repeatedly and at reasonable speed, and the effects of pain, fatigue, etc. You can use this information to gather good medical evidence (see below) and to help you clarify to the tribunal exactly where in the assessment you should score points.
- ❑ If you think one of the circumstances applies in which you can be treated as having a limited capability for work (see Chapter 10(2)) seek medical evidence to confirm which one applies.
- ❑ If your medication affects your ability to complete tasks, or your physical condition affects your alertness, check whether this has been properly assessed under the mental, cognitive and intellectual functions assessment. Perhaps you have a mental health problem that has not been taken into account. For example, you may suffer from depression or anxiety but have not seen your GP about it. If so, you will stand more chance of having this taken into account if you have evidence, preferably medical evidence, to back you up.

Get medical evidence – Seek medical evidence in advance of the hearing. An advice centre may be able to help you with this. Your doctor may want to charge a fee for providing evidence for you, so check on this first – you may be able to get Legal Aid to pay for it (see Chapter 61(2)).

Ask your doctor, consultant, physiotherapist, etc to comment on the practical and functional problems you have regarding each descriptor that is at issue in your appeal.

- ❑ Where there is a dispute, what descriptors do they think should apply?
- ❑ Is your assessment of your limitations consistent with their understanding of your condition?
- ❑ Do any of the circumstances apply in which you can be treated as having limited capability for work?

It is important that your evidence focuses on these things, not simply on what condition you have and the treatment you receive.

If your condition has changed since the decision that you are appealing against was made, the tribunal cannot take that into account. So make sure that your evidence is about your condition as it was at the time of the decision.

Remember, however, that you know your abilities better than anyone. The DWP healthcare professional will only have seen you briefly so cannot know everything about you. What you say will count as evidence as long as it is not self-contradictory or implausible (R(I)2/51, R(SB)33/85). Your statements will, however, carry even more weight when supported by medical evidence.

At the tribunal hearing – The tribunal should be conducted in an informal manner and should consider all the medical and other evidence in making its decision, and reach its own conclusions on each descriptor that is at issue in the appeal, not simply adopt the report of the DWP healthcare professional (CIB/14722/96). If you think you need more evidence from your own doctor, ask for an adjournment. However, you do not have an automatic right to an adjournment for this reason, so it is best to get all of your medical evidence ready before the hearing.

- on exceptional circumstances.

The appeals process is described in Chapter 60.

Appeals over the limited capability for work assessment

If it is decided that you do not have a limited capability for work and none of the exceptional circumstances apply (see 7 above), you will not be entitled to ESA. You can appeal against this decision. The appeal tactics you can use in such cases are described in Box D.6.

While you are appealing – You can continue to claim the basic allowance of ESA (see Chapter 9(8)) while you are appealing against a decision that you do not have a limited capability for work. This applies if you are making a new claim for ESA or if your existing entitlement has been reassessed. If your appeal is successful, you will receive full arrears for any additional component that has not been paid.

ESA Regs, reg 6

What if you get worse before the appeal is heard? – A tribunal can look at your situation only as it was at the time of the decision you are appealing against. If your condition has deteriorated since then, they cannot take this into account.

To make sure you do not lose out while your appeal is pending, you should consider making a new claim if the change in circumstances means you should be entitled to ESA. If the new claim is unsuccessful, it is important to appeal against the new decision. If you do not, you will find that the tribunal hearing your first appeal cannot consider the period covered by your second unsuccessful claim, so that even if you win the first appeal, you will still be treated as not having a limited capability for work from the date of the later unsuccessful claim. Although a decision maker can revise the decision on the new claim following the successful first appeal, there is no guarantee this will happen or that they will revise the decision in your favour. To be on the safe side, lodge a second appeal.

Note: If you are still within six months of the date of the decision, a new claim will normally be refused unless your condition is significantly worse than before or you have a different condition (see 10 below).

Appeals over the limited capability for work-related activity assessment

If it is decided that you do not have a limited capability for work-related activity, you will be placed in the work-related activity group (see 3 above). If you consider that at least one of the descriptors listed in Box D.5 applies to you or alternatively one of the circumstances where you can be treated as having a limited capability for work-related activity applies to you (see 3 above), then you may wish to appeal against the decision.

If you appeal against the decision that you do not have a limited capability for work-related activity, you will continue to be paid the lower level of ESA for claimants placed in the work-related activity group. If the tribunal decides that you do have a limited capability for work-related activity, you can be placed in the support group and become entitled to the higher level of ESA. The difference between the two levels of benefit can be backdated to the time that the additional component for the support group would have become payable (which would normally be once the assessment phase of ESA was completed – see Chapter 9(4)).

The general advice provided in Box D.6, which applies to appeals over the limited capability for work assessment, also applies to appeals over the limited capability for work-related activity assessment. Any medical evidence you obtain should focus on confirming which Box D.5 descriptor applies to you or which circumstance where you can be treated as having a limited capability for work-related activity applies. In the former case, you could ask your doctor, consultant or physiotherapist, etc to comment on the practical and functional problems you have with respect to the descriptor in question.

10. What if your condition deteriorates?

After a decision that you do not have a limited capability for work – If you re-claim ESA within six months of a decision that you do not have a limited capability for work, medical certificates from your doctor will be sufficient evidence of your limited capability until you are assessed under a WCA, provided:

- you have a different condition; *or*
- your condition has significantly worsened since the decision.

It would be helpful if your medical certificates clearly showed this was the case. This allows benefit to be paid pending a new decision under the WCA.

ESA Regs, reg 30

If you re-claim within six months for the same condition, you will not get paid while waiting to be assessed. The decision maker may decide not to reassess you immediately. This cannot be appealed, but after six months has passed, you should be paid on the basis of your medical certificates. Alternatively, the decision maker may decide that you do not have a limited capability for work, without obtaining any further evidence. Since this is a new decision, you have the right to appeal against it. If you missed the deadline for appealing against the earlier decision, this gives you another chance, although you may not get full arrears if successful.

After a decision that you do not have a limited capability for work-related activity – If you are placed in the work-related activity group and your condition has recently got worse such that you now feel you should be placed in the support group, you can ask for the decision to be revised. You can do this at any time.

Contact your local Jobcentre Plus office and explain that your condition has recently got worse, and tell them which of the descriptors also now apply to you (see Box D.5). If you do this by phone, follow it with a letter to the office confirming your request. If you can, obtain medical evidence to back up your case, eg a letter from your doctor, consultant or specialist nurse, confirming the descriptor that applies to you. Attach a copy of this evidence to your revision request.

You can appeal against a decision that you do not have a limited capability for work-related activity. For details of the appeals process, see Chapter 60.

11 Contributory ESA

1. What is contributory ESA?

Contributory employment and support allowance (ESA) is payable if you have paid sufficient national insurance contributions. You can also qualify in certain circumstances if your period of limited capability for work began before the age of 20, or 25 in some cases.

Contributory ESA is not affected by savings or most other income, except for occupational or personal pensions. It is taxable.

You should claim contributory ESA if you cannot get statutory sick pay because, for example, you are not working, you are self-employed or your statutory sick pay has run out. You cannot work and receive contributory ESA, unless the work is treated as 'permitted work' (see Chapter 16(3)).

2. Do you qualify?

To be entitled to contributory ESA you need to satisfy one of the following conditions, as well as the basic conditions laid out in Chapter 9(9).

- ❑ You satisfy the national insurance contribution conditions (see 5 below).
- ❑ Your limited capability for work began before the age of 20 (or 25 in some cases), you claim in time and satisfy other conditions, or you were under 20 (or 25) in a previous linked claim (see 8 below).

WRA, S.1(2)(a)

3. National insurance contributions

There are six different classes of national insurance (NI) contributions, but only Classes 1 and 2 count towards contributory ESA. Voluntary Class 3 contributions only count towards bereavement benefits and the basic state pension. Classes 1A and 1B are paid by employers only and do not count towards benefit entitlement. Class 4 contributions are normally paid by self-employed people on profits or gains above a certain level.

Class 1 contributions

Class 1 contributions are paid by employees and employers. You pay these, and hence build up entitlement to contributory ESA, on any earnings above the 'primary threshold' of £110 a week (for the tax year 2009/10).

If you are not contracted out of the state second pension scheme (see Box O.2, Chapter 43), your contribution will be 11% on earnings between £110.01 and £844 a week. The contribution on earnings over £844 a week, the 'upper earnings limit', is just 1%.

If you earn less than the primary threshold, but more than the 'lower earnings limit' of £95 a week (for the tax year 2009/10), you will still be treated as having paid Class 1 contributions even though you do not actually have to pay any contributions.

SSCBA, Ss. 6(1), 6A & 8(1)-(2)

Earnings per week	Level of NI contribution
Below £95	Nil
From £95 – £110	Nil (but treated as paid)
From £110.01 – £844	11%
£844.01 and above	1%

Reduced rate for married women – If you are a married woman or widow and have kept your right to pay reduced-rate contributions and you earn over £110 a week, you will pay Class 1 contributions of 4.85% on your earnings between £110.01 and £844 and 1% on earnings above £844.

SSCBA, S.19(4) & Cont. Regs, regs 127(1)(a) & 131

Reduced-rate contributions do not count towards contributory ESA, so it is worth considering giving up your right to pay reduced-rate contributions, particularly if you are not contracted out of the state second pension. Ask for advice from a Citizens Advice Bureau or the NI Contributions Office (see inside back cover).

Class 2 contributions

Class 2 contributions are flat-rate contributions of £2.40 a week (2009/10) paid by self-employed people.

If your net profits or gains are below (or you expect them to be below) £5,075 in the 2009/10 tax year, you can apply for a certificate of exception on form CF10, available from your local Jobcentre Plus office or HMRC Enquiry Centre. If (and only if) you get this certificate, you do not have to pay Class 2 contributions. However, even if your net profits are below £5,075 and you have the certificate, you still have the right to pay Class 2 contributions. If you have low earnings from self-employment and want to pay contributions voluntarily, it is sensible to pay Class 2 rather than Class 3 contributions.

SSCBA, S.11 & Cont. Regs, reg 46

A married woman or widow who has kept her reduced-rate election, does not have to pay Class 2 contributions (although if her taxable profits from self-employment are £5,715 a year or more, she will be liable to pay Class 4 contributions).

Cont. Regs, reg 127(1)(b)

Class 3 contributions

Class 3 contributions are completely voluntary, flat-rate contributions. In the 2009/10 tax year they are £12.05 a week. You may want to pay them if the other contributions you have paid (or been credited with) in a tax year are not enough to make that year count as a 'qualifying year' for state pension or bereavement benefits (see Box O.1, Chapter 43). If you are covered by home responsibilities protection for that complete tax year, you may not need to pay Class 3 contributions (see Chapter 44).

SSCBA, S.13

If you reach state pension age on or after 6.4.08 and have not paid enough contributions for the tax years from 1975/76 onwards to get a full state pension, you may be able to make up the deficit for up to six of those years in certain cases, which may allow for a late claim of state pension.

Pension Act 2008, S.135

4. Contribution credits

There are situations when you are not in a position to pay national insurance (NI) contributions, but are awarded NI 'credits' instead. These only count towards the second contribution condition for contributory ESA (see 7 below). There are different ways of receiving such credits. For instance, you are awarded a Class 1 credit for each week you receive jobseeker's allowance or are entitled to carer's allowance. If you are awarded a Class 1 credit, you are treated as if you had earnings equal to the lower earnings limit for that week. If you are a married woman and have kept your right to pay the reduced-rate NI contributions, you cannot get Class 1 contribution credits. Widows in this position, however, can get credits. The different ways that you can be awarded NI credits are listed in Box D.7.

5. Contribution conditions

There are two national insurance (NI) contribution conditions, both of which you must meet to be entitled to contributory ESA. The first condition depends on the NI contributions that you have actually paid in the relevant tax year (see 6 below). For the second condition, credited NI contributions, as well as paid NI contributions, count (see 7 below). In both cases, there is a relationship between 'tax years' and 'benefit years', so it is important to know the difference between them.

Tax years – A tax year runs from 6 April to 5 April the following year.

Benefit years – Benefit years start on the first Sunday in January and end on the Saturday before the first Sunday in January the following year. The 2009 benefit year started on Sunday 4.1.09 and will end on Saturday 2.1.10.

SSCBA, S.21(6)

The 'relevant benefit year' is usually the year that includes the start of your 'period of limited capability for work'.

WRA, Sch 1, para 3(1)(f)

Period of limited capability for work – This is the period throughout which you have, or are treated as having, a limited capability for work. It usually begins once you have made a claim for ESA. There are linking rules that mean, in some circumstances, your period of limited capability for work begins before you actually claim.

Linking rules

These rules link together two or more periods of limited capability for work and treat them as one. They are important because it is the beginning of the period of limited capability for work that determines which tax years are relevant.

12-week linking rule – Any two periods of limited capability for work separated by no more than 12 weeks are treated as one single period.

Work or training linking rules – If you are covered by the extended linking rules for 'work or training beneficiaries' (see Chapter 16(12)), any two periods of limited capability for work separated by no more than 104 weeks are treated as one single period.

If, during the 104-week period from starting work or training, your condition deteriorates and you can no longer continue, the new period of limited capability for work links back to the pre-work or training period. Consequently, you can re-claim contributory ESA at the same rate as before without re-satisfying the contribution conditions.

Tax credits and training linking rules – If you were in a period of limited capability for work before going on a training course or getting the working tax credit disability element, a similar 104-week linking rule provides a bridge between your earlier period of limited capability for work and a new claim for ESA. See Chapter 16(12) for details.

ESA Regs, reg 145

Waiving the linking rules

The above linking rules can be waived if they act to your disadvantage. If two periods of limited capability for work could be linked *and*

- you would not satisfy the contribution conditions based on the tax years related to the first period of limited capability for work, *but*
- you would satisfy the contribution conditions based on the tax years related to the second period of limited capability for work,

the link is not made, thus allowing you to meet the contribution conditions.

ESA Regs, reg 13

6. The first condition – paid contributions

You must have paid Class 1 or Class 2 national insurance (NI) contributions on earnings 25 times the lower earnings limit in one of the last three complete tax years before the start of the relevant benefit year. For instance, if you make your ESA claim in the 2009 benefit year, you need to have paid the contributions in one of the following tax years: 2005/06, 2006/07 or 2007/08 (unless one of the exceptions listed below applies).

WRA, Sch 1, para 1

Lower earnings limits – These are uprated each year. For the last nine years they were:

Lower earnings limits

2001/02	**£72**	2004/05	**£79**	2007/08	**£87**
2002/03	**£75**	2005/06	**£82**	2008/09	**£90**
2003/04	**£77**	2006/07	**£84**	2009/10	**£95**

Example: If you claim ESA in the 2009 benefit year, you pass the first condition if you paid NI contributions on earnings of £2,050 between April 2005 and April 2006 (which is 25 times £82, the lower earnings limit for that year); or £2,100 between April 2006 and April 2007; or £2,175 between April 2007 and April 2008.

Exceptions

There are exceptions for some people whose circumstances may have prevented them from working or paying enough contributions in the usual three-year period. You will satisfy the first condition with NI contributions paid in *any* complete tax year if you are in one of the following groups.

- ❑ **Carers** – You were entitled to carer's allowance for at least one week in the last complete tax year before the start of the relevant benefit year. For example, if you claim ESA in the 2009 benefit year and you were getting carer's allowance at any time between 6.4.07 and 5.4.08, you can pass the first condition based on contributions paid in any tax year.
- ❑ **Low-paid disabled workers** – You were working and entitled to the disability or severe disability element of working tax credit. You must have been working for at least two years immediately before the first day of your period of limited capability for work. This helps you claim contributory ESA when your earnings were below the limit for NI contributions. Note that if you were working for less than two years, one of the linking rules may allow you to go back onto your pre-work ESA at the same rate without needing to re-satisfy the contribution conditions (see 5 above).
- ❑ **Previous ESA claimants** – You received contributory ESA for at least one day in the last complete tax year before the benefit year in which you again become entitled to contributory ESA.
- ❑ **In prison or detention but conviction or offence quashed** – You are entitled to an NI credit for a period in prison or detention, or would be if you applied, for at least one week in any tax year before the relevant benefit year.

ESA Regs, reg 8

7. The second condition – paid or credited contributions

You must have paid or been credited with Class 1 or Class 2 national insurance contributions on earnings 50 times the lower earnings limit in each of the last two complete tax years before the start of the relevant benefit year. For example, if your benefit year is 2009, you meet this condition if you paid contributions on earnings of £4,200 in the 2006/07 tax year, and of £4,350 in the 2007/08 tax year.

WRA, Sch 1, para 2

8. Claiming under age 20 (or 25)

People who have had a limited capability of work since before the age of 20, or 25 if they have been in education or training, can get contributory ESA without needing to satisfy the national insurance (NI) contribution conditions: 'contributory ESA in youth' (CESA(Y)).

Do you qualify? – Jobcentre Plus will first check to see if you satisfy the usual NI contribution conditions for contributory ESA (see 5 above). If you do not, you can qualify for CESA(Y) if you meet all of the following conditions:

- you are aged 16 or over (or 19, generally, if you are in full-time education); *and*
- you are aged under 20 (under 25 if you were in education or training) at the start of your period of limited capability for work; *and*
- you have had a limited capability for work for a continuous period of 196 days (28 weeks), the 'qualifying period', immediately before the first day your entitlement can begin and you still have a limited capability for work; *and*
- you satisfy the residence and presence conditions (see Chapter 50).

WRA, Sch 1, para 4

Age limits

There is a lower age limit of 16 and an upper age limit of 20 (or 25 in some cases). You are eligible for CESA(Y) if you claim within these limits (see below for the latest you can start your claim). Once you have served the 196-day qualifying period, CESA(Y) is paid from the first day of entitlement (there are no waiting days) and you can stay on ESA right up until state pension age if you remain in the same period of limited capability for work. There are linking rules that allow you to re-claim if your benefit stops while you try out employment or training (see 5 above).

Aged 16 or over – You must be at least 16 when you claim. If you are 16, 17 or 18 you will usually be excluded if you are at school or in full-time education of 21 hours or more a week (see Chapter 39(3) for details). If you are 19 or over, you cannot be excluded from claiming CESA(Y) solely because you are in full-time education.

To avoid missing out on CESA(Y) if you are excluded while aged under 19, claim as soon as you leave school or college, or on your 19th birthday if you are still in education. ***Note:*** The kinds of activities involved in attending the course may be taken into account in the work capability assessment.

ESA Regs, reg 12

D.7 Contribution credits

Credits for incapacity or limited capability for work

You will be credited with a Class 1 contribution for each complete week of incapacity for work – ie on each day of the week you are entitled to:

- incapacity benefit; *or*
- statutory sick pay (SSP); *or*
- severe disablement allowance; *or*
- income support on the ground of incapacity for work; *or*
- maternity allowance.

You will be credited with a Class 1 contribution for each complete week you have a limited capability for work – ie on each day of the week you are entitled to employment and support allowance (ESA).

If you are not entitled to any of these benefits or you claim late, you can still get credits if you are accepted as being incapable of work or having a limited capability for work. The rules for assessing incapacity for work are described in Chapter 13; the rules for assessing limited capability for work are described in Chapter 10. You should apply for your credits before the end of the benefit year after the tax year in which you were incapable of work or had a limited capability for work.

If you were getting SSP, you will have paid or been treated as having paid Class 1 contributions if your employer also has an occupational sick pay scheme that brings your SSP to the lower earnings limit. But if you only got SSP, and therefore did not earn enough to pay or be treated as paying contributions and your national insurance (NI) contribution record is deficient, you should apply for credits.

You can also get a credit for each week for any part of which you received a war pensions or industrial injuries unemployability supplement. A week for NI contribution purposes begins on a Sunday and ends on a Saturday.

Incapacity and limited capability for work credits can help meet the second contribution condition for any benefit.

Credit Regs, reg 8B

Credits for unemployment

You will be credited with a Class 1 contribution for each complete week you are paid jobseeker's allowance (JSA).

If you are not entitled to JSA, you can protect your NI contribution record by signing on at the Jobcentre Plus office for credits only. You will get a credit for each week in which you meet the basic JSA rules (other than the specific contribution-based or income-based conditions for receipt of benefit) – see Chapter 15(2). You do not have to sign a jobseeker's agreement when you are signing on for credits only. If you are incapable of work or have a limited capability for work for part of the week, you are still entitled to a credit.

However, you may not get a credit for any week in which your JSA is not paid (or joint-claim JSA reduced) because of a sanction, or you get JSA hardship payments or you are on strike. If there is a gap in your contribution record, you can protect your state pension entitlement by paying voluntary Class 3 contributions.

Unemployment credits help meet the second contribution condition for any benefit.

Credit Regs, reg 8A

Carer's allowance credits

You get a Class 1 credit for each week in which you are paid carer's allowance, or in which you would be paid carer's allowance if you were not receiving bereavement benefit instead. Carer's allowance credits count for any benefit.

Credit Regs, reg 7A

Credits for tax credits

You get a Class 1 credit for each week in which you receive the disability element or severe disability element of working tax credit (WTC). These credits count for any benefit. You may also get a Class 1 credit, which counts for state pensions and bereavement benefits, for any week you receive WTC. In each case you must be either:

- employed and earning less than the lower earnings limit for that year; *or*
- self-employed and exempt from having to pay Class 2 contributions (see Chapter 11(3)).

If you are a couple, the credit is awarded to the one who is earning. If you are both earning, it is awarded to the one being paid WTC.

Credit Regs, regs 7B & 7C

Aged under 20 – Your period of limited capability for work must begin before your 20th birthday and you must have had a limited capability for work for 196 days in a row before you become entitled. The latest you can start your entitlement is immediately after the end of the 196-day qualifying period that began no later than the day before your 20th birthday; the latest you can make your claim is up to three months after the 196th day.

C&P Regs, Sch 4

You can make a claim for CESA(Y) up to the age of 25 if you have been in education or training under the rules explained below. If you do not claim in time to qualify for CESA(Y), you can only get contributory ESA in future if you have paid enough NI contributions.

Age exception for under-25-year-olds

The age limit can be extended to under 25 if the following conditions are met:

- you were on a course of education or training for at least three months before your 20th birthday (you must have started your course within the first academic term after registration unless the delay was because of illness or a domestic emergency); *and*
- the course was one of:
  - full-time education of any level from secondary school to postgraduate, or part-time if you couldn't attend full time because of your disability; *or*
  - vocational or work-based training (this includes courses such as life skills for disabled trainees of at least 16 hours a week, as long as their primary purpose is to teach occupational or vocational skills); *and*
- you finished attending the course within the last two complete tax years (6 April to 5 April) before the 'benefit year' in which you claim; *and*
- you claim before your 25th birthday, or immediately after the end of 196 days of limited capability for work that began before your 25th birthday.

ESA Regs, reg 9

You must have had a limited capability for work for 196 consecutive days before your claim. Generally, these days can fall while you are still attending the course, unless it is a training course for which you are paid a training allowance (other than one that just covers travel or meal expenses).

ESA Regs, reg 32(2)

Training and education credits

Termination of full-time education/training credits – To help meet the second contribution condition for contribution-based JSA or contributory ESA only, you can get Class 1 credits for one of the two tax years before your benefit year if in that tax year you were aged 18 or over and in full-time education or on a training course or in an apprenticeship, and the course or apprenticeship, which must have begun before you became 21, has now ended. In the other year, you must have passed the second contribution condition in a different way.

Credit Regs, reg 8

Approved training credits – To help you meet the second contribution condition for any benefit, you can get Class 1 credits for each week you are on an approved training course. The course must be full time, or 15 or more hours a week if you are disabled, or be an introductory course to one of those courses. It must not be part of your job. It must be intended to run for no longer than one year (unless it is a course provided by or on behalf of Jobcentre Plus and a longer period is reasonable because of your disability). Jobcentre Plus training courses automatically count, but for other courses you must apply for credits. You must have reached 18 before the start of the tax year in which you require the credits.

Credit Regs, reg 7

Others

Maternity and adoption pay period credits – If you were getting statutory maternity pay (SMP) or statutory adoption pay (SAP) and did not earn enough to pay or be treated as paying contributions on your SMP or SAP, you can apply for Class 1 credits if you need them. These credits count for any benefit.

Credit Regs, reg 9C

Jury service credits – If you were on jury service for all or part of any week, you can apply for Class 1 credits if you need them. These credits count for any benefit.

Credit Regs, reg 9B

Credits following official error – Due to an error in passing information between the DWP and HMRC between 1993 and 2007, some people have been over-credited with contributions for incapacity. These credits will be removed and claimants will be offered the opportunity of paying voluntary contributions instead (at the same rate they would have paid if voluntary contributions had been made at the time of the error). They will have until 5.4.14 to do this.

Anyone receiving a contributory benefit (incapacity benefit, bereavement benefits, state pension or contribution-based JSA) due to this error will continue to receive the benefit even though entitlement is based on incorrect information. A review will be carried out to check if anyone has been underpaid and they will be contacted.

Credit Regs, reg 8D-8F

Starting credits – To help meet the second contribution condition for basic state pension and bereavement benefits, you can get Class 3 credits for the tax year in which you reached 16 and for the two following years.

Credit Regs, reg 4

60 or older credits – Men can get credits automatically for the tax year in which they reach 60 and the following four years, provided they are not out of the UK for six months or longer in the year. These credits cover gaps in your NI record for these years and count for all benefits. If you are unemployed, you don't have to sign on to get these credits. You must continue to pay Class 1 or Class 2 contributions for weeks where you are liable. When the state pension age is equalised, women will also become eligible for these credits.

Credit Regs, reg 9A

Bereavement credits – To help meet the second contribution condition for JSA or contributory ESA when your bereavement benefit or widowed mother's allowance ceases, you can get Class 1 credits for each year up to the year in which your bereavement benefit or widowed mother's allowance ended, except where your benefit stopped because of remarriage, forming a civil partnership or cohabitation. Women who were getting widow's allowance or widowed mother's allowance are also deemed to satisfy the first contribution condition for contributory ESA (again, except where the benefit stopped because of remarriage etc).

Credit Regs, reg 8C & Statutory Instrument 1974/2010, reg 3(a)

Credits for periods in prison – You can apply for credits for any weeks in which you were imprisoned or detained in legal custody for convictions or offences which were subsequently quashed by the courts, provided there were no other reasons for you being in prison or custody at that time. These credits count for all benefits.

Credit Regs, reg 9D

196-day qualifying period

You must have had a limited capability for work for a continuous period of 196 days (28 weeks) before the first day you can be paid CESA(Y). These can be days before your 16th birthday. Days of entitlement to statutory sick pay can also be included.

When you are serving the qualifying period, a break of just one day (perhaps a day trying to see if you can manage a job) is enough to put you back to the beginning and start the 196 days all over again.

Once you have served the initial qualifying period, you will not have to serve it again while your ESA is in the same period of limited capability for work.

WRA, Sch 1, para 4(1)(d) & ESA Regs, reg 33(1)

Re-claiming CESA(Y)

If you have previously qualified for CESA(Y), and you re-claim ESA within 12 weeks of the earlier claim or while covered by the extended linking rules for work or training (see Chapter 16(12)), you can re-qualify for CESA(Y) on the same basis even if you are now over 20 or 25.

If you are not covered by one of these linking rules, you can still re-qualify for CESA(Y) if all the following conditions are satisfied:

- you previously qualified for CESA(Y);
- your previous entitlement did not end because of a determination that you did not have a limited capability for work;
- you are now over 20 (or 25);
- your previous entitlement to CESA(Y) ended solely with a view to you taking up employment or training;
- your earnings were too low to meet the first contribution condition for contributory ESA (see 6 above);
- you meet the second contribution condition for contributory ESA (see 7 above); *and*
- you re-claim no later than 12 weeks after your last job ended.

ESA Regs, reg 10

9. How much do you get?

For the first 13 weeks of your claim, you are paid the assessment phase rate, which depends on your age.

Contributory ESA (assessment phase)	per week
Aged under 25 years	£50.95
Aged 25 years and over	£64.30

Following the 13-week assessment phase, if you are assessed as having a limited capability for work (see Chapter 10(2)), you receive the basic allowance plus an additional component depending on whether you are placed in the support group or the work-related activity group (see Chapter 10(3)).

Contributory ESA (main phase)	per week
Basic allowance	£64.30
Support component	£30.85
Work-related activity component	£25.50

ESA Regs, reg 67(2)-(3) & Sch 4, paragraph 1(1) & Part 4

10. Does anything affect what you get?

Other benefits

To be entitled to ESA you must not be entitled to either income support or jobseeker's allowance. Additionally, you cannot receive contributory ESA as well as state pension, maternity allowance, carer's allowance, bereavement benefits and unemployability supplement, as these are 'overlapping benefits'. This means you cannot claim more than one of any of these benefits, but you receive an amount equal to the highest amount of whichever benefit you are entitled to.

WRA, S.1(3)(e)-(f) & OB Regs, reg 4

You can receive other benefits such as disability living allowance and industrial injuries disablement benefit without contributory ESA being affected. You may also be able to claim income-related ESA to top up contributory ESA if you are on a low income (see Chapter 12(5)).

Statutory payments – Statutory maternity pay, statutory adoption pay and statutory paternity pay also 'overlap' with contributory ESA. Consequently, if you are entitled to contributory ESA and claim one of these statutory benefits, you will receive whichever is the higher (which will usually be the statutory benefit).

ESA Regs, regs 80-83

Occupational and personal pension

If you receive an occupational or personal pension (including permanent health insurance payments, Pension Protection Fund periodic payments and Financial Assistance Scheme payments – but see below) that pays more than £85 a week, then your contributory ESA payment is reduced by half of the amount over this limit. For example, if you receive £105 a week before tax from a personal pension, your ESA is reduced by £10 a week, ie half of the excess figure of £20. If you receive more than one pension, they are added together for this calculation.

Some payments are ignored for this purpose, ie:

- a pension payment (or Pension Protection Fund periodic payment or a Financial Assistance Scheme payment) that you receive as the beneficiary upon the death of the pension scheme member;
- a pension payment in respect of death due to military or war service;
- a permanent health insurance payment if you paid more than 50% of the premium.

ESA Regs, regs 72, 74 & 75

Hospital and care homes

You can continue to receive contributory ESA while in hospital or a care home.

Prison

You are generally disqualified from receiving contributory ESA for any period during which you are in prison or legal custody.

WRA, S.18(4)(b)

Payment of contributory ESA is suspended if you are on remand awaiting trial or sentencing. Full arrears of benefit are payable if you do not receive a penalty (such as a fine or imprisonment) at the end of proceedings. No arrears are payable if you do receive a penalty.

If you are detained in a hospital or similar institution following a criminal conviction as a person suffering from a mental disorder, contributory ESA is payable for the length of the sentence unless you are detained under section 45A or 47 of the Mental Health Act 1983 (or equivalent Scottish legislation).

ESA Regs, regs 160 & 161

Councillor's allowance

If you receive a councillor's allowance that pays more than £92 a week (excluding expenses), an amount equal to the extra money will be deducted from your contributory ESA.

ESA Regs, reg 76

12 Income-related ESA

1. What is income-related ESA?

Income-related employment and support allowance (ESA) is the means-tested element of ESA. It provides for basic living expenses for you and your partner, if you have one. In this sense, it is similar to income support, the benefit it replaces. Like income support, income-related ESA does not depend on your national insurance contributions. It can be paid on its own if you have no other income, or it can top up contributory ESA (see 5 below and Chapter 11) or earnings from permitted part-time work.

Income-related ESA reflects contributory ESA in that it is paid at a higher rate after the 13-week assessment phase, when one of two additional components can be included in the calculation. Which component you are eligible for is determined by whether you are placed in the support group or the work-related activity group (see Chapter 10(3) and 7 below).

Income-related ESA can help towards mortgage interest payments and certain other housing costs. If you get income-related ESA, you may also be entitled to housing benefit and council tax benefit, and will not have to go through a separate means test (see Chapter 20).

Getting income-related ESA may entitle you to other types of benefit, eg:

- free prescriptions and dental treatment (Chapter 55);
- housing grants (Chapter 31);
- help from the social fund (Chapters 22 and 23);
- free school meals (Chapter 37);
- help with hospital fares (Chapter 35).

Income-related ESA only covers the needs of you and your partner. If you have dependent children, you must claim child tax credit to cover their needs (see Chapter 18).

2. Do you qualify?

To be entitled to income-related ESA you must satisfy all the following conditions, as well as the basic conditions laid out in Chapter 9(9).

- ❑ You must have no income, or your income is below your 'applicable amount' (a set amount that depends on your circumstances) – see 6 below.
- ❑ Your capital must be no more than £16,000. See Chapter 27(3).
- ❑ You must not be entitled to pension credit.
- ❑ If you are a member of a couple, your partner must not be entitled to income-related ESA, pension credit, income support or income-based jobseeker's allowance.
- ❑ You must not be in remunerative work (see 3 below).
- ❑ If you are a member of a couple, your partner must not be working for 24 hours or more a week (see 3 below).
- ❑ You are not in full-time education (see 4 below).
- ❑ You are not subject to immigration control (see Chapter 50(3)).
- ❑ You satisfy the habitual residence test (see Chapter 50(2)).

WRA, Sch 1, para 6(1) & Sch 3, para 19; ESA Regs, reg 70 & Sch 5, para 11

Couples

You are treated as a couple if you and your partner are in any of the following categories:

- a man and woman who are married to each other and living in the same household;
- an unmarried man and woman who are living together as husband and wife;
- two people of the same sex who have entered into a civil partnership and live in the same household;
- two people of the same sex who have not entered a civil partnership but who live together as if they were civil partners.

ESA Regs, reg 2

3. Full-time or part-time work

You are excluded from income-related ESA if you or your partner are in 'remunerative work', which is work done for payment or in expectation of payment. You are not entitled to income-related ESA if you, the claimant, do any such work (except in some limited circumstances – see Chapter 16(3)). If you have a partner, you are not entitled to income-related ESA if they work for 24 hours or more a week, unless one of the exceptions listed in Chapter 14(6) applies to them. If one of these exceptions does apply, any earnings are taken into account in the usual way (see Chapter 26(3)-(5)).

ESA Regs, regs 41(1) & 42(1)

4. Full-time education

You cannot usually undertake full-time education and receive income-related ESA (unless you are entitled to disability living allowance). Whether your course is classed as full time or part time usually depends on the academic institution that you attend.

If you are on a government-funded further education course in England or Wales, it is full time if it involves 16 or more hours of guided learning a week.

In Scotland, it is full time if structured learning packages make up the hours to over 16 a week, up to a maximum of 21 hours a week.

ESA Regs, regs 14 & 18

Under 19

If you are aged under 19 but not a 'qualifying young person' for child benefit purposes (see Chapter 38(1)), you are not treated as in full-time education if the course of study is not:

- a course leading to a first degree or postgraduate degree (or comparable qualifications), a higher education or higher national diploma; *or*
- any other course of a standard above advanced GNVQ or equivalent.

ESA Regs, reg 16

Any student grants or loans you receive while in education can be taken into account as income when determining how much income-based ESA you will be entitled to. See Chapter 40(3) for details.

5. How do you work out your entitlement?

The amount of income-related ESA you are entitled to depends on your income and capital, whether you have a partner, whether you (or your partner) have a severe disability or are a carer, whether you have certain housing costs, whether you are in the assessment phase or the main phase and, in the latter case, whether you have been placed in the support group or the work-related activity group.

If you are a single person, only your needs and resources are relevant. If you are one of a couple (see 2 above), the needs and resources of both of you are relevant.

Set amounts for different needs are added together to reach the total amount the law says you need to live on. This is called your 'applicable amount'. Any income worked out under set rules is deducted from your applicable amount. This leaves the amount of income-related ESA you are entitled to. The calculation is as follows:

Step 1: Add up your total capital resources – You will not be entitled to income-related ESA if your capital, and any capital belonging to your partner, is more than £16,000. See Chapter 27.

Step 2: Work out your applicable amount – See 6 below.

- ❑ Identify your 'prescribed amount' (see 7 below).
- ❑ Add any entitlement to the support component or the work-related activity component (see 7 below).
- ❑ Add any entitlement to the premiums (see 8 below).
- ❑ Add any allowable housing costs (see Chapter 25).

The sum total of all these is your applicable amount.

Step 3: Add up your total income resources – See Chapter 26. Do not forget the tariff income if you have capital over £6,000, or £10,000 if you are in a care home (see Chapter 27(4)).

Step 4: Deduct your income from your applicable amount – If your income is less than your applicable amount, income-related ESA makes up the difference in full, provided you meet the other qualifying conditions (see 2 above and Chapter 9(9)).

WRA, S.4, ESA Regs, reg 67

What happens if you are also entitled to contributory ESA?

If you have no other income that should be taken into account, the amount of ESA you are entitled to will be equal to whichever is the higher: the contributory ESA or the applicable amount (as worked out in Step 2 above).

If you have income that should be taken into account, the amount of ESA you get will be whichever is the higher: contributory ESA or the amount by which your applicable amount exceeds your income (the result of Step 4 above).

In each case, if ESA is payable at a rate greater than the contributory ESA rate, your payments of ESA will consist of two combined elements:

- contributory ESA; *and*
- a top-up of income-related ESA.

WRA, S.6

6. What is your applicable amount?

The applicable amount is the amount of money the law says you need to live on. It consists of:

- a prescribed amount – for either a single claimant or a couple (see 7 below);
- an additional component, depending on whether you are in the work-related activity group or support group (see 7 below);
- premiums – flat-rate extra amounts if you satisfy certain conditions (see 8 below);
- certain housing costs (see Chapter 25).

ESA Regs, reg 67

7. The prescribed amount and additional components

The prescribed amount

The prescribed amount is part of your applicable amount. The rate that applies to you depends on your age and whether or not you are part of a couple. There are lower rates of prescribed amount for people aged under 25, although these only apply during the 13-week assessment phase. After this, if you have established your entitlement to ESA, the higher rate applies regardless of your age.

Prescribed amount		per week
Single person	25 or over	£64.30
	under 25 (assessment phase)	£50.95
	under 25 (main phase)	£64.30
Lone parent	18 or over	£64.30
	under 18 (assessment phase)	£50.95
	under 18 (main phase)	£64.30
Couple	both 18 or over[1]	£100.95
	both under 18 (assessment phase)[2]	£76.90
	both under 18 (main phase)[2]	£100.95
	one 25 or over[3]	£64.30
	one 18-24 (assessment phase)[3]	£50.95
	one 18-24 (main phase)[3]	£64.30

ESA Regs, Sch 4, Part 1

Couples (where one partner is aged under 18) – In the table of rates above, the reference numbers mean:

1: includes couples where one is under 18 but would be eligible for either income-related ESA or income support if they were single, or is eligible for income-based jobseeker's allowance (JSA) or severe hardship payments;

2: only if one is responsible for a child; or each would be eligible for income-related ESA if they were single; or the claimant's partner would be eligible for income support if they were single or is eligible for income-based JSA or severe hardship payments. If none of these conditions are met, the single person's amount will apply (£50.95 during the assessment phase, £64.30 after this);

3: only if the other is under 18 and would not be eligible for either income-related ESA or income support (even if they were single), income-based JSA or severe hardship payments.

The additional component

Following the 13-week assessment phase, you are paid an additional component depending on whether you are placed in the work-related activity group or the support group (see Chapter 10(3)).

Components	per week
Work-related activity component	£25.50
Support component	£30.85

ESA Regs, Sch 4, Part 4

8. The premiums

There are four different premiums, each with specific qualifying conditions, as detailed in Chapter 24. The premiums are included as part of your applicable amount (see 6 above). Unless otherwise specified in Chapter 24, each premium to which you are entitled is added to the total of your applicable amount.

Premiums		per week
Severe disability	single	£52.85
	couple (one qualifies)	£52.85
	couple (both qualify)	£105.70
Enhanced disability	single	£13.40
	couple	£19.30
Pensioner (single)	work-related activity group	£40.20
	support group	£34.85
	assessment phase	£65.70
Pensioner (couple)	work-related activity group	£72.00
	support group	£66.65
	assessment phase	£97.50
Carer		£29.50

ESA Regs, Sch 4, Part 3

9. Other matters

Care homes – For how income-related ESA is calculated for care home residents, see Chapter 33(5).

Hospital – For how income-related ESA is affected by a stay in hospital, see Box M.1, Chapter 35.

Going into prison – You are generally disqualified from receiving income-related ESA for any period during which you are in prison or legal custody. However, if you are detained in custody awaiting trial or sentence you can continue to receive an amount of income-related ESA to cover housing costs.

ESA Regs, Sch 5, Part 1, para 3

13 Incapacity benefits: pre-November 2008

1. What happened to incapacity benefit and income support?

Incapacity benefit (IB) and income support (IS) paid on the basis of incapacity were abolished for new claims from 27.10.08 and replaced by employment and support allowance (ESA: see Chapter 9). If you were already in receipt of IB or IS paid on the basis of incapacity on that date, you can remain on these benefits for the time being if you continue to satisfy the rules of entitlement. Your continued eligibility for IB or IS will be assessed under the personal capability assessment (PCA: see 3 below) rather than the new work capability assessment (WCA: see Chapter 10). The PCA will not apply if you can be treated as incapable of work (see 2 below). Between 2009 and 2013, existing IB/IS claimants will moved onto the WCA. Once they have established an ongoing entitlement to benefit under this, they will be moved onto ESA.

Income support is covered in Chapter 14. Incapacity benefit is covered briefly in 7 below.

Linking claims – A period of incapacity for work in a later claim links to an earlier one where the gap is no more than eight weeks, or 104 weeks/two years if the extended linking rules for work and training apply (see Chapter 16(12)). So you can have a break in your claim of either IB or IS paid on the basis of incapacity for up to eight weeks for any reason, or longer if the extended linking rules apply, and still reclaim your IB or IS.

2. Treated as incapable of work

You are treated as incapable of work on any day:

- you are an inpatient in hospital;
- you are pregnant and, to avoid serious risk of damage to your health or the baby's health, you must not work;
- you are pregnant or have recently given birth but are not entitled to maternity allowance or statutory maternity pay, from six weeks before the baby is due to two weeks after the birth;
- for up to 91 days if your benefit is protected under the 'welfare to work' linking rules (see Chapter 16(12)) and you are re-claiming benefit within your 104-week linking period. If you had previously passed or been exempt from the PCA, it doesn't apply to you again for 91 days of a new claim; just send in medical certificates;
- you receive regular weekly peritoneal or haemodialysis for chronic renal failure; or weekly parenteral nutrition for gross impairment of enteric function; or treatment by plasmapheresis, parenteral chemotherapy with cytotoxic drugs, anti-tumour agents or immunosuppressive drugs or radiotherapy.

  Days of treatment can include any necessary recuperation specified in the treatment. If you are not able to work on the other days in the week, your incapacity on those days is assessed under the PCA. If you are receiving dialysis or other treatment only on a limited number of days in a week, and could not pass the appropriate test on the other days, you might still be treated as incapable of work for the whole of the week. This is because you can benefit from the approach in R(IB) 2/99, which allows a 'broad view' to be taken that considers the overall severity of the disablement and the frequency of occurrence of good and bad days (CIB/2397/2002).

  If you work on other days of the week, you are only treated as capable of work on the days you work, not for the whole week;
- you have been requested or given notice, under specific legislation, to refrain from work because you are a carrier of, or have been in contact with, an infectious disease.

You must still satisfy all the other conditions for benefit. You must not work on the days for which you are claiming benefit unless it is exempt work (see Chapter 16(3)).

IW Regs, regs 11-14

3. What is the personal capability assessment?

The personal capability assessment (PCA) is a points-related assessment of the extent to which your condition affects your ability to perform a range of activities. Each activity is divided into a list of related tasks of varying difficulty; these are called 'descriptors'. You score points when you are not able to perform a task described. The assessment is divided into two parts: a physical/sensory assessment and a mental health assessment.

How many points do you need? – On the physical/sensory assessment, each descriptor is allocated a fixed number of points, ranging from 0 to 15. To pass the assessment you need a score of at least 15 points. If more than one descriptor applies to you within an activity, you only include the one with the highest score.

You don't have to score points in every activity. You will pass the assessment if you score 15 points in just one activity; or if points under two or more activities add up to 15 or more. Note that only the higher score from the two activities 'walking' and 'walking up and down stairs' may be counted.

For the mental health assessment, you pass if you score 10 points or more when you add all the points from any of the descriptors that apply.

If you score at least 6 points in the mental health assessment these can be combined with the physical/sensory assessment: 9 points are added from the mental health assessment (whatever your actual score was) to the total score on your physical/sensory assessment to see if you meet a combined threshold of 15 points.

For a list of all the activities and points allocated to each descriptor, see Box D.8.

How is the PCA applied?

Jobcentre Plus will check to see if they have enough information in their records and from your medical certificates to decide if you are exempt from the PCA (see 4 below); they

D.8 Personal capability assessment

Physical disabilities

To pass the test you need 15 points. Add together the highest score from each activity that applies to you. The first two activities (walking on level ground and walking up and down stairs) count as one activity so if you score on both, just count the highest.

Descriptors	Points
Walking on level ground with a walking stick or other aid if such aid is normally used	
■ Cannot walk at all	15
■ Cannot walk more than a few steps without stopping or severe discomfort	15
■ Cannot walk more than 50 metres without stopping or severe discomfort	15
■ Cannot walk more than 200 metres without stopping or severe discomfort	7
■ Cannot walk more than 400 metres without stopping or severe discomfort	3
■ Cannot walk more than 800 metres without stopping or severe discomfort	0
■ No walking problem	0
Walking up and down stairs	
■ Cannot walk up and down one stair	15
■ Cannot walk up and down a flight of 12 stairs	15
■ Cannot walk up and down a flight of 12 stairs without holding on and taking a rest	7
■ Cannot walk up and down a flight of 12 stairs without holding on	3
■ Can only walk up and down a flight of 12 stairs if he goes sideways or one step at a time	3
■ No problem in walking up and down stairs	0
Sitting in an upright chair with a back but no arms	
■ Cannot sit comfortably	15
■ Cannot sit comfortably for more than 10 minutes without having to move from the chair because the degree of discomfort makes it impossible to continue sitting	15
■ Cannot sit comfortably for more than 30 minutes without having to move from the chair because the degree of discomfort makes it impossible to continue sitting	7
■ Cannot sit comfortably for more than one hour without having to move from the chair because the degree of discomfort makes it impossible to continue sitting	3
■ Cannot sit comfortably for more than 2 hours without having to move from the chair because the degree of discomfort makes it impossible to continue sitting	0
■ No problem with sitting	0
Standing without the support of another person or the use of an aid except a walking stick	
■ Cannot stand unassisted	15
■ Cannot stand for more than a minute before needing to sit down	15
■ Cannot stand for more than 10 minutes before needing to sit down	15
■ Cannot stand for more than 30 minutes before needing to sit down	7
■ Cannot stand for more than 10 minutes before needing to move around	7
■ Cannot stand for more than 30 minutes before needing to move around	3
■ No problem standing	0
Rising from sitting in an upright chair with a back but no arms without the help of another person	
■ Cannot rise from sitting to standing	15
■ Cannot rise from sitting to standing without holding on to something	7
■ Sometimes cannot rise from sitting to standing without holding on to something	3
■ No problem with rising from sitting to standing	0
Bending and kneeling	
■ Cannot bend to touch his knees and straighten up again	15
■ Cannot either, bend or kneel, or bend and kneel as if to pick up a piece of paper from the floor and straighten up again	15
■ Sometimes cannot either, bend or kneel, or bend and kneel as if to pick up a piece of paper from the floor and straighten up again	3
■ No problem with bending or kneeling	0
Manual dexterity	
■ Cannot turn the pages of a book with either hand	15
■ Cannot turn a sink tap or the control knobs on a cooker with either hand	15
■ Cannot pick up a coin which is 2.5 cm or less in diameter with either hand	15
■ Cannot use a pen or pencil	15
■ Cannot tie a bow in laces or string	10
■ Cannot turn a sink tap or the control knobs on a cooker with one hand, but can with the other	6
■ Cannot pick up a coin which is 2.5 cm or less in diameter with one hand, but can with the other	6
■ No problem with manual dexterity	0
Lifting and carrying by the use of upper body and arms (excluding all other activities specified in Part I of this Schedule [ie this box])	
■ Cannot pick up a paperback book with either hand	15
■ Cannot pick up and carry a 0.5 litre carton of milk with either hand	15
■ Cannot pick up and pour from a full saucepan or kettle of 1.7 litre capacity with either hand	15
■ Cannot pick up and carry a 2.5 kg bag of potatoes with either hand	8
■ Cannot pick up and carry a 0.5 litre carton of milk with one hand, but can with the other	6
■ Cannot pick up and carry a 2.5 kg bag of potatoes with one hand, but can with the other	0
■ No problem with lifting and carrying	0
Reaching	
■ Cannot raise either arm as if to put something in the top pocket of a coat or jacket	15
■ Cannot raise either arm to his head as if to put on a hat	15
■ Cannot put either arm behind his back as if to put on a coat or jacket	15
■ Cannot raise either arm above his head as if to reach for something	15
■ Cannot raise one arm to his head as if to put on a hat, but can with the other	6
■ Cannot raise one arm above his head as if to reach for something, but can with the other	0
■ No problem with reaching	0

Speech

■ Cannot speak	15
■ Speech cannot be understood by family or friends	15
■ Speech cannot be understood by strangers	15
■ Strangers have great difficulty understanding speech	10
■ Strangers have some difficulty understanding speech	8
■ No problems with speech	0

Hearing with a hearing aid or other aid if normally worn

■ Cannot hear sounds at all	15
■ Cannot hear well enough to follow a television programme with the volume turned up	15
■ Cannot hear well enough to understand someone talking in a loud voice in a quiet room	15
■ Cannot hear well enough to understand someone talking in a normal voice in a quiet room	10
■ Cannot hear well enough to understand someone talking in a normal voice on a busy street	8
■ No problem with hearing	0

Vision in normal daylight or bright electric light with glasses or other aid to vision if such aid is normally worn

■ Cannot tell light from dark	15
■ Cannot see the shape of furniture in the room	15
■ Cannot see well enough to read 16 point print at a distance greater than 20 cm	15
■ Cannot see well enough to recognise a friend across the room at a distance of at least 5 metres	12
■ Cannot see well enough to recognise a friend across the road at a distance of at least 15 metres	8
■ No problem with vision	0

Continence (other than enuresis (bed wetting))

■ No voluntary control over bowels	15
■ No voluntary control over bladder	15
■ Loses control of bowels at least once a week	15
■ Loses control of bowels at least once a month	15
■ Loses control of bowels occasionally	9
■ Loses control of bladder at least once a month	3
■ Loses control of bladder occasionally	0
■ No problem with continence	0

Remaining conscious without having epileptic or similar seizures during waking moments

■ Has an involuntary episode of lost or altered consciousness at least once a day	15
■ Has an involuntary episode of lost or altered consciousness at least once a week	15
■ Has an involuntary episode of lost or altered consciousness at least once a month	15
■ Has had an involuntary episode of lost or altered consciousness at least twice in the 6 months before the day in respect to which it falls to be determined whether he is incapable of work for the purposes of entitlement to any benefit, allowance or advantage	12
■ Has had an involuntary episode of lost or altered consciousness once in the 6 months before the day in respect to which it falls to be determined whether he is incapable of work for the purposes of entitlement to any benefit, allowance or advantage	8
■ Has had an involuntary episode of lost or altered consciousness once in the 3 years before the day in respect to which it falls to be determined whether he is incapable of work for the purposes of entitlement to any benefit, allowance or advantage	0
■ Has no problems with consciousness	0

IW Regs, Sch, Part 1

Mental disabilities

Add all the points together for each descriptor that applies to you. To pass the test you need 10 points. If your score is between 6 and 9 points, you'll still pass if you also score at least 6 points for physical disabilities (see above).

In the table below we give the codes that will be used by the DWP in any report about you. For example, if you are awarded 2 points because you need alcohol before midday, this will be referred to as descriptor DL(b).

Descriptors	Points
Completion of tasks (CT)	
a Cannot answer the telephone and reliably take a message	2
b Often sits for hours doing nothing	2
c Cannot concentrate to read a magazine article or follow a radio or television programme	1
d Cannot use a telephone book or other directory to find a number	1
e Mental condition prevents him from undertaking leisure activities previously enjoyed	1
f Overlooks or forgets the risk posed by domestic appliances or other common hazards due to poor concentration	1
g Agitation, confusion or forgetfulness has resulted in potentially dangerous accidents in the 3 months before the day in respect to which it falls to be determined whether he is incapable of work for the purposes of entitlement to any benefit, allowance or advantage	1
h Concentration can only be sustained by prompting	1
Daily living (DL)	
a Needs encouragement to get up and dress	2
b Needs alcohol before midday	2
c Is frequently distressed at some time of the day due to fluctuation of mood	1
d Does not care about his appearance and living conditions	1
e Sleep problems interfere with his daytime activities	1
Coping with pressure (CP)	
a Mental stress was a factor in making him stop work	2
b Frequently feels scared or panicky for no obvious reason	2
c Avoids carrying out routine activities because he is convinced they will prove too tiring or stressful	1
d Is unable to cope with changes in daily routine	1
e Frequently finds there are so many things to do that he gives up because of fatigue, apathy or disinterest	1
f Is scared or anxious that work would bring back or worsen his illness	1
Interaction with other people (OP)	
a Cannot look after himself without help from others	2
b Gets upset by ordinary events and it results in disruptive behavioural problems	2
c Mental problems impair ability to communicate with other people	2
d Gets irritated by things that would not have bothered him before he became ill	1
e Prefers to be left alone for 6 hours or more each day	1
f Is too frightened to go out alone	1

IW Regs, Sch, Part II

may write to your doctor for more details of your condition. If you are not exempt, you will be sent a questionnaire (form IB50) to fill in. The form is mostly in multiple-choice format; for each different activity (walking, sitting etc) you are asked to tick whichever box applies to you. The boxes correspond to the descriptors for that activity. The IB50 form has much in common with the ESA50 form used to assess eligibility for employment and support allowance (ESA). Although the activities, descriptors and scores differ in the ESA assessment, the general advice we provide for completing the ESA50 form is equally applicable to completing the IB50 form (see Chapter 10(6) for details).

What happens next? – Your completed IB50 is usually then sent to a DWP-approved healthcare professional. They will consider the evidence on your claim and may request further information from your doctor and/or ask you to attend a medical assessment. The general advice we provide with respect to ESA medical assessments is applicable here (see Chapter 10(7) for details). At the assessment the healthcare professional should also consider whether any of the 'exceptional circumstances' apply (see 5 below).

4. Are you exempt?

When applying the personal capability assessment (PCA), Jobcentre Plus checks to see if you are in an exempt group.

❑ **You are exempt from the PCA if you satisfy any one of these conditions:**

- you get highest rate care component of disability living allowance (DLA), or constant attendance allowance (intermediate or exceptional rate);
- you are assessed (or passported) as 80% disabled for severe disablement allowance (SDA), or are entitled to industrial injuries disablement benefit or war pension on the basis of at least 80% disablement;
- you are terminally ill and your death can *'reasonably be expected within 6 months'*;
- you are registered blind;
- you have any of these conditions: tetraplegia; persistent vegetative state; dementia; paraplegia or *'uncontrollable involuntary movements or ataxia which effectively renders [you] functionally paraplegic'*.

❑ **You are exempt if there is medical evidence that you are suffering from any of the following conditions:**

- severe learning disability – this is defined as a *'condition which results from the arrested or incomplete physical development of the brain, or severe damage to the brain, and which involves severe impairment of intelligence and social functioning'*;
- severe and progressive neurological or muscle wasting disease (eg advanced conditions of: multiple sclerosis; Huntington's chorea; Parkinson's disease; motor neurone disease; muscular dystrophy);
- active and progressive form of inflammatory polyarthritis;
- progressive impairment of cardio-respiratory function which severely and persistently limits effort tolerance (eg from heart disease, emphysema);
- dense paralysis of the upper limb, trunk and lower limb on one side of the body (eg from a severe stroke);
- multiple effects of impairment of function of the brain or nervous system causing severe and irreversible motor, sensory and intellectual deficits (eg from a severe stroke, brain tumour, head injury);
- manifestations of severe and progressive immune deficiency states characterised by the occurrence of severe constitutional disease (eg loss of weight, CD4 count below 400, fever, night sweats) or opportunistic infections or tumour formation;
- severe mental illness involving the presence of mental disease which severely and adversely affects mood or behaviour, and severely restricts social functioning or awareness of immediate environment.

IW Regs, Reg 10

❑ **Exemption for those receiving SDA before 13.4.95**

You are exempt if you were in receipt of SDA on 12.4.95. The exemption continues if you have a break in your claim, as long as the two periods of incapacity are no more than eight weeks apart, or 104 weeks if your benefit is protected under the 'welfare to work' linking rules (see Chapter 16(12)).

Social Security (Incapacity Benefit) (Transitional) Regs 1995, reg 31

D.9 Severe disablement allowance

What happened to SDA?

Severe disablement allowance (SDA) was abolished on 6.4.01. If you were already getting, or were treated as getting, SDA by 5.4.01, you can continue to receive it, although SDA claimants under 20 on 5.4.01 were moved onto long-term incapacity benefit on 6.4.02.

IB Regs, reg 19

Staying on SDA

If you are on SDA, your entitlement will continue indefinitely, as long as you continue to be incapable of work and satisfy the SDA conditions. All the old SDA rules continue to apply, although the amount of benefit, earnings limits, etc will be uprated each year.

Linking claims – A period of incapacity for work in a later claim links to an earlier one where the gap is no more than eight weeks, or longer if the 'welfare to work', tax credits or training linking rules apply (see Chapter 16(12)). So you can have up to eight weeks off SDA for any reason (or up to 104 weeks/two years off under the welfare to work/tax credits/training linking rules) and still re-claim your SDA.

How much do you get?

SDA rates		per week
For yourself		£57.45
Age addition	higher rate	£15.65
	middle rate	£9.10
	lower rate	£5.35
Adult dependant		£31.90
Child dependant	first child	£8.20
	each other child	£11.35

Earnings – Your partner's earnings do not affect your basic benefit but can affect entitlement to dependants' additions. The rules are the same as for incapacity benefit (for details see the *Disability Rights Handbook* 33rd edition, page 87).

SDA is not affected by any wages, sick pay or occupational or personal pension you get. However, it is only possible to do limited work and still be counted as incapable of work for SDA (see Chapter 16(3)).

Other benefits – If you get SDA, you may get a disability premium included in income support, council tax benefit and housing benefit. SDA overlaps with other benefits such as carer's allowance, maternity allowance, state pension, bereavement benefits and unemployability supplement. If you are entitled to more than one, you are paid the one worth most.

Other SDA rules – More information about SDA can be found in Chapter 15, *Disability Rights Handbook*, 25th edition. If you do not have a copy, send us an A4-sized, stamped addressed envelope and we will send you a photocopy.

If it is decided you are not exempt but you think you are, write to Jobcentre Plus explaining which of the exempt categories you fit into. It would help to have a letter from your doctor to support you; show your doctor the list of exemptions so they can focus specifically on how you fit into the relevant category. In the meantime, make sure you send back the IB50 questionnaire within the deadline. If you are ultimately found capable of work, you can also argue in your appeal that you should be exempt.

Reviews of exemption – A DWP-approved healthcare professional gives advice on prognosis to help the decision maker decide when (if at all) there might be a significant improvement in your condition. The exemption may not last indefinitely, but could be reconsidered after a period depending on the medical advice.

5. Exceptional circumstances

Even if you do not score enough points to satisfy the personal capability assessment, you will be treated as incapable of work if any of the following circumstances apply to you.

- You have a severe life-threatening disease and there is medical evidence that it is uncontrollable, or uncontrolled, by recognised therapeutic procedure, and if uncontrolled there is reasonable cause for this.
- You have some specific disease or bodily or mental disablement and because of this there would be a substantial risk to the mental or physical health of anyone if you were found capable of work. The risk should be linked to the work, and any work considered should be work you could realistically do according to your education and skills (CIB/143/2007).
- You have a previously undiagnosed potentially life-threatening condition that was discovered during the examination by the DWP-approved healthcare professional.
- There is medical evidence that you are due to have a major surgical operation, or other major therapeutic procedure, and it is likely this will be within three months of the DWP-approved healthcare professional's examination. It does not matter if the DWP-approved healthcare professional or the decision maker do not consider the operation to be required if you have your consultant's opinion that it is (CIB/1381/2008).

IW Regs, reg 27

Decisions on exceptional circumstances – The decision maker decides if any of the exceptional circumstances apply, based on the report from the DWP-approved healthcare professional who examined you. But if there is also medical evidence from your own doctor they must consider this too and decide on the basis of *'the most reliable evidence available'*. You can appeal against the decision.

6. PCA Appeals

You can appeal against a decision to stop benefit (or national insurance (NI) credit entitlement) when you are found to be capable of work under the personal capability assessment (PCA). If you are only receiving income support (IS) because incapacity benefit or severe disablement allowance (SDA) cannot be paid, you should receive two decisions when you are found capable of work; one on your IS and one on your NI credits. You should appeal against the decision that you are no longer entitled to NI credits; if you win this, the tribunal decision will be binding on your IS as well (CIB/2338/2000).

See Box D.6 in Chapter 10 for ideas of points to consider in your appeal; most of the advice will be equally valid for PCA appeals. Chapter 60 gives more general information on appeals.

While you are appealing – You can sign on as available for work for jobseeker's allowance (see Chapter 15). This does not prejudice your chance of winning an appeal on incapacity for work. By signing on, you will protect your right to NI credits, whether or not your appeal is successful.

You may be able to claim IS instead without signing on while you are waiting for your appeal, but there are disadvantages. Your IS personal allowance is reduced by 20% while you are awaiting an appeal against a decision under the PCA (if you win the appeal the reduction will be repaid to you). The disability premium will not be included in your IS either, unless you still qualify for it via one of the 'disability conditions' – see Chapter 24(2). (Again, if you win the appeal any disability premium due will be repaid to you.) Furthermore, your right to NI credits is not protected unless your appeal is successful. See Box E.1 in Chapter 14.

What if you get worse? – Bear in mind that the appeal tribunal can only look at your situation as it was at the time of the decision you are appealing against. If your condition gets worse later, they can't take that into account. To make sure you don't lose out while you have an appeal pending,

D.10 Transferred from invalidity benefit

Invalidity benefit was abolished on 13.4.95 and replaced by incapacity benefit (itself now replaced by employment and support allowance). If you were entitled to invalidity benefit on 12.4.95, the amount of your benefit is protected (your award is a 'transitional award'). This protection continues to apply until you have a break in your claim of over eight weeks. Your award is also protected if the 'welfare to work', tax credits or training linking rules apply (see Chapter 16(12)).

Social Security (Incapacity Benefit)(Transitional) Regs 1995, reg 17(1)

Amounts for 2009/10		**per week**
Long-term incapacity benefit		£89.80
Invalidity allowance	higher rate	£15.65
	middle rate	£9.10
	lower rate	£5.35
Dependants' addition		£53.10
Additional pension (SERPS)*		

* The amount of any additional SERPS pension is based on your contribution record and is frozen at your 1994/95 level.

Dependant's addition – You can no longer claim an addition for a wife or husband under the age of 60 unless you have children. But if an addition for an adult dependant was payable with your invalidity benefit at any time in the eight weeks immediately before 13.4.95, you could keep the addition. This protection is lost if the addition is not payable for more than eight weeks (eg if payment of the addition is extinguished because your dependant receives a benefit of their own (R(IB)7/04)). If you are covered by the 'welfare to work', tax credits or training linking rules (see Chapter 16(12)), you also keep protection for the dependant's addition on a new claim.

Social Security (Incapacity Benefit)(Transitional) Regs 1995, regs 24 & 25

Industrial injuries – If you received invalidity benefit on the grounds of industrial injury or disease, ie without having to pass any national insurance contribution conditions, your protected award ends if your incapacity for work is no longer a result of that injury or disease. But you can pick up the protected award again if you become incapable of work within eight weeks through the same injury or disease.

Social Security (Incapacity Benefit)(Transitional) Regs 1995, reg 21

A B C D E F G H I J K L M N O P Q R S T U

you should consider making a new claim for employment and support allowance (this may be treated as a claim for incapacity benefit, SDA or IS if no more than eight weeks separate the two periods of incapacity for work).

7. Incapacity benefit – how much do you get?

For the first 28 weeks you get the short-term lower rate of incapacity benefit (IB). After 28 weeks on the lower rate, you move onto the short-term higher rate. After 52 weeks the long-term rate becomes payable, unless you are over state pension age (see Chapter 41(3)). If you are entitled to disability living allowance (DLA) highest rate care component or you are terminally ill, you are paid at the long-term rate after 28 weeks.

Incapacity benefit		**per week**
Short term		weeks 1-28
lower rate		£67.75
adult dependant		£41.35
Short term		weeks 29–52
higher rate		£80.15
adult dependant		£41.35
child dependant	first child	£8.20
child dependant	each other child	£11.35
Long term		after 52 or 28* weeks
basic rate		£89.80
adult dependant		£53.10
child dependant	first child	£8.20
child dependant	each other child	£11.35
age addition	under 35	£15.65
age addition	35-44	£6.55

SSCBA, S.30B & Sch 4(Parts I & IV)

*Long-term rate is payable after 28 weeks if you are entitled to DLA highest rate care component or are terminally ill.

If you are over state pension age, the rates are different (see Chapter 41(3)).

Additions for dependants

Adult dependants – You qualify for an adult dependant's addition if:

- your spouse/civil partner is aged 60 or over and either lives with you, or you contribute to their maintenance at least to the level of the adult dependant's addition; *or*
- you live with your spouse/civil partner (of any age) and you are also entitled to child benefit for a dependent child or young person; *or*
- you live with an adult (who may be your unmarried or same-sex partner, or a relative or friend) who looks after a child or young person for whom you are entitled to child benefit; *or*
- you contribute to the maintenance of, or employ, an adult who does not live with you, to look after a child or young person for whom you are entitled to child benefit, and you pay at least the amount of the adult dependant's addition to the person's maintenance or for caring for the child.

Note: You are treated as entitled to child benefit if you live with the child or young person and their parent who gets child benefit for them, and you are either also their parent, or wholly or mainly maintaining the child or young person.

SSCBA, S.86A & Statutory Instrument 1994/2945, reg 9(1) & 9(2B)

Child dependants – You can only qualify for an addition for a dependent child or young person if you were already receiving the increase on 5.4.03. You also need to continue meeting the following conditions:

- you are entitled to child benefit for that child or young person and either the child or young person lives with you or you contribute to their maintenance at least to the amount of the addition plus the amount of child benefit; *or*
- you live with the child or young person and their parent who gets child benefit; *and*
  - you are also the child or young person's parent; *or*
  - you maintain the child or young person at least to the level of the addition and before you were incapable of work you contributed more than half the actual cost of maintenance for the child or young person if they were a dependant (eg you are a step-parent).

See Chapter 38 for details of child benefit entitlement.

SSCBA, Ss.80 & 81

Age addition

Age additions are payable only with the long-term rate. It is your age on the first day of your period of incapacity for work (PIW) that counts for determining whether an age addition is payable. If you are under 35 on the first day of your PIW, you get the higher amount of £15.65. If you are at least 35 but have not reached your 45th birthday on the first day of your PIW, you get the lower amount of £6.55. These amounts have been reduced this year, and reductions are likely to occur in future years. This is being done to align the rates of IB and employment and support allowance (ESA).

SSCBA, S.30B(7)

Occupational and personal pensions

Occupational and personal pensions affect your incapacity benefit in a similar way to contributory ESA (see Chapter 11(10)).

Other benefits

You cannot get IB as well as state pension, jobseeker's allowance, maternity allowance, carer's allowance, bereavement benefits and unemployability supplement, as these benefits 'overlap'. You can only receive an amount equal to the highest of any of these benefits to which you are entitled.

Other benefits can be paid on top, including disability living allowance, attendance allowance and industrial injuries disablement benefit. Working tax credit can be paid on top, but IB is taken into account in the tax credit assessment unless it is short-term lower rate IB or you previously got invalidity benefit and are still in the same period of incapacity for work.

Work

Generally, if you do any work you are treated as capable of work and cannot get IB. But some work is exempt from this rule (see Chapter 16(3)).

You may be able to protect your entitlement to IB while you try out a job (see Chapter 16(12)). You may also qualify for a 'return to work credit', based on your receipt of IB prior to returning to work, which is ignored as income for means-tested benefits and tax credits (see Chapter 17(2)).

Your partner's earnings do not affect your basic benefit, but can affect additions for children and dependent adults. For details see the *Disability Rights Handbook* 33rd edition, page 87.

Disqualification

You can be disqualified from IB or severe disablement allowance, or treated as capable of work for other purposes (eg for disability premium), for up to six weeks. The rules are the same as for ESA but there are no exemptions for 'persons in hardship' (see Chapter 9(16)).

This section of the Handbook looks at:

Out of work

E

14 Income support

1. What is income support?

Income support (IS) is a means-tested or income-related benefit intended to provide for basic living expenses for you and your partner, if you have one. It does not depend on your national insurance contributions. It can be paid on its own if you have no other income, or it can top up other benefits or earnings from part-time work up to the basic amount the law says you need to live on. IS has been replaced by pension credit for people aged 60 or over (see Chapter 42) and by income-related employment and support allowance for those with a limited capability for work (see Chapter 9). If you have children, their basic living expenses can be met by child tax credit (see Chapter 18).

IS is for people not required to sign on for work – eg people who are carers or lone parents. Box E.1 lists the groups of eligible people. If you are not in one of these groups, you are not eligible for IS and should claim income-based jobseeker's allowance (see Chapter 15) or income-related employment and support allowance (see Chapter 9).

IS can help towards mortgage interest payments and certain other housing costs. If you get IS, you may also get housing benefit and council tax benefit to help with your rent and council tax. You won't have to go through a separate means test (see Chapter 20(21)).

Getting IS may entitle you to other types of benefit, eg:

- free prescriptions and dental treatment (Chapter 55);
- housing grants (Chapter 31);
- help from the social fund (Chapters 22 and 23);
- free school meals (Chapter 37);
- help with hospital fares (Chapter 35).

This chapter deals with the conditions of entitlement to IS, the way it is calculated and how to claim it. The premiums that make up part of the calculation of IS are covered in Chapter 24. The way in which housing costs can be met by IS is covered in Chapter 25. For the way income, including part-time earnings, is treated for IS purposes, see Chapter 26; for the way capital and savings are treated, see Chapter 27.

2. The starting conditions

To qualify for IS there are eight key starting conditions. You are generally eligible for IS if you meet all these conditions:

- you must be in Great Britain (see 3 below); *and*
- you must be aged 16 or over (see 4 below); *and*
- you must be aged under 60. If you are aged 60 or over, claim pension credit instead (see Chapter 42). If your partner receives pension credit you cannot claim IS; *and*
- you must not be in full-time education, though there are exceptions (see 4 and 5 below); *and*
- you must not be working 16 or more hours a week (see 6 below); *and*
- if you have a partner, they must not be working 24 or more hours a week (see 6 below); *and*
- your capital (and any belonging to a partner, but not to a dependent child) must be no more than £16,000 (see Chapter 27); *and*
- you must be in one of the categories of people who can claim IS (see Box E.1).

If you meet these eight conditions, you'll be entitled to IS if your income, worked out under IS rules, is less than your 'applicable amount' (the amount the law says you need to live on – see 9 below). Note the following points.

- ❑ If you have no income at all, you'll be paid the full amount of your IS applicable amount.
- ❑ If you have some income, but it is less than your IS applicable amount, IS is payable to bridge the gap between that income and your IS applicable amount.
- ❑ If your income is higher than your IS applicable amount, you won't be entitled to IS, but you may be entitled to housing benefit and/or council tax benefit (see Chapter 20).
- ❑ If you are classed as a person 'subject to immigration control', you are generally not entitled to IS, although there are limited exceptions (see 7 below).
- ❑ For some groups of people there are special rules. IS rules for those in care homes are explained in Chapter 33.

Claiming jobseeker's allowance or employment and support allowance? – If you are claiming either jobseeker's allowance (JSA) or employment and support allowance (ESA) or your partner is claiming income-based JSA or income-related ESA, you cannot get IS at the same time. You can switch claims if you find you have made the wrong choice (see 14 below).

3. Presence in Great Britain (GB)

IS can only be paid for the first four or eight weeks of a temporary absence from Great Britain (see Chapter 51(5)).

As well as being present in GB, you must also be 'habitually resident' in the UK, Channel Islands, Isle of Man or Republic of Ireland (see Chapter 50(2)).

4. Aged 16 or over

If you are under 16 you cannot get IS in your own right in any circumstances.

If you are under 20 and still at school or doing a non-advanced course at college or certain types of unwaged work-based training, you are usually excluded from IS; your parents

A B C D E F G H I J K L M N O P Q R S T U

E.1 Who can claim income support?

You can only claim IS if one of the categories below applies to you. You are eligible for the whole benefit week if the category applies for at least one day. You must also pass the entitlement conditions listed in (2). If none of the categories below apply, claim either jobseeker's allowance (JSA) or employment and support allowance instead.

The categories marked with an asterisk* do not apply to new claims from 27.10.08, unless they can be linked back to an earlier claim (see Chapter 13(1)).

Sickness or disability

- ❑ You are entitled to statutory sick pay (SSP).
- ❑ You are incapable of work.*
  This is assessed under the 'personal capability assessment' (PCA) (see Chapter 13(3)). You must send in medical certificates until you are assessed under (or exempted from) the PCA. You can be treated as incapable of work even if you are able to work in some circumstances (see Chapter 13(2)). You are also eligible for IS when you are treated as capable of work during a 6-week disqualification (see Chapter 13(7)).
- ❑ You have appealed against a decision under a determination that you are capable of work following a personal capability assessment (PCA).
  This category continues to apply until the final decision on your appeal. IS will be reduced by 20% of the single person's personal allowance for your age group (unless you are eligible for IS under one of the other categories in this box, eg you are a carer). If you win your appeal, the reduction will be repaid. See Chapter 15(8), as you may be better off claiming JSA.
  IS Regs, reg 22A
- ❑ You are registered as blind (in Scotland, certified as blind). If you regain your sight, you don't have to sign on during the 28 weeks after you are taken off the register.*
- ❑ You are mentally or physically disabled and are not treated as being in remunerative work because your hours or earnings are 75% or less than that of a person without your disability in the same job (see 6).*
- ❑ You are in employment while living in (or temporarily absent from) a care home, an Abbeyfield Home or an independent hospital in which you receive care.

Caring

- ❑ You are *'regularly and substantially engaged in caring for another person'* and either you are getting carer's allowance, or the person you are looking after gets attendance allowance (AA) or constant attendance allowance, or the middle or highest rate of disability living allowance (DLA) care component.
  If the person you are looking after has claimed DLA or AA, you'll be eligible for up to 26 weeks while you are waiting for their claim to be processed. You are eligible if they have an advance award of DLA middle or highest rate care component or AA but are still in the qualifying period. If carer's allowance entitlement stops, or the person you are looking after stops getting AA or the middle or highest rate of DLA care component, you continue to be eligible for eight weeks.
- ❑ If you would have been eligible for IS as a carer had you made a claim for IS, then you are eligible for IS for eight weeks from the date your carer's allowance and/or the disabled person's qualifying benefit stops.
- ❑ You are looking after your partner or a child or qualifying young person (see Chapter 38(1)) who is *'temporarily ill'* and for whom you are responsible.

Childcare responsibility

- ❑ You are a lone parent and responsible for a child under 12 (reduced to 10 from 26.10.09; however, this will not apply to certain lone parents who are also full-time students, completing full-time New Deal for Lone Parents courses or participating in approved schemes) who is a member of your household.
- ❑ You are taking unpaid statutory parental leave to look after a child who lives with you. You must have been entitled to housing benefit (HB), council tax benefit (CTB), working tax credit (WTC) or child tax credit (CTC – payable at a higher rate than the family element) on the day before your leave began.
- ❑ You are taking statutory paternity leave and you do not receive statutory paternity pay or any payment from your employer, and/or you were entitled to HB, CTB, WTC or CTC (payable at a higher rate than the family element) on the day before your leave began.
- ❑ You are single or a lone parent and are fostering a child under 16 through a local authority or voluntary organisation.
- ❑ You are looking after a child under 16 because the child's parent, or the person who usually looks after the child, is temporarily ill or away from their home.
- ❑ Your partner is temporarily outside the UK and you are responsible for a child under 16 who is a member of your household.

Education and training

- ❑ You are at school, in full-time non-advanced education or approved unwaged training and in one of the categories not excluded from IS (see 5).
- ❑ You are under 21, on a full-time non-advanced educational course which began before you were 19, and you are either an orphan or living away from your parents in one of the circumstances listed in 5.
- ❑ You are on a full-time course and eligible for IS as a disabled student (see Chapter 40(2)).*
- ❑ You are on Work-Based Learning for Young People (see Chapter 17(3)).
- ❑ You are a refugee and start attending an English course for over 15 hours a week during your first year in Great Britain (to help you obtain employment); you are eligible under this category for up to nine months only.

Pregnancy

- ❑ You are pregnant and incapable of work because of your pregnancy.
- ❑ You are pregnant and due to have your baby within the next 11 weeks.
- ❑ You have had a baby within the last 15 weeks.

Other

- ❑ You are getting IS urgent cases payments as a *'person subject to immigration control'* (see Chapter 50(3)).
- ❑ You have started work and are eligible for the first four weeks of housing costs run-on (see Chapter 16(4)).
- ❑ You are required to attend court or a tribunal as a JP, juror, witness, defendant or plaintiff.
- ❑ You are remanded or committed in custody for trial or sentencing (however, you can only get IS to cover housing costs; see Chapter 25).
- ❑ You are held to be involved in a trade dispute.

IS Regs, Sch 1B

can claim child benefit and child tax credit for you instead. But in some circumstances you can claim IS in your own right while you are at school (see 5 below).

If you are under 20 and on a full-time advanced course, see Chapter 40(2) for details of IS entitlement.

Once you've left school, you are eligible to claim IS from the 'terminal date' (see Chapter 38(1)) if you fit into one of the groups listed in Box E.1. If you don't fit into one of these groups, you should claim employment and support allowance (if you have a limited capability for work) or jobseeker's allowance (JSA) instead. There are additional conditions for 16/17-year-olds claiming JSA (see Chapter 15(19)).

Care leavers – If you are a care leaver, your local authority has a duty to support you until your 18th birthday. In most cases you would be excluded from IS. This does not apply, however, if you are a lone parent or a single foster parent.

Children (Leaving Care) Social Security Benefits Regs 2001, reg 2

5. Full-time education

You are normally excluded from IS if you are aged 16-19 and are at school or doing a non-advanced course at college for 12 or more hours a week or participating in approved unwaged training (and are thus treated as a qualifying young person for child benefit purposes – see Chapter 38).

IS Regs, reg 12

However, you won't be excluded from IS in this way if you:

- qualify for the disability or severe disability premium; *or*
- have been incapable of work for more than 28 weeks, ignoring gaps of up to eight weeks (this category only applies to IS claims made prior to 27.10.08); *or*
- have limited leave to enter or remain in the UK and you are dependent on funds from abroad that have been temporarily disrupted; *or*
- get child benefit for a child living with you (provided no one gets child benefit for you); *or*
- are a refugee on an English course (see Box E.1); *or*
- are an orphan and no one is legally responsible for you or acting in place of your parents; *or*
- are living away from your parents (and anyone acting in their place) and they cannot support you as they are chronically sick or disabled (mentally or physically), in custody, or prohibited from coming into Great Britain; *or*
- have to live away from your parents (and anyone acting in their place) because:
  - you are estranged from them; *or*
  - you are in physical or moral danger; *or*
  - there is a serious risk to your physical or mental health; *or*
- have left local authority care and have to live away from your parents (and anyone acting in their place).

IS Regs, reg 13

If you are aged 20 or over and on a full-time course, you will be treated as a student whether your course is advanced or non-advanced. Chapter 40(2) explains which students are entitled to IS.

6. Full-time or part-time work

You are excluded from IS if you or your partner are in 'remunerative work'. This means you are not entitled to IS if you, the claimant, work for 16 hours or more a week or if your partner works for 24 hours or more a week. But there are exceptions (see below).

To count as 'remunerative' it must be work *'for which payment is made or which is done in expectation of payment'*.

Lunch breaks, if you are paid for them, count towards the 16 or 24 hours.

Some people may be treated as being in full-time work, eg if they are off work because of a holiday. But if you are off work because you are ill or on maternity leave, you are not treated as being in remunerative work, even if you are getting sick pay or maternity pay from your employer. You are also not treated as being in remunerative work if you are off work because you are on paternity or adoption leave.

IS Regs, reg 5

Exceptions to the 16-hour/24-hour rule

If you come within one of the exceptions listed below, you can qualify for IS even if you are working for 16 hours or more a week. If your partner is working 24 hours or more a week, they must come within one of these exceptions.

Although you are not excluded from IS on account of the number of hours you work in these cases, any earnings are taken into account in the usual way (see Chapter 26(3)).

Unless you are a carer (see below), if you have an additional occupation that is not in one of these exceptions, the hours you work in that occupation count towards the 16-hour or 24-hour remunerative work limit.

You are not treated as being in remunerative work in the following circumstances.

❑ **Less hours or pay because of disability** – Because of your disability, physical or mental, *either*:

- your earnings are reduced to 75% or less of what someone without your disability would reasonably be expected to earn if they worked the same number of hours in your type of job or in a comparable job in the area; *or*
- your hours of work are 75% or less of what someone without your disability would reasonably be expected to undertake in your type of job, or in a comparable job in the area. DWP guidance advises that your own evidence of reduced earnings or hours should normally be accepted. But the decision maker may get more evidence from employment agencies, social services departments or disability charities if they need this to make a comparison.

❑ **Living in a care home** – You are in employment and live in, or are temporarily away from, a care home, an Abbeyfield Home or an independent hospital, in which you receive care due to your old age, disability, terminal illness or (past or present) mental disorder, drug or alcohol dependence.

❑ **Volunteering** – You are a volunteer or working for a charity or voluntary organisation, but only if the payment you receive or expect to receive is solely a payment to cover your actual expenses. If you are paid anything else, even if it is below your earnings disregard, all your hours of work count. If your average hours are 16 or more a week, you'll be excluded from IS. If the decision maker is not *'satisfied that it is reasonable for [you] to provide [your] services free of charge'*, they may treat you as having 'notional' earnings (see Chapter 26(20)).

❑ **Caring** – You are eligible for IS because you are caring for a person who gets attendance allowance (AA), or the middle or highest rate of disability living allowance care component, or you get carer's allowance (see Box E.1). If this exception applies, you are not excluded from IS even if you have another job. For example, if you care for your mother during the day and she gets AA, and you also work 20 hours a week in a supermarket in the evenings, because you are a carer none of your hours count, not even the 20 hours' evening work.

❑ **Foster or respite care** – You are a foster carer or you are paid by a health body, local authority or voluntary organisation to provide respite care in your own home for someone who does not normally live with you.

❑ **Childminding** – You are working as a childminder in your home.

❑ **Other** – You are not treated as being in remunerative work if you are:

- engaged on a scheme for which a training allowance is being paid;
- receiving assistance through the New Deal self-employment

route or a similar scheme;
- starting work and eligible for the first four weeks' housing costs run-on (see Chapter 16(4));
- working as councillor;
- engaged as a part-time firefighter, auxiliary coastguard or lifeboat person, or are a member of the territorial or reserve forces;
- held to be involved in a trade dispute (but not during the first seven days after the day you stopped work);
- engaged in an activity in respect of which a sports award has been, or is to be, made and no other payment is expected.

IS Regs, reg 6

7. Subject to immigration control

With very few exceptions, if you are 'subject to immigration control' you are not entitled to ordinary IS, although some people may be able to get an urgent cases payment. People who have been granted refugee status, or indefinite or exceptional leave to remain or enter, are not subject to immigration control and are eligible for ordinary IS. See Chapter 50(3) for more details.

8. How do you work out your entitlement?

The amount of IS you get depends on your income and capital, whether you have a partner, your age, whether you (or your partner) have a disability or are a carer, and whether you have certain housing costs. If you are a single person, only your needs and resources will be relevant. If you are one of a couple, the needs and resources of both of you will be relevant. You are considered to be one of a couple if you are married, in a civil partnership, or cohabiting (whether with someone of the opposite or the same sex). If you have dependent children living with you, their needs and resources will be ignored because support for children is provided through child tax credit (see Chapter 18).

Set amounts for different needs are added together to reach the total amount the law says you need to live on. This is called your 'applicable amount'. Any income worked out under IS rules is deducted from your applicable amount. This leaves the amount of IS you are entitled to.

Step 1: Add up your total capital resources – You will not be entitled to IS if your capital, and capital belonging to your partner, is more than £16,000. See Chapter 27.

Step 2: Work out your applicable amount – See 9 below.

- ❑ Add up all your personal allowances (see 10 below).
- ❑ Add up your entitlement to the premiums (see 11 below).
- ❑ Add up any IS housing costs (see Chapter 25).

The sum total of all these is your IS applicable amount.

Step 3: Add up your total income resources – See Chapter 26. Don't forget the tariff income if you have capital over £6,000, or £10,000 if you are in a care home (see Chapter 27(4)).

Step 4: Deduct your income from your applicable amount – If your income is less than your applicable amount, IS makes up the difference in full, provided you meet the other qualifying conditions (see 2 above).

Example: Mr Porter, aged 37, cares for his mother, who lives with him. Mr Porter receives carer's allowance.

His applicable amount is:	
Personal allowance	£64.30
Carer premium	£29.50
Applicable amount	*£93.80*
His income is:	
Carer's allowance	£53.10
Applicable amount	£93.80
Less income	£53.10
IS entitlement	*£40.70*

Mr Porter will be paid IS of £40.70 as well as carer's allowance of £53.10.

9. What is your applicable amount?

The applicable amount, set by Parliament, is the amount the law says you need to live on. It consists of:
- personal allowances – for a single claimant or for a couple (see 10 below);
- premiums – flat-rate extra amounts if you satisfy certain conditions (see 11 below);
- certain housing costs (see Chapter 25).

IS Regs, reg 17

Your entitlement to all of these is taken into account when your claim is assessed. Jobcentre Plus will add up your total applicable amount. Any income worked out under set rules is deducted from your applicable amount (see Chapter 26). This leaves the amount of IS that you are entitled to.

To check that your IS has been correctly worked out, you should ask for a detailed notice of assessment (on form A124).

Special groups

In some circumstances your IS may be worked out differently or paid at a reduced rate.

Children: pre-April 2004 claims – If your claim for IS began before April 2004 and you have dependent children living with you, your IS may still include amounts payable for the children. These will include personal allowances for each child, as well as a family premium, and possibly disabled child premiums and enhanced disability premiums for any disabled children.

The child allowances are similar to those that still exist for housing benefit and council tax benefit (see Chapter 20(25)). The premiums are covered in Chapter 24.

At some date in the future, amounts payable in IS for children will be removed and child tax credit will become payable instead.

Care homes – If you live permanently in a care home, the lower capital limit is higher (see Chapter 27(3)).

Hospital – If you or a member of your family are in hospital, your applicable amount may be reduced (see Box M.1, Chapter 35).

Urgent cases – If you are subject to immigration control (see Chapter 50(3)) or treated as possessing income not readily available to you (notional income – see Chapter 26(20)), you can sometimes claim 'urgent cases' payments. These are payments of IS made at a reduced rate. Ask your local Jobcentre Plus office for details.

IS Regs, regs 70-71

Incapacity appeals – Generally, IS is reduced while you are appealing against a decision under the 'personal capability assessment' that you are capable of work (see Chapter 13(6)).

Jobcentre Plus interviews – You (or your partner) may be asked to attend a work-focused interview with a personal adviser. If you fail to attend without good cause, your IS will be paid at a reduced rate. See Box T.1 in Chapter 59.

Housing costs run-on – For the first four weeks after starting work, you may continue to get housing costs, including mortgage interest, met by IS (see Chapter 16(4)).

Sanctions – IS can be paid at a reduced rate for 13 weeks through sanctions, which can be applied if either you or your partner are convicted of more than one benefit offence within a 5-year period.

10. The personal allowances

The personal allowances are part of your applicable amount (see 9 above). For IS, the decision maker takes into account your age and whether you are part of a couple.

Personal allowances		per week
Single person	aged 25 or over	£64.30
	aged under 25	£50.95
Lone parent	aged 18 or over	£64.30
	aged under 18	£50.95
Couple	both aged 18 or over [1]	£100.95
	both under 18 [2]	£76.90
	one aged 25 or over [3]	£64.30
	one aged 18-24 [3]	£50.95

Couples (where one partner is under 18) – In the table of rates above, the reference numbers mean:
1: includes couples where one is under 18 but is: eligible for IS or would be if they were single; or eligible for income-based jobseeker's allowance (JSA) or severe hardship payments (see Chapter 15(19));
2: only if one is responsible for a child; or each would be eligible for IS if they were single; or the claimant's partner is eligible for income-based JSA or severe hardship payments. If only one of the couple is eligible for IS, etc, the single person's allowance of £47.95 would apply;
3: only if the other is under 18 and would not be eligible for IS (even if they were single), income-based JSA or severe hardship payments.
IS Regs, Sch 2, Part I

11. The premiums

There are five premiums, each with specific qualifying conditions. These are detailed in Chapter 24. The premiums are part of your applicable amount (see 9 above). Unless otherwise specified, each premium to which you are entitled is added to the total of your applicable amount.

Premiums		per week
Disability	single	£27.50
	couple	£39.15
Enhanced disability	single	£13.40
	couple	£19.30
Severe disability	single	£52.85
	couple (one qualifies)	£52.85
	couple (both qualify)	£105.70
Pensioner	couple	£97.50
Carer		£29.50

IS Regs, Sch 2, Parts III & IV

12. How do you claim income support?

You can start your claim for IS by ringing the Jobcentre Plus claim-line (0800 055 6688; textphone 0800 023 4888). The claim-line will put you through to your nearest Jobcentre Plus contact centre. The contact centre will take your details and go through your claim over the phone. This will take about 45 minutes. In some cases, they may need to ring you back for additional information. They may also arrange a date for you to attend a Jobcentre Plus interview with a personal adviser about work prospects (see Box T.1, Chapter 59).

You will then be sent a statement containing the information you provided over the phone. You need to sign that the statement is correct and return it in the envelope provided or take it to the Jobcentre Plus interview, if one has been arranged. You may be asked to provide supporting documents, such as payslips or proof of savings, with the statement; these will be necessary for your claim to be accepted as properly made. If you do this within one month of the date you first notified the Jobcentre Plus of your intention to claim, your date of claim will be the date of that first contact. If you have problems getting the necessary information or evidence within one month, tell Jobcentre Plus straightaway and send the statement anyway. If your difficulty is for certain specified reasons, your claim can still be treated as made on the date of your first contact. For more details see Chapter 59(2).
C&P Regs, reg 6(1A)

If you are not able (or it is inappropriate for you) to use the telephone, a claim can be made on a paper form – the A1. You can obtain this from your local Jobcentre Plus office or download it from www.dwp.gov.uk/advisers/claimforms.

If you re-claim IS after a break in benefit of no more than 12 weeks, you can re-claim the benefit under a rapid reclaim process using a much shorter claim-form.

13. Backdating

If you think you were entitled to IS before you put in your claim, ask, in writing, for your claim to be backdated. IS can be backdated for up to three months if there are 'special reasons' why you couldn't reasonably have been expected to claim earlier (see Chapter 59(3)).

Waiting for a decision on another benefit?

Entitlement to another benefit may entitle you to IS, or to more IS, because your applicable amount (see 9 above) goes up. For example, if you or your partner get disability living allowance (DLA), that qualifies you for a disability premium.

If you already get IS – Ask for your award to be revised or superseded once you get the decision on DLA or other qualifying benefit. Arrears of any extra IS you are entitled to are paid for the same period as the award of the qualifying benefit.

If you do not already get IS – To make sure you do not miss out on benefit, you may need to make two IS claims. (We use the example of DLA here, but the process is the same for any other benefit that allows you to qualify for IS.)

Do not delay making an IS claim while you are waiting for a decision on the DLA claim, as DLA claims can sometimes take a long time to be decided. This IS claim will be turned down if entitlement depends on DLA being awarded (eg without a disability premium, your income is higher than your applicable amount). If you are later awarded DLA, and then claim IS again within three months of the date of the decision to award DLA, IS can be backdated to the date from which DLA was first payable (or the date of the first IS claim if that is later).

If the DLA claim is made more than ten working days after your first IS claim, the second IS claim cannot be backdated in this way. If you did not make an IS claim at the right time, claim as soon as you can and ask for it to be backdated for up to three months if there are 'special reasons' (see Chapter 59(3)).
C&P Regs, reg 6(16)-(18)

If your IS is stopped – Where IS entitlement depends on getting another qualifying benefit like DLA, and the qualifying benefit is stopped, your IS will also stop. But if you challenge the decision on the qualifying benefit and it is reinstated, claim IS again within three months and it will be fully backdated.
C&P Regs, reg 6(19)-(22)

Conversely, if your IS is stopped and following this a decision is made to award you a qualifying benefit, a further IS claim can be backdated to the date the earlier claim was stopped (or the date the qualifying benefit became payable, if that is later), as long as it is made within three months of the decision on the qualifying benefit.
C&P Regs, reg 6(30)

14. Who should make the claim?

You should normally make the claim yourself; if you are unable to act for yourself, a decision maker can appoint someone else (eg a parent, carer or close friend) to take over the management of your claim (see Chapter 59(4)).

Couples

A married couple, a man and woman living together as husband and wife, and same-sex partners (whether registered as civil partners or not), all count as couples for IS.

If one is eligible for IS – If you are eligible for IS but your partner would be required to sign on for benefit, you can choose which of you should make a claim. Either you claim IS or your partner claims jobseeker's allowance (JSA). However, if you are in the joint-claim age group for JSA (see Chapter 15(2)), either you claim IS or you both claim JSA jointly. You can't get IS and JSA at the same time unless your partner is only claiming contribution-based JSA. In this case, you can claim IS to top up the JSA.

Whether you claim IS or JSA, the amount of benefit is usually the same. But note that:

- IS is tax free, whereas JSA is taxable;
- JSA is not payable for the first three 'waiting days' at the start of the claim;
- you avoid the risk of JSA sanctions if you claim IS instead (see Chapter 15(9)).

If you claim IS, your partner can sign on voluntarily at the Jobcentre Plus office to secure national insurance credits.

If you find you've made the wrong choice, simply put in a claim for IS. Jobcentre Plus will stop the JSA award if your IS claim is successful.

If you are eligible for IS and your partner is eligible for employment and support allowance (ESA), you can choose which of you should make the claim; ie either you claim IS or your partner claims income-related ESA. If a disability premium is payable with the IS (which, for instance, would be the case if your partner is in receipt of disability living allowance – see Chapter 24(2)), you will usually be better off claiming IS. If a disability premium is not payable with the IS, you will probably be better off if your partner claims income-related ESA.

If both are eligible for IS – You can choose which of you should make the claim. You can switch roles at any time. Your partner just has to put in a claim for IS with your agreement that they should make the claim, or vice versa.

C&P Regs, reg 4(3) & (4)

15. How is income support paid?

IS is usually paid into a bank, building society or Post Office account (see Chapter 59(5)). If you need money urgently at the start of your claim, Jobcentre Plus should make the first payment by cheque. Payment is usually made weekly in arrears, but if you are getting certain other benefits, it may be paid in advance (see 16 below).

It is intended that over a 2-year period, starting from 6.4.09, claimants will be moved onto a new arrangement, where they will be paid fortnightly in arrears. If you are left without money for a week due to the changeover, you will be eligible for a loan from the social fund equivalent to that week's IS.

Small payments – If you are entitled to less than £1 a week in IS, it will be paid to you weekly or fortnightly only if it can be paid along with another benefit. Otherwise, it will usually be paid in one sum at intervals of no more than 13 weeks.

C&P Regs, Sch 7, para 5

The minimum payment of IS is 10p a week. If you are entitled to IS of 9p or less a week, it can only be paid to you if it can be paid along with another benefit. If you cannot be paid IS because of this minimum payment rule, you don't count as being 'on IS' for housing benefit or council tax benefit purposes; you have to go through the separate benefit assessments (see Chapter 20).

C&P Regs, reg 26(4)

Third-party deductions from benefit – IS for mortgage interest is paid to the lender if it is a member of the Mortgage Interest Direct scheme. For other costs, part of your benefit (up to a ceiling) may be deducted and paid to a third party if you have enough benefit, and usually if you have a debt.

C&P Regs, regs 34A & 35

The order of priority for direct payment deductions is: child maintenance payments (new rules), housing costs, rent arrears and service charges, fuel costs, water charges, council tax, court fines and compensation orders, child maintenance payments (old rules), refugee integration loans and Eligible Loans Deduction scheme payments.

C&P Regs, Sch 9, para 9

16. Benefit weeks and pay days

IS is normally paid on the same day and at the same intervals as other benefits you get. In most cases, it is paid in arrears. It is only paid in advance if you are getting widows' or bereavement benefits (but not if you are providing medical evidence of incapacity) or returning to work after a trade dispute.

C&P Regs, Sch 7, para 2

When you are paid in arrears, your 'benefit week' is the period of seven days ending with your IS pay day, and you can be paid from the date your claim was received (or treated as received) in the Jobcentre Plus office. If there is a change of circumstances, your IS will alter from the first day of the week in which the change occurs.

C&P Regs, Sch 7, para 6 & D&A Regs, Sch 3A, para 1(a)

Over a 2-year period, starting from 6.4.09, claimants will be moved onto fortnightly payments in arrears. Once you are on the new arrangement, you will have a standard pay week ending with a day linked to your national insurance number.

17. Revisions and appeals

When you first claim, or when there is a major change in your applicable amount or resources, and thus a change in the amount of benefit you get, you will be sent a short notice of assessment. You can ask for a more detailed notice of assessment (on form A124) at any time.

If your IS claim is turned down, or you think you've been awarded the wrong amount, you can ask for the decision to be revised and/or lodge an appeal to an independent tribunal. The time limit in either case is one month from the date the decision was sent to you. If the decision did not include a written statement of reasons, you can ask for one; if you do this within the month, the time limit can then be extended by at least 14 days (see Chapter 60(3) for details).

A phone call to your local Jobcentre Plus office can set up a revision. If the decision maker revises the decision you will be given a new decision with new appeal rights; if they don't revise the decision, you will be informed and told you have one month in which to appeal against the original decision.

You should appeal on form GL24 (see Chapter 60(8)).

If you are out of time, you can still ask for the past decision to be revised or superseded (see Box T.5, Chapter 60). However, unless there are special circumstances for admitting your late application (see Chapter 60(5)), the decision maker will only change the decision from the date of your request (thus limiting any arrears payable to this date; see Box T.4, Chapter 60 for exceptions). You will have the right of appeal against the new decision.

15 Jobseeker's allowance

In this chapter we look at: page

A. GENERAL CONDITIONS

1. What is jobseeker's allowance?

Jobseeker's allowance (JSA) is for people who are unemployed or working less than 16 hours a week and who are seeking work. People who have a limited capability for work due to illness or disability should claim employment and support allowance instead (see Chapter 9). Others who do not have to sign on for work (eg carers or lone parents with responsibility for young children) should claim income support instead (see Chapter 14). There are two forms of JSA.

- **Contribution-based JSA:** this is a personal flat-rate allowance with entitlement based on your national insurance contribution record; it is payable for up to six months (182 days) and is taxable.
- **Income-based JSA:** this is means tested, taxable, and payable if you have no income or a low income and no more than £16,000 in savings. Your partner (if you have one) cannot work 24 hours a week or more.

One set of general labour market conditions of entitlement applies to JSA as a whole, so you must be available for work, take active steps to look for work and have a current jobseeker's agreement.

2. The basic conditions

You are entitled to jobseeker's allowance if you:

- are available for work (see 4 below); *and*
- are actively seeking work (see 5 below); *and*
- have entered into a jobseeker's agreement that remains in force (see 6 below); *and*
- are not working 16 hours or more a week (see 7 below); *and*
- are capable of work (see 8 below); *and*
- are under state pension age (currently 60 for women, 65 for men); *and*
- are not in full-time education – see Chapter 40(4) for exceptions; *and*
- are in Great Britain (GB) – see Chapter 51(7) for exceptions; *and*
- for contribution-based JSA, pass the contribution-based conditions (see 11 below); *or*
- for income-based JSA, pass the income-based conditions (see 16 below).

If you satisfy the conditions for both, you may be entitled to contribution-based JSA topped up with income-based JSA (see 21 below).

JSA, Ss.1-3

Couples

For contribution-based JSA, both members of a couple can claim separately based on their own contribution records. For income-based JSA, unless you are in a joint-claim couple (see below), one of you must claim for both partners. The person who claims must sign on as available for work and meet all the other conditions for benefit.

Joint-claim couples – Some couples must make a joint claim for income-based JSA. This applies to couples without dependent children, where one or both of the couple is aged at least 18 and was born after 28.10.47. If you are one of a joint-claim couple, you and your partner must both be available for work and meet all the other basic conditions above, unless one of you is 'excused'. You and your partner need to decide which one of you receives payment of JSA.

If one of you does not meet all the conditions, JSA is paid at the single person rate. But if one of you would be eligible for income support (see Box E.1, Chapter 14) or employment and support allowance (ESA – see Chapter 9) instead, that person is excused from meeting the JSA conditions. In this case, there is a choice; the eligible partner can claim income support or income-related ESA for both of you (and the other can sign on voluntarily for national insurance credits), or you claim JSA jointly and get paid the full couple rate but only one of you needs to meet the JSA conditions.

There are a few further circumstances in which only one member of the couple is expected to meet JSA conditions, including if one of you is a full-time student, is or has been pregnant (for the same period that maternity allowance is payable), is not habitually resident in GB, or is working at least 16 hours but less than 24 hours a week.

JSA Regs, regs 3A, 3D, 3E & Sch A1

Lone parents

For new claims from 24.11.08, lone parents who are able to work and whose youngest child is over the age of 12 (age 10 from 26.10.09) must claim JSA rather than income support.

As income support is normally paid weekly in arrears and JSA fortnightly, there is protection for lone parents who are moved from one benefit to the other. At the start of the JSA claim they will be able to take out a repayable 'transition loan' from the social fund to cover them until they receive the first JSA payment.

3. How do you claim?

On the first day you become unemployed, you should make a claim for JSA. Don't delay, otherwise you will lose benefit unless you can show you have 'special reasons' for delaying (see Chapter 59(3)).

JSA is administered by Jobcentre Plus. Most contact will be with a personal adviser at the local office where you sign on. Decisions on your claim will normally be made at a processing centre, which you can only contact by phone.

Waiting days – The first three days of your claim are 'waiting days', during which you cannot usually be paid either type of JSA. You do not have to serve waiting days if your claim is linked to a previous 'jobseeking period' (see 12 below), a decision maker elects to move you to JSA from income support, or you claim within 12 weeks of the end of a previous entitlement to employment and support allowance, incapacity benefit, income support or carer's allowance.

JSA, Sch 1, para 4 & JSA Regs, reg 46

Starting your claim – To make a claim, ring the national claim number (0800 055 6688; textphone 0800 023 4888). Call centre staff will take your details, and book an appointment for you to see a financial assessor and a personal adviser. These interviews will take place consecutively at your local Jobcentre Plus office, normally within a week. The call centre will send you claim documents, which you should complete and bring to the interviews. The documents will either be a claim-pack for you to complete (see below) or a 'customer statement', a computer printout of the information you provided over the phone, which you need to check and sign. Jobcentre Plus prefers claims to be completed by phone. However, heavy demand on the call centres sometimes means they have to send out paper claim-packs. If you find it hard to use the phone for any reason, you have a right to ask for a claim-pack to be sent to you and Jobcentre Plus should work with you to overcome your communication difficulties. Whether you make a statement by phone or complete a claim-pack you will be asked for the same information.

The claim-pack – This consists of two forms. The first, the JSA1, asks for details to check whether you satisfy the contribution-based and income-based conditions. The form must be completed by the time of your interview for the claim to be paid from the time you first contacted Jobcentre Plus. If you do not complete it properly, your claim may only date from when you do so (see Chapter 59(2)). If you need help to complete the form, tell the Jobcentre.

The second form (ES2, *Helping you back to work*) asks detailed questions about the work you are looking for; the hours you are available for work; the pay you will accept; the distance you are prepared to travel to work and the steps you will take to find work. You should take care when filling in this form, because if you put restrictions on what you are prepared to accept, your answers could lead to doubts about whether you are available for work (see 4 and 5 below).

Under the 'rapid reclaim' process, if you are re-claiming JSA after a break of no more than 26 weeks, you should be interviewed the same or the next day, and you will not have to complete a full claim-pack.

The interviews – The financial assessor will discuss your benefit entitlement and confirm the information on your JSA1 or customer statement. The personal adviser will ask questions to check whether you are capable of and available for work and what you intend to do to look for work. You will also be asked to discuss, agree and sign the jobseeker's agreement (see 6 below). Once it has been established that you meet the basic labour market conditions for benefit, your claim will be assessed for both contribution-based and income-based JSA. If your health or disability means you need specialist advice and help, you can be referred to a disability employment adviser.

Problems? – If there is a delay in your claim being decided, or benefit is suspended or disallowed, a sanction is applied, or you are told you can't claim, seek advice. You should continue to sign on if possible while you are challenging a decision. You might be able to get hardship payments in the meantime (see 10 below). For how to challenge a decision about your entitlement to benefit, see Chapter 60.

If you find it difficult to make phone calls, you should be able to visit your local Jobcentre Plus office, where you will be able to phone the call centre or processing centre free of charge and use computer terminals to look for jobs. Staff should also be able to meet any access needs arising from your disability.

During your claim – JSA is paid every two weeks in arrears, usually directly into a bank or building society account (see Chapter 59(5)).

Normally, you will have to sign on at Jobcentre Plus every fortnight. You can be asked to sign on more frequently, even daily, if, for example, you are suspected of working without declaring it, or as a way of keeping in contact with you if you are homeless. Once you have been claiming JSA for 13 weeks you must sign on weekly for the next six weeks and need to widen the scope of your search to 'any suitable job'.

JSA, S.8 & JSA Regs, reg 24(6)

If you miss your signing-on day, your benefit entitlement will stop, unless you show within five working days that you had 'good cause' for not signing (eg you had a doctor's appointment or job interview). If one of the circumstances in which you are 'treated' as though you are available for work apply (see 4 below, under 'Absences, emergencies and other circumstances'), you will have 'good cause'.

JSA Regs, regs 25(1)(c) & 27

Each time you sign on you will be asked to explain what you have done to look for work or improve your prospects of finding work. Keep a record of your jobseeking steps (including any use of the internet and email) so you can show that you are 'actively seeking work' (see 5 below).

There will also be more in-depth interviews where your jobseeker's agreement will be reviewed and updated if necessary. This will happen after 13 weeks, then 26 weeks, and thereafter once every six months, but you can be called in for an interview at any time. If you do not attend, your benefit entitlement will stop, unless you can show within five working days that you had 'good cause'.

Jobseeker's direction – At an in-depth interview, your personal adviser may issue a 'jobseeker's direction', requiring you to take a specific step to improve your job prospects. For example, you could be directed to attend a course or to improve the way you present yourself to employers. If you don't comply with a jobseeker's direction, unless you have good cause, a sanction is applied (see 9 below).

JSA, S.19(5)(a) & JSA Regs, reg 72

New Deal – If you are aged 18-24 and have been claiming JSA for six months, you will be referred to the New Deal (see Chapter 17(4)). If you are 25 or over, you will be referred after claiming JSA for 18 months. You may be referred more quickly. Once on the New Deal, failure to comply with the requirements can result in your benefit being sanctioned. From October 2009, a 'Flexible New Deal' comes in, under which personalised 'intensive' back-to-work help will be offered after 12 months. Failure to attend 'back to work' sessions could lead to sanctions (see also Chapter 17(4)).

4. Available for work

You must be willing and able to take up immediately any paid employment of at least 40 hours a week (see below for restrictions you are allowed to make).

JSA, S.6 & JSA Regs, reg 6

Treated as unavailable for work – You are not regarded as available for work and therefore not entitled to JSA if you:

- get maternity allowance or statutory maternity pay; *or*
- are on paternity or adoption leave; *or*
- are a full-time student – there are limited exceptions (see Chapter 40(4)); *or*
- are a prisoner on temporary release.

JSA Regs, reg 15

At the start of your claim – For a 'permitted period' of up to 13 weeks from the beginning of your claim, you may be allowed to restrict your availability and jobseeking to your usual occupation and/or to your usual pay. After this you must be prepared to widen your availability for work and job searching activity. You are still allowed to restrict your availability under the rules described below if (in most cases) you have reasonable prospects of securing employment.

JSA Regs, reg 16

Can you restrict the hours you are available for work?

The 40-hours rule – You must be prepared to take up employment of at least 40 hours a week, or less than 40 if required to do so. In most cases, you do not have to accept a job of less than 24 hours a week (see 'What is good cause' in 9 below).

JSA is a 7-day benefit, so you must fulfil the conditions of entitlement on each day of the week. This does not mean you must be prepared to work seven days a week. You can restrict the times in the week you are available to take up work (eg Monday to Saturday, 9am to 6pm) provided your 'pattern of availability' would give you 'reasonable prospects of employment' (see below), your job prospects are not considerably less than they would be if you were available at all times, and your available hours are at least 40 a week. You can specify fewer than 40 hours a week if that is reasonable in the following situations.

JSA Regs, reg 7

Carers – If you care for a child or an elderly person or someone *'whose physical or mental condition requires [him or her] to be cared for'* who is a *'close relative'* or a member of your household, you may restrict the hours you are available for work to less than 40 hours, but not less than 16 hours a week. A 'close relative' means a partner, parent, parent-in-law, step-parent, son, daughter, son/daughter-in-law, stepson/daughter, grandparent, grandchild, brother or sister, or the partner of any of those. You must be available for as many hours and at the times that your caring responsibilities allow, taking into account the times you spend caring, whether the caring is shared, and the age and physical and mental condition of the person you care for. You must normally show you have 'reasonable prospects of securing employment' (see below). However, if you care for a child, Jobcentre Plus may accept that you do not have to have reasonable prospects of securing employment in light of the type and number of employment vacancies within daily travelling distance of your home.

JSA Regs, regs 4 & 13(4)-(6)

Laid off or short-time working – For the first 13 weeks you are treated as available for work, provided you are available to take on casual employment to top up any hours you actually work to at least 40 a week, and you are prepared to resume immediately the work you were laid off from, or return full time to the job in which you are being kept on short time. After 13 weeks, you must show you have reasonable prospects of employment if you want to continue to restrict the hours you are available for work.

JSA Regs, reg 17

Can you put any other restrictions on the type of work you'll accept?

Provided you can show you have 'reasonable prospects of securing employment' (see below), you can restrict:

- the nature of the employment (eg due to sincerely held religious or conscientious objections);
- the terms and conditions of employment;
- the rate of pay – but only for the first six months of your claim (after six months you can't insist on a rate of pay higher than the relevant national minimum wage);
- the areas you will work in – generally, you are expected to be prepared to travel for up to 1½ hours both to and from work, although you may restrict this to one hour for the first 13 weeks of your claim.

JSA Regs, regs 8 & 9

Disability-related restrictions – You can restrict your availability in any way (eg pay, hours, travel time, type of work), providing the restrictions are reasonable given your physical or mental condition. In this case, it is not relevant whether the restrictions affect your employment prospects, providing you do not put other non-disability-related restrictions on your availability as well. If you do, you will have to show you have reasonable employment prospects given all the restrictions. If you restrict the rate of pay you are prepared to accept, this is not subject to the general 6-month limit, but applies for as long as the restriction is reasonable given your physical or mental condition. If you refuse a job offer where the hours of work or other conditions of the job are beyond your agreed restrictions, you won't generally be sanctioned for this (see 9 below).

JSA Regs, reg 13(3)

Reasonable prospects of employment

If you put any restrictions on your availability, unless these are solely disability-related, you must show you have reasonable prospects of securing employment. The decision maker must consider all the evidence, and in particular:

- your skills, qualifications and experience;
- the type and number of vacancies within daily travelling distance;
- how long you have been unemployed;
- your job applications and their outcome; *and*
- if the restrictions are on the nature of the work, whether you are prepared to move home to take up work.

It is important to think carefully before you put restrictions on your availability. If you can't show you have reasonable employment prospects, your benefit could be disallowed.

JSA Regs, reg 10

Can you delay taking up an offer of employment?

Generally, you must be able to take up employment immediately. However, if you are a carer (see above) or a volunteer, you must be able to take up employment given one week's notice and attend any employment opportunity interview given 48 hours' notice. If you care for a child, you can be given up to 28 days' notice to take up employment and seven days' notice to attend an interview, as long as you can show that this is reasonable.

If you are providing a service (paid or unpaid) you must be able to take up work given 24 hours' notice. If you are employed for less than 16 hours a week, you must be able to take up work immediately after the statutory minimum notice period (rather than any contractual notice) that your employer is entitled to – usually one week.

JSA Regs, reg 5

Absences, emergencies and other circumstances

You may be treated as available for work in the following situations. You are also treated as actively seeking work for the week if the situation applies to you for at least three days in the week.

❑ **Absences from home**

- you are at a work camp – for up to two weeks, once in 12 months;
- you are on a Venture Trust programme – for up to four weeks, once in 12 months;
- you are on an Open University residential course – for up to one week per course;
- you are absent from Great Britain (GB) to attend a job interview (up to one week), or for a child's medical treatment (up to eight weeks), or your partner is over 60 or disabled and you are both abroad (up to four weeks) – see Chapter 51(7).

❑ **Emergencies**

- you need time to deal with a death or serious illness or funeral of a close relative or close friend, or a domestic emergency affecting you, a close relative or close friend; or the person you have been caring for has died – for up to one week, no more than four times in 12 months (or, if you care for a child, in the case of a death, serious illness or domestic emergency, up to eight weeks once every 12 months);
- you are working as a part-time firefighter, or helping to run or launch a lifeboat;
- you are part of a group of people organised to respond to an emergency – eg part of a search for a missing person.

❑ **Other circumstances**

- you are sick for a short while, and treated as capable of work (see 8 below);

- you are a full-time student on an employment-related course and have prior approval from the employment officer – for up to two weeks, once in 12 months;
- you are looking after your child while your partner is temporarily absent from the UK – for up to eight weeks;
- you are temporarily looking after a child because the usual carer is ill, temporarily away from home, or looking after a member of your family who is ill – for up to eight weeks;
- you are looking after your child during the child's school holidays (or similar vacations) and it would be unreasonable to make other care arrangements;
- you are looking after your child who has been excluded from school and it would be unreasonable to make other care arrangements;
- you are a party to court or tribunal proceedings – for up to eight weeks;
- you are temporarily detained in police custody – for up to 96 hours;
- you have been discharged from prison – for one week from the date of release.

JSA Regs, reg 14

If you are on holiday in GB, you must still be available for work (although you might not have to be actively seeking work – see below). You must show you can be contacted regularly while away, and be willing to return at once to start work. Before you go, send form ES674 *Going on holiday within Great Britain* to the Jobcentre Plus office. If you go abroad on holiday, you are not usually entitled to JSA (see Chapter 51(7)).

5. Actively seeking work

As well as being available for work, you are expected to take such steps, usually at least three a week, as you can *'reasonably be expected to have to take'* in order to have the best prospects of getting employment, eg:

- applying for jobs;
- looking for vacancies, including via the internet;
- registering with an employment agency;
- on referral from an employment officer, seeking specialist advice on improving your prospects with regard to your particular needs or disability;
- drawing up a CV or getting a reference;
- drawing up a list of relevant employers and seeking information from them;
- seeking information on an occupation.

Even if you've taken reasonable steps to look for work, they can be disregarded if, by your *'behaviour or appearance [you] otherwise undermined [your] prospects of securing the employment in question'*, or you acted in a violent or abusive way or spoiled a job application. But it can't be held against you if these were due to circumstances beyond your control (eg because of mental health problems).

JSA, S.7(1) & JSA Regs, reg 18

Absences, emergencies and other circumstances

In some circumstances for a limited time, you can be treated as actively seeking work. The circumstances in which you are treated as both actively seeking work and available for work are listed in 4 above, under 'Absences, emergencies and other circumstances'. There are other times when you are not expected to take any steps to look for work, although you must still be available to take up work.

JSA Regs, reg 19

If you are absent from home – In any 12-month period, you may be treated as actively seeking work for a maximum of:

- two weeks for any reason (eg a holiday) as long as you are away from home for at least one day each week; *or*
- six weeks if you are blind: the six weeks consists of a maximum of four weeks during which you are attending, for at least three days a week, a training course in using a guide dog, and a further two weeks for any reason as long as you are away from home for at least one day each week; *or*
- three weeks if you are attending an Outward Bound course for at least three days a week.

In each case, you must give written notice that you intend to stay away from home for at least one day in each week and that you do not intend to actively seek work in that week.

The weeks don't have to be consecutive. You can't use more than one provision in any one 12-month period. For example, if you have had one week away on holiday and then within 12 months you go on an Outward Bound course, you can only have one more week in which you are treated as actively seeking work.

For the 2-week 'any reason' provision, once you've notified your intention, you'll be treated as actively seeking work. If you change your mind and don't go anywhere you must give written notice withdrawing your intention before the start of the week you were due to be away to make sure you don't use up a week unnecessarily.

JSA Regs, reg 19(1)(p) & (2)

Becoming self-employed – You are treated as actively seeking work for up to eight weeks during which you are taking steps to establish yourself in self-employment, starting with the week you are accepted on a government scheme for helping people into self-employment.

JSA Regs, reg 19(1)(r)

6. Jobseeker's agreement

This contains a description of the type of work you're looking for, the hours you are available and any 'pattern of availability', the action you're expected to take to look for work and to improve your job prospects, details of any restrictions on your availability for work and the dates of any 'permitted period' (see 4 above). It is a condition of entitlement to JSA that you and your personal adviser agree and sign the jobseeker's agreement (joint-claim couples must each sign a jobseeker's agreement).

If you don't accept the proposed agreement, you have the right to ask your personal adviser to refer it to a decision maker who should make a decision *'so far as practicable'* within 14 days. In the meantime, you are not entitled to benefit. You may qualify for hardship payments of reduced-rate income-based JSA (see 10 below). The decision maker may decide to backdate the jobseeker's agreement, but not necessarily back to your date of claim.

JSA, S.9 & JSA Regs, regs 31 & 32

Varying an existing jobseeker's agreement – Either you or the adviser can propose to vary the agreement. If there is a dispute, the proposed agreement may be referred to a decision maker as above. Your benefit will continue to be paid while the decision maker is considering a variation. If the agreement is varied, you must sign within 21 days, otherwise the jobseeker's agreement may be terminated and your entitlement to benefit will stop.

JSA, S.10 & JSA Regs, regs 37-40.

7. Working full time or part time

You are excluded from JSA if you are in 'remunerative work' of (on average) 16 hours a week or more. Work counts if you are paid or if you work 'in expectation of payment'. The rules closely follow the income support rules and provide for specific circumstances in which work can be ignored or, conversely, in which you can be treated as working even when you're not (see Chapter 14(6)). If you stop work because of a trade dispute at your workplace, you are not eligible to claim JSA; your partner could claim income-based JSA or you could claim income support, but payment will be at a reduced rate.

JSA Regs, regs 51, 52 & 53 and JSA, S.14

Partners – For contribution-based JSA it makes no difference to your entitlement whether or not your partner works or how much they earn. For income-based JSA, see 19 below.

8. Capable of work

Generally, you only need to state that you are capable of work, which is sufficient to satisfy the entitlement condition.

If you are disabled or ill – If you are incapable of work through ill health (unless it is a short illness – see below) or disability, you are not eligible for JSA, but you may be able to claim employment and support allowance (ESA) (see Chapter 9).

If you are already claiming ESA and believe you are now capable of work and wish to claim JSA, you will need to show that you have *'a reasonable prospect of obtaining employment'*. This will be the case even if there has recently been a determination that you have (or can be treated as having) a limited capability for work. A similar rule exists if you are still claiming incapacity benefit, in which case you can also be treated as capable for work if you have worked or been in education or training to prepare for work while you had the same illness or disability, which has not worsened since then. Once you have shown that you are eligible for JSA, any restrictions you wish to place on your availability for work because of your health or disability are treated as a separate issue.

ESA Regs, reg 31 & IW Regs, reg 17A

What if you are ill for a short while? – If you fall ill, you may choose to stay on JSA for up to two weeks: you must fill in a form to declare that you are unfit for work and for how long. You may only do this twice in each 'jobseeking period' (ie period of entitlement to JSA – see 15 below). Or, if you are entitled to JSA for over a year (ignoring breaks in entitlement of 12 weeks or less) you can only choose this option twice in each year. If you fall ill a third time or are ill for longer than two weeks, you should claim ESA instead.

If you fall ill within 12 weeks of an end of entitlement to ESA or eight weeks of the end of an entitlement to incapacity benefit, statutory sick pay, severe disablement allowance or income support based on incapacity, you cannot stay on JSA. You should re-claim your previous benefit and, in most cases, you'll be entitled to your previous rate of benefit without re-serving any qualifying period (see Chapter 16(12)).

JSA Regs, reg 55

Incapacity cut-offs – If your incapacity benefit (IB), severe disablement allowance (SDA) or income support (IS) has been cut off because of a determination that you are capable of work, you may claim JSA instead. You will be regarded as capable of work until the decision is overturned, whether at review or appeal. This does not prevent you making a claim for ESA if your condition gets significantly worse or if you begin to suffer from a different illness or disability (this may be treated as a claim for IB, SDA or IS if no more than eight weeks separate the two periods of incapacity for work).

D&A Regs, reg 10; SSCBA, S.30C(1)(c)

Claiming JSA while you are appealing the decision on incapacity does not prejudice your chances of winning the appeal. However, you may claim income support instead (without signing on but at a reduced rate and without national insurance credits) while you are appealing (see Box E.1, Chapter 14). If you claim JSA, there will be no question about your capacity for work but you will be asked about your availability for work and the sort of work you are looking for. The rules allow you to impose any restrictions that are reasonable given your disability (see 4 above). It might be useful to talk to a disability employment adviser.

9. Sanctions

If you don't fulfil the basic labour market conditions, JSA is disallowed altogether (or paid at a single person's rate if one member of a joint-claim couple fails to meet the conditions – see 2 above).

Even if you satisfy the basic conditions, in some circumstances your JSA may be sanctioned. In this case you remain entitled to JSA but payments stop for a limited period. The sanction period normally runs from the beginning of the benefit week following the decision to apply the sanction. If a sanction is applied (or your JSA is disallowed), you may be eligible for hardship payments (see 10 below). For a joint-claim couple, if one of you is subject to a sanction, JSA is reduced to the rate for a single person (a lower reduction will be made if you are eligible for hardship payments).

2- or 4-week sanctions

JSA is not payable for two weeks, or four weeks if this is the second sanction within 12 months (except that a first New Deal sanction and any sanction under Gateway to Work is always for two weeks), in the following circumstances.

- ❑ You refuse or fail to carry out a reasonable jobseeker's direction (see 3 above).
- ❑ You neglect to avail yourself of a reasonable place on a training scheme or employment programme.
- ❑ You refuse or fail to apply for, or take up a place on, a training scheme or employment programme notified to you by an employment officer.
- ❑ You give up a place on, or fail to attend, a training scheme or employment programme.
- ❑ You lose your place on a training scheme or employment programme through misconduct.

In any case other than misconduct, a sanction will not be applied if you can show you had 'good cause' for your action (see below).

JSA, Ss.19(2)&(5) & 20A(2)&(3) and JSA Regs, reg 69(1)(a)&(b)

Training schemes and employment programmes – Although these sanctions only apply to certain schemes, such as Gateway to Work or any of the options in the New Deal for Young People, you could also be sanctioned for not attending other schemes if you've been referred under a jobseeker's direction and you don't comply with it. If you are aged 25 or over and in full-time education or training under the New Deal provisions, you can be sanctioned if, once you have accepted the course, you do not fulfil the requirements of this option or you leave without good cause or due to misconduct.

'Good cause' – The following circumstances count as good cause (unless you refused or failed to carry out a reasonable 'jobseeker's direction', when the test is the same as for the 26-week sanction – see below).

- ❑ You could not attend because of your disability or ill health, and attendance would put your health, or that of others, at risk.
- ❑ You have caring responsibilities, you could not make alternative arrangements and the person has no 'close relative' (see 4 above) or member of their household available to care for them.
- ❑ Travel time would be more than an hour either way, or if there is no scheme within this travel time, the travel time would be longer than to the nearest appropriate scheme.
- ❑ You had to deal with a domestic emergency or were running or launching a lifeboat, on duty as a part-time firefighter, or part of a group organised to provide assistance in an emergency.
- ❑ You were arranging or attending the funeral of a close friend or relative.
- ❑ You did not participate due to a sincerely held religious or conscientious objection.
- ❑ You were attending court as a party to the proceedings, a witness or juror.
- ❑ For the New Deal for Young People, you were not given prior written notice about the relevant option, warning of the actions that could lead to a sanction.
- ❑ For full-time education and training under the New Deal 25 Plus, you were within the first four weeks, or you left because of a lack of ability or the course was not 'suitable'.

If none of these apply, other reasons can also be considered.
JSA Regs, reg 73

26-week sanction

JSA is not payable for up to 26 weeks in the following circumstances.

- You lose your job through misconduct.
- You voluntarily leave your job without 'just cause'.
- You refuse or fail to apply for a vacancy or accept a job offer, notified to you by an employment officer, without 'good cause' (see below).
- You do not take up a job opportunity with an employer for whom you worked within the last 12 months, where the terms and conditions of employment are at least as good as before (eg you do not exercise your right to return to work after maternity leave), without 'good cause' (see below).
- You have already been sanctioned twice under the New Deal, and this is the third or subsequent sanction without good cause, each sanction being within 12 months of the previous one.

JSA, Ss.19(3)&(6) & 20A(2)&(4) and JSA Regs, reg 69(1)(c)&(d)

Entitlement to contribution-based JSA lasts for a maximum of 26 weeks. Since you continue to be entitled during the period of a sanction you could be left with no payment at all if the maximum 26-week sanction is applied. The 26-week maximum period is discretionary and the decision maker must consider all your circumstances, including:

- any physical or mental stress connected with a job you left voluntarily or with a job for a previous employer;
- the rate of pay and hours of work in a job you left voluntarily, if you worked 16 hours or less a week;
- the length of time a job was likely to have lasted, if this would be less than 26 weeks.

JSA Regs, reg 70

You can appeal against the decision (see Chapter 60); a tribunal could reduce the period of sanction. The minimum sanction is one week.

If you lose your job through misconduct – Being dismissed does not necessarily lead to a benefit sanction. When you claim benefit, your ex-employer will be sent a standard form asking whether you were sacked and why. If it looks as though a sanction may be applied, you will be sent a copy of your employer's reply. It is important to comment on this reply in detail. Your ex-employer will also see what you have said and can add further comments. You may also be making a claim of unfair dismissal to an Employment Tribunal. If someone is helping with this (eg your union representative) you should ask them for advice. If a sanction is applied, you can appeal (see Chapter 60).

If you leave your job voluntarily – The decision maker has to show that you left your job voluntarily, but once this is shown you must show you had 'just cause' for leaving if you want to avoid a sanction. This is not the same as having a good reason for leaving. Your state of health (or the health of a close relative (R(U)14/52)) may help you show just cause. Generally, there must be something in the nature of your job or your domestic circumstances that meant it was no longer reasonable for you to continue working.

If you can, show that handing in your notice was the only thing you could do given all the circumstances, including your attempts to resolve the problems. This may enable you to escape the sanction altogether. You should therefore try and resolve work-related problems (using the firm's grievance procedures if they have any) before handing in your notice. You should also look for other work before leaving, or find out if you can be transferred to lighter work. If possible, discuss your personal or domestic difficulties with your employer to see if you can resolve the difficulty without handing in your notice.

You should not normally be sanctioned for agreeing to take voluntary redundancy, as you are not regarded as having left your job voluntarily. Nor should you be sanctioned if you left because your employer paid you less than the national minimum wage and you had tried unsuccessfully to get them to pay it.

JSA Regs, reg 71 & Decision Makers Guide, Vol 6, Chap 34, para 34284

When considering whether you had just cause for leaving a job, the decision maker should take into account any childcare responsibilities that made it unreasonable for you to stay in your job and any childcare expenses that were unreasonably high when compared with your pay.

JSA Regs, reg 73A

Employment on Trial – Although you would normally be sanctioned for leaving a job without good reason, Employment on Trial allows you to leave a job and still claim JSA if you have been in the job at least four weeks and one day, and you have left before you have been there for 13 weeks. You must have worked at least 16 hours in each complete week. Dismissal or leaving the job through misconduct could still lead to sanctions. Jobcentre Plus can provide more details.

JSA, Ss. 20(3) & 20B(3) and JSA Regs, reg 74

What is 'good cause'? – In deciding if you have 'good cause' for failing to carry out a jobseeker's direction, or not applying for or accepting a job notified to you by an employment officer, or not taking up a job opportunity with a previous employer (see above), the decision maker must take all your relevant personal circumstances into account.

You are not expected to accept a job of less than 24 hours a week unless it has been agreed you may restrict the hours you are available for work to less than 24 hours a week (eg because of a disability or caring responsibilities – see 4 above). In this case, you won't be sanctioned for refusing a job of less than 16 hours a week.

The level of pay (if it's at least the national minimum wage) cannot usually be taken into account in deciding whether you have good cause for refusing a job, even if the pay would not cover your financial commitments or would be less than your benefits. The only exception is if, under the availability for work rules, it has been agreed that you may restrict the level of pay you are prepared to accept (eg if this is reasonable given your disability, or during the 'permitted period' at the start of your claim – see 4). See below if there are high work-related expenses.

You will have good cause if your reason for refusing a job or not carrying out a jobseeker's direction is that you are only looking for work in your usual occupation during your 'permitted period' or that you are not required to be able to take up a job at once – eg you are a carer or a volunteer (see 4). When deciding whether you have good cause, the decision maker must take certain other factors into account:

- any personal circumstances that suggest a particular job or jobseeker's direction might cause significant harm to your health or subject you to excessive physical or mental stress;
- any responsibility for caring for a 'close relative' (see 4) or someone in your household that might make it unreasonable for you to do a particular job or carry out a jobseeker's direction. If you care for a child, the availability and suitability of childcare should be considered;
- travel time to and from work, or to a place mentioned in the jobseeker's direction; but it won't count as good cause if the travel time is normally less than 1½ hours (one hour during the first 13 weeks of your claim) each way unless the time is unreasonable due to your health or caring responsibilities;
- any agreed restrictions on your availability for work (see 4), and differences between the work you are available for given those restrictions and the job requirements;
- any sincerely held religious or conscientious objections to

taking the job or carrying out the jobseeker's direction;

- childcare expenses, travel expenses and other necessary, exclusively work-related expenses if these are an unreasonably high proportion of the income from the job, or your income while carrying out a jobseeker's direction. However, nothing else to do with your (or your family's) income and outgoings can be taken into account, unless you have been allowed to restrict the level of pay you are prepared to accept because of your disability, or you are still in the 'permitted period' at the start of your claim (see 4), or if the job is paid only by commission or pays below the national minimum wage.

JSA Regs, reg 72

10. Hardship payments

If your benefit is sanctioned, suspended or disallowed, or there is a delay in making a decision on your claim, you may be entitled to reduced-rate hardship payments of income-based JSA. Payment is not automatic, and in most cases you must show that you or your family will suffer hardship unless benefit is paid. Unless you fall into a particular vulnerable group, no benefit will be paid for the first two weeks.

The applicable amount is reduced by 40% of the single person's personal allowance. However, if you, your partner or your child are seriously ill or pregnant, the reduction is 20%. If your partner is entitled to income support, they can claim it for both of you. It is not subject to any reduction.

JSA Regs, regs 145 & 146G

You may be entitled to hardship payments if you have no JSA in payment for one of the following reasons.

- There is a delay in the decision on your claim for JSA because of a question about whether you satisfy the availability, actively seeking work and jobseeker's agreement conditions for benefit.
- Your benefit has been sanctioned. During a New Deal sanction of two, four or 26 weeks, you can only get hardship payments if you are considered to be 'vulnerable' (see below).
- Your benefit has been suspended because of a doubt about whether you satisfy the availability, actively seeking work or jobseeker's agreement conditions.
- If you are not available for work or actively seeking work or do not have a current jobseeker's agreement, you may still get hardship payments, but you must be considered to be vulnerable (see below) even after the first two weeks. However, this reason will not apply if you are 'treated' as unavailable for work (see 4 above).

JSA Regs, regs 141 & 146C

For the first two weeks – Hardship payments are not payable for the first two weeks unless you or your partner are considered to be vulnerable, ie are:

- responsible for a child or qualifying young person (see Chapter 38(1)); *or*
- pregnant; *or*
- a carer looking after someone who gets attendance allowance or disability living allowance middle or highest rate care component (or has claimed but is waiting for a decision), and you cannot continue to care for them unless you receive hardship payments. In this case you need not show hardship would result; *or*
- qualify for a disability premium; *or*
- suffering from a *'chronic medical condition which results in functional capacity being limited or restricted by physical impairment'* that has lasted, or is likely to last, for at least 26 weeks, and during the first two weeks the disabled person's health would probably decline more than that of a healthy person; *or*
- under 18 and fall within one of the groups eligible for JSA while age 16 or 17 (see 20 below); *or*
- under 21 and have recently left local authority care.

In each case, other than the exception for carers, you must satisfy the decision maker that the vulnerable person will suffer hardship unless payments are made.

JSA Regs, regs 140(1) & 146A(1)

After two weeks – If you are not considered 'vulnerable', you are eligible for hardship payments only after the first two weeks after the sanction has been applied, or suspension made, etc. You must show that you or your partner will suffer hardship unless payment is made.

JSA Regs, regs 142 & 146D

What is 'hardship'? – You must fill in an application form and set out your grounds for applying for a hardship payment. In deciding whether or not you will suffer hardship if no payment is made, the decision maker must take into account any resources likely to be available to you. They must also look at whether there is a substantial risk that you will have much-reduced amounts of, or lose altogether, essential items such as food, clothing, heating and accommodation. It is also relevant whether a disability premium, or disabled or severely disabled child elements of child tax credit, are payable. But they may also take other factors into account.

JSA Regs, regs 140(5) & 146A(6)

B. CONTRIBUTION-BASED JSA

11. Do you qualify?

To qualify for contribution-based JSA you must meet the national insurance conditions (see 12 below). You must also satisfy the basic conditions for JSA (see 2 above).

Contribution-based JSA is a flat-rate personal benefit and is payable for a maximum of six months (182 days). If you don't meet the national insurance conditions, you may be entitled to income-based JSA instead. You may also be entitled to income-based JSA to top up your benefit (eg if you have a dependent partner or certain housing costs such as a mortgage) – see 16 below.

12. National insurance contribution conditions

There are two contribution conditions for contribution-based JSA. Both need to be satisfied. The first condition depends on contributions you have actually paid in the relevant tax year. For the second condition, credited contributions as well as paid contributions count. The different classes of national insurance (NI) contribution are covered in Chapter 11(3). Credited contributions are covered in Chapter 11(4).

With both conditions, there is a relationship between 'tax years' and 'benefit years', so it is important to know the difference between them.

Tax years – A tax year runs from 6 April to 5 April the following year.

Benefit years – A benefit year starts on the first Sunday in January and ends on the Saturday before the first Sunday in January the following year. The 2009 benefit year started on Sunday 4.1.09 and will end on Saturday 2.1.10.

SSCBA, S.21(6)

The 'relevant benefit year' is usually the benefit year that includes the start of your 'jobseeking period'.

JSA, S.2(4)

The first condition – paid contributions

You must have paid Class 1 NI contributions on earnings 25 times the lower earnings limit for that tax year (see Chapter 11(6)) in either one of the two complete tax years before the start of the benefit year in which you make your claim or in which your jobseeking period (or linked period) began (see below). So if you claim in the 2009 benefit year, you meet the first condition if you paid Class 1 contributions on earnings of £2,100 between April 2006 and April 2007, or on earnings of £2,175 between April 2007 and April 2008.

JSA, S.2

The second condition – paid or credited contributions
You must have paid or been credited with Class 1 NI contributions on earnings 50 times the lower earnings limit for that tax year (see Chapter 11(6)) in each of the last two complete tax years before the start of the benefit year in which you make your claim or in which your jobseeking period (or linked period) began (see below). So if you claim in the 2009 benefit year, you meet the second condition if you paid or had been credited with contributions on earnings of £4,200 in the 2006/07 tax year and of £4,350 in the 2007/08 tax year. A credited contribution counts as having earnings at the amount of the lower earnings limit for that tax year. You can combine credits and paid contributions.

SSCBA, Sch 3, para 2(3) & (5) and JSA, S.2

Jobseeking period and linking rules
The jobseeking period is any period for which you claim and satisfy the basic conditions of entitlement to JSA (see 2 above), or you get a hardship payment, or you are signing on to protect your NI contribution record. A period in which you lose entitlement because of failure to sign on or attend an appointment, or you are not entitled because you are involved in a trade dispute, is not included in the jobseeking period.

Any two jobseeking periods link together and are treated as one single jobseeking period if they are separated by:

- 12 weeks or less; *or*
- one or more linked periods (periods when you are incapable or have a limited capability of work, or entitled to maternity allowance, or training and getting a training allowance, or on certain New Deal options); *or*
- a period on jury service.

Gaps of 12 weeks or less between jobseeking periods and linked periods, or in between linked periods, are ignored.

For JSA, the beginning of the jobseeking period or any linked period is used to decide the tax years for which you must satisfy the contribution conditions. For example, if your employment and support allowance (ESA) ends and you sign on for JSA instead, and you claim JSA within 12 weeks of the end of your ESA claim, the relevant tax years for your JSA claim will be the same as the ones used for your earlier ESA claim.

Another linking rule helps people who give up work to care for someone to qualify for JSA on the basis of the contributions they paid when they were working. If you were getting carer's allowance and this ended within 12 weeks of the beginning of your jobseeking period (or linked period), the period of carer's allowance entitlement also links to the jobseeking period, if this would help you satisfy the contribution conditions for JSA. So your benefit year would be the year in which your carer's allowance entitlement began.

JSA Regs, reg 48

Linking rules before 7.10.96 – Jobseeking periods were introduced on 7.10.96. For a note on linking rules before this, see *Disability Rights Handbook* 25th edition, page 80.

13. How much do you get?

Contribution-based JSA	per week
Aged under 25	£50.95
Aged 25 or over	£64.30

JSA Regs, reg 79

14. Does anything affect what you get?

The amount you get may be affected by earnings or by an occupational or personal pension. Only your earnings (not those of your partner or other family members) are taken into account. Payment is not affected by other income or savings you have. If one or more of these sources of money mean you are not paid benefit you will still remain entitled (unless your earnings exceed your 'prescribed amount' – see below). Any day for which you are entitled but not paid will count towards your 182 days of entitlement (see 15 below).

Earnings – Your weekly earnings from employment or self-employment are deducted in full from the amount of benefit due, apart from an earnings disregard of £5 (or £20 if you are working as a part-time firefighter, auxiliary coastguard, lifeboat operator or member of a territorial or reserve force). Except for this earnings disregard, the assessment of earnings is essentially the same as for means-tested benefits – see Chapter 26(3)-(5).

JSA Regs, regs 98-102 & Sch 6

On days in any week when your earnings exceed your 'prescribed amount' (which is the amount of contribution-based JSA payable for your age plus your earnings disregard minus one pence) you are not entitled to contribution-based JSA and these days do not count towards your 182 days of entitlement (see 15 below).

JSA, S.2(1)(c) & JSA Regs, reg 56

Occupational or personal pensions – Income from an occupational or personal pension or from the Pension Protection Fund or the Financial Assistance Scheme of over £50 a week is deducted from the amount of benefit due – eg, if your pension is £55 a week, £5 is deducted from your benefit. Days when no contribution-based JSA is payable because the level of your pension reduces it to nil, count towards your 182 days of entitlement. A one-off lump-sum payment does not affect your benefit.

JSA Regs, reg 81(1)

Other benefits – You cannot get more than one contributory benefit at the same time, nor can you get income support or income-related employment and support allowance (ESA) while claiming contribution-based JSA, although you may be entitled to income-based JSA paid as a top-up. However, if you have a partner they may be entitled to claim income support (if they come within one of the groups listed in Box E.1) or income-related ESA (if they have a limited capability for work) for both of you, provided you only get contribution-based JSA. If this applies, you should check whether you will be better off if you claim income-based JSA or if your partner claims income support or ESA.

15. How long does contribution-based JSA last?

Entitlement to JSA lasts for a total of six months (182 days). This can be in one spell of unemployment lasting for six months or in more than one spell of unemployment where you make shorter claims for JSA but your entitlement in each of those claims is based on the same two tax years. Once your 182 days are exhausted, you can only re-qualify when you begin a new jobseeking period and your new JSA claim is based on different tax years (at least one of which is a later year). See 12 above for details of the tax years on which your claim is based.

JSA, S.5

Jobseeking period – This is the period when you meet the conditions for JSA or a hardship payment, including time when you are sanctioned. Two jobseeking periods can be linked in certain circumstances (see 12 above). If your new claim is linked to your previous jobseeking period, you will not have to wait another three waiting days but will only be entitled to what remains of your 182 days of contribution-based JSA.

JSA Regs, regs 47(1)&(2)

C. INCOME-BASED JSA

16. Do you qualify?

To qualify for income-based JSA, you must satisfy the basic conditions for JSA set out in 2 above. In addition you must satisfy the following income-based conditions.

- ❑ You must have no income, or your income is below your 'applicable amount' (a set amount that depends on your circumstances) – see 17 below.
- ❑ Your capital must be no more than £16,000 (see 18 below).
- ❑ If you have a partner they must not be working for 24 hours or more a week (see 19 below).
- ❑ You must be aged 18 or over; or aged 16 or 17 and pass other tests (see 20 below).
- ❑ You must be 'habitually resident' and not subject to immigration control (see Chapter 50(2 and 3)).

Income-based JSA is means tested and taxable. You claim for yourself and your partner. If you are one of a couple, you can choose who should make the claim. The one who claims must sign on and satisfy all the basic conditions. (If you are part of a joint-claim couple, see 2 above.) Income-based JSA can be paid in addition to contribution-based JSA.

Income-based JSA can help towards mortgage interest payments and certain other housing costs. If you get income-based JSA, you may also be entitled to housing benefit and council tax benefit, and will not have to go through a separate means test (see Chapter 20).

Getting income-based JSA may entitle you to:

- free prescriptions and dental treatment (Chapter 55);
- housing grants (Chapter 31);
- help from the social fund (Chapters 22 and 23);
- free school meals (Chapter 37);
- help with hospital fares (Chapter 35).

17. If you have any income

If you are one of a couple (married or in a civil partnership, or living together as spouses/civil partners), your partner's income is added to yours. Otherwise, only your income is taken into account. Some types of income and part of any earnings may be ignored or disregarded. See Chapter 26 for details of how your income is worked out.

JSA Regs, regs 93-97, 103-105 & Sch 7

18. If you have savings or other capital

If you or your partner have capital of over £16,000 you won't be entitled to income-based JSA. If your capital is between £6,000.01 and £16,000, it is treated as producing a 'tariff income' – ie, £1 a week for every £250 or part of £250 that you have in capital above £6,000 is deducted from your benefit entitlement. If you live in a care home, tariff income starts at capital above £10,000. Some types of capital are ignored partly or completely and others count towards the capital limit. See Chapter 27 for details of how your capital is worked out.

JSA Regs, regs 107-116 & Sch 8

19. If your partner is working

You are not entitled to income-based JSA if your partner is in 'remunerative work' of (on average) 24 hours or more a week. Work counts if it is paid or done *'in expectation of payment'*. The rules closely follow the income support rules (see Chapter 14(6)) and provide for specific circumstances in which work can be ignored or, conversely, in which your partner can be treated as working even when they're not. If your partner's work does not exclude you from entitlement, their earnings are taken into account in the assessment of your benefit.

JSA Regs, regs 51(1)(b) & (2)-(3), 52 & 53

20. If you are aged 16 or 17

If you are aged 16 or 17, you are only entitled to JSA if you are in certain specified groups, eg people estranged from their parents. You must register for work and training with the Careers Service or Connexions Service. You must also satisfy all the basic conditions of entitlement (set out in 2 above) including being available to take up work and taking active steps to look for work and training. Provided you haven't been subject to a JSA sanction in the past, you can restrict your availability to jobs where the employer is providing suitable training – ie you can turn down a job if no such training is offered.

JSA Regs, regs 62 & 64

Severe hardship payments – If you don't fit into any of the circumstances outlined below in which JSA can be paid to people aged 16/17, you can be paid JSA on a discretionary basis if you would otherwise suffer severe hardship. The direction to pay JSA will be for a temporary period (usually eight weeks) and you must also satisfy the basic conditions of entitlement (set out in 2 above). Factors such as your health, vulnerability, threat of homelessness, training or job prospects should be taken into account. In some situations (eg if you fail to complete a course of training without good cause) the amount you get is reduced for the first two weeks by 40% of the personal allowance (or 20% if you are seriously ill or pregnant).

Who is eligible? – You are eligible for income-based JSA while aged 16/17 if you fall into one of the specified groups of people who are eligible for income support (see Box E.1, Chapter 14) or employment and support allowance (see Chapter 9(9)), but you choose to claim JSA instead. You are also eligible if you are one of a couple and are treated as responsible for a child who lives with you, or if you are laid off or on short-time working (up to a maximum of 13 weeks).

JSA Regs, reg 61

21. How much do you get?

The amount you get is based on your 'applicable amount' and on your income and capital. Your applicable amount is made up of:

- **a personal allowance:** for yourself or for a couple (these are the same as those of income support – see Chapter 14(10)); *plus*
- **premiums:** (see below); *plus*
- **certain housing costs** (eg mortgage interest) – see Chapter 25.

JSA Regs, reg 83, Sch 1 & Sch 2

Your income or capital will be assessed and may affect how much of your applicable amount you are entitled to (see Chapters 26 and 27).

Premiums – There are five premiums, each one with specific qualifying conditions (see Chapter 24 for details). Unless otherwise specified, each premium to which you are entitled is added to the total of your applicable amount.

Premiums		**per week**
Disability	single	£27.50
	couple	£39.15
Enhanced disability	single	£13.40
	couple	£19.30
Severe disability	single	£52.85
	couple (one qualifies)	£52.85
	couple (both qualify)	£105.70
Pensioner	single	£65.70
	couple	£97.50
Carer		£29.50

IS Regs, Sch 2, Parts III & IV

If you satisfy the contribution-based conditions

You are paid contribution-based JSA if you satisfy the conditions. Your entitlement to income-based JSA is also calculated and if this amount exceeds the contribution-based JSA the extra amount is paid as a top-up.

F Going back to work

This section of the Handbook looks at:

16 Benefits and work

1. Going back to work

This chapter looks at the effect on benefit entitlement of doing paid or voluntary work and the linking rules that can help you return to benefit without losing out.

2. What happens to your DLA?

Disability living allowance (DLA) and attendance allowance are payable whether or not you are working. They are not means tested, so earnings do not affect the amount of your benefit (see Chapters 3 and 4).

Note: Starting a job may suggest that your care or mobility needs have changed, so your benefit entitlement could be reconsidered. The DWP views starting or leaving work as a potential 'change of circumstance' for DLA. You may be asked to explain your care needs in work. When doing this, consider carefully what 'attention' (see Chapter 3(11)) you need to do your job.

3. Can you work while claiming ESA or benefits for incapacity?

Generally, if you do any work, whether or not you expect to be paid, you are treated as capable of work for the week in which you do the work (Sunday to Saturday) and thus are not entitled to the following benefits:

- employment and support allowance (ESA);
- incapacity benefit or severe disablement allowance;
- income support based on incapacity for work (see Box E.1, Chapter 14);
- disability premium under the 'incapacity condition' (see Chapter 24(2));
- national insurance incapacity or ESA credits.

IW Regs, reg 16(1); ESA Regs 40(1)

If you come off one of these benefits to start paid work, you can protect your right to return to benefit for up to two years (see 12 below).

Exempt work – You are allowed to do the kinds of work described below while remaining on benefit, although that work might not be ignored completely. The sort of activities or tasks you are able to do, whether connected with the work or not, could be taken into account when deciding whether you pass the personal capability or work capability assessments (for incapacity benefits and ESA respectively). When you start work your case may be referred to a DWP healthcare professional for an opinion and you may be subject to another medical examination, but this should not happen routinely. You do not have to undergo a medical examination just because you are doing permitted work, but any medical examination that may be due during a period of permitted work will go ahead.

Caring for a relative (in your own home or elsewhere) and domestic tasks in your own home are not regarded as work. A relative is a parent (or in-law or step-parent), son/daughter (in-law/step), brother, sister, or the partner of any of them; or a spouse or partner, grandparent, grandchild, uncle, aunt, nephew or niece.

IW Regs, reg 16(3)(c); ESA Regs, reg 40(2)(c)

Negligible amounts of work can be ignored, eg someone who occasionally does small jobs for a business (eg signing cheques).

Decision Makers Guide, Vol 3, Chap 13, para 13857

Permitted work

You are allowed to do the following types of 'permitted' work. You do not need to tell Jobcentre Plus that you are working as a condition for doing the permitted work. However, as you should notify them of any change of circumstances that could affect your benefits, it is best to let them know as soon as you start the work.

Permitted work lower limit – You can earn no more than £20 a week. You can do such work even between periods when you are on the other forms of permitted work described below. The £20 limit means that such work should not interfere with your entitlement to means-tested benefits such as income support, housing benefit (HB) or council tax benefit (CTB), if you qualify for the disability premium.

Supported permitted work – This is work carried out as part of your treatment programme under medical supervision while you are an inpatient or regular outpatient of a hospital or similar institution, or work done under the supervision of a person employed by a public or local authority or voluntary organisation that provides or arranges work opportunities for disabled people. The support must be ongoing and regular, but the frequency of contact can vary depending on the needs. The means of contact can vary, and be either face to face or by phone. The work can be in the community or a sheltered workshop. Your earnings must not exceed £92 a week, which is roughly equivalent to 16 hours work at the national minimum wage.

Permitted work higher limit – This is designed to test your ability to work before you move permanently into employment. You can earn up to £92 a week and you must work less than 16 hours a week.

If you are in the support group of ESA claimants (see Chapter 9(6)) or are an incapacity claimant exempt from the personal capability assessment (PCA, see Chapter 13(4)), you can do this work for an unlimited period.

If you are in the work-related activity group of ESA claimants (see Chapter 9(7)) or if you are an incapacity claimant who is not exempt from the PCA, you can only do this work for a maximum of 52 weeks. If you have a break in your claim of more than 12 weeks, you can repeat the 52-week period of permitted work higher limit. Otherwise, you can do further permitted work higher limit only after a gap of more than 52 weeks since you last did it.

IW Regs, reg 17(2)-(4); ESA Regs, reg 45(2)-(4)

16-hour limit – You must work for less than 16 hours a week. Your hours are averaged over the current week and the four preceding weeks, or over the period of a 'recognisable cycle' of work.

IW Regs, reg 17(8); ESA Regs, reg 45(8)

Effect of earnings – For ESA, earnings for permitted work are calculated in the same way as they are under the income assessment for income-related ESA (see Chapter 26(3) and (4)). For benefits paid for incapacity, earnings for permitted work are calculated in the same way as they are for carer's allowance dependant's addition (see Chapter 6(5)).

ESA Regs, reg 88; R(IB)1/06 (CoA: 'Doyle') & CE Regs

If your earnings from permitted work are below the £20 or £92 limit (whichever is appropriate), your ESA, incapacity benefit or severe disablement allowance (SDA) will not be affected. But if you get income support, HB or CTB, earnings over £20 are taken into account as income and may reduce that benefit (see Chapter 26(5)). However, if you get income-related ESA, you can earn up to £92 a week and keep your ESA and this will also have no effect upon HB and CTB or other 'passported' benefits.

Other kinds of work

The following kinds of work are also allowed:

- work done as a councillor. If you receive a councillor's allowance that pays more than £92 a week (excluding expenses), an amount equal to the extra money will be deducted from your contributory ESA, incapacity benefit or SDA;
- an approved work trial arranged in writing with the employer by Jobcentre Plus (or an organisation providing services to them) for which you will receive no wages;
- any activity in an emergency, to protect another person, or to prevent serious damage to property or livestock;

IW Regs, reg 16(3)(a), (b) & (d); ESA Regs, regs 40(2)(a)&(e) & 45(7)

- self-employed work done while you are 'test trading' for up to 26 weeks with help from a self-employment provider arranged by Jobcentre Plus;
- voluntary work (not for a close relative) – see 11 below;
- duties undertaken as a 'disability member' of an appeal tribunal or the DLA Advisory Board – but only one full day or two half days a week is allowed.

IW Regs, reg 17(5), (6) & (7), ESA Regs, regs 45(5)-(6) & 40(2)(b)

Dialysis, radiotherapy and other treatments

If you receive certain specified types of treatment for two or more days in a week, you can work on the other days and continue to receive incapacity benefit or SDA for the days of treatment (including days of preparation and recuperation specified as part of the treatment). If you receive such treatment and can thus be treated as having a limited capability for work for the week (see Chapter 10(2)) you can work on the other days and continue to receive contributory ESA for the days of treatment and recovery.

IW Regs, reg 13, ESA Regs, reg 46

If your partner works

Your partner's earnings do not affect the basic amount of contributory ESA, incapacity benefit or SDA you get, but for incapacity benefit and SDA they can affect an adult dependant's addition (see Chapter 13(7)). Your partner's earnings affect income support, income-related ESA and income-based jobseeker's allowance (see 4 and 7 below).

4. What happens to income support?

If you get income support on the grounds of incapacity for work, you may do permitted work of less than 16 hours a week or other exempt work (see 3 above). If you get income support on any other grounds (eg because you are registered blind or a carer) you can work for less than 16 hours in any job.

In some cases there is no limit on the hours you can work – eg if your earnings or hours are 75% or less of what someone without your disability would expect to earn or to work in a comparable job (see Chapter 14(6)).

If you are the claimant and your partner works, their hours must be less than 24 a week, although there are some exceptions (see Chapter 14(6)).

In each case, you can keep only a maximum of £20 of your earnings or joint earnings for a couple (see Chapter 26(5)).

Housing costs run-on – If your income support, income-based jobseeker's allowance (JSA) or income-related employment and support allowance (ESA) stops because you or your partner get a job or more hours or more pay, any housing costs (including payments to cover mortgage interest) you were getting can be paid for an extra four weeks at the existing rate whatever your earnings, provided your job is expected to last at least five weeks. You may be able to get this help if you or your partner were getting benefit continuously for at least 26 weeks and you received housing costs immediately before starting (or extending) the work. You do not have to make a separate claim. Simply inform Jobcentre Plus that you are starting work or increasing your hours/earnings.

IS Regs, reg 6(5)-(8)

Job grant – This helps to bridge the gap between leaving benefit and receiving a wage. It is a one-off tax-free payment for people who have been claiming income support, JSA, ESA, incapacity benefit or severe disablement allowance (or New Deal allowances based on these) for at least 26 weeks and who are moving into remunerative work of at least 16 hours a week, provided the job is expected to last five weeks or more. The grant is for £100, or £250 if you have children.

5. What about carer's allowance?

You can work and claim carer's allowance at the same time if your earnings (less any allowable deductions) are no more than £95 a week. There is no limit on the number of hours you can work, although you must continue to provide care for at least 35 hours a week. Work during breaks from caring (see Chapter 6(10)) does not affect carer's allowance.

Carer's allowance is not means tested. Provided your earnings are below the limit, the full amount of carer's allowance is payable. Caring costs of up to half your net earnings can be disregarded if you pay someone other than a close relative to look after the disabled person you care for or a child under 16 (for whom you get child benefit). Your partner's earnings do not affect the basic amount of carer's allowance you get but can affect an adult dependant or child dependant's addition. See Chapter 6(5) for details.

Income support to top up your carer's allowance is affected in a different way. For carers, there is no limit on the number of hours you work, but only £20 of your net earnings can be disregarded (see Chapter 26(5)).

6. Getting housing and council tax benefit

You can claim housing benefit (HB) and council tax benefit (CTB) whether or not you are in work (see Chapter 20). They are means tested, so the amount you get depends on the level of your (and your partner's) income and savings. See Chapter 26 for the way earnings are assessed.

Extended payments – If your income-related employment and support allowance (ESA), income support or income-based jobseeker's allowance (JSA) stops because you (or your partner) get a job or more hours or pay, your HB and CTB may carry on for an extra four weeks at the existing rate whatever your earnings, provided the job is expected to last five weeks or more. To be eligible, you or your partner must have been getting income support, income-related ESA or contribution- or income-based JSA, or a combination of these, for at least 26 weeks.

A similar extended payment can be made if you have received contributory ESA, incapacity benefit or severe disablement allowance continuously for at least 26 weeks before you get a job or your pay or hours increase. You do not have to make a separate claim. Simply inform Jobcentre Plus or your local authority within four weeks that you or your partner have started or are about to start work or that your earnings or hours have increased.

HB Regs, reg 72 & 73 & Sch 7 and CTB Regs, reg 60 & 61& Sch 6

F.1 Going back to work – a checklist

This is a guide to the main help available if you are in work or looking for work. To find out more about other kinds of help, ask at your local Jobcentre Plus office. A disability employment adviser can provide specialist advice on employment and training.

It is worth asking for a 'better-off' calculation before taking a job. Ask a local advice agency or a Jobcentre Plus adviser. They can work out how much benefit you might get at a given level of earnings or other income. You can then compare your income in and out of work.

Working 16 hours a week or more

Tax credits – Top up earnings if you are in low-paid work, with extra support for disabled people, those with children, and those over 50 starting work (see Chapter 18).

Income support (IS) – You can stay on IS in some circumstances – eg, your hours or earnings are reduced to 75% or less than those of a person without your disability in the same job; you live in a care home; or you are a carer. Keep up to £20 a week of earnings. IS helps with mortgage interest (tax credits do not). See Chapter 14(6).

Housing benefit (HB) and council tax benefit (CTB) – Help with rent and council tax. See Chapter 20.

Working under 16 hours a week

Permitted work – Employment and support allowance (ESA), incapacity benefit (IB) and severe disablement allowance (SDA) can be paid on top of agreed permitted work earnings of up to a maximum of £92 a week (see 3).

IS – You can stay on IS if work is permitted or you are eligible for a reason other than incapacity for work. Keep up to £20 a week of earnings. See 4.

Jobseeker's allowance (JSA) – Keep up to £20 a week of earnings. You must still look for full-time work. See Chapter 15.

HB and CTB – Help with rent and council tax. See Chapter 20.

When you start work

HB and CTB extended payments – Existing rate paid for first four weeks of coming off IS, income-based JSA, ESA, IB or SDA. See 6.

Housing costs run-on – Existing housing costs paid for the first four weeks of coming off IS, income-related ESA or income-based JSA. See 4.

Benefit linking rules – Various linking rules help you re-claim benefit on the same terms as before if you have to stop work again. See 12.

Job grant – One-off payment if you start full-time work after at least 26 weeks on IS, JSA, ESA, IB, or SDA (or New Deal allowances based on these). See 4.

Equipment and support at work

Access to Work – Can help pay for equipment and adaptations at work and cover extra disability-related costs such as travel to work and support workers. See Chapter 17(2).

Workstep – Provides job support for disabled people who face more complex barriers to finding and keeping work. See Chapter 17(2).

Trying out a job

Benefit linking rules – Various linking rules help you re-claim benefit without losing out after a trial period at work. See 12.

Work trials – Allow you to remain in receipt of benefit and receive travel and meal allowances for up to 30 working days while you and the employer see whether you will be suitable for a job.

Work Preparation – For people out of the job market for some time due to ill health or disability, this is a programme to build confidence and work skills. You may be able to stay on your existing benefits or claim an allowance. See Chapter 17(2).

Employment on Trial – Your JSA will not be sanctioned for leaving a job voluntarily during the trial period. See Chapter 15(9).

Job Introduction Scheme – Your new employer applies to the Jobcentre for payments towards your wages for the first few weeks to give you a trial period in the job. See Chapter 17(2).

Return to work credit or in-work credit – £40 or £60 weekly, payable for a year to help people on benefits move into work. See Box F.2 and Chapter 17(2).

Starting a business

Jobcentre Plus can put you in touch with Businesslink in England (www.businesslink.gov.uk), Business Gateway in Scotland (www.bgateway.com) or in Wales, Flexible Support for Business (www.business-support-wales.gov.uk).

Looking for work

JSA – Weekly benefit providing a basic income if you have to sign on as available for work. See Chapter 15.

Access to Work – Help with the cost of travel, support workers and communication support at interviews paid through the Access to Work scheme. See Chapter 17(2).

Social fund budgeting loan – A loan to help with the expenses of looking for work or starting work if you have been getting IS, income-based JSA or income-related ESA for at least 26 weeks. See Chapter 23(5).

Work-related activity premium – £20 premium available for up to six months to lone parents with children aged 11 and over who have been on IS or income-based JSA for over 26 weeks.

A similar premium is paid to partners of working tax credit claimants in pilot areas. See Chapter 17(2).

Childcare costs

Working tax credit – Includes a childcare tax credit of 80% of certain childcare costs. See Chapter 18(7).

HB and CTB – Certain childcare costs can be ignored from your earnings in the benefit assessment. See Chapter 26(5).

Employment rights

Disability Discrimination Act – See Chapter 56.

Minimum wage – £5.73 an hour for workers aged 22, £4.77 if aged 18-21 and £3.53 if aged 16/17.

Other rights at work – Contact your trade union or ACAS (Advisory, Conciliation and Arbitration Service, tel: 0845 747 4747, Minicom 0845 606 1600).

Once the extended payments come to an end, HB and CTB are based on your new circumstances.

7. Jobseeker's allowance

If your income-based jobseeker's allowance (JSA) stops because you or your partner get a job or more hours or earnings, you may continue to get housing costs paid for up to four weeks under the housing costs run-on (see 4 above).

If you are working less than 16 hours a week, you are eligible for JSA. If your partner works and you get income-based JSA, they must work less than 24 hours a week. You must still sign on for work and actively look for, and be available to take up, a full-time job. Earnings above the earnings disregard affect the amount that you get. For income-based JSA only, your partner's earnings also affect the amount of your benefit (see Chapter 15(19)).

8. Tax credits

You may qualify for tax credits if you are in work or have dependent children and your income is low enough (see Chapter 18). If you qualify for tax credits you are unlikely to be worse off in work, but it is worth getting advice before taking a job so you know just how your income would be affected. Although tax credits include elements that reflect individual and family needs, including disabilities, they do not help with mortgage interest, unlike income support, income-related employment and support allowance and income-based jobseeker's allowance.

If you stop work again and were getting the disability element of working tax credit (WTC) included in the calculation of your tax credits, a special linking rule may allow you to return to benefit on the same terms as before (see Chapter 18(8)). For all WTC claims, if you stop work or your normal working hours fall below 16 hours a week, you will be treated as being in work for a further four weeks (see Chapter 18(6)).

9. Health benefits

You may qualify for help with prescription charges, hospital travel costs, dental treatment and glasses. If your income and savings are low, claim on form HC1, available from the doctor, dentist or optician or by ringing 0845 850 1166. You qualify automatically if you get income support, income-related employment and support allowance or income-based jobseeker's allowance. If you get tax credits you may qualify, depending on the level of earnings. See Chapter 55.

10. Industrial injuries benefit

Industrial injuries disablement benefit is not affected by any work or earnings you might have.

11. Voluntary work

If you get employment and support allowance (ESA), incapacity benefit, severe disablement allowance or any other incapacity-related benefit you are allowed to do voluntary work for anyone other than a close relative (parent (or in-law or step-parent), son/daughter (in-law/step), or the brother, sister or partner of any of them), or, for ESA, a relative (see 3 above). You must not be paid for your work, other than expenses *'reasonably incurred by [you] in connection with that work'*. Permitted expenses could include travel, meals, childminding, the costs of caring for a dependant, equipment needed for work and use of a telephone. There is no limit on the number of hours you can volunteer.

IW Regs, regs 2 & 17(6); ESA Regs, regs 2 & 45(6)

If you get income support you can do voluntary work without your income support being affected. See Chapter 14(6) for details. If you get income support on the basis of being incapable of work, the work must be for someone other than a close relative, otherwise you will be regarded as capable of work. Care you provide for a relative will not count as work (see 3 above).

12. Stopping work again

If you stop claiming benefits to begin work, but then stop working and re-claim benefit, there are linking rules that may allow you to go back to your previous benefit on the same terms as before. We outline some of the main rules below. There may be other linking rules that apply to your benefit entitlement. More than one linking rule may apply to you at the same time; use whichever is most beneficial.

Rapid reclaim – There is a 'rapid reclaim' process for income support (IS), income-based jobseeker's allowance (JSA), employment and support allowance (ESA), incapacity benefit (IB), housing benefit (HB) and council tax benefit (CTB). This can help if you have to reclaim these benefits within 26 weeks of a previous claim (eg if you started work but then couldn't cope with it). You are allowed to complete shorter claim-forms. Your circumstances must be broadly the same as when you made your previous claim.

Incapacity-related benefits

8-week linking rule – Two periods of incapacity separated by a gap of eight weeks or less can be linked together and treated as one period of incapacity. This means that if you are off work because of illness or disability within eight weeks of the end of your last severe disablement allowance (SDA) or incapacity benefit (IB) award, you'll go back onto your SDA or IB at the same rate and on the same terms as before.

For IB, if the gap in your period of incapacity for work is eight weeks or less, you are not required to satisfy or re-satisfy the contribution conditions.

This rule also applies to the disability premium paid within IS, HB or CTB. If you become incapable of work again within eight weeks, you'll go straight back onto the disability premium without having to serve the 52-week qualifying period again. If you hadn't served the full 52 weeks on your earlier claim, you don't have to start at the beginning again but will pick up where you left off. See Chapter 24(2).

There is a similar 8-week linking rule for statutory sick pay (SSP). See Chapter 8(3).

SSCBA, S.30C(1)(c)

'Welfare to work' linking rule – If you start work or training, the welfare to work linking rule allows you to return to your incapacity-related benefit at the same rate as before if you become incapable of work again within a period of 104 weeks. You have this protection as long as you are considered to be a 'welfare to work beneficiary'. This will apply if:

- you have been incapable of work for more than 196 days – including periods on SSP (gaps of up to eight weeks are ignored); *and*
- your entitlement to any *'benefit, allowance or advantage'* awarded on the basis of incapacity for work (other than SSP) stops at the end of your period of incapacity; *and*
- you start work or training (see below) within one month of entitlement to this benefit ending.

IW Regs, reg 13A

The linking rule applies to full-time or part-time work for which you are paid or which you do in expectation of payment and to government training programmes for which a training allowance is paid. There is also a 2-year linking rule covering these training programmes and some non-government programmes (see Chapter 17(5)).

The protection applies to any number of repeat claims made during the 104-week linking period, so you could try a number of different jobs or move from training into work and your benefit is protected each time you claim. For income-based JSA claimants to benefit from this linking rule, it must be the claimant's partner who meets the above conditions.

You are not covered by the welfare to work linking rule if your last period of incapacity ended because you were found to be (or treated as being) capable of work (unless you successfully appeal the decision).

If you are off work or stop work within your 104-week linking period, get a medical certificate from your doctor and put in a claim for the benefit or benefits that you were getting before. The linking rule means that:

- Any two or more periods of incapacity for work that are no more than 104 weeks apart are linked and count as one period of incapacity.
- IB is paid at the same rate as before, including any age addition and dependants' additions. You won't need to re-satisfy the national insurance contribution conditions. If you had been getting 'IB in youth' (IB(Y)) for those incapable of work since before age 20 (or 25), you go back on without re-serving the qualifying period.
- You can re-claim SDA and it is paid at the same rate as before, including the age addition and any dependants' additions (see Box D.9, Chapter 13).
- The disability premium is included in your IS, HB or CTB immediately without serving the qualifying period again. If you were part-way through the qualifying period you pick up where you left off (Chapter 24(2)).
- You will normally be accepted as incapable of work for the first 13 weeks of your claim provided you send in medical certificates from your doctor.
- If you were getting an age addition with your IB within 104 weeks of reaching state pension age, it is paid with your state pension (Chapter 43(4)).

In general, your benefits are protected only if you become incapable of work again. However, for HB, you also regain transitional protection from rent restrictions (Chapter 20(9)) if you claim within the 104-week linking period for another reason – eg your wages decrease.

Employment and support allowance

12-week linking rule – Any two periods of limited capability for work separated by no more than 12 weeks are treated as one single period. Hence, you can go back onto your previous rate of ESA if you have had break in your claim of 12 weeks or less.

'Work or training beneficiary' linking rule – If you are a 'work or training beneficiary', any two periods of limited capability for work separated by no more than 104 weeks are treated as a single period. You are classed as a work or training beneficiary if you had a limited capability for work for more than 13 weeks in a previous ESA award and you started work or training within one month of the end of that period of limited capability for work. The rule does not apply if the reason for your previous award of ESA ending was that you were found not to have a limited capability for work. You will be treated as having a limited capability for work (or will be placed in the support group if you were in it previously) for the first 13 weeks of your new ESA claim (the 'assessment phase'). This way you will go back onto the same rate of ESA you were getting in the previous award.

ESA Regs, regs 145(1)-(2) & 148-50

Other linking rules

Check first to see if the linking rules above might apply. Often this will give you a better deal.

2-year training linking rule – You may return to the rate of ESA, IB or SDA you received previously if you had a break in your claim of less than two years while participating in certain types of training courses (see Chapter 17(5)).

2-year working tax credit (WTC) disability element linking rule – If you are receiving tax credits (apart from just the family element of child tax credit) and the WTC disability element has been included in your tax credit calculation when you stop work, you may be able to go back onto ESA, IB or SDA under the WTC disability element 2-year linking rule. See also Chapter 18(8).

SSCBA S.30C(5) & (5A); ESA Regs, reg 145(3)&(4)

Contributory ESA and IB in youth – You may be able to re-claim benefit on the same no-contribution basis as a previous claim made before the age of 20 or 25 that ended because you took up work or training and your earnings were below a certain limit (see Chapter 11(8) for the ESA rules; for the IB rules, see the *Disability Rights Handbook* 33rd edition, page 89).

ESA Regs, reg 10

IS/ESA/JSA housing costs – For linking rules and other help, see Chapter 25(5).

Housing benefit – If you have been claiming HB continuously since before 1996, you are exempt from the rent restrictions described in Chapter 20(9). To keep the exemption, any break in claim must be no longer than four weeks.

If no linking rule applies

If you are not covered by any of the above linking rules and you fall sick again, you may get SSP from your employer if you are still employed. If you can't get SSP or are self-employed, you cannot go back to IB or IS but you may get ESA (see Chapter 9). You are not excluded from ESA while you are off work sick even if you normally work 16 hours or more a week. If you are claiming tax credits, you can ask for your award to be adjusted to reflect any loss in income. You must still be treated as being in work to qualify for WTC.

17 Employment and training

1. Introduction

In this chapter we look at some of the services and programmes designed to help you get and remain in work.

2. Jobcentre Plus

Jobcentre Plus is the DWP agency providing benefits and services for people of working age. Everyone who claims benefits from Jobcentre Plus has a personal adviser to deal with benefit claims and provide information on work and training opportunities. If you are between 16 and 60 and claiming income support, employment and support allowance (ESA), incapacity benefit or severe disablement allowance (SDA) you will be required to have a work-focused interview. Your partner can also be required to have a work-focused interview if your benefit is paid at a higher rate because they are included in the claim. These requirements, however, can sometimes be waived or deferred if it would not be of assistance to you (or your partner) or it would not be appropriate in the circumstances of your case. See Box T.1 in Chapter 59 for details. The rules for ESA are slightly different (see Chapter 9(15)).

Disability employment advisers – Disability employment advisers (DEAs) can be contacted through your local Jobcentre Plus office and can provide employment assessment, job-seeking advice and referral to training courses, as well as advice and information on Jobcentre Plus programmes for disabled people. The personal adviser and DEA roles are complementary. If you wish to be referred to a DEA, who may have more specialist experience, make this clear; your request should not be refused. Advice and support from a DEA is not dependent on receipt of benefits.

Welfare to work – Jobcentre Plus administers the welfare to work strategy, a package of schemes and rules designed to encourage claimants to find jobs. Some schemes pay allowances or provide services to make finding work easier, others seek to compel you to find work by cutting or removing your benefit if you do not take particular actions recommended by your personal adviser.

The strategy is evolving and there are pilot schemes in different parts of the country. Depending on where you live, you may be compelled to take actions or may be offered services that do not apply in other areas. We cover the most important schemes in some detail, others we simply make reference to.

Job Introduction Scheme

The Job Introduction Scheme is for disabled people who, in the opinion of the DEA, are suited to a job but need to demonstrate their capabilities to a new employer. The scheme pays £75 a week to your employer during your initial period of employment – usually six weeks, but in some cases up to 13. The employment must be expected to last at least 26 weeks, including the scheme period, and you or your employer must apply before you start work.

Access to Work

Access to Work provides practical advice to help overcome work-related obstacles resulting from disability and grants towards extra employment costs, including:

- special aids or equipment for employment;
- adaptations to premises and existing equipment;
- help with travel to work if public transport can't be used because you are disabled;
- a support worker (eg a reader) to provide help in the workplace;
- a communicator for support at job interviews.

The programme is flexible to meet your needs in your job. Contact Jobcentre Plus and ask to talk to a DEA for details or check the website (www.direct.gov.uk/en/DisabledPeople/Employmentsupport).

Who can get help? – You may be eligible if you are unemployed with a job to start, employed or self-employed, and you are disabled. Access to Work defines 'disability' as in the Disability Discrimination Act (see Chapter 56) but extends it to include disabilities that are only apparent in the workplace. The amount of support depends on what is needed because of your disability, and is granted for a maximum 3-year period, after which you can re-apply. If you have been in a job for less than six weeks or are about to start work, Access to Work will cover up to 100% of approved costs. If you have been in your job for six weeks or more when you first apply for help, Access to Work will cover up to 80% of approved costs above a threshold of £300 and below a ceiling of £10,000, and all costs above £10,000 over the 3-year period. All the extra costs of travel to work, support workers and communicator support for job interviews, and all the extra costs if you are self-employed, are met under Access to Work. In autumn 2009, there will be Access to Work pilots in London to help people with mental health problems to enter or to stay in work.

Work Preparation

Work Preparation (WP) provides individually tailored programmes to assess and address needs related to your disability that prevent you from taking up employment or training that would otherwise be suitable. WP can also help if you are at risk of losing your job because you are disabled.

A WP course normally lasts from a few hours up to six weeks, but can be longer if necessary. You can stay on your existing benefits (if you are claiming) or claim an allowance and travel expenses. Your DEA can advise you further. If you are due to attend on a residential basis, ask for clarification of the effect on your benefits. If you claim the allowance, you can re-claim benefit at the end of the programme and regain your former rate of payment without having to serve any qualifying periods, provided you are still incapable of, or a have a limited capability for, work (see 'The 2-year linking rule' under 5 below).

Residential training programme

This programme aims to help long-term unemployed adults overcome disability-related barriers to employment. It provides a combination of guidance, learning in the workplace, work experience and training. The programme will be tailored to your needs and can run for a maximum of 52 weeks, although it will usually be much shorter. You can apply if you are in receipt of any benefit, or just signing on for national insurance credits. Referral to residential training can only be made by a DEA.

Workstep

Workstep provides tailored support for disabled people who face more complex barriers to finding and keeping a job but who can work effectively with the right support. It enables eligible disabled people to realise their full potential to work in a commercial environment, giving them, wherever possible, the opportunity to progress into unsupported employment.

You will get the same wage as colleagues doing the same or similar work. You agree a development plan with your employer to ensure you have the necessary training and support to learn to do your job and to develop to the best of your ability.

A DEA can explain the entry conditions and discuss whether Workstep would be the right choice for you.

Work-related activity premium

If you are a lone parent and your children are aged 11 or over and you have been on benefits for over six months, you may be eligible for a 'work-related activity premium'. This is £20 a week on top of your benefits, payable for up to six months provided you attend four work-focused interviews a year (see Box T.1, Chapter 59) and undertake work-related activity agreed with your personal adviser.

Return to work credit and in-work credit

Return to work credit – If you take a job of at least 16 hours a week after claiming ESA, incapacity benefit, income support (paid on the basis of incapacity) or SDA for 13 weeks, you may be paid a 'return to work credit' for up to 52 weeks. Your earnings (but not any other income) must be less than £15,000 and your job should be expected to last at least five weeks. The £40 a week credit will be disregarded for tax credits and means-tested benefits.

In-work credit – This is paid to lone parents who have been on income support or income-based jobseeker's allowance (JSA) for 52 weeks and have started working at least 16 hours a week. It is £40 a week (£60 in London) for the first year of the new job and is ignored for means-tested benefits and tax credits. In London and 'New Deal Plus' pilot areas, in-work credit has been extended to cover couples with children in addition to lone parents and the eligibility criteria also include periods on incapacity benefit, SDA or carer's allowance.

Employment Zones

There are several Employment Zones around the country where personal advisers from private and public sector contractors run intensive programmes for jobseekers. It is compulsory to participate if you live in the Employment Zone and have claimed JSA for 18 out of the last 21 months. If you are under 25, you must participate if you have claimed JSA for six months after leaving the New Deal for Young People (see 4 below). Other claimants, including disabled people and lone parents, can choose to join the programme, but in some cases your benefit can be sanctioned if you leave. For further information, go to www.jobcentreplus.gov.uk.

Employment Zone Regs 2003

3. Training

There are a variety of government training programmes; we focus below on 'Work-Based Learning for Young People'. However, as new training initiatives are often launched, the rules for existing programmes can change at short notice. You can find out about other options from Jobcentre Plus or, if you are under age 20, from the Careers or Connexions services.

Support for disabled people – Various types of help are available to enable you to participate in a government training programme, including individually tailored programmes, aids, equipment, adaptations to premises and equipment, a readership service for blind people and an interpreter service for deaf people. Contact a disability employment adviser or, for young people, your local Careers Service or Connexions Service.

Minimum wage – Trainees aged 18 or over who receive wages from the employer must be paid at least the national minimum wage (see Box F.1). The trade union in your workplace can tell you which rate applies, or you can call the national minimum wage helpline (0845 600 0678).

National Minimum Wage Act, S.54(3)

Work-Based Learning for Young People

Recruitment to Work-Based Learning (WBL), or Skillseekers in Scotland, is usually through the Connexions Service or Careers Service. The training provided by WBL should lead to a recognised vocational qualification.

Most 16/17-year-olds are excluded from jobseeker's allowance (JSA) as they are expected to take up a 'guaranteed' place in WBL. You may be offered a place in WBL if you are aged 18-24 and your health or disability meant you could not join or didn't complete a course. In Scotland, the rules are different: contact your local Careers Service for information.

In WBL, you may be a trainee or you may have employed status. Being an employee could give you far more legal rights than a trainee and you will receive wages instead of the basic training allowance.

Training allowance – For those who are not employed while training, the minimum training allowance is £40 a week. In many cases, the levels are higher because of employer contributions.

Benefits – A trainee can claim income support to top up their training allowance.

IS Regs, Sch 1B, para 28

The whole £40 is taken into account as income. Once you leave the programme you are no longer eligible for income support unless you are covered by one of the other situations listed in Box E.1, Chapter 14. You should claim JSA instead. If you don't complete the programme and don't have 'good cause' for leaving, your JSA may be paid at a reduced rate (see Chapter 15(9)).

4. New Deal

There are six main New Deal programmes:

- New Deal for Young People;
- New Deal 25 Plus;
- New Deal 50 plus;
- New Deal for Partners;
- New Deal for Disabled People;
- New Deal for Lone Parents.

New Deal for Young People and New Deal 25 Plus are compulsory if you have been claiming jobseeker's allowance (JSA) for 26 weeks or more (if you are aged 18-24), or 18 months or more or 18 out of the last 21 months (if you are aged 25-60). Your benefit could be suspended under a sanction if you do not comply (see Chapter 15(9)). All other New Deals are voluntary.

We focus below on the New Deal for Young People and New Deal for Disabled People. Basic information about the other schemes is available at www.jobcentreplus.gov.uk.

Flexible New Deal – From 6.4.09, new claimants in 28 Jobcentre Plus districts will have access to a new 'Jobseeker's Regime' and 'Flexible New Deal'. This scheme will apply nationally from April 2010. It is aimed at giving you help and support in finding employment from the start of your claim, if Jobcentre Plus thinks that you need it. The amount of support increases in stages during the first 12 months of your claim, and you will be expected to increase your own efforts at the same time.

If you are still unemployed after 12 months, you will be referred to the Flexible New Deal, to be introduced in October 2009. It will replace the first three New Deal programmes listed above, together with the New Deals for musicians and the self-employed and Employment Zones.

New Deal for Young People

If you are aged 18-24 and you have been claiming JSA continuously for six months you will be required to enter the New Deal Gateway, a period of up to 16 weeks of support from a personal adviser to help you find a job. If you don't find a job in this period, you will be offered an 'option period', lasting between 13 and 52 weeks, designed to help you get into work. Your options could involve paid employment or self-employment, work with a voluntary or community organisation, or education or training to N/SVQ Level 2. Depending on the option, you could be paid a wage by an employer (when you will be an employed earner for benefit purposes) or a New Deal allowance (plus a token 10p a week income-based JSA to give you access to passported benefits).

If you can't attend your chosen option because of your disability, this should be accepted as good cause for leaving. You will be expected to take up an alternative.

JSA Regs, reg 73(2)(a)

If you have not found a job after your option period, you will need to re-claim JSA and enter the follow-through stage of the New Deal programme with further job search help.

New Deal for Disabled People

The New Deal for Disabled People (NDDP) is a voluntary programme available through a network of 'job brokers' drawn from the private, public and voluntary sectors. Job brokers help people to find, prepare for and stay in work. The way they do this varies and should depend on your needs. They may offer training, work experience, work trials, help with job applications and interviews, or help to become self-employed. Once you start work, you can continue to get in-work support for the first six months of employment.

While on the NDDP, you have access to other Jobcentre Plus programmes and services if you meet the eligibility criteria for the particular programme.

You can apply to join the NDDP if you receive employment and support allowance, incapacity benefit (or a European equivalent), severe disablement allowance, a disability premium (with income support, housing benefit or council tax benefit), disability living allowance, unemployability supplement, or national insurance credits for incapacity for work. You must not be receiving JSA or doing more than 16 hours paid work a week. You can choose which job broker you use.

To check if NDDP is available in your area and to find out more, contact Jobcentre Plus or go to www.jobbrokersearch.co.uk.

5. Benefits and training allowances

Disability living allowance (DLA)

DLA mobility component is not affected if you get a training allowance. DLA care component is not affected if you are living at home and attending the training programme daily. However, you will not be able to get the care component for the days you stay in a care home in order to attend the programme, nor if your training allowance includes a 'living away from home' allowance. The care component stops after 28 days in such accommodation (see Chapter 3(8)). You can get the care component for any days spent at home.

Although DLA can be paid at the same time as a training allowance, your ability to start a programme may suggest a lessening in your care or mobility needs, so your benefit may be reconsidered.

Disability premium

If you were getting a disability premium before beginning the programme, it won't be withdrawn even though you may now no longer be receiving the qualifying benefit. At the end of the programme, you will only continue to receive the disability premium if you satisfy the entitlement criteria (see Chapter 24(2)).

IS Regs, Sch 2, para 7(1)(b)

Employment and support allowance (ESA) and incapacity benefits

A day in receipt of a state training allowance (other than just travel and meals expenses) cannot count as a day of incapacity for work or limited capability for work. This means you will cease to be entitled to ESA, incapacity benefit or severe disablement allowance (SDA) on starting your programme (but see 2 above if you are going on a Work Preparation course). At the end of your programme, you may be able to get benefit at the rate you were getting before your course started (see below).

IB Regs, reg 4(1)(c) & (2)(a)&(c); ESA Regs, reg 32(2)&(3)

A day in receipt of an Adult Learning Option scheme training premium can count as a day of incapacity for work, as long as the training premium is not intended to meet the cost of everyday living expenses (see Chapter 26(11)).

IB Regs, reg 4(1)(d)

If you do not find a job at the end of your programme, and are capable of work, you can sign on and claim jobseeker's allowance (JSA) – see Chapter 15.

2-year linking rule – If you are unable to work because of illness or disability at the end of your programme, there is a 2-year linking rule that enables you to go back onto the same level of ESA, incapacity benefit or SDA. To qualify you must have been entitled to ESA, higher rate short-term or long-term incapacity benefit or SDA for at least one day during the eight weeks before your programme started, and be accepted as incapable of work or having a limited capability for work on the day after your programme stops, and this day must be within two years of the last day you were entitled to benefit.

The 2-year rule applies to certain Jobcentre Plus programmes including Work Preparation, New Deal, and Work-Based Learning. But it also applies to non-government courses if the primary purpose is the teaching of occupational or vocational skills and which you attend for 16 or more hours a week.

SSCBA, S.30C(6) & IB Regs, reg 3; ESA Regs, regs 2 & 145(5)

Non-government training courses

On a non-government training course you may be paid an allowance, but it is treated in a different way from a state training allowance. It will be taken into account in full as income for income support and other means-tested benefits unless some or all of it can be disregarded under the normal rules.

You may be regarded as a student for benefit purposes. Most full-time students are excluded from income-related ESA, income support and JSA (see Chapter 40). The rules are complicated, so seek advice on how your benefit rights might be affected.

There are no specific rules to prevent someone from studying or training on a non-government course and receiving contributory ESA, incapacity benefit or SDA. However, the assessment of your ability to undertake the activities in the work capability or personal capability assessments will take into account how you manage on your course. Starting a course may lead to your incapacity or limited capability for work being reassessed.

If your course is funded by the European Social Fund, seek advice.

A B C D E F G H I J K L M N O P Q R S T U

G Tax credits

This section of the Handbook looks at:

18 Tax credits

1. What are tax credits?

Tax credits are administered by HMRC. There are two types:

Child tax credit (CTC) – is a means-tested or income-related tax-free payment for people, whether working or not, who are responsible for children. It replaces the child allowances in income support and income-based jobseeker's allowance (JSA), and the increases for child dependants paid with non-means-tested benefits. See Box G.1 for transitional rules.

Working tax credit (WTC) – is a means-tested or income-related tax-free payment for those in low-paid work.

Will you be better off going back to work?

Going back to work usually means some benefits may stop (eg employment and support allowance (ESA)), some carry on as normal (eg disability living allowance) and others continue at a reduced rate depending on income (eg housing benefit (HB) and council tax benefit (CTB)). Box F.1 in Chapter 16 outlines benefits and other help available when you start work. To work out whether you might be better off on tax credits, note the following points.

- ❑ You may be able to earn up to £92 a week from 'permitted work' on top of ESA, incapacity benefit or severe disablement allowance. You may be better off doing this (see Chapter 16(3)). However, if you also get income support, HB or CTB, only a maximum of £20 of such earnings can be disregarded for these benefits (see Chapter 26(5)).
- ❑ Income-related ESA, income support and income-based JSA may include an amount to cover mortgage interest payments, while tax credits do not.
- ❑ You keep the full amount of child maintenance payments on top of your tax credits, whereas on income-related ESA, income support or income-based JSA you will usually only keep up to £20 a week of such payments (see Chapter 26(8)).
- ❑ Depending on your level of tax credits, you may be entitled to free prescriptions and other health benefits (see Chapter 55), free legal help (see Chapter 61(2)) and home repair assistance (see Chapter 31).
- ❑ Tax credits (above the basic CTC family element or WTC that includes the disability or severe disability element) may give you access to the Sure Start maternity grant and social fund funeral payment (see Chapter 22).
- ❑ Income-related ESA and income support entitle your children to free school meals, and free milk or fresh fruit and vegetables under the Healthy Start scheme if they are under 4. With tax credits, you are entitled to these if you receive CTC only and your income is below a certain level (see Chapter 55(6)).

2. Do you qualify for CTC?

You can get CTC if you meet all the following conditions when you make your claim:

- you are at least 16 years old;
- you, or your partner, are responsible for a child or young person who normally lives with you (see 3 below);
- you satisfy the residence and presence conditions and are not subject to immigration control (see Chapter 50);
- your income is within a set limit, which varies according to your family circumstances (see 9 below).

If you are one of a couple you claim jointly and your claim is called a 'joint claim'. Otherwise, you claim as a single person. Your entitlement will end immediately if you are a couple who separate or one of you dies, or a single claimant who becomes part of a couple. Your entitlement will also usually end if you cease to be responsible for any children or young people (see 3 below). A couple is defined as: a married couple, civil partners, or two people living together as though they were either a married couple or civil partners.

TCA, S.3

3. Responsible for a child or young person

A child is someone aged under 16. Once a child reaches 16 they will continue to be treated as a child for tax credit purposes until 31 August following their 16th birthday.

CTC Regs, regs 2 & 4

A young person is someone over 16 but under 20 who is in full-time, non-advanced education or approved training. If they are 19 they must have started the course of education or training before that age (or were accepted or enrolled to undertake it). Young people continue to count for tax credit purposes for the first 20 weeks after they leave full-time education or approved training if they are under the age of 18 and registered for work or training with the Careers Service, Connexions Service, the Department for Children, Schools and Families or Skillseekers in Scotland. Young people will no longer count for tax credit purposes once they start work or undertake training provided under a contract of employment, or claim income-related employment and support allowance (ESA), income support or income-based jobseeker's allowance in their own right.

CTC Regs, reg 5

If two or more households make a claim in respect of the same child (eg the child of separated parents spends time with both), the two households may agree and jointly elect who will receive CTC for that child. If they cannot agree, HMRC will decide which parent has main responsibility for that child.

CTC is not normally payable in respect of a child who:

- has been placed by a local authority in certain types of accommodation paid for by that local authority;
- has been placed for adoption with you by a local authority who are making payments under s.3 of the Children Act 1989 (and Scottish and Northern Irish equivalents);
- is serving a custodial sentence of more than four months;
- is 16 or older and claiming CTC themselves for their own child, WTC, contributory ESA or incapacity benefit;
- is living with a spouse or partner (opposite or same sex) who is not in full-time education or approved training.

CTC is not payable if you are the partner of the young person and you live together, unless you were living together on 31.8.08.

CTC Regs, reg 3

If a qualifying child or young person dies during the period of an award, CTC will continue in respect of them for eight weeks following their death (or until a 19-year-old would have become 20, if that is earlier).

CTC Regs, reg 6

4. CTC elements

CTC is made up of a number of elements.

Family element – This is included in the calculation for all who qualify for CTC.

Family element (baby addition) – This extra amount is included if the family has any children under the age of one.

Child element – This is included for each child or young person in your family (see 3 above) at a single fixed rate regardless of the age of the dependent child or young person.

Disabled child element – This is included if any child or young person:

- receives either element of disability living allowance (DLA) at any rate (or would do but for the fact that they are a hospital inpatient); *or*
- is registered as blind, or has ceased to be registered within 28 weeks of the claim to CTC being made.

Severely disabled child element – This is included if any child or young person receives DLA highest rate care component (or would do but for the fact that they are a hospital inpatient).

CTC Regs, regs 7 & 8

5. Do you qualify for WTC?

You can get WTC if you meet the following conditions at the time you make your claim:

- ❑ You are at least 16 years old; *and*
  either you or your partner are working for 16 or more hours a week, *and*
  - you are responsible for a dependent child or young person; *or*
  - you have a physical or mental disability that puts you at a disadvantage in getting a job and you were previously receiving some form of disability benefit; *or*
  - you or your partner are aged 50 or over and qualify for the 50-plus element (see 7 below); *or*

  you or your partner are aged 25 or over and work at least 30 hours a week.
- ❑ You satisfy the residence and presence conditions and are not subject to immigration control (see Chapter 50).
- ❑ Your income is within a set limit, which varies according to your family circumstances (see 9 below).

If you are part of a couple, you claim WTC jointly and your claim is called a joint claim. Otherwise, you claim as a single person. Your entitlement will end immediately if you are a couple who separate or one of you dies, or a single claimant who becomes part of a couple. It will also usually end immediately if you cease working the right number of hours to qualify (see 6 below).

TCA, S.10 & WTC(E&MR) Regs, reg 4

6. What does and does not count as work?

In order to be treated as being in *'qualifying remunerative work'* you must *either*:

- be working at the date of your claim, and the work must be expected to continue for at least four weeks after you have made the claim; *or*
- have an offer of work which you are expected to start within seven days of making your claim, and the work must be expected to last for a total of at least four weeks.

'Work' means work done for, or in expectation of, payment. If you are an employee, the number of hours that count are the number of hours you normally work each week,

G.1 Tax credits transitional rules

CTC replacing child allowances and premiums

CTC will eventually replace existing child allowances and premiums paid to families with children within income support and income-based jobseeker's allowance (JSA) – ie, the personal allowances for dependent children, the family premium, disabled child premiums and enhanced disability premiums for children. Families should receive the same amount for their children through CTC as they did through income support/JSA.

New claims for income support or income-based JSA – There is no provision for children within these benefits now. You need to claim CTC if you have not already done so.

Already getting income support or income-based JSA – It has long been planned that families still receiving child allowances or premiums within these means-tested benefits would be transferred onto CTC but there is no date set for this transfer. Legislative provision has been made to treat those who are still getting such child allowances or premiums as if they had made a claim for CTC, and to ensure that once they are transferred they cannot backdate any claim for this (to prevent them receiving both for the same period). The legislation has extended the time limit for the transfer to 31.12.11. Once transferred, the money may initially go to the income support/JSA claimant but at a later stage couples should be asked to make their own choice.

'Floating off' income support – When you claim CTC you may 'float off' income support. This could happen if your income from other sources comes to more than your income support applicable amount. For example, maintenance is not treated as income for CTC purposes but is for income support purposes, so if you claim CTC your income from maintenance and other sources of income may be higher than your income support applicable amount.

Child dependant increases

Increases for child dependants within non-means-tested benefits such as incapacity benefit (IB), severe disablement allowance (SDA), bereavement benefits and state pension were abolished for new claimants from 6.4.03. Instead, you claim CTC for your dependent children. However, if you were getting such an increase on 5.4.03 you will continue receiving it until you no longer meet the qualifying conditions. If you get such an increase with IB or SDA and you lose it because of the way the increase is means tested against the earnings of your partner, you can have it restored to you if, within 58 days of you last having got it, your partner stops working or starts earning below the figure at which the increase would be removed.

including any overtime you do regularly. If you are self-employed, the number of hours that count are those that you actually work in your self-employed capacity, including time spent on *'activities necessary to'* your self-employed activity, eg essential bookkeeping, distributing advertising flyers, etc. In calculating the number of hours you work towards the 16 or 30 hours a week limit you cannot include time spent in unpaid meal breaks or periods of customary or paid holiday.

WTC(E&MR) Regs, reg 4

Exceptionally, if you work in a school or otherwise work on a seasonal basis and you have a recognisable pattern of employment over the year, you may ignore the school holidays or other holiday periods. This rule benefits people like school dinner ladies who might otherwise be found not to be working enough hours to qualify.

WTC(E&MR) Regs, reg 7

When you are not treated as being in work – Some kinds of work do not count:

- work for a charitable or voluntary organisation or otherwise as a volunteer if you are only paid expenses;
- work on a training scheme where you are paid a training allowance (unless taxable as trade profit);
- work as part of intensive activity period activities or Employment Zone Programmes as a jobseeker;
- work while you are serving a custodial sentence or remanded in custody awaiting trial or sentence;
- activities when you are in receipt of a sports award and no other form of payment is made to you;
- work where you are caring for someone who is temporarily living with you if the only payment you get is from a local authority, health authority, primary care trust, voluntary organisation or the cared-for person, and your income is below the taxable limit for this sort of work. However, foster carers and adult placement carers are able to claim WTC in respect of their caring activities.

WTC(E&MR) Regs, reg 4(2)

When you are treated as being in work – You can qualify for WTC during certain interruptions in your working pattern, provided you were in qualifying remunerative work immediately before the interruption. Your working hours will be treated as being the same as they were before. This applies in the following circumstances.

- ❑ You are not working because you are off sick. You will continue to be treated as being in work for a period of up to 28 weeks while you are receiving statutory sick pay (SSP), short-term lower rate incapacity benefit, employment and support allowance, income support (on the basis of incapacity) or national insurance contribution credits only (on the basis of being incapable of work or having a limited capability for work). If you are self-employed and off sick you will continue to be treated as being in work if you would have got SSP but for the fact that as a self-employed person you are not entitled to it.
- ❑ You have recently finished working or started to work for less than the required 16 or 30 hours a week. You can still be treated as being in qualifying remunerative work for up to four weeks. This allows for a 4-week run-on of WTC.
- ❑ You are off work and getting maternity allowance or statutory maternity, paternity or adoption pay, or you are on ordinary maternity, paternity or adoption leave, including the first 13 weeks of any additional maternity or adoption leave.
- ❑ You are temporarily suspended from work while complaints or allegations against you are being investigated.
- ❑ You are on strike, but only for a period of up to ten consecutive days on which you would normally have been working.

WTC(E&MR) Regs, regs 4-7C

7. WTC elements

WTC is made up of a number of elements. If you are a couple and qualify for more than one disability, severe disability or 50-plus element, then more than one will be included in the calculation.

Basic element – This will be included in the calculation for all who qualify for WTC.

TCA, S.11

Couple element – This will be included if you are one of a couple (see 2 above).

WTC(E&MR) Regs, reg 11

Lone parent element – This will be included if you are single and have a dependent child or young person.

WTC(E&MR) Regs, reg 12

30-hour element – This will be included if you are treated as working enough hours, which will be the case when:

- one person works enough hours because you and/or your partner work at least 30 hours a week; *or*
- you are part of a couple and together you work enough hours because:
  - you have a dependent child or young person; *and*
  - between you, you work at least 30 hours a week in total; *and*
  - at least one of you works at least 16 hours a week.

WTC(E&MR) Regs, reg 10

Severe disability element – This will be included if you get either higher rate attendance allowance or disability living allowance (DLA) highest rate care component (or would but for the fact that you are in hospital). If you are part of a couple and one of you meets this test, you get one severe disability element. If both of you meet this test, you get two severe disability elements. The person who meets this test does not have to be the person who is working. A common error is claiming the severe disability element when only entitled to the disability element; resulting overpayments can be high.

WTC(E&MR) Regs, reg 17

50-plus element – You will qualify for this if you or your partner are aged at least 50 and start working at least 16 hours a week. If you are part of a couple and one of you meets this test you get one 50-plus element; if you both meet it you get two 50-plus elements. For at least six months before starting this work, you or your partner must have been getting:

- income support; *or*
- jobseeker's allowance (either contribution- or income-based); *or*
- incapacity benefit; *or*
- severe disablement allowance (SDA); *or*
- state pension topped up by pension credit; *or*
- a training allowance paid under Training for Work; *or*
- another person was getting one of those benefits and claiming for you as their dependant; *or*
- employment and support allowance; *or*
- you were getting national insurance contributions credits (eg if you were signing on as unemployed).

If you or your partner were getting carer's allowance, bereavement allowance or widowed parent's allowance before claiming one of the benefits listed above, you can combine the time spent on the two sets of benefits to count towards the six-month qualifying rule.

There are two rates to the 50-plus element:

- a lower rate if you work at least 16 hours but less than 30 hours a week;
- a higher rate if you work at least 30 hours a week.

The 50-plus element is payable for no more than 12 months if your employment is continuous, or, if your employment is not continuous, for a total of no more than 12 months if gaps between periods of entitlement are no more than 26 weeks.

WTC(E&MR) Regs, reg 18

Childcare element – You get a tax credit equal to 80% of eligible childcare costs, which are £175 maximum a week for one child and £300 maximum a week for two or more children. So, the highest childcare tax credit you could get is £140 a week for one child or £240 for two or more children.

You include a childcare tax credit if you are:

- a lone parent working at least 16 hours a week; *or*
- one of a couple and both of you work at least 16 hours a week; *or*
- one of a couple and one of you works at least 16 hours a week and the other is 'incapacitated', a hospital inpatient, or in prison.

If you are on maternity or adoption leave, the statutory period you are away from work will count as though you were still working (see 6 above). So you will be able to claim help with childcare costs for the new child provided you were working the hours as set out above before your break from work.

You count as 'incapacitated' if you receive:

- housing benefit (HB) or council tax benefit (CTB) that includes a disability or higher pensioner premium, or if you have already been held to be incapacitated for the purposes of HB/CTB childcare costs; *or*
- short-term higher rate or long-term incapacity benefit, contributory employment and support allowance (providing you have been entitled to it for at least 28 weeks – including linked periods and periods on statutory sick pay when you otherwise satisfied the contribution conditions), attendance allowance, SDA, DLA, constant attendance allowance (payable with the Industrial Injuries or War Pensions schemes), or war pensions mobility supplement (or would get one of these benefits but for the fact that you are a hospital inpatient).

In order to qualify, your child or children must be aged 15 or younger, or aged 16 or younger if they meet the same rules as for the disabled child element within CTC (see 4 above). You can claim a childcare element up to the last day of the week containing the 1st September following their 15th birthday, or for a disabled child, their 16th birthday.

Childcare must be provided by a registered childminder (or equivalent), a childminder approved by an accredited organisation or an out-of-school-hours scheme run by a school or local authority. If you've arranged the childcare but it hasn't started by the time you make your claim, the amount is based on an estimate provided by the childcare provider.

If your childcare costs vary (eg you pay more during school holidays), it is the average weekly costs over the period covered by your award that will be taken into account in the calculation. If there is a change in the childcare provided while you are getting WTC and your childcare charges go down by £10 a week or more, or stop altogether, you must report this promptly (see Chapter 19(4)). Your WTC will then be recalculated.

WTC(E&MR) Regs, regs 13-16

8. WTC disability element

This element is a significant one for disabled people. In addition to working at least 16 hours a week, you have to satisfy two other tests, one relating to your disability and one to your recent receipt of a qualifying benefit. It is the person who meets the work conditions who also has to meet the disability and qualifying benefit tests. So, if you are working and not disabled, but have a disabled partner who is not working, you will not receive the disability element. Conversely, if both you and your partner meet the rules about working and about disability and qualifying benefits, you can receive two disability elements.

The 'disability' test

To get the disability element of WTC included in your assessment, you must have a *'physical or mental disability which puts [you] at a disadvantage in getting a job'*. How

G.2 The 'disability' test

Disability that puts you at a disadvantage in getting a job

These are the ways you can pass the disability test for working tax credit (WTC).

On an initial claim, you will pass the disability test if any one (or more) of the conditions in Parts 1 or 2 apply to you.

On a renewal claim, you will pass the test if any one (or more) of the conditions in Part 1 apply to you.

Part 1

- ❑ When standing you cannot keep your balance unless you continually hold on to something.
- ❑ Using any crutches, walking frame, walking stick, prosthesis or similar walking aid which you habitually use, you cannot walk a continuous distance of 100 metres along level ground without stopping or without suffering severe pain.
- ❑ You can use neither of your hands behind your back as in the process of putting on a jacket or of tucking a shirt into trousers.
- ❑ You can extend neither of your arms in front of you so as to shake hands with another person without difficulty.
- ❑ You can put neither of your hands up to your head without difficulty so as to put on a hat.
- ❑ Due to lack of manual dexterity you cannot with one hand pick up a coin which is not more than 2.5 cm in diameter.
- ❑ You are not able to use your hands or arms to pick up a full jug of one litre capacity and pour from it into a cup, without difficulty.
- ❑ You can turn neither of your hands sideways through 180 degrees.
- ❑ You are registered as blind or partially sighted.
- ❑ You cannot see to read 16 point print at a distance greater than 20 centimetres, if appropriate, wearing the glasses you normally use.
- ❑ You cannot hear a telephone ring when you are in the same room as the telephone, if appropriate, using a hearing aid you normally use.
- ❑ In a quiet room you have difficulty hearing what someone talking in a loud voice at a distance of 2 metres says, if appropriate, using a hearing aid you normally use.
- ❑ People who know you well have difficulty in understanding what you say.
- ❑ When a person you know well speaks to you, you have difficulty in understanding what that person says.
- ❑ At least once a year during waking hours you have a coma or fit in which you lose consciousness.
- ❑ You have a mental illness for which you receive regular treatment under the supervision of a medically qualified person.
- ❑ Due to mental disability you are often confused or forgetful.
- ❑ You cannot do the simplest addition and subtraction.
- ❑ Due to mental disability you strike people or damage property or are unable to form normal social relationships.
- ❑ You cannot normally sustain an 8-hour working day or a 5-day working week due to a medical condition or intermittent or continuous severe pain.

Part 2

- ❑ As a result of an illness or accident you are undergoing a period of habilitation or rehabilitation.

WTC(E&MR) Regs, Sch 1

this is assessed depends on whether you are making an initial claim or a renewal claim.

Initial claims – If you are claiming WTC for the first time you need to meet the rules set out in *either* Part 1 *or* Part 2 of Box G.2.

Renewal claims – When making a WTC renewal claim you need to meet the rules set out in Part 1 of Box G.2.

The 'qualifying benefit' test

To get the disability element of WTC included in your assessment, you must also meet *one* of the following conditions.

- ❑ **Condition A** – At any time in the last 26 weeks before you claim WTC you were getting: higher rate short-term or long-term incapacity benefit, severe disablement allowance (SDA) or employment and support allowance (ESA: providing you have been entitled to it for at least 28 weeks – including linked periods and periods on statutory sick pay (SSP)).
- ❑ **Condition B** – At any time in the last 26 weeks before you claim WTC you were getting the disability or higher pensioner premium in income support, income-based jobseeker's allowance, housing benefit or council tax benefit.
- ❑ **Condition C** – You get disability living allowance (DLA – either component, any rate) or attendance allowance (or an Industrial Injuries or War Pensions scheme equivalent). You must meet this condition throughout the period of your claim, not just at the start of it (CTC/643/2005).
- ❑ **Condition D** – On the date of your claim, and (following CTC/643/2005) throughout your claim, you have a Motability car.
- ❑ **Condition E: the 'Fast Track'** – This route to the disability element is referred to as the 'Fast Track' because it allows some of those who have been off work for a while to return to work without having either to have been off sick for a prolonged period or to fit the qualifying rules for DLA, etc (as in Conditions A to D).

  At any time *in the last eight weeks* before you claim WTC you had been getting, for at least 20 weeks:
  - SSP, occupational sick pay, lower rate short-term incapacity benefit or income support on the basis that you were incapable of work; *or*
  - ESA; *or*
  - Class 1 or Class 2 national insurance (NI) contribution credits on the basis that you were incapable of work or had a limited capability for work; *and*
  - at the date of claim you have a disability likely to last at least six months (or for the rest of your life if your death is expected within that time); *and*
  - your gross earnings are less than they were before your disability began, by at least 20% or £15 a week, whichever is greater.
- ❑ **Condition F** – At any time in the last eight weeks before you claim WTC you:
  - had been undertaking training for work (which means certain government training courses or a course of 16 hours or more a week learning occupational or vocational skills); *and*
  - within the eight weeks prior to the start of the training course, had been getting higher rate short-term or long-term incapacity benefit, SDA or contributory ESA (providing you have been entitled to it for at least 28 weeks – including linked periods and periods on SSP when you otherwise satisfied the contribution conditions).
- ❑ **Condition G** – You will be treated as qualifying for the disability element if, within the eight weeks before you make your claim (including renewal claims), you were entitled to the disability element of tax credits by virtue of Condition A, B, E or F. This allows those who were getting a qualifying benefit such as incapacity benefit, etc to continue to get the WTC disability element for long after they stopped receiving that benefit. If you got the disability element because you met Condition C or D, as you were in receipt of, for example, DLA, you need to be getting that benefit when you make your new, or renewal claim.

WTC(E&MR) Regs, reg 9

WTC disability element 2-year linking rule

There is a special WTC disability element 2-year linking rule that may help you return to your former incapacity benefit or SDA on the same basis as before. It does not help you return to the disability premium with income support, housing benefit or council tax benefit; you must re-qualify for this.

For this linking rule to apply, you must:

- give up or lose your job (for any reason at all) or be off work sick; *and*
- be entitled to have the WTC disability element included in your tax credits assessment; *and*
- receive some tax credits (apart from just the family element of CTC) for the week that includes your last working day (eg the day before you went off sick); *and*
- be incapable of work on the first day after your last working day; *and*
- have a gap of no more than two years between your last day of entitlement to your pre-tax credits incapacity benefit or SDA and the first day after giving up your job or self-employment.

If you meet these conditions, your days in receipt of tax credits count as days of incapacity for work. If your period of incapacity for work (PIW), including these days, links back to your previous award of incapacity benefit or SDA, you go onto the level of benefit you had before. PIWs link if the gap between them is no more than eight weeks (or 104 weeks if you are covered by the 'welfare to work' linking rules – see Chapter 16(12)).

SSCBA S.30C(5) & (5A)

9. Income and savings

CTC and WTC have no system of capital limits. There is thus no upper limit on savings above which CTC and/or WTC is not payable. However, income from savings is taken into account in the calculation (see below).

Income for tax credit purposes is similar to that counted for means-tested benefits but not identical. The rules are largely based on income tax legislation. The broad principle is that all taxable income will be taken into account and other income will be ignored.

TC(DCI) Regs 2002

Income that has the first £300 ignored

The following types of income will be included in the calculation, but the first £300 a year of the total of such income will be ignored:

- pension income, including taxable income from annuities and pensions paid by the Crown or a former employer, but excluding war disablement pensions, war pensioners mobility supplement and certain other war service pensions that are exempt from income tax;
- investment income, including taxable income from stocks and shares;
- property income, including taxable income from rents;
- foreign income, including income arising from a source outside the UK or from foreign holdings, whether or not this was remitted to the UK, converted into British pounds. This excludes pensions or annuities paid under German or Austrian law to victims of National Socialist persecution and certain other non-taxable receipts. If you receive a

foreign pension, whether or not it was remitted to the UK, 90% of the full amount received will be taken into account (in British pounds, not the foreign currency);
- notional income, including:
  - various forms of income treated as notional income under tax legislation, eg stock dividends;
  - income of which you have deprived yourself to gain entitlement to, or increase the amount of, tax credit;
  - income that would be available to you if you applied for it;
  - income you have done without because you have provided a service to another person but not been paid for it or been paid less than the going rate for it;
  - trust income that, under the income tax rules, is treated as your income, eg investment income of a child where the trust funds have been provided by the parent and the amount exceeds £100.

TC(DCI) Regs, regs 5, 10, 11, 12 & 13-17

Employment income

All taxable income from employment is usually taken into account. In contrast to means-tested benefits, income from employment is taken into account gross, that is, before income tax and national insurance (NI) contributions have been deducted. Such income includes:
- PAYE income from an office or employment, including pay, holiday pay, bonus and commission;
- payment made in respect of expenses not *'wholly, exclusively and necessarily incurred'* in the performance of the job;
- cash vouchers, non-cash vouchers or credit tokens (but not if for eligible childcare – see below);
- the value of a car made available for private use and of car fuel (but not if you are a disabled employee with an adapted or automatic company car);
- goods or assets your employer gave you that you could sell for cash (eg gifts of food, drink, clothes, cigarettes) or payments made by your employer that you should have paid yourself (eg if they paid your rent to your landlord or paid your gas or personal phone bills);
- redundancy payments to the extent they are subject to income tax;
- statutory sick pay. Statutory maternity, paternity or adoption pay in excess of £100 a week;
- certain retainer fees or similar compensation for a restrictive undertaking;
- strike pay received as a member of a trade union;
- taxable gains from security options (eg company shares, bonds, government gilts) acquired as a result of your employment.

Some tax exempt payments made from your earnings are ignored in reckoning your gross income, including:
- the gross amount of contributions you make to a pension scheme or retirement annuity contract;
- fees and subscriptions to professional bodies and learned societies, employee liabilities and indemnity insurance;
- contributions to charity made under Gift Aid and Give-As-You-Earn payroll deduction schemes.

Disregarded employment income – The following types of income are disregarded as employment income. As such, they are not treated as any form of income:
- payments in respect of expenses wholly, exclusively and necessarily incurred in the performance of the duties of the employment or which are qualifying travelling expenses for tax purposes;
- the provision of transport to a disabled employee, if it is exempt from income tax;
- payment or reimbursement of expenses in connection with the use of a car parking space at your place of work, or for certain overnight expenses or for removal expenses;
- cash vouchers or equivalents that you are to use to pay for childcare costs of the sort which would be included for WTC purposes (see 7 above);
- the value of meal vouchers received as an employee;
- certain taxable benefits provided by an employer that do not have to be reported for tax credit purposes, eg the provision of living accommodation and cheap loans;
- operational allowances paid to members of HM Forces in respect of service in certain operational areas, eg Iraq and Afghanistan;
- the provision by an employer of one mobile phone to an employee, if it is exempt from income tax.

TC(DCI) Regs, reg 4

Self-employment income

Your taxable profit for income tax purposes, as a sole trader or a partner in a business, is taken into account. You can deduct the following items from your taxable profit:
- the gross amount of contributions you made to a pension scheme or retirement annuity contract;
- current year trading losses and those brought forward from a previous year under the tax credit rules (if you have insufficient other income to cover a current year loss, it must be set against your partner's income);
- the gross amount of Gift Aid payments you made.

If your business made a loss you should contact the Tax Credit Helpline (see 10 below), as there are special rules dealing with losses.

TC(DCI) Regs, reg 4

Benefit income

All benefit income is taken into account in full as income, except:
- attendance allowance and disability living allowance;
- back-to-work bonus, return to work credit or better off in work credit;
- bereavement payment;
- child benefit and guardian's allowance;
- Christmas bonus;
- housing benefit, council tax benefit and discretionary housing payments (see Chapter 20(17));
- income support, except to strikers;
- incapacity benefit which is either the short-term lower rate or that paid to people previously in receipt of invalidity benefit and still in the same period of incapacity for work;
- industrial injuries benefits (except industrial death benefit);
- income-based jobseeker's allowance (JSA);
- income-related employment support allowance
- maternity allowance and health in pregnancy grant;
- pension credit;
- severe disablement allowance;
- social fund payments;
- certain compensation payments, including compensation payments for the non-payment of income support, JSA, or housing benefit; *and*
- payments in lieu of milk tokens or vitamins.

TC(DCI) Regs, reg 7

Student grants

Student grants and loans (except grants for adult dependants and lone parents) are ignored.

TC(DCI) Regs, regs 8 & 9

Other income

Most other forms of taxable income are to be included in the calculation. The following are ignored:
- mandatory top-up payments (and discretionary payments to help meet special needs) to those taking part in certain training or employment programmes;

- payments made to disabled people to help them obtain or retain employment;
- adoption allowances;
- fostering allowances (and, in practice, allowances paid to adult placement carers) to the extent that they do not exceed certain tax-exempt limits;
- maintenance payments;
- apart from notional income from trusts (described above), the income of any children or young people for whom you claim CTC.

This is not an exhaustive list.

TC(DCI) Regs, reg 19

10. Claiming tax credits

Claims for CTC or WTC are made on claim-form TC600. This can be obtained by ringing the Tax Credit Helpline (0845 300 3900; Minicom 0845 300 3909) or by calling in at an HMRC enquiry centre or Jobcentre Plus office.

You must produce a valid national insurance number, or provide information or evidence to enable one to be traced. If you are unable to make a claim on your own behalf, it can be done by your appointee or someone else legally empowered to act on your behalf.

TC(C&N) Regs, Regs 5, 17 & 18

Backdating claims

If you meet the qualifying conditions, tax credits can be backdated for a maximum of three months. If you were not awarded tax credits or did not get the disability, severe disability, disabled child or severely disabled child element in your tax credit award because you were waiting to hear the result of a claim for a qualifying benefit (eg disability living allowance), there are special backdating rules. See Chapter 59(3) under 'Exceptions' for details.

TC(C&N) Regs, Reg 7

Renewal claims

If you got tax credits in 2008/09, HMRC will send renewal papers early in the 2009/10 tax year. The renewal process involves establishing your final entitlement for 2008/09 by establishing your actual income and circumstances in that year. Your 2008/09 income and current circumstances are used as the basis for your initial award in 2009/10. If you are required to complete and return the forms, you must do so by 31.7.09. If you have difficulty giving details for 2008/09 (eg because you were self-employed and do not yet have your accounts available), you will have until 31.7.09 to provide an estimate of your 2008/09 income, and until 31.1.10 to provide your actual details. If you miss the deadline, but either renew within 30 days of the notice stating your payments will stop, or show good cause outside of the 30 days, HMRC may allow you to backdate your claim to the start of the tax year; otherwise, you may have to make a new claim, which can be backdated by three months only.

11. Payment of tax credits

CTC and WTC payments towards childcare costs will normally be paid direct to the main carer by HMRC. WTC, apart from any help with childcare costs, will normally be paid direct to the worker by HMRC.

Payments are normally made by credit transfer to a bank account or similar account. Payments into your account will be made weekly or 4-weekly, at your choice, unless the amount due is less than £2 a week, when payment may be made by lump sum.

The Tax Credits (Payments by the Board) Regulations 2002

12. Penalties

Tax credits contain a system of financial penalties.

A penalty of up to £3,000 can be imposed if you *'fraudulently or negligently'* make an incorrect statement or declaration or give incorrect information or evidence either in connection with your claim or when you are informing HMRC of a change of circumstances. If you claim as a couple, the penalty can be imposed on either of you, unless one of you can show you were not aware and could not *'reasonably have been expected'* to be aware that your partner was making a false statement or providing incorrect information or evidence about your claim. You can also be subject to this penalty if you make a false statement when you are acting for someone else.

A penalty of up to £300 can be imposed if you fail to provide information or evidence that HMRC has asked you to provide in connection with your claim, or if you fail to notify HMRC of a change of circumstances which it is obligatory to report. This penalty can be increased by up to £60 a day for each day that you continue to fail to provide the required information, but will not be imposed if you have a reasonable excuse for not providing it.

TCA, Ss.31 & 32

13. Revisions, appeals and complaints

HMRC can end or amend your tax credit award at any time. They can do so if you have told them of a change in circumstances (see Chapter 19(4)) or if they have 'reasonable grounds' for believing you should be getting a different amount, or even no tax credits at all. If there has been an official error by HMRC or the DWP, HMRC can revise a decision in your favour up to five years after the end of the tax year to which the decision relates.

The rules on appeals are similar but not identical to those for other social security benefits. Chapter 60 gives details of how to challenge a decision. Some specific differences are:

- ❑ You have 30 days to appeal to the First-tier Tribunal against a tax credit decision; notice of appeal must be sent to HMRC. There are certain circumstances in which appeals up to a year late may be allowed.
- ❑ Your notice of appeal must give the grounds of appeal. The tribunal may allow you to put forward grounds that were not specified in that notice, and take them into consideration, if they think the omission was *'not wilful or unreasonable'*.
- ❑ There is no right of appeal against a decision to recover an overpayment, so arguments about *'misrepresentation'* or *'failure to disclose'* are irrelevant. However, you may be able to appeal against the underlying decision(s) that led HMRC to believe they overpaid you.

It is standard practice for HMRC to contact you by phone to settle with you if you submit a valid appeal. You may persist with your appeal if you do not wish to negotiate in this way.

TCA 2002, Ss.38 & 39; The Tax Credits (Appeals) Regs 2002; The Tax Credits (Notice of Appeals) Regs 2002

Complaints

The HMRC complaints procedure is set out in the factsheet *Complaints and putting things right.* If you are dissatisfied with the result, you can refer the matter to the Adjudicator. Beyond the Adjudicator, you have the right to approach the Parliamentary and Health Service Ombudsman through your MP, but the Ombudsman will normally expect you to have exhausted all other routes, including the Adjudicator, before considering your complaint.

19 Calculating tax credits

1. Introduction

Child tax credit (CTC) and working tax credit (WTC) are paid by reference to an 'award period'. This usually reflects the tax year (6 April to the following 5 April), unless HMRC terminates it earlier (see Chapter 18(13)). Entitlement, however, is calculated on the basis of daily, not annual, rates. You can be entitled to tax credits at different rates for different periods (known as 'relevant periods') during the course of the tax year. If that is the case, entitlement is calculated (or recalculated) separately for the number of days in each relevant period.

Initially, the income taken into account is your income in the tax year preceding that for which you are awarded WTC/CTC. So if you are awarded WTC/CTC in 2009/10, it is initially assessed on your income in 2008/09. Your award can be altered if your income has decreased, or increased by more than a certain amount, since the year used in the assessment.

2. Rates of CTC and WTC

The various elements described in Chapter 18(4) and (7) are.

CTC elements 2009/10	yearly amount
Family element (normal)	£545
Family element (baby addition)	£545
Child element	£2,235
Disabled child element	£2,670
Severely disabled child element	£1,075

WTC elements 2009/10	yearly amount
Basic element	£1,890
Couple element	£1,860
Lone parent element	£1,860
30-hour element	£775
Severe disability element	£1,075
50-plus element (16- to 30-hours rate)	£1,300
50-plus element (30-hours rate)	£1,935
Disability element	£2,530
Childcare element*	(weekly amount)
maximum eligible cost for 1 child	£175
maximum eligible cost for 2 or more children	£300

*Childcare element is paid at 80% of actual childcare costs

CTC Regs, reg 7; WTC(E&MR) Regs, reg 20 & Sch 2

3. The steps in tax credit calculations

You work out your entitlement to tax credits for a whole award period (assuming no changes of circumstances):

Step 1: Work out the maximum tax credits for yourself and for your family – This will be the combination of all of the above CTC and WTC elements that apply to you, leaving the family element aside for now.

Step 2: Work out your annual income (see Chapter 18(9)) – There is no income calculation for periods when you are receiving income-related employment and support allowance, income-based jobseeker's allowance, income support or pension credit. Receipt of each of these benefits is a passport to the maximum tax credits award.

Step 3: Find the appropriate income threshold figure (see below).

Step 4: Compare the income to the threshold figure – If your income is below or the same as the first income threshold, you'll get the maximum tax credit for your family. If your income is above the first income threshold, deduct the threshold figure from the income: the result will be your 'excess income'. Then apply the correct taper (see below) to the resulting excess income. If your income exceeds the second income threshold, a much gentler taper applies to the family element which constitutes the excess (see below).

Step 5: Deduct the result at Step 4 from your maximum tax credits (see Step 1) – and add back the family element, which is not tapered away until your income is above the second income threshold. The amount you are left with is your tax credit entitlement.

Note: This calculation gives only a provisional entitlement figure, as your true entitlement is based on a comparison of your actual income in the year of the award and your income in the previous tax year. This will not be known until after the year has ended. See 6 below.

TC(IT&DR) Regs, reg 7

Income thresholds and tapers

The threshold figures used in the process described are:

2009/10	income threshold figure
1st income threshold WTC	£6,420
1st income threshold CTC (only)	£16,040
2nd income threshold CTC (family element only)	£50,000

If you qualify for both CTC and WTC, the WTC threshold figure is used in the calculation.

You apply a taper to work out how much of any excess income above the first income threshold should be taken from your maximum tax credit entitlement. This taper is 39% in 2009/10 (also 39% in 2008/09; 37% in 2007/08 and earlier years). However, the family element of CTC is retained until income exceeds the second income threshold, which is a minimum of £50,000 a year or, if higher, the point at which

G.3 Calculating tax credits

Shirley is a lone parent with two children aged 4 and 10. She works 20 hours a week and her gross annual income is £9,000. She gets disability living allowance highest rate care component for one child. Childcare costs are £30 a week (£1,560 a year).

Step 1: work out maximum tax credits	
WTC basic element	£1,890.00
WTC lone parent element	£1,860.00
WTC childcare (£1,560 x 80%)	£1,248.00
CTC child element x 2	£4,470.00
CTC disabled child element	£2,670.00
CTC severely disabled child element	£1,075.00
Maximum tax credits	*£13,213.00*
Step 2: annual income	
Annual income	£9,000.00
Step 3: find income threshold	
1st income threshold (WTC)	£6,420.00
Step 4: compare income to threshold	
Difference between steps 2 and 3	£2,580.00
Tapered at 39%	£1,006.20
Step 5: deduct 4 from 1	
£13,213 less £1,006.20	£ 12,206.80
Add family element	£545.00
Tax credit entitlement	*£12,751.80*

Note: This example is simplified by using annual rather than daily rates, which, with rounding, gives a slightly lower result than the claimant's actual entitlement. The discrepancy is marked when relevant periods are computed separately, so Box G.4 uses daily rates ascertained by dividing the annual figure by 365 and rounding up the result to the nearest penny.

all elements of WTC and CTC, apart from the family element of CTC, are completely tapered away. At that point the family element starts to be tapered away at a rate of 6.67% (roughly £1 for every £15 of gross income above the second income threshold). If your family has a baby under one, you get a higher family element with the baby addition.

When doing these calculations, HMRC must apply the taper in the following order: first to the WTC elements, then to the WTC childcare elements, then to the CTC child elements and finally to the CTC family elements. The effect of this is that payments made to the employee (the non-childcare elements of WTC) are reduced before those made to the main carer (the childcare elements of WTC and CTC).

TC(IT&DR) Regs, regs 7 & 8

G.4 Calculating tax credits: effect of change of circumstances

Farouk is single, 35, works full time and has a disability. His salary is £10,220 a year. At the start of the year he does not meet the conditions for the disability element, but after five months is awarded disability living allowance mobility component. He is not entitled to the disability element for the first 150 days of the year (first relevant period), but is for the remaining 215 (second relevant period).

First relevant period	
Step 1: work out maximum tax credits at daily rates	
WTC basic element: £5.18* x 150	£777.00
WTC 30-hour element: £2.13* x 150	£319.50
Maximum tax credits	*£1,096.50*
Step 2: income	
Income: £10,220 x 150/365	£4,200.00
Step 3: income threshold	
1st income threshold (WTC)	
£6,420 x 150/365	*£2,638.36
Step 4: compare income to threshold	
Difference between steps 2 and 3	£1,561.64
Taper excess income: £1561.64 x 39%	£609.03
Step 5: deduct 4 from 1	
£1,096.50 less £609.03	
Tax credit entitlement for 1st relevant period	*£487.47*
Second relevant period	
Step 1: work out maximum tax credits at daily rates	
WTC basic element: £5.18* x 215	£1,113.70
WTC disability element: £6.94* x 215	£1,492.10
WTC 30-hour element: £2.13* x 215	£457.95
Maximum tax credits	*£3,063.75*
Step 2: income	
Income: £10,220 x 215/365	£6,020.00
Step 3: income threshold	
1st income threshold (WTC)	
£6,420 x 215/365	*£3,781.65
Step 4: compare income to threshold	
Difference between steps 2 and 3	£2,238.35
Taper excess income: £2,238.35 x 39%	£872.95
Step 5: deduct 4 from 1	
£3,063.75 less £872.95	
Tax credit entitlement for 2nd relevant period	*£2,190.80*
Actual tax credits payable for both relevant periods	
First relevant period	£487.47
Second relevant period	£2,190.80
Total	*£2,678.27*

* these figures are rounded up to nearest penny (see note in Box G.3)

4. Changes in your circumstances

Normally, CTC and WTC awards run for a full tax year. However, if you fail to meet the qualifying conditions at some point your entitlement ends immediately. On the other hand, if your income goes up or down, even very substantially, there is usually no statutory requirement to notify HMRC, although it may be advisable to do so (see 5 below).

You *must* report the following changes of circumstances:

- a change to your status as a single person or couple;
- you cease to meet the residence conditions (eg you move abroad);
- your childcare costs end, or go down by £10 a week or more;
- your work hours change so that you no longer meet a 16- or 30-hours a week qualifying rule (see Chapter 18(5)-(6));
- you cease to be entitled to the 30-hour element;
- you stop being responsible for a child or qualifying young person, or one you are responsible for dies, or a qualifying young person stops counting as such (eg because they leave college and start work).

You must report the change within one month of the change occurring or of you becoming aware of it (whichever is later). Failure to do so may result in a penalty (see Chapter 18(12)).

TC(C&N) Regs, Reg 21

A change of circumstances that increases your maximum tax credit (such as the birth of a child) should be reported within three months to allow a full backdate.

5. The £25,000 disregard

Since April 2006 your income can increase by up to £25,000 in a tax year before it affects your tax credit entitlement for that year. In 2005/06 and earlier years, the amount of that disregard was £2,500.

The £25,000 disregard is applied in the following way.

- ❑ If the current year's income is greater than the previous year's income by £25,000 or less, the previous year's income is used to assess the current year's entitlement.
- ❑ If the current year's income is less than the previous year's income, the current year's income is used.
- ❑ If the current year's income is greater than the previous year's income by more than £25,000, the current year's income less £25,000 is used.

For example, if your income in 2008/09 was £10,000 but in 2009/10 it is £30,000, your 2009/10 award will be based on your 2008/09 income of £10,000; if your income in 2008/09 was £10,000 but in 2009/10 is £40,000, your 2009/10 award will be based on your income of £40,000 less the disregard of £25,000, ie £15,000. But note that the disregard applies for one year only – your initial 2010/11 award will be based on the actual income figure for 2009/10, ie £40,000. Thus, it is advisable to give HMRC up-to-date income data before the year-end, otherwise substantial overpayments can mount up in the very early months of the new tax year before the renewal papers are processed and the initial award is set.

You should be wary of entering into financial commitments, such as a mortgage or other loan, when you are receiving a high payment of tax credits as the result of the £25,000 disregard. Although with the £25,000 disregard, the high payment is much less likely to be an overpayment than previously, it is *still* a higher payment of tax credits than you will be entitled to in future years.

If you think the current year's income is likely to vary from that of the previous year by being either lower or more than £25,000 higher, you can ask for a reassessment so that your award is based on the likely income in the current tax year. However, if your income subsequently rises again to a level below the previous year's income, an overpayment will still accrue, as the disregard applies only when comparing current year to previous year income.

6. Overpayment or underpayment of tax credit

Because tax credits are assessed by reference to the tax year and are provisional in nature, being paid throughout the year but not determined until after the year-end, it is inevitable that overpayments and underpayments will sometimes arise. In addition, the system is designed to be flexible and to respond to changes in your circumstances. Consequently, a change in circumstances that affects the tax credits to which you are entitled is bound to give rise, even if only for a limited period, to overpayments and underpayments. Finally, errors – whether your error or official (ie HMRC or other government) error – can lead to too much or too little tax credit being paid.

7. Overpayments

An overpayment arises when the amount of a tax credit paid to you for a tax year exceeds the amount of your entitlement. For the reasons given in Chapter 19(6), it is not until after the end of a tax year that your entitlement for that year can be ascertained, and only then can it be established whether you have been paid the right amount, been underpaid or been overpaid.

If it appears to HMRC during a tax year that there is likely to be an overpayment at the end of it, HMRC may adjust the ongoing award with a view to reducing or eliminating the overpayment. This is generally a computer-generated operation, triggered by you reporting a change of circumstances that reduces entitlement.

TCA, S.28(1)&(5)

Methods of recovery

The usual methods of recovery are by:

- direct assessment; *or*
- deduction from payments under future awards.

A third, deduction via PAYE, is currently being piloted for small overpayments.

TCA, S.29(1), (3)&(4)

Under the second method, the amount by which payments can be reduced is limited, depending on your award. The reduction is at 10% if you receive the maximum tax credit award; 25% if you receive less than the maximum award but more than the family element of CTC; or 100% if you receive only the family element of CTC or less.

If you do not have an ongoing award because you no longer qualify, or if you have to make a new claim because your household unit has changed, HMRC will send you a demand for payment within 30 days. HMRC allows repayment in 12 monthly instalments, or even longer if you have little disposable income. In cases of hardship, it is possible for overpayments to be written off.

If HMRC is recovering an overpayment incurred by a couple who have split up, official policy is to try initially to recover equally from each former member of the couple; but the law makes each member responsible for the whole overpayment, and HMRC can, if they choose, pursue one member for the entire bill ('joint and several' liability).

When will an overpayment not be recovered?

Official error – HMRC has complete discretion whether or not to recover an overpayment in whole or in part. There is no right of appeal against a decision by HMRC to recover an overpayment, but there is a right of appeal against an award notice showing an overpayment (eg if it has been calculated incorrectly). HMRC practice on recovery is set out in code of practice COP26. If you fulfil all your responsibilities as listed in COP26, but HMRC has not fulfilled all of its responsibilities as listed, overpayments generated by official error are generally written off. Otherwise, they are generally recovered. An earlier test, that official error overpayments would be recovered unless you *'could reasonably have thought (your) award was correct'*, ceased to apply from 31.1.08.

In practical terms, it is essential to check your award notices carefully and compare the payment schedules on your award notices with the entries on your bank statements, then report within 30 days of the date of the notice any discrepancy, mistake or oddity that you observe. In addition, changes of circumstances should be reported as soon as they happen.

If you dispute recovery of an overpayment on grounds of official error, you must do so in writing, preferably using form TC846 (available on the HMRC website: www.hmrc.gov.uk). On receiving your written dispute, HMRC should immediately suspend collection of your overpayment. The suspension remains in force while HMRC considers your case, but is released if HMRC finds against you, even if you subsequently complain to HMRC or refer the matter to the Adjudicator or Parliamentary and Health Service Ombudsman (see Chapter 18(13)).

Since most business with the Tax Credit Office is done by phone, it is advisable to keep a note of every call you make or receive, the date and time, who you spoke to and what was said. HMRC generally keeps tape recordings of calls to the helpline, and either the Tax Credit Office or the HMRC Data Protection Unit will send you tape recordings on request.

Hardship – If repaying the overpayment would cause hardship to you or your family, you can ask HMRC to reduce or cancel the overpayment.

The effect of overpayments on other benefits

Means-tested benefits – If your payment of tax credit is reduced or stopped by HMRC because of overpayment recovery, your means-tested benefit (income-related employment and support allowance, income support or income-based jobseeker's allowance) will not be increased to make up for the drop in tax credits. At worst, this could leave you living on an income below the normal means-tested benefit level. However, if they are recovering an overpayment from an ongoing award, HMRC should pay full CTC to people in receipt of a means-tested benefit with only a 10% reduction to cover the overpayment.

Housing benefit (HB) and council tax benefit (CTB) – What counts for HB and CTB is the amount of tax credit that you actually *receive*. So, if you are being overpaid tax credit you may receive less HB and/or CTB than you would if you were getting the right amount, but the payment is nevertheless correct. When your tax credit award is lowered to recover an overpayment from a previous year or to avoid you being overpaid in the current year, your HB and/or CTB *must* be increased to compensate.

8. Underpayments

If you are underpaid tax credit (eg because your family income goes down) and the underpayment comes to light 'in year', the award can be changed to reflect your new circumstances, but any accrued underpayment will be held back until the end of the year. If the underpayment comes to light at the end of the year, the award will be corrected to reflect your circumstances and, providing there are no outstanding overpayments on other awards, a one-off arrears payment will be made to you.

The effect on HB and CTB – If you are being underpaid tax credit and receive a lump-sum payment that makes up for the accumulated underpayment you will receive a higher award of HB/CTB in this period because of your low actual income from tax credit. In contrast, if you opt to have the underpayment corrected in the course of the year, then 85% of the additional income is likely to be lost due to reduced HB/CTB payable.

H Help with rent and council tax

This section of the Handbook looks at:

20 Housing benefit and council tax benefit

1. What is housing benefit?

Housing benefit (HB) helps people pay their rent. It can also be known as rent rebate or rent allowance. In Northern Ireland, where the rates scheme still applies, it helps people pay their rates. Council tax was not introduced in Northern Ireland (see 28 for details of the rate rebate scheme).

In nearly all cases, local authorities run the HB scheme. But in a few cases, other organisations run the scheme and some authorities have contracted out part of the administration to private firms. In Northern Ireland, the Northern Ireland Housing Executive and the Land & Property Services administer the scheme for tenants and owner occupiers respectively.

2. Who can get HB?

You can get HB if you satisfy all the following conditions:

- you are not excluded from getting HB (see below and Box H.1);
- you are liable to pay rent on your normal home (see 5 below);
- with the exception of some people aged 60 or over, your capital is no more than £16,000 (see 23 below);
- you are on income support, income-based jobseeker's allowance, income-related employment and support allowance or the guarantee credit of pension credit, or you have a fairly low income (see 21 & 24 below); *and*
- you claim and provide the information requested (see 14 below).

People who cannot get housing benefit

If you are in any of the groups below, you cannot get HB.

- ❑ **Care leavers under 18** – if social services are responsible for accommodating you. There are rare exceptions: seek further advice if you are in this situation.
- ❑ **People in care homes** – There are rare exceptions (see Chapter 33(3)).
- ❑ **'Persons from abroad' or 'subject to immigration control'** – This does not cover every non-UK national, and it does cover some UK nationals who do not habitually reside in the UK. See Chapter 50 for details.
- ❑ **Many full-time students** – Full-time students cannot get HB unless they fall within certain groups – eg disabled students (see Chapter 40(2) for details). If you are in a couple and only one of you is a full-time student, the other one can get HB for you both.
- ❑ **Members of religious orders** – if you are maintained by the order.
- ❑ **Other groups** – See Box H.1 for details of other people who cannot get HB.

3. What is rent?

You can get HB towards almost any kind of rent, whether you pay it to a local authority (including a health authority), the Northern Ireland Housing Executive, a housing association, a co-op, a hostel, a bed and breakfast hotel, a private company or a private individual (including a resident landlord – but see Box H.1). This is true whether your letting is a 'tenancy' or 'licence'; whether your payments are for 'rent' or for 'use and occupation' or for 'mesne profits' or 'violent profits'; and whether you have a written or a verbal letting agreement. If you are buying a share of your home through a shared ownership scheme but still pay rent, you can get HB towards the rent (and you may be able to get income-related employment and support allowance, income support, income-based jobseeker's allowance or pension credit towards the mortgage interest). You can also get HB towards the following, which all count as 'rent' for HB purposes:

- mooring charges and/or berthing fees for a houseboat (as well as your rent, if you do not own it);
- site fees for a caravan or mobile home (as well as your rent, if you do not own it);
- payments to a charitable almshouse;
- payments under a 'rental purchase' agreement;
- payments (in Scotland) on a croft or croft land.

HB Regs, reg 12(1)

4. Housing costs that HB cannot meet

You cannot get HB towards any of the following costs, although some may be met by income-related employment and support allowance, income support, income-based jobseeker's allowance or pension credit (see Chapter 25):

- payments you make on your home if you own it or have a long lease (over 21 years; this includes a life tenancy if created in writing), except for a shared ownership lease;
- payments you make in a co-ownership scheme where, if you left, you would be entitled to a sum based on the value of your home;
- rent if you are a Crown tenant (there is a separate scheme for Crown tenants). But tenants of the Crown Estate Commissioners and the Duchies of Cornwall and Lancaster can get HB;
- hire purchase or credit sale agreements;
- conditional sale agreements (unless for land);
- payments on a tent;
- payments in respect of a dwelling owned by your partner.

HB Regs, reg 12(2)

5. Liability for rent on your normal home

To get HB, the general rule is that you must be personally liable to pay the rent on your home. You can usually only get HB on one home at a time, which is the dwelling *'normally occupied'* by yourself and any members of your family. (Seek advice if you live in more than one dwelling due to the size of your family.) However, there are exceptions to these points, as described in the next few paragraphs.

Couples – Either one of you can get HB towards the rent on your normal home. Even if the letting agreement is in one name only, the other person is treated as liable to make payments.

HB Regs, Reg 8(1)(b)

If you take over paying someone else's rent – If the person liable for the rent on your home stops paying it, and you take over the payments to continue living there, you can get HB even though you are not legally liable for the rent. This applies if your partner has left you, and in any other reasonable case, including if the 'person' is a limited company.

HB Regs, Reg 8(1)(c)

Repairs to your home – If your landlord agrees not to collect rent while you do repairs to your home, you can carry on getting HB for the first eight weeks. After that, you cannot get HB until you start paying rent again.

HB Regs, Reg 8(1)(d)

If you have to move into temporary accommodation while essential repairs are being carried out to your normal home, you can get HB on the property for which you are liable to make payments – but only if you are not liable for payments on the other home.

HB Regs, Reg 7(4)

Joint occupiers – 'Joint occupiers' means two or more people (other than a couple) who are jointly liable to pay rent on their home. If you are a joint occupier, you can get

H.1 Who cannot get HB?

The rules in this box apply in addition to those in the main text (see 2). If you have difficulties getting HB because of these rules, seek advice.

Your letting is not on a commercial basis – You cannot get HB if your letting is not on a commercial basis.

This rule applies whether you live with your landlord or somewhere else. Factors to be considered when deciding this include: the relationship and agreement between the parties; the living arrangements; the amount of rent; and whether the agreement contains terms enforceable by law.

You live with your landlord who is a close relative – You cannot get HB if you live with your landlord and they are a 'close relative'. Sharing just a bathroom, toilet, hallway, stairs or passageways does not count as living with your landlord, but sharing rooms might. A 'close relative' means only a parent, parent-in-law, step-parent, son, daughter, son/daughter-in-law, stepson/daughter, sister, brother or the partner of any of those.

Your landlord is an ex-partner – You cannot get HB if you rent your home from:

- your ex-partner, and you used to live there with that ex-partner; *or*
- your (current) partner's ex-partner, and your (current) partner used to live there with that ex-partner.

Your landlord is the parent of your child – You cannot get HB if you or your partner are responsible for a child whose father or mother is your landlord. You (or your partner) count as 'responsible' for any child who normally lives with you.

Your landlord is a company or a trust connected with you – You cannot get HB if your landlord is a company or a trust of which any of the directors or employees (of the company), or trustees or beneficiaries (of the trust) is:

- you or your partner, or an ex-partner of either of you; *or*
- a person who lives with you and who is a 'close relative' of you or your partner (see above).

But this rule does not apply if your letting agreement was created for a genuine reason (rather than to take advantage of the HB scheme). What counts as 'taking advantage of the HB scheme' can be open to argument.

Your landlord is a trust connected with your child – You cannot get HB if your landlord is a trust of which your, or your (current) partner's, child is a beneficiary. For this rule, you cannot get HB even if your letting agreement was created for a genuine reason.

You used to be a non-dependant – You cannot get HB if:

- you lived in your home before you began renting it; *and*
- at that time you were a non-dependant (see 22) of a person who then lived in your home; *and*
- that person still lives in your home.

But this rule does not apply if your letting agreement was created for a genuine reason (rather than to take advantage of the HB scheme). What counts as 'taking advantage of the HB scheme' can be open to argument.

You used to own or have a long tenancy of the home you rent – You cannot get HB if you or your partner used to own or have a long tenancy of the home you are now renting. But this rule only applies if you owned it or had a long tenancy of it within the past five years and have lived there continuously since you owned or had a long tenancy of it. It does not apply if you or your partner would have to have left your home if it was not sold or the tenancy given up. For example, this rule should not apply if you are renting your home under a 'mortgage rescue scheme'.

Tied accommodation – You cannot get HB if you or your partner are employed by your landlord and have to live in your home as a condition of that employment.

Contrived lettings – In addition to all the above rules, you cannot get HB if your or your landlord's principal or dominant purpose in creating your letting agreement was to take advantage of the HB scheme. The motives and intentions of landlord and tenant may be considered in order to determine this.

HB Regs, reg 9

HB towards your share of the rent. This share is assessed by taking into account the number of joint occupiers, how much each of you pays and how many rooms you each occupy.

HB Regs, reg 12(5)

Bail or probation hostels – If you are required to reside in a bail or probation hostel, you will not be treated as occupying that dwelling as your home, and so will be unable to claim HB for any rent charged.

HB Regs, reg 7(5)

6. Temporary absence

You can continue to get HB while you are temporarily absent from your normal home in the circumstances described below.

The 13-week rule

You can get HB for up to 13 weeks during a temporary absence from your normal home if:

- you intend to return to occupy it as your home; *and*
- the part you normally occupy has not been let or sub-let; *and*
- your absence is unlikely to exceed 13 continuous weeks.

This rule applies to all absences (including absences outside the UK). In calculating the length of a prison sentence, the length of the sentence includes periods of temporary release, but should be reduced by any remission allowable for good behaviour.

HB Regs, reg 7(13)-(15)

The 52-week rule

You can get HB for up to 52 weeks during a temporary absence from your normal home if:

- you intend to return to occupy it as your home; *and*
- the part you normally occupy has not been let or sub-let; *and*
- your absence is unlikely to exceed 52 weeks or, in exceptional circumstances, is unlikely to substantially exceed 52 weeks; *and*
- your absence is for any of the reasons listed below.

Who the rule applies to – You can get HB under this rule if you are:

- a patient in a hospital or similar institution;
- receiving medical treatment or medically-approved care or convalescence (other than in a care home) in the UK or abroad;
- accompanying your child or partner who is receiving the above (but not care);
- providing care to a child whose parent or guardian is absent from home due to receiving medically approved care or medical treatment;
- providing medically approved care to anyone in the UK or abroad;
- receiving care in a care home (but not for a trial period – see below);
- on an approved training course in the UK or abroad;
- on remand awaiting trial or sentencing or required to reside in a hostel or property other than your home as a condition of bail;
- a student who is eligible for HB/council tax benefit (see Chapter 40(2));
- in fear of violence but only if you are not liable for rent on your other home (the conditions are the same as in the rule for getting HB on two homes in such cases – see 7 below).

HB Regs, reg 7(16) & (17)

Your period of absence

If your absence is likely to exceed 13 or 52 continuous weeks, you cannot get HB for any time you are away. If you cannot estimate the length of your absence, you are unlikely to get HB during any of it. So, if possible, always give your local authority an estimate. Your intention to return must be a realistic possibility.

Any re-occupation of the home (other than a prisoner's temporary release) will break the period of absence – a stay of 24 hours is usually enough, although the authority has to be satisfied that your stay at home was genuine.

As soon as it becomes likely that the absence will exceed the 13- or 52-week limit, your HB entitlement will stop.

Trial periods in care homes

You can get HB for up to 13 weeks during an absence from your normal home if:

- you are trying out a care home to see whether it suits your needs; *and*
- you intend to return to your normal home if it does not; *and*
- the part you normally occupy has not been let or sub-let.

HB Regs, reg 7(11) & (12)

7. Moving home and getting HB on two homes

The general rule – When you move from one rented home to another, you can get HB on both homes for up to four weeks if you have moved into the new home but your local authority agrees you could not reasonably have avoided liability for rent on both the new and the old home (eg because you had to move unexpectedly and had to give notice on your old home). This general rule applies only if you have actually moved into the new home. Exactly what it means to *'move in'* can be interpreted in different ways. It could be enough if you have moved some furniture and personal possessions into the property (R(H)9/05). This 4-week rule also applies if you move to a new home where you are not liable for rent but continue to have a rental liability on your old property.

HB Regs, reg 7(6)(d) & (7)

Different rules apply if you move for one of the following reasons.

Fear of violence – This rule applies if you move because of fear that violence may occur:

- in your old home – in this case, the rule applies regardless of who might cause the violence; *or*
- in the locality – in this case, only if the violence would be caused by a former member of your family.

In either case, you can get HB on both homes for up to 52 weeks, as long as you intend to return to your old home at some point and your local authority agrees it is reasonable to pay HB on both. You do not have to say exactly when you intend to return: it should be sufficient if you intend to return when it is safe to do so. If you do not intend to return, you continue to get HB on your former property for up to four weeks – if the continuing liability was unavoidable.

HB Regs, reg 7(6)(a) & (10)

Waiting for your new home to be adapted – If you do not move into a new rented home straight away because you have to wait for it to be adapted to meet your disablement needs or those of any member of your family, and your local authority agrees the delay is reasonable, you can get HB for up to four weeks before you actually move in. If you are liable for rent on your old home, you can get HB on both during those four weeks.

HB Regs, reg 7(8)(c)(i) & 7(6)(e)

Waiting for a social fund payment before moving – If you do not move into a new rented home straight away because you have asked for a social fund payment to help with the move or with setting up home, and your local authority agrees the delay is reasonable, you can get HB for up to four weeks before you move in. But this rule only applies if there is a child under the age of 6 in your family, or if you or your partner are aged 60 or over, or if you qualify for one of the HB disability, severe disability or disabled child premiums (see Chapter 24(2), (3) and (8)). Under this rule you cannot get HB on your old home at the same time.

HB Regs, reg 7(8)(c)(ii)

When you leave hospital or a care home – If you do not move into a new rented home straight away because you are waiting to leave hospital or a care home, and your local authority agrees the delay is reasonable, you can get HB for up to four weeks before you actually move in.

HB Regs, reg 7(8)(c)(iii)

Claiming on time – In the above three cases, you must claim straight away; do not wait until you have moved in. If the authority rejects the claim, but you re-apply within four weeks of moving in, the rejected claim must be reconsidered. If you move within a local authority area, you will qualify if you notify them of the new tenancy before the move.

HB Regs 7(8)(b)

Large families – If your local authority has arranged for you to be housed in two homes, you can get HB on both.

HB Regs, reg 7(6)(c)

Students – Some students with partners who have to maintain two homes can get HB on both (if they are eligible for HB in the first place) – see Chapter 40(2).

HB Regs, Reg 7(6)(b)

8. How much of your rent is taken into account?

Your rent may include charges for water, fuel, meals or other services; or you may rent a garage with your home. As detailed below, HB cannot be awarded towards all of these.

Eligible rent – The HB calculation is based on your weekly 'eligible rent'. This means:

- the actual rent on your home,
- plus in some cases the rent on a garage,
- minus amounts for water, fuel, meals and certain other services.

To convert monthly rent to a weekly figure, multiply by 12 then divide by 52.

Exceptions – In certain cases, the HB calculation is based instead on a different figure. In particular, if you rent from a private sector landlord, a new claim would be based on a standard local housing allowance (LHA) amount or your ongoing claim may be subject to restrictions (see 9 below).

Non-LHA tenancies – The following applies only to LHA-exempt tenancies and those claims not yet subject to the LHA. For a list of LHA exempt tenancies, see 9 below.

Garages

If you rent a garage, it is included as part of the rent on your home only if you were obliged to rent the garage from the beginning of your letting agreement, or you are making (or have made) all reasonable efforts to stop renting it.

HB Regs, reg 2(4)(a)

Water charges and council tax included in your rent

If your rent includes water or sewerage charges, the actual amount of the charge for your home (or if your water is metered, an estimate) is deducted. If your rent includes a contribution towards the council tax because your landlord pays it, this is included as part of your eligible rent.

HB Regs, reg 12(3)(b)(i) & (6)

Service charges: general conditions

The rules for several types of service charge are given below, saying whether they can be taken into account as part of your eligible rent. But even when they can, there are two further conditions:

- ❑ The amount of the charge must be reasonable for the service provided. If it is not, the unreasonable part is deducted.
- ❑ Payment of the charge must be a condition of occupying your home, whether from the beginning of your letting agreement or from later on. If it is not a condition, the whole charge is deducted.

HB Regs, Sch 1, para 4 & reg 12(1)(e)

Exception – If the rent officer fixes a maximum rent for your home, they also fix a value for some of the services (see 9 below).

Fuel and related charges

If your rent includes fuel of any kind, the fuel charge is deducted if there is evidence of the amount (eg in your rent book or letting agreement). If there is no evidence of the amount, a flat-rate amount is deducted for the various things the fuel is for; the amounts are given below.

Whenever your local authority makes flat-rate deductions, it must write inviting you to provide evidence of the actual amount. If you can provide reasonable evidence (which need not be from your landlord), the authority must estimate the actual amount and deduct that instead of the flat rate.

Exceptions – A fuel charge for a communal area (including communal rooms in sheltered accommodation) is included as part of your eligible rent if it is separately specified in your rent book or letting agreement. The same is true for a separately specified charge for providing a heating system.

Flat-rate deductions – If you rent more than one room (not counting any shared accommodation), these are:

Deductions	per week
Heating	£21.55
Hot water	£2.50
Lighting	£1.75
Cooking	£2.50

If you rent only one room (not counting a shared kitchen, bathroom or toilet), the flat-rate deduction for heating is £12.90. If you get a flat-rate deduction for heating, there is no further deduction for hot water or lighting, but the figure for cooking is as above.

HB Regs, Sch 1, paras 5 & 6

Meal charges

If your rent includes meals (the preparation of food or the provision of food) a flat-rate amount is deducted for these. The flat rate is always used, regardless of how much you are actually charged. One flat-rate deduction is made for each person (even if not a member of your family) whose meals are included in your rent. The amount for each person depends on their age and what meals they get.

Weekly deductions per person	aged 16+	under 16
For at least 3 meals every day	£22.95	£11.60
For breakfast only	£2.80	£2.80
For any other arrangement	£15.25	£7.65

H.2 Why housing benefit may not cover all your rent

Your HB may not cover all of your rent. This could be because:

- your rent includes service charges or other things that must be deducted in the calculation of HB (see 8);
- you have one or more non-dependant(s) in your home and a deduction must be made because of this (see 22);
- your HB is restricted (eg because a standard local housing allowance or 'maximum rent' applies) (see 9);
- the level of your income means you do not qualify for the whole of your rent to be met (see 21).

A B C D E F G H I J K L M N O P Q R S T U

For these purposes, a person does not count as aged 16+ until the first Monday in the September following their 16th birthday.

HB Regs, Sch 1, paras 1(a)(i) & 2

Other services

Cleaning and window cleaning – A charge for cleaning and window cleaning of communal areas is included in your eligible rent; so is a charge for exterior window cleaning if neither you nor anyone in your household can do it. A charge (estimated if necessary) is deducted for any other cleaning and window cleaning.

Furniture and household equipment – A charge for these is included in your eligible rent if your landlord has not agreed they will become your personal property.

General support charges – Before April 2003, 'support charges' could be included in your eligible rent if you lived in supported accommodation. This has now ceased but you may be able to get help from the Supporting People scheme (see Chapter 28(5)).

Medical, nursing and personal care – A charge for any of these (estimated if necessary) is deducted.

Communal or accommodation-related services – Most charges for these are included in your eligible rent. Examples are: TV/radio aerial and relay, refuse removal, lifts, communal telephones, entry phones, children's play areas, garden maintenance necessary for the provision of adequate accommodation and communal laundry facilities.

Day-to-day living expenses, etc – Charges for these (estimated if necessary) are deducted. Examples are: TV rental, subscription and licence fees, laundering (ie if washing is done for you), transport, sports facilities, leisure items and any other service not related to the provision of adequate accommodation.

Staffing and administration charges – These are covered only if they are connected with the provision of adequate accommodation. To determine this, it is necessary to look at the number of hours a week spent by employees on providing accommodation-related services.

HB Regs, Sch 1, para 1

9. HB restrictions

There are several rules about how your local authority can restrict (in other words, reduce) your eligible rent. They depend on whether you rent from the local authority, from a housing association, or from any other landlord (including a private landlord).

Note: When you look at the following, don't forget the rules about joint occupiers (see 5 above); and don't forget to convert your rent (and the other figures mentioned below) to a weekly amount.

If you rent from your local authority

If you rent from the local authority, it will administer your HB claim, and it is very unlikely that your eligible rent will be restricted. If you rent from any other authority (such as a non-metropolitan county council), see below 'If you rent from any other landlord, including a private landlord'.

If you rent from a housing association

If you rent from a registered housing association (or any other registered social landlord), it is possible (though fairly unlikely) that your eligible rent will be restricted. If your local authority considers that your rent is unreasonably high or your accommodation unreasonably large, they may refer your details to the rent officer.

- ❑ If they do this, all the rules relating to people who rent from a private landlord will apply to you (see below).
- ❑ If they do not do this, they should not restrict your eligible rent.

If you rent from an unregistered housing association (which is not a registered social landlord), all the rules about renting from a private landlord will apply to you (see below).

HB Regs, Sch 2, para 3

Note: Don't forget to look at the exceptions given later: they can mean you qualify for more HB.

If you rent from any other landlord, including a private landlord

In this case, your eligible rent is restricted to a figure called your 'maximum rent' – unless you fall within certain protected groups (see below).

If you have moved or started to claim HB from 7.4.08, your maximum rent will be set at a standard rate: the local housing allowance (see below).

Before 7.4.08, maximum rents were set at rates that followed determinations by rent officers. Rent officers are independent of the local authority; they look at your rent and various other factors (eg what is a reasonable market rent for your home and what is the midpoint of all rents in your area) before providing the authority with various figures that are used to calculate your maximum rent. Once your maximum rent has been set at a rate following a rent officer's determination, it will continue to be based on this determination. Your claim can be referred back to the rent officer for a redetermination if:

- ■ there has been a relevant change of circumstances; *or*
- ■ 52 weeks have passed since the last referral.

For further details on this type of rent restriction, see *Disability Rights Handbook* 32nd edition, page 41. Note, however, that, following the House of Lords judgment in *Heffernan v The Rent Service* (30.7.08), the Government amended the local reference rent rules. From 5.1.08, the criteria for establishing the local reference rent relates to a 'broad market rental area' rather than 'locality'. The definition of broad market rental area is the same as that applied to the local housing allowance (see below).

The Rent Officer (Housing Benefit Functions) Order 1997, Sch 1

Local housing allowance

If you have moved or started to claim HB from 7.4.08, your maximum rent will be set at a standard rate, the local housing allowance (LHA).

The LHA is a standard amount of maximum HB (eligible rent), set according to the area you live in and who is in your household, including non-dependants (see 'Rate of LHA' below). This figure is used whatever the actual amount of your rent. However, the amount is restricted so it can never be more than £15 above the rent you pay. This means your HB may not be the same amount as your rent, even if you are entitled to maximum benefit. Claimants are expected to make up any shortfall or seek cheaper accommodation or, alternatively, keep up to £15 of any benefit in excess of rent.

HB Regs, regs 12D & 13D

The LHA rules apply to most private sector tenancies. They may not apply to you if:

- ■ your HB claim is backdated to a date earlier than 7.4.08; *or*
- ■ your tenancy is exempt (see 'Exempt tenancies' and 'Exceptions to the above rules' below); *or*
- ■ you are in a protected category and your LHA would be less than your eligible rent (see 'Protections for certain people' below).

Exempt tenancies – These are:

- ■ registered social landlord tenancies (eg local authority or housing association);
- ■ protected cases – such as supported housing provided by certain local authorities, housing associations, registered charities or voluntary organisations;
- ■ protected tenancies with a registered fair rent;

- exceptional cases such as caravans, houseboats, mobile homes and hostels;
- board and attendance cases if the rent officer judges that a substantial part of the rent is for board and attendance.

HB Regs, reg 13C(5)

Rate of LHA – If the LHA applies, the amount of eligible rent is the standard LHA, determined by a local authority rent officer according to:

- the broad market rental area where the dwelling is situated; *and*
- the size of the household and number of bedrooms required.

HB Regs, reg 13D

Broad market rental area – This is made up of two or more distinct areas of residential accommodation within which a person could reasonably be expected to live, having regard to facilities and services, and including a variety of types of accommodation and tenancy. The LHA is based on the median (middle) rent (rather than the average) for properties of the relevant size within the broad market rental area. These standard amounts are published each month by every local authority.

HB Regs, reg 13E

Size criteria – The LHA is based on the number of occupants in the benefit household. Restrictions apply to single claimants under 25 and those in shared accommodation. One bedroom each is allowed for:

- every adult couple;
- any other adult aged 16 or over;
- any two children of the same sex;
- any two children regardless of sex if under age 10; *and*
- any other child.

No other type of room is taken into account.

Since 6.4.09, the LHA is 'capped' at the 5-bedroom rate for new claimants from the date of claim and for pre-existing claimants from 26 weeks after the first annual review date.

Young people – Single claimants under 25 years old have an LHA based on one bedroom in shared accommodation. This does not apply if they qualify for a severe disability premium or are a care leaver aged under 22.

Single claimants over 25 and couples without children – Claimants over 25 years old without children are allowed the normal one-bedroom rate unless they live in shared accommodation, in which case the rate for one bedroom shared accommodation is used.

Protections for certain people

Your local authority may not use the maximum rent figure described above in the following two cases. (For how your eligible rent is calculated in these cases, see 8 above.)

- ❑ If you and/or any member of your household could afford the financial commitments of your home when you first entered into them, and you (or your partner) have not received HB during the 52 weeks before your current claim, your authority may not use the maximum rent figure for the first 13 weeks of your claim.
- ❑ If a member of your household has died, and you have not moved since then, the authority may not use the maximum rent figure until a year after the date of that death (unless there was already a maximum rent figure that applied before that death, in which case that continues).

However, if your LHA rate would be higher than your 'protected' rate, you can receive the LHA rate instead.

Although your local authority may not use the maximum rent figure in the above two cases, it can restrict your eligible rent if it considers it is unreasonable in all the circumstances of your case. If this happens, seek advice.

For the purposes of the above protections, all the following count as members of your household:

- each member of your family: you, your partner, children under 16 and young people aged 16-19 for whom child benefit is payable (see 25 below, under 'Your family');
- any other relative of yours (or your partner) who lives with you but does not have an independent right to do so. A 'relative' means a parent, parent-in-law, step-parent, son, daughter, son- or daughter-in-law, stepson or stepdaughter, sister, brother or the (married or unmarried) partner of any of those, grandparent, grandchild, uncle, aunt, niece or nephew.

HB Regs, reg 12D, 13(11) & (14)-(17)

Exceptions to the above rules

The following exceptions to the rent restriction rules may apply to you if you rent from a housing association or from any other private landlord. If you fall within more than one of the following exceptions, just look at the first one that applies to you.

The exceptions can be complicated in some cases (and in rare cases there are yet further rules). It is often worth seeking advice. Don't forget to also check the points in 'Protections for certain people' above.

Pre-January 1989 tenancies – This applies to you if your letting began before 15.1.89 in England and Wales or 2.1.89 in Scotland. In these cases it is very unlikely your local authority will restrict your eligible rent.

HB Regs, Sch 2, para 4

People in accommodation where care, support or supervision is provided – This applies to you if:

- your home is provided by a non-metropolitan county council, housing association, registered social landlord, registered charity, non-profit-making voluntary organisation or certain similar bodies; *and*
- your landlord provides you with 'care, support or supervision' or has arranged for you to be provided with this. For this to apply there must be some contractual obligation between the landlord and the care provider.

This exception also applies to you if your home is a resettlement hostel.

In these cases, your local authority can only restrict your eligible rent if it has evidence that your rent is unreasonably high or your home unreasonably large.

There are several further rules that give protection to certain vulnerable people – if you have difficulties seek further advice.

HB & CTB (Consequential Provisions) Regs 2006, Sch 3(4)(1)(b)&(10)

If you have been on HB since 1.1.96 – This applies to you if you:

- were getting HB on 1.1.96 (in Northern Ireland on 1.4.96); *and*
- have been on HB continuously since that date, ignoring gaps of either no more than 52 weeks if you or your partner are covered by the 'welfare to work' linking rules (see Chapter 16(12)) or no more than four weeks for anyone else; *and*
- have not moved since that date (unless as a result of a fire, flood, explosion or natural catastrophe).

If your partner or another member of your household previously satisfied these conditions, you may be able to take advantage of these rules. Seek further advice.

In the above cases, your local authority can only restrict your eligible rent if it has evidence that your rent is unreasonably high or your home unreasonably large.

There are further rules that give protection to certain vulnerable people; if you have difficulties seek advice.

HB & CTB (Consequential Provisions) Regs 2006, Sch 3(4)(1)(a)&(10)

If you have been on HB since 5.10.97 – This applies if:

- you were getting HB on 5.10.97; *and*
- you have been on HB continuously since that date, ignoring gaps of no more than 52 weeks if you or your partner are covered by the 'welfare to work' linking rules (see Chapter

16(12)). No gaps are allowed for anyone else; *and*

- you have not moved since that date (regardless of the reason for the move); *and*
- the rent officer has provided a local reference rent for your claim.

In these cases, your local authority may have to use a higher maximum rent when it assesses your eligible rent. If this applies to you, seek further advice.

HB & CTB (Consequential Provisions) Regs 2006, Sch 3(8)

People who pay caravan/mobile home site rent or mooring fees – This applies to you if you:

- pay a county council for the rent of a caravan or mobile home or its site for Gypsies and Travellers; *or*
- pay a housing authority for the rent of a site for a caravan or mobile home or for houseboat mooring charges, and housing benefit is payable as a 'rent allowance'.

From 06.4.09, these tenancies are excluded from rent restrictions in the same way as housing association tenancies, see above. They should only be referred to the rent officer if accommodation is considered to be unreasonably large or expensive.

HB Regs, Sch 2, para 3

Getting information before you sign up for a letting

LHA rates for each size category of property should be available from every local authority. These rates should be reviewed each month and can help you to know how much HB you would receive if you moved to a new address.

10. What is council tax benefit?

Council tax benefit (CTB) helps people pay their council tax. There are two types of CTB, but you can only get one type at a time. 'Main CTB' is the more common type and is described below. 'Second adult rebate' is much less common (see 27 below).

In all cases, local authorities run the CTB scheme, although some have contracted part of the administration to private firms. (There is no council tax, and so no CTB, in Northern Ireland.)

11. Who can get Main CTB?

You can get Main CTB if you satisfy all the following conditions:

- you are not excluded from getting Main CTB (see below);
- you are liable to pay council tax on your normal home (see 12 below);
- you claim and provide the information requested (see 14 below);
- you are on income support, income-based jobseeker's allowance, income-related employment and support allowance, the guarantee credit of pension credit, or you have a fairly low income (see 21 below);
- with the exception of some pensioners, your capital is no more than £16,000 (see 23 below).

People who cannot get Main CTB

The following groups are excluded from getting Main CTB.

- ❑ **'Persons from abroad' or 'persons subject to immigration control'** – This does not include every non-UK national, but covers some UK nationals who do not habitually reside in the UK. See Chapter 50 for details.
- ❑ **Many full-time students** – Full-time students cannot get Main CTB unless they fall within certain groups (although they can get second adult rebate). Many students with disabilities fall within one of those groups. See Chapter 40(2) for details. If you are in a couple and only one of you is a full-time student, the other can get Main CTB for you both. If your residence is occupied solely by students, you should be exempt from council tax (see Box H.4, Chapter 21).

12. Liability for council tax on your normal home

To claim CTB, you must be personally liable to pay the council tax on your normal home. For most purposes, your 'normal home' means wherever you are treated as being *'resident'* under council tax rules (see Chapter 21(6)). Most home owners and rent payers are liable for council tax and so can claim CTB. But note the following points.

- ❑ **Exempt dwellings** – If your dwelling is exempt from council tax (see Chapter 21(4)), you cannot get CTB on it
- ❑ **If you rent non-self-contained accommodation** – You are not liable for council tax (your landlord is), so you are not eligible for CTB.
- ❑ **Water charges** – You cannot get CTB towards water charges or (in Scotland) towards the council water charge.
- ❑ **Couples** – If you are in a couple and you are jointly liable for council tax on your home, either one of you can get CTB towards this. If only one of you is liable, that person can get CTB on behalf of you both (see Chapter 21(5)).
- ❑ **Joint occupiers** – 'Joint occupiers' means two or more people (other than a couple) who are jointly liable to pay council tax on their home (see Chapter 21(5)). If you are a joint occupier, you can get Main CTB towards your share of the council tax. This share is found by dividing the council tax bill by the number of people who are liable.
- ❑ **Absences from home** – The rules for whether you can get CTB during a temporary absence from home are the same as those for HB (see 6 above).
- ❑ **Moving home and occupying two homes** – You can only get CTB on one home at a time, which is wherever you are treated as being resident under the council tax rules (see Chapter 21(6)).

13. How much of your council tax is taken into account?

The CTB calculation is based on your weekly *'eligible council tax'*. For Main CTB, this means whatever you are liable to pay after you have been awarded a reduction for disabilities or discount (see Chapter 21(7), (8) and (9)).

CTB is worked out on a weekly basis, so your council tax liability has to be converted. Divide the annual figure by 365 (giving a daily figure), then multiply by 7. If your bill is not for a full year, divide it by the number of days it covers, then multiply by 7.

14. How to claim HB and CTB

The following applies to HB for rent and CTB (both Main CTB and second adult rebate). For HB help with rates in Northern Ireland, see 28 below.

Getting someone to claim for you – If you are incapable of managing your own affairs, an appointee can take over the responsibilities of claiming for you and dealing with any further matters relating to your claim. That person (who must be aged 18 or over) should write to your local authority to request approval to act as your appointee. Permission should not be withheld unreasonably.

Paper claims

If you are claiming employment and support allowance (ESA), income support, jobseeker's allowance (JSA) or pension credit, you will normally be sent a claim-form for HB and CTB, usually the HCTB1. A shorter version, the HBRR1 or 'rapid reclaim' form, will be used if you reclaim one of these benefits within 26 weeks of last receiving it. Complete the form and send it to your local authority.

If you are not claiming one of these benefits, you should ask your local authority for an HB/CTB claim-form, complete it and send it back to them within one month. Most (if not all) authorities have one combined form for claiming both HB and CTB. You can phone and ask for the form. If you cannot easily get the claim-form, write to your local authority:

give your name and address, say you wish to claim HB and/ or CTB, and date it. The authority should then send you the claim-form. Make sure you get it back to the authority within one month of the date it was sent to you.

Keeping a record – If possible keep a copy, or at least a record including the date, when you send the claim-form or any information you have been asked for. If you take in forms instead of posting them, get a receipt or written acknowledgement from whoever you give them to.

What do you need to send with the claim? – The claim-form asks you to provide various documents (eg your rent book in the case of a claim for HB). If you do not have all the information or documents requested, send the form back as soon as possible, and write on it that you will send the further information or documents as soon as you can. Explain any reasons for the delay. Sometimes your local authority may write with further questions. Always ensure your reply reaches them within one month of when they sent the letter to you.

If you do not keep to the one-month time limit for sending information to your local authority (or for sending in the form if you originally sent a letter), they can agree a delay of whatever period is *'reasonable'*. This will mean you are treated as having claimed within the time limits (see below).

HB Regs, reg 86(1) & CTB Regs, reg 72(1)

Telephone claims

You can now claim HB and CTB over the phone at the same time that you make a claim for ESA, income support, JSA or pension credit. The relevant DWP office will take your details over the phone and send you a statement of your circumstances to sign and return to them. They will then forward the details to your local authority.

Date of claim

If you make a claim for a means-tested benefit (income-related ESA, income support, income-based JSA or the guarantee credit of pension credit) that is successful, and your HB/CTB claim is received within one month of this claim, your HB/CTB will start from the same date as the means-tested benefit.

If you notify either the HB office or an authorised DWP office of your intention to claim HB/CTB, your date of claim will be that date if you return the form within one month. For HB only, the one-month time limit can be extended if the HB office thinks it is 'reasonable'.

If you have separated from your partner or your partner has died, and they were receiving HB/CTB, your claim for HB/CTB will start from the date of the change as long as you claim within one month.

In all other cases, your claim begins on the day your claim-form is received by the HB office. However, in all cases you may qualify for your claim for HB/CTB to be backdated under the 'good cause' rule (see 17 below).

HB Regs, reg 83(5) & CTB Regs, reg 69(5)

15. When your HB/CTB starts, changes and ends

Your first day of entitlement

HB and/or CTB usually start on the Monday after the date of your claim (this date is described above). Even if that date was itself a Monday, HB and/or CTB start the following Monday.

The exception is if the date of your HB/CTB claim is in the same benefit week (Monday to Sunday) as you moved into your home (or first became liable for rent or council tax for any other reason). In that case, your CTB starts on the exact day you became liable for council tax; your HB starts on the day your rent liability began (whether your rent is due daily, weekly or monthly).

HB Regs, reg 76 & CTB Regs, reg 64

When your benefit ends

You cease to be entitled to HB/CTB if a change in your circumstances means you no longer qualify. If you are moving into work and qualify for extended payments of HB/ CTB, you no longer need to reclaim HB/CTB (see Chapter 16(6) for details).

Change of circumstances

Although HB/CTB is awarded for an indefinite period, you still have a duty to notify your local authority about any change in circumstances that may affect your entitlement. The authority will advise you of changes you should notify.

HB Regs, reg 88(1) & CTB Regs, reg 74(1)

If a change in circumstances means you qualify for more HB/CTB, write to your local authority promptly. If you take more than one calendar month and you have no good reason for the delay, you will lose money because the increase will only be given to you from the Monday following the day your letter reached them. If you have a good reason for delaying more than a month, explain this in your letter, as otherwise it may not be taken into account. In all cases, 13 months is the absolute limit for notifying changes.

HB&CTB(D&A) Regs, regs 8(3) & 9

If a change in your circumstances means you qualify for less HB/CTB, write to the authority promptly, or you will probably be asked to repay any overpayment (see 19 below).

16. How your HB/CTB is paid

HB if you pay rent to the local authority

HB is awarded as a rebate towards your rent account, which is why it is also called a 'rent rebate'. In other words, the rent you have to pay will be reduced. This also applies if you pay rent to the Northern Ireland Housing Executive.

HB for everyone else

HB is usually paid straight into your bank account, although it can be paid by cheque, which is why it is also called a 'rent allowance'. Your local authority must take into account your *'reasonable needs and convenience'* in choosing the method of payment, so should not insist on paying you by crossed cheques if you do not have a bank account.

Your first payment of HB – Your authority should make your first payment within 14 days of receiving your properly completed claim or *'if that is not reasonably practicable, as soon as possible thereafter'*. This must be either the correct amount of your entitlement or, if that is not yet known, an estimated amount, known as a 'payment on account', which will be adjusted when the correct amount is known. You should not have to ask the authority for a prompt first payment, but if you do not get one, contact them and remind them of their duties. Authorities do not, however, have to make a prompt first payment if you have not supplied the information and documents they have requested, unless you can show that your failure to do so is 'reasonable' (eg if the delay in providing these is outside your control).

HB Regs, regs 91(3) & 93

Paying HB to your landlord – HB is paid to your landlord instead of to you if:

- you request or consent to this; *or*
- it is in your or your family's best interests; *or*
- you have left the dwelling with rent arrears (but payment will only be made up to the level of rent owing); *or*
- an amount of a means-tested benefit (income support, jobseeker's allowance, income-related employment and support allowance (ESA) or pension credit) is being paid direct to the landlord to cover rent arrears, or if you have at least eight weeks of rent arrears (six weeks in Northern Ireland).

In the first three cases, the authority does not have to agree. In the fourth case, they must pay the landlord (until the rent arrears reduce to below eight weeks) unless there are overriding reasons for refusing, or if the landlord is deemed not to be a 'fit and proper' person to receive payment. The authority can also choose to pay your first payment of HB to your landlord (regardless of whether you agree) if they consider this appropriate.

HB Regs, regs 95 & 96

Local housing allowance (LHA) cases – Payments of LHA are normally made direct to you. Payments can be made direct to the landlord if:

- the authority believes you are likely to have difficulty managing your affairs; *or*
- the authority considers it improbable that you will pay your rent; *or*
- for eight weeks, if the authority suspects that either of the above may apply and is considering this; *or*
- the authority has previously had to pay the landlord direct; *or*
- you have left the property and there are rent arrears of less than eight weeks.

The local authority must pay LHA direct to the landlord when you have rent arrears of at least eight weeks or when an amount of a means-tested benefit is being paid direct to the landlord to cover rent arrears.

HB Regs, regs 96(3A) & (3B)

Council tax benefit

CTB is awarded as a rebate towards council tax liability. In other words, your council tax bill will be reduced. If, however, at the end of the financial year (31 March) your authority owes you any CTB, you can ask for it to be paid to you by cheque. Otherwise, it is usually carried over and rebated against the new financial year's council tax bill.

17. Getting more benefit

Discretionary housing payments

Discretionary housing payments (DHPs) are technically not a kind of HB or CTB, but they are administered by the same authorities and can only be given to people who qualify for at least some HB or Main CTB.

The local authority can give you a DHP if you *'appear to [the] authority to require some further financial assistance... in order to meet housing costs'*. DHPs are discretionary (no one has a right to one) – as is the amount of DHP (if any) and the period it is granted for. The combined amount of your HB, CTB and DHP in any one week cannot usually exceed your 'eligible rent' (see 8 above) and 'eligible council tax' (see 13 above). However, a DHP can exceed the current amount of eligible rent in some circumstances, eg if you have rent arrears and the DHP covers the past period.

DHPs cannot be used if benefit has been reduced or suspended (eg for failure to attend a work-focused interview), or for any of the following:

- service charges (including support charges) that HB cannot meet (see 8 above);
- water and sewage charges;
- your rent liability if you qualify only for CTB;
- your council tax liability if you qualify only for HB, or only for second adult rebate.

In Northern Ireland, a DHP is paid only to claimants whose rent has been restricted and who seem to need further financial assistance. It is intended to meet only the shortfall between the rent being requested by a landlord and the restricted rent. It does not apply to the rate rebate scheme.

Most local authorities have a form on which to request a DHP. If your authority does not, write a letter instead. The authority may ask for detailed information about your circumstances and those of your household. Explain these fully, eg the authority could take into account your disability needs and the fact that you receive state benefits, such as disability living allowance, for these (even if the HB rules would normally ignore these). The availability of DHPs varies widely from authority to authority. The HB and CTB appeals system does not apply to DHPs, but you have the right to ask the authority to look again at its decision if you are dissatisfied. It is your duty to report changes in your circumstances that could affect the payment of a DHP.

The Discretionary Financial Assistance Regs

Getting your benefit backdated

If you are aged under 60, HB and CTB can be backdated for up to six months if you have continuous 'good cause' for the delay in claiming. If you are aged 60 or over (and not claiming income support or income-based jobseeker's allowance), HB and CTB can be backdated for up to three months without you having to show good cause.

HB Regs, reg 83(12), HB(SPC) Regs, reg 64(1), CTB Regs, reg 69(14) & CTB(SPC) Regs, reg 53(1ZA)

Good cause – This means some fact or facts which *'having regard to all the circumstances (including the claimant's state of health and the information which he had received and that which he might have obtained) would probably have caused a reasonable person of his age and experience to act (or fail to act) as the claimant did'*.

R(S)2/63(T)

For example, you may have good cause if you are ill and have no one to help you make the claim, or if you are unable to manage your own affairs and you don't have an appointee. Ignorance of the law on its own is not normally good cause unless there are exceptional circumstances (eg mental health or learning disabilities, educational limitations, youthfulness, language difficulties, or a combination of these and other factors). Generally, you are expected to make reasonable enquiries about your right to benefit. You will normally be able to show good cause if you ask the DWP or local authority for advice and then act on the basis of their wrong or misleading advice, or if you reasonably misunderstood the advice you were given.

Ex-gratia payments – If your claim was delayed for over three or six months and the delay was the local authority's fault, you can ask for an ex-gratia compensation payment to cover the period remaining after the maximum 3- or 6-month backdate.

18. Underpayments

If your local authority has awarded you less HB or CTB than they should have, due to official error, they must make up the difference. An *'official error'* means a mistake by the authority, Jobcentre Plus, Pension, Disability & Carers Service or HMRC. There is no limit to the period for which arrears may be paid in these cases.

However, if you were awarded less HB or CTB because you failed to tell the authority something, see 15 above.

HB&CTB(D&A) Regs, reg 4(2)

19. Overpayments

Overpayments are amounts of HB/CTB you were awarded but which you weren't entitled to – perhaps because you did not tell the local authority something you should have, or because the authority or Jobcentre Plus office made a mistake, or for some unavoidable reason. Different rules apply to different types of overpayment, as follows.

Overpayments of CTB due to a change in council tax liability – If you get a backdated reduction for disabilities or discount (see Chapter 21), and you were getting CTB, you will have been overpaid CTB. When the authority adjusts your council tax bill, it will adjust your CTB entitlement at the same time to recover the overpayment. Overpayments caused by such adjustments are always recoverable.

CTB Regs, regs 82 & 83

Overpayments of HB payments on account – If you were granted a payment on account (see 16 above) and it turned out to be greater than your actual entitlement to HB, the overpayment will be recovered from your future HB entitlement. If it turns out you were not entitled to any HB, the following rules apply.

HB Regs, reg 93(3)

Overpayments of HB or CTB due to official error – An 'official error' means a mistake, to which you did not contribute, by your local authority, Jobcentre Plus, Pension, Disability & Carers Service or HMRC.

An example of a mistake made by a Jobcentre Plus office that counts as official error is when they tell your local authority that you qualify for income-related employment and support allowance (ESA) when in fact you do not.

If your Jobcentre Plus office does not tell your local authority that you have come off income support, income-based jobseeker's allowance or income-related ESA (or started receiving any other benefit), this may count as an official error, but because the law says it is your duty to tell the authority about changes in circumstances that may affect benefit they should not be deemed as having caused the overpayment. If the error does not cause the overpayment it will be recoverable from you.

Your local authority must not recover an overpayment due to official error unless you (or someone acting for you, or the person who received the payment, eg your landlord if your HB is paid to them) could *'reasonably have been expected to realise that it was an overpayment'* at the time the payment or any notification about it was received. The authority should take into account what you (or the other person) personally could have been expected to realise.

HB Regs, reg 100(2)-(3) & CTB Regs, reg 83(2)-(3)

Overpayments due to a mistake about capital – An overpayment of more than 13 weeks of HB or CTB due to a mistake about capital may not be recoverable in full. There are 'diminishing capital' rules that treat the capital as gradually reducing (described in Chapter 59(6)).

All other overpayments – Any overpayment of HB or CTB not mentioned above may be recovered by your local authority. This includes overpayments due to a failure or mistake by you, and even overpayments that were unavoidable (such as overpayments due to a backdated pay rise or a backdated social security benefit).

HB Regs, reg 100(1) & CTB Regs, reg 83(1)

How much is the overpayment?

If you qualified for at least some HB or CTB during the period for which you were overpaid, your local authority should allow you to keep that (even if you didn't claim it or tell them everything you should have at the time). It should normally only recover the difference between what you were paid and what you should have been paid. If the authority does not do this, seek advice.

HB Regs, reg 104 & CTB Regs, reg 89

Discretion and hardship

Even if an overpayment is recoverable, your local authority can exercise its discretion not to recover it (eg if you can show that you would otherwise suffer hardship).

SSAA, S.75(1)

Notifications and appeals

In all cases, if your local authority decides to recover an overpayment, it must write notifying you of all the details and of your appeal rights. You can use the appeal procedure (see below) if you are dissatisfied with its decision.

How are overpayments recovered?

If an overpayment is recoverable, it can be recovered from you or your partner (as long as they caused the overpayment or, where recovery is by deductions from HB, you were a couple at the time of both the overpayment and the recovery) or (in most cases) the person who received the payment (eg your landlord) or the person who caused the overpayment. It can be recovered as follows:

- by reducing your future HB entitlement but not, in most cases, if you are a local authority or Northern Ireland Housing Executive (NIHE) tenant, by simply turning the amount into arrears of rent. The most the authority can recover in this way is £9.75 a week (although this can be increased in certain cases if you are working or receive a war widow's or war disablement pension or charitable or voluntary income, have committed fraud or have moved);
- by adding the amount back to your council tax account. Therefore, you will have more council tax to pay;
- if the above methods are not possible, by making deductions from almost any other social security benefit.

In all cases, you can agree to repay the overpayment in cash or by cheque, giro, etc. As a last resort, the authority can take action in the courts to recover an overpayment.

If an HB overpayment is recovered from your landlord, then (unless you rent your home from the local authority or NIHE), your landlord is legally allowed to treat the amount repaid as rent arrears due from you.

HB Regs, regs 101-102 & CTB Regs, regs 84-86

20. Decisions, revisions and appeals

The following rules apply to HB and CTB. For more detail, see Chapter 60.

Notice of decisions

Your local authority has a duty to send you a written notice about the decision it makes on your HB and/or CTB claim. If you do not qualify, the notice will say why not. If the authority makes further decisions during the course of your claim (eg about a change of circumstances or an overpayment), it must send you a written notice about that. In each case, it will also explain your right to get more information and to appeal.

If you want more information about how your entitlement to HB or CTB (or lack of it) was worked out, write to the authority and ask for a written statement. You can do this at any time (but if you are also thinking about asking the authority to revise its decision or lodging an appeal, bear in mind the time limits mentioned below). You can ask about specific things or ask for full details of how your claim was assessed. The authority should reply in writing within 14 days, or as soon as possible after that.

HB Regs, reg 90 & CTB Regs, reg 76

Exceptions – In certain circumstances, the authority does not have to make a decision, and the tribunal does not have to deal with an appeal. This is called 'staying' a decision or appeal. It arises when a test case is pending, the result of which could affect your case (see Chapter 60(6)).

Asking the authority to revise their decision

You have the right to ask your local authority to revise its decision on almost any matter relating to your HB and/or CTB claim (eg, how much you qualify for, whether you should have to repay an overpayment, etc). If your letter arrives within the 'dispute period' (see below), the authority must reconsider its decision, taking account of what you say. It should give you a written notice saying whether it is revising or sticking to its original decision, and giving the reasons. If you are requesting a revision of a maximum rent fixed by the rent officer (see 9 above), it will take longer because it will be sent to the rent officer to consider.

HB&CTB(D&A) Regs, reg 4

Appeals to a tribunal
Either instead of, or after, asking your local authority to revise a decision (see above), you can appeal to an independent appeal tribunal; see Chapter 60 for details.
Exceptions – There is no right of appeal to a tribunal about:

- most administrative decisions about HB/CTB claims and payments, although you can appeal to a tribunal about when HB/CTB should begin and whether your claim should be backdated;
- whether your local authority should run a local scheme for war widow/widower's pensions and war disablement pensions (see Chapter 26(6) under 'Benefits that are partly disregarded');
- your maximum rent if the rent officer or Northern Ireland Housing Executive (NIHE) fixed one for your home (see 9 above);
- discretionary housing payments (see 17 above).

In each case, however, you can ask the local authority to revise its decision.
HB&CTB(D&A) Regs, reg 16 and Sch

The dispute period
Whether you are asking the local authority to revise a decision or asking for an appeal, your letter should reach the authority within one calendar month of the day it sent the decision notice. If you are asking for a revision of the decision and have asked for a written statement, the time the authority took to deal with that is ignored when calculating the month. If you are appealing the decision, you have 14 days from the date the written statement is sent to ask for an appeal.

Your local authority (or the tribunal, in the case of an appeal) can agree to extend the one-month time limit if the delay was caused by special circumstances or, if you are appealing, the tribunal judge agrees (see Chapter 60(3) and (7)). If this is the case, explain what the special circumstances are when you write, otherwise they may not be taken into account. In all cases, 13 months is the absolute limit for asking for the decision to be changed.
HB&CTB(D&A) Regs, regs 4(1), 5, & 19

The Ombudsman
You can make a complaint to the Ombudsman if you feel the local authority or NIHE administered your claim unfairly or caused unreasonable delays. This is separate from the appeal process. See Chapter 62(5).

21. How much benefit?

We explain below how to work out entitlement to HB and Main CTB. We give the rules if you are on a means tested benefit (income support (IS), income-based jobseeker's allowance (JSA), income-related employment and support allowance (ESA) or the guarantee credit of pension credit) first, then the rules for if you are not. For how to work out second adult rebate, see 27 below. For how to calculate HB for rates in Northern Ireland, see 28 below.

If you are on a means-tested benefit
If you (or your partner) are on a means-tested benefit, there are a few simple steps to follow.
Step 1: Work out your eligible rent and council tax
HB is worked out on your weekly eligible rent. This can be less than your actual rent (see 8 and 9 above). Main CTB is worked out on your weekly eligible council tax (see 13 above).
Step 2: Deduct amounts for non-dependants
If you have one or more non-dependants in your home, your HB and Main CTB are reduced by flat-rate amounts (though there are exceptions to this). For who counts as a non-dependant and the other details, see 22 below.
Step 3: Amount of benefit per week
HB equals your weekly eligible rent minus any amounts for non-dependants. Main CTB equals your weekly eligible council tax minus any amounts for non-dependants.

Examples
HB: If your weekly eligible rent is £90 and you have no non-dependants, the weekly amount of your HB is £90. But if you have one non-dependant, and a flat-rate deduction of £47.75 applies, the weekly amount of your HB is £42.25.
Main CTB: If your weekly eligible council tax is £15 and you have no non-dependants, the weekly amount of your Main CTB is £15. But if you have one non-dependant and a flat-rate deduction of £6.95 applies, the weekly amount of your Main CTB is £8.05.

If you are not on a means-tested benefit
If you (or your partner) are not on a means-tested benefit, there are several steps to follow.
Step 1: Your capital
If your capital (including your partner's) is more than £16,000 you cannot get HB or Main CTB. Not all capital counts. For how to work out your capital, see 23 and 26 below. Even if your capital is over £16,000, you may be able to get second adult rebate (see 27 below).
Step 2: Your eligible rent and council tax
HB is worked out on your weekly eligible rent. This can be less than your actual rent (see 8 and 9 above). Main CTB is worked out on your weekly eligible council tax (see 13 above).
Step 3: Deduct amounts for non-dependants
If you have one or more non-dependants in your home, your HB and Main CTB are reduced by flat-rate amounts (though there are exceptions to this). For who counts as a non-dependant and the other details, see 22 below.
Step 4: Work out your weekly income
This includes your (and your partner's) income from some, but not all, sources. For how to work out your weekly income, see 24 and 26 below.
Step 5: Work out your applicable amount
This figure represents your weekly living needs. For how to work out your applicable amount, see 25 and 26 below and Chapter 24.
Step 6: Have you got 'excess income'?
If your income is *less* than, or equal to, your applicable amount, you do not have 'excess income'. See Step 7.

If your income is *greater* than your applicable amount, you have 'excess income'. The amount of the excess income is the difference between your income and your applicable amount. See Step 8.
Step 7: Amount of benefit per week if you do not have excess income
HB equals your weekly eligible rent less any amounts for non-dependants.

Main CTB equals your weekly eligible council tax less any amounts for non-dependants.

This is exactly the same as for people who are on a means-tested benefit. For examples, see above.
Step 8: Amount of benefit per week if you have 'excess income'
HB equals your weekly eligible rent less any amounts for non-dependants and less 65% of your excess income. If the result is less than 50p you will not be awarded HB. See below, 'Points to note'.

Main CTB equals your weekly eligible council tax less any amounts for non-dependants and less 20% of your excess income. You might get more using the second adult rebate calculation (see 27 below).

For other points to note, see below.

Examples if you have excess income

HB: If your weekly eligible rent is £90, you have no non-dependants and you have excess income of £20, the weekly amount of your HB is:

Eligible rent	£90.00
Less 65% of £20 excess income	£13.00
Weekly HB	*£77.00*

But if you have one non-dependant and a flat-rate deduction of £7.40 applies, the weekly amount of your HB is:

Eligible rent	£90.00
Less non-dependant deduction	£7.40
Less 65% of £20 excess income	£13.00
Weekly HB	*£69.60*

Main CTB: If your weekly eligible council tax is £15, you have no non-dependants and you have excess income of £20, the weekly amount of your Main CTB is:

Eligible council tax	£15.00
Less 20% of £20 excess income	£4.00
Weekly Main CTB	*£11.00*

But if you have one non-dependant and a flat-rate deduction of £2.30 applies, your weekly Main CTB is:

Eligible council tax	£15.00
Less non-dependant deduction	£2.30
Less 20% of £20 excess income	£4.00
Weekly Main CTB	*£8.70*

Points to note

The percentages (65% in HB and 20% in Main CTB) are also called 'tapers' because of how they work: as your excess income goes up, your benefit goes down. You can have so much excess income that you do not qualify for any benefit. The amount(s) of your non-dependant deduction(s) can also mean you do not qualify for any benefit.

HB Regs, reg 71 & CTB Regs, reg 59

The minimum HB award is 50p a week. So if the calculation comes out at less than 50p, you will not get any HB. There is no minimum award of Main CTB: you can get as little as 1p a year.

HB Regs, Reg 75

22. Non-dependants

Deductions are made from your HB and/or Main CTB if you have one or more non-dependants, even if you are on income-related employment and support allowance (ESA), income support (IS), income-based jobseeker's allowance (JSA) or the guarantee credit of pension credit. The law assumes they will contribute towards your rent and/or council tax, whether or not they do. A deduction cannot be cancelled on the grounds that your non-dependant pays you nothing. But there are cases when no deduction can be made.

HB Regs, reg 74 & CTB Regs, reg 58

Who is a non-dependant?

A non-dependant is someone who normally lives in your home on a non-commercial basis – usually an adult son, daughter, friend or relative. None of the following are your non-dependants (so there is no deduction for any of them):

- your *'family'* (see 25 below). For example, an 18-year-old who is still included in your family is not your non-dependant;
- foster children;
- someone with whom you share just a bathroom, toilet, communal area (or in sheltered accommodation, a communal room);
- your joint occupier(s), tenant(s) or sub-tenant(s), resident landlord (and members of their households);
- your or your partner's carer if they are provided by a charity or voluntary organisation that charges you for this (even if someone else pays the charge for you).

Almost anyone else who lives with you is your non-dependant.

HB Regs & CTB Regs, reg 3

No non-dependant deduction

Your (or your partner's) circumstances – There is no deduction for any non-dependants you have (no matter how many) if you or your partner:

- are registered as blind or ceased to be registered within the last 28 weeks; *or*
- get the care component of disability living allowance (DLA; any rate) or attendance allowance (AA) or constant attendance allowance.

Your non-dependant's circumstances – There is no deduction for a non-dependant if they:

- are under 18; *or*
- in calculating HB, are under 25 and on IS, income-based JSA or assessment-phase income-related ESA; *or*
- are on pension credit; *or*
- in calculating Main CTB, are any age and on income-related ESA, IS or income-based JSA; *or*
- get a Work-Based Learning for Young People training allowance; *or*
- have been in an NHS hospital for over 52 weeks; *or*
- are detained in prison or a similar institution; *or*
- have their normal home elsewhere; *or*
- are a full-time student (see Chapter 40(2)) – but in calculating HB only, there is a deduction in the summer vacation if they take up remunerative work (see below), unless they (or their partner) are 65 or over; *or*
- in calculating Main CTB only, are in any of the groups who are 'disregarded' for the purposes of the council tax discount rules (see Box H.5).

HB Regs, reg 74(6)-(8) & (10) and CTB Regs, reg 58(6)-(8)

The amounts of the deductions

- ❑ **Non-dependants aged 25 or over on income-related ESA, IS or income-based JSA** – The weekly amount in calculating HB is £7.40, but there is no deduction in calculating Main CTB.
- ❑ **Non-dependants on pension credit** – No deduction.
- ❑ **Other non-dependants not in remunerative work** – Regardless of the level of your non-dependant's income, the weekly amount is £7.40 in HB and £2.30 in Main CTB.
- ❑ **Non-dependants in remunerative work (excluding those on pension credit** – The weekly amount depends on the level of your non-dependant's weekly gross income.

Weekly gross income	HB	Main CTB
£382 or more	£47.75	£6.95
£306 to £381.99	£43.50	£5.80
£231 to £ 305.99	£38.20	£4.60
£178 to £230.99	£23.35	£4.60
£120 to £177.99	£17.00	£2.30
Under £120	£7.40	£2.30

HB Regs, reg 74(1)-(2) & CTB Regs, reg 58(1)-(2)

If you cannot provide evidence of your non-dependant's gross income (and they are in remunerative work and not receiving pension credit, your local authority must consider all the circumstances of the case before making the highest of the above deductions. If you later provide evidence showing that the deduction should have been lower, the authority should award you arrears of HB/Main CTB as you have been underpaid (but act quickly – see 15 above).

A B C D E F G H I J K L M N O P Q R S T U

Which non-dependants are in remunerative work?
'Remunerative work' means work that averages 16 or more hours a week. If your non-dependant is on maternity, paternity, adoption or sick leave, they do not count as being in remunerative work (even if paid full pay or statutory maternity, paternity, adoption or sick pay). If your non-dependant gets income-related ESA, IS or income-based JSA for more than three days in any benefit week (Monday to Sunday) they do not count as being in remunerative work.

HB Regs & CTB Regs, reg 6

Your non-dependant's gross income
Your non-dependant's income is relevant if they are in remunerative work. It is assessed gross, which, in the case of earnings, means before tax, national insurance and other deductions are made. All other income is counted, except DLA, AA, constant attendance allowance and payments from the Macfarlane Trusts, the Eileen Trust, the Independent Living Fund and the Fund. If your non-dependant has capital, only the interest is counted as gross income. If your non-dependant is in a couple, add their partner's gross income (but see below).

HB Regs, reg 74(9) & CTB Regs, reg 58(9)

Other points about non-dependants
You get a deduction for each non-dependant you have (apart from those for whom no deduction applies). But if you have non-dependants who are a couple, you get only one deduction for the two of them. This is the higher figure of the two amounts that would have applied to them if each was single and each had the income of both.

If you are a joint occupier (see 5 and 12 above), and your non-dependant is also a non-dependant of the other joint occupier(s), the deduction is shared between you and the other joint occupier(s).

HB Regs, reg 74(3)-(5) & CTB Regs, reg 58(3)-(4)

Concession if you are aged 65 or over
If you or your partner are 65 or over, special non-dependant deduction rules apply. If a non-dependant comes to live with you, their income will be ignored for HB/CTB purposes for 26 weeks. If you already have a non-dependant living with you and their circumstances or income change (meaning a higher deduction applies), the local authority will not increase the amount of the deduction for a 26-week period. If changes occur more than once, the 26-week period runs from the date of the first change. If your non-dependant's income decreases, the authority should reduce the deduction immediately if appropriate.

HB(SPC) Regs, reg 59(10)-(12) & CTB(SPC) Regs, reg 50(10)-(12)

23. Capital

Your local authority needs to assess your capital if you are not on income-related employment and support allowance, income support, income-based jobseeker's allowance or the guarantee credit of pension credit. If you are in a couple, your partner's capital is included with yours. For how capital is assessed for HB and Main CTB purposes, see Chapter 27.

There are different capital rules for claimants aged 60 or over that are intended to reflect the more generous provisions of pension credit (see 26 below).

If your capital is over £16,000, you cannot get HB or Main CTB (but you may still get second adult rebate – see 27 below). If your capital is £6,000 or less, it is ignored in assessing your HB/CTB. If it is a higher figure (but not over £16,000), you are treated as having income – known as 'tariff income' (see Chapter 27(4). In rare cases, some people in care homes are entitled to HB (see Chapter 33(3)), and the first £10,000 (instead of £6,000) of their capital is ignored.

If a child in your family has capital of their own, it is disregarded.

24. Income

Your local authority needs to assess your income if you are not on income-related employment and support allowance, income support, income-based jobseeker's allowance or the guarantee credit of pension credit. If you are in a couple, your partner's income is included with yours. For how income is assessed for HB and Main CTB purposes, see Chapter 26. Income rules for claimants aged 60 or over are intended to reflect the more generous provisions of pension credit and differ in some respects (see 26 below).

If your income is greater than your applicable amount, this affects the amount of HB and Main CTB you get (see 21 above). It does not affect second adult rebate (see 27 below).

25. Applicable amounts

Your local authority needs to assess your applicable amount if you are not on income-related employment and support allowance (ESA), income support (IS), income-based jobseeker's allowance (JSA) or the guarantee credit of pension credit. An 'applicable amount' is a figure set by Parliament that is intended to reflect your weekly living needs and those of your family. If you (or your partner) are aged 60 or over, see 26 below. If you are under 60, your applicable amount is made up of:

- **personal allowances** – you get one or more of these for various members of your family, including children; *plus*
- **premiums** – many, but not all, people get one or more premiums to take account of family responsibilities, age, disabilities and responsibilities as a carer; *plus*
- **additional components** – which apply only if you are entitled to main-phase ESA.

HB Regs, reg 22 & CTB Regs, reg 12

You must satisfy conditions for each part of the applicable amount. You can ask for a written statement from the authority about what premiums you have been awarded and why. If you think any have been missed, you should ask for a revision or lodge an appeal (see 20 above).

Your family
Applicable amounts are based on the circumstances of your 'family'. 'Family' is used in a technical sense in HB/CTB. It means:

- you (the claimant); *and*
- your partner. This can be your spouse or civil partner, as long as you are living in the same household. It can also include your partner if you are unmarried or have not entered into a civil partnership if you are effectively living together as husband and wife or civil partners; *and*
- any dependent child(ren) or young people who are members of your household, and are under the age of 16 (or under the age of 20 if they are a 'qualifying young person' for child benefit purposes – see Chapter 38(1)). The definition of a dependent child includes your natural and adopted children and other children for whom you are responsible (eg a grandchild). Foster children are not usually included. If a child who is normally in local authority care spends time with you at home, your local authority can either include that child or not as a member of your family for the benefit week(s) (Monday to Sunday) when the child stays with you. This is an 'all or nothing' rule: the authority cannot give you just part of a personal allowance or family premium.

HB Regs, regs 19-21 & CTB Regs, regs 9-11

Personal allowances
Lower personal allowances apply to people under 18, unless the claimant is entitled to main-phase ESA.

Allowances for children, although removed from IS and JSA following the introduction of child tax credit, have been retained in the applicable amounts for HB and CTB. They are paid for each dependent child or qualifying young person under the age of 20 for whom you are responsible (see above).

Personal allowances		per week
Single person	aged 25 or over	£64.30
	aged 16-24	£50.95
	entitled to main-phase ESA*	£64.30
Lone parent	aged 18 or over	£64.30
	aged under 18	£50.95
	entitled to main-phase ESA	£64.30
Couple	one or both aged 18 or over	£100.95
	both under 18	£76.90
	entitled to main-phase ESA	£100.95
Dependent child		£56.11

HB Regs, Sch 3, Part 1 & CTB Regs, Sch 1, Part 1

*Includes claimants receiving national insurance credits only.

The premiums

There are six premiums, each with specific qualifying conditions (see Chapter 24). Unless otherwise specified in that chapter, each premium to which you are entitled is added to the total of your applicable amount.

Premiums		per week
Family	ordinary rate	£17.30
	lone parent rate	£22.20
	child under one	£10.50
Disability	single	£27.50
	couple	£39.15
Disabled child		£51.24
Severe disability	single	£52.85
	couple (one qualifies)	£52.85
	couple (both qualify)	£105.70
Enhanced disability	single	£13.40
	couple	£19.30
	child	£20.65
Carer		£29.50

Additional components

If you are entitled to main-phase ESA, you are entitled to an additional component depending on whether you are placed in the work-related activity group or the support group (see Chapter 9(6) and (7)).

Components	per week
Work-related activity component	£25.50
Support component	£30.85

26. Rules for people in receipt of pension credit or aged 60 or over

The rules for claimants aged 60 or over are different and intended to reflect the more generous provisions of pension credit (see Chapter 42). The main changes are listed below.

Your applicable amount

Your personal allowance will be based on the 'standard minimum guarantee' and, if you or your partner are aged 65 or over, the 'maximum savings credit' (see Chapter 42(3) and (4)). For a single claimant the personal allowance is £130 or £150.40 if you are aged 65 or over. For a couple it is £198.45 or £225.50 if either of you is 65 or over.

The following extra sums can be included in your applicable amount following the usual HB/CTB rules:

- personal allowances for dependent children and young people (see 25 above);
- family premium (see Chapter 24(7));
- severe disability premium (see Chapter 24(3));
- enhanced disability premium (for any qualifying dependent child or young person, not for yourself or your partner) (see Chapter 24(4));
- disabled child premium (see Chapter 24(8));
- carer premium (see Chapter 24(6)).

Income and capital

There are different rules about how income and capital affect the amount of HB/CTB you get, depending on whether or not you receive pension credit and which elements of it are in payment.

Guarantee credit – If you or your partner receive the guarantee credit of pension credit, the whole of your capital and income will be disregarded and you will receive full HB/CTB. This applies even if your capital exceeds the usual HB/CTB limit of £16,000. Since there is no capital limit for pension credit, it is possible to receive the guarantee credit even though your savings would exceed the HB/CTB limit.

HB(SPC) Regs, reg 26 & CTB(SPC) Regs, reg 16

Savings credit only – If you or your partner are aged 65 or over and receive the savings credit but not the guarantee credit of pension credit and do not have more than £16,000 capital, then the local authority will use the assessment of your income and capital that the DWP used to calculate your savings credit (see Chapter 42(4)). The authority will then adjust this figure to reflect the following special rules.

- ❑ Any of your partner's income or capital that was not taken into account in the pension credit calculation will be taken into account.
- ❑ Any income of a non-dependant that can be treated as yours under HB/CTB regulations will be included.
- ❑ Any pension credit savings credit will be taken into account.
- ❑ The higher HB/CTB disregards of lone parent's earnings and maintenance payments and the '16- or 30-hours' disregard (see Chapter 26(5)) will apply.
- ❑ The normal HB/CTB disregard of childcare costs will apply (see Chapter 26(5)).
- ❑ Any discretionary disregard of war pensions allowed by your local authority will be applied to your income.

HB(SPC) Regs, reg 27 & CTB(SPC) Regs, reg 17

No pension credit payable – If you or your partner are aged 60 or over but do not receive pension credit (savings credit or guarantee credit), your income and capital will be assessed by the local authority in much the same way as it is for pension credit (see Chapter 42(5) and (6)).

HB(SPC) Regs, reg 28 & CTB (SPC) Regs, reg 18

27. Second adult rebate

This type of CTB is known in the law as *'alternative maximum council tax benefit'*, but we use the more common term 'second adult rebate'. You can get it regardless of how much income and capital you have. You cannot get second adult rebate and Main CTB at the same time, but if you satisfy the rules for both, your local authority will grant whichever is the higher amount.

CTB Regs, regs 62-63 & Sch 2

Claims

You should not have to make a separate claim for second adult rebate: your claim for CTB should be treated as a claim for both Main CTB and second adult rebate. However, some local authorities have a special claim-form to use if you want to be considered for second adult rebate only (eg if your capital is considerably more than £16,000).

Who is eligible?

You can get second adult rebate if you satisfy all the following conditions:

- you are not excluded from getting CTB by the rule about 'persons from abroad' (see 11 above);
- you are liable to pay council tax on your normal home (see Chapter 21(5));
- there are one or more 'second adult(s)' in your home (see below);
- the second adult(s) is on income-related employment and support allowance (ESA), income support, pension credit or income-based jobseeker's allowance (JSA), or has a fairly low income (see below);
- you meet conditions relating to certain types of households (see below);
- your entitlement to second adult rebate is greater than any entitlement to Main CTB (see below, 'The better buy');
- you claim and provide the information requested (see 14 above).

Note: If you are a student, you can get second adult rebate even if you are excluded from getting Main CTB (see Chapter 40(2)).

Who is a 'second adult'?

You must have at least one 'second adult' in your home to get second adult rebate. A person is a 'second adult' if they are:

- aged 18 or over; *and*
- your non-dependant (see 22 above); *and*
- not in any of the groups who are 'disregarded' for the purposes of the council tax discount rules. Those groups are listed in Box H.5.

If your non-dependant is in one of the 'disregarded' groups, this should have been taken into account in considering whether you qualify for a council tax discount (see Chapter 21(9)); this is why you can only get second adult rebate if you have a non-dependant who is not 'disregarded'. (The note on carers under 'Extra rules' below gives the one exception to the above definition of a 'second adult'.)

Extra rules for certain types of households

Couples – Either you or your partner (or both of you) must be 'disregarded' for the purposes of the council tax discount rules (see Box H.5). If you are jointly liable for council tax with someone other than just your partner, see below.

Jointly liable for council tax – If you and others are jointly liable for council tax, either all, or all but one, of the jointly liable people must be 'disregarded' for the purposes of the council tax discount rules. The amount of second adult rebate is worked out for the whole dwelling and you will get a share, which is calculated by dividing the total amount by the number of jointly liable people.

All claimants who have tenants, sub-tenants or boarders in their home – In addition to the rules mentioned above, there is an overriding rule that you cannot get second adult rebate if you personally receive rent from a tenant, sub-tenant or boarder aged 18 or over in your home.

Carers – Many carers are 'disregarded' for the purposes of the council tax discount rules so they cannot be second adults. But if you or your partner have a carer who is not 'disregarded' and who is provided by a charity or voluntary organisation that charges you for this, the carer is a 'second adult'. This is the only case in which someone who is not a non-dependant can be a 'second adult'.

Students – A 100% rebate is sometimes payable, see below.

Amount of second adult rebate

The amount of your second adult rebate depends only on the income of your second adult(s).

- ❑ If you have just one second adult, you get the highest amount of second adult rebate if they are on a relevant means-tested benefit (income-related ESA, income support, pension credit or income-based JSA). In all other cases, the amount depends on their gross income.
- ❑ If you have two or more second adults, you get the highest amount of second adult rebate if they are all on a relevant means-tested benefit. In all other cases, the amount depends on the combined gross income of all of them apart from those on a relevant means-tested benefit.
- ❑ If you are a student and share the house only with other students or people on a relevant means-tested benefit, the rebate is payable at 100%.

Income of second adult(s)	rebate
Second adult(s) is on a relevant means-tested benefit	25%
Weekly gross income of second adult(s) is:	
Under £175	15%
£175 to 227.99	7½%
£228 or more	nil

Your second adult rebate is shown in the above table as a percentage of your eligible council tax. For example, if the 15% figure applies to you, your second adult rebate is 15% of your eligible council tax – ie your bill is cut by 15%.

Your eligible council tax – For second adult rebate purposes, your eligible council tax is the same as for Main CTB purposes (see 13 above).

Exceptions if you also qualify for a discount – There is one rule that applies only for second adult rebate (not Main CTB) and only if you qualify for a council tax discount (see Chapter 21(9)). If this applies to you, your eligible council tax is worked out as though you did not get that discount. (You do not lose the discount: it is ignored only for the purposes of calculating your second adult rebate.) The following example may explain this.

Example: Mr Young owns his home. He is 'severely mentally impaired'. He has savings over £16,000 and so cannot get Main CTB. His adult son lives with him (but does not provide personal care). His son works and has a gross income of £110 a week. The home falls in council tax band D: this year the full council tax for band D in his area is £800.

Mr Young asks for a council tax discount. His local authority agrees he is a 'disregarded person' (see Box H.5, Chapter 21), but his son is not. So Mr Young qualifies for a 25% council tax discount (see Chapter 21(9)), which is £200 a year.

Mr Young also claims second adult rebate. The authority agrees that he qualifies for second adult rebate: his son is the 'second adult'. Based on his son's gross income, the amount of the second adult rebate is 15% of his eligible council tax. This means 15% of his council tax before the discount is awarded, in other words 15% of £800. This is £120 a year.

Mr Young's council tax reduction:	per year	per week
Total council tax bill	£800	£15.34
Less 25% discount	£200	£3.84
Less 15% second adult rebate	£120	£2.30
Amount of council tax due £480		*£9.20*

Your second adult's gross income

The second adult's income is relevant whether or not they are in remunerative work (but not if they are on income-

H.3 For more information

Your local Citizens Advice Bureau has detailed information on housing benefit, council tax benefit and council tax rules and should be able to advise you. If you want to look at the law, see CPAG's *Housing Benefit and Council Tax Benefit Legislation.* For further information see the *Guide to Housing Benefit and Council Tax Benefit* and other publications listed in Chapter 63.

related ESA, IS, pension credit or income-based JSA). It is assessed gross, which, in the case of earnings, means before tax, national insurance and other deductions are made. All other income is counted, except disability living allowance, attendance allowance, constant attendance allowance and payments from the Macfarlane Trusts, the Eileen Trust, the Independent Living Fund and the Fund. If the second adult has capital, only the actual interest is counted as gross income. If they are in a couple, add in their partner's gross income (even if the partner is not classified as a second adult).

The 'better buy'

If you qualify for both second adult rebate and Main CTB, there is one final step, often known as a 'better buy' calculation. Because you cannot get both Main CTB and second adult rebate at the same time, you will get the one that is worth most. You should get a full notification explaining this if it applies to you, and can ask for a written statement if you want more information (see 20 above).

28. Rate rebates in Northern Ireland

Rates are payable on domestic properties in Northern Ireland: there is no council tax. You can get help through HB towards the rates you are liable to pay on your normal home – whether you pay rent for your home (in which case you can get a rate rebate as well as HB for your rent) or whether you own your home (in which case you can get only a rate rebate).

The conditions for getting a rate rebate are similar to those for getting HB for rent, described at the start of this chapter. The method of claiming a rate rebate is also similar to that for HB for rent (see 14 above). Your rate rebate is awarded towards your rates liability.

If you rent from a private landlord or housing association, and your landlord (not you) pays the rates, the amount of your rate rebate is usually paid to you, along with your HB for rent, in a cheque, giro, etc. Recoverable overpayments may be recovered by adding the amount back to your rates bill. Other rules (eg about appeals) are the same as the rules about HB for rent (see 20 above).

Amount of rebate

If you (or your partner) are on income-related employment and support allowance (ESA), income support, income-based jobseeker's allowance (JSA) or the guarantee credit of pension credit, your rate rebate equals:

- the weekly amount of your rates liability;
- less any amount for non-dependants.

The amounts for non-dependants are the same as the figures used in England and Wales for CTB (see 22 above).

If you (or your partner) are not on income-related ESA, income support, income-based JSA or pension credit (guarantee credit), your rate rebate equals:

- the weekly amount of your rates liability;
- less any amount for non-dependants;
- less 20% of your excess income.

The amounts for non-dependants are the same as for CTB (see 22 above). For whether you have excess income, see 21 above.

Housing Benefit Regs (Northern Ireland)

21 Council tax

1. What is council tax?

Council tax is a domestic property-based tax paid to the local authority to help pay for the services it provides. It applies only in England, Scotland and Wales. Domestic rates are payable in Northern Ireland (see Chapter 20(28)).

2. Your dwelling

Council tax is only charged on domestic properties or 'dwellings'. A 'dwelling' is a self-contained unit of living accommodation, such as a house, flat, bungalow, houseboat or mobile home. It does not matter whether the dwelling is owned or rented. One council tax bill is due on each dwelling, unless it is exempt (see 4 below). If a property is divided into self-contained units (eg flats), each unit is a separate dwelling and gets a separate bill (unless exempt). If a property contains non-self-contained units (eg a house with a number of rooms with different people in each, but they all share some accommodation) the property is one dwelling and gets one bill (unless exempt). A self-contained unit is defined as *'a building or part of a building which has been constructed or adapted for use as separate living accommodation'*. If a property contains living and business accommodation, council tax is due for the domestic part (unless exempt) and the business part is subject to non-domestic rates.

Council Tax (Chargeable Dwellings) Order

3. How much council tax?

Council tax bands

Every property in each local authority area is placed into a valuation band, labelled from A (the lowest) to H (the highest) (or A to I in Wales), depending on its value. The higher the band, the more council tax you are liable to pay.

Values – The value of a dwelling does not relate to its current market value. In England and Scotland, it is based on April 1991 property values and on several other assumptions, eg that it is in a reasonable state of repair. In Wales, it is based on April 2003 property values.

In England and Wales, dwellings are valued by the Valuation Office Agency (VOA), and in Scotland by the local assessor. (The VOA or local assessor also decides what counts as a dwelling and how many dwellings there are in a property.)

LGFA, Ss.5(2)-(3) & 74(2)

Challenges and appeals

You have the right to challenge the valuation of your dwelling if within six months you have become newly liable for council tax there (eg through moving) or if there has been a material reduction in its value (eg through partial demolition or its adaptation for use by a disabled person). You can also ask for a change if part of the property begins to be used for business purposes. If the VOA or local assessor does not agree to the change an appeal can be made to the independent Valuation Tribunal (England and Wales) or Valuation Appeal Committee (Scotland). An appeal must be made within three months of receiving the decision.

You can also appeal within six months of a successful challenge on a comparable dwelling (eg another property on the same street or on a new estate) if this suggests that the value of your own property should be changed.

In other circumstances, you can ask the VOA or local assessor to reconsider the band for your dwelling and, if it is wrong, they may alter it. But if they do not agree, you do not have the right of appeal.

4. Exempt dwellings

If your home is an exempt dwelling, no council tax is due on it. Most exemptions are for unoccupied dwellings. The main conditions for exemptions are given in Box H.4.

Getting an exemption, and backdating – If your local authority has not awarded an exemption you can ask for one. The authority may have a standard form you can fill in. An exemption can be backdated to the date it should have first applied. There is no time limit and no need to show 'good cause' for applying late but you will need to produce evidence that the exemption has applied throughout the period.

Appeals – Appeals about whether a dwelling is exempt go first to your local authority. There is no time limit for lodging the appeal. If this is refused you can make a further appeal, to the Valuation Tribunal (England and Wales) or Valuation Appeal Committee (Scotland), within two months of receiving the decision.

5. Who is liable to pay?

Unless a dwelling is exempt, someone will be liable to pay council tax on it. This usually depends on who is *'resident'* there (see 6 below). The rules for the dwelling in which you are resident are given below. If you own or rent a dwelling that has no residents, you are usually liable for council tax there (whether or not you are also liable on the dwelling in which you are resident).

Backdating – If you were liable for council tax in the past but were not billed, a bill can be backdated. There is no time limit, but local authorities must issue bills as soon as is reasonably practicable.

Appeals – Appeals about who is liable for council tax go first to your local authority. There is no time limit for lodging the appeal. If this is refused you can make a further appeal, to the Valuation Tribunal (England and Wales) or Valuation Appeal Committee (Scotland), within two months of receiving the decision.

General rules for the dwelling in which you reside

The following rules apply to the dwelling in which you are 'resident' (see 6). A partner as referred to below includes a partner of the same sex.

If you own it – You are liable for council tax. Your partner, if resident with you, is jointly liable with you (even if not a joint owner). Any other joint owners resident with you are also jointly liable.

If you rent it and do not have a resident landlord – You are liable for council tax. Your partner, if resident with you, is jointly liable with you (even if not included on the letting agreement). Any other residents who rent it on the same letting agreement are also jointly liable.

If you rent from a resident landlord – Your landlord is liable.

If you rent non-self-contained accommodation and/or any others who rent it have separate letting agreements – Your landlord is liable, even if they are not resident there.

If it is a care home or (in most cases) a hostel – The landlord is liable.

If you are an asylum seeker receiving asylum support (other than temporary support) from either the National Asylum Support Service or your local authority – The landlord is liable.

LGFA, Ss.6, 8, 75 & 76

Special cases

If you and any other occupiers are *'severely mentally impaired'* (see Box H.5) or are students, the dwelling in which you are resident is exempt (see Box H.4). If anyone else lives with you, including carers, the property will not be exempt, but you may be eligible for a discount (see 9 below).

If you are under 18 you are not liable for council tax on any dwelling in which you are resident. Other resident(s)

H.4 Summary of council tax exemptions for dwellings

Note: Authorities are required to take reasonable steps to check whether any discounts apply before deciding on the chargeable amount.

❑ **A substantially unfurnished, unoccupied dwelling is exempt if:**

- structural or major repair works are needed, are in hand, or have been completed recently (for up to 12 months in total); *or*
- it is unoccupied for any other reason (which could be that it has just been built), and has been for less than six months.

❑ **An unoccupied dwelling (whether furnished or not) can be exempt if it is:**

- left empty by persons in prison or a similar institution;
- left empty by persons now resident in a hospital, a care home or a hostel where personal care is provided;
- left empty by persons now resident elsewhere for the purpose of receiving or providing personal care due to old age, disablement, illness, past or present alcohol or drug dependence, or past or present mental disorder;
- left empty by deceased persons where probate or letters of administration have not been granted, or less than six months have passed since the granting of probate or letters of administration;
- the responsibility of a bankrupt's trustees;
- to be occupied by ministers of religion; *or*
- a pitch or mooring that is not occupied by a caravan or boat.

❑ **A dwelling is also exempt if it is:**

- wholly occupied by a person (or persons) who is *'severely mentally impaired'* (see Box H.5) and no one else could be liable. (Note: You do not lose the exemption if a student or students also occupy the dwelling);
- wholly occupied by people under the age of 18;
- unoccupied, and is part of a single property containing another dwelling where someone resides, and letting it separately would be a breach of planning control;
- in Scotland and is a housing association trial flat for pensioners or for people with disabilities;
- unoccupied and occupation is prohibited by law (eg it is unfit for habitation or subject to a compulsory purchase order);
- unoccupied and a planning condition prevents occupancy;
- under charitable ownership and has been unoccupied for less than six months;
- an armed forces barracks or married quarters or used as visiting forces accommodation;
- a repossessed property where the property is unoccupied;
- a student hall of residence; *or*
- currently wholly occupied by students (including students temporarily absent from their course).

❑ **In England and Wales only**

There is a further exemption where there are at least two dwellings (ie two self-contained units) within a single property and one occupant is a *'dependent relative'* of someone who is resident in another part of the property. The exemption applies only to the part of the property where the dependent relative is resident. The definition of 'relative' is quite straightforward and includes quite distant relatives (eg great-great-grandchild) and common-law relations. If there is a dispute about your status as a relative you should seek advice. The dependent relative must be:

- aged 65 or over; *or*
- *'severely mentally impaired'* (see Box H.5); *or*
- *'substantially and permanently disabled'*, the definition of which is open to wide interpretation.

Council Tax (Exempt Dwellings) Order1992 (as amended); & Council Tax (Exempt Dwellings)(Scotland) Order 1997, Sch 1 aged 18 or over are liable instead. If there are none, the dwelling is exempt (see Box H.4).

6. Who is a resident of a dwelling?

You are a *'resident'* of a dwelling if it is your *'sole or main residence'*. You can only be a resident of one dwelling at a time. Deciding where you are resident is usually straightforward. In difficult cases, your local authority should take into account how much time you spend at different addresses, where you work, where your children go to school, how much security of tenure you have at different addresses, and other relevant information.

LGFA, Ss.6(5) & 99(1)

Appeals – Appeals about where you are resident go first to your local authority. There is no time limit for lodging the appeal. If it is refused you can make a further appeal, to the Valuation Tribunal (England and Wales) or Valuation Appeal Committee (Scotland), within two months of receiving the decision.

7. How to pay less council tax

There are three different schemes for reducing council tax bills. You can get help through all three schemes at the same time if you satisfy the relevant conditions for all of them. The three schemes are:

- the Disability Reduction scheme (see 8 below);
- the discount scheme (see 9 below);
- the council tax benefit scheme (see Chapter 20).

Some dwellings are exempt from council tax (see 4 above).

H.5 People who are disregarded for council tax discount purposes

People who are 'severely mentally impaired'

This means anyone who:

- *'has a severe impairment of intelligence and social functioning (however caused) which appears to be permanent'; and*
- has a certificate from a registered medical practitioner confirming this (which may cover a past, present or future period); *and*
- is entitled to one of the following benefits:
  - disability living allowance (DLA) middle or highest rate care component;
  - attendance allowance, constant attendance allowance (or an equivalent benefit);
  - employment and support allowance;
  - incapacity benefit (any rate);
  - severe disablement allowance;
  - income support including a disability premium due to incapacity, or whose partner has a disability premium for them included in their income-based jobseeker's allowance;
  - the disability element of working tax credit; *or*
  - is over state pension age and would have been entitled to one of the above benefits if under state pension age.

Carers

There are two different types of carer who are disregarded.

First type of carer – All the following conditions must be met. The carer:

- provides care for at least 35 hours a week on average. The law refers to *'care'*, not *'support'*;
- is 'resident' (see 6) in the same dwelling as the person cared for;
- is not the partner of the person cared for (ie neither married, nor living together as husband and wife, nor a same-sex partner);
- is not the parent of the person cared for, if the person cared for is aged under 18;
- cares for a person who is entitled to one of the following: the highest rate DLA care component, the higher rate of attendance allowance or constant attendance allowance.

Second type of carer – All the following conditions must be met. The carer must be:

- providing *'care or support'* on behalf of a local authority, government department or charity, or through an introduction by a charity where the person being cared for is the carer's employer;
- employed for at least 24 hours a week;
- paid no more than £44 a week;
- resident where the care is given or in premises that have been provided for the better performance of the work.

People in a hospital, a care home, or certain kinds of hostel

People whose sole or main residence is a hospital or care home are disregarded (ie a short stay does not count). People in hostels who have no residence elsewhere are also disregarded; this includes bail or probation hostels along with night shelters and other similar accommodation.

Anyone whose 'sole or main residence' is elsewhere

People whose sole or main residence is with someone else or who are living in another institute (not a hospital or care home) in order to receive care are disregarded. For where someone is 'resident', see 6.

Young people, students, student nurses, youth trainees, apprentices, and others

The following individuals or groups are ignored:

- everyone aged 17 or under;
- 18/19-year-olds for whom child benefit is payable (see Chapter 38);
- education-leavers under 20 (but only if they left on or after 1 May, and then only until 31 October inclusive that year);
- school or college-level students aged under 20, if their term-time study normally amounts to 12 or more hours a week;
- students, if their study amounts to at least an average of 21 hours a week for periods of at least 24 weeks a year;
- student nurses whose academic course means they count as a 'student', or who are studying for their first nursing registration;
- foreign language assistants;
- trainees under the age of 25 on training funded by the Learning and Skills Council for England;
- apprentices undertaking training that leads to an accredited qualification (eg an NVQ), subject to limitations on pay;
- people in prison or similar institutions;
- members of a religious community where the community provides for all the individuals' needs;
- members of some international organisations or visiting forces;
- foreign spouses and dependants of students;
- diplomats and their spouses.

Council Tax (Discount Disregards) Order 1992;
Council Tax (Additional Provisions for Discount Disregards) Regs 1992;
Council Tax (Discounts)(Scotland) Order 1992;
Council Tax (Disregards)(Scotland) Regs 1992 - each as amended

8. The Disability Reduction scheme

You can get a disability reduction if you or any other *'resident'* (see 6 above) in your dwelling is *'substantially and permanently disabled'*. This can be an adult or a child of any age, whether or not they are related to you. At least one of the next three conditions must also be met:

- you have an additional bathroom or kitchen needed by the disabled person; *or*
- you have a room (other than a bathroom, kitchen or toilet) needed by and predominantly used by that person; *or*
- you have enough space in your dwelling for that person to use a wheelchair indoors.

Disability reductions are available in all types of dwellings, including care homes and hostels.

In Scotland, the council water charge can also be reduced under this scheme.

Council Tax (Reductions for Disabilities) Regs

Comments

There is no general test of who counts as *'substantially and permanently disabled'*, although it is clear that it includes people who have been disabled for life and also those who have become disabled later in life. There is also no general test of what it means for the disabled person to 'need' the room or the wheelchair, except that they must be *'essential or of major importance to [his or her] well-being by reason of the nature and extent of [his or her] disability'*.

However, it is clear that disability reductions are not limited to dwellings specially constructed or adapted to provide a room or wheelchair space.

Guidance given to local authorities suggests they should consider how difficult life would be for the disabled person without the facilities being available.

Practice Note No 2 (para 40)

The *Sandwell* High Court judgment has been misinterpreted by many authorities as denying a reduction to disabled people who use another room instead of a dedicated bedroom. In fact, the judgment simply emphasised that there must be an *'appropriative causative link between the disability and the requirement of the use of the room, because the use has to be essential or of major importance, because of the nature and extent of the disability'*. This has been further clarified in a more recent decision, which states that the room must be extra or additional, in the sense that it would not be required for the relevant purpose if the person were not disabled.

R (Sandwell Metropolitan District Council) v Perks [2003]
South Gloucestershire Council v Titley & Clothier HC [2006]

How much is it worth?

If you qualify for a disability reduction, your council tax bill is reduced to the amount payable for a dwelling in the valuation band below yours. So if your home is in band F, the bill will be reduced to the amount for band E. Since 1.4.00, if your dwelling is in band A, you get a reduction of one-sixth of your bill.

Getting a reduction, and backdating

The person liable for council tax (not necessarily the disabled person) has to make an application. The authority may have a standard form for this (and in some areas you may have to make a separate application for each financial year). If you should have been given a disability reduction in the past, but were not, it should be backdated. There is no time limit.

Council Tax (Reductions for Disabilities) Regs, reg 3(1)(b)

Appeals

Appeals about disability reductions go first to your local authority. There is no time limit for lodging the appeal. If it is refused you can make a further appeal, to the Valuation Tribunal (England and Wales) or Valuation Appeal Committee (Scotland), within two months of receiving the decision.

9. The discount scheme

The council tax discount scheme is applied to dwellings where less than two adults are 'resident' (see 6 above). You can get a discount if:

- there is only one resident in your dwelling: in this case your discount equals 25% of your council tax liability; *or*
- there are no residents in your dwelling: in this case your discount may be up to 50% of your council tax liability (but see 10 below). If your home is empty, you may be able to qualify for exemption instead of a discount (see 4).

LGFA, Ss.11 & 79

Counting the residents

Several groups of people are disregarded when counting the number of residents in your dwelling; they are sometimes called 'invisible'. The groups are outlined in Box H.5. This is important because it can mean you qualify for a discount even if there are several people in your dwelling, as long as enough of them are 'disregarded'.

Example: If you are in a couple and have two children aged 17 and 20 at home, you might not expect to get a discount. But if your partner is severely mentally impaired or is a carer (as defined in Box H.5), and the 20-year-old is a student, they will both be 'disregarded'. So will the 17-year-old (because of being under 18). That will leave you as the only resident who will be counted. Your council tax bill will be reduced by 25%.

Getting a discount, and backdating

Your local authority may automatically grant a discount, but you can also apply for one. The authority may have a standard form for this. A discount can be backdated to the date it should have first applied. There is no time limit within which you can apply for the discount.

Appeals

Appeals about discounts go first to your local authority. There is no time limit for lodging the appeal. If this is refused you can appeal to the Valuation Tribunal (England and Wales) or Valuation Appeal Committee (Scotland), within two months of receiving the decision.

10. Second homes and long-term empty properties

In England and Scotland, local authorities have the power to reduce the discount offered on furnished second homes from 50% to just 10%. In Wales, authorities have discretion to reduce the discount below 50% or to offer no discount at all.

Local authorities also have the power to reduce or remove completely the discount offered on long-term empty properties that are substantially unfurnished.

The Council Tax (Prescribed Classes of Dwellings) Regs

Social fund

22 Regulated social fund

1. What is the regulated social fund?

The regulated social fund is a government fund that makes payments to people in need to cover specific costs. It provides Sure Start maternity grants and funeral, cold weather and winter fuel payments. You are legally entitled to a payment if you satisfy the regulations.

2. Sure Start maternity grants

You are entitled to a Sure Start maternity grant of £500 for each child if:

- you (or a member of your family) are pregnant, have given birth in the last three months (including stillbirth after 24 weeks of pregnancy), have adopted a child (or, in certain circumstances, been granted a residence order for a child) under the age of one, or have been granted a parental order for a child born to a surrogate mother; *and*
- you or your partner have been awarded one of the following qualifying benefits in respect of the day you claim the maternity grant: income support, pension credit, income-based jobseeker's allowance, income-related employment and support allowance, child tax credit paid at a rate that exceeds the family element or working tax credit that includes the disability or severe disability element; *and*
- you have received health and welfare advice about child health matters and, if applying before the birth, advice about maternal health (see below); *and*
- you claim within the time limits (see below).

SFM&FE Regs, reg 5

Claim on form SF100, available from Jobcentre Plus or your antenatal clinic. You must claim in the 11 weeks before your expected week of confinement, or in the three months following the date of the birth or adoption, residence or parental order. If you are waiting for a decision about a qualifying benefit, you must still claim within the time limits and if your claim is refused because you are not getting a qualifying benefit, re-claim within three months of being awarded the qualifying benefit.

C&P Regs, Sch 4, para 8

The form must be signed by a health professional to confirm you have received health and welfare advice about child health matters and, if appropriate, maternal health.

3. Funeral payments

You are entitled to a funeral payment if:

- you or your partner accept responsibility for the costs of a funeral (ie you have paid or are liable to pay them) that takes place in the UK (or in another European Economic Area country (see Chapter 50(1)) or Switzerland, if you or a member of your family are classified as a 'worker' or have the right to reside in the UK under European Community law – see Chapter 50(2)); *and*
- you or your partner have been awarded one of the following qualifying benefits in respect of the day you claim a funeral payment: income support, pension credit, income-based jobseeker's allowance, income-related employment and support allowance, child tax credit paid at a rate that exceeds the family element, working tax credit that includes the disability or severe disability element, housing benefit or council tax benefit; *and*
- the deceased was ordinarily resident in the UK when they died; *and*
- you claim within the time limits (see below); *and*
- you fall into one of the groups of people who are eligible to claim (see below).

SFM&FE Regs, reg 7

Who can claim?

You can only get a funeral payment if you fall into one of the following groups.

- ❑ You were the partner of the deceased when they died or immediately before either of you moved permanently into a care home. 'Partner' includes both opposite and same-sex couples whether or not you were married or civil partners.
- ❑ The deceased was a child for whom you were responsible and there is no 'absent parent' (unless they were getting one of the above qualifying benefits when the child died), or the deceased was a stillborn child.
- ❑ You were a 'close relative' or close friend of the deceased and it is reasonable for you to accept responsibility for the funeral costs, given the nature and extent of your contact with the deceased. Close relative means parent (or parent-in-law), son (-in-law), daughter (-in-law), brother (-in-law), sister (-in-law), stepson/daughter (-in-law) or step-parent.

You cannot get a payment as a close relative or friend of the deceased if:

- the deceased had a partner when they died; *or*
- there is a parent, son or daughter of the deceased who is not:
  - getting a qualifying benefit (see above); *or*
  - in prison or hospital immediately following a period on a qualifying benefit; *or*
  - under 18; *or*
  - aged 18 or 19 and a qualifying young person for child benefit (see Chapter 38(1); *or*
  - aged 18 or over and in full-time education; *or*
  - a fully maintained member of a religious order; *or*
  - someone who was estranged from the deceased; *or*
  - receiving asylum support from the National Asylum Support Services (see Chapter 50(4)); *or*
  - ordinarily resident outside the UK; *or*
- there is a close relative (see above) of the deceased, other than a person who falls into one of the groups above, who was in closer contact with the deceased than you were, or had equally close contact and is not getting a qualifying benefit.

SFM&FE Regs, reg 7 & 8

How much do you get?

The following costs can be met:

- the necessary costs of purchasing a new burial plot with exclusive rights plus necessary burial fees, or the necessary costs of cremation including medical fees;
- the cost of documentation required to release the deceased's assets;

- the reasonable costs of transport for the portion of journeys in excess of 50 miles, undertaken to transport the body within the UK to a funeral director's premises or a place of rest and to transport the coffin, bearers and mourners in two vehicles to the funeral;
- the necessary costs of one return journey from your home for you or your partner to arrange or attend the funeral if you are responsible for the funeral costs;
- up to £700 for other funeral expenses (or £120 if you have a pre-paid funeral plan that does not cover these expenses).

The following amounts are deducted from an award of a funeral payment (note that a funeral payment is recoverable from the deceased's estate):

- any of the deceased's assets that are available to you without probate or letters of administration;
- any lump sum due to you or a member of your family on the death of the deceased from an insurance policy, occupational or war pension, burial club or similar scheme;
- any contribution towards the funeral costs from a charity or relative of yours or the deceased's;
- any amount from a pre-paid funeral plan or similar scheme.

Payments from the Macfarlane, variant CJD, or Eileen Trusts, the Fund or Skipton Fund, or the London Bombings Relief Charitable Fund are ignored.

SFM&FE Regs, regs 9 & 10

How and when to claim

You must claim within three months of the date of the funeral (on form SF200, available from the DWP). If you are waiting for a decision on a qualifying benefit, you must still claim within the time limit and if your claim is refused because you are not getting a qualifying benefit, re-claim within three months of being awarded the qualifying benefit.

C&P Regs, Sch 4, para 9

4. Cold weather payments

These are automatic payments (you do not need to make a claim) of £8.50 (£25 for winter 2008/09) for each qualifying week made by the DWP if:

- the average temperature recorded or forecast over seven consecutive days at the designated weather station for your area is zero degrees Celsius (freezing) or less; *and*
- you have been awarded income support (IS), income-based jobseeker's allowance (JSA) or income-related employment and support allowance (ESA) for at least one of those days and you are responsible for a child under the age of 5, or you are getting child tax credit that includes a disabled or severely disabled child element, or your IS, JSA or ESA includes one of the disability or pensioner premiums; *or*
- you have been awarded pension credit or income-related ESA that includes a work-related activity or support component for at least one of those days; *and*
- you are not resident in a care home.

Social Fund Cold Weather Payments Regs

5. Winter fuel payments

This is a lump-sum payment (for winter 2009/10) if you are 60 or over in the 'qualifying week' (week beginning 21.9.09).

You are not entitled to a payment if during that week you:

- are subject to immigration control or not ordinarily resident in Great Britain (see Chapter 50(2) and (3)); *or*
- have been receiving free inpatient treatment in hospital (or similar institution) for more than 52 weeks; *or*
- are in custody serving a sentence imposed by a court; *or*
- have a partner aged 60 or over who gets pension credit (PC), income-based jobseeker's allowance (JSA) or income-related employment and support allowance (ESA) – they will receive the payment instead.

Social Fund Winter Fuel Payment Regs

How much do you get? – If you or your partner do not receive PC, income-based JSA or income-related ESA and you are aged:

- 60 to 79, you will get £250 if you are the only person in the household entitled to a payment, or £125 if you share a household with one or more other people entitled to a payment – eg a married couple or two friends living together will each receive £125;
- 80 or over, you will get £400 if you are the only person in the household aged 80 or over, or £200 each if there are more people aged 80 or over entitled to a payment. If one of you is 80 or over and the other aged 60-79 you will get £275 and £125 respectively.

If you are receiving PC, income-based JSA or income-related ESA you will get £250 (or £400 if you or your partner are aged 80 or over) regardless of who else is in the household. If you are one of a couple and your partner receives PC, income-based JSA or income-related ESA, they will receive the payment instead.

If you have been living in a care home for 13 weeks or more at the end of the qualifying week and are not getting PC, income-based JSA or income-related ESA, you are entitled to £125 if you are aged 60-79, or £200 if you are aged 80 or over.

How do you claim? – You should automatically receive a payment without making a claim if you received a payment last year and your circumstances have not changed, or you are getting a state pension or other social security benefit (excluding child benefit, housing benefit or council tax benefit) in the qualifying week. Otherwise, you must make a claim, which must be received by the Winter Fuel Payment Centre by 30.03.10. Ring the winter fuel payment helpline (08459 151 515) to get a claim-form and other information.

6. Appeals

If you disagree with a decision relating to the regulated social fund, you can ask for a revision or appeal to a tribunal (see Chapter 60).

23 Discretionary social fund

1. What is the discretionary social fund?

The discretionary social fund provides grants and interest-free loans for a variety of needs that are difficult to meet from weekly benefits. There are three types of payments.

- ❑ **Community care grants** are intended to promote community care by assisting people on a qualifying benefit (see below) to live independently in the community, ease exceptional pressure on families and help with certain travelling expenses.
- ❑ **Budgeting loans** are interest-free loans to help people who have been on a qualifying benefit (see below) for at least 26 weeks to meet intermittent expenses for specified items for which it may be difficult to budget, enabling the cost to be spread over time.
- ❑ **Crisis loans** are interest-free loans for people (on benefit or not) who are unable to meet their immediate short-term needs in an emergency or as a result of a disaster, or, in certain circumstances, for rent in advance.

There are eligibility rules for each type of payment (see 4, 5 and 6 below). There is no legal entitlement to a payment if the rules are satisfied. Payments are discretionary. Each DWP district has an annual budget for grants and another for loans. These must not be overspent and must be managed on a monthly basis so that funds are available throughout the financial year. Decisions are subject to review rather than appeal (see 7 below).

Qualifying benefits – these are: income-related employment and support allowance, income support, income-based jobseeker's allowance and pension credit.

2. Applying for a payment

Apply for a community care grant on form SF300 and a budgeting loan on form SF500; these are available from your local Jobcentre Plus office or can be downloaded from the DWP website (www.dwp.gov.uk). See 4 and 5 below for more on claiming. For how you apply for a crisis loan, see 6 below. In each case, an appointee, or someone with your written authority, can apply for a payment on your behalf.

Always apply for a community care grant rather than a budgeting or crisis loan if you might be eligible. You can apply for a grant and a loan for the same item, although if the loan is awarded first it may lessen your chance of getting a grant. An application for a crisis loan can be treated as an application for a community care grant (and vice versa).

Social fund direction 49

You cannot get a community care grant or crisis loan for an item if you have already received or been refused a grant or crisis loan for that item on an application made within the previous 28 days, unless there has been a relevant change of circumstances, eg a change in your circumstances or a change in the budget.

Social fund direction 7

Certain items are excluded from grants or crisis loans (see Box I.1). There are no restrictions on re-applying for budgeting loans, but you can only apply for specified items (see 5 below).

3. How decisions are made

Decisions are made by social fund decision makers. Although payments are discretionary, decision makers are required to take the following into account:

- for community care grants and crisis loans, all the circumstances of each case and, in particular, the nature, extent and urgency of the need, and whether it can be met by other resources (excluding the disability living allowance mobility component) or by another person or body;
- for budgeting loans, specified personal circumstances only;
- the likelihood and timescale of repayment of a budgeting loan or crisis loan;
- the amount in the district budget (see 1 above);
- legally binding social fund 'directions' that set out the eligibility conditions for each type of payment, the criteria for managing the district budget (see below) and the procedure for reviews;
- national guidance on how to prioritise applications, exercise discretion and interpret the social fund directions set out in the *Social Fund Guide* (see page 6) (the guidance is *not* legally binding, however, and although it gives examples of when payments may be appropriate, it stresses that the absence of guidance relating to a particular situation or item does not mean that a payment cannot be considered);
- local guidance issued to decision makers in each DWP district giving monthly information about the district budget and the priority of applications it can afford to meet. Ask your local Jobcentre Plus office for a copy.

SSCBA, S.140

Decisions should be made without delay and notified to you in writing with confirmation of your right to request a review. If there are unreasonable delays, complain to the social fund district manager. Payments should normally be made to you, but the DWP can decide to pay a supplier directly.

4. Community care grants

To be eligible for a community care grant you must satisfy all the following conditions.

- ❑ You must be in receipt of (ie be the claimant of) a qualifying benefit (see 1 above) when you apply for a grant (or be leaving institutional or residential care within six weeks and likely to get a qualifying benefit when you leave). You satisfy this condition if you receive a backdated award of a qualifying benefit that covers the date of your grant application. For JSA joint-claim couples, only the partner who is paid JSA is eligible for a grant.

Social fund direction 25 and Social fund direction General

- ❑ The item you apply for is not excluded (see Box I.1).
- ❑ You or your partner must not be involved in a trade dispute, unless the claim is for travel expenses to visit a sick person.

Social fund direction 26

- ❑ You must not have too much capital. The amount of any award you get will be reduced on a pound-for-pound basis by any savings you or your partner have over £500 (£1,000 if you or your partner are aged 60 or over). Capital is worked out in the same way as for the qualifying benefit depending on which benefit you are getting (but disregard any Family Fund payments or refugee integration loans).

Social fund direction 27

- ❑ You must need the grant for one or more of the purposes listed below.

Leaving institutional or residential care

A grant can be given to help you, a member of your family, or someone you or a member of your family are caring for to *'establish yourself or themselves in the community following a stay in institutional or residential accommodation in which you or they received care'*.

Social fund direction 4(a)(i)

The *Social Fund Guide* advises that 'institutional or residential' care means places like hospitals, care homes, hostels, supported lodgings, prisons, youth centres and foster care, where there is significant and substantial care, protection or supervision provided to residents because they cannot live independently or might be a danger to others. If your accommodation would not usually be classed as institutional or residential care you may qualify on the grounds that a grant will help you to stay in the community (see below).

The *Social Fund Guide* says that a 'stay' in care normally means at least three months or a pattern of frequent or regular admission, but the High Court has ruled that *'Undue importance should not be attached to the reference to a 3-month period in... the guidance'*.

R v Secretary of State, ex parte Stitt, Sherwin and Roberts, 21.2.90

To qualify, you must be moving into the community. Therefore, you cannot get a grant under this provision if you are transferring from one care institution to another.

You should apply for what you need to set up home and live independently – eg furniture, household equipment, connection charges, bedding, clothing, removal expenses, storage charges or items needed because of a disability (as long as it is not an excluded item – see Box I.1).

Staying out of institutional or residential care

A grant can be given to help you, a member of your family, or someone you or a member of your family are caring for *'to remain in the community rather than enter institutional or residential accommodation in which you or they will receive care'*.

Social fund direction 4(a)(ii)

The grant does not have to prevent you going into care, and the risk of care does not have to be immediate, but you should show how a grant would improve your independence in the community and therefore reduce or delay the risk of admission into care. See above for what counts as institutional or residential care. The *Social Fund Guide* suggests that a higher priority should be given to applications if the threat of care is immediate or imminent or there is a direct link between the threat of care and the need in question.

If you have a history of admission into care, it should be easier to argue that the risk is significant. If you are elderly or have a disability and your medical condition or home circumstances are deteriorating, a grant should be considered.

The *Social Fund Guide* says a grant may be appropriate to help you improve your living conditions, or move to more suitable accommodation or nearer to people who will be supporting you (or whom you will be supporting). These are only examples, however, and you can ask for whatever you need to help you to remain independent (as long as it is not an excluded item – see Box I.1).

For example, to improve living conditions you may get a grant for redecoration, refurbishment, bedding (particularly for those who are housebound and need extra warmth or who are incontinent), reconnection charges, heaters, a washing machine (particularly for those who are bedridden or incontinent or can't do laundry by hand because of a disability), minor repairs and improvements. You may also get a grant for disability-related items such as a stairlift, a wheelchair, an orthopaedic mattress or an upright armchair. If you are moving home, you may get a grant for removal expenses, fares, furniture and household equipment, connection charges and installation charges.

I.1 Which items are excluded?

You cannot get a community care grant or crisis loan for the following items (the exclusions do not apply to budgeting loans):

- maternity or funeral expenses (see below);
- needs occurring outside the UK;
- educational or training needs, including clothing and tools;
- distinctive school uniform or equipment, or sports clothes for school use;
- travelling expenses to or from school;
- school meals taken during school holidays by children who are entitled to free school meals;
- expenses in connection with court (legal) proceedings (including a community service order) such as legal fees, court fees, fines, costs, damages, subsistence or travelling expenses (other than a crisis loan for emergency travelling expenses if an applicant is stranded away from home);
- removal or storage charges if an applicant is rehoused following the imposition of a compulsory purchase order or a redevelopment or closing order or a compulsory exchange of tenancies, or pursuant to a housing authority's statutory duty to the homeless under Part VII of the Housing Act 1996 or Part II of the Housing (Scotland) Act 1987;
- domestic assistance and respite care;
- repair to property of any body mentioned in section 80(1) of the Housing Act 1985 or section 61(2)(a) of the Housing (Scotland) Act 1987 and, in the case of Scotland, any repair to property of any housing trust in existence on 13.11.53;
- work-related expenses;
- debts to government departments;
- investments;
- council tax, council water charges or community water charges;
- costs of purchasing, renting or installing a telephone or call charges;
- medical, surgical, optical, aural or dental items or services (see below).

Maternity expenses – This only includes maternity expenses to meet the immediate needs of a recently born baby (*Social Fund Commissioner's Advice on Maternity Expenses*, 2/1/02). You could apply for clothing for a pregnant woman or a growing baby, or for items such as a high chair, stair gate, pram, or even a cot if the baby slept in something else initially.

Medical items – Medical items are not defined, but an item of ordinary everyday use cannot be regarded as a medical item (*R v SFI ex parte Connick*, 8.6.93). This includes items such as cotton sheets, non-allergic bedding or curtains, built-up shoes, incontinence pads, beds with adaptations or lactose-free foods. If an item is not one of ordinary everyday use, it should only be treated as a medical item if its sole purpose is to cure, alleviate, treat, diagnose or prevent a medical condition, eg a nebuliser or insulin gun (*Social Fund Commissioner's advice on excluded items*, 18/6/01). Under this test, wheelchairs or stairlifts should not be treated as medical items. You will not get help, however, if they are available from the NHS or elsewhere.

Community care grants only

In addition, you cannot get a community care grant for:

- expenses which the local authority has a statutory duty to meet;
- costs of fuel consumption and any associated standing charges;
- housing costs – including repairs and improvements to the dwelling occupied as the home (including any garage, garden and outbuildings), deposits to secure accommodation, mortgage payments, water rates, sewerage rates, service charges, rent and all other charges for accommodation (whether or not such charges include payment for meals and/or services), other than:
  - minor repairs and improvements; *or*
  - charges for accommodation applied for under direction 4(b) (ie overnight accommodation included in a grant for travel expenses (see 4));
- daily living expenses such as food and groceries, except if:
  - such expenses are incurred in caring for a prisoner or young offender on release on temporary licence; *or*
  - a crisis loan cannot be awarded for such expenses because the maximum loan limit has been reached.

Crisis loans only

In addition, you cannot get a crisis loan for:

- mobility needs;
- holidays;
- a television or radio, or licence, aerial or rental charges for a television or radio;
- garaging, parking, purchase and running costs of any motor vehicle except if payment is being considered for emergency travelling expenses;
- housing costs (as for community care grants), other than:
  - payments for intermittent housing costs not met by housing benefit, income support, income-related employment and support allowance, income-based jobseeker's allowance or pension credit, or for which direct payments cannot be implemented, such as the cost of emptying cesspits or septic tanks; *or*
  - rent in advance which is payable to secure fresh accommodation where the landlord is not a local authority; *or*
  - charges for board and lodging accommodation and residential charges for hostels (but not deposits, whether included in the total charge or not); *or*
  - minor repairs and improvements.

Social fund directions 23 & 29

Families under exceptional pressure

A grant can be given *'to ease exceptional pressures'* on you and your family.

Social fund direction 4(a)(iii)

There is no legal definition of 'exceptional pressures'. You should always fully explain in your application all the pressures your family is experiencing and their cumulative effects. These could include problems relating to your physical or mental health, any disabilities you have, your accommodation, your finances or your children (eg behavioural problems or difficulties at school). The *Social Fund Guide* advises that the term 'family' generally means couples (same- or opposite-sex) with or without children, people caring for children, or women over 24 weeks pregnant; it can also mean an extended family. There is no legal definition of 'family', but the Social Fund Commissioner has advised that it could include relationships of long-term interdependence even if there are no blood or marriage ties (eg a disabled person and their carer). Decision makers are advised to be flexible in their interpretation, and to give higher priority to cases involving domestic violence.

Examples of circumstances in which a grant may be appropriate include where there are high washing costs or excessive wear and tear on clothing because of a disabled child, or where minor structural repairs are needed to keep a home habitable, or for the safety of a child. You can ask for any item that will ease the pressures on your family (as long as it is not an excluded item – see Box I.1).

Setting up home in the community as part of a planned programme of resettlement

A grant can be given to someone *'to set up home in the community as a part of a planned resettlement programme following a period during which he has been without a settled way of life'*.

Social fund direction 4(a)(v)

The *Social Fund Guide* advises that being *'without a settled way of life could include being in a night shelter, a hostel, sleeping rough, temporary supported lodging, or temporary accommodation provided by the Home Office for asylum seekers'*. But this list is not exhaustive and it could include, for example, a situation where someone had been moving around between friends and relatives. 'Setting up home' is more than just moving into a property. 'Planned resettlement programmes' may be run by local authorities, voluntary organisations, housing associations and registered charities, but it can include anyone, including yourself, who has planned a programme of support (incuding budgeting and literacy skills tuition and benefits and careers advice).

Other purposes for which a grant can be awarded

A grant can be given to:

- allow you or your partner to care for a prisoner or young offender on temporary release;
- help you or your family with travel expenses within the UK (including overnight accommodation) to visit a sick person, attend a relative's funeral, ease a domestic crisis, move to suitable accommodation, or visit a child who is with the other parent pending a court decision.

Social fund direction 4(a)(iv)&(b)

Decision making and priorities

A decision maker should first decide whether you are eligible for a grant under one of the purposes listed above, and if so, the priority of your application. Local guidance (see 3 above) must specify whether the district budget can afford to meet high-, medium- or low-priority applications (usually only high).

The *Social Fund Guide* states that an application should normally be given high priority if a grant will have a substantial effect in the immediately foreseeable future in resolving or improving the circumstances of the applicant and meeting one of the purposes listed above. Medium priority should normally be given if a grant will have a noticeable (but not substantial or immediate) effect in meeting one of the above purposes, and low priority should normally be given if a grant will only have a minor effect in meeting one of the above purposes.

The *Social Fund Guide* gives examples of situations that would affect priority, including if a person has:

- restricted mobility or a physical disability;
- mental health problems or learning difficulties;
- chronic physical or mental illness;
- behavioural problems often associated with drug or alcohol abuse;
- unstable family circumstances or experience of abuse.

How much do you get?

The *Social Fund Guide* says the amount you ask for should normally be allowed if it is within the range of prices charged for the item in question by high street chain retailers and national catalogue outlets. If you need a specialist item, eg a supportive mattress, you need to explain why it is needed and, if possible, provide evidence. There is no maximum amount that can be awarded. The minimum is £30, but this does not apply to grants for travelling and daily living expenses.

Social fund direction 28

Applying for a community care grant

Apply on form SF300, giving full details of your needs and circumstances. You must show that you need a grant for one of the purposes listed above and why your application should be given high priority, bearing in mind the guidance on priorities referred to above.

When listing the items you need, be as specific as possible. If, for example, you need bedding, specify what you need (eg two single sheets, one single duvet cover, two pillows, etc), giving the cost of each item. If you need carpets, state which rooms they are for, the size of the rooms, the condition of any existing carpet and why you need it (eg you have fits or falls or need to keep warm). If you need curtains, specify the size, the rooms they are needed for and whether the rooms are overlooked. For less common items, such as an orthopaedic mattress and other disability-related items, back up your application with an estimate from a specialist supplier.

5. Budgeting loans

To be eligible for a budgeting loan you must satisfy all the following conditions.

- ❑ You must be in receipt of (ie be the claimant of) a qualifying benefit (see 1 above) when your application for a budgeting loan is decided, and you and/or your partner must have been receiving a qualifying benefit throughout the 26 weeks before the decision (ignoring breaks of 28 days or less). The three waiting days at the start of a JSA claim do not count. For joint-claim couples (see Chapter 15(2)), only the partner who is paid JSA is eligible for a budgeting loan.
- ❑ You or your partner must not be involved in a trade dispute.

Social fund direction 8

- ❑ You must not have too much capital. The amount of any loan you get will be reduced on a pound-for-pound basis by any savings you or your partner have over £1,000, or £2,000 if you or your partner are aged 60 or over. Capital is worked out in the same way as for the qualifying benefit depending on which benefit you are getting (except that Family Fund payments and refugee integration loans are disregarded).

Social fund direction 9

- ❑ Your application must be for one of the categories of expenses listed below.

What can you get a budgeting loan for?

You do not have to specify what item(s) you need the loan for, but it must fall into one of the following categories:

- furniture and household equipment;
- clothing and footwear;
- rent in advance and/or removal expenses to secure new accommodation;
- improvement, maintenance and security of the home;
- travelling expenses;
- expenses associated with seeking or re-entering work;
- HP and other debts for expenses associated with the above categories.

Social fund direction 2

How is the amount of the loan calculated?

The maximum loan that can be awarded depends on whether you are single, a couple or have children. Each district is guided to use the same maximum amount for a single person. This amount may vary during the year. Your local Jobcentre Plus office should be able to tell you the current amount. If you are not single, the maximum loan is calculated as follows:

- a couple will get 1⅓ times a single person amount;
- someone with children will get 2⅓ times a single person amount.

Social fund direction 52

How much do you get? – The lowest award that can be made is £100 (so you should not ask for less than this) and the highest is £1,500. The actual amount you are offered may be less than the maximum for the following reasons.

- ❑ The repayment rules may prevent full payment (see below).
- ❑ The amount of the award is reduced if you have capital or savings over the limit (see above).
- ❑ If you or your partner have another budgeting loan outstanding, the maximum amount you can get is reduced by the amount of your outstanding loan.
- ❑ If you asked for less than the maximum that you can be awarded, you will only get the amount you asked for.

Social fund directions 10 & 53

Repayment of budgeting loans

A decision maker can only award an amount you are likely to be able to repay. The loan will be scheduled for repayment within 104 weeks. If you have asked for a loan (within your maximum amount) that cannot be repaid within 104 weeks at standard repayment rates, the decision maker will give you up to three repayment options, worked out using combinations of different repayment rates, amounts or number of weeks, and could include varying repayment rates on outstanding loans. Standard repayment rates are 5%, 10% or 12% of your income-related employment and support allowance (ESA), income support (IS) or income-based jobseeker's allowance (JSA) applicable amount or pension credit appropriate minimum guarantee (excluding, in each case, housing costs) plus any child tax credit or child benefit, depending on whether you have other financial commitments. The maximum repayment rate is 20%.

Social fund direction 11

Decisions about repayment are not subject to review. If you have difficulty repaying the loan you can, however, ask for it to be rescheduled by writing to your local Jobcentre Plus office.

Loans are normally repaid by deductions from your or your partner's income-related ESA, IS, pension credit or income-based JSA. If you don't get enough benefit, or your benefit stops, deductions can be made from most other social security benefits. Deductions cannot be made from disability living allowance, attendance allowance or child benefit.

The Social Fund (Recovery by Deductions from Benefits) Regs 1988

Applying for a budgeting loan

Apply on form SF500, making sure that you include all the information requested about your personal circumstances.

6. Crisis loans

To be eligible for a crisis loan you must satisfy all the following conditions.

- ❑ You must be aged 16 or over.
- ❑ You must be without sufficient resources to meet the immediate short-term needs of yourself and/or your family.

Social fund direction 14

- ❑ The item you apply for must not be excluded (see Box I.1).
- ❑ The amount to be awarded must not be more than you can afford to repay.

Social fund direction 22

- ❑ You must need the loan because of an emergency or disaster (if the loan would be the only means of preventing serious damage, or serious risk to the health or safety of yourself or a member of your family), or to pay rent in advance (see below 'When can you get a crisis loan?').

Social fund direction 3

You do not have to be in receipt of a qualifying benefit to get a crisis loan but all your available resources are taken into account, including most types of savings, if it is reasonable to do so in the circumstances.

The *Social Fund Guide* gives examples of resources that normally should be ignored, including housing benefit, other social fund payments, business assets, personal possessions and payments from the Independent Living Fund, the Macfarlane and Variant CJD Trusts and the Skipton Fund. Disability living allowance mobility component must be ignored. Help from any other source can be taken into account if there is a realistic expectation that it would be available in time. Decision makers should not routinely refer applicants to charities, employers, relatives, close friends or social services, unless there is reason to believe that an offer of help will be forthcoming. Credit facilities should only be taken into account if you are not getting income-related employment and support allowance (ESA), income support (IS), income-based jobseeker's allowance (JSA) or pension credit and are likely to be able to afford the repayments.

Who cannot get a crisis loan?

You cannot get a crisis loan if you are:

- in a care home or hospital, unless discharge is planned within the following two weeks;
- a prisoner or in custody or released on temporary licence;
- a member of, and fully maintained by, a religious order;
- under 20 and in full-time non-advanced education and as a result not entitled to income-related ESA, IS or income-based JSA.

Social fund direction 15

When can you get a crisis loan?

A crisis loan may be paid to meet expenses *'in an emergency, or as a consequence of a disaster, provided that the provision of such assistance is the only means by which serious damage or serious risk to the health or safety of that person, or to a member of his family, may be prevented'*.

Social fund direction 3(1)(a)

If you are awarded a community care grant to enable you to return to the community after a stay in institutional or residential care, you may get a crisis loan to cover rent in advance (without having to show there is an emergency or disaster, or a risk to your health or safety).

The need for help will generally be for a specific item or service or for immediate living expenses for a short period not normally exceeding 14 days.

The *Social Fund Guide* does not define the terms 'emergency', 'disaster' or 'serious risk to health or safety'. The cause of the crisis is irrelevant and 'health' includes both physical and mental health. It is important to argue that your individual circumstances should be considered fully, as people may be affected differently by the same situation. Supporting evidence from a social worker, doctor or other professional may be helpful but you should not delay your application to get it. The guidance gives a number of examples where a crisis loan may be considered, including:

- loss of money;
- hardship due to payment of regular income in arrears;
- a disaster (eg fire or flood) that caused significant damage;
- emergency travel expenses (eg if you are stranded away from home);
- hardship due to compulsory unpaid holiday;
- fares to hospital for patients;
- fuel reconnection charges;
- homelessness.

Restrictions for certain groups

- If you are not entitled to income-related ESA, IS, pension credit or income-based JSA because you are a full-time student or a *'person from abroad'* (ESA, IS and JSA) or a *'person not in Great Britain'* (pension credit), you can only get a crisis loan to alleviate the consequences of a disaster.
- If you or your partner are involved in a trade dispute, you can get a crisis loan only for items needed for cooking or heating, or to meet expenses arising from a disaster.
- If your JSA is sanctioned or disallowed and you are not getting hardship payments, or you have been sanctioned for not taking part in a work-focused interview, you can only get a crisis loan for items needed for cooking or heating or to meet expenses arising from a disaster for the first two weeks of the sanction period, or for the whole sanction period in the case of a New Deal or work-focused interview sanction. Your partner can claim a crisis loan in the normal way but cannot get living expenses for you.

Social fund directions 16 & 17

How much do you get?

The amount of any crisis loan awarded is the smallest amount needed to tide you over or remove the crisis. There is no minimum amount. The maximum that can be paid is £1,500, less any other social fund loan outstanding.

If you are applying for immediate living expenses (eg because of lost or stolen money) the maximum loan is:

- 75% of the ESA/IS/JSA personal allowance (single or couple rate); *plus*
- £56.11 for each dependent child.

Social fund directions 18 & 21

Repayment of crisis loans

The rules are similar to budgeting loans (see 5 above), with most loans being recovered by weekly deductions from benefit over 104 weeks at the rate of 5%, 10% or 12% of your ESA/IS/JSA applicable amount or pension credit appropriate minimum guarantee (excluding, in each case, housing costs).

Applying for a crisis loan

Apply for a crisis loan by ringing the Freephone number, which you can get by ringing the Jobcentre Plus claim-line (0800 055 6688) or by calling in at the local Jobcentre Plus office where the need arises. You have the right to make a paper claim if you do not want to claim by phone or find it difficult to do so. You should insist on making a formal application and being given a written decision (it is common for counter staff to put off potential applicants by telling them they will not be given a loan). If you claim by phone, you will normally be given the decision in the same call.

7. Reviews

Internal reviews

You can ask for a review of any decision made by a decision maker, including the refusal of a payment or the amount awarded (you can accept the payment pending review of the amount). You must do this in writing within 28 days of the date the decision was issued to you. The time limit can be extended if there are 'special reasons'. There is no definition of, or guidance on, what counts as special reasons so each case should be considered on its merits. Your application must explain why you disagree with the decision. The review is carried out by a reviewing officer in the office that made the decision. A decision can also be reviewed at any time at the discretion of a decision maker. As an alternative to a late review, or if one is refused, you can make a repeat application instead.

The Social Fund (Application for Review) Regs 1988

If the decision is not revised in your favour, you will usually be asked if you want an interview by telephone. If it is difficult or inappropriate for you to use the telephone, you can be interviewed at the local office, and you can take a representative with you to help present your case. The interview can be held at your home if you cannot attend the office or deal with it by phone. Due to a backlog in reviews, temporary measures have been introduced where only one attempt will be made to contact you. If it is not successful, the review will be carried out without you.

Social fund direction 33

For reviews concerning budgeting loans, the reviewing officer will only look at your circumstances at the time of the original decision (you can submit new evidence relating to the time of the decision). For other reviews, changes of circumstances since the decision can be taken into account, including changes in the level of the district budget.

Social fund direction 32

There are no legal time limits for carrying out reviews but if there are unreasonable delays, you should complain to the social fund manager or ask your MP to intervene. You are entitled to a written decision, which must include confirmation of your right to request a further review (by the Independent Review Service).

Social fund direction 36

Independent Review Service

If you are not happy with a review decision made by a reviewing officer, you can ask for a further review by a social fund inspector based at the Independent Review Service in Birmingham. The inspectors are independent from the DWP but must take into account the same matters as decision makers when deciding whether to change a decision (see 3 above).

SSA, S.38

Apply direct to the Independent Review Service on form IRS1 within 28 days of the day the decision was issued to you. The social fund inspector can accept a late application if there are special reasons (see above under 'Internal reviews').

Your application must explain why you are unhappy with the review decision. You can accept any grant or loan already offered while you are asking for a further review.

The Independent Review Service should write to you within a few days of receiving your application, setting out the main issues and asking you for further information or comments before a decision is made by an inspector. The decision will be notified to you in writing and may confirm or revise the original decision or (exceptionally) refer the case back to the DWP for re-determination. A review for a crisis loan for urgent living expenses should be carried out within 24 hours. If you are dissatisfied with an inspector's decision, you can ask the inspector to reconsider it, or you can apply for a judicial review in the High Court (you will need legal advice to do this and must act quickly).

J Means-tested benefits: common rules

This section of the Handbook looks at:

24 Premiums

1. Introduction

This section covers the common rules for means-tested benefits, which provide a basic amount of money for you and your partner to live on. Support for children is now usually provided by child tax credit (see Chapter 18). This section covers the common rules for:

- income-related employment and support allowance (ESA);
- income support;
- income-based jobseeker's allowance (JSA);
- housing benefit;
- council tax benefit; *and*
- pension credit.

Each of these benefits is calculated with reference to an applicable amount, which is the amount of money the law says you need to live on. The applicable amount is made up of a number of different elements, including flat-rate amounts known as 'premiums'; these are covered in this chapter. Another element can cover certain housing costs; this is covered in Chapter 25. Your means-tested benefit could be affected by your earnings or other income; this is covered in Chapter 26. Finally, capital and savings can affect your benefit; we cover this in Chapter 27. Since income and savings are treated in a different manner for pension credit, we cover the separate rules for this benefit in Chapter 42.

The premiums

There are seven different types of premium:

- disability premium;
- severe disability premium;
- enhanced disability premium;
- pensioner premium;
- carer premium;
- family premium; *and*
- disabled child premium.

You are entitled to these premiums if you satisfy certain conditions, detailed in 2 to 8 below. The eligibility rules for these premiums are generally the same for each benefit; where there are differences, we will point this out. However, not all the premiums apply to each means-tested benefit. The family premium, disabled child premium and the enhanced disability premium (for a child) usually only apply to housing benefit and council tax benefit. They can only apply to income support or income-based JSA if your claim for either of these benefits began before April 2004 and you continue to receive support for your children through that benefit rather than through child tax credit. The disability premium does not apply to income-related ESA (and has a limited application to housing benefit and council tax benefit). Only the severe disability premium and the carer premium apply to pension credit (and are named 'amounts' rather than premiums, although the eligibility rules are similar).

For the sake of simplicity, we generally confine the legal references to those applicable to income-related ESA and income support.

2. The disability premium

The disability premium does not apply to either income-related employment and support allowance (ESA) or pension credit. Nor does it apply to housing benefit (HB) or council tax benefit (CTB) if you are claiming ESA once you have established an entitlement to ESA (through being found to have, or treated as having, a limited capability for work).

HB Regs, Sch 3, para 13(9); CTB Regs, Sch 1, para 13(10)

For a single claimant aged 16 or over, the disability premium is £27.50. For a couple, the disability premium is £39.15, whether one or both of the couple count as disabled.

The disability premium can be awarded on top of an enhanced disability premium, carer premium and severe disability premium. The disability premium is payable only while the person who qualifies is aged under 60.

There are two ways of qualifying for the premium:

- you (or your partner) must meet at least one of the disability conditions; *or*
- the person who is, or becomes, the claimant meets the incapacity condition.

IS Regs, Sch 2, paras 11-12

The disability conditions (claimant or partner)

You (or your partner) must be:

- registered as blind, or taken off that register in the past 28 weeks; *or*
- receiving one of the following qualifying benefits:
  - attendance allowance
  - disability living allowance (DLA)
  - long-term incapacity benefit (IB)
  - severe disablement allowance (SDA)
  - the disability element or severe disability element of working tax credit
  - war pensioner's mobility supplement
  - constant attendance allowance

(but you or your partner must satisfy the conditions for getting that benefit yourselves; it doesn't count if you are paid someone else's benefit as an appointee).

IS Regs, Sch 2, para 12(1)(a) & (2)

Points to note – If your DLA stops when you are in hospital, you won't lose the disability premium as well; it can continue for up to 52 weeks of the hospital stay.

IS Regs, Sch 2, para 12(1)(d)

If you have been getting long-term IB or SDA, and have already qualified for the disability premium, the premium won't be withdrawn if you go on a government training course such as Work-based Learning for Adults or for any period in which you receive a training allowance. Nor will the premium be withdrawn if the overlapping benefit rules mean that you cannot be paid your long-term IB or SDA (eg because you start to receive a bereavement allowance).

IS Regs, Sch 2, paras 7(1)

As mentioned above, the disability premium does not apply to a claim you make for HB or CTB if you are claiming ESA once you have established an entitlement to ESA. However, if you are the ESA claimant and you have a partner who claims HB or CTB instead, and one of you gets a qualifying benefit (eg DLA), then the disability premium could be awarded.

Backdating the premium – If you get one of these qualifying benefits backdated, you should ask for the disability premium to be backdated to either the start of your means-tested benefit claim or the start of your award of the qualifying benefit, whichever is the later.

If you claim income support (IS) or income-based jobseeker's allowance (JSA) and this is turned down while you are still waiting for a decision on a claim for one of these qualifying benefits, you must make sure that you make another IS/JSA claim within three months of the decision awarding the qualifying benefit so that you don't lose out on backdated IS/JSA.

The incapacity condition (claimant only)

Now that ESA has been introduced, this route will be limited in scope. It will still be relevant to people who have made claims on the basis of incapacity prior to the date that ESA was introduced: 27.10.08.

To qualify under the incapacity condition, you must:

- have been incapable of work or entitled to statutory sick pay during the qualifying period of 52 weeks (or 28 weeks if you are terminally ill); *and*
- still be incapable of work. See Chapter 13 for details of the assessment of incapacity for work.

You must be the claimant. If you are one of a couple, you must become the claimant. But you don't have to have been the claimant during the qualifying period.

IS Regs, Sch 2, para 12(1)(b)

During the qualifying period – You don't have to be in receipt of the means-tested benefit during the 52-week qualifying period, so if you have already been incapable of work for 52 weeks before you claim, the disability premium will be included immediately. There are linking rules that allow gaps in your incapacity during the qualifying period to be ignored (see below). The qualifying period is 28 weeks if you are terminally ill. You count as terminally ill if you *'suffer from a progressive disease and [your] death can reasonably be expected within 6 months'*.

After you have qualified – If you stop being incapable of work, you will lose the disability premium unless you can pass the 'disability condition' (eg you get one of the qualifying benefits) – see above. But you will be able to go straight back onto the disability premium if you become incapable of work again and the two spells of incapacity are linked (see below).

If you go on a government training course or receive a training allowance you will not lose the disability premium.

IS Regs, Sch 2, paras 7(1)(b)

8-week linking rule – Gaps of up to eight weeks in your incapacity (for any reason) are ignored. When you become incapable of work again, the two spells of incapacity are linked together. If you had already served the qualifying period, the disability premium is included again immediately. If you are still in the qualifying period, you pick up where you left off.

IS Regs, Sch 2, para 12(1)(b)(ii)(bb)

Welfare to work linking rule – If your incapacity stops because you begin work or training, you may be covered by a 104-week 'welfare to work' linking rule – see Chapter 16(12) for the qualifying conditions. The 104-week linking period starts from the day after your last day of incapacity. During this period your entitlement to the disability premium is protected if you become incapable of work again. If you are part-way through the qualifying period when you start work or training, you only need to serve the remainder of the qualifying period before the disability premium is included.

IS Regs, Sch 2, para 12(1A)

3. The severe disability premium

The severe disability premium (SDP) can be awarded on top of any disability premium, enhanced disability premium or pensioner premium that may be payable. It is £52.85 for each person who qualifies. To qualify:

- you must receive disability living allowance (DLA) care component at the middle or highest rate, or attendance allowance (AA) (or constant attendance allowance); *and*
- no one gets carer's allowance for looking after you; *and*
- you technically count as living alone (see below).

Couples – If you are one of a couple, you can qualify for the SDP if:

- both you and your partner get DLA care component at the middle or highest rate, or AA (or constant attendance allowance); *and*
- you technically count as living alone (see below); *and either*
- someone gets carer's allowance for looking after just one of you; *or*
- no one gets carer's allowance for looking after either of you.

If your partner is registered blind or severely sight impaired (or been taken off that register in the past 28 weeks), you can still qualify for the SDP even if they do not get DLA or AA. You are treated as if you were a single person.

If you both get middle or highest rate care component or AA and no one gets carer's allowance for looking after either you or your partner, your SDP will be £105.70.

If you both get middle or highest rate DLA care component or AA, and one person gets carer's allowance for looking after you (or your partner), your SDP will be £52.85. If two people are getting carer's allowance for looking after you and your partner, you won't get any SDP. It is possible for you and your partner to each get carer's allowance for looking after each other. Normally, this would disqualify you both from getting the SDP. However, when carer's allowance cannot actually be paid because of the overlapping benefit rules (which restrict you to getting paid just one type of non-means-tested benefit when you may be entitled to more than one), then the SDP would not be affected. If you both have overlapping benefits such that neither of you are actually paid carer's allowance, then not only could you get the higher SDP of £105.70, but you could also get two carer premiums (see 6 below).

ESA Regs, Sch 4, paras 6 & 11(2); IS Regs, Sch 2, para 13 & 15(5)

Is someone caring for you?

If someone gets carer's allowance for looking after you, you are excluded from the SDP. If carer's allowance is not actually payable to your carer, for whatever reason, you can get the SDP. For example, if carer's allowance cannot be paid to your carer because they get another non-means-tested benefit that cancels out carer's allowance under the overlapping benefit rules, you will be entitled to the SDP. In this example, your carer may also qualify for a carer premium (see 6 below). If your carer stops being paid carer's allowance, but it is some time before the office administering your means-tested benefit becomes aware of that fact, arrears of the SDP can be paid from the date that the carer's allowance stopped.

D&A Regs, reg 7(2)(bc)

Your carer cannot be forced to claim carer's allowance. The DWP will ask if anyone is caring for you, and will send you the carer's allowance claim-form to give to your carer, but nothing should happen if a non-resident carer decides not to claim carer's allowance. If your carer does claim carer's allowance, they will need you to confirm on the claim-form that they are caring for you for at least 35 hours a week.

Note that the deprivation of income and notional income rules apply also to carer's allowance (see Chapter 26(20)). Seek advice if you or your carer fall foul of these rules (see also para 28608, Vol 5, *Decision Makers Guide*).

Arrears of carer's allowance – Your premium is only affected once carer's allowance is actually awarded. Arrears of carer's allowance for any period before the date of the award will not affect your SDP.

ESA Regs, Sch 4, para 6(6); IS Regs, Sch 2, para 13(3ZA)

Living alone?

You cannot qualify for the SDP if you have a partner who is not also getting the middle or highest rate of DLA care component or AA (unless your partner is registered blind or severely sight impaired), or if you have people living with you who are classed as 'non-dependants'. A non-dependant is someone who lives in your home – usually an adult son or daughter, friend or relative. The following are not classed as non-dependants and their presence in your home is ignored:

- anyone aged under 18;
- anyone aged 18 or 19 who is part of your family and counts as a 'qualifying young person' for child benefit purposes (see Chapter 38(1));
- someone who is not a *'close relative'* of you (or your partner) and *'jointly occupies'* your dwelling as a co-owner or who is sharing legal liability to make 'rent' payments – a joint occupier, such as a joint tenant, cannot count as a non-dependant. If a co-owner or joint tenant is a close relative of you (or your partner), they will count as a non-dependant (and so exclude you from the SDP) unless the co-ownership or joint liability began:
  - before 11.4.88; *or*
  - after 11.4.88 but began *'on or before the date upon which [you or your] partner first occupied the dwelling in question'*;
- someone who is not a close relative of you (or your partner) and who is your resident landlord sharing living accommodation with you – to whom you or your partner are *'liable to make payments on a commercial basis in respect of [your] occupation of [his or her] dwelling'*;
- someone who is not a close relative of you (or your partner) and who shares living accommodation with you and is *'liable to make payments on a commercial basis to [you or your partner] in respect of [his or her] occupation of [your] dwelling'*. A licensee, tenant or sub-tenant cannot count as a non-dependant;
- a live-in helper (and, for income-related employment and support allowance, income support and income-based jobseeker's allowance, their partner) who has been placed with you by a charitable or voluntary body (not by a public or local authority), where the organisation (not the helper) charges you for that help. The charge need only be nominal.

ESA Regs, reg 71, IS Regs, reg 3

The presence of the following are also ignored:

- someone who gets the middle or highest rate DLA care component or AA (or constant attendance allowance);
- anyone who is registered blind or severely sight impaired (or been taken off that register in the past 28 weeks).

ESA Regs, Sch 4, para 6(4)(a) & (c); IS Regs, Sch 2, para 13(3)(a) & (d)

If someone does not *'normally'* reside with you because they normally live elsewhere, they cannot count as a non-dependant (there is no definition of 'normally resides' in terms of time, frequency or anything else – see CSIS/100/93 and CIS/14850/96).

If you are already getting the SDP and someone else joins your household *'for the first time in order to care for [you or your partner]'*, the SDP continues for up to 12 weeks after the date they join your household to give them time to claim carer's allowance. Once carer's allowance is awarded, the SDP stops.

ESA Regs, Sch 4, para 6(4)(b) & (7); IS Regs, Sch 2, para 13(3)(c) & (4)

Close relatives and living arrangements

A 'close relative' is a parent, parent-in-law, son, daughter, son-in-law or daughter-in-law, step-parent, stepson or stepdaughter, brother, sister or the partner of any of those.

ESA Regs, reg 2(1); IS Regs, reg 2(1)

If you have a licence or tenancy agreement with a relative who is not a close relative, you (or they) would only be excluded from the SDP while you were residing with them if your occupancy agreement was not on a commercial basis.

Living independently? – If you have entirely separate living accommodation, you cannot be said to 'normally reside' with other people living under the same roof. For example, if you live in a separate granny flat, your right to the SDP is not affected, even if a close relative lives under the same roof. If you are living under the same roof as other people, with a separate bedroom, kitchen and living room, you won't count as residing with those other people so you can qualify for the SDP. It makes no difference if you share a bathroom, lavatory or communal area (which does not include any communal rooms, unless you are living in sheltered accommodation).

Separate liability – If you share a living room or kitchen with other people but are *'separately liable to make payments in respect of [your] occupation of the dwelling to the landlord'*, you won't count as residing with those other people even if they are close relatives. This would typically cover someone in supported lodgings.

ESA Regs, reg 71(6); IS Regs, reg 3(4)

Protecting pre-21.10.91 SDP

If you are a co-owner or joint tenant with a close relative and had an award of income support, including an SDP, in the week before 21.10.91, your position is protected. Protection will survive changes in the type of agreement, in the parties to the agreement, and even a move of home. It cannot survive a carer getting carer's allowance or a non-dependant joining your home. If you have a break off income support, you can regain your protected SDP if:

- the break is no more than eight weeks or less (for any reason); *or*
- the break is no more than 12 weeks (covered by the work 'trial period' provisions); *or*
- you have just finished employment training or an employment rehabilitation course and you re-claim income support immediately.

IS (General) Amdt No.6 Regs 1991, regs 4-6

Hospital

If you enter hospital, the SDP will be withdrawn once your DLA care component or AA is withdrawn – usually once you've been in hospital for four weeks.

For couples, if both of you get DLA care component or AA, and one or both of you enters hospital, you will still get the SDP even after the care component or AA is withdrawn, but the SDP will only be paid at the rate of £52.85.

ESA Regs, Sch 4, paras 6(5) & 11(2)(b)(i); IS Regs, Sch 2, paras 13(3A) & 15(5)(b)(i)

If your carer enters hospital and loses carer's allowance, you may qualify for the SDP while they are in hospital.

4. The enhanced disability premium

The enhanced disability premium does not apply to pension credit. It is £13.40 for a single person and £19.30 for a couple where one or both qualify. You or your partner qualify for the enhanced disability premium if you or they are paid disability living allowance (DLA) highest rate care component or you have been found to have, or are treated as having, a limited capability for work-related activity. It can be awarded on top of any disability premium or severe disability premium that may be payable. The enhanced disability premium is payable only while the person who qualifies is aged under 60.

If your DLA stops when you are in hospital, you won't lose

the enhanced disability premium. It can continue for up to 52 weeks of the hospital stay.

ESA Regs, Sch 4, para 7; IS Regs, Sch 2, para 13A

The enhanced disability premium (child) – This premium generally applies only to housing benefit and council tax benefit. It can still be paid with income support or income-based jobseeker's allowance if your claim began before April 2004 and you continue to receive support for your children through one of those benefits rather than child tax credit. The enhanced disability premium is paid at the rate of £20.65 for each child who qualifies.

A child qualifies for the enhanced disability premium if they are paid DLA highest rate care component. It can be awarded on top of a disabled child premium. If a child is in hospital, you keep the enhanced disability premium for as long as the child is treated as a member of your family.

HB Regs, Sch 3, para 15 & CTB Regs, Sch 1, para 15

5. The pensioner premium

The pensioner premium does not apply to pension credit, nor to housing benefit (HB) or council tax benefit (CTB) if you or your partner are aged 60 or over and not claiming income support or income-based jobseeker's allowance (JSA). There are only limited circumstances in which the pensioner premium will be relevant to an income support claim. It is payable only when the income support claimant is under 60 and their partner reaches the age of 60 first and chooses not to claim pension credit instead. Since pension credit has a number of features that make it more attractive than income support (particularly with respect to the way in which capital and savings are treated), this is not likely to occur very often.

The pensioner premium is paid if you or your partner are aged 60 years or over. It can be awarded in addition to the severe disability premium and the carer premium.

The pensioner premium is normally £65.70 for a single person and £97.50 for a couple. For income-related employment and support allowance, however, these figures are then reduced by any work-related component or support component that may be payable (this ensures that your applicable amount, before any other premiums are added on, is equivalent to the standard rate of pension credit: £130 a week for a single person and £198.45 a week for a couple).

ESA Regs, Sch 4, paras 5 & 11(1)

Enhanced and higher pensioner premiums – For income support, income-based JSA, HB and CTB, the pensioner premium was originally paid at three different levels: the pensioner, enhanced, and higher pensioner premiums. Although these separate premiums still technically exist, they are now all paid at the same rate – ie the amount you get is the same whichever one you qualify for. The difference occasionally becomes important (we point out when it does).

- ❑ **Pensioner premium** – You qualify for this if you or your partner are aged 60-74 (inclusive).
- ❑ **Enhanced pensioner premium** – You qualify for this if you or your partner are aged 75-79 (inclusive).
- ❑ **Higher pensioner premium** – You qualify for this if you or your partner are aged:
  - 80 or over; *or*
  - 60 or over and also satisfy the 'disability condition' for a disability premium (see 2 above).

  There are other ways to qualify for the higher pensioner premium. For details see *Disability Rights Handbook* 25th edition, page 20.

IS Regs, Sch 2, paras 9-10

6. The carer premium

The carer premium can be awarded in addition to any of the other premiums covered in this chapter. It is £29.50 a week for each person who qualifies.

You'll qualify for a carer premium if you or your partner:

- are actually paid an amount of carer's allowance; *or*
- have an underlying entitlement to carer's allowance: ie you are entitled to it but it cannot be paid because of the overlapping benefit rules (see Chapter 6(6)).

8-week extension – The carer premium can continue for eight weeks after you stop getting carer's allowance or lose an underlying entitlement to it. Your caring role can have ended temporarily or permanently and for any reason, with one exception: where the person you are caring for dies, in which case, since carer's allowance can also be extended for eight weeks, the carer premium can continue during the same period and is limited to that period. Thus, it must stop being paid eight weeks after the death of the cared-for person.

ESA Regs, Sch 4, para 8; IS Regs, Sch 2, para 14ZA

7. The family premium

This premium generally applies only to housing benefit (HB) and council tax benefit (CTB). It can still be paid with income support or income-based jobseeker's allowance (JSA) if your claim began before April 2004 and you continue to receive support for your children through one of those benefits rather than child tax credit.

The family premium is awarded if you have a dependent child or 'qualifying young person' (see Chapter 38(1)) aged under 20. You only get one family premium, regardless of the number of children you have. The ordinary rate of £17.30 is awarded if you are one of a couple or a lone parent, unless you have transitional protection for the HB/CTB higher lone parent rate of £22.20 (see below). For HB and CTB, if your family includes a child under the age of one, you will receive an additional £10.50. The ordinary rate can be awarded in addition to any other premium.

Protected lone parent rate – The lone parent rate was abolished on 6.4.98 but existing HB/CTB claimants can continue to get it. You must have been a lone parent entitled (or treated as entitled) to HB or CTB on 5.4.98 and have continued to be entitled to it. You must not cease to be or become entitled to either income support or income-based JSA. If you are or become entitled to a disability premium or any pensioner premium, your family premium switches to the ordinary rate. But you regain the lone parent rate if the disability premium or pensioner premium stops.

HB Regs, Sch 3, para 3 & CTB Regs, Sch 1, para 3

8. The disabled child premium

This premium generally applies only to housing benefit and council tax benefit. It can still be paid with income support or income-based jobseeker's allowance if your claim began before April 2004 and you continue to receive support for your children through one of those benefits rather than child tax credit. The disabled child premium can be awarded in addition to any of the other premiums. The disabled child premium is £51.24 for each child who lives with you and counts as disabled. Your child counts as disabled if they:

- are registered blind, or were taken off that register within the past 28 weeks; *or*
- get disability living allowance (DLA); *or*
- no longer get DLA because they are in hospital – as long as they are still treated as a member of your family.

HB Regs, Sch 3, para 16 & CTB Regs, Sch 1, para 16

25 Housing costs

1. The basic rules

Income-related employment and support allowance (ESA), income support, income-based jobseeker's allowance (JSA) and pension credit can all help with mortgage interest payments and certain other housing costs. If you pay rent, you may be able to get housing benefit (HB) instead (see Chapter 20). For help with the cost of a care home, see Chapter 33.

Housing costs can be included in your applicable amount if:

- you or your partner are liable for the housing costs at the home you normally live in (see 2 below); *and*
- the type of housing costs is covered (see 2 and 3 below); *and*
- your mortgage was not taken out while you or your partner were on income-related ESA, income support, income-based JSA or pension credit or, in some cases, between claims for one or more of these benefits (there are some exceptions) – see 3 below.

The amount of housing costs met is worked out taking into account the following:

- whether your housing costs are 'excessive' (see 3 below);
- an upper limit or 'ceiling' on loans (there are some exceptions) – see 4 below;
- a standard rate of interest applied to loans (see 4 below);
- deductions for 'non-dependants' living with you (eg adult son or daughter, friend or relative). It is assumed they contribute towards your housing costs, whether they do or not. Unless your or your non-dependant's circumstances exempt you from the deduction, an amount is deducted from your assessed housing costs. The rules are almost the same as for HB (see Chapter 20(22)). No deduction is made, however, if a deduction for that non-dependant is already being made from your HB;

ESA Regs, Sch 6, para 19; IS Regs, Sch 3, para 18

- a waiting period (ie a number of weeks you must be entitled to the means-tested benefit before housing costs are included in your applicable amount) – see 5 below.

Jobseeker's allowance – If your claim for JSA began on or after 5.1.09, any help with interest on qualifying mortgages or loans will be limited to a period of 104 weeks. This limit will not apply if you (or your partner in the case of a joint claim) were claiming either income support or ESA in the 12 weeks prior to your JSA award. In calculating the 104-week period, any linked periods when you come off JSA (see Chapter 15(2)) are disregarded.

JSA Regs, Sch 2, para 4A; Statutory Instrument 2008/3195, para 11

Absence from home – Generally, you can only get help on one home at a time and this must be the home you occupy. In some situations you are treated as occupying your home when you are not actually present there – eg during a temporary absence or when moving home; the rules are almost the same as for HB (see Chapter 20(6) and (7)).

ESA Regs, Sch 6, para 5; IS Regs, Sch 3, para 3

2. Housing costs you can get help with

Liability for housing costs

You (or your partner) must be liable for housing costs for the home you live in. The liability cannot be to a member of your household. If it is reasonable to do so, you can be treated as liable if the person normally liable for the costs is not meeting them and you have to meet them in order to carry on living in your home.

If someone living with you is liable for the housing costs and that person is not a close relative of you or your partner, you can be treated as sharing the costs if it is reasonable to do so. A 'close relative' is a parent, parent-in-law, son, daughter, son-in-law or daughter-in-law, step-parent, stepson or stepdaughter, brother, sister or the partner of any of those.

ESA Regs, reg 2 & Sch 6, para 4; IS Regs, reg 2 & Sch 3, para 2

Housing costs covered

The following housing costs can be included as part of your applicable amount:

- mortgage interest payments and interest on other loans taken out to buy your home (see 3 and 4 below);
- interest on loans for certain repairs and improvements (see below);
- some service charges payable as a condition of your occupancy (eg under a lease) relating to the provision of adequate accommodation. House insurance can be included if payments are made under the terms of the lease, rather than as a condition of the mortgage (R(IS)4/92). Service charges for repairs and improvements listed below are not met, although you can get help to pay interest on a loan taken out to pay these charges. Service charges are not met if they would be ineligible under the housing benefit rules (see Chapter 20(8));
- ground rent or other rent payable under a long lease of over 21 years;
- payments under a co-ownership scheme;
- rent if you are a Crown tenant;
- payments for a tent and site fees;
- rentcharges – nominal charges sometimes due as a condition of a freehold.

ESA Regs, Sch 6, paras 16-18; IS Regs, Sch 3, paras 15-17

Interest on mortgages, higher purchase agreements or other loans is only covered if used:

- to buy your home – including buying your home jointly with others, buying the freehold if you are a leaseholder (R(IS)7/93) or buying out a joint owner;
- to pay off an earlier loan, but only to the extent that the earlier loan would have already been met. For example, if your outstanding mortgage was £10,000 and you borrow £12,000 to repay it, only the interest on £10,000 of the second loan is covered;
- for certain repairs and improvements (see below).

If part of a loan is taken out for a different purpose (eg a business loan), that part of the loan will not be covered.

ESA Regs, Sch 6, paras 16 & 17; IS Regs, Sch 3, paras 15 & 16

If your loan is covered, an amount is added to your applicable amount, worked out according to the rules in 4 below. (See 5 below for when entitlement to housing costs can begin.) If your lender is part of the Mortgage Direct scheme, this amount is deducted from your benefit and paid 4-weekly in arrears directly to your lender.

Loans for repairs and improvements

The interest on loans taken out and used within six months (or longer if reasonable) to pay for repairs and improvements to your home is covered. These must be *'undertaken with a view to maintaining the fitness of the dwelling for human habitation'* and fall within the following categories:

- adapting your home for *'the special needs of a disabled person'*. See below for who counts as *'a disabled person'* for this rule;
- provision of a bath, shower, sink or lavatory (and associated plumbing);
- provision of ventilation, natural lighting, insulation or electric lighting and sockets;
- provision of facilities for preparing and cooking food, storing fuel or refuse, or for drainage;
- provision of separate bedrooms for children or young

people of different sexes aged 10 or over but under 20 who live with you and for whom you are responsible;

- repairs to existing heating systems or of unsafe structural defects; *or*
- damp proofing.

Loans to pay service charges for any of these works are covered, as are loans used to pay off an existing loan for repairs, but only to the extent that the existing loan would have qualified.

ESA Regs, Sch 6, para 17; IS Regs, Sch 3, para 16

Who counts as a 'disabled person'? – Someone is considered to be 'a disabled person' if, at the date the loan is taken out:

- they satisfy the conditions for a disability premium, disabled child premium, enhanced or higher pensioner premium (for income support (IS) and income-based jobseeker's allowance (JSA), but they don't actually have to be getting any of these premiums or be entitled to IS or JSA); *or*
- they are being paid main phase employment and support allowance (ESA); *or*
- had they been entitled to IS, they would have qualified for the disability premium (for ESA); *or*
- they would qualify for the disabled or severely disabled child elements of child tax credit (for income support, JSA and ESA).
- they are aged 75 or over (for pension credit and ESA); *or*
- had they been entitled to IS, they would have qualified for the higher pensioner or disability premium (for pension credit); *or*
- they are under 20, you or your partner are responsible for them and they get disability living allowance (or would get it were they not in hospital) or are registered as blind (for pension credit).

The disabled person could be you (the claimant) or a member of your family or someone else who lives with you or who will be living with you.

ESA Regs, Sch 6, para 1(3); IS Regs, Sch 3, para 1(3); SPC Regs, Sch 2, para 1(2)(a)

3. Housing costs you cannot get help with

Housing costs not covered

Your personal allowances are intended to cover day-to-day living expenses, including the cost of water and fuel. For this reason, water and fuel charges cannot be included as housing costs. Other housing costs not covered include:

- housing costs covered by housing benefit;
- ineligible service charges – see Chapter 20(8);
- capital repayments, endowment premiums, or arrears payable on a loan or mortgage;
- mortgage interest on a new or additional loan taken out while you were on income-related employment and support allowance (ESA), income support (IS), income-based jobseeker's allowance (JSA) or pension credit, or in some cases between claims for one or more of these benefits – see below;
- excessive housing costs – see below.

Following changes to the rules on 2.10.95, some housing costs previously covered by IS can no longer be met: arrears of mortgage interest payments; loans for certain repairs and improvements; and extra help to separated couples with loans secured on the home. If, in the benefit week including 1.10.95, your applicable amount included interest for such a loan, it will continue to be met as long as you or your partner remain on IS or JSA, disregarding any breaks in entitlement of 12 weeks or less. If you separate from your partner, you keep this protection. If you start work or training and are covered by the welfare to work linking rule (see Chapter 16(12)), this protection should be maintained on a new claim where you become incapable of work again within your 104-week linking period.

Income Support (Gen.) Amdt. and Transitional Regs 1995

Mortgages taken out while on specified benefits or between claims

The general rule is that mortgage interest is not met on a loan taken out to buy a home while you or your partner were on a specified benefit (income-related ESA, IS, income-based JSA, pension credit or on certain New Deal options); or within a break in entitlement to a specified benefit of 26 weeks or less. The intention is to restrict your entitlement to the level of help (if any) to which you were already entitled.

If a restriction is made, it applies until you have a break in entitlement of over 26 weeks to a specified benefit. Some loans may not be restricted in this way (see below). These restrictions do not apply to loans for repairs and improvements.

ESA Regs, Sch 6, para 6(2) & (4); IS Regs, Sch 3, para 4(2) & (4)

Replacement or additional loans – If you already have a mortgage and you increase it or take out an additional loan while on a specified benefit (or between claims), the additional amount is not met. You can replace one mortgage with another provided the new mortgage is for the same amount or less.

If your new mortgage is used to buy a home and you pay off all or part of the mortgage on your old home from the sale of that property, payment for the new mortgage is restricted to the amount of the earlier loan. Arguably, this could allow a separated couple who sell their home to each have mortgage interest covered on a new home at the full amount of the previous mortgage (CIS/11293/1995).

ESA Regs, Sch 6, para 6(8); IS Regs, Sch 3, para 4(6)

If you were previously getting housing benefit – If you take on a mortgage while on a specified benefit (or between claims), the payment for mortgage interest and for other housing costs (such as service charges and ground rent) is restricted to the level of housing benefit payable to you or your partner in the week before the week you buy the home. If you were getting both housing benefit and housing costs in that week, perhaps because you were on a shared ownership scheme, the restriction is applied to the total of housing benefit payable plus the housing costs included in your applicable amount. The restricted amount can only then increase if the standard interest rate (see 4 below) goes up or there is an increase in service charges or ground rent, etc.

ESA Regs, Sch 6, para 6(10); IS Regs, Sch 3, para 4(8)

If your applicable amount previously included only housing costs other than loan interest (eg service charges or ground rent) – If you take on a mortgage while on a specified benefit (or between claims), the level of housing costs included in your applicable amount is restricted to that already included in the week before the week you buy the home. The restricted amount can only then increase if the standard interest rate goes up or there is an increase in service charges or ground rent, etc.

ESA Regs, Sch 6, para 6(13); IS Regs, Sch 3, para 4(11)

Loans exempt from these restrictions – In the following cases, loans are exempt from the restrictions described above and housing costs are worked out under the usual rules:

- the loan was taken out before 3.5.94;
- the loan was taken out, or an existing loan increased, to buy *'alternative accommodation more suited to the special needs of a disabled person'* (see 2 above for who counts as a disabled person). This could include moving home to be nearer a carer (CIS/14551/96) or moving to sheltered housing;
- an additional or increased loan was taken out because you've sold your home to buy another solely to provide separate bedrooms for children or young people of different sexes aged 10 or over but under 20 for whom you are responsible.

ESA Regs, Sch 6, para 6(2), (11) & (12); IS Regs, Sch 3, paras 4(2), (9) & (10)

Even if a loan is exempt from these restrictions, a ceiling may still be applied to it (see 4 below).

Excessive housing costs

The amount of housing costs met may be restricted if they are regarded as 'excessive', eg your home is larger than you need for your household, the area is more expensive than other areas where there is suitable alternative accommodation, or your housing costs are higher than those for suitable alternative accommodation in the area.

No restriction is made if it is not reasonable to expect you to move, taking into account the availability of suitable alternative accommodation, the level of housing costs in the area, and the circumstances of you and your family. In particular, the age and health of you and your family must be considered, as well as your employment prospects and the effect of a move on a child or young person's education. Other factors may also be relevant – eg whether you provide care, or rely on the care or support of someone nearby.

No restriction is made for the first 26 weeks of your claim or after a decision is made to introduce a restriction if you could afford the costs when you took them on; nor for a further 26 weeks if you're doing your best to find cheaper accommodation. The 26 weeks continues to run during a break in the means-tested benefit of 12 weeks or less.

If a restriction is applied, the amount of loan to be met is restricted to the amount you need to obtain suitable alternative accommodation.

ESA Regs, Sch 6, para 14; IS Regs, Sch 3, para 13

4. Calculating your housing costs

The outstanding balance of your qualifying mortgage(s) and/or loan(s) is multiplied by a standard interest rate to give a qualifying amount of interest for the year. A weekly rate of qualifying interest is calculated by dividing the yearly figure by 52. Other qualifying housing costs (eg service charges) are calculated at a weekly rate and added to this figure. The result is added to your applicable amount.

ESA Regs, Sch 6, paras 11, 13 & 18; IS Regs, Sch 3, paras 10, 12 & 17

Deductions from your housing costs are made for non-dependant contributions (see 1 above).

In most cases, there is a waiting period before the loan interest is included in your applicable amount (see 5 below).

Once loan interest is included, reductions to the amount of eligible capital owing (eg if you make capital repayments) are only taken into account one year from the date the costs were first included in your applicable amount and then annually thereafter. If you move between employment and support allowance (ESA), income support, income-based jobseeker's allowance (JSA) or pension credit, reductions in the outstanding balance are taken into account on the anniversary of the housing costs first being included in any of these benefits.

ESA Regs, Sch 6, para 8(2) & (3); IS Regs, Sch 3, para 6(1A) & (1B)

The ceiling on mortgages and loans

If your loan (or the total of your loans) is above a certain set level or ceiling, the interest met is worked out only on the part of the loan up to the level of this ceiling. The ceiling is currently £100,000. A higher ceiling of £200,000 applies to claims of income-related ESA, income support and income-based JSA made on or after 5.1.09 (and which do not link back to a previous claim made before 5.1.09 – see 5 below). The higher ceiling also applies if you were entitled to one of these benefits but you are still serving the waiting period (see 5 below) on 4.1.09. The higher ceiling continues to apply if you move onto pension credit, if no more than 12 weeks separate the last day of your claim for ESA, income support or JSA and the first day of your entitlement to pension credit. If you are eligible for housing costs to be covered on two homes, the ceiling is applied separately to each home. The higher ceiling will be reviewed once the housing market recovers.

ESA Regs, Sch 6, para 12(3)-(5); IS Regs, Sch 3, para 11(4)-(6); Statutory Instrument 2008/3195

Any loan taken out to adapt your existing home *'for the special needs of a disabled person'* (see 2 above) is ignored when working out whether your loans exceed the ceiling.

ESA Regs, Sch 6, para 12(8); IS Regs, Sch 3, para 11(9)

The £100,000 ceiling applies to claims made from 10.4.95. If you have been on income support or JSA continuously since before this, existing loans will be met up to the level of the ceiling that applied at the time the claim was made. For claims made:

- prior to 2.8.93, there was no ceiling;
- between 2.8.93 and 10.4.94, the ceiling was £150,000;
- between 11.4.94 and 9.4.95, the ceiling was £125,000.

Loans you take out or increase while on a means-tested benefit are subject to whichever ceiling applies at the time you take out or increase the loan. In this case, the loan is met to the level of the ceiling that applied at the time the first claim was made. Generally, a break in your claim(s) of just one day is enough to end this protection. However, if you start work or training and are covered by the welfare to work linking rule (see Chapter 16(12)), you keep the protection during a break in your claim(s) of up to 104-weeks.

ESA Regs, Sch 6, para 20; IS Regs, Sch 3, para 14(3AA)

See Chapter 26(13) for the way in which payments from a mortgage protection insurance policy to cover the interest on the part of a loan above the ceiling are treated when your income is assessed.

The standard interest rate

The DWP uses a standard interest rate to calculate the amount of interest that is added to your applicable amount. From 5.1.09 it is 6.08%. It will be reviewed in July 2009.

ESA Regs, Sch 6, para 13; IS Regs, Sch 3, para 12

Before 2.10.95, housing costs were worked out using actual interest rates. There is transitional protection (called 'add back') for those who have received housing costs with a means-tested benefit since this date and who would otherwise have lost out when the rules changed. See *Disability Rights Handbook* 24th edition, page 23.

ESA Regs, Sch 6, para 20(1)(b); IS Regs, Sch 3, para 7

5. Waiting periods

In most cases, there is a 13-week waiting period at the start of your entitlement to a means-tested benefit before housing costs are included in your applicable amount. The 13-week waiting period was introduced on 5.1.09. Prior to this, longer waiting periods were in place, for details see *Disability Rights Handbook* 33rd edition, page 22. The waiting period length will be reviewed once the housing market recovers.

If you are not entitled to contribution-based jobseeker's allowance (JSA) or contributory employment and support allowance (ESA) and, without the inclusion of housing costs, your income would exceed your applicable amount, a 39-week waiting period will apply instead (during this period you can be treated as entitled to the means-tested benefit once you have claimed it – see below). This could be the case if you were already receiving incapacity benefit on 4.1.09 and had claimed income support, in which case you would need to re-apply for income support once you have completed the 39-week qualifying period. The qualifying period can only begin once you put in a claim for the means-tested benefit.

The waiting period at the start of your benefit entitlement begins even if you have no housing costs at the time. So, if you take out a loan while on benefit, having already served the waiting period, and you are eligible for help with the costs, housing costs can be included immediately.

ESA Regs, Sch 6, paras 8(1) & 9(1); IS Regs, Sch 3, paras 6(1) & 8(1); Statutory Instrument 2008/3195

No waiting period

Pension credit – The waiting period does not apply to claims for pension credit.

If your partner is aged 60 or over – Eligible housing costs are included in your applicable amount from the beginning of your benefit entitlement, or from the day your partner reaches 60 if you are part-way through the waiting period.

Certain housing costs – There is no waiting period for payments under a co-ownership scheme, rent for a Crown tenant or payments on a tent.

ESA Regs, Sch 6, para 10; IS Regs, Sch 3, para 9

If you are not entitled to the means-tested benefit during the waiting period

Throughout the waiting period, you must usually be entitled to the means-tested benefit, although breaks in entitlement of up to 12 weeks are ignored.

During a break in claims, or a change of claimant – You are treated as entitled to the means-tested benefit:

- during a gap in entitlement to the benefit of 12 weeks or less;
- during a gap between claims of up to 52 weeks if you are protected under the back-to-work linking rule, or up to 104 weeks if you are covered by the welfare to work/work or training linking rules (see below);
- for any period in which it is decided retrospectively that you were entitled to the benefit (eg following an appeal);
- during any time your partner was getting (or treated as getting) the benefit for both of you if you swap to become the claimant instead;
- during a gap between claims of 26 weeks or less where your last claim included full housing costs, your benefit stopped because of child support payments and you re-claim later because the child support payments either stop or are reduced;
- during a gap between claims while you or your partner were on certain government training schemes or New Deal options;
- for any period your ex-partner was getting (or treated as getting) the benefit for both of you, if you claim within 12 weeks of separating;
- for any time someone was claiming the benefit for you as their dependent child, if you claim within 12 weeks of the end of the claim and your claim includes a child who was also their dependant; *or*
- for any period that your new partner was getting (or treated as getting) the benefit as a single person or lone parent, if you claim within 12 weeks of becoming a couple.

In the last three cases, the 12-week linking period is extended to 52 weeks if the back-to-work linking rule applies, or to 104 weeks if you (or, in the last case, your partner) are covered by welfare to work/work or training linking rules (see below).

ESA Regs, Sch 6, para 15; IS Regs, Sch 3, para 14

You are treated as receiving income-related ESA during any time you have received income support, income-based JSA or pension credit or during any break in entitlement to those benefits (as listed above). You are treated as receiving income-based JSA during any time you have received income support or income-related ESA (including entitlement breaks listed above). You are treated as receiving income support during any time you have received income-based JSA (including entitlement breaks listed above).

ESA Regs, Sch 6, para 20(1)(c); Stat. Instrument 1996/206, reg 32

If your income or capital is over the limit – If you cannot get the means-tested benefit only because your income is higher than your applicable amount and/or your capital is over £16,000, you are treated as entitled to the benefit for up to 39 weeks if you satisfy one of the following conditions on each subsequent day (but gaps of up to 12 weeks are allowed):

- you are entitled to contributory ESA, contribution-based JSA, statutory sick pay or incapacity benefit; *or*
- you are entitled to national insurance credits for incapacity for work, limited capability for work or unemployment; *or*
- you are treated as entitled to the benefit during a break in claims, or because of a change in claimant (see above); *or*
- you are a lone parent or eligible for income support as a carer (even though you do not claim it) – provided you are not working 16 hours or more a week, your partner (if you are a carer) is not working 24 hours or more a week, you are not a full-time student excluded from the benefit and are not absent from the UK other than in circumstances described in Chapter 51(5). The 39 weeks runs from when your unsuccessful claim is made, so don't delay claiming.

If you also have a mortgage protection policy, the 39 weeks is extended to cover the period that payments are made under the policy, provided your capital is within the limit of £16,000 throughout.

ESA Regs, Sch 6, para 15(8)-(12); IS Regs, Sch 3, para 14(4)-(6)

Once you have qualified for housing costs

You will not have to serve the waiting period again if you have a break in your claim of 12 weeks or less, or longer if you are still treated as entitled to benefit (see above).

Back-to-work linking rule – If your means-tested benefit stops because you or your partner start work (employed or self-employed) or your working hours or earnings increase, you do not have to serve the waiting period again on a new claim if the break in claims is no longer than 52 weeks. Housing costs can be included from the start of your new claim. Similar protection will be afforded if your participation in certain government training schemes or New Deal options takes you off the benefit.

ESA Regs, Sch 6, para 15(16) & (17); IS Regs, Sch 3, para 14(11) & (12)

Welfare to work/work or training linking rules – If you have previously been incapable of work and are moving into work or training you may be covered by the more generous 104-week 'welfare to work' linking rule. A similar 'work or training' linking rule exists for ESA if you previously had a limited capability for work. See Chapter 16(12) for details.

Starting work – When you start work, you may continue to get housing costs, payable as income support, for the first four weeks (see Chapter 16(4)).

Insurance payments – If you have a break in claim of 26 weeks or less and payments from an insurance policy for unemployment have run out, your two claims are linked and the period in between during which you were receiving the insurance payments is ignored. Consequently, housing costs will resume from the start of your linked claim.

ESA Regs, Sch 6, paras 15(13) & (14); IS Regs, Sch 3, para 14(8) & (9)

26 Income

In this chapter we look at: page

1. Introduction

In this chapter we look at how the income you receive is treated when means-tested benefits are being calculated. The rules in this chapter apply to the following benefits:

- income-related employment and support allowance (ESA);
- income support;
- income-based jobseeker's allowance (JSA); *and*
- housing benefit and council tax benefit – as long as you (and your partner) are under 60 or still claiming one of three benefits listed above (otherwise the rules are similar to pension credit – see Chapter 42(5)).

Where there are significant differences in the way that income is treated for different benefits, we say so. As income is treated in a substantially different way for pension credit, we describe this separately in Chapter 42(5).

For the sake of simplicity, we generally confine the legal references to those applicable to income-related ESA and income support.

Disregarded income – All income is considered, including earnings, benefits and pensions, but your income may then be disregarded, partially disregarded or taken fully into account. If you have earnings, we outline how these are assessed, and how much is disregarded, in 3 to 5 below. If you have income other than earnings, see 6 to 16 below to check if any (or all) of it may be disregarded.

Income or capital? – Generally, it will be clear if a particular resource is income or capital, although the distinction is not defined in the regulations. Where it is unclear, the general principle (developed in case law) is that payments of income recur periodically and do not include ad hoc payments, whereas capital payments are one-off and not linked to a particular period (although capital may be paid in instalments). In some cases, the rules treat capital as income (see 18 below) and vice versa (see Chapter 27(8)).

In some cases you can be treated as possessing income that you don't actually have (see 20 below).

2. Whose income is included?

If you are one of a couple (married or living together as husband and wife, or in a same-sex partnership whether registered or not), your partner's income is added to your own. Otherwise, only your own income is taken into account; any income belonging to dependent children is disregarded (unless you have a claim for income support or income-based jobseeker's allowance that began before April 2004 and you continue to receive support for your children through one of those benefits rather than child tax credit – see *Disability Rights Handbook* 28th edition, page 25).

ESA Regs, reg 83; IS Regs, reg 23

3. Earnings from employment

How earnings from employment are assessed

The income assessment is normally related to your actual earnings in respect of a particular week. If you are paid monthly, that month's pay is multiplied by 12 and then divided by 52 to provide a weekly amount. If your income varies from week to week, there is discretion to take a more representative period and work out your average earnings over that period. If you have a regular pattern of working some weeks on, some weeks off, your average weekly earnings may be worked out over your working cycle: that average is then also taken into account in your off weeks.

ESA Regs, reg 94(1) & (6); IS Regs, reg 32(1) & (6)

If you are not being paid, or are underpaid for a service, 'notional' earnings may be taken into account (see 20 below).

Final earnings – If you have just retired, or your job has ended or been interrupted for some other reason (but not if you have been suspended), your last normal earnings as an employee will usually be disregarded. This includes pay in lieu of notice, holiday pay (payable within four weeks of the employment ending or being interrupted) and pay in lieu of remuneration (but not periodic redundancy payments). These disregards only apply when the job ends or is interrupted before the first day of entitlement to the means-tested benefit. Retainer payments and payments received under employment protection legislation will, however, be taken into account.

ESA Regs, reg 95(1) & Sch 7, para 1; IS Regs, reg 35(1) & Sch 8, para 1

Housing benefit (HB)/council tax benefit (CTB) – Your average weekly earnings are estimated over the five weeks before your HB/CTB claim if you are paid weekly, or the two months before your claim if you are paid monthly. But in either case, your local authority should average them over another period if that would give a more accurate estimate.

HB Regs, reg 29; CTB Regs, reg 19

Working out net earnings

Do not count any payment in kind (see 10 below) or *'any payment in respect of expenses wholly, exclusively and necessarily incurred in the performance of the duties of the employment'*. Occupational pensions are not treated as earnings, but are normally taken into account in full (as income) less tax payable (see 6 below).

ESA Regs, Sch 8, para 3; IS Regs, Sch 9, para 3

For income support, income-based jobseeker's allowance and income-related employment and support allowance do not count as earnings any sick pay, maternity pay, paternity pay or adoption pay from your employer, nor any statutory sick pay (SSP), statutory maternity pay (SMP), statutory paternity pay (SPP) or statutory adoption pay (SAP). Instead, these are counted in full (as income) less tax, national insurance contributions and half of any contributions you make towards an occupational or personal pension.

ESA Regs, regs 95(2)(b) & Sch 8, paras 1 & 4; IS Regs, reg 35(2)(b) & Sch 9, paras 1 & 4

For HB and CTB, the following are all counted as earnings: sick pay, maternity pay, paternity pay or adoption pay from your employer and SSP, SMP, SPP and SAP.

HB Regs, reg 35(1)(i)-(j) & CTB Regs, reg 25(1)(i)-(j)

An advance of earnings or a loan counts as capital.

ESA Regs, reg 112(5) & IS Regs, reg 48(5)

Count any other payment from your employer as earnings: eg bonuses, commission, payments towards travel expenses between your home and workplace or towards childminding fees and retainers (from your employer or from a boarder). Also count pay in lieu of notice and holiday pay, unless your job has ended or been interrupted for some other reason – see 'Final earnings' above. Most non-cash vouchers, but not childcare vouchers, count as earnings.

ESA Regs, reg 95(1) & (3); IS Regs, regs 35(1) & (2A)

Deduct from your earnings income tax, national insurance contributions and half of any contribution you make towards an occupational or personal pension scheme.

ESA Regs, reg 96; IS Regs, reg 36

4. Earnings from self-employment

There are specific rules for working out income from self-employment related to the net cash flow of your business or your share of the business. If you get royalties or copyright payments, seek advice.

Step 1: Take full gross receipts of the business

This is all the money you receive in respect of and generated by the business over a specific trading period. This is normally one year, but if you have recently started self-employment or there has been a change that is likely to affect the normal pattern of business, Jobcentre Plus can pick a different period more representative of your average weekly earnings.

ESA Regs, reg 92; IS Regs, reg 30

For housing benefit and council tax benefit, earnings are usually assessed over the period covered by your last year's trading accounts. A different period can be used if appropriate, if it is no longer than one year.

HB Regs, reg 30 & CTB Regs, regs 20

Step 2: Work out net profit – deduct:

- *'any expenses wholly and exclusively defrayed [ie actually paid] in that period for the purposes of that employment'*: this is subject to some exceptions and extra rules, eg the expenses must be 'reasonably incurred', and business entertainment is specifically excluded. Expenses can be apportioned between business and personal use (see R(FC)1/91 and R(IS)13/91);
- a repayment of capital on any loan used for replacing equipment or machinery, or for repairing existing business assets (less any insurance payments);
- the excess of VAT paid over VAT received;
- expenditure out of income to repair an existing business asset (less any insurance payment);
- interest (but not capital) payments on a loan taken out for the purposes of the employment.

The sum left after these deductions is your net profit. However, if you work as a childminder, simply deduct two-thirds of those earnings.

ESA Regs, reg 98(3)(a) & (5)-(9); IS Regs, reg 38(3)(a) & (5)-(9)

Step 3: From your net profit, deduct:

- income tax – this is based on your appropriate personal tax allowances, on a pro rata basis if necessary (see Chapter 52(3));
- Class 2 and Class 4 national insurance contributions;
- half of any contribution to a personal pension scheme (including annuity contracts or trust schemes approved under tax law).

ESA Regs, regs 98(3)(b)-(c) & 99; IS Regs, regs 38(3)(b)-(c) & 39

Step 4: See which earnings disregards apply

Check to see which, if any, earnings disregards apply (see below).

5. Earnings disregards

Once you have worked out your total earnings, as above, deduct the appropriate 'earnings disregard'. This applies to the earnings of employed earners and the self-employed. The level of the disregard will depend on which benefit you are claiming.

Employment and support allowance (ESA) – If you are doing 'permitted work' (see Chapter 16(3)) all your earnings up to the permitted work earnings limit that applies in your case will be disregarded. This will be £20 a week if you are doing lower limit permitted work, or £92 a week if you are doing either higher limit or supported permitted work.

If you are doing any other kind of work that is allowed (see Chapter 16(3)), up to £20 a week of earnings will be disregarded.

If you are earning less than the above limits, and your partner is in part-time work, the difference between your earnings and the appropriate limit can be disregarded from your partner's earnings (up to a limit of £20).

ESA Regs, Sch 7, paras 5-7

Other means-tested benefits – For income support, income-based jobseeker's allowance, housing benefit (HB) and council tax benefit (CTB), disregard £20 a week of your earnings or joint earnings with your partner if any of the following apply.

- ❑ You qualify for a disability premium or, for HB/CTB, a severe disability premium, work-related activity component or support component.
- ❑ You qualify for a carer premium. The disregard applies to the earnings of the carer; if you are the carer and your earnings are less than £20, up to £5 (or £10 for HB/CTB) can be disregarded from your partner's earnings, subject to the overall £20 maximum.
- ❑ You are a lone parent. For HB/CTB only, the disregard for lone parents is £25.
- ❑ You qualify for the higher pensioner premium – but only if you or your partner were working part time immediately before reaching 60 and were then entitled to the £20 disability premium earnings disregard. Since then, you or your partner must have continued in part-time employment, although breaks of up to eight weeks when you were not getting the means-tested benefit are ignored.
- ❑ You are one of a couple and your means-tested benefit would include a disability premium but for the fact that the higher pensioner premium is applicable. Either you or your partner must be under 60 with either one of you in part-time employment.
- ❑ If you are working in one of the jobs listed below, up to £20 of those earnings are disregarded:
- part-time firefighter;
- auxiliary coastguard on coast rescue activities;
- part-time crewing or launching of a lifeboat;
- member of any territorial or reserve force.

  If you are part of a couple and you are both doing one of those jobs, you are still restricted to the joint earnings disregard of £20. If you are doing one of those jobs, your earnings are less than £20 and either you or your partner are also doing an ordinary part-time job, up to £5 (or £10 for HB/CTB) can be disregarded from the earnings of the ordinary job, subject to the overall £20 maximum.

If you do not qualify for the £20 earnings disregard, disregard £5 from earnings if you are single. Disregard £10 from joint earnings if you are in a couple, whether one or both of you are working.

IS Regs, Sch 8, paras 4-9; HB Regs, Sch 4, paras 3-10; CTB Regs, Sch 3, paras 3-10

For HB and CTB there are two extra disregards: the 'childcare costs' and the '16- or 30-hours earnings' disregards.

Childcare costs earnings disregard in HB/CTB

For HB and CTB only, you may get an extra earnings disregard for childcare costs.

- ❑ You must be:
- a lone parent working at least 16 hours a week; *or*
- in a couple and you both work at least 16 hours a week; *or*
- in a couple and one of you works at least 16 hours a week and the other counts as 'incapacitated', is a hospital inpatient or is in prison. You count as 'incapacitated' if:
  - you get main phase ESA, short-term higher rate or long-term incapacity benefit or severe disablement allowance; *or*

– you get attendance allowance, disability living allowance, constant attendance allowance or mobility supplement (or payment has stopped because you are an inpatient); *or*
– your HB/CTB includes a disability premium (on account of your incapacity) or a support component or work-related activity component (on account of your limited capability for work); *or*
– you are the claimant and have been incapable of work for at least 28 weeks (ignoring gaps of eight weeks or less) or have had a limited capability for work for at least 28 weeks (ignoring gaps of 12 weeks or less).

In each of these three categories you are still treated as working for up to 28 weeks when you are off sick and claiming statutory sick pay, ESA, short-term lower rate incapacity benefit, and income support or national insurance credits on the grounds of incapacity or limited capability for work. You will also still be treated as working when you are on maternity, paternity or adoption leave, as long as you are entitled to statutory maternity, paternity or adoption pay, maternity allowance or income support while on paternity leave. In each case, you must have been previously working for at least 16 hours a week.

❑ Your child must be aged 15 or under, or aged 16 or under if they are eligible for a disabled child premium (see Chapter 24(8)). The disregard is available until the day before the first Monday in September after their 15th or 16th birthday.
❑ The childcare must meet certain requirements. You must be paying an approved or registered childcare provider, including out-of-school-hours schemes run on school premises or provided by local authorities. If a relative of the child is providing the care, it needs to be done away from your home.

Disregard from your earnings childcare payments up to a maximum of £175 weekly for one child, or £300 weekly for two or more children.

HB Regs, regs 27(1)(c) & 28; CTB Regs, regs 17(1)(c) & 18

If you get working tax credit (WTC) or child tax credit and your earnings, once other earnings disregards have been taken off, are less than the disregard for childcare costs, then the disregard is made from the total of your earnings and your tax credits added together.

HB Regs, reg 27(2) & CTB Regs, regs 17(2)

16- or 30-hours disregard in HB/CTB

There is an extra earnings disregard, only in HB/CTB, for certain groups of people who work on average either 16 or 30 hours or more a week. Disregard an extra £16.85 from earnings if you (or your partner):

- receive the 30-hour element within your WTC – see Chapter 18(7); *or*
- are aged at least 25 and work at least 30 hours a week; *or*
- work at least 16 hours a week; *and*
  – your HB/CTB includes a family premium (see Chapter 24(7)); *or*
  – are a lone parent; *or*
  – your HB/CTB includes a disability premium, work-related activity component or support component. If you are the one eligible for the premium or component, then you must be the one who is working for at least 16 hours a week; *or*
  – are at least 50, have recently started work and would satisfy the conditions for the 50-plus element of WTC (see Chapter 18(7)).

Only one such £16.85 disregard can be made from earnings or from a couple's joint earnings. If your earnings are less than the sum of all the relevant earnings and childcare costs disregards, then £16.85 can be disregarded from any WTC that is taken into account instead.

HB Regs, Sch 4, para 17; CTB Regs, Sch 3, para 16

6. Income from benefits, tax credits and pensions

Most benefits are taken into account in full (less any income tax payable). However, some benefits are either completely or partly disregarded.

Benefits that are completely disregarded

The following benefits are completely disregarded:

- guardian's allowance;
- child benefit (this will not apply to housing benefit (HB) or council tax benefit (CTB) claims until October 2009. Nor does it apply to income support (IS) and income-based jobseeker's allowance (JSA) claims that began before April 2004, where you continue to receive support for your children through one of those benefits rather than child tax credit – see Chapter 14(9));

ESA Regs, Sch 8, paras 6 & 7(2); IS Regs, Sch 9, paras 5A & 5B

- disability living allowance (DLA) mobility component;
- war pensioners' mobility supplement;
- DLA care component, attendance allowance and constant attendance allowance, severe disablement occupational allowance, exceptionally severe disablement allowance (payable under the War Pensions or Industrial Disablement schemes);
- any ex-gratia payment made to compensate for the non-payment of DLA, attendance allowance, employment and support allowance (ESA), IS or JSA;

ESA Regs, Sch 8, paras 8-11; IS Regs, Sch 9, paras 6-9

- any social fund payment;
- any payment(s) of the Christmas bonus;
- any payment or repayment of health benefits and any payment made instead of Healthy Start vouchers, milk tokens or vitamins;

ESA Regs, Sch 8, paras 35, 37 & 45-46; IS Regs, Sch 9, paras 31, 33 & 48-49

- certain supplementary payments or pensions for war widows, widowers or surviving civil partners;
- dependants' additions to non-means-tested benefits if the dependant is not a member of your family;

ESA Regs, Sch 8, paras 49-52; IS Regs, Sch 9, paras (54-56) & 53

- HB and CTB.

ESA Regs, Sch 8, paras 64 & 65; IS Regs, Sch 9, paras 5 & 52

If you save your benefit – Although these benefits are disregarded as income in the assessment, if there is any money left over after the end of the period for which the benefit is paid, it will be regarded as capital and, in most cases, will then count in with any other savings. (Benefit can be disregarded as capital in limited cases – see Chapter 27(6).) For example, if you save up your mobility component towards a wheelchair, the savings will count as capital. This will only affect your benefit if it takes your capital above the lower limit for tariff income (see Chapter 27(4)).

Benefits that are partly disregarded

For income-related ESA, IS and income-based JSA, disregard up to £10 of:

- widowed parent's or widowed mother's allowance;
- a war disablement pension (including a 'service attributable pension' or tax-free service invaliding pension);
- a guaranteed income payment made under the Armed Forces and Reserve Forces Compensation scheme (including payment abated by a pension paid under the scheme);
- war widow's, widower's or surviving civil partner's pension;
- comparable pensions paid under non-UK social security legislation, or to victims of Nazi persecution.

ESA Regs, Sch 8, para 17, IS Regs, Sch 9, para 16

For HB/CTB, the rule is the same except that £15 is disregarded from the widowed parent's or widowed mother's allowance. Local authorities can choose to run a local scheme under which they disregard more than £10 of a war pension (or Armed Forces and Reserve Forces Compensation scheme payment) in HB/CTB. Your local authority can tell you if it runs a scheme and how much it disregards.

HB Regs, Sch 5, paras 15 & 16; CTB Regs, Sch 4, paras 16 & 17

Tax credits

Working tax credit (WTC) is taken into account in full for income-related ESA, IS, and income-based JSA. Child tax credit (CTC) is disregarded.

ESA Regs, Sch 8, para 7(1); IS Regs, Sch 9, para 5B

For HB/CTB, both WTC and CTC are taken into account in full. They will be reduced, however, by any deduction that is being made to recover an overpayment of tax credit which arose in a previous year.

HB Regs, reg 40(6); CTB Regs, reg 30(6)

Additionally, if your earnings are less than the sum of all the relevant earnings and childcare costs disregards, the WTC taken into account can be reduced by the £16.85 16- or 30-hours disregard (see 5 above).

Statutory sick pay and statutory maternity/paternity/ adoption pay

ESA/IS/JSA – Statutory sick pay (SSP), statutory maternity pay (SMP), statutory paternity pay (SPP) and statutory adoption pay (SAP) are taken into account in full for income-related ESA, IS and income-based JSA, less any Class 1 national insurance contributions, tax and half of any contributions you make towards an occupational or personal pension scheme.

ESA Regs, reg 95(2)(b) & Sch 8, paras 1 & 4; IS Regs, reg 35(2)(b) & Sch 9, paras 1 & 4

HB/CTB – SSP, SMP, SPP and SAP are counted as earnings for HB/CTB. So when you go on sick leave, maternity leave, paternity leave or adoption leave, your SSP, SMP, SPP or SAP are added in with any actual earnings you continue to receive. All the rules on assessing earnings then apply. In particular, you get an 'earnings disregard' (see 5 above) even if you receive only SSP, SMP, SPP or SAP.

HB Regs, reg 35(1)(i); CTB Regs, reg 25(1)(i)

Occupational and personal pensions

Occupational, personal and state pensions are normally taken into account in full, less any tax payable. If you are aged 60 or over, income from an occupational or personal pension or the Pension Protection Fund that would be available to you on application, or from a pension fund that could be turned into an annuity, may be taken into account as 'notional income' (see 20 below). The same applies to your partner.

ESA Regs, reg 104(8); IS Regs, reg 40(4)

ESA reductions

For IS and income-based JSA, if your partner is receiving contributory ESA that has had a reduction imposed upon it (because of a failure to take part in either a work-focused interview or health-related assessment), then the contributory ESA will be taken into account in full as if it had not been reduced. The same rule will apply for HB/CTB if either you or your partner are receiving such a reduction in contributory ESA.

IS Regs, reg 40(6)

7. Charitable, voluntary and personal injury payments

Regular payments

Regular charitable and voluntary payments are usually disregarded. Charitable payments are payments made under a charitable trust at the discretion of the trustees. Voluntary payments are similar, but are not usually made from charitable trusts; they are payments that have a benevolent purpose and are given without anything being given in return (R(IS)4/94). Regular payments are those that are paid or due to be paid at recurring intervals, such as weekly, monthly, annually or following some other pattern. For income support and income-based jobseeker's allowance, the disregard does not apply to such payments made to strikers.

For maintenance payments, see 8 below.

ESA Regs, Sch 8, para 16; IS Regs, Sch 9, para 15

Irregular payments

If charitable or voluntary payments are not made or not due to be made to you (rather than to a third party – see 9 below) at regular intervals, they will be treated as capital. Irregular gifts in kind from a charity are disregarded.

ESA Regs, reg 112(7); IS Regs, reg 48(9)

Payments from specific trusts

Payments in kind or cash made by the Macfarlane Trusts, the Fund, the Eileen Trust or the Independent Living Fund are disregarded.

Payments made by or on behalf of a person with haemophilia (or their partner) who received money from any of these trusts or funds are disregarded in full if they originate from that trust or fund. Payments deriving from the Skipton Fund or the London Bombings Relief Charitable Fund are treated in the same way. To qualify for the disregard, the payment must be made to (or for the benefit of) the partner or former partner of the person who is making the payment (unless you are estranged, divorced or out of a civil partnership), or to dependent children or young people (if they are a member of the donor's family, or were, but are now a member of the claimant's family). If the person making the payment has no partner or dependent children, a payment (including a payment from their estate if they are now dead) to their parent, step-parent or guardian is disregarded for a period of two years after their death, as long as the payment originates from any of these trusts.

ESA Regs, Sch 8, para 41; IS Regs, Sch 9, para 39

Personal injury payments

Payments that are made, or due to be made, at regular intervals, are disregarded, as long as they are:

- from a trust set up from an award made because of any personal injury to you;
- under an annuity purchased from funds derived from an award made because of any personal injury to you; *or*
- received under any agreement or court order to pay you because of any personal injury to you.

Personal injury payments include vaccine damage payments (Chapter 48) and criminal injuries compensation payments (Chapter 47), as well as payments from insurance companies and damages awards by the courts.

ESA Regs, Sch 8, para 16(3); IS Regs, Sch 9, para 15(5A)

8. Maintenance payments

A maximum of £20 a week will be disregarded from child maintenance payments (including those made voluntarily). Payments for more than one child (or different payments for the same child) will be added together and treated as a single payment, so only one disregard can apply. Other maintenance payments are taken fully into account.

ESA Regs, Sch 8, para 60; IS Regs, Sch 9, para 73

For housing benefit and council tax benefit, child maintenance payments are disregarded. Other maintenance payments are taken fully into account, unless a family premium is included in the applicable amount, in which case £15 will be disregarded. If more than one payment is made in any week, they will be added together and treated as a single payment, so only one disregard can apply.

HB Regs, Sch 5, para 47-47A & CTB Regs, Sch 4, para 48-48A

If you pay maintenance, there is no disregard for your payments.

9. Payments to third parties

A payment of income made to a third party in respect of you or your partner can be taken into account but only to the extent that it is used for everyday living expenses (see below). If it is not used for everyday living expenses (eg paying a garage for your car to be repaired or adapted), its value will be disregarded. If the payments are used to provide benefits in kind, see 10 below.

Any payment made to a third party towards the cost of your care home is treated as your income. This may be partly disregarded under other rules (see 15 below).

A payment to a third party from an occupational or personal pension or the Pension Protection Fund is normally taken into account even when it is not used for everyday living expenses.

ESA Regs, reg 107(3); IS Regs, reg 42(4)

Everyday living expenses – These are defined as: food, ordinary clothing or footwear, household fuel, council tax, water charges, rent (for which housing benefit could be payable) or any housing costs (which could be met by employment and support allowance, income support or jobseeker's allowance).

Ordinary clothing or footwear includes items for normal daily use, but does not include school uniforms, or clothing or footwear used solely for sporting activities.

ESA Regs, regs 2(1) & 107(3)(c); IS Regs, reg 42(9)

10. Payments in kind

Any income in kind, eg a free bus pass, food, cigarettes, petrol, etc, is disregarded unless (for income support and income-based jobseeker's allowance) you are involved in a trade dispute. However, payments made to third parties to provide benefits in kind to you are treated as your income.

ESA Regs, Sch 8, para 22; IS Regs, Sch 9, para 21

Non-cash vouchers liable for Class 1 national insurance contributions are not treated as payments in kind, but vouchers not liable for contributions (eg certain childcare and charitable vouchers) are, and are thus disregarded.

ESA Regs, reg 95(3); IS Regs, reg 35(2A)

11. Training and employment schemes

If you are on a government training programme or employment scheme (under either s.2 of the Employment and Training Act 1973 or s.2 of the Enterprise and New Towns (Scotland) Act 1990) any payment is disregarded unless it is:

- made as a substitute for the means-tested benefit (eg the basic rate of New Deal allowance);
- intended to meet the cost of everyday living expenses (see 9 above) while you are participating in the programme or scheme; *or*
- intended to meet the cost of living away from home, if the payment is to cover rent charged for the accommodation where you are staying, for which housing benefit is payable.

ESA Regs, Sch 8, para 15: IS Regs, Sch 9, para 13

The following are also disregarded:

- return to work credit, in-work credit and lone parent work-search premium;
- payments to help a disabled person get or keep work, made under the Disabled Persons (Employment) Act 1944 – eg Access to Work payments – but not if it is a government training allowance;
- special account payments made under the New Deal self-employment route to meet necessary expenses or maintain loan repayments taken out to support the business;
- Employment Zone discretionary payments.

ESA Regs, Sch 8, paras 15, 48, 55 & 59; IS Regs, Sch 9, paras 13, 51, 64 & 72

12. Payments towards education

The following are disregarded:

- education maintenance allowance;
- repayments of student loans to certain newly qualified teachers;
- maintenance payments to the school or college for a dependent child or young person from someone outside your family (income-related employment and support allowance, income support and income-based jobseeker's allowance only);

ESA Regs, Sch 8, paras 13, 14 & 27; IS Regs, Sch 9, paras 11, 11A & 25A

- if you make assessed parental contributions to a student son or daughter, the amount you pay is disregarded from your income – unless the student is under 25, in advanced education and receives only a discretionary grant or gets no grant or loan, in which case the disregard is limited to £50.95 a week, less the amount of any discretionary grant (housing benefit and council tax benefit only).

HB Regs, Sch 5, paras 19 & 20; CTB Regs, Sch 4, paras 19 & 20

Certain amounts of a student grant or loan, Access Fund payment or Career Development Loan can be disregarded (see Box N.3, Chapter 40).

13. Payments for your home

ESA/IS/JSA – For income-related employment and support allowance (ESA), income support (IS) and income-based jobseeker's allowance (JSA), the following payments related to your home are disregarded:

- payments under a mortgage protection policy used to meet repayments on a mortgage or on a loan for eligible repairs and improvements (see Chapter 25(2)) up to the amount of loan interest not met in your applicable amount, plus the amount due in capital repayments or endowment premiums, premiums on the mortgage protection policy and premiums on a buildings insurance policy;
- payments (from any source) made to you that are intended and used as a contribution towards:
  - payments due on a loan secured on your home that are not covered by income-related ESA, IS or income-based JSA – see Chapter 25(3);
  - housing costs covered by income-related ESA, IS or income-based JSA but not met in your applicable amount;
  - capital repayments or endowment premiums on loans covered by income-related ESA, IS or income-based JSA;
  - premiums on a policy taken out to meet any of the above costs or for buildings insurance;
  - any rent not met by housing benefit;

  (unless these are already covered by an insurance policy).

ESA Regs, Sch 8, paras 31 & 32; IS Regs, Sch 9, paras 29 & 30

Housing benefit (HB)/council tax benefit (CTB) – For HB and CTB, disregard payments under an insurance policy taken out against the risk of being unable to maintain repayments on a loan secured on your home, and used to maintain repayments and premiums on that policy and any premiums for buildings insurance if this is a requirement of the loan.

HB Regs, Sch 5, para 29; CTB Regs, Sch 4, para 30

14. Income from tenants and lodgers

Disregard the following income from tenants and lodgers:

- contributions towards living and accommodation costs made to you by someone living as a member of your household (but not if they are a commercial boarder or a sub-tenant);
- if you have sub-let part of your home (under a formal contract), a maximum of £20 will be disregarded from the weekly payment received from each sub-tenant;
- if you provide board and lodging in your own home, £20 and half of the remainder of the weekly charge paid by each person provided with such accommodation (even if that person lodges with you for just one night).

ESA Regs, Sch 8, paras 19-21; IS Regs, Sch 9, paras 18-20

15. Payments for care homes

Some payments towards the cost of your care are disregarded for income-related employment and support allowance, income support and income-based jobseeker's allowance. See also Chapter 33(5).

If the local authority arranged your care – Payments made by the local authority towards the cost of care home charges are fully disregarded.

ESA Regs, Sch 8, para 56; IS Regs, Sch 9, para 66

If the local authority did not arrange your care – Any payment intended for and used to meet the care home charge is partly disregarded (unless it is a regular charitable or voluntary payment when it is fully disregarded – see 7 above). The amount disregarded is the weekly accommodation charge less your applicable amount.

ESA Regs, Sch 8, para 34; IS Regs, Sch 9, para 30A

16. Payments for children

The following payments for children or young people in your care are disregarded:

- adoption and residence order allowances and special guardianship payments. However, for housing benefit and council tax benefit (and income support and income-based jobseeker's allowance if your claim began before April 2004 and you continue to receive support for your children through one of those benefits rather than child tax credit), only the amount of allowance or payment that exceeds the child's personal allowance and disabled child premium is disregarded;
- fostering allowances (for official arrangements only);
- discretionary payments from social services or social work departments to help children in need or to provide help to young care leavers.

ESA Regs, Sch 8, paras 26, 28 & 30; IS Regs, Sch 9, paras 25, 26 & 28

17. Income generated from capital

Income derived from capital is generally not treated as income but is added to your capital from the date it is normally due to be credited to you. However, income derived from the following items of disregarded capital (see Chapter 27(6)) is treated as income:

- your home;
- premises you've acquired to live in, but have not yet been able to move in to;
- premises occupied by a partner or relative who is aged 60 or over or incapacitated, or an ex-partner (but not if estranged, divorced or out of a civil partnership);
- your former home if you are estranged, divorced or out of a civil partnership;
- premises you are taking reasonable steps to sell;
- premises you intend to occupy and are taking legal steps to obtain possession of;
- premises you intend to occupy but which need essential repairs or alterations;
- business assets;
- a trust fund from compensation for personal injury;
- capital administered by the courts from damages awarded for personal injury or, for under-18s, compensation for the loss of a parent.

ESA Regs, reg 112(4); IS Regs, reg 48(4)

During the period in which you receive income from any of the premises listed above (other than the home you live in), any mortgage payments made, or council tax or water charges paid, in respect of the disregarded premises can be offset against that income. The amount above this is taken into account as income.

ESA Regs, Sch 8, para 23(2); IS Regs, Sch 9, para 22(2)

If you let out your property and it is not covered under one of the disregards above, rent is treated as capital not income. The full amount is taken into account as capital without any deductions for mortgage payments, etc.

18. Capital treated as income

If any capital is payable by instalments, each instalment outstanding when your claim is decided (or on the first day for which the means-tested benefit is paid if this is earlier), or at a later supersession, is treated as income if the total of all your capital, including the outstanding instalments, adds up to more than the upper capital limit. If your total capital adds up to less than or equal to the upper capital limit, each instalment is treated as a payment of capital (see Chapter 27(3) for details of the upper capital limits).

Any periodical personal injury payments made under an agreement or court order to you count as income (see 7 above for when these can be disregarded).

Any payment under an annuity is treated as income.

Any capital treated as income is disregarded as capital.

ESA Regs, reg 105; IS Regs, reg 41

19. Miscellaneous income

The following types of income are also disregarded:

- expenses paid to a volunteer, including advance payments to cover expenses – but only if you are paid nothing else by the charity or organisation and aren't treated as having 'notional' earnings (see 20);
- Victoria Cross/George Cross annuities and analogous payments;
- income abroad while transfer to the UK is prohibited;
- charges for currency conversion if income is not paid in sterling;

ESA Regs, Sch 8, paras 2, 12, 24 & 25; IS Regs, Sch 9, paras 2, 10, 23 & 24

- payments in respect of a person not normally a member of your household but temporarily in your care, made by a health body, voluntary organisation or local authority (or by a person placed with you by the local authority). This covers respite care payments for overnight (or longer) stays or for just a few hours in the day. It does not cover any direct payments of housing benefit made to you;

ESA Regs, Sch 8, para 29; IS Regs, Sch 9, para 27

- payments under an insurance policy taken out against the risk of being unable to maintain repayments under a credit agreement, hire purchase or conditional sale agreement, up to the amount used to maintain the repayments and pay premiums on that policy;
- payments to a juror or witness in respect of attendance at court (but not if they are to compensate for loss of earnings or loss of benefit);
- payments under the Assisted Prison Visits scheme;

ESA Regs, Sch 8, paras 33, 43 & 47; IS Regs, Sch 9, paras 30ZA, 43 & 50

- community care direct payments;
- Sports Council National Lottery award, except for amounts awarded for everyday living expenses (see 9 above, although 'food' in this case does not include vitamins, minerals or other special dietary supplements intended to enhance performance);
- discretionary housing payments made under the Discretionary Financial Assistance Regulations 2001;
- payments from a local authority under the Supporting People scheme.

ESA Regs, Sch 8, paras 53, 57, 62 & 63; IS Regs, Sch 9, paras 58, 69, 75 & 76

20. Notional income

Income that you do not actually possess may be taken into account in some circumstances.

- ❑ **Deprivation of income** – You are treated as possessing income of which you have deprived yourself in order to get a means-tested benefit or increase it.

ESA Regs, reg 106(1), IS Regs, reg 42(1)

- ❑ **Income available if applied for** – You are treated as possessing income from the date that you could expect to receive it. This also applies to most social security benefits (but only up until the time you put in a claim). The rule does not apply to:

- jobseeker's allowance (for income support and income-related employment and support allowance only);
- working tax credit and child tax credit;
- payments from a discretionary trust or a personal injury compensation trust;
- compensation administered by the courts for personal injury;
- employment rehabilitation allowances;
- income from a personal pension scheme (including an annuity contract or trust scheme approved under tax law), occupational pension scheme or the Pension Protection Fund (PPF), as long as you are aged under 60. If you are 60 or over and fail to draw an income from the pension or PPF, you are assumed to have notional income. Income that could be obtained from money purchase benefits under an occupational or personal pension scheme will be treated in the same way;

ESA Regs, reg 106(2)-(8); IS Regs, reg 42(2)-(2CA)

- any Category A or B state pension, additional state pension or graduated retirement benefit that has been deferred (but not if you choose to have a lump-sum payment in preference to an increased pension) – see Chapter 43(4) (for housing benefit and council tax benefit only).

HB(SPC) Regs, reg 41(2)-(3); CTB(SPC) Regs, reg 31(2)-(3)

- **Notional earnings** – If you are a volunteer, or engaged by a charitable or voluntary organisation, notional earnings cannot be assumed if it is reasonable for you to provide your services free of charge. (A carer may count as a 'volunteer' – see CIS/93/91, but see CIS/701/94 for exceptions.)

  If it is reasonable to expect you to charge for your services, or you are performing a service for someone else in some other capacity, you are treated as having *'such earnings (if any) as is reasonable for that employment unless [you] satisfy [the decision maker] that the means of that person are insufficient for him to pay, or to pay more, for the service'*. Decision makers are advised to assume earnings of at least the relevant national minimum wage. If notional earnings are assumed, seek expert help with your appeal.

ESA Regs, reg 108(3) & (4)(a); IS Regs, reg 42(6) & (6A)(a)

- **Income owed** – For income-related employment and support allowance, income support and income-based jobseeker's allowance, you are treated as possessing any income owing to you, but there are exceptions (eg income from a discretionary or personal injury trust, or delays in social security benefits).

ESA Regs, reg 107(1); IS Regs, reg 42(3)

- **Care homes** – Any payment made towards the cost of your care home is treated as your income, but some of this may be disregarded (see 15 above).

27 Capital

In this chapter we look at:

1. Introduction

In this chapter we look at the way that any capital you have is treated when means-tested benefits are being calculated. The rules in this chapter apply to the following benefits:

- income-related employment and support allowance (ESA);
- income support;
- income-based jobseeker's allowance;
- housing benefit and council tax benefit – if you (and your partner) are under 60 or still claiming one of three benefits listed above (otherwise the rules are similar to pension credit – see Chapter 42(6)).

Where there are significant differences in the way that capital is treated for different benefits, we say so. As capital is treated in a substantially different way for pension credit, we describe this separately in Chapter 42(6).

For the sake of simplicity, we generally confine the legal references to those applicable to income-related ESA and income support.

Any capital that you possess can affect your entitlement to means-tested benefits when it is more than certain set limits (see 3 below). Capital includes savings, investments, some lump-sum payments and the value of property and land (but if you own the home you live in, the value of your home, garden, garage and outbuildings is not taken into account). Certain types of capital can be disregarded (see 6 below). Sometimes capital can be treated as income and vice versa (see 8 below).

2. Whose capital is included?

If you are one of a couple (married or living together as husband and wife, or in a same-sex partnership whether registered or not), your partner's capital is added to your own. Otherwise, only your own capital is taken into account; any capital belonging to dependent children is disregarded (unless you have a claim for income support or income-based jobseeker's allowance that began before April 2004 and you continue to receive support for your children through one of those benefits rather than child tax credit – see *Disability Rights Handbook* 28th edition, page 25).

ESA Regs, reg 83; IS Regs, reg 23

3. Capital limits

There is a lower capital limit and an upper capital limit. You cannot get any of the means-tested benefits listed in 1 above if your capital is above the upper limit of £16,000.

ESA Regs, reg 110; IS Regs, reg 45

If your capital is at or below the lower limit of £6,000, your means-tested benefit is unaffected. If you move permanently into a care home, an Abbeyfield Home or an independent hospital, this lower limit goes up to £10,000 (see Chapter 33(5)). If your stay is only temporary, the £6,000 limit still applies.

If your capital is between the lower and upper limits, an amount of 'tariff income' is assumed (see 4 below).

Some types of capital are disregarded for these capital limits (see 6 below). You can also be treated as having capital that you may not actually possess: this is called 'notional capital' (see 9 below).

4. Tariff income

If your capital is between the lower and upper limits, a 'tariff income' is assumed, ie your capital is treated as if it were generating income. Normally, £1 a week for every £250 (or part of £250) above the lower limit is included as your income in this way (but see below for an exception). For instance, if you have capital of £6,300, £2 a week is included. Each time capital moves into the next block of £250 (even by as little as one penny) an additional £1 is included as income. This tariff income is added to your other income when calculating your entitlement to the means-tested benefit.

ESA Regs, reg 118; IS Regs, reg 53

For housing benefit and council tax benefit, if you or your partner are aged 60 or over (and not claiming income-related employment and support allowance, income support or income-based jobseeker's allowance), the assumed tariff income is £1 for every £500 (or part of £500) above the lower limit.

HB(SPC) Regs, reg 29(2); CTB(SPC) Regs, reg 19(2)

If tariff income is included in your assessment, notify Jobcentre Plus if the amount of your capital changes. If your savings drop to the next lower tariff income band and you have not told Jobcentre Plus, you will be getting too little of the means-tested benefit. If your savings have increased to the next higher tariff income band and you have not told Jobcentre Plus, you will have been overpaid benefit. Watch out for the 'notional capital' rule (see 9 below). You should keep records and all receipts to show how and why you spent your savings.

5. How is capital valued?

Capital is calculated at its current market or surrender value, less 10% if there would be costs involved in selling and less any mortgage or debt secured on the property.

ESA Regs, reg 113; IS Regs, reg 49

Jointly owned capital – If you own property or other capital jointly with one or more others so that each person owns the whole asset jointly with no separate or distinct shares, then you are treated as though you own an equal share. Thus, if four people jointly own a capital asset as joint tenants, each of you will be treated as possessing 25% of that capital. However, if you share the property as tenants-in-common rather than as joint tenants, the share you are treated as owning should reflect the actual split.

ESA Regs, reg 117; IS Regs, reg 52; R(IS)4/03

The decision maker must establish the market value or price that a willing buyer would pay to a willing seller for the share that you possess. The market value could be low or even nil if other joint owners would not be prepared to sell the property as a whole or to buy the share themselves.

6. What capital is disregarded?

Benefits

Arrears (or an ex-gratia payment) of the following benefits are disregarded for 52 weeks after you get them: disability living allowance and attendance allowance (or equivalents under the Industrial Injuries or War Pensions schemes), housing benefit, council tax benefit, income-related employment and support allowance (ESA), income support, income-related jobseeker's allowance, child tax credit and working tax credit.

If arrears made to rectify or compensate for an official error amount to £5,000 or more, and have been awarded in full since 14.10.01, they can be disregarded for 52 weeks from the date of receipt or for the remaining period of the award of the means-tested benefit, whichever is the longer period.

ESA Regs, Sch 9, para 11; IS Regs, Sch 10, para 7

Social fund payments are disregarded. Payments or repayments of a health benefit in respect of NHS prescription charges, dental charges or hospital travelling expenses are disregarded for 52 weeks after you receive the money. Payments made instead of Healthy Start vouchers, milk tokens or free vitamins are disregarded for 52 weeks after receipt.

ESA Regs, Sch 9, paras 23, 37 & 38; IS Regs, Sch 10, paras 18, 38 & 39

Personal possessions

The value of personal possessions is disregarded, except those bought to reduce your capital in order to get more benefit. A compensation payment for loss of or damage to personal possessions that is to be used for repair or replacements is disregarded for 26 weeks, or longer if that is reasonable.

ESA Regs, Sch 9, paras 14 & 12(a); IS Regs, Sch 10, paras 10 & 8(a)

Trust funds and personal injury payments

Personal injury payments – When a trust fund is created from payments for a personal or criminal injury to you or your partner, the value of the fund is disregarded indefinitely. 'Personal injury' includes a disease and injury suffered as a result of a disease (R(SB)2/89). Trusts created from vaccine damage payments are covered, so too may a trust of funds collected for a person because of their personal injuries. Actual payments from a trust fund for a personal or criminal injury can count in full as capital, but may be disregarded as income (see Chapter 26(7)).

If a lump-sum payment for a personal or criminal injury to you or your partner has not been put into a trust, it can be disregarded for up to 52 weeks from the date of receipt (to allow you time to set up a trust). However, this only applies to an initial payment; subsequent lump-sum payments made in consequence of the same injury count in full.

ESA Regs, Sch 9, paras 16 & 17; IS Regs, Sch 10, paras 12 & 12A

If capital is administered by the courts, damages awarded for personal injury and, for under-18s, compensation for the loss of a parent are disregarded.

ESA Regs, Sch 9, paras 43 & 44; IS Regs, Sch 10, paras 44 & 45

Life interest – The value of the right to receive any income under a life interest or from a life rent (this is a type of trust in Scotland) is disregarded. Actual income received counts in full as income.

ESA Regs, Sch 9, para 18; IS Regs, Sch 10, para 13

Specific trusts – Payments made under the Macfarlane Trusts, the Fund, the Eileen Trust, the Skipton Fund, the London Bombings Relief Charitable Fund or the Independent Living Fund are disregarded. Payments made by or on behalf of a person with haemophilia may be disregarded under the same rules as income (see Chapter 26(7)).

ESA Regs, Sch 9, para 27; IS Regs, Sch 10, para 22

A payment from the government-funded trust for people with variant Creutzfeldt-Jakob disease (vCJD) paid to a person with vCJD or their partner is disregarded for life. If the trust payment is made to a parent or child of a person with vCJD (including payment from the estate if they are now dead), it is disregarded for two years from the date it is paid or until the child reaches age 20 or leaves full-time education, whichever is the latest.

ESA Regs, Sch 9, para 53; IS Regs, Sch 10, para 64

Training and employment

Disregard the following:

- business assets while you are '*engaged as a self-employed earner*'. If you've ceased that self-employment, the assets will be disregarded for as long as is reasonable in the circumstances to allow you to dispose of them. However, if sickness or disability means you cannot work as a self-employed earner, your business assets will be disregarded for 26 weeks from your date of claim, or longer if that is reasonable in the circumstances. You must intend to start or resume work in that business as soon as you are able to or as soon as you recover;
- business assets while you are on the self-employment route of the New Deal, and for as long as is reasonable after the self-employment ends;

ESA Regs, Sch 9, para 10; IS Regs, Sch 10, para 6

- payments (but not a government training allowance) made under the Disabled Persons (Employment) Act 1944 to help a disabled person get or keep work;
- start-up capital under the Blind Homeworkers' scheme.

ESA Regs, Sch 9, paras 41 & 42; IS Regs, Sch 10, paras 42 & 43

Disregard for 52 weeks from the date of receipt:

- any payment from a government training programme or employment scheme (under either s.2 of the Employment and Training Act 1973 or s.2 of the Enterprise and New Towns (Scotland) Act 1990);
- any New Deal self-employment route business capital;
- any discretionary payment or arrears of subsistence allowance from an Employment Zone contractor.

ESA Regs, Sch 9, paras 32, 46 & (48 & 49); IS Regs, Sch 10, paras 30, 52 & (58 & 59)

Your home

The following items are disregarded:

- the value of your own home;
- the value of premises you've acquired, if you intend to move in within 26 weeks of the date of purchase. More time is allowed if that is reasonable in the circumstances to enable you to get possession and move in;
- any sum directly attributable to the proceeds of the sale of your former home that you intend to use to buy another home within 26 weeks of that sale. More time is allowed if that is reasonable in the circumstances to enable you to complete the purchase;

ESA Regs, Sch 9, paras 1, 2 & 3; IS Regs, Sch 10, paras 1, 2 & 3

- the value of premises occupied wholly or partly by your partner or by a relative, if they are aged 60 or over, or incapacitated; or former partner if you are not estranged, divorced or out of a civil partnership;
- the value of your former home for 26 weeks after you left it because of divorce, civil partnership dissolution or estrangement from your former partner. If the former partner is a lone parent, the value is disregarded for as long as they occupy your former home;
- the value of premises you are taking reasonable steps to dispose of, for 26 weeks from the date on which you first took such steps. More time is allowed if that is reasonable in the circumstances to dispose of the premises;

ESA Regs, Sch 9, paras 4, 5 & 6; IS Regs, Sch 10, paras 4, 25 & 26

- the value of premises you intend to occupy as your home if you are taking steps to obtain possession and have either sought legal advice or commenced legal proceedings in order to obtain possession. The value is disregarded for 26 weeks from the date on which you first sought such advice, or started proceedings (whichever is earlier), but it may be disregarded for a longer period if that is reasonable in the circumstances;
- the value of premises you intend to occupy as your home once *'essential repairs or alterations'* make the premises *'fit for such occupation'*, for 26 weeks from the date on which you first took steps to get the premises repaired or altered, or such longer period as is reasonable in the circumstances to enable the works to be carried out and for you to move in. This can help if you need to make adaptations because of a disability (eg install a ground floor bathroom);

ESA Regs, Sch 9, paras 7 & 8; IS Regs, Sch 10, paras 27 & 28

- any sum paid to you because of damage to, or loss of, the home or any personal possession and intended for its repair or replacement, or any sum given or loaned to you expressly for essential repairs or improvements to the home, will be disregarded for 26 weeks if you are going to use that sum for its intended purpose, or for longer if that is reasonable in the circumstances;
- any sum deposited with a housing association as a condition of occupying the home. If you've removed that deposit and intend to use it to buy another home it can be disregarded on the same basis as the proceeds of the sale of a former home;

ESA Regs, Sch 9, paras 12 & 13; IS Regs, Sch 10, paras 8 & 9

- any grant made by a local authority (if you are one of its tenants) to be used to buy premises you intend to live in as your home, or to do repairs or alterations needed to make the premises fit for you to live in. The grant is disregarded for 26 weeks, or such longer period as is reasonable in the circumstances, to enable you to complete buying, repairing or altering the premises;
- arrears of discretionary housing payments made under the Discretionary Financial Assistance Regulations 2001 for 52 weeks from the date received.

ESA Regs, Sch 9, paras 36 & 11(1)(c) ; IS Regs, Sch 10, paras 37 & 7(d)

Right to receive income or payment in future

Certain forms of capital can be released at some stage in order to provide you with income or payment in the future. The following types are disregarded:

- any future interest in property other than land or premises on which you have been granted a lease or tenancy;
- the capital value of the right to receive any income under an annuity, and the surrender value of an annuity;
- the capital value of the right to receive any income that is disregarded because it is frozen abroad;

ESA Regs, Sch 9, paras 9, 15 & 19; IS Regs, Sch 10, paras 5, 11 & 14

- the full surrender value of a life insurance policy;
- the value of the right to receive an occupational or personal pension, and the value of funds held under a personal pension scheme (including annuity contracts and trust schemes approved under tax law);
- the value of the right to receive any rent, except where you have a future interest in the property.

ESA Regs, Sch 9, paras 20, (28 & 29) & 30; IS Regs, Sch 10, paras 15, (23 & 23A) & 24

Other capital

The following types of capital are disregarded:

- where any payment of capital *'falls to be made by instalments, the value of the right to receive any outstanding instalments'* (see also Chapter 26(18));
- discretionary payments from social services or social work departments to help children in need or to provide help to young care leavers;
- a refund of tax deducted on loan interest if that loan was taken out in order to buy the home or to carry out repairs or improvements to the home;

ESA Regs, Sch 9, paras 21, 22 & 24; IS Regs, Sch 10, paras 16, 17 & 19

- any charge for currency conversion if your capital is not held in sterling;
- payments in kind made by a charity, the Macfarlane Trusts, the Fund, the Eileen Trust (for income-related ESA) or the Independent Living Fund;
- payments made to a juror or witness in respect of attendance at a court (but not if it was to compensate for loss of earnings or loss of benefit);

ESA Regs, Sch 9, paras 26, 31 & 34; IS Regs, Sch 10, paras 21, 29 & 34

- payment to you as holder of the Victoria Cross or George Cross;
- a Sports Council National Lottery award, less everyday living expenses (see Chapter 26(9)), although 'food' in this case does not include vitamins, minerals or other special dietary supplements intended to enhance performance, for 26 weeks after you receive payment of the award;
- £10,000 special payment made to you or your partner (or for a deceased spouse/civil partner or partner's deceased spouse/civil partner) because of internment by the Japanese during the Second World War;

ESA Regs, Sch 9, paras 45, 47 & 50; IS Regs, Sch 10, paras 46, 56 & 61

- education maintenance allowance paid to you or your dependent child;
- payments made to you or your partner (or for a deceased spouse/civil partner or partner's deceased spouse/civil partner) to compensate for being a slave labourer or a forced labourer, suffering property loss or personal injury or being the parent of a child who had died, during the Second World War;
- payments from local authorities under the Supporting People scheme;

ESA Regs, Sch 9, paras 52, 54 & 55; IS Regs, Sch 10, paras 63, 65 & 66

- community care direct payments;
- a payment made under s.2(6)(b), 3 or 4 of the Adoption and Children Act 2002;
- a special guardianship payment.

ESA Regs, Sch 9, paras 56, 57 & 58; IS Regs, Sch 10, paras 67, 68 & 68A

Disregard the following for 52 weeks after you receive them:

- payments made under the Assisted Prison Visits scheme;
- arrears of supplementary pensions to widows, widowers and surviving civil partners.

ESA Regs,Sch 9, paras 39 & 40; IS Regs, Sch 10, paras 40 & 41

7. Loans

If you borrow money, it will almost always count as money you possess (generally as capital if it is a one-off loan or, in some cases, as income if it is part of a series of payments). If you intend to borrow a sum to use for a specific purpose, wait until you actually need to spend that money.

8. Income or capital?

There is usually no problem deciding whether a particular resource is income or capital. However, the distinction is not defined in the regulations. Where it is unclear, the general principle (developed in case law) is that payments of income recur periodically and do not include ad hoc payments, whereas capital payments are one-off and not linked to a particular period (although capital may be paid in instalments). In some cases, the rules treat income as capital. For the circumstances in which capital is treated as income, see Chapter 26(18).

Income treated as capital

The following payments of income are treated as capital:

- income derived from capital (but see Chapter 26(17));
- income tax refunds;*
- irregular charitable or voluntary payments (other than payments made under the Macfarlane Trusts, the Fund, the Eileen Trust or the Independent Living Fund);*
- holiday pay payable more than four weeks after the employment ends or is interrupted;*
- advance of earnings or a loan from an employer;*
- payment for a discharged prisoner (for income-related employment and support allowance, income support (IS) and income-based jobseeker's allowance (JSA));
- lump-sum payment of arrears of Employment Zone subsistence allowance;
- a bounty paid no more than once a year to a part-time firefighter, for coast rescue duties or running a lifeboat, or to a member of the Territorial Army or reserves.

* except for those involved in a trade dispute (for IS/JSA)

ESA Regs, reg 112; IS Regs, reg 48

In addition to the above, the following payments are treated as capital for housing benefit and council tax benefit:

- arrears of child tax credit and working tax credit;
- gross business receipts payable into New Deal self-employment route special accounts.

HB Regs, reg 46; CTB Regs, reg 36

9. Notional capital

If you are held to have deprived yourself of some capital in order to get or increase a means-tested benefit, the law says that capital must be treated as if you still had it. This is called 'notional' capital. In some cases, the amount of notional capital along with your actual capital will exclude you from the benefit. Or, you may be entitled to the benefit, but because of your notional capital the assessment is related to a higher tariff income than your actual capital warrants (see 4 above).

If there were good and sensible reasons for spending your capital, and getting the means-tested benefit (or more of it) wasn't a significant motive for spending part of your savings, you should be alright. It is worth appealing if capital you no longer have is taken into account, but do seek expert advice and check Commissioners' decisions R(IS)1/91, R(SB)11/82, R(SB)38/85, R(SB)40/85, R(SB)9/91 and CIS/242/93.

If you are held to have notional capital on this basis, you won't be excluded from the means-tested benefit permanently, nor will a tariff income be related permanently to the higher amount of notional capital. Jobcentre Plus will apply the 'diminishing capital rule', which reduces the amount of notional capital over time (see below). It is not possible to deprive yourself of notional capital – only actual capital is subject to this rule.

ESA Regs, reg 115; IS Regs, reg 51

Reducing 'notional' capital

Your notional capital is treated as having been reduced by the amount of the means-tested benefit 'lost' over a set period. If you are held to have deprived yourself of an amount of capital, Jobcentre Plus will work out:

- how much benefit you would have been entitled to in the normal way if you had no notional capital – (A)
- how much benefit, if any, you are entitled to on the basis of your notional capital (as well as actual capital) – (B)
- (A) minus (B) = the benefit you have lost – (LB 1).

If you have also lost any of the other means-tested benefits, Jobcentre Plus (or the local authority) will add on those amounts of lost benefit, eg LB 1 (income support) + LB 2 (housing benefit) + LB 3 (council tax benefit) = total lost benefit (TLB). Your notional capital is treated as being reduced each week by your total lost benefit.

When you claim the means-tested benefit, the decision on your claim will include the amount of that benefit you have lost because of notional capital. Keep that decision letter. You may need to produce it if you claim another means-tested benefit and you are held to have deprived yourself of some capital in order to get that benefit as well. For example, if you are excluded from income support because of notional capital and you are also held to have deprived yourself of some capital to get housing benefit (HB) and/or council tax benefit (CTB), you will need to show the income support decision letter to the local authority sections dealing with your HB/CTB claims. It is quite possible to have completely different decisions on deprivation of capital, and different amounts of notional capital, for each benefit.

If you still get the means-tested benefit – Each time your notional capital goes below another tariff income step, you will be entitled to more benefit. A change of circumstances may also increase or reduce your benefit. Both (A) and (B) will be re-calculated, giving you a new amount of lost benefit (LB 1.2). For other means-tested benefits, the amount of lost benefit may also change – so you will add these on (LB 1.2 + LB 2.2, etc). Your notional capital will now be treated as being reduced by your current total lost benefit (TLB 2).

If you don't get the means-tested benefit – Once your total lost benefit is worked out, it cannot be reduced. It can only be increased so as to enable your notional capital to diminish faster. Unless you have a change of circumstances, your total lost benefit can only be re-calculated after 26 weeks. The onus is on you to make a fresh claim for each benefit affected by the deprivation of capital rule and to produce the decision letters showing the amount(s) of the other lost benefit(s). If there is only a small amount of notional capital, you may become entitled to some benefit within a matter of weeks.

You do not have to wait 26 weeks before making a fresh claim. That time limit is only relevant for re-calculating total lost benefit if there have been no changes of circumstances affecting your entitlement beforehand.

More deprivation? – If you have actual capital as well as notional capital, you should still be careful about how you spend your actual capital. Obviously, you will have to draw on actual capital to help supplement your income and cover expenses not met by benefit. But the deprivation of capital rule can be re-applied to the actual capital spent.

ESA Regs, reg 116; IS Regs, reg 51A

K Practical help at home

This section of the Handbook looks at:

28 Care services

1. What is community care?

Community care is defined as *'providing the right level of intervention and support to enable people to achieve maximum independence and control over their own lives'*. The objective of the 1993 community care reforms was for fewer people to go into care homes because there would be a greater range of care in the community.

In England, there are plans to transform social care radically to give people easy access to services and choice and control over how the services are provided. The first part of these changes is the 'Personalisation Agenda', launched in a 2007 Green Paper and to be implemented by 2011 (see 3 below).

NHS and Community Care Act 1990, LAC(DH)(2009)1

Healthcare and social care

There is no obvious dividing line between a social care need and a healthcare need. Legislation allows social services and health bodies to work together using pooled budgets and joint commissioning of services. Health bodies might not provide services they consider are not reasonably required, taking into account their own resources.

England and Wales – In some areas, care trusts combine the functions of health and social services. It is important to know if your care is considered to be under the NHS, as most healthcare is free at the point of delivery, but people are charged for most social care.

Local authorities in England and Wales can only provide social care packages. Since April 2003 the NHS is responsible for meeting the cost of registered nursing care in care homes that provide it, as well as all other reasonably required healthcare (see Chapter 32(3)). Both England and Wales have a *National Framework for Continuing NHS Care* outlining the criteria under which the NHS should fund care. The criteria were developed as a result of the *Grogan* High Court case, which established that where a person's primary need is a health need, the NHS should fully fund care.

Grogan v Bexley NHS care trust (C012008/2005)

Scotland – Local authority social work departments have key duties for providing help to 'persons in need' and are responsible for the provision of a range of care services. There have been moves in recent years towards joint working between social work departments and health boards, with an expansion of local pooled budget arrangements and the setting up of community healthcare partnerships and single shared assessments. There has also been an increase in the number of people eligible for direct payments and the introduction of free nursing and personal care for people over 65.

Northern Ireland – Health and social care are provided by health and social care trusts, commissioned by four joint Health and Social Care Boards. The structure of health and social care is being reorganised and the four boards will be replaced by one board and local support services agencies.

Intermediate care services

England – Intermediate care services promote independence by helping people to either leave hospital quicker or avoid admission to hospital. Intermediate care tries to maximise independence by allowing someone to continue living at home or to return home. One or several services may be offered as part of your intermediate care plan and are usually provided by teams other than those who provide services as part of a normal ongoing care plan. Intermediate care is an intensive service normally lasting no longer than six weeks and often arranged very quickly; although it covers both health and social care, it should be free (see 6 below). Support can be provided in your home, housing schemes, day centres, hospitals or rehabilitation centres. Services can include homecare, nursing and intensive rehabilitation. Health and social services should work in partnership to provide these services using a single assessment process and shared protocols. After intermediate care services finish, you should have an assessment to see if you require any ongoing care or health services.

LAC (2001)1; LAC (2003)14

Wales – There is a system of short-term support referred to as '6-weeks support at home for vulnerable people', to aid those being discharged from hospital and to prevent those at risk from entering hospital.

NAFWC 43/02

Scotland – People 65 or over can have free home care for up to four weeks following a period in hospital, whether overnight or for surgery as a day patient, and this also includes equipment provided during that time. Home care includes meals on wheels, laundry and shopping needed during a period of recovery, and so is wider in definition than 'personal care'.

CCD 2/2001; CCD 5/2003

Northern Ireland – There is an intermediate care system similar to England.

HSS(ECCU) 2/2005

Setting eligibility criteria

England –The criteria are contained within *The National Framework for NHS Continuing Health Care and NHS funded Nursing Care*. This sets out the principles and processes to be followed when establishing primary health needs. A person with a primary health need is eligible for continuing NHS care.

Each local authority must publish its joint plans for services and must have a publicly available long-term care charter, *Better care, higher standards*, setting out its service standards in health, housing and social services.

LAC(DH) (2008)1

Wales – There are common eligibility criteria for continuing healthcare based on national guidance (produced in 2004, supported by further advice in 2006); these are incorporated into local implementation plans produced by local health boards. There was a consultation on the development of a national framework in 2008 and a revised continuing NHS healthcare framework will be issued in spring 2009.

WHC (2004)54; NAfWC 41/04: WHC (2006)46; NAfWC 32/06

Scotland – New guidance, published in February 2008, sets out the criteria for receiving continuing NHS care, which could be in hospital, a care home or a person's own home. An additional assessment tool to promote consistency across health boards is to be developed. See Chapter 32(3).

NHS Scotland Continuing Health Care CEL6 (2008)

Delayed discharges

England and Wales – The NHS and local authorities have an obligation to work together on discharge arrangements. In England, the NHS has a duty to inform social services of patients likely to require community care services, and social services then have a duty to assess that person and provide services within certain strict time limits. The local authority must reimburse an NHS acute trust if a delay in organising a community care assessment (or the setting up of services) is the sole reason that discharge is delayed. You should not be pressured into leaving hospital until suitable care arrangements are in place. If you are returning home, social services must review your case within two weeks to ensure the care package is adequate.

Community care (Delayed Discharges etc) Act 2003; LAC (2003)21

Scotland – An action plan on delayed discharges, published by the Scottish Executive Health Department in 2002, led to local joint action plans by Community Health Partnerships to reduce delayed discharges against targets set by the Government. The key target for local authorities and NHS boards is for a maximum 'reasonable' period of six weeks to assess, make plans for and then arrange the discharge of someone who needs community support or nursing home care after leaving hospital.

CCD 8/2003

2. Where do you go for help?

Go first to the local area office of the social services department, or in Scotland, the social work department. Sometimes NHS staff undertake the community care assessment at the request of social services. For help with housing, you may be referred to the housing department.

Discuss your needs with a social worker (or care manager). Otherwise, look up the address of your nearest office in the phone book, under the name of your local authority. For example, look up 'Essex County Council' and find the heading 'Social Services Department, Area Office'. If you outline the type of help you want, they can put you through to the right section and arrange for you to have an assessment. Your health visitor, GP or occupational therapist might also help arrange the services you need.

See Chapter 29 for help available to buy care at home.

3. Getting an assessment of your needs

If you have difficulty managing at home because of age, illness or disability, you can ask for an assessment of your needs. If it is apparent to the local authority that you might have a need for services, you should not have to ask for it. However, it is not only disabled people who can get a local authority assessment. See Box K.1 for the law on assessments. The Community Care Assessment Directions 2004 (LAC (2004)24) give a legal framework to good practice on assessments and care planning.

The form your assessment takes will largely depend upon the complexity of your needs. However, even if the local authority is unlikely to provide a service because of its resource constraints, you should not be denied an assessment.

R v Bristol City Council ex p Penfold [1998] (1CCLR 315)

People often complain of having to wait before they receive an assessment and there are no national rules about how quickly assessments must take place. However, many local authorities have their own targets for assessing people and these should be laid out in their charters; the Government has also produced performance targets for local authorities. If you experience unreasonable delay, use the complaints procedure first and then the appropriate Ombudsman (see 7 below under 'Further steps').

If you need assistance urgently, your local authority can temporarily provide or arrange community care services before an assessment is carried out. Once temporary services are in place, the authority is required to assess you as soon as practicable.

Assessments for older people

England – Under the Government's single assessment process (SAP) for older people, agencies responsible for assessing your social, health, housing and other needs should work together to reduce multiple assessments. Local authorities and health bodies should have worked out procedures for sharing information so you will not have to keep providing the same information. Guidance states that the views and wishes of the older person must be kept at the centre of the decisions made under the SAP process.

Under the SAP process there are four types of assessment, depending on what your needs appear to be. These are: a simple 'contact assessment', a more complex 'overview assessment', a 'specialist assessment' and a 'comprehensive assessment'.

LAC (2002)1; HSC 2002/001

Wales – There is single 'unified assessment process'. Guidance is holistic, person-centred and designed to be applied to the assessment and care management of all adult service user needs and to promote more effective joint working. There are some differences from the process in England.

NAfWC 09/02; WHC (2002)32; NAfWC12/2006

Scotland – The SAP process is called 'single shared assessment' and there are some slight differences from the process in England.

CCD 8/2201; CCD 2/2003; CCD 10/2004

Northern Ireland – A single assessment process is being developed, to include all service users.

Eligibility criteria guidance

In deciding whether you will be provided with services, the local authority will compare your assessed needs with the eligibility criteria it has set for community care services. Eligibility criteria set out the circumstances that must be present in any particular case before a person is considered eligible for services. Local authorities publish information about their assessment procedures and their eligibility criteria.

England – Guidance is contained within *Fair Access to Care Services.*

Wales – Guidance is contained within *Creating a Unified and Fair System for Assessing and Managing Care.*

Scotland – The Single Shared Assessment IoRN (or Indicator of Relative Need), previously know as the 'Resource Use Measure' was introduced in 2006 as a national tool to support professionals and managers in decisions about the use of resources and the planning of services.

Northern Ireland – *Fair Access to Care Services* is applied.

LAC (2002)13; NAfWC 09/02; CCD 10/2004; CCD 5/2004

The assessment result

You should be informed in writing of the result of your assessment and eligibility for services. A care plan is drawn

K.1 The law and community care

The law on assessments set out in this box applies equally if you want an assessment of your need for care in a care home. The duties and powers of statutory authorities come from Acts, regulations and Orders, as interpreted by case law. In following the law, authorities must act in accordance with Directions and mandatory guidance, and take account of other guidance (see Box L.1, Chapter 32).

Most of the provisions in Scotland come under different legislation. Although broadly equivalent to the law in England, Wales and Northern Ireland, there are some important differences. Guidance in the different nations may indicate differing application or interpretation of principles.

Assessments legislation

NHS & Community Care Act 1990 – S.47(1) states: *'... where it appears to a local authority that any person for whom they may provide or arrange for the provision of community care services may be in need of any such services, the authority (a) shall carry out an assessment of his needs for those services, and (b) having regard to the results of that assessment, shall then decide whether his needs call for the provision by them of any such services.'*

Disabled Persons (Services, Consultation & Representation) Act 1986 – S.4 states: *'When requested to do so by – (a) a disabled person [...] or (c) any person who provides care for him [...] a local authority shall decide whether the needs of the disabled person call for the provision by the authority of any services in accordance with s.2(1) of the [Chronically Sick & Disabled Persons Act 1970 (CSDPA)] (provision of welfare services).'*

Carers (Recognition & Services) Act 1995 – S.1(1) states: *'...in any case where – (a) a local authority carry out an assessment under s.47(1)(a) of the NHS & Community Care Act 1990 of the needs of a person for community care services, and (b) an individual (carer) provides or intends to provide a substantial amount of care on a regular basis for the [...] person, the carer may request the local authority, before they make their decision as to whether the needs of the [...] person call for the provision of any services, to carry out an assessment of his ability to provide and to continue to provide care for the [...] person; and if he makes such a request, the local authority shall carry out such an assessment and shall take into account the results of that assessment in making that decision.'*

Carers & Disabled Children Act 2000 (Not applicable in Scotland) – S.1(1) states: *'If an individual aged 16 or over ('the carer') – (a) provides or intends to provide a substantial amount of care on a regular basis for another individual aged 18 or over ('the person cared for'), and (b) asks a local authority to carry out an assessment of his ability to provide and to continue to provide care for the person cared for, the local authority must carry out such an assessment if it is satisfied that the person cared for is someone for whom it may provide or arrange for the provision of community care services.'*

S.2(1) states: *'The local authority must consider the assessment and decide: (a) whether the carer has needs in relation to the care which he provides or intends to provide; (b) if so, whether they could be satisfied (wholly or partly) by services which the local authority may provide; and (c) if they could be so satisfied, whether or not to provide services to the carer.'*

The services must *'help the carer care for the person cared for, and may take the form of physical help or other forms of support'*. Although provided to the carer it may take the form of a service delivered to the cared-for person if both agree and it does not include anything of an intimate nature.

Scotland

Section 12 of the Social Work (Scotland) Act 1968 sets out local authorities' duty to give help to persons in need. The Disabled Persons (Services, Consultation & Representation) Act 1986 sets out local authorities' duties to assess the needs of disabled people. Under the CSDPA, brought into effect by the Chronically Sick & Disabled Persons (Scotland) Act 1972, local authorities must provide disabled people with the services they have been assessed as needing. Also of importance is the duty on local authorities to carry out an assessment of need under s.55 of the NHS & Community Care Act 1990. Sections 8-11 of the Community Care & Health (Scotland) Act 2002 set out carers' entitlements to assessments.

Northern Ireland

In addition to the above, the CSDPA(NI) 1978, Disabled Person's (NI) Act 1989, Carers & Direct Payments (NI) Act 2002, Health & Social Services (NI) Act 2002 contain the relevant legislation.

Children

The assessment of, and provision of services to, children, including disabled children, comes under (as far as most services are concerned) the Children Act 1989 (in Scotland, the Children (Scotland) Act 1995). Assessment of need is undertaken under s.17(2) and Schedule 2, para. 3 (s.23 in Scotland) using the *Framework for the Assessment of Children in Need and their Families* issued in 2000 (2001 Wales). (An assessment under the NHS & Community Care Act 1990 – see above – is also available for services under the NHS Act 1977.) S.17 (s.22 in Scotland) places on local authorities a general duty to safeguard and promote the welfare of children in need. In meeting this duty they may provide services in kind or, in exceptional circumstances, in cash.

Children in need are those who are disabled and those who require the provision of services to achieve a reasonable standard of health or development or to prevent impairment of health or development. 'Disabled' is defined in the same terms as s.29 of the National Assistance Act 1948, below, except for being '18 or over'. (In Scotland, s.23 of the 1995 Act allows for the assessment and provision of services not only to children who are disabled but also to any child adversely affected by the disability of another family member.) Disabled children are also entitled to all services available under s.2 CSDPA by virtue of s.28A of that Act.

Providing community care services

Following an assessment, the local authority must decide how it will meet identified needs of the following people:

- provision of residential accommodation to *'persons aged 18 or over who by reason of age, illness, disability or any other circumstances are in need of care and attention which is not otherwise available to them'* – s.21(1)(a) National Assistance Act 1948 (NAA) (see Chapter 32(3));
- *'persons aged 18 or over who are blind, deaf or dumb or who suffer from mental disorder of any description, and other persons aged 18 or over who are substantially and permanently handicapped by illness, injury, or congenital deformity or such other disabilities as may be prescribed'*. S.29 NAA gives a general provision to promote the welfare of the above people including workshops, suitable work in their own homes or elsewhere, recreational facilities, information on services and keeping a register;
- those above (to whom s.29 NAA applies) who are

'ordinarily resident in their area'. The local authority has a duty under s.2 CSDPA to make arrangements for the provision of a range of services. Chapter 28(5) lists these services;
- old people – a general power, under s.45 Health Services & Public Health Act 1968, to promote welfare by providing services;
- *'a person who is suffering from illness, lying in, an expectant mother, aged, handicapped as a result of having suffered an illness or by congenital deformity'*. Local authorities have a duty, under s.21 and Schedule 8 National Health Service Act 1977, to provide adequate home help and may provide laundry services for households when such help is required owing to the presence of the above. This schedule also places a duty to provide day and training centres for those with a 'mental disorder';
- *persons who were detained or admitted to hospital under ss.3, 37, 47 or 48 of the Mental Health Act 1983*. S.117 Mental Health Act 1983 places a duty to provide aftercare services. In Scotland under ss.25-27 of the Mental Health (Care & Treatment) (Scotland) Act 2003 local authorities have a duty to provide services for people with a mental disorder regardless of whether they have been in hospital. These include care and support services, services to promote well-being and social development, and assistance with travel in connection with these;
- in Scotland, the Social Work (Scotland) Act 1968 also requires local authorities to make available advice, guidance and assistance to *'persons in need'*. It produces many of the same effects as the legislation above. Section 7 of the Community Care & Health (Scotland) Act 2002 gives local authorities wider powers to make direct payments to people to arrange and purchase their community care.

Also, s.2 of the Local Government Act 2000 gives local authorities the power to promote well-being in their area and to provide financial assistance, facilitate activities and provide accommodation.

Registered nursing care

(Not applicable in Scotland)

The Health & Social Care Act 2001 – S.49 removes the power of local authorities to provide nursing care by a registered nurse, defined as: *'Any services provided by a registered nurse and involving: (a) the provision of care; or (b) the planning, supervision or delegation of the provision of care, other than the services which, having regard to their nature and the circumstance in which they are provided, do not need to be provided by a registered nurse.'*

Free personal and nursing care

(Only applicable in Scotland)

The Community Care & Health (Scotland) Act 2002 – defines the care for which local authorities should not charge as:
- *'personal care as defined in s.2(28) of the Regulation of Care (Scotland) Act 2001;*
- *personal support as so defined;*
- *whether or not such personal care or personal support, care of the kind for the time being mentioned in schedule 1 to this Act; or*
- *whether or not from a registered nurse, nursing care.'*

'Personal care' relates to day-to-day physical tasks and the mental processes related to those tasks. *'Personal support'* means counselling or other help provided as part of a planned care programme – see Chapter 28(6) for items included in schedule 1.

Charges

Local authorities can charge for domiciliary services. They *'may recover such charge (if any) for it as they consider reasonable'*. If you satisfy your local authority that your *'means are insufficient for it to be reasonably practicable for [you] to pay'* what it has asked, it *'shall not require [you] to pay more for it than it appears to them that it is reasonably practicable for [you] to pay'* (s.17(3) Health & Social Services and Social Security Adjudications Act 1983/s.87 Social Work (Scotland) Act 1968). See Chapter 28(6). There are different rules for charges for services provided under the Children Act 1989 or Children (Scotland) Act 1995.

Those whose domiciliary or residential services are provided under s.117 Mental Health Act 1983 cannot be charged. In Scotland, charges can be made for such aftercare services, but this should not be for personal care provided to a person aged 65 or over. See Chapter 28(6) for details of the Mental Health (Care & Treatment) (Scotland) Act.

Information

Various pieces of legislation lay a duty on authorities to publish information.

NHS & Community Care Act 1990 – S.46(1)(a) and (c) and s.5A of The Social Work Scotland Act (1968) state: *'Each local authority (a) shall [...] prepare and publish a plan for the provision of community care services in their area.'*

Chronically Sick & Disabled Persons Act 1970 – S.1 states: *'(2) Every [local] authority (a) shall cause to be published from time to time [...] general information as to the services provided... under s.29, which are for the time being available in their area; and (b) shall ensure that any [...] person [...] who uses any other service provided by the authority [...] is informed of any other of those services which in the opinion of the authority is relevant to his needs and of any service provided by any other authority or organisation which in the opinion of the authority is so relevant...'*

Carers (Equal Opportunities) Act 2004 – S.1 requires local authorities to inform carers of their right to an assessment.

Complaints

Local Authority Social Services Act 1970 – S.7 establishes the requirements for complaints procedures. In England, new procedures are established in The Local Authority Social Services and NHS Complaints (England) Regulations 2009 (see Chapter 28(7)). For Scotland, see SWSG 5/96; S.7 gives ministers powers to hold an inquiry into a local authority's exercise of its social services functions, including any breach of its statutory duties. It also gives the Secretary of State 'default powers' to enforce action on a local authority.

If you are challenging a decision about the help you get or need at home or about care in a care home, the following may be useful.

- ❑ *Paying for Care Handbook* (2009, Child Poverty Action Group)
- ❑ *Community Care and the Law* by Luke Clements and Pauline Thompson (2007, Legal Action Group)
- ❑ *Community Care Law Reports* (Legal Action Group) – a quarterly digest of case law
- ❑ *Encyclopaedia of Social Services and Child Care Law (Volume 3)* (Sweet and Maxwell) – community care legislation including amendments to Acts and regulations
- ❑ *Social Work Law in Scotland* by Mays, Smith and Strachan (2006, W Green & Son)
- ❑ *Community Care Practice and the Law* by Michael Mandelstam (2008, Jessica Kingsley)
- ❑ *Health and Social Care Handbook* by Bielanska and Scolding (2006, Law Society)

up, and you should be given a copy of it. If you are not given a written result, you should ask for one. If your needs are urgent, services can be provided before an assessment, which should then be carried out as soon as possible. It is important that your care plan is detailed so you can see which of your needs have been taken into account, what services you should be getting and who will provide them.

Unhappy with the result? – If you are refused an assessment, or feel it has not taken account of your needs, or there is a delay in carrying it out, you can use the complaints procedure (or seek legal advice if it is urgent) – see 7 below. In England and Wales, practice guidance makes it clear that the carrying out and completion of a community care assessment should not be contingent on whether or not you can pay for care services, be they provided in a care home or your own home. With respect to services in your own home, a local authority should arrange those services irrespective of resources or capacity, if that is what you are assessed as needing. A local authority has been criticised by the Ombudsman where inadequate assessment caused loss to services users and their families.

Complaint against Wandsworth LBC (05/B/02414)

England – Personalisation Agenda

Personalisation is being implemented gradually by social services in England in 2009-10; by 2011 all services users must have a personalised plan. Personalisation should radically change your experience of social care and give you control of how your needs are met. Under the Personalisation Agenda, you will self-assess your needs and produce a care plan, with support from social care staff if necessary. As well as covering care issues, the care plan can include quality of life issues, eg work, leisure, domestic and family tasks. Social services will allocate funding, called a 'personal budget', either by direct payments (see Chapter 29(3)) or by arranging services for you (or a combination of the two). You should have total control over how you use these monies to meet your needs. It is planned that some health services will also come under personal budgets and this will be piloted over the next year.

Review of services

Local authorities should review the needs of service users annually and new service users should be reviewed after three months. A review can also be requested if you feel your needs warrants it, eg if your circumstances have changed.

Local authorities cannot reduce or remove services without a reassessment, and if your needs fall within their eligibility criteria they must provide the services. If the authority changes its criteria and becomes more restrictive (eg because of financial restraints), it would have to reassess you under the new criteria to see what services will be provided.

Carers

Carers can request that an assessment of their ability to continue providing care be carried out at the same time that the person for whom they are caring is assessed for services. The assessment of the carer should be taken into consideration in the decisions made as a result of the disabled person's assessment.

England and Wales – Local authorities are required to inform carers of their rights to an assessment and to promote equality of opportunity for carers. A carer's employment, educational and recreational intentions must be taken into account by social services. Authorities should co-ordinate a multi-agency approach if they believe a carer's ability to provide care might be enhanced by health, housing or education services.

Carers (Equal Opportunities) Act 2004

Carers have the right to be assessed independently. A carer's assessment may result in services being provided to the person cared for, or, additionally, the carer may receive services in their own right. They can choose to receive a direct payment for services they are assessed as needing (see Chapter 29(3)). Local authorities in England should now be setting up voucher schemes to help carers access short-term breaks. Authorities can charge carers for services provided directly to them. See Box K.1 for more on these rights under the Carers and Disabled Children Act 2000.

Scotland – The definition of carers includes those under the age of 16. Local authorities have a duty to inform carers of their right to an assessment (but not to paid carers). Although the law does not provide explicitly for services to carers, a carer's assessment can result in additional help being provided to the person cared for. Local authorities are also required to take into account the contribution of carers and the views of the person being cared for and their carer before deciding on services to be provided. A carer may receive support from the authority directly (in the form of information, advice or access to other resources) to assist them in their caring role. Guidance is clear that authorities should not charge carers for support provided to them in their caring role (CCD2/2003).

The Community Care and Health (Scotland) Act 2002

Northern Ireland – There are similar provisions.

Carers and Direct Payments (Northern Ireland) Act 2002

4. How can you register as disabled?

England and Wales – Anyone whose disability is 'substantial and permanent' can register with their local authority. But you don't have to register to qualify for an assessment or obtain services.

To register, contact the area office of your social services department. They will arrange for someone, usually a social worker or occupational therapist, to visit you and complete a registration form. Registering may not have any immediate benefit, but the more accurately the register reflects the number of disabled people in the community, the better services can be tailored to meet their needs.

Scotland – Although there is no requirement to keep registers, some local authorities do so, particularly for blind and visually impaired people. To qualify for services, you must fit the definition of disability under the Community Care and Health (Scotland) Act 2002.

Sight impairment – If you have a sight impairment, your ophthalmologist or hospital eye specialist will advise if you are able to register as sight impaired. There are two levels of registration: blind/severely sight impaired and partially sighted/sight impaired. Every local authority in the UK has a duty to keep a register of sight-impaired people in their area. There are a number of concessions available to people who are registered – contact RNIB for details (see Address List).

5. What help can be provided?

Local authorities have a legal duty to provide certain services. Other services may be provided, but there is no requirement to do so. See Box K.2 for some types of services that may be available. All these services may not be available in your area and the list is not exhaustive. Under the Personalisation Agenda in England there will much more flexibility as to what social services can fund through your 'personal budget' (see 3 above).

What are your rights to services?

If you are disabled and assessed as needing one of the services listed in section 2 of the Chronically Sick and Disabled Persons Act 1970 (CSDPA), your local authority has a duty to make arrangements for the provision of the services, which are:

- practical help in the home (eg a home help);
- providing, or help in getting, a radio or television or access to a library or similar recreational facilities;
- lectures, games, outings or other recreational facilities

outside your home and any help needed to take advantage of educational facilities;

- help with travelling to any of these or similar activities;
- any adaptations (eg a ramp or lift or special equipment) needed in the home *'for greater safety, comfort or convenience'*; this can even include building an extra room on the ground floor;
- holidays;
- meals, either in the home or a local centre;
- a telephone, and any special equipment necessary to use the phone (eg Minicom).

See Box K.1 for the definition of disability and the legal provisions to provide services.

CSDPA, S.2

Scotland – Key sections of the CSDPA were brought into effect through the Chronically Sick and Disabled Persons (Scotland) Act 1972. The Community Care and Health Act (Scotland) 2002 also extended the range of duties on local authorities and NHS boards through joint working and locally pooled budgets.

Northern Ireland – The legislation is contained within the Chronically Sick and Disabled Person's (Northern Ireland) Act 1978.

Supporting People services

In England, the Supporting People programme is *'committed to providing better quality of life for vulnerable people to live more independently and to maintain their tenancies'*. It provides housing-related support to prevent problems that can lead to hospitalisation, institutional care or homelessness and to support people leaving an institutional environment. It is available to people in all types of housing, is run by Communities and Local Government, and is administered by 150 agencies.

The Local Government Act, S.93(8)

In Wales, Supporting People is funded through two streams. Funding for community-care type services is administered by local authorities, and homelessness services are administered by the Welsh Assembly Government.

In Scotland, ring-fenced funding for Supporting People has been removed.

Supporting People services should complement community care and health services. Examples include support to keep older people in their own homes, wardens in sheltered schemes, supporting and training care leavers, and providing ongoing support for people adjusting to independent living.

Your needs and local authority resources

Local authorities may wish to refuse or withdraw services because of a shortage of resources. They may tighten eligibility criteria defining needs they will meet and services they will provide.

Although a local authority can take its resources into account when setting its eligibility criteria (so the criteria might be tightened when resources are short), if you come within the criteria, and a decision is made that you need services, it cannot use lack of resources as a reason not to provide the services to meet your assessed need. However, when meeting your assessed needs the authority is entitled to exercise flexibility and can take resources into account when deciding how your needs are met, eg it may provide the cheaper option. It cannot take its resources into consideration if you would be left at severe physical risk if services were not provided.

R v Kirkless MBC ex p Daykin

Once services are provided, an authority may not withdraw or reduce them (whether or not as a result of introducing stricter eligibility criteria) without conducting a review of your community care assessment.

Seek advice (see 7 below) if you are not getting the services you need because of local authority resources problems. Resources issues are repeatedly coming before the courts, which have been consistent in finding that authorities cannot take resources into account once you have been assessed as needing services.

6. Do you have to pay for your care?

A local authority may charge for domiciliary services (ie services provided at home) and other services in the community (eg day centres) that it either provides or arranges for you. Carers may be charged for services they receive direct. You cannot be charged for services provided by the NHS, eg district nurses. If you are getting intermediate care services (see 1 above) you may not be charged for them for an initial 6-week period.

England – Community equipment is free and minor adaptations that you or your carer are assessed as needing will be provided free by social services, as long as the cost is less than £1,000. (Free-standing equipment does not have a £1,000 cap, although some local authorities have tried to cap equipment at £1,000.) Social services have the discretion to charge for minor adaptations costing over £1,000. In some cases, you may be able to get a disabled facilities grant (see Chapter 31). The system for charging for care in a care home is explained in Chapter 34.

LAC (2003)14

Wales – Local authorities have the power to charge for the provision of community equipment but presently do not choose to do so. In some cases, you may be able to get a disabled facilities grant (see Chapter 31).

Scotland – There is no charge for advice and information about availability of services and assessment of care needs. People aged 65 or over are not charged for personal care; the amount of free care you will receive is determined by a local authority assessment and there is no set limit to the amount authorities can provide if you live at home. Limits apply if you live in a care home (see Chapter 32(3)). Free personal care services may be arranged by the authority, or you can ask for a direct payment (see Chapter 29(3)). Receipt of free personal care while living at home does not adversely affect entitlement to attendance allowance (AA), disability living allowance (DLA) or any other state benefit. Conversely, if you are aged 65 or over and live in a care home, you will not be entitled to AA or DLA if you receive payment for free personal care. If you are under 65, you will receive both benefits if the only help you get is free nursing care. See Chapter 33(2). Free personal care is defined in the Community Care and Health (Scotland) Act 2002 and includes help with:

- personal assistance – eg help with dressing, getting up and going to bed, using a hoist, help with surgical appliances and manual aids;
- personal hygiene – eg bathing, washing hair, shaving, nail care, oral hygiene;
- continence management – eg toileting, catheter/stoma care, skin care, bed changing, incontinence laundry;
- dealing with problems arising from immobility;
- simple treatments – eg assistance with medication (including eye drops), simple dressings, oxygen therapy and the application of creams and lotions;
- counselling and psychological support including behaviour management and the provision of reminding and safety devices;
- food and diet – eg help with the preparation of food and assistance with special dietary needs.

Despite the fact that the legal definition of personal care includes *'assisting with the preparation of food'*, guidance issued by the Scottish Executive states that food preparation (other than specialised meals, eg pureed foods) and the provision of meals is not covered. Seek further advice if you are charged for help with meal preparation.

The definition of free personal care covers physical assistance with care and help with the mental processes related to that care – eg helping someone to remember to wash.

Free personal care payments start from the date the assessed service is provided and cannot be backdated (eg to the date of referral or date of assessment). If you are assessed as requiring free personal care but told you will have to wait before it can be provided, seek advice. On admission to hospital, you become responsible for the full cost of your care after two weeks.

You may be charged for shopping, domestic chores or other forms of non-personal care. A recent Court of Session judgment has set out that a local authority is only obliged to provide free personal care if it is providing the service, and that it is at the authority's discretion whether to provide the payment to a private care provider, if it is not care that the authority is providing.

CCD 1/2008; Argyll & Bute Council – Judicial review of Decision of Scottish Public Services Ombudsman [2007] CSOH 168

Northern Ireland – If you are 75 or over, you are not charged for your home help service. Charges for people under 75 are explained in circular HSS1/80, which has been regularly amended.

Health and Personal Social Services (Assessment of Resources) Regulations 1993; HSS1/80

How much can you be charged?

England – Local authorities have the power to charge for home care services. Charging policies for domiciliary and day care vary considerably. *Fairer Charging for Other Non-Residential Social Services* (LAC 2001/32) and associated practice guidance lay down a framework as to how authorities should charge for services.

Fairer Charging instructs local authorities on minimum levels for charging. Authorities can decide not to charge at all or can have policies that are more generous than the guidance. If there are charges (which is the case in nearly all authorities), each person's circumstances must be considered individually. The authority should give you written details of how much you will be charged, a breakdown of how this has been worked out and details of what to do if you think you cannot afford the charge.

The guidance states that disability-related benefits (defined as the severe disability premium, DLA care component, AA, constant attendance allowance and exceptionally severe disablement allowance) may be taken into account as income. The DLA mobility component is disregarded. If disability-related benefits are taken into account, the local authority should assess your disability-related expenditure; guidance gives examples of the main types, including expenditure on additional clothing or heating, private care or complementary therapies. Some authorities have decided to allow a set amount for normal disability-related costs in order to avoid intrusive questions; it varies from authority to authority. Local authorities have their own lists of disability-related expenditure but these might not be comprehensive and you can ask for a review for other expenditures to be taken into account. Payments to relatives might be disallowed as disability-

K.2 Checklist of care services

Where to get help

Practical help with caring may be available from a number of sources: relatives, friends and neighbours; private organisations or individuals; voluntary organisations; local authorities or the NHS.

To find out what help is available, first contact your area social services department. If they do not provide a particular service, they should be able to put you in touch with the right organisation. Your area may not have all the services listed below. Authorities have a legal duty to provide information about services available (see Box K.1).

Getting services into the home

Adaptations – see Chapter 31.

Alarm system – allows you to get emergency help via an alarm button. Contact social services for advice.

Benefits – see Benefits Checklist.

Care Attendant scheme – voluntary schemes to help give carers of disabled and older people a break. There may be a local scheme. If not, contact Crossroads (see Address List).

DIAL – see Address List for the nearest Disablement Information and Advice Line (DIAL) group and other sources of telephone advice.

Direct payments – made by social services departments (health and social service boards or trusts in Northern Ireland) (see Chapter 29(3)) for you to purchase care to meet your care needs.

District/community nurses – may provide nursing care at home or in a care home, or arrange to supply equipment to help with nursing care, as well as incontinence aids.

Energy efficiency schemes – see Chapter 31(4).

Equipment – see Chapter 30.

Good neighbour scheme – volunteers who will socially visit older people or people with a disability.

GPs – your general practitioner is the key person in ensuring you get, or are referred to, the services you need. If you are really dissatisfied with your GP you should consider transferring to another doctor.

Health visitors – can provide information and advice on local services and act as a liaison or referral point between disabled people and social services departments. Health visitors automatically visit families with children under 5. They also offer practical advice and support. You can get in touch with a health visitor through your GP, health centre or child health clinic.

Home helps or domestic help workers – can provide practical help in the home – eg domestic tasks, including shopping or housework. Some social services departments no longer provide this help but it may be provided by a private agency instead. There is a home help service in Northern Ireland.

Home carers – can provide personal care assistance in the home such as help with getting up, washing and getting dressed.

Home visits – you can arrange a home visit from a chiropodist, dentist, doctor, hairdresser, occupational therapist, optician or a physiotherapist. A Citizens Advice Bureau worker will try to visit you at home if you are housebound and it is not possible to advise you over the phone or by letter.

Hospital after-care schemes – see 'intermediate care' below.

Incontinence – for continence services, see Chapter 30(3).

Independent Living Funds – see Chapter 29(2).

Intermediate care – intensive therapeutic care aimed at avoiding the need to go into hospital, or to enable you to leave hospital earlier. It usually lasts for up to six weeks and may be free (in Wales it is called '6-weeks support at home for vulnerable people') – see Chapter 28(1).

Laundry service – see Chapter 30(3).

Library – if you are housebound, you can get home visits from the library service. Check the Address List for organisations such as Listening Books.

Meals on Wheels – meals delivered to your house, run by social services or by local voluntary or commercial agencies. Contact social services for details.

Occupational therapists – can help you learn or relearn the related expenditure (*R on the application of Stephenson v Stockton on Tees BC (Admin)*, 7 CCLR December 2004), but the Court of Appeal stated that local authorities should look at each case on its merits.

If you get higher rate AA or highest rate DLA care component (ie for both daytime and night-time care needs) but you receive only day services, the local authority should not take all of your benefit into account, just the part for daytime care (*R v Coventry City Council ex p Carton*). DLA mobility component should not be taken into account as income.

SSCBA, S.73(14)

Your income should not be reduced below the basic level of income support (ie personal allowance and appropriate premium(s) – excluding the severe disability premium) or pension credit through charges, and there should be a buffer of 25% above this level.

Importantly, earnings are disregarded. If the local authority takes your capital into account, the minimum limit above which you can be charged the full cost of the service should be the same as for care in a care home (£23,000) and they can use the same tariff income. Authorities can be more generous if they wish.

Only the person receiving the service can be charged, and if carers receive services they should be charged according to the guidance.

The guidance states that benefits advice should be provided at the time of the charges assessment. This should include advice about entitlement, help with completing claim-forms and follow-up action if the user wishes.

Wales – Similar arrangements apply, although the *Fairer Charging* guidance issued in 2002 was revised in April 2007. The buffer above basic levels of income support or pension credit is 35%, not 25%. All users are also given a flat-rate disability-related expenditure disregard in charge assessments of at least 10% of their equivalent basic level of income support or pension credit. The maximum capital limit in Wales for 2009-10 is £22,000.

Scotland – The level of charge will be determined by the local authority, but in 2006 the Convention of Scottish Local Authorities (CoSLA) produced its own guidance on charging older people for 'non-personal' care services. CoSLA guidance recommends the following.

- Earnings, pensions and social security benefits (except DLA mobility component) should be taken into account as income, and this includes the resources of a partner.
- A minimum earnings disregard of £20 should be applied.
- There is an income disregard of all benefits paid for dependent children for whom you are responsible.
- Local authority charging should not reduce your income below a threshold of the standard minimum guarantee of pension credit plus a 16.5% buffer.
- The level of charge is based on a percentage of your excess income. Each local authority is free to determine its own percentage figure.
- Tariff income should be £1 for every £500 from £6,000, but with no upper limit.
- Local authorities should use their powers to abate or

skills of independent self-care and personal management in all aspects of everyday life. They can also offer advice on, or arrange the provision of, necessary equipment or adaptations to your home. Contact them through social services or the primary care trust.

Odd job schemes – sometimes called Handy Person schemes, give practical help with tasks you cannot manage (eg decorating, gardening, etc) and are usually run by a voluntary group.

Physiotherapists – provide treatment and advice to relieve pain and help restore and maintain mobility. This includes advice about equipment. Contact your GP for a referral.

Recreational facilities – radio, TV, etc.

Rehabilitation – many district general hospitals have well-equipped rehabilitation departments with a variety of services and techniques to help patients develop their maximum ability. Treatment may also be provided at health centres, at home or at other suitable centres.

Self-help and socialising – check Address List. You could, for example, join a PHAB club.

Sheltered or supported housing – provides a range of options, from an on-call warden to extra care housing.

Sitting in service – see 'Care Attendant scheme'.

Sleeping in service – allows your carer a night or weekend away.

Social workers or care managers, community care practitioners – play a key role in getting services into your home and offering advice.

Social fund – discretionary one-off payments (see Chapter 23).

Speech and language therapists – for all forms of communication disorders. Available through the NHS.

Support for a carer – contact Carers UK or Crossroads (see Address List).

Supporting people services – see Chapter 28(5).

Telephone – if you can't handle and/or read a printed phone book, register for free use of Directory Enquiries (ring 195 for details).

Telecare – passive sensors around your home can alert someone if you need urgent help: eg if you fall or if you leave the gas on or the tap running. This is becoming an increasingly popular service provided by many local authorities – sometimes by social services and sometimes by housing services.

Services away from the home

Adult education – Contact your local authority or library.

Advice – contact your local council for a list of local advice centres. See also Chapter 61.

Care homes – can be provided by local authorities, the NHS, private and voluntary organisations (see Chapters 32, 33 and 34).

Day centres – provided by the local authority (or in some cases by voluntary organisations) as places where elderly people or those with disabilities can meet. Meals, therapies and activities are usually available.

Day hospital care – some hospitals offer hospital stays during the day but you return home at night. This can be done on a regular basis or just in emergencies.

Emergency overnight stay – in hospital or a care home.

Employment schemes – contact social services and/or the disability employment adviser (see Chapter 17(2)).

Holiday/Short-term care – a 'foster' scheme with volunteer families.

Respite or short-stay care – can be in a hospital or a care home. Allows carers a break or holiday and may help you to remain at home longer (see Chapters 3, 33 and 35 for the benefit implications).

Transport – most social services departments arrange transport to clubs, day centres and workshops for people with disabilities who are unable to use public transport. The British Red Cross offers a transport and escort service for people unable to use public transport or travel alone. In some areas there are voluntary schemes, such as Dial-a-Ride. For information on free local bus travel for older and disabled people, see Box B.6 in Chapter 5.

waive charges if you would have difficulty paying the assessed charge.

- ❑ Local authorities should consider not charging for day care services and for aids and adaptations.
- ❑ Charging policies that reduce a person's income below 'basic' levels should not be acceptable.

This guidance builds on the Scottish Executive guidance on charging (SWSG1/1997) and also on domiciliary care (CCD 5/2004 and CCD 12/2004).

When can charges not be made?

The local authority cannot charge:

- anyone (family, carer or friend) other than the person using the service. They can only take into account your own income and capital when deciding how much you should pay (although for couples, guidance indicates they can take into account a partner's income and capital if the user has a legal entitlement or if benefit is paid to one of a couple for both). In Scotland, the CoSLA guidance recommends the assessment of a partner's resources, as both are perceived to benefit from the non-personal care services for which they are being charged;
- the parent or guardian, for children's services provided under the Children Act 1989 (Children (Scotland) Act 1995) if the child is under 16 and the parent or guardian is on income support or receiving any element of child tax credit other than the family element;
- a young person, for services under the Children Act 1989 (Children (Scotland) Act 1995) if the young person is aged 16-18 and on income support or income-based jobseeker's allowance (JSA);
- for intermediate care services in England;
- you, if you have any form of Creutzfeldt-Jakob disease (CJD), as you should be exempt from charges;
- in England, for equipment. Minor adaptations costing less than £1,000 are also free;
- in England and Wales, for services provided under section 117 of the Mental Health Act 1983.

Scotland – People 65 or over can have free home care for up to four weeks following a period in hospital (see 1 above under 'Intermediate care services'). Local authorities must not charge for care provided to people 65 or over that comes under the definition of 'personal care' (see 6 above). They must not charge for training and occupation (eg day centres) provided for adults with learning disabilities. There is a duty on local authorities to provide services to those who have, or who have had, a 'mental disorder' under the Mental Health (Care and Treatment) (Scotland) Act 2003. Authorities can charge for aftercare services.

Charges for Supporting People services

People can be charged for Supporting People services, but they should not be worse off than under the pre-April 2003 support services system. Tenants on housing benefit, people in short-term schemes (for developing independent living) and owner occupiers on means-tested benefits will not be charged. People not on means-tested benefits will be charged in accordance with the *Fairer Charging* guidance. There is protection to ensure that people who lost means-tested benefits when support services charges were removed are no worse off. Council tenants in pooled accommodation who previously had support costs pooled should also be offered protection to ensure their support costs do not increase.

In Wales, the charging framework follows the English structure. However, a key difference is that the Welsh Assembly Government funds some services directly (mostly for younger people and homeless people) and these will be exempt from charges.

Ring-fenced funding under the Supporting People programme is no longer available in Scotland.

More details on Supporting People and charges can be found at www.spkweb.org.uk for England and www.wales.gov.uk for Wales.

If you cannot afford to pay the charge

The local authority has a duty to decide how much you can afford to pay and reduce the charge, or not charge you, if it is not reasonable for you to pay the charge. It may not withdraw a service because you fail to pay the charge. This is because the decision to meet a need is separate from, and comes before, any decision to charge for the service. This does not appear to apply, however, to Supporting People services.

The local authority or the provider of housing support services can use debt enforcement proceedings (eg taking you to court) for the recovery of arrears. If you cannot afford the charge, ask for it to be reduced or waived.

Complaints – You can complain about the amount you are being charged and have your case heard by a review panel. Some local authorities have a separate charges complaints procedure, which is shorter than the standard complaints procedure described below.

7. If you are not satisfied with your care services

Complaints

Each local authority in England, Wales and Scotland has a complaints procedure. Each must publicise its complaints procedure and provide you with information regarding the action you can take if you are unhappy about the assessment or the services to be provided at the time of the care assessment or when you are informed of any charge.

England – From April 2009, a new combined health and social services complaints procedure was introduced. It is a two-stage system with an emphasis on local resolution and a simpler, less bureaucratic, more personal and comprehensive way of handling complaints. A local authority complaints officer should ensure that people making complaints get adequate support. If complaints are not resolved locally, they will be referred to the Local Government Ombudsman (see Chapter 62(5)).

Complaints started before April 2009 will continue under the old three-stage system of local resolution, investigation and review panel (see *Disability Rights Handbook* 33rd edition, page 156).

There is now a one-year time limit for considering complaints, although older complaints can be considered in some special circumstances, eg if the person was too frightened to complain earlier.

The Local Authority Social Services Complaints (England) Regs 2006; The Local Authority Social Services & NHS Complaints (England) Regs 2009

Wales – The complaints procedure has three stages: 'local resolution', 'formal consideration' and 'independent panel'. It is hoped that most complaints will be resolved at the local resolution stage. This should happen within ten days, although it can be extended by another ten days if you request or agree to it. If the matter is not dealt with after the maximum of 20 days, it should move to the next stage: formal consideration. This stage should be completed within 25 days. It need not be a formal investigation but can be resolved in another way, eg through mediation. If you are still not happy, or if the council has not responded to your complaint within three months, you can ask for an independent panel. A panel should be arranged within 20 days of your request, a report of the finding produced within five days, and a decision by the authority within 15 working days. The panel is independent of the authority and consists of people selected and trained by the Welsh Assembly Government. If you are still not happy, you can take your case to the Public Services Ombudsman. The Ombudsman can also consider complaints directly after local authority consideration.

The Social Services Complaints Procedures (Wales) Regs 2005

Scotland – The procedure is similar to Wales but with different time limits. A third-stage 'review panel' has 56 days to provide written recommendations and the local authority has 42 days to decide on action. The right to complain extends to carers. The authority should provide information on the procedural steps of the assessment and care plan and, if it is relevant to the complainant, on how an independent advocate can be made available.

Social Work Representations Procedure (Scotland) Order 1990 and Social Work Representation Procedure (Scotland) Directions 1996

Further steps

You may wish to take your complaint to local councillors or your MP (MSP in Scotland and National Assembly Member in Wales) if you feel it would be helpful for them to know the system is not working for you. If you have exhausted the complaints procedure you can contact the relevant Ombudsman: Local Government Ombudsman in England, Northern Ireland Ombudsman in Northern Ireland, Scottish Public Services Ombudsman in Scotland and Public Service Ombudsman for Wales in Wales (see Address List). The Ombudsman can investigate complaints against local authorities if there has been maladministration.

Local Authority Social Services Act 1970

If it is not possible to resolve your dispute via the complaints procedure, you may wish to consider a legal remedy such as judicial review. You can also complain to the local authority's Monitoring Officer (usually the Chief Executive or Borough Solicitor) who is responsible for ensuring that decisions are lawful and procedures correctly followed. It is also possible to ask the Secretary of State to use their default powers, but these extend only to statutory duties, not to discretionary powers – ie if you feel the local authority has withdrawn or failed to provide a service that it has a duty under law to provide.

It may be useful to contact a national organisation or seek legal advice to discuss ways of pursuing your case. You must act quickly. Contact a law centre or the Disability Law Service (see Address List).

Scotland – The rules applicable to judicial review and involvement of the Monitoring Officer apply as above. You can also ask the Scottish Government to order the authority to provide a statutory duty under section 65A of the Social Work (Scotland) Act 1968. If you need community care help because of mental health problems, learning disability or dementia, contact the Mental Welfare Commission (see Address List). The Commission cannot force changes, but can make recommendations and carry out enquiries.

29 Buying care

1. Introduction

Local authorities have the main responsibility for directly providing or arranging services for disabled people and others who are assessed as needing them (see Chapter 28). In this chapter, we look at some of the cash help available to help pay for care. There are three main sources.

Social security benefits – If you are under 65, you may be able to get disability living allowance care component (see Chapter 3). If you are 65 or over, you may be able to get attendance allowance (see Chapter 4). Carers who spend at least 35 hours a week caring for a severely disabled person may be able to get carer's allowance (see Chapter 6). There are also premiums within means-tested benefits and additional amounts in pension credit for carers and disabled people (see Chapter 24).

Independent Living Fund – The Independent Living Fund (see 2 below) makes cash payments directly to you to pay for care to help you live independently in your own home. It is a government-funded but independent and discretionary trust fund, governed by a board of trustees. A legally binding trust deed sets out the powers and procedures of the trustees and the eligibility criteria for help from the Fund.

Direct payments – Local authorities have direct payment schemes whereby social services departments make cash payments to you so you can make your own arrangements to meet your assessed needs (see 3 below).

2. Independent Living (2006) Fund (ILF)

Since October 2007 the ILF has operated a single fund – the Independent Living (2006) Fund. ILF is a national resource providing financial support for disabled people to live independently. There are two main groups of ILF users.

Group 1 (former Extension Fund users) – The role of Group 1 is to maintain payments made to people who applied under the pre-1993 system. No new applications are accepted. Money from ILF is wholly ignored when means-tested benefits are being calculated. For details of employment issues, contributions and appeals, see below.

If you go into hospital or a care home, your payments from ILF may be suspended. However, if you privately employ a carer, an appropriate retainer can be paid for up to four weeks to avoid disruption to care. The rules are the same as those for Group 2.

ILF may consider increases for people who have *'experienced a significant change in their circumstances'* – eg if total care needs or costs have increased. In these circumstances, ILF may ask your local authority to review its contribution. The maximum award payable is £815 a week.

Group 2 (new applicants and former 1993 Fund users) – ILF works in partnership with local authorities to devise joint care packages. These are a combination of services or direct payments from the local authority and cash from the ILF. ILF payments are made 4-weekly in arrears and normally paid into your bank account. Money from the ILF is wholly ignored when means-tested benefits are being calculated and when your local authority assesses your charges for home care services.

Who can get help?

Awards are discretionary, but there are basic guidelines that the trustees must consider. To qualify for help from the ILF, you should normally fulfil all of the following conditions. You must:

- be severely disabled to the extent that extensive help with personal care or household duties is needed to maintain an independent life in the community; *and*
- be at least 16 and under 65 years of age when you make the application; *and*
- be receiving disability living allowance (DLA) highest rate care component; *and*
- be receiving (or it is planned that you will receive) services or cash to a value of at least £320 a week from your local authority; *and*
- have less than £23,000 savings; *and*
- be living alone or with people who are unable to fully meet your care needs.

The ILF will give priority to applications from people working at least 16 hours a week, whether employed or self-employed. Applications are normally accepted from people receiving income-related employment and support allowance, income support, income-based jobseeker's allowance or pension credit guarantee credit (or people whose income is no more than 25% above the level of these benefits) if the ILF/local authority joint package costs are likely to be at least £500 a week. Other applications will not normally receive an offer of financial assistance.

How to apply for help
If you think you may be eligible for help from the ILF, you should do the following:

- ❑ Ask your local authority social services department for an assessment of your needs, and say you want to apply to the ILF.
- ❑ If the social worker decides the care package you need will involve at least £320 worth of services and/or cash from the local authority, they will support your application to the ILF.
- ❑ Once the ILF has accepted your application, one of its visiting assessors will visit you and the local authority social worker together. At this visit, your care needs can be discussed by all three parties and an agreement reached about the amount and type of care you need.
- ❑ The ILF assessor will then send a written report making recommendations about the care package needed.
- ❑ If your application is successful, the ILF will make you a cash award of up to £475 a week. It will be paid once the ILF receives details from you of how you will use the money (eg who your care/personal assistants will be or what care agency you will be using).

If you cannot apply to the ILF yourself or manage the money from the ILF, or manage using it to buy part of your care package, someone else can do so on your behalf. Note that the rules for direct payments from the local authority are different (see 3 below).

How much will you have to contribute?
You will always be expected to put at least half of your DLA care component towards the cost of your care. The exact amount will depend on a financial assessment, based on income support rules (see Chapter 14(8)). If you are one of a couple, your capital and income will be counted jointly, except that earnings are always disregarded. If you lose your DLA highest rate care component, the ILF payments can continue if you are asking for a review of the decision or are in the process of appealing to a First-tier Tribunal. Payments will be suspended for the duration of any subsequent appeals.

If you get a means-tested benefit – If you get a means tested benefit (income-related employment and support allowance, income support, income-based jobseeker's allowance or pension credit guarantee credit), you are expected to contribute any severe disability premium (or pension credit equivalent).

If you do not get a means-tested benefit – The extra amount you are expected to contribute is calculated by working out your income (excluding earnings), and deducting from this any allowances (see below) and the amount you would get if you were on income support (excluding the severe disability premium).

The allowances deducted from your income are based on those for income support but some are more generous. All mortgage payments and endowments are taken into account. Earnings are disregarded. Tariff income is assumed from £14,000.

If you are charged by your local authority at the time of application for the care they are providing, the charge will be deducted from the amount the ILF will expect you to contribute.

The ILF contribution rules cover the UK, so in Scotland you may be charged by the ILF for personal care if you are under 65. People 65 or over who receive ILF payments can seek advice about whether their local authority would provide them with an equivalent amount of free personal care; as this may be a complex area, contact the ILF for advice.

What if you need more care?
If your care needs increase or you need more money, you can apply for an increase in your payments at any time. If you need an increase, your local authority will normally have to contribute at least £320 before the ILF will consider paying one. If you receive direct payments, the ILF will normally match those payments.

Going into hospital or a care home
If you are admitted to hospital or another type of residential or institutional care, ILF payments will be suspended. But payments may continue for up to four weeks if they are needed to pay a retainer to directly employed staff. Your case can be kept open for 13 weeks (or longer at the discretion of the ILF) and your payments reinstated if you return to live independently in the community within that time.

Employment issues
It is important to check the status of the care/personal assistants who work with you. Each case is different and is judged on its merits by HMRC. If you employ a worker directly, you should assume you are the employer unless you have checked that the assistant is self-employed. You have all the responsibilities of an employer – eg paying employer's national insurance contributions, etc. HMRC has a simplified way of collecting tax in these situations. If the decision causes any difficulty, you could discuss it with the local tax office. In addition, you can contact the ILF for general advice (0845 601 8815).

The National Centre for Independent Living has details of books and pamphlets to help people who employ their own care workers, and other support organisations can offer practical assistance to people who employ their own staff through direct payments (see Address List).

Appeals
For complaints about social services, see Chapter 28(7). If you are dissatisfied with any aspect of how the ILF has dealt with your application, set out your reasons in a letter to the ILF Complaints and Decision Review Manager (see Address List), who will review the case and then may refer it to the Senior Management Panel and, where appropriate, the Trustees, for a decision.

3. Social services direct payments

Direct payments allow a person who has been assessed as needing particular services to receive cash to arrange and pay for those services. You can have a combination of some services provided directly by social services and others arranged by yourself with direct payments. Direct payments may give you more control over the way your care needs are met.

Health and Social Care Act 2001; Community Care (Direct Payments) Act 1996

Who can have a direct payment?
In England, Wales and Scotland local authorities have a duty to offer direct payments to people who fall within the rules below. The Government has launched an initiative to increase take-up of direct payments over the next year and has produced new support to authorities to develop local schemes.

England and Wales – To get a direct payment, you must be over the age of 16 and be a disabled person, carer or someone with parental responsibility for a disabled child. You must have been assessed as needing community care services or services as a carer. Currently, you must have the mental capacity to agree to and manage direct payments, but there are plans to extend this in England to people who lack such capacity. Although you should be offered direct payments, you cannot be forced to have them.

You cannot have direct payments if you are subject to certain mental health or criminal justice legislation.

The Health and Social Care Act 2008

Disabled parents can use direct payments to purchase children's services. The High Court has ruled it is lawful to pay an independent trust set up for a user (in this case with trustees composed of the parents and representatives of a disability organisation and the local authority).

R(A&B, X&Y) v East Sussex CC

Scotland – Disabled people over 16 assessed as needing services can receive direct payments; people with parental responsibility can give consent for disabled children to receive direct payments. People over 65 who, due to age or frailty, may have community care needs can get direct payments. In addition, non-disabled people receiving care services, eg people who are homeless, refugees or ex-offenders, or those fleeing domestic abuse or recovering from drug or alcohol dependency are also eligible.

Carers do not receive services in their own right so cannot get direct payments unless they are assessed as needing them. If someone cannot give consent or manage their affairs, a representative can receive and manage direct payments on their behalf. Guidance suggests this will be limited to attorneys and guardians granted the relevant powers. Entitlement to free personal care is not affected unless you are under 65 or live in a care home. A new guide is being developed by the Scottish government: *Directing your own support: a user's guide to self-directed support in Scotland.*

CCD 7/2007

Northern Ireland – You are eligible to receive direct payments if you are over 16 and have been assessed as needing personal social services. This includes carers.

What can direct payments be used for?

England, Wales and Northern Ireland – Direct payments can be used to arrange services (including equipment) to meet your assessed needs. Local authorities should allow you to choose how best to meet your assessed needs. Direct payments cannot be used, however, to purchase care in a care home, apart from periods up to four weeks (120 days for children) in any one year. Separate periods in a care home of less than four weeks are added together towards the maximum only if you are at home for 28 days or less in between.

Direct payments cannot normally be used to pay for services from your spouse, partner or a close relative (or their spouse or partner) living in your household, other than in exceptional circumstances agreed with the local authority. You can use your direct payment to employ a relative if they are not living with you. You cannot use a direct payment to purchase services from the local authority.

Guidance to local authorities encourages them to ensure that support is available for users of direct payment. Authorities must check that the money you have been given is spent on the care you have been assessed as needing. If not, they could ask for it to be paid back.

The National Centre for Independent Living (see Address List) gives advice on direct payments as well as general advice and information about local independent living organisations.

Scotland – Similar rules apply, with an emphasis on flexibility, choice and control for the eligible group seeking a direct payment. You can use direct payments to purchase wide-ranging services from the local authority, eg help with going shopping or accessing community psychiatric nursing. Normally, direct payments cannot be used to pay for the services from others living in the same household, although in exceptional circumstances a local authority can make direct payments to employ live-in relatives if the authority is *'satisfied that securing the service from such a person is necessary to meet the beneficiary's need for that service'*. You can, however, use your direct payment to employ a relative who is not living with you.

Local direct payment support organisations can give advice and practical assistance. For details, ring your local authority or Update on 0131 669 1600.

CCD 7/2007

How much are you paid?

Local authorities must make direct payments equal to their estimate of the reasonable cost of the service to meet your assessed needs and fulfil your legal obligations if you employ your carer/s (eg national insurance payments, employers' liability insurance, holiday and sick pay). If you choose a more expensive way to meet your assessed needs than is *'reasonable'*, you will have to pay the extra cost yourself. Payments made will not affect your benefits.

You may be asked to contribute towards the cost of your care. The amount of your contribution will be calculated using the same charging rules as for care arranged by the local authority (see Chapter 28). You will either be paid your direct payment net (with the charge taken off) or gross (where you pay the amount you are assessed to pay in the same way as if you were getting a service).

If you are unhappy with the amount you are offered or any other aspect of the direct payment, you should use the complaints procedure (see Chapter 28(7)).

The Personalisation Agenda

In England there are plans to bring the Personalisation Agenda to all community care service users by 2011. This system will allow you to write your own care plans and decide how your needs will be met (see Chapter 28(3)). The system will incorporate direct payments and individual budgets. Similar provisions were introduced recently in Scotland.

LAC(DH)(2008)1; CCD 7/2007

30 Help with equipment

1. Items for daily living

Under section 2 of the Chronically Sick & Disabled Persons Act 1970 (CSDPA) covering England, Scotland and Wales (and the Chronically Sick & Disabled Persons (Northern Ireland) Act 1978), local social services (or in Scotland, social work) authorities have a duty in some circumstances to arrange for the provision of equipment or to assist with home adaptations for disabled people. This duty arises when the authority has assessed you and decided your needs are sufficiently high to qualify for assistance – an 'eligible need'. However, the threshold varies between local authorities, who are increasingly restricting its scope.

Once an eligible need has been determined, the local authority has an absolute duty to arrange to meet it in some way within a reasonable period of time. On request by a disabled person or their carer, the authority has a duty to make a decision about your possible needs under the CSDPA.

Disabled Persons (Services, Consultation & Representation) Act 1986, S.4 (England, Scotland & Wales); Disabled Persons (Northern Ireland) Act 1989, S.4.

Equipment – The CSDPA refers to additional facilities concerned with your safety, comfort and convenience, including communication facilities. It also refers to practical assistance in the home, outings, educational opportunities, holidays, etc – all of which could involve a need for equipment.

Home adaptations – The CSDPA contains a duty to arrange for assistance with carrying out home adaptations. Typically, this duty will apply to so-called minor adaptations, but may also cover expensive major adaptations that are not (easily) removable. The authority must decide whether the cost of major adaptations (eg provision of an extra bathroom or toilet) falls within the criteria for provision of a housing grant under housing legislation (see Chapter 31), whether it comes within social services criteria under the CSDPA, or whether a housing grant may be topped up to meet eligible needs. Not all social services are fully aware of their duties in this respect.

Landlords and the Disability Discrimination Act – Public and private landlords must make reasonable adjustments for disabled tenants. This could include provision of auxiliary aids and adaptations (eg signs, notices, taps, door handles, doorbells and door entry systems) but not involving removal or alteration of a building feature or fixtures.

DDA, S.24 & the Disability Discrimination (Premises) Regs 2006 (SI 2006/887)

Restrictive policies – Social services often operate restrictive policies, eg some say as a matter of policy they don't provide certain types of equipment. Such blanket policies may be unlawful if they are applied without taking your individual needs into account. Some authorities may refuse to provide equipment on the grounds that they lack the resources. This, too, is unlawful if you have already been assessed as having an eligible need.

Carers – In England and Wales, social services have a duty to assess informal carers and provide services for them (see Chapter 28(3)). These services are not defined but could in principle cover equipment used by the carer (rather than the cared for person). Although Scottish legislation does not provide explicitly for services to carers, local authorities must take account of their contribution. The views of the person in need and their carer should also be considered during the assessment before deciding what services to provide.

Charges – In England, legislation prevents social services from charging for equipment provided under the CSDPA or under section 2 of the Carers & Disabled Children Act 2000, or for minor adaptations costing less than £1,000 provided under either of those Acts. Guidance says the cost of a minor adaptation is to be calculated in terms of both its purchase and installation expenses. Some authorities are now trying to charge people for maintaining the equipment; it is unclear whether this is lawful.

In Wales, social services have a legal power to make charges for equipment but in practice might not exercise it – eg personal reminder systems for taking medicines may be provided free of charge by community pharmacists for people assessed as qualifying if, in the pharmacist's opinion, the medication regime is suitable.

In Scotland, under the Community Care & Health (Scotland) Act 2002 certain personal care equipment must be free for people aged 65 or over, although what is covered is limited. 'Personal care' would include such things as memory and safety devices, eg sound/movement alarms linked to light controls to guide people with dementia to the toilet and to minimise the risks related to wandering at night. It does not include community alarms and other associated devices. Scottish guidance states *'frail older people'* should not be charged for equipment and minor adaptations provided by social services if these are supplied and fitted either immediately prior to hospital discharge, or within the following four weeks.

For the charging rules generally, see Chapter 28(6).

Self-assessment – Social services and the NHS increasingly operate self-assessment or self-selection schemes, enabling you to choose some items of equipment yourself. In some areas of England from 2009, a needs assessment will result in an equipment prescription being issued. This prescription may be taken to a retail outlet and the equipment will be supplied. Service users may choose a more expensive variation of their prescribed equipment if they top up the price difference themselves. Your right to a formal assessment should not be affected in any instance. In practice, some local authorities take shortcuts and will seek to whittle away your right to assessment – typically by screening you out.

Direct payments – If certain conditions are met, social services have a duty to make direct payments (see Chapter 29(3)) for equipment as well as for other community care services. Direct payments are not available through the NHS for healthcare equipment.

Buying your own equipment

Specially designed equipment (sometimes called assistive technology or AT) can be a key factor in enabling people to live as independently as possible. Before buying, check whether the equipment you need is available on long-term loan through social services or the NHS. If you are unsure about what to buy, get expert advice and always ask to use the equipment on a trial basis. Many items are small, relatively inexpensive and can make an enormous difference. Consider carefully more expensive items, eg electric scooters, riser/recliner electric wheelchairs, walk-in baths or special beds. These can cost thousands of pounds and may not be what you require, so you will need expert objective advice. Look for supply companies who are recommended or who are members of a recognised and regulated organisation.

Occupational therapists may be able to give advice, as may other health and social care professionals such as physiotherapists, district nurses, health visitors and social

K.3 For more information

Equipment

Contact the Disabled Living Foundation for general information, advice and factsheets on equipment, and to use their online self-assessment tool, 'AskSARA' (380-384 Harrow Road, London W9 2HU; 0845 130 9177; textphone 020 7432 8009; www.dlf.org.uk).

Disabled Living Centres and Communication Aids Centres – have a range of equipment on show, and some sell equipment. You can often try out equipment as well as get advice about what might help you best. Contact Assist UK for a list of local centres (see Address List).

Ask your doctor, social worker or health visitor for advice. See also Age Concern factsheets FS6 *Finding help at home*, FS24 *Direct payments from social services* and FS42 *Disability equipment and how to get it*.

Social services and the NHS

You can get specialist information on all aspects of community care from organisations such as Age Concern, Carers UK, Counsel and Care, Help the Aged, Mind and RADAR (see Address List). They can offer practical suggestions if you haven't been able to resolve the problem locally (see Chapter 28(7) 'Further steps' for some suggestions). In Scotland, the Scottish Helpline for Older People may be helpful (0845 125 9732). For information and links regarding provision of equipment, go to www.direct.gov.uk/en/DisabledPeople/index.htm.

workers. Independent Living Centres display and demonstrate equipment/assistive technology and are an important source of impartial advice; some are now also retail outlets.

For information about VAT relief on equipment, see Chapter 53. If the occupational therapist recommends an item of equipment, ask if there is a centre where you can see it (see Box K.3) or look at a website that displays alternatives (eg www.dlf.org.uk). Equipment provided by social services is generally considered to be on long-term loan.

2. Healthcare equipment

The NHS may provide equipment for particular health conditions, eg beds, hoists, wheelchairs, commodes, urinals and continence pads. However, as some are also aids to daily living, NHS and social services providers may not be able to agree who is responsible for providing equipment. Increased financial pressure in the NHS and social services is escalating this difficulty and there is a risk that neither service will accept responsibility.

Legally, it is not easy to challenge non-provision of equipment by the NHS if it argues it is short of money; however, blanket policies on provision are illegal. Every equipment package should be provided on the basis of individual assessment and need.

In the first instance, apply for items via your doctor, district nurse/health visitor, continence adviser, occupational therapist, physiotherapist or social worker. GPs can prescribe equipment on an approved list (the 'Drug Tariff'), including catheters, elastic hosiery, supports, etc, which have standard prescription charges.

In Wales, prescriptions for equipment listed in the Drug Tariff no longer attract a prescription charge, provided the equipment is prescribed on a Welsh prescription form and dispensed in a Welsh pharmacy.

An NHS consultant may prescribe equipment necessary for a patient's treatment – eg walking aids, orthotics, supports and prosthetics. Depending on the patient's condition, these may be free or there may be special prescription charges. Standard prescription charges apply to Drug Tariff items for outpatients.

Hearing aids are supplied on the prescription of a consultant, or patients can be referred by their GP to the audiology department. Hearing aids are supplied on free long-term loan from NHS Hearing Aid Centres. Hospital ophthalmologists can prescribe items varying from low-vision aids to more complex items like eye prostheses. Visual assessments and the provision of aids are also available from accredited optometrists, although there may be a charge for consultation.

3. Services to help with incontinence

Incontinence has physical, mental and social consequences. It is important to get advice from an NHS continence adviser, GP, practice nurse or physiotherapist to see if there is treatment that might help. Your need for assistance should be taken into account during a social services community care assessment. There are several types of provision: advice about management of incontinence, treatment (eg drugs, physiotherapy and surgery), supplies and equipment, laundry services and disposal of waste. However, these provisions may vary between different local authorities.

How to get help

The NHS may supply, free of charge, continence aids and equipment – including commodes, bed linen, continence pads, protective pants, inter-liners, disposable draw sheets, bedpans, etc. For an individual, the NHS decides on the quantity and quality of items, and sometimes decides not to supply any. Although this may seem unfair, it is not normally easy to challenge this legally. However, for residents in nursing homes (ie those that provide registered nursing) the NHS should provide incontinence aids free of charge (in England and Wales). Protective pants and pads are not available on GP prescription (except in Scotland). If you cannot get an item through the NHS, you can buy it from chemists (although the range may be limited) or from specialist mail order firms. Body-worn urinary appliances can be prescribed by GPs, but take the prescription to a chemist or surgical supplier that has a skilled fitting service. For more information on aids, equipment and services, ring PromoCon (0161 834 2001) or the Bladder and Bowel Foundation (0870 770 3246).

How to obtain a laundry service

If a laundry service is available in your area, it will normally be run by the social services department, probably attached to the home help service, or by the NHS. In some areas there is no laundry service, but extra help may be given through the home help service. For families with very severely disabled children, the Family Fund can provide washing machines and/or dryers (see Chapter 37(8)). If you cannot cope with the practical problems arising because of incontinence, you may qualify for disability living allowance care component or attendance allowance (see Chapters 3 and 4).

4. Environmental control systems and communication aids

Environmental controls enable people with severe disabilities to operate electrical appliances and equipment from a central control, with switching mechanisms adapted to meet their needs; contact an occupational therapist or your doctor. For more sophisticated equipment, an NHS specialist will assess your needs and arrange for installation. The equipment is provided on loan and serviced free of charge. Simpler environmental control systems can be provided by social services, although they are not always aware of their potential obligations under section 2 of the Chronically Sick & Disabled Persons Act 1970 (see 1 above).

People with severe difficulties in speaking or writing can be helped by a range of communication aids – from charts with pictures to specially adapted computers and electronic voice output devices. These can be provided by social services or schools, or through the Access to Work scheme run through your local Jobcentre Plus office (see Chapter 17(2)). NHS speech and language therapists can refer you to a communication aids centre for advice and assessment. However, communication aids are subject to significant rationing and may not be easy to get.

5. Wheelchairs

Under the NHS, wheelchairs (manual and electrically powered) are supplied and maintained free of charge to a disabled person whose need for such a chair is permanent.

If you are severely disabled, electrically powered indoor/outdoor wheelchairs can be provided if you are unable to walk or to propel an ordinary wheelchair. The NHS locally applies eligibility criteria, along the lines that you are unable to propel a manual wheelchair and are able to benefit from an improved quality of life and handle the chair safely. In Scotland, similar criteria are set nationally for powered wheelchairs.

Attendant-controlled powered wheelchairs are issued when it is difficult for the disabled person to be pushed out of doors – eg when the attendant is aged, the district is hilly, or the person cannot operate a powered indoor/outdoor wheelchair by themselves.

NHS trusts in England have a voucher scheme. Users can top up an NHS voucher with their own financial contribution towards a more expensive or sophisticated wheelchair. You may be unable to use the voucher scheme to get a powered wheelchair, but you could use the Motability scheme to hire purchase an electric wheelchair (see Box B.6, Chapter 5).

Anyone who thinks they might need a wheelchair should be referred to their local wheelchair centre for assessment. Your GP, local health centre, physiotherapist or occupational therapy department can tell you where your local wheelchair centre is, or you can ring NHS Direct (0845 4647). In principle, any wheelchair available may be supplied by the NHS to meet assessed individual need. However, you should be aware that, locally, NHS wheelchair services are significantly under-resourced and operate restrictive eligibility criteria as well as waiting times. This means you may not get the wheelchair you need, or you may have to wait an undue length of time to get it.

6. Community alarms and Telecare

Community alarms are used to call for help and are particularly useful to people who live alone or who are on their own for substantial periods of the day or night, or if both partners are frail. Some local authorities provide community alarms through their housing or social services departments, or they can be supplied by private companies. There is a charge for this service.

Telecare

Telecare is an extension of the community alarm system and provides a way of discreetly monitoring the home environment, for example by means of sensors (eg for gas, smoke or movement). Should an emergency occur, a signal is sent automatically to a call centre, which in turn will take appropriate action. Telecare is particularly appropriate to people who have a tendency to fall, who have health problems that require monitoring or who are at significant risk through forgetfulness. There is a charge for this service.

7. Other sources of equipment

Although social services and the NHS are the main statutory providers of equipment, you can obtain equipment through other channels.

The Access to Work scheme, run via your local Jobcentre Plus office, may fund equipment needed for work (see Chapter 17(2)).

Schools or local authorities can provide equipment needed for education, and local authorities sometimes have an absolute duty to do so if the need is specified in the educational section of a child's statement of special needs.

The social fund (see Chapter 23) has been used to help people get items ranging from wheelchairs to continence pads.

Local and national voluntary organisations (including the Family Fund (Chapter 37(8)) can help by lending or hiring equipment or providing a grant to buy it (see Box K.3).

Specific charities for medical conditions often provide equipment help and advice, as do umbrella charities with websites and helplines such as the Disabled Living Foundation, Assist UK, etc.

31 Housing grants

1. The housing renewal grants system

Local authorities in England and Wales have a general discretionary power to help with adaptation or improvement of living conditions by providing grants, loans, materials or other forms of assistance.

Community equipment, aids and minor adaptations that assist with living at home or aiding daily living and cost less than £1,000 should be provided free of charge in England. In Wales, the Rapid Response Adaptations Programme aims to provide adaptations costing up to £350 within 15 days of a referral by your local authority or health worker.

In Scotland, the housing grants system is different (see Box K.4).

2. Disabled facilities grants

A mandatory disabled facilities grant is designed to help with the cost of adapting a property for the needs of a disabled person.

Who is eligible for a grant?

To be eligible for a disabled facilities grant, you must be:

- an owner occupier; *or*
- a private tenant; *or*
- a landlord with a disabled tenant; *or*
- a local authority tenant; *or*
- a housing association tenant.

Some occupiers of caravans and houseboats are also eligible.

HGCRA, S.19

You are treated as disabled if:

- your sight, hearing or speech is substantially impaired; *or*
- you have a mental disorder or impairment of any kind; *or*
- you are physically substantially disabled by illness, injury, impairment present since birth, or otherwise; *or*
- you are registered (or could be registered) disabled with the social services department.

HGCRA, S.100

What can you get a grant for?

A grant can be awarded for:

- facilitating a disabled occupant's access to and from the dwelling;
- making the dwelling safe for the disabled occupant and others residing with them;
- facilitating a disabled occupant's access to a room used or usable as the principal family room;
- facilitating a disabled occupant's access to or providing a room used or usable for sleeping in;
- facilitating a disabled occupant's access to or providing a room in which there is a lavatory, bath or shower and wash-hand basin, or facilitating the use of any of these;
- facilitating the preparation and cooking of food by the disabled occupant;
- improving the heating system to meet the disabled occupant's needs, or providing a suitable heating system;
- facilitating a disabled occupant's use of a source of power, light or heat;
- facilitating access and movement around the home to

enable the disabled occupant to care for someone dependent on them, who also lives there;

- facilitating access to and from a garden by a disabled occupant; *or*
- making access to a garden safe for a disabled occupant.

HGCRA, S.23

The test of financial resources

Disabled facilities grants for adults are means tested. There is no means test if an application is made for the benefit of a disabled child or young person.

The relevant person – For applications from owner occupiers and tenants, a test of resources is applied to the person with disabilities and their partner, if they have one. This is so even if the disabled person is not the grant applicant. For example, a disabled person lives with his brother, who has sole ownership of the property. The brother can apply for a disabled facilities grant to carry out adaptations for the benefit of his disabled brother. The test of resources applies only to the disabled brother (known as the relevant person) not to the brother who made the application.

HRG Regs, reg 5

The test – The test of resources is similar, but not identical, to that for housing benefit or, if the relevant person is aged 60 or over, pension credit, but there are a number of important differences.

- There are no non-dependant deductions.
- There is an extra premium (the 'grant premium', sometimes called the 'housing allowance') designed to reflect housing costs, currently £61.30. This is added to the total applicable amount for every grant application.
- If the relevant person receives income support, income-based jobseeker's allowance, the guarantee credit of pension credit, housing benefit, council tax benefit or working tax credit (WTC) or child tax credit (CTC) with a gross taxable income of less than £15,050, the applicable amount is automatically £1 and all their income and capital are disregarded, giving a zero contribution. Income-related employment and support allowance (ESA) is expected to be added to this list of benefits in April 2009.
- There is no capital cut-off point. The first £6,000 of capital is disregarded. Weekly tariff income is assumed on capital over £6,000.
- There is a system of stepped tapers on 'excess income'.

K.4 Grant system in Scotland

In Scotland local authorities are allowed to provide grants, loans, subsidised loans, practical assistance and information or advice to home owners for repairs, improvements, adaptations and the acquisition or sale of a house.

HSA, S.71

Grants – Assistance *must* be by way of a grant if the adaptations are essential to the disabled person's needs and the work is structural or involves permanent changes to the house (except extensions to provide living accommodation in the existing structure or any other structure). A grant must also be given for work to provide a standard amenity to meet the needs of a disabled person, ie: a fixed bath or shower, wash-hand basin or sink (in each case with a hot and cold water supply) or a toilet.

The grant will be 100% of approved costs if the applicant or a member of their household receives income support, income-based jobseeker's allowance, the guarantee credit of pension credit or income-related employment and support allowance. In other cases the grant will be 80%.

Housing (Scotland) Act 2006 (Scheme of Assistance) Regs 3 & 4

Guidance – The local authority must publish a statement of its criteria for deciding whether to provide assistance and in what form. The statement must also set out any circumstances in which it would cap the costs of work for which a grant or loan is available, and the rate of interest or other charges on loans.

HSA, S.72

Tenants – Tenants are not eligible for a grant or loan unless the work to which the grant or loan relates:

- has, for a period of two years preceding the tenant's application, been the tenant's responsibility under the tenancy;
- is for the adaptation of a disabled person's house to make it suitable for their accommodation, welfare or employment, or for the reinstatement of any house adapted; *or*
- is required as a matter of urgency for the health, safety or security of the occupants of a house, including, in particular, work to repair it or provide means of escape from fire or other fire precautions.

HSA, S.92

Applications – A grant or loan application must include full details of the proposed work, including plans, specifications, location of the work, an estimate of the cost and other information the authority may reasonably require. An authority may require information to support the accuracy of such details.

HSA, S.74

Decisions on applications – The local authority has discretion to approve or refuse an application for a grant or loan. If one is approved, the authority must work out the approved expense and, where the application is made for a grant or subsidised loan, the applicant's contribution. The authority may only approve a grant or loan application if it considers that:

- the owners of all the land on which the work is to be carried out have given written consent to the application and to being bound by the conditions of the grant or loan;
- the house will provide satisfactory accommodation for a reasonable time and meet reasonable standards of physical condition and amenities; *and*
- the work will not prevent the improvement of any other house in the same building. The authority must not approve an application if the work has already begun, unless there were good reasons for starting the work early.

HSA, S.75

Energy Assistance Package

The Energy Assistance Package, introduced in April 2009 to help maximise incomes, reduce fuel bills and improve energy efficiency in homes, has four stages:

- an initial energy audit: ring the Energy Savings Scotland Advice Centre network (0800 512 012);
- help with improving incomes and reducing energy bills for people vulnerable to fuel poverty;
- a package of standard insulation measures (cavity wall and loft insulation). These will be provided free to those on income-related benefits or aged 70 or over, and at a subsidised rate to others;
- more enhanced energy efficiency measures in private sector homes for: pensioner households who have never had central heating installed; pensioners in energy-inefficient homes who receive the guarantee element of pension credit or are aged 75 or over; low-income families in energy-inefficient homes with a child under 5 or a disabled child under 16; and those living permanently in mobile homes.

- Personal allowances and premiums are sometimes not uprated at the same time as those for housing benefit or pension credit. The last uprating was on 22.05.08.
- WTC and CTC are disregarded as income from 31.12.08 in England.
- It is expected that, in England, there will be no ESA additional components as part of the applicable amount but receipt of contributory ESA will be a qualifying benefit for the disability premium.

Working out your contribution

The test of resources is designed to calculate how much, if anything, you can afford to contribute towards the cost of the works. This is done by calculating the value of a notional standard repayment loan you could afford to take out using a proportion of your 'excess income' (see below) to repay the loan. If you have no excess income, your contribution will be zero. Owner occupiers, including leaseholders, are expected to be able to repay a loan over ten years; tenants, over five years. The higher the amount of excess income, the higher the proportion expected to be used towards repaying the notional loan. To work out your contribution, see below.

Step 1: Work out your capital

Your capital, together with your partner's, is taken into account. Certain types of capital are disregarded. The rules are similar to those for income support (see Chapter 27). However, the capital value of the dwelling to which your application relates is disregarded whether or not you live there. The first £6,000 of your capital is ignored. Tariff income of £1 per £250 (or part thereof) over £6,000 is assumed if the relevant person is aged under 60 and £1 per £500 (or part thereof) if the relevant person is 60 or over.

HRG Regs, reg 40

Step 2: Work out your income

Your average earnings and other income are based on your income over the 12 months before your application or a shorter period if that gives a more accurate figure. The earnings and income disregards are similar to those for housing benefit (see Chapter 26).

HRG Regs, regs 20, 21 & 22

K.5 For more information

Guidance on assistance with repairs, improvements and adaptations is in Circular 05/2003, *Housing Renewal* (Office of the Deputy Prime Minister, 17.06.03) and in *Delivering Housing Adaptations for Disabled People: A good practice guide* (Communities and Local Government – C&LG, June 2006). Equivalent guidance for Wales is in National Assembly for Wales Circular 20/02; Annex D, on disabled facilities grants, was revised in April 2007.

The law and guidance are available from The Stationery Office (see page 6).

A C&LG leaflet on disabled facilities grants is available on their website (www.communities.gov.uk) and can be ordered in alternative formats.

Independent home improvement agencies offer advice about grants and help people apply for grants, obtain other sources of finance to help pay for works, find good builders and ensure works are properly carried out. Ask your local authority if there is one in your area or contact your national co-ordinating body: Foundations (in England), Care & Repair Forum Scotland, or Care & Repair Cymru (Wales) – see Address List.

For information about VAT relief on building works, see leaflet 701/7, *VAT reliefs for people with disabilities,* available from HMRC (0845 010 9000).

Step 3: Work out your applicable amount

This represents your weekly living needs and those of your family (see Chapter 20(25) or Chapter 42(3)). Add on the grant premium (see above).

HRG Regs, reg 14

Step 4: Work out your excess income

If your income is less than or equal to your applicable amount, you have no excess income. Your contribution is zero. If your income is greater than your applicable amount, the excess income is the difference between the two figures.

Step 5: Work out your contribution

Excess income is apportioned into a maximum of four bands and multiplied by the relevant loan generation factor(s). For applications made after 22.05.08, the bands and multipliers are shown below.

HRG Regs, reg 12

Loan generation factors			owner occupiers	tenants
Band 1	First £47.95	factor	18.85	11.04
Band 2	£47.96 to £95.90	factor	37.69	22.09
Band 3	£95.91 to £191.80	factor	150.77	88.34
Band 4	£191.81 or more	factor	376.93	220.86

The aggregate of Bands 1-4 is the value of the notional loan the relevant person is expected to contribute towards the cost of the works.

Example: An applicant who is an owner occupier with an excess income of £100 would calculate their contribution as follows:

Band 1	£47.95	x	18.85	=	£903.86
Band 2	£47.95	x	37.69	=	£1,807.24
Band 3	£4.10	x	150.77	=	£618.16
Applicant's contribution					*£3,329.26*

The applicant's contribution would therefore be £3,329.26. If the total cost of the works were £11,000 the grant would be calculated as follows:

Total cost of works	£11,000.00
Less applicant's contribution	£3,329.26
Grant amount	*£7,670.74*

Subsequent grants

If a relevant person has had to make a contribution to a previous grant on the same dwelling (in the last ten years for owner occupiers or five years for tenants), the value of that contribution is deducted from the assessed contribution on a subsequent grant application. The works under the first grant must have been carried out to the local authority's satisfaction for this offsetting to apply. If the contribution on the earlier grant was more than the cost of the works, leading to a 'nil-grant approval', the value of the works properly carried out can be offset against a subsequent grant contribution.

HRG Regs, reg 13

Applying for a disabled facilities grant

Disabled facilities grants are administered by the local housing authority rather than the social services department if these are different. An application form should be available from the housing authority. It must be supported by a certificate stating that the disabled occupant intends to live in the property for at least five years after the works are completed, or for a shorter period if there are health or other special reasons.

HGCRA, Ss.21 & 22

Approval of a disabled facilities grant

The maximum grant payable under a mandatory disabled facilities grant is £30,000 in England, £25,000 in Northern Ireland and £36,000 in Wales. Local authorities could provide further assistance for extra costs under their discretionary power (see 3 below).

The Disabled Facilities Grants (Maximum Amounts & Additional Purposes) (England) Order 2008, Reg 2;

In order to approve an application for a disabled facilities grant, the local housing authority must be satisfied that the works are both necessary and appropriate for the needs of the disabled person, and reasonable and practicable in relation to the property. In determining whether the works are necessary and appropriate, the housing authority must consult with the social services authority. This is why some local authorities direct people to the social services department first for an occupational therapy assessment.

HGCRA, S.24

However, it is important to make a formal application for a grant, because the 6-month time limit for the local authority to make a decision only begins from the date of the formal application. The authority cannot refuse to allow you to make a formal application or refuse to give you an application form.

HGCRA, S.34

If you do not get a decision within six months of applying, write and ask why and request that a decision be made. Seek legal advice if you still do not get a decision, or if you have been prevented from applying in the first place. Alternatively, you can make a complaint of maladministration to the relevant Ombudsman (see Chapter 62(5)). If approved, the adaptations should usually be completed within one year by one of the contractors who supplied an estimate for the application. The local housing authority has a discretion to approve a mandatory grant but to stipulate that it won't be paid for up to 12 months from the date of application.

HGCRA, Ss.36, 37 & 38

If, after the application has been approved, the disabled person's circumstances change in some way before the works are completed, the local housing authority has a discretion as to whether to proceed with paying for all, part or none of the works. It must take into account all the circumstances of the situation before deciding how to proceed.

HGCRA, S.41

From April 2008 in England, local authorities may place a charge against a property if a disabled facilities grant exceeds £5,000. The maximum charge is £10,000 and would apply for ten years. This means the value of the charge could be repayable if the adapted property is sold within ten years. Authorities should decide whether to place a charge on a property on a case-by-case basis considering the individual circumstances of each applicant. In Wales, the charge is determined by the local authority.

3. Discretionary power to assist with housing repairs, adaptations and improvements

Local housing authorities in England and Wales have a discretionary power to provide financial and other assistance for repairs, improvements and adaptations. In Northern Ireland, the discretionary grants are different. Details are available from the Northern Ireland Housing Executive, The Housing Centre, 2 Adelaide Street, Belfast BT2 8PB (028 9024 0588; www.nihe.gov.uk).

Scope of the power

Under this discretionary power, local authorities can set their own conditions for assistance, such as whether to perform a means test and the circumstances under which financial assistance should be repaid. Assistance may be given in the form of grants, loans, labour, materials, advice or in any combination of these. Accommodation may be acquired, adapted, improved or repaired, demolished or replaced (if it has been demolished). Local authorities may take security, including a charge on a person's home. People in all tenures may be helped, including owner occupiers, tenants and landlords (including companies and registered social landlords). To find out what is available in your area, contact your local housing authority, who must make available a summary of its scheme.

RR(HA)(E&W) Order, art 3

When providing assistance, the local authority must set out in writing the terms and conditions that apply and must take into account a person's ability to afford any repayment or contribution towards the costs.

Even if the help you need appears not to be available you can ask the local authority to consider your needs. An application for assistance may be legitimately turned down if it falls outside the published policy, but an authority cannot refuse to consider an application or turn down an application that does not fit the published policy without there being a mechanism in place to determine such cases.

If you are refused assistance, you should ask for the decision to be confirmed in writing and ask what system of review or appeal the authority operates. If you are still not happy with the decision, you should seek advice and/or consider making a complaint to the relevant Ombudsman (see Chapter 62(5)).

4. Energy efficiency grants

England – Under the Warm Front Grant scheme, help towards improvements in insulation, room heating and water heating is available to disabled people, families with children who get a qualifying benefit or tax credit, and people aged 60 or over who get a means-tested benefit. Warm Front provides maximum grants of £3,500 for installing insulation and improving heating for households using mains gas, solid fuel, oil or off-peak electricity for heating (or £6,000 if oil central heating is installed or repaired). Enquire about eligibility on Freephone 0800 316 2805.

The Warm Front £300 Heating Rebate Scheme can help with the cost of installing central heating for pensioners not eligible for Warm Front qualifying benefits. Apply via the Eaga Contact Centre (0800 316 2805).

Wales – The Home Energy Efficiency Scheme (HEES) provides grants of up to £2,000 on a similar basis to Warm Front Grant. HEES Plus provides up to £3,600 for central heating (or £5,000 if oil central heating is installed or repaired) for householders who are over 80, or who are receiving a qualifying benefit *and* are over 60 or disabled or chronically sick, or a lone parent with children under 16. It may provide £500 to people aged 60 or over and not on a qualifying benefit. For applications/enquiries ring 0800 316 2815.

Northern Ireland – The Warm Homes scheme provides insulation grants of up to £850 to owner occupiers and private tenants who are disabled, over 60 or with children under 16, and who are in receipt of a qualifying benefit. Warm Homes Plus provides grants of up to £4,300 for insulation and repair or installation of central heating for householders over 60 in receipt of a qualifying benefit. For enquiries and applications, ring 0800 181 667.

Scotland – See Box K.4.

5. Alternative housing

Many people prefer to move to a property designed to be accessible for a disabled person rather than undertaking major adaptations to their present home. However, even an accessible property may require some adaptations to suit your particular needs.

If you are seeking social housing (ie council or housing association properties), contact your local authority and make sure you go on the housing register. It is important to stress your housing requirements. Most housing association properties are allocated via local authorities but some associations operate their own waiting lists, particularly for wheelchair users, so it is worthwhile contacting housing associations directly.

L Care homes

This section of the Handbook looks at:

32 Help with care home fees

In this chapter we look at: page

1. Who can get help with care home fees?

If you require help with care home fees you need to approach your local authority social services departments. Help will be provided only on the basis of a professional assessment of your needs (see Chapter 28(3) and Box K.1). Some people will be entitled to full NHS funding within a nursing home. Contact your primary care trust or health board for details (see 3 below).

- **England and Wales** – The NHS is responsible for your registered nursing costs in a home providing nursing care after a determination of how much care you need by a registered nurse, even if you do not need help with the rest of your fees. You should be assessed by an NHS nurse if you want the NHS to contribute towards your nursing care (see 3 below).
- **Scotland** – Social work departments will pay a set amount (£216 a week) for both nursing and personal care if you are 65 or over; you should only be asked to contribute towards accommodation and living costs (see 3). If you are under 65, the local authority will pay a fixed amount towards nursing care only (£67 a week).
- **Northern Ireland** – Payments for nursing costs are made by Health and Personal Social Services.

If you get help from social services, the amount you pay normally depends on an assessment of your means. Chapter 33 covers the benefits you can receive in a care home and Chapter 34 covers the way local authorities assess how much you should pay if they are helping with funding your place.

The system of assessing needs and charging is the same whether your accommodation is provided in a home managed or owned by a local authority, or in a home managed or owned by a voluntary or private organisation (sometimes described as the independent sector).

NAA, Part III

If you enter a care home and don't want or need help with the fees, you should still ask for an assessment of your needs, as the local authority may make other suggestions and could advise whether the type of home you plan to go into is suitable for your needs, and whether, once your capital is below the capital limit for your country (see Box L.2, Chapter 34), they will agree to help with the funding.

It is useful to find out what fee level the local authority is prepared to pay for someone with your needs. You can then compare it to prices quoted by homes you visit. Many homes charge people who pay for themselves more than they charge local authority-funded residents, and some are prepared to reduce this charge if you later need help from the local authority. This is important if you think you might need local authority funding in the future.

Children – Care in care homes for children aged under 18 is provided under the Children Act 1989 (or in Scotland, the Children (Scotland) Act 1995).

Hospices – Care in hospices is free at the point of use.

Aftercare services – In England and Wales, care in care homes must be free of charge for people who have previously been detained in hospital for treatment under certain sections of the Mental Health Act 1983 and who are entitled to aftercare services under that Act.

Mental Health Act 1983, S.117

The Local Government Ombudsman in 2003 found that a failure to provide s.117 services was maladministration and instructed local authorities to identify and reimburse residents who have previously been incorrectly charged for aftercare services.

York City Ombudsman (04/B/01280); R v Manchester CC ex p Stennett HoL [2002] (5 CCLR 500); LAC 2000/11

In Scotland, there should be no charge for services provided under the Mental Health (Care and Treatment) (Scotland) Act 2003. However, charges can be made for other aftercare services; the charges omit a set amount for personal care or nursing if you are 65 or over, or for just nursing if you are under 65.

In Northern Ireland aftercare services, which can include care homes, are provided free.

Mental Health Order (NI) 1986

2. Different types of care homes

Care homes are run by a range of providers. Health bodies as well as local authorities can arrange care in homes that provide nursing. We use the term 'care home' when talking about any of the types of homes listed below. All homes must be registered as 'fit for the purpose' for the care they intend to provide.

- In England, the Care Quality Commission registers and inspects homes and reports are available on its website (www.cqc.org.uk).

CSA (England and Wales)

- In Scotland, homes are registered and regulated by the Scottish Commission for the Regulation of Care (www.carecommission.com).

RC(S)A (Scotland)

- Care homes in Wales are registered and regulated by the Care and Social Services Inspectorate Wales (www.wales.gov.uk/cssiw).
- Homes in Northern Ireland are registered and inspected by the Regulation and Quality Improvement Authority and homes are called nursing and residential care (www.rqia.org.uk).

The Health and Personal Social Services (Quality, Improvement and Regulation) (Northern Ireland) Order 2003

Although all homes that must be registered are called care homes (except in Northern Ireland), some also provide nursing care. There are regulatory bodies in each UK country to ensure homes meet required standards. Homes must produce a statement of intent, a service users' guide giving details about the home, and a copy of the most recent inspection report. You will also get a statement of terms and conditions (or written contract) describing the services covered by the fee, services not included in the fee, and terms and conditions of occupancy.

Care Homes Regs 2001

Homes providing personal care – These can be run by private or voluntary organisations or private individuals. Personal care is not defined, but to trigger the need for registration, it means assistance with bodily functions such as feeding, bathing, toileting, etc. If healthcare is needed it should be provided by the local community health services in the same way as for a person in their own home. Non-physical care such as advice, encouragement and prompting do not trigger a requirement to register. This is so that sheltered housing schemes do not have to be registered. There is no longer a requirement for homes to provide board as well as personal care, although most do. Some local authorities provide care homes, mostly for older people, but also hostels for people with learning disabilities and for those with, or recovering from, a mental illness. Some local authority and independent hostels, which tend to be for younger people, do not provide board as they want to encourage independence. In this case you may count as a 'less dependent resident' (see Chapter 34(3)).

Homes providing nursing care – These may be run by NHS bodies or independent organisations. They provide nursing care as well as personal care, and as part of their registration criteria must have a suitably qualified registered nurse working at the home at all times. Health services such as continence advice, stoma care, physiotherapy, chiropody, specialist feeding equipment, etc should be provided to residents by the NHS, as well as free continence products.

3. How to get help with care home fees

Most people who need help to pay for their care get it from the local authority. However, for those people with many or complex healthcare needs the NHS will be responsible for the full cost of their fees in a home providing nursing care. The NHS is also responsible (in England and Wales) for paying for the care you receive from a registered nurse in a home that provides nursing.

In Scotland, the local authority remains responsible for nursing costs but cannot charge you the £67 considered to be the cost of nursing care (see below).

Continuing NHS healthcare

Continuing care means care provided over an extended period of time to those aged 18 or over to meet physical and mental health needs that have arisen as a result of disability, an accident or illness. It may require services from the NHS and/or social services. Individuals with complex, intense or unpredictable healthcare needs, or whose primary need for accommodation arises from their health needs and who are assessed as meeting the eligibility criteria for continuing NHS healthcare should be funded by the NHS. Care home residents who are fully funded by the NHS do not contribute towards their care home fees but are treated as hospital inpatients for benefits purposes. The overriding test for continuing care is whether a person's primary need is for healthcare. You can request an assessment for continuing care wherever you are – whether at home, in hospital or in a care home.

England – Eligibility for fully funded NHS care in a care home is established using *The National Framework for NHS Continuing Healthcare and NHS-funded Nursing Care*. This lays out the principles and processes that should be followed when deciding whether someone has a 'primary health need' and is therefore eligible for continuing care funding. The framework aims to reduce previous problems and inconsistencies that led to several critical Ombudsman reports.

If you think you are eligible for continuing care, you should get a copy of this framework and contact your primary care trust for an assessment. The framework states that the assessment should be person-centred and understandable, and that your carers and other agencies should be involved. The framework advises that the following things should be considered when reaching a decision as to whether your primary need is a health need:

- the nature of the needs, including the type of interventions and help required;
- intensity – the extent and severity of needs, including the need for sustained care;
- complexity – how the needs arise, whether they are stable or require monitoring;
- unpredictability – the degree to which needs fluctuate and the level of risk if adequate and timely care is not provided.

The framework advises that the decision should generally be met within two weeks.

Wales – Common eligibility criteria based on Welsh Assembly national guidance are incorporated into local implementation plans by local health boards. There are plans to introduce a revised national framework in 2009. To request an assessment, contact your local health board. It may be useful to get a copy of your local criteria.

WHC (2004) 54, NAfW 41/2004; WHC (2006) 46, NAfWC 32/2006

Scotland – In February 2008 new national guidance on continuing care was published to improve transparency in decision making. It indicates that establishing eligibility requires *'a clear reasoned decision based on evidence of needs from a comprehensive assessment'*. The following key aspects should be considered when assessing eligibility:

- the complexity, nature or intensity of the patient's health need;
- the need for frequent, not easily predictable, clinical interventions;
- the need for routine use of specialist healthcare equipment or treatments requiring supervision from specialist NHS staff; *or*
- a rapidly degenerating or unstable condition requiring specialist medical or nursing supervision.

Your consent is required, although special rules apply if you are incapable of making a decision. If you think you might be eligible, get a copy of the guidance.

NHS Scotland Continuing Health Care CEL6 (2008)

Problems with continuing care

If you feel your need for nursing home care is primarily due to health needs, but you have been refused NHS full funding, there are a number of steps you can take.

England – Contact your primary care trust (PCT) and request a review of your decision. If you are receiving any NHS funding, your case should be routinely reviewed after three months. The PCT should apply their local resolution process and, if necessary, hold a PCT review panel.

If you disagree with the type and location of the NHS care offered, or the treatment received, you should complain using the normal social services and NHS complaints procedure (see Chapter 28(7)).

If you disagree with the actual decision about whether you are entitled to NHS funding and you are still unhappy with the decision after the local review, you can apply to your local strategic health authority for an independent review panel (IRP). At this stage, you should consider getting advice or an advocate from a voluntary agency or your local Patient Advocacy and Liaison Service. The IRP will review your case and make recommendations to your PCT. The national framework states that in all but exceptional circumstances the PCT should accept the recommendations.

If after this you still disagree with a decision, you can have your case referred to the Health Care Commission. Contact their complaints helpline (0845 601 3012). You could also contact the Parliamentary and Health Service Ombudsman (0845 015 4033) for advice or to ask them to investigate your case.

Wales – Ask your local health board for a copy of their criteria. If you disagree with the way the criteria has been applied in your case, request a review. A review may involve an IRP. If you are in hospital, you can remain there while the review is considered; this normally should be within 14 days.

If you disagree with the review decision or the local criteria, use the NHS complaints procedure (see Chapter 62(4)). Finally, you can contact the Public Service Ombudsman for Wales. At any time you can contact your Community Health Council for advice.

Scotland – First, request a review by your health board. This will seek a second assessment/review by another medical practitioner. Such reviews should normally be heard within two weeks. If you remain unhappy with the decision, you can use the NHS Scotland complaints procedure, which normally you must do within six months. If after that you still disagree, you can ask to have your case considered by the Scottish Public Services Ombudsman (0800 377 7330). Full details are contained in the guidance (CEL6 (2008)).

Intermediate care

Intermediate care is any extra care you may need to recover after hospital treatment or to prevent admission to hospital (see Chapter 28(1)).

England – If your intermediate care has been arranged in a care home, it should be free for up to six weeks.

Scotland – If there is a need for intermediate care under the continuing care provisions, that care should last as long as there is an assessed need for it; also, people aged 65 or over can have free home care for up to four weeks following a period in hospital, either overnight or for surgery as a day patient.

Registered nursing care

In England and Wales, even if you do not qualify for fully funded NHS continuing care, the NHS is responsible for funding the cost of nursing provided by a registered nurse. This is determined by a framework that should now be part of the continuing care assessment. If your condition is such that you have complex, intense or unpredictable healthcare needs, you should continue to be able to access full funding from the NHS under continuing care. From April 2009 in England, this is effectively payable at a single standard rate of £106.30 (for people on the earlier 'high band' rate, there is a transitional rate of £146.30).

In Wales, nursing rates are set by individual local health boards, who have agreed a standard rate of £117.66 a week for 2008/9. This is subject to annual review.

In Northern Ireland, care is free when provided by the Health and Social Services Department. There is a single band of £100 for nursing care.

In Scotland, your local authority pays £67 towards nursing care (see below).

Payment is made to the home, which must pass it on to you or reduce your fees by that amount or explain how the

L.1 Directions, guidance and circulars

Directions, guidance and circulars are issued by ministers in the devolved governments and must be followed by local authorities and health bodies. Your local authority or health authority will have copies, and they are usually available on the internet.

- **England:** Health Service Directions, Guidance and Circulars (HSGs and HSCs); Local Authority Circulars (LACs) (www.dh.gov.uk)
- **Scotland:** Community Care Circulars (CCDs) replaced the previous Social Work Services Group (SWSGs); in the NHS, Chief Executive Letters (CELs) have replaced Health Department Letters (HDLs), previously Management Executive Letters (MELs) (www.show.scot.nhs.uk/sehd/hdl.asp and www.show.scot.nhs.uk/sehd/ccd.asp or for previous guidance www.scotland.gov.uk/library/swsg/contents.htm)
- **Wales:** Welsh Assembly Government Circulars (WAGCs) previously National Assembly for Wales Circulars (NAfWCs) and Welsh Office Circulars (WOCs); Welsh Health Circulars (WHCs) (www.wales.gov.uk)
- **Northern Ireland:** Bills and statutory rules plus Health Service Circulars (HSS) (www.dhsspsni.gov.uk or www.hscni.net)

Challenging decisions

If you are challenging a decision about residential care, the following may be particularly useful:

- DMG: *Decision Makers Guide* issued by the DWP for DWP staff (www.dwp.gov.uk)
- CRAG: *Charging for Residential Accommodation Guide* explains the basic charging rules for residential care; a new version is issued each April. The latest English amendment is LAC (2007)4. The latest Welsh amendment is NAfWC 19/07. CRAG for England is available to download from (www.dh.gov.uk) or for Wales (www.wales.gov.uk). In Scotland, the latest guidance on residential care charging is to be found in CCD 4/2007

Other useful circulars:

- 'Ordinarily resident' rules are contained in LAC 93/7, WOC 25/93 and SWSG 11/93
- Choice of Accommodation Directions: LAC (2004)20, SWSG 5/93, NAfWC 46/04, WHC066/2004
- Responsibilities for meeting continuing care: *The NHS Continuing Healthcare (responsibilities) Directions* (2007), *The National Framework for NHS Continuing Care and NHS Nursing Care* (2007) supersedes previous circulars in England. In Scotland guidance is contained in MEL (1996)22, *NHS Scotland Continuing Health Care* CEL6 (2008) and in Wales in WHC (2004) 54/NAfWC 41/04, WHC(2006) 046/NAfWC 32/06
- Deferred Payments: LAC (2001)25, LAC (2001)29 (England), CCD 7/2002, CCD 13/2004 (Scotland) and NAfWC 21/03 (Wales)
- NHS funded nursing care: HSC 2003/06, LAC (2003)7 (England) and NAfWC 25/04/WHC (2004) 024 (Wales)
- Free personal care (Scotland): CCD 4/2002, CCD 5/2003
- Intermediate care: LAC (2001)1, LAC (2003)14 (England) and NAfWC 43/02 (Wales)
- Fairer charging for non-residential services: LAC (2001)32 (England) and NAfWC 11/07 NAfWC, 10/04 (Wales)
- Single assessment process for older people: LAC (2002)1, HSC 2002/01 (England) and NAfWC 09/02 (Wales)

Further information

See Box K.1 in Chapter 28 for books on community care law. See Box T.7 in Chapter 60 for information on Commissioners' decisions and pages 6-7 on where to find the law. Age Concern, Counsel and Care, and Help the Aged are among a number of organisations that produce excellent factsheets covering all aspects of community care. See the Address List at the back of this Handbook.

amount has been taken into account in calculating your fees. You should be given a statement specifying the fees payable for your nursing, personal care and accommodation. If you are being charged for nursing costs covered by the NHS payment, take this up with the care home manager. If you are not satisfied with the explanation, you could raise the matter with the PCT or local health board responsible for the nursing payment. You can also request an independent review (see above).

People who are funded by the local authority also have their nursing costs met by the NHS, but this does not affect the level of charges unless your income is such that the authority charges meant you were paying for part of your nursing costs.

Your benefits are not affected by receiving free nursing care.

The responsibility of the local authority to fund care

England and Wales – Local authorities have a duty to provide residential care for all those who *'by reason of age, illness, disability, or any other circumstances are in need of care and attention which is not otherwise available to them'*. Authorities can meet this duty by providing it in one of their homes or arranging it in an independent sector care home.

NAA, Part III, S.21(1)(a)

Scotland – A similar duty to provide care home placements is in section 59 of the Social Work (Scotland) Act 1968.

If you are 65 or over and assessed as requiring personal care (see Box K.1, Chapter 28) in a care home, you can receive a fixed payment of £149 a week, with a further payment of £67 if you require nursing care (£216 in total), from your local authority. Care home residents who are under 65 can only be considered for a payment of £67 towards their nursing care costs. These payments are made regardless of your income and capital and are issued by the authority direct to the care home.

CCH(S)A; CCD 5/2003

You can choose whether to take the payments for your care; if you do not, you can continue to make your own arrangements direct with the home. If you access payments, you can decide whether you want the local authority to contract with the home for just the payments it is making (with you contracting separately with the home for your accommodation and living expenses) or for the authority to make the contract with the home on your behalf for all of the costs. There may be advantages in the latter arrangement, since the authority's standard contract may restrict increases in the care home fees and may also include provisions for monitoring the quality of care. A Court of Session judgment has set out that a local authority is only obliged to provide free personal care if it is providing the service, and that it is at the authority's discretion whether it provides the payment to a private care provider, if it is not care that the authority is providing.

Argyll & Bute Council – Judicial review of Decision of Scottish Public Services Ombudsman [2007] CSOH 168

If you are admitted to hospital, your local authority will continue to make payments (including direct payments) at the full flat rate for two weeks after admission and at 80% for a subsequent month, or until your future placement arrangements are confirmed. You will still need to pay for accommodation and living costs. You may get assistance with these costs, but this will depend on a financial assessment carried out by the authority (see Chapter 34).

Northern Ireland – The duty is in Article 15 of the Health and Social Services (NI) Order 1972.

Deciding if you need care in a care home

If you think you might need care in a care home, either on a temporary or permanent basis, ask your local authority for a needs assessment (see Chapter 28(3)). Funding will only be given if the authority thinks your needs can be best met in a care home. Guidance advises that *'the law does not allow authorities to refuse to undertake an assessment of care needs for anyone on the grounds of the person's financial resources'* – eg because you have capital above the capital limit. They should advise you about the type of care you require and what services are available.

LAC (98)19

Local authorities have been reluctant, in some cases, to provide expensive packages of care for people to remain in their own homes. It is often cheaper for them to arrange for people to go into a care home. Case law has established that it may be lawful to provide care in a care home rather than meet 24-hour needs at home. However, a 2004 Health Service Ombudsman ruling agreed that a person with dementia should be entitled to constant care at home, and that their psychological needs should have been taken into account in NHS and social services assessments (*Pointon*, E22/02-03). Following a High Court decision in 2005 it was noted that assessors should also consider aspects under Article 8 of the Human Rights Act (concerning the right to a home life).

Rachel Gunter v SW Staffs PCT (EWHC1894)

Some local authorities have a lower ceiling on the amount of care they will provide for older people in their own homes than that for younger disabled people. This might, in England and Wales, contravene both the *National Service Framework for Older People* and the *Fair Access to Care Guidance*, which aim to end age discrimination and ensure equality of access to care for all client groups. See Chapter 28(7) for details of what to do if you disagree with the local authority.

R v Lancashire County Council ex p RADAR & Gilpin (1 CCLR 19)

If it is agreed you need care in a care home, and you need help with the funding because you cannot afford the fees, the local authority enters into a contract with the home and is liable for the full cost of your care home. It will recover from you any contribution you are assessed as having to pay, according to national rules (see Chapter 34). Registered nursing costs are the responsibility of the NHS as described above.

Even if you can pay the fees yourself, this does not necessarily mean the local authority should not arrange your care. If your capital is over the capital limits and you are liable to pay for yourself, a local authority *'must satisfy itself that [you are] able to make [your] own arrangements, or have others who are willing and able to make the arrangements for [you]'*. If you are too frail physically or mentally to make your own contract with the home, and others are not willing or able, the authority must make the arrangements and charge the full cost. If you are managing someone's affairs it may also be advisable to refuse to make the arrangements if the person would get the same care home cheaper through a local authority contract.

LAC (98)19

Urgent cases

If your need is urgent, the local authority can arrange for care in a care home without carrying out a formal needs assessment. The assessment should be done as soon as possible. If you urgently need to go into a home providing nursing, the authority does not have to get the health body's consent beforehand, but should do so as soon as possible. Contact your social services (or social work) department, explain your crisis and ask for a social worker to visit you urgently. If necessary, ask your GP for help when contacting the social services department.

Local authorities deferring provision or funding

Some local authorities, because of their lack of resources, place people on waiting lists for funding after they have been assessed as needing care in a care home. This could mean you have a long wait in hospital or at home. Other people may already be in a care home but waiting their turn for funding, and so may be running their capital down below the national limits. Some authorities suggest that people may wish to make their own arrangements for care while waiting for local authority funding.

Such waiting lists are arguably unlawful. The local authority may take its resources into account to a limited extent in deciding whether you need care, but it may not do so if you fall within its own eligibility criteria. Once it has decided that you need care in a care home, it has an immediate duty to make some provisions to ensure that you are cared for (subject to the statutory means test – see Chapter 34).

NAA, S.21(2A); See also R v Wigan MBC ex p Tammadge [1998] (1 CCLR 581); R v Kensington & Chelsea RLBC ex p Kujtim [1999] (2 CCLR 340); R v Islington LBC ex p Batantu; MacGregor v South Lanarkshire

The local authority must ignore capital within the upper capital limit when deciding if it needs to make arrangements for care in a care home. The value of your own home should not be included in the decision about whether the authority needs to make the arrangements for you if you are going to enter into a 'deferred payment agreement' (see Chapter 34(6)). They disregard the property for the first 12 weeks of a permanent stay. Guidance states that once the local authority has decided you need care and attention that is not otherwise available, it should make arrangements for you *'without undue delay'*. If it is unable to do so, the authority should *'ensure that suitable arrangements are in place to meet the needs of [you and your] carer'*. If you are already in a care home, the local authority should take over the arrangements to ensure you are not forced to use up capital below the upper capital limit for your country (see Box L.2, Chapter 34). Guidance in England has strengthened this and authorities are reminded that they *'need to ensure that they are in a position to provide Part III accommodation as soon as they are aware that the resident needs it. Once the council is aware of the resident's circumstances, any undue delay in undertaking an assessment and providing accommodation if necessary would mean that the council has not met its statutory obligations. Consequently, the council could be liable to reimburse the resident for any payment he has made for the accommodation which should have been met by the council pursuant to its statutory duties.'*

LAC (98)19; SWSG 2/99; LAC (2001)25

You are in a care home and your capital is reaching the capital limit

If you are already in a care home but have not needed help because your capital was above the capital limit, you will need to contact the social services department where the care home is situated when your capital nears the figure set for that year. It will then assess whether you actually need care in a care home, and whether it will meet the cost in that particular home. The help you receive should start from the time your capital reaches the upper capital limit – but see above, 'Local authorities deferring provision or funding'.

Note for couples with joint capital – If you have a joint account in excess of £46,000, it may be worth splitting your account so that you do not have to wait until your joint account is down to this figure. For example, if you have £55,000 in a joint account, your partner will only get help after £9,000 has been paid in fees and your account is down to £46,000. If you split the account so you each have £27,500, help will be available after spending only £4,500 in fees. The example uses the capital limits for England and Northern Ireland; in Scotland and Wales different amounts will apply.

4. Choice of home

If the local authority decides, after the needs assessment, to offer you a permanent or respite place in a care home, it may suggest a particular home or give you advice on homes to choose from. In all cases where a local authority is making the arrangements, you have the right to choose your own care home ('preferred accommodation').

However, if a health body places you in a home providing nursing care and pays the full fee, you do not have the same right to choose a particular home, although the Government has said a health body in England and Wales should take account of patients' wishes. You will not be liable to meet any of that home's charges. Although your health body must consent to a local authority placing you in a home providing nursing care, the health body *'would be expected not to interfere with an individual's choice of nursing home'* (HSG 92/54).

Preferred accommodation

England and Wales – If you tell your local authority you want to enter a particular care home, that home is called 'preferred accommodation'. There are legally binding directions and regulations intended to ensure you have a genuine choice over where you live. In reality, this choice may be restricted, as described below. The guidance *New Choice of Accommodation* (LAC (2004)20) and similar guidance in Wales (NAfWC 46/2004 and WHC (2004) 066) states that there should be a presumption in favour of individuals being able to exercise reasonable choice in the care they receive. It states that if a local authority cannot provide a place in your preferred home, it must give clear and reasonable justification (in writing) that relates to the directions on choice. It also states that if a person needs to be placed in another area that is more expensive than their normal costs, the authority should pay more.

If you have preferred accommodation, the local authority must arrange for care in that accommodation, as long as:

- it is suitable in relation to your assessed needs. The assessment should be individual and a home should not be deemed suitable for a person just because it satisfies registration for that type of person;
- it is available. If a place is not available in your preferred home, you may have to wait. The authority should ensure that adequate and suitable care is available while you wait, taking account of your needs and wishes. If you unreasonably refuse to move to a suitable interim arrangement, the authority can decide it has reasonably met its statutory duties and may ask you to make your own arrangements. Seek advice if this happens;
- the home is willing to provide a place subject to the authority's usual terms and conditions for such accommodation;
- the accommodation would not cost the authority more than it would usually expect to pay for accommodation for someone with your assessed needs; *and*
- your authority has legal power to make such a placement.

Protocols have been developed regarding placements and funding structures in homes providing nursing care across the UK. Seek advice if you plan to move between countries.

NAA (Choice of Accommodation) Directions 1992; LAC (2004)20
In Wales: NAfWC 46/2004 & WHC (2004) 066

Scotland – If you wish to move into a preferred home in Scotland, the social work service must give you a choice about the home you move into, even though it will generally be paying at least some of the costs. You can choose to move into any home if:

- there is a place available;
- the social work service has decided the home is suitable for your needs;
- the social work service and the owner of the home can agree a contract;
- the home you have chosen will not cost the social work service more than it usually expects to pay for a home providing the sort of care you need; *and*

- the home is willing to accept you.

If there is no place available in the home you have chosen, you can ask the social work staff to provide you with help to stay in your own home until there is a suitable vacancy.

SWSG5/93; CCD 13/2004; CCD 4/2007

More expensive homes

If you have chosen a home that costs more than your local authority would usually expect to pay for someone with your needs, the authority can make arrangements for your preferred home (given that it satisfies the other conditions above) if a third party will meet the shortfall and continue doing so for as long as you are likely to be in that care. This is usually known as a top-up or third-party payment. If the third party is unable to keep up payments, you may have to move to a cheaper home; seek advice if this is likely to happen. You should not be asked for a top-up if you moved into a more expensive home for necessity, eg it was the only home available that met your care needs. If there are not suitable homes available at the local authority's funding level, you should take advice and challenge this. Authorities must ensure that a third party is reasonably able to pay top-up fees for the time you are in the home.

As a resident you are not usually allowed to make your own top-up payment, eg by using your personal allowance, disregarded income or capital. This was confirmed in *R v E Sussex ex p Ward* (3 CCLR 132). It is permissible, according to the Department of Health, for you to pay for 'extras' that are outside of the care package. As long as you do not feel pressured by the home owner or the local authority, there is no reason why you should not enter into a contract with the home owner for extra services.

People who are either within the period of the 12-week disregard of their property or using the provisions for a 'deferred payment agreement' can use their own money to pay for a more expensive home (see Chapter 34(6)). This is to cover people who will only receive temporary funding until they sell their home.

LAC (2004)20

People in Scotland who are better off as a result of receiving free personal or nursing care can use some of their money to pay for a more expensive care home.

Additional Payments (Scotland) Regs 2002; CCD 7/2002 & CCD 2/2005

The local authority cannot use the direction on the choice of accommodation or the regulations to set arbitrary ceilings on the amount it will contribute towards care in a care home and to routinely require third parties to make up the difference. Only when a person has expressed a choice of preferred accommodation should the authority consider a third-party top-up arrangement.

The local authority must be able to justify its usual cost and show that it is enough to buy a reasonable level of service without contributions from third parties. If the authority places you in more expensive accommodation because there are no vacancies in 'usual cost' homes, the local authority, not a third party, should meet the additional cost. Nor should the authority seek a top-up payment if an individual's physical, psychological or other needs are such that they can only be met in a more expensive home. This could be because of language, culture, religion or the need to be near family so that regular visits can be made. In some areas it is difficult to find a home that will accept you at the price the local authority is prepared to pay. Homes might say they will accept you quicker if you pay a top-up, but you will have to wait longer if the home is only going to be paid the local authority rate. You should complain if there are too few homes in the area with vacancies at the local authority's usual rate, as your choice is therefore restricted. See Chapter 28(7).

England and Wales – Guidance is clear that the local authority remains responsible for the home's full fees, even if a third party is making a contribution. Authorities should not encourage homes to make separate arrangements with relatives for top-up payments that are not included in the local authority's contract with the home. If your relatives are asked to make a separate payment to the home, you should refer the homeowner to the local authority. Third parties may have to meet the greater share of any subsequent fee increases.

Scotland – Guidance states that the local authority has discretion to collect top-up payments and contract with the care home, or to leave the third party to make top-up payments direct to the care home. If a home's fees rise above the level of the third-party agreement, the authority should consider the impact of moving the person to a cheaper room or home and take steps, where possible, to enable the resident to remain in their current home.

CCD 6/2002 and CCD 5/2003, CCD 4/2007 (contains CRAG)

What sort of home?

It is very important to choose a home where you think you could be happy and comfortable. Certain standards have to be met because of registration (see 2 above), but services and facilities may vary greatly from home to home. You should visit homes before you make a decision. Your social worker or GP may give you a checklist of questions, as may some local and national charities, such as Age Concern or Counsel and Care. Don't take anything for granted. For example, how often will it be possible for you to have a bath? Can you take your favourite armchair or pet with you? Given the increase in home closures, you should try to establish the financial viability of the home, or whether there are any plans to sell it. You might want to enter the home for a short stay before committing yourself to a permanent stay. You should be given a written contract or statement of terms and conditions if you are being funded by the local authority. Check what the fees cover, what are 'extras', what happens if you are absent from the home, or what period of notice is required. This is especially important if you are making your own contract with the home. If the local authority has made the contract, it is still useful for you to know exactly what is covered. Do not be rushed into things. See Box L.1 and the Address List for organisations that can support you.

Complaints

All care homes must have a complaints procedure that is accessible and explained to you. Initially, you should complain to the manager of the home. Complaints should be responded to within 28 days. The complaints procedure for the home should also make it clear how to complain to the registration body (see 2 above). If the NHS or local authority is involved in any way with your care – eg the NHS is paying for your nursing and you have a complaint about the standards of the nursing, or the local authority has arranged your care and you are unhappy with it – you can use the social services and NHS complaints procedures (see Chapters 28(7) and 62(4)).

33 Benefits in care

In this chapter we look at: page

1. What benefits are you entitled to?

If you have moved into a care home (either temporarily or permanently), with or without help from the local authority, the only social security benefits that may be affected are:

- disability living allowance (DLA) care component;
- attendance allowance;
- constant attendance allowance and exceptionally severe disablement allowance;
- income support, income-based jobseeker's allowance, income-related employment and support allowance;
- pension credit;
- housing benefit;
- council tax benefit.

All other social security benefits can be claimed and paid in the normal way, subject to the standard rules outlined in the rest of this Handbook. It normally makes no difference whether the care home you are in is owned or managed by a local authority or by a private or voluntary organisation.

NHS-funded healthcare in a care home

If you have moved into a care home you may be eligible for fully funded NHS continuing healthcare to meet the costs of your accommodation and care. In these circumstances, you will normally be treated as if you are in hospital for benefit purposes (see Chapter 35). *The National Framework for NHS Continuing Healthcare and NHS-funded Nursing Care*, implemented on 1.10.07, contains guidance on the main NHS and local authority responsibilities that are contained in primary legislation and explains the influence of key court cases. It also provides new national assessment tools.

There are some outstanding applications for retrospective NHS funding by residents in care homes that provide nursing, following earlier revised guidance on NHS continuing healthcare funding. In these circumstances, any retrospective NHS funding will not mean that you have to repay any social security benefits you have received, even though any charges you have paid to the local authority or to the care home should be refunded to you.

Decision Makers Guide Memo Vol 3 08/04

If you are not eligible for fully funded NHS healthcare in a care home, you may be entitled to NHS funding for the nursing element of your care. *The National Framework* (see above) provides for 'funded nursing care' at one rate of £106.30 a week or the transitional higher rate of £146.30 (England: 2009/10 rates) (see Chapter 32(3)). In these circumstances, if you cannot meet the remaining costs of your accommodation and care, the local authority can provide the additional funding, subject to a charging assessment (see Chapter 34). The payment of funded nursing care on its own does not affect entitlement to social security benefits. You are still entitled to receive attendance allowance/DLA care component if you are self-funding (or if you are only receiving interim funding from the local authority – see 2 below) even though you receive funded nursing care.

AA Regs, reg 7(5)(f) & DLA Regs, reg 9(6)(f)

It is not always clear which body, under which power, is or should be funding your stay in a care home and which benefits are payable as a result. A Tribunal of Commissioners held that funding responsibility for residents living in a nursing home lies with the local authority under Part III of the National Assistance Act 1948 if the nursing needs are *'incidental and ancillary to other care needs'* and with the appropriate health body if they are not. In the view of the tribunal, it was therefore for the NHS to pay the full cost of their accommodation and care, and not rely on part of the cost to be paid by the residents from their own resources.

R(DLA)2/06

2. Attendance allowance and disability living allowance

Normally, you cannot be paid attendance allowance, disability living allowance (DLA) care component, constant attendance allowance or exceptionally severe disablement allowance after the first four weeks in a care home (see Chapter 3(8)). However, if you pay the fees for the care home without funding (or only with interim funding) from the local authority, you will be able to keep your attendance allowance or DLA care component (see below).

You should also be able to keep your attendance allowance or DLA care component if you are in a care home that receives a section 256 (NHS Act 2006) (previously section 28A (NHS Act 1977)) grant from the NHS to help towards the general running costs of the home and you are able to meet the fees of the care home (charged at a reduced rate due to the NHS grant payable) from your benefits or other income and/or capital. In these circumstances, you, rather than the local authority and the NHS, would be contracting with the care home for the provision of your specific accommodation and care – therefore you would not be treated as being 'resident in a care home' (see below) or as a hospital inpatient for the purposes of payment of attendance allowance or DLA care component. This would still be the case even if the local authority or NHS helped with finding a suitable care home to meet your needs, as long as they were not involved in the contract.

DLA mobility component is affected only if your stay is in hospital or a similar institution (a similar institution includes a nursing home where your placement is fully funded by the NHS under the continuing healthcare provisions). It is not affected by a stay in a care home, even if you are funded by the local authority.

Resident in a care home – You will be considered to be resident in a care home, and therefore not entitled to payment of attendance allowance or DLA care component, when any of the costs of any qualifying services (accommodation, board and personal care) provided for you are paid for out of public or local funds under specified legislation (see Chapter 3(8) under 'What is a care home'). 'Qualifying services' do not include services such as domiciliary services, including personal care, provided to you in your own home. If you go into a care home from the community, the days you enter and leave are counted as a days in the community. If you go into hospital from a care home (or vice versa), the days you enter and leave are counted as days in the care home.

AA Regs, reg 7; DLA Regs reg 9

Paying your own fees

If you are paying your own fees, you are a self-funder and can receive attendance allowance or DLA care component as long as you:

- do not get any funding from the local authority; *or*
- are only getting funding on an interim basis from the local authority and will be paying it back in full; ie you are a 'retrospective self-funder'. This is most likely to apply if you are in the process of selling your home and

you have a 'deferred payment agreement' with the local authority (see Chapter 34(6)).

AA Regs, reg 8(6); DLA Regs, reg 10(8); R(A)1/02 & Decision Makers Guide, para 61735

You can also receive attendance allowance or DLA care component if you are in a nursing home getting NHS-funded nursing care only and not fully funded NHS continuing healthcare (see Chapter 32(3)) and the above two points apply.

AA Regs, reg 7(3)(f); DLA Regs reg 9(6)(f)

Scotland – If you are 65 or over you will not be entitled to attendance allowance or DLA care component if you are receiving local authority help with the cost of your care under the 'free personal care' arrangements (see Chapter 28(6)). If you are under 65, you will be paid DLA care component if the only help you get is for 'free nursing care'.

Direct payments

Local authorities can give you direct payments so that you can arrange your own care at home or buy up to four weeks respite care in any one year (see Chapter 29(3)). Therefore, attendance allowance and DLA care component will not normally be affected. But they could be affected if you need another period of care or hospital treatment within the linking period (see Chapter 3(7 and 8)).

Example: You use your direct payment to buy four weeks in a care home, then two weeks later your carer falls ill, so you return to the care home. This time your stay is funded by the local authority under a contract with the home. Your attendance allowance or DLA care component is affected immediately as it links with a period when your care was funded by local authority money because you were using the payment from the authority to buy your respite care.

3. Housing benefit

Registered care homes

You cannot usually get housing benefit (HB) for the costs of a registered care home. See below for help with meeting the costs of your own home.

Homes that do not need to register

From 24.10.05, for HB and council tax benefit, 'residential accommodation' has been defined as accommodation provided in a care home or an independent hospital. Care homes, including local authority care homes, that provide *'accommodation with nursing or personal care'* are required to be registered with the Care Quality Commission even if they do not also provide board. This means some homes not required to register previously, and where residents were able to claim HB, are now registered as care homes. In these situations you will not usually be able to claim HB. You should therefore have any contribution reassessed by the local authority (see Chapter 34).

HB Regs, reg 9(4)

Some care homes have deregistered and become 'Supported Living' accommodation. In this situation you will be able to claim HB.

Adult placement schemes (England only) – Adult placement schemes are no longer required to register. This means if you are in an adult placement you no longer fall within the HB definition of 'residential accommodation' and therefore you are eligible to claim HB.

HB/CTB Circular A20/2005, para 12

Help with meeting the costs of your own home

If you go into a care home for a temporary stay or for respite care, you can continue to receive HB – or help to cover mortgage interest payments with income support, income-based jobseeker's allowance (JSA), income-related employment and support allowance (ESA) or the guarantee credit of pension credit – for up to 52 weeks, as long as it is clear that:

- your stay is not likely to last longer, or in exceptional circumstances substantially longer, than this;
- you intend to return to your own home; *and*
- you have not rented your normal home to someone else.

HB Regs, reg 7(16)

However, if you go into a care home for a trial period with a view to a permanent admission but you intend to return to your home if the care home does not suit you, then HB (or mortgage interest payment in income support, income-based JSA, income-related ESA or pension credit) is only paid for up to 13 weeks (see Chapter 20(6)). If you decide the care home suits you and you are not going to return home, then, as long as the other conditions continue to be satisfied, you will continue to be eligible for HB for the whole 13-week period. This will enable you to give appropriate notice of the termination of your tenancy as long as your liability for rent will come to an end within the 13-week period.

HB Regs, reg 7(11) & (12); R(H)4/06; HB/CTB Bulletin G4/2006

If you move to a care home on a permanent basis from a home where you remain liable for the rent because a notice period for the termination of the tenancy is being served, you can be treated as occupying your former home for up to four weeks, as long as that liability could not reasonably have been avoided. Hence, HB can be paid on your former home for that period.

HB Regs, reg 7(7)

4. Council tax benefit

You can get council tax benefit only if you are liable to pay council tax. Your former home is exempt from council tax if it is unoccupied *and* you are now solely or mainly resident in any type of care home. Before this is the case, your former home, even though it may be unoccupied, will still be treated as your 'sole or main' home and you can get council tax benefit in the normal way (see Chapter 20(11)).

5. Income support/income-based JSA/income-related ESA

Capital limits in care homes

For all types of registered care homes mentioned in this section of the Handbook, if you are a resident aged under 60, you can claim income support, income-based jobseeker's allowance (JSA) or income-related employment and support allowance (ESA) if your capital is £16,000 or less. Tariff income of £1 for every £250 or part thereof starts at £10,000 for permanent residents and £6,000 for temporary residents (see Chapter 27(4)).

If you know you want to stay in a care home, your admission can be permanent from the start. Most local authorities, however, prefer you to have a trial period to see if you like it. During a trial period (and for temporary stays), the lower capital limit for IS, income-based JSA and income-related ESA is £6,000. This only goes up to £10,000 when your stay is permanent. The upper capital limit is £16,000 for both temporary and permanent residents. You are still considered to be a permanent resident if you are temporarily absent from the care home for up to 13 weeks.

Income support/income-based JSA/income-related ESA in care homes

If you are a resident in a care home and you are over 16 and under 60, your income support, income-based JSA or income-related ESA is worked out in the standard way (see Chapters 12(6), 14(9) and 15(21)) by adding together:

- your personal allowance/prescribed amount; *and*
- any premiums to which you are entitled (which can

include severe disability premium (SDP) while disability living allowance (DLA) care component is payable). There is no disability premium for income-related ESA (see Chapter 24); *and*

- for income-related ESA, any additional component.

Even if you are not entitled to income support, income-based JSA or income-related ESA in your own home, you may be entitled when you go into a care home.

Temporary admission (single person) – If you go into a care home for a temporary period, the amount of income support, income-based JSA or income-related ESA you receive will usually not change because you will be treated as normally residing in your own home (but see note below).

Temporary admission (couple) – If one of you goes into a care home or if you go into different rooms in the same care home or into different care homes for a temporary period, for income support, income-based JSA or income-related ESA purposes you will still be assessed as a couple, but you will each get the appropriate single person rate in your applicable amount if this amount is more than the couple rate. If the appropriate single person rate is the greater amount, the person at home (or in a different room in the same care home or in a different care home) will get a single rate personal allowance/prescribed amount plus any appropriate premiums and any housing costs (and any additional component for income-related ESA), and the person in care will get a single rate personal allowance/ prescribed amount plus any appropriate premiums (and any additional component for income-related ESA), at the single rate amount. These are then added together, and your combined income is taken from this figure to give the amount of income support, income-based JSA or income-related ESA to be paid to the claimant.

If you go into the same room in the care home, you will receive the couple rate of income support, income-based JSA or income-related ESA plus any appropriate premiums (and any additional component for income-related ESA). Housing benefit (HB)/council tax benefit (CTB) will continue to be paid for your housing costs at home.

IS Regs, Sch 7, para 9; JSA Regs, Sch 5, para 5; ESA Regs Sch 5, para 4(a)

Note: If the SDP and, for income support and income-based JSA only, the enhanced disability premium, are included in the calculation, they will no longer be included if payment of DLA care component ceases. The enhanced disability premium will continue to be included in the applicable amount for income-related ESA if you are in receipt of the support component.

SDP and temporary admissions – There is often confusion about the payment of the SDP if one of a couple goes into a care home for a temporary period. If carer's allowance is paid to a carer, SDP will not be paid. However, in other circumstances, a Commissioner's Decision held that the SDP should be included in the calculation of income support, income-based JSA or income-related ESA for each qualifying person, even where a partner in the community may have prevented its inclusion previously.

R(IS)9/02 & Decision Makers Guide, Vol 4, paras 23231-33

In practice, SDP is often left out of the calculation for both temporary and permanent admissions, and if you are being assessed by the local authority you do not see any benefit from the extra money anyway. In this case, you should check that the authority is not assuming you are getting SDP and therefore including it in the calculation of your charge, even if you are not being paid it.

Some local authorities do not assess the charge for temporary stays and charge a flat rate instead. Where this is the case, if no one receives carer's allowance for looking after you and the DWP has not included SDP as part of their calculation, seek advice, since any additional benefit you receive will not be taken away in local authority charges.

Permanent admission (single person) – If you are a single person going into a care home on a permanent basis, the amount of any income support, income-based JSA or income-related ESA will usually only change in the following circumstances (but see note below):

- ❑ If you have capital between £6,000 and £10,000, an increase in the amount of income support, income-based JSA or income-related ESA will be payable, as there will no longer be a tariff income applied because of the increased lower capital limit from £6,000 to £10,000 (see above). If you have capital between £10,000 and £16,000, a reduction in the amount of tariff income will be applied (and therefore an increase in income support, income-based JSA or income-related ESA), due to the increased lower capital limit.
- ❑ If you are a single person and have a carer receiving carer's allowance, or you are living with a non-dependant in the community, you may become entitled to, or there may be an increase in the amount of, income support, income-based JSA or income-related ESA payable when you enter a care home permanently. This is because carer's allowance will no longer be payable to your carer and your non-dependant will no longer count as a non-dependant. Therefore, the SDP will be included in the income support, income-based JSA or income-related ESA calculation for any period in which attendance allowance/DLA care component remains in payment.

IS Regs, Sch 2, para 13(2)(a); JSA Regs, Sch 1, para 15(1); ESA Regs, Sch 4, para 6(2)(a)

If you are retrospectively self-funding (see 2 above) you will still be entitled to income support, income-based JSA or income-related ESA if you are selling your property.

Permanent admission (couple) – If you are one of a couple permanently in a care home, each of you will be treated as separate single claimants.

IS Regs, reg 16(1) & (3)(e); JSA Regs, reg 78(1) & 3(d); ESA Regs, reg 156(1) & 4(d)

Any jointly-owned capital will be split, and the income support, income-based JSA or income-related ESA calculation should be based solely on each of your individual capital and income. See Chapter 32(3) for information about joint capital. If you both enter the same care home you may still be assessed by the DWP as a couple, although case law (R(IS)1/99) has now established that most people should be assessed as separate individuals even if they share a room. Seek advice if you are treated as a couple in this situation.

Note: If the SDP and, for income support and income-based JSA only, the enhanced disability premium, are included in the calculation, they will no longer be included if payment of DLA care component ceases. The enhanced disability premium will continue to be included in the applicable amount for income-related ESA if you are in receipt of the support component.

6. Income support/income-based JSA/income-related ESA and maintenance

Liable relatives – The income and capital of the non-resident spouse or civil partner cannot be taken into account in determining a permanent resident's claim to income support, income-based jobseeker's allowance (JSA) or income-related employment and support allowance (ESA). However, spouses or civil partners are each liable to maintain the other and the non-resident spouse/civil partner can be asked to make a contribution. The non-resident should not feel pressured into paying more than they can reasonably afford given their actual resources and expenses. Unless the DWP obtains a court order, payment is voluntary. In practice, legal proceedings are rarely undertaken, although the DWP may put pressure on the non-resident spouse/civil partner to make 'voluntary' payments. Normally, payments made by the non-resident spouse/civil partner are taken into account as the resident spouse's/civil partner's income. But if you are receiving payments to help meet the costs of more expensive 'preferred' accommodation (see Chapter 32(4)), they are ignored for income support, income-based JSA and income-related ESA.

Note: These liable relative rules do not apply to pension credit.

7. Pension credit

Capital limits in care homes

Capital under £6,000 for temporary (or trial period) residents, or £10,000 for permanent residents, does not attract any deemed or assumed income. You are still considered to be a permanent resident if you are temporarily absent from the care home for up to 52 weeks. Assumed income from capital above £6,000 (or £10,000) is £1 a week for every £500 or part thereof. There is no upper capital limit.

Pension credit in care homes

If you are a resident in a care home and aged 60 or over, your pension credit guarantee credit element is worked out in the usual way, by adding together your standard minimum guarantee and any additional amounts to which you are entitled (which can include the severe disability additional amount while disability living allowance (DLA) care component or attendance allowance is payable). The pension credit savings credit element is also worked out in the usual way. See Chapter 42.

For people aged 65 or over, both elements will normally have an 'assessed income period' of up to five years (these can be indefinite if you are aged 75 or over). During a typical 5-year award period, certain elements of your income are treated as constant with deemed annual increases built in. It is not a fixed award, as the deemed increases will alter the amount of the award from year to year. This will usually mean that if you are going temporarily into a care home there will be no need to notify the DWP. However, if you are in receipt of attendance allowance or DLA care component, you will still need to inform the Disability Contact & Processing Unit (see inside back cover) if your temporary stay will be for more than 28 days (or less if you have been in hospital or a care home within the previous 29 days, as this period will be linked – see Chapter 3(8) and Box B.3). If you are going into a care home on a permanent basis, any assessed income period will end and therefore you will need to inform the DWP.

SPCA, S.9(4)(b); SPC Regs, reg 12(c)

Temporary admission (single person) – There will usually be no change in the amount of pension credit you receive because you will be treated as normally residing in your own home (but see note below).

Temporary admission (couple) – There is no provision for the treatment of couples as two single people in terms of the appropriate minimum guarantee if one is going into a care home on a temporary basis. This means the amount of pension credit payable will usually be the same as the amount payable when you were both living at home in the community.

However, if the severe disability additional amount is included in the calculation at the single or couple rate, it will no longer be included if attendance allowance or DLA care component in payment to the resident has been suspended. This is the case even if your partner is living at home in the community and in receipt of attendance allowance or DLA care component themselves. This is because you, as the resident, are treated as still being in the household and not disregarded for the purposes of qualifying for the severe disability additional amount. A similar situation occurs when one of a couple is temporarily in hospital, but the pension credit regulations provide for this by allowing a single severe disability additional amount to continue in payment for the partner at home. In practice, however, the DWP also appears to apply this hospital provision to a care home situation, perhaps because it was not intended to treat one of a couple temporarily in a care home differently in these circumstances to one of a couple temporarily in hospital.

SPC Regs, reg 6(5) & Sch 1, para 1(2)(b)

The treatment of couples as couples for pension credit appropriate minimum guarantee purposes in these circumstances instead of as single people also has problematic knock-on effects for local authority charging (see Chapter 34(5)).

Permanent admission (single person) – If you are a single person going into a care home on a permanent basis, the pension credit amount will usually only change in the following circumstances.

- If you have capital between £6,000 and £10,000 there will be an increase in pension credit payable, as there will no longer be an assumed income applied because of the increased assumed income threshold from £6,000 to £10,000 (see above). If you have capital between £10,000 and £16,000, there will be a reduction in the amount of assumed income applied (and therefore an increase in pension credit) due to the increased threshold.
- If you are a single person living with a non-dependant in the community or you had a carer in receipt of carer's allowance, you may become entitled to pension credit, or there may be an increase in the amount of pension credit, due to the severe disability additional amount being included in the appropriate minimum guarantee for any period that attendance allowance or DLA care component remains in payment.

SPC Regs, reg 5(1)(b) & Sch 1, para 1(1)(a)

You may still be entitled to pension credit while living in a care home even if you have more than the local authority charging capital limit and are therefore self-funding and not receiving financial help from the authority. This is because there is no upper capital limit for pension credit; therefore, as long as your income, including the assumed income, is below your pension credit appropriate amount, you will be entitled to pension credit.

You will also be entitled to pension credit if you are retrospectively self-funding (see 2 above) because you are selling your property.

Permanent admission (couple) – If you are one of a couple permanently in a care home, each of you will be treated as separate single claimants. Any jointly owned capital will be split, and the pension credit calculation should be based solely on each of your individual capital and income (see Chapter 32(3) for information about joint capital). If you both enter the same care home you may still be assessed by the DWP as a couple, although case law (R(IS)1/99) has established that most people should be assessed as individuals even if they share a room. Seek advice if you are treated as a couple in this situation.

SPC Regs, reg 5(1)(b)

Note: If the severe disability additional amount was included in the calculation of pension credit when you were in the community, it will no longer be included if payment of attendance allowance or DLA care component has ceased.

8. Special help for war pensioners

If you get a war disablement pension or have had a gratuity for your disability, you may qualify for help with your care home fees from the Service Personnel and Veterans Agency. It can cover medical treatment, nursing home fees and respite breaks that you need wholly or mainly because of that disability. You are not means tested for these services but you must apply before arranging them. For more information, see Chapter 46(11).

34 Charging for care

1. The legal basis of the financial assessment

Section 22(1) of the National Assistance Act 1948 provides for local authorities to charge for the accommodation and care they provide under the Act, whether in a care home owned by a local authority or in an independent care home.

Local authorities must provide care in care homes for those who need it unless it is *'otherwise available to them'*. The Health and Social Care Act 2001 and its subsequent regulations reaffirm that a local authority cannot say that accommodation is *'otherwise available'* because of your capital if you have less than the upper capital limit for your country (see Box L.2). While it is clear that in Scotland the provision of services to a person assessed as being in need of them is not related to that person's ability to meet the costs, because of slightly different wording in the English legislation, it is unclear whether this applies across the rest of the UK.

Robertson v Fife, HoL (25.7.02)

If you are entering into a deferred payments agreement (see 6 below), your former home is not included by the local authority in deciding whether accommodation is otherwise available.

HSCA, S.55; CCH(S)A

The standard rate – The local authority must fix a standard rate for the accommodation. The standard rate for local authority care homes is the full cost to the authority of providing your place in that accommodation. The standard rate for independent care homes is the gross cost to the authority of providing or paying for your place in that accommodation under a contract with the independent care home.

NAA, Ss.22(2) & 26(2)

If your income or capital is sufficient for you to pay the standard rate, you can still, in some circumstances, have the local authority make the arrangements for you but you will be assessed to pay the full cost less any NHS-funded nursing care (see Chapter 32(3)).

If you cannot pay the standard rate, the local authority must assess your ability to pay under national rules and calculate what lower amount to charge you.

NAA, S.22(2)

The basis of that assessment is in the National Assistance (Assessment of Resources) Regulations 1992, as amended. These rules are explained in the *Charging for Residential Accommodation Guide* (CRAG). Local authorities must take account of the CRAG because it is statutory guidance issued by the Secretary of State. It is updated and amended, and circulars are issued with each amendment. There are separate guides for England, Scotland and Wales (see Box L.1). Following the financial assessment, you will be left with at least the amount of the personal expenses allowance (see 5 below).

NAA s22(4)

Capital – If you are in a care home (on either a permanent or temporary basis) and your savings are over the upper capital limit for your country, you will have to pay the standard rate for your accommodation until your capital drops to this limit. Some items of capital are ignored or disregarded in the assessment. If you have capital over the lower capital limit for your country, a tariff income is assumed. See Box L.2 and 6 below for details (including about how your property is treated).

Income – In general, assume all income counts unless it, or a part of it, is specifically ignored. The 'income disregards' are similar to those for income support (see Chapter 26). Note that pension credit, income support, income-based jobseeker's allowance and income-related employment and support allowance are taken into account as income by the local authority (except for any element for housing costs and the savings disregard applied to the savings credit element of pension credit). See Box L.2 for details.

2. Key points

- The local authority does not have to carry out a charging assessment for the first eight weeks of a temporary stay in care; it can charge what is reasonable.

  NAA, S.22(5A)
- If you count as a 'less dependent resident', the local authority can ignore the whole of the charging assessment if reasonable in your situation (see 3 below).
- If you are a temporary resident in the care home, the charging assessment is slightly different in order to allow for your costs at home (see 8 below).
- If you are one of a couple, the law does not allow a joint charging assessment; only the resident's own income and capital affects the assessment. However, see 4 below for when the non-resident partner is the claimant of benefit paid in respect of both members of the couple.

  CRAG, para 11.005
- Whatever your source(s) of income, you'll generally be left with no less than the personal expenses allowance (PEA) of £21.90 a week (£22 in Wales). Except for any income ignored in the assessment, such as a savings disregard in certain circumstances if you are aged 65 or over (see Box L.2), the rest of your income goes towards meeting the standard rate for your accommodation.
- Any difference between what you pay and the standard rate is met by the local authority, which is liable for the full cost of the fees (although see Chapter 32(4) if you have chosen more expensive accommodation than the authority thinks you need).
- If the application of the law affects you unfairly, urge the local authority to use its discretion to correct that unfairness by letting you keep more than £21.90 (£22 in Wales) a week of your income for your PEA (see 5 below).

  NAA, S.22(4)
- The assessment is largely based on income support rules but there are some important differences, and the local authority has some discretion (see Box L.2).
- In England and Wales only, if your accommodation is provided as part of your aftercare package under section 117 of the Mental Health Act 1983, you should not be charged for your accommodation.

  LAC 2000/3; R v Manchester CC ex p Stennet [2002]

  You should seek urgent advice if you are being charged or have been charged in the past and have not received a refund. If you receive aftercare under s.117 you will still be entitled to benefits (including income support, income-based jobseeker's allowance, income-related employment and support allowance and pension credit) in the normal way. However, disability living allowance (DLA) care component and attendance allowance will not be payable, as case law (CDLA/870/2004) suggests that s.117 is an *'enactment relating to persons under disability'* for the purposes of defining those people in 'certain accommodation' for whom DLA care or attendance allowance is not payable.

  Decision Makers Guide, Chapter 61, Appendix 1

3. Less dependent residents

If you count as a 'less dependent resident' – ie you live in an establishment not registered with the Care Quality Commission, the local authority has complete discretion to ignore the whole of the charging assessment if *'reasonable in the circumstances'*.

CRAG, para 2.008

This is because it has been recognised that to live as independently as possible you will need to be left with more than the personal expenses allowance.

AOR Regs, reg 5; CRAG, para 2.007

A similar effect can be achieved if you live in registered accommodation and do not qualify as a 'less dependent resident' by a variation of the personal expenses allowance in the charging assessment (see 5 below).

CRAG, para 5.005

4. Couples

Couples and maintenance

The local authority has no power under the National Assistance Act (NAA) to assess couples jointly. The financial assessment should be of the income and assets of the resident only (including any entitlement to pension credit, income support, income-based jobseeker's allowance or income-related employment and support allowance). The spouse remaining at home has no obligation to fill in any sections of the assessment form asking about their income and assets. Indeed, the guidance underlines this, stating that *'local authorities should not use assessment forms for the resident which require information about the means of the spouse'*.

CRAG, para 11.005

Liable relatives – From April 2009 the liable relative provision should have been abolished. This means that a local authority no longer has the power to approach your spouse for any contribution to the cost of care and accommodation unless they are receiving a benefit that is paid to them in respect of both of you as a couple. In Scotland, the liable relatives legislation was repealed in 2008.

Benefit paid to non-resident partners in respect of couples

If you are one of a couple (including same-sex couples) going temporarily into a care home and your partner is the claimant of income support or pension credit in respect of both of you, guidance states that *'it would be reasonable to expect the partner receiving the income support/pension credit to contribute to the charge for accommodation for the other partner a sum equivalent to the income support/pension credit payable for that partner'*.

CRAG, para 4.005

The issue that arises for local authorities is what constitutes a reasonable amount. For couples in receipt of income support, the situation is quite straightforward, as, in most cases, the applicable amount in these circumstances is usually calculated using two single people's applicable amounts added together (see Chapter 33(5)), which can be apportioned easily to find out the amount paid in respect of the resident. However, for couples in receipt of pension credit, the situation is complicated by the fact that pension credit is calculated using the couple appropriate minimum guarantee (see Chapter 33(7)).

The same apportionment issue arises for local authorities when they are deciding how much to increase the personal expenses by to allow an amount for the partner in the community when it is the resident who is the claimant of pension credit for both members of the couple. See 5 below for a common approach taken by authorities to this issue.

5. The personal expenses allowance

You will get the same £21.90 (£22 in Wales) personal expenses allowance (PEA) whether you are in a local authority or independent care home on a temporary or permanent basis. Your PEA should be spent as you wish on personal items. Neither the care home nor the local authority can require you to spend your PEA in any particular way.

If you are not able to manage your PEA because of ill health, the local authority may (subject to your agreement, or that of your personal representative) deposit it in a bank account on your behalf, and use it to provide for your smaller needs. Money unspent on your death will form part of your estate.

Guidance reminds local authorities that the PEA should not be used for care that is contracted for because it has been assessed by the local authority or the NHS as needed.

CRAG, para 5.001

Campaigns by voluntary organisations and local government bodies to substantially raise the level of the PEA have not achieved any success to date.

Increasing the PEA

Local authorities have discretion to allow more PEA in 'special circumstances' – eg if you need to keep more of your income to lead a more independent life or pursue a hobby that is important to you. Guidance reminds authorities that if a resident is temporarily absent there is a discretion to vary the PEA to enable the resident to have more money while staying with family or friends.

NAA, S.22(4); LAC 97/5

If you are one of a couple, the PEA may be increased so that you can help support your partner at home, perhaps because you are not married or registered as civil partners and so cannot have half of your personal or occupational pension disregarded (see Box L.2), or because, as the resident, you are in receipt of a means-tested benefit (income support (IS), income-based jobseeker's allowance (JSA), income-related employment and support allowance (ESA) or pension credit) paid in respect of both of you.

CRAG, para 5.005

Basically, the local authority should not require a charge that would leave your partner without enough money to live on. However, the authority could consider being on a means-tested benefit as 'having enough to live on'.

If you are one of a couple going temporarily into a care home and you are the claimant of IS, income-based JSA, or income-related ESA in respect of both of you, then the local authority usually has a straightforward task of apportioning the benefit according to your individual incomes because it is usually calculated using two single people's applicable amounts added together (see Chapter 33(5)). However, if you are one of a couple going temporarily into a care home and you are the claimant of pension credit in respect of both of you, then the position is far less straightforward because pension credit is calculated using the couple appropriate minimum guarantee rather than two single people's appropriate minimum guarantees added together (see Chapter 33(7)). This means that local authorities must decide how to carry out an apportionment. In most cases, it seems that as a starting point authorities are either:

- dividing the couple rate standard minimum guarantee equally (ie £198.45 divided by 2 = £99.23) and adding any additional amount included in the appropriate minimum guarantee to the amount for the person for whom it is paid. Then they deduct any assessable income received by the partner in order to reach an amount by which to vary the PEA; *or*
- allowing the amount that would be paid by way of the guarantee element of pension credit to the partner as if they were a single person and varying the PEA by this amount.

L.2 Capital and income

General

Local authority assessments of capital and income under the National Assistance (Assessment of Resources) Regulations 1992 are closely based on the assessment for income support – see Chapter 42(5)-(6). There are differences, however.

In this box we outline how local authority assessments of capital and income differ from those of means-tested benefits, including income support, income-related employment and support allowance (ESA), income-based jobseeker's allowance (JSA) and pension credit.

Capital limits

For local authority charging purposes these are:

- in England and Northern Ireland, £23,000 upper limit, and £14,000 lower limit for tariff income purposes; in Scotland, £22,500 and £13,750; and Wales £22,000 and £20,750 – for both temporary and permanent residents.

For ESA/income support/JSA, the capital limits are:

- £16,000 upper limit and £6,000 lower limit (for tariff income) for temporary residents;
- £16,000 upper limit and £10,000 lower limit (for tariff income) for permanent residents.

For pension credit, the capital limits are:

- no upper limit for temporary or permanent residents;
- £6,000 limit (for tariff income) for temporary residents;
- £10,000 limit (for tariff income) for permanent residents.

Note: The tariff income for local authority charging purposes and ESA/income support/JSA purposes is calculated using £1 a week for every £250 or part thereof in excess of the lower limits.

For pension credit purposes, tariff income (or 'deemed income') is £1 a week for every £500 or part thereof in excess of the limits.

Arrears of benefits

There is a 52-week limit on the disregard of arrears of some benefits for charging assessments. For means-tested benefits, this period is extended in certain circumstances (see Chapters 27(6) and 42(6)).

Your home

See also Chapter 34(6). If you are a 'temporary resident', the value of 'one dwelling' is ignored if:

- you intend to return to live in it as your home; *and*
- it is still available to you; *or*
- your property is up for sale and you intend to use the proceeds to buy a more suitable property to return to.

AOR Regs, Sch 4, para 1

You count as a 'temporary resident' if your stay is unlikely to last more than 52 weeks or *'in exceptional circumstances (is) unlikely substantially to exceed that period'*.

AOR Regs, reg 2(1)

If you are unsure of your long-term plans, it is usually best to say you intend to return to your own home. However, if you are one of a couple going into a care home on a trial basis with a view to a permanent stay, then for pension credit purposes you will still be treated as a couple, whereas if you are one of a couple going permanently into a care home, you will be treated as two single people and any pension credit entitlement will be paid to each of you based on your individual resources. Therefore, it may be financially beneficial in these circumstances to be permanent from the day of entering the care home (see Chapter 34(4) and (5)).

You count as a 'permanent resident' if you are not a temporary resident and the agreed intention is for you to remain in a care home.

AOR Regs, reg 2; LAC (2002)11, para 25; CRAG, para 3.001A

The local authority has discretion, not found in means-tested benefits, to disregard the value *'of any premises occupied in whole or in part by a third party where the local authority considers it would be reasonable to disregard the value of those premises'*.

AOR, Sch 4, para 18

Examples are given where a carer has given up their own home in order to care, or the person remaining is an elderly companion of the resident, particularly if they have given up their own home.

CRAG, para 7.007

The examples are not exhaustive. If you think a disregard should apply to your property, and it has not been, use the complaints procedure (see Chapter 28(7)).

While your home is up for sale – Unlike for means-tested benefits, if you are a permanent resident when your old home is up for sale, the local authority does not ignore the value for 26 weeks or longer where reasonable. It counts as capital from the 13th week after you have become a permanent resident. See also Chapter 34(6).

AOR Regs, Sch 4, para 1A

Although the local authority may help towards your care home fees while your home is up for sale, you will have to pay back the full amount once the home is sold. See also Chapter 34(6) for information about deferred payment agreements.

If you jointly own property – Only *your* actual interest is valued. It is recognised that it might be hard to find a willing buyer for a part-share in a property (CRAG 7.012). An Ombudsman decision makes it clear that a local authority should deal with the question of the valuation of a property in accordance with the guidance and without delay.

Lincolnshire County Council (03/C/9384) [28.6.04]

Seek advice if you disagree with how your share is valued. ESA/income support/JSA has used a 'deemed' share based on the number of owners rather than the actual share in the property (see Chapter 27(5)).

If you jointly own a property with your spouse or civil partner who decides to sell in order to move (eg to a smaller house), you can give them some of your share of the proceeds to help buy the new home. The local authority should not consider this as deprivation of your capital.

CRAG, para 6.063

Jointly owned capital

If you jointly own capital (other than property) with your partner (or any other person), the local authority, to avoid administrative difficulties, will divide it into equal shares in the charging assessment regardless of what your actual share is. Once you are in sole possession of your actual share, you will be treated as owning that actual amount.

AOR Regs, reg 27(1); CRAG, para 6.013

This applies whether you are a temporary or permanent resident, unlike the means-tested benefit rules for couples, which count your capital together until you become a permanent resident, when they divide your capital.

Personal possessions

The value of these is ignored unless you acquired them with the intention of reducing your capital in order to satisfy a local authority that you are unable to pay for your accommodation at the standard rate or to reduce the rate at which you would otherwise be liable to pay for your accommodation.

AOR Regs, Sch 4, para 8

Deprivation of capital

Local authorities have powers that may be used to treat you as having notional capital, ie as possessing capital that you have given away. Chapter 34(7) explains the deprivation of capital rule. However, there is also an additional power under section 21 of HASSASSA (Health and Social Services and Social Security Adjudication Act 1983) – the '6-month rule' – which has different conditions.

The 6-month rule

Section 21 of HASSASSA may be applied if you:

- transferred cash or any other asset, which would have affected the charging assessment, to someone else; *and*
- did this *'knowingly and with the intention of avoiding charges for the accommodation'*; *and either*
- transferred the asset six months or less before the day the local authority has arranged a placement in a care home; *or*
- transferred the asset while you were being funded by the local authority in a care home; *and either*
- were not paid anything, or given anything, in return for the transfer; *or*
- were paid, or given something, less than the value of the asset in return for the transfer.

If a resident is self-funding in an independent sector home, has not been assessed nor had their placement arranged by a local authority, the 6-month rule applies only if the local authority takes over the arrangements within that time.

CRAG, Annex D(2.1)

If section 21 of HASSASSA applies, the person to whom you transferred the asset is *'liable to pay ... the difference between the amount assessed as due to be paid for the (residential) accommodation ... and the amount (which you are paying)'*. In this case, the local authority may:

- use the deprivation of capital rule (see Chapter 34(7)) to base the charging assessment on the amount of 'notional capital' you gave away, as well as on your actual capital and income; *or*
- if you cannot pay the assessed charge, use section 21 of HASSASSA to transfer the liability for the part of the charges assessed as a result of the notional capital from you to the person(s) to whom you transferred the asset, up to the value of the transferred asset.

Some people mistakenly think if they have given away assets more than six months before entering a care home, that cannot affect the amount they would have to pay for a care home. However, if a significant purpose of giving away an asset was to get help, or more help, from the local authority with the cost of a care home, the deprivation of capital rule may be applied – even if the transfer took place over six months before (see Chapter 34(7)).

AOR Regs, reg 25(1); CRAG, paras 6.057 to 6.066

Obviously, if you have given away something that would not have affected the charging assessment at all, the deprivation of capital rule cannot apply, nor can section 21 of HASSASSA. If the local authority refuses to arrange a place for you in a care home because the asset you gave away, together with other savings, was worth more than the capital limit in your country (see above), seek urgent advice.

See also Robertson v Fife Council (25.7.02)

Charitable and third party payments

The way charitable, voluntary and personal injury payments are treated in the local authority's charging assessment has been changed to reflect the way they are treated for means-tested benefits (currently in England only but due to be amended in Wales and Scotland). See Chapters 26(7) and 27(6).

Third party payments to meet a shortfall for more expensive accommodation are always taken fully into account as your income by the local authority. This is not the case for means-tested benefits.

Income

- ❑ Attendance allowance and disability living allowance (DLA) care component are only disregarded if you are a 'temporary resident' (see above).
- ❑ DLA mobility component is disregarded.
- ❑ income support, income-related ESA, pension credit and income-based JSA are taken fully into account but payments in these benefits made towards housing costs (eg payments toward mortgage interest) are disregarded. See below for the savings disregard applied to the savings credit element of pension credit.
- ❑ Housing benefit and council tax benefit being paid in relation to your usual home are disregarded.
- ❑ Supporting People payments are disregarded.
- ❑ The local authority can disregard any payments you are making towards your housing costs as a temporary resident (see Chapter 34(8)).
- ❑ If you get a child or adult dependant's addition to a contributory benefit (eg as part of your incapacity benefit or state pension), it is disregarded if it is paid to the person for whom it is intended.
- ❑ Working tax credit is taken fully into account.
- ❑ Child tax credit is disregarded.
- ❑ Child support maintenance payments, child benefit and guardian's allowance are disregarded (unless the child is in the accommodation with you).

AOR Regs, Sch 3

- ❑ If you do not live with your spouse/civil partner, half your personal or occupational pension or payment from a retirement annuity contract will be disregarded if you pass at least this amount to your spouse/civil partner. If you pass nothing or less than half, there is no disregard. The disregard is for both temporary and permanent residents. (The means-tested benefit rules do not have a similar disregard.)

AOR Regs, reg 10A

Savings disregard

The Department of Health and devolved governments apply a savings disregard for residents aged 65 or over.

NA(AOR)(A)(NO2)(England) Regs 2003 & similar provisions in Scotland & Wales

The amounts below are for 2009/10. References to couples include civil partners.

- ❑ If you are a resident in receipt of pension credit savings credit element with pre-pension credit qualifying income of between £96 (savings credit threshold; £0.75 more than basic state pension) and £130 (standard minimum guarantee) a week (or between £153.40 and £198.45 for couples) you will have a disregard of an amount equal to the savings credit award or £5.65 a week (£8.45 for couples), whichever is less.
- ❑ If you are a resident in receipt of pension credit savings credit element with pre-pension credit qualifying income in excess of £130 a week (£198.45 for couples) you will have a disregard of £5.65 a week (£8.45 for couples).
- ❑ If you are a resident who is not in receipt of pension credit savings credit element because, although you have qualifying income, your total income is in excess of £181 a week (£266.03 for couples), you will have a disregard of £5.65 a week (£8.45 for couples).

These different approaches produce significant variations across the country in the amounts allowed in charging assessments for partners in the community. If the amount allowed for your partner leaves them without enough money to live on, you should seek advice with a view to using the complaints procedure (see Chapter 28(7)).

6. Treating your home as capital

The value of your previous home will be ignored when the local authority assesses your resources:

- if you are temporarily resident in a care home; *or*
- for the first 12 weeks of being a permanent resident in a care home provided by the local authority under Part III of the National Assistance Act 1948, irrespective of whether you were already in a care home as a self-funder (seek advice if your local authority does not apply the disregard because you have been self-funding in a care home. New Department of Health guidance is due to clarify this issue); *or*
- if the home is occupied by your partner/or former partner (unless you are estranged or divorced from them) – this includes same-sex partners (whether registered or not); *or*
- if your home is occupied by your estranged or divorced partner and they are a lone parent with a dependent child; *or*
- if the home is occupied by a relative of yours or a relative of a member of your family who is:
  - aged 60 or over; *or*
  - incapacitated; *or*
  - aged under 16 and a child for whom you are liable to maintain.

A 'relative' is your parent, parent-in-law, son, daughter, son/daughter-in-law, step-parent, stepson/daughter, brother, sister, or the partner (including civil partner) of any of the above, grandparent, grandchild, uncle, aunt, nephew or niece.

'Incapacitated' is not defined but guidance says you count as incapacitated if you get incapacity benefit, severe disablement allowance, disability living allowance (DLA), attendance allowance or constant attendance allowance, or you would satisfy incapacity conditions for any of these.

Local authorities have discretion to ignore the value of the property if anyone else lives there. Box L.2 gives the legal basis for this discretion and explains when it is likely to be used.

AOR Regs, Sch 4

If your home is taken into account, its value will be based on the current selling price, less any debts (such as a mortgage) charged on it, and less 10% in recognition of the expenses that would be incurred in selling it. Its value should be reassessed periodically. The capital value of your home is assessed in this way until it is sold and added to any other capital you have; the local authority may help towards your fees while your home is being sold. Seek advice if you are refused help with funding pending the sale of your home if the authority has assessed you as needing care in a care home. Once your home is sold, the actual capital realised less any debts and the actual expenses involved in the sale are taken into account.

AOR Regs, reg 23; CRAG, 6.011a and 6.015

The local authority cannot make you sell your home to pay the assessed charge for your accommodation, other than through the courts. However, under section 22 of the Health and Social Services and Social Security Adjudication Act 1983 (HASSASSA), and section 23 for Scotland, the authority can place a legal charge on the property so that it can recover outstanding debts when the property is eventually sold. If the property is jointly owned, the authority is advised to put a caution (or security) on it, which has a similar effect.

CRAG, Annex D(3.5) – similar provisions apply to Scotland

The method of valuing your interest or share in joint property is outlined in Box L.2.

The value of any other property you own will usually be taken into account as capital.

Deferred payment agreements

Deferred payment agreements are available to people in care homes who do not wish to sell their home (for whatever reason), or who face a delay in selling it, and have:

- less than the upper capital limit in England and Wales and the lower capital limit in Scotland (disregarding the value of their home); *and*
- insufficient income to meet the cost of their placement.

HSCA 2001, S.55; CCH(S)A 2002, S.6

The scheme allows the local authority to enter into a written agreement with the resident whereby:

- the authority places a legal charge on the resident's property, or in Scotland has a standard security granted in the agreement;
- the authority contracts to pay the full fees of the placement to the home;
- the resident is assessed to pay a weekly charge to the authority based on their weekly income (less the personal expenses allowance); *and*
- payment by the resident of the balance of the weekly cost of the placement is deferred until the resident dies or the property is sold.

Local authorities have discretion as to whether to enter into an agreement in individual cases.

Guidance to local authorities about operating the scheme is set out in LAC (2001)25 (see Box L.1), which says caution should be exercised if there is an outstanding mortgage on the property or the amount of the deferred payment is very high. If a local authority refuses to enter into an agreement, it should put the refusal in writing. You should use the complaints procedure if you wish to challenge the decision (see Chapter 28(7)).

Further guidance (LAC (2002)15) (England only) has been issued, as a number of local authorities had only made limited use of the power to make deferred payments. In Scotland, guidance is contained in CCD13/2004; in Wales in NAfWC 21/2003.

Points to note:

- ❑ Deferred payments should not be used if the value of your home should be disregarded under the Assessment of Resources Regulations (see Box L.2).
- ❑ Residents should be given full information about the scheme and advised to seek independent financial advice before entering an agreement.
- ❑ If you enter into an agreement you may have to pay for land registry searches and other legal expenses relating to placing a legal charge on your property.
- ❑ Deferred payments are interest free, although local authorities can charge interest, at a reasonable rate, on the debt from 56 days after your death or after you terminate the agreement.
- ❑ Local authorities can still use section 22 of the HASSASSA to place a legal charge (or charging order in Scotland), a type of secured loan, on your property. However, this provision should only be used if residents are unwilling to pay their assessed contribution and a debt arises. Your consent is not required.

  CRAG, para 7.019; LAC (2002)15

  If the local authority uses its ordinary debt recovery powers to put a charge on your property, section 24 of the HASSASSA places a duty on the authority to charge reasonable interest on any sum owed after the day of death. Before then, the authority cannot charge you interest.
- ❑ In certain situations, you can change from being subject to the provisions of section 22 of the HASSASSA to having a deferred payment agreement.

- ❑ Local authorities have a discretion to make allowances for ongoing expenses relating to the property, but this may increase the debt repayable when the property is sold.
- ❑ If you enter a deferred payment agreement you should note the following effects on your benefit entitlement:
- ■ if you are under 60, you will not be entitled to income support or income-related employment and support allowance (ESA) while the property is not up for sale if your interest in the property is worth more than £16,000. If you are aged 60 or over it is also unlikely that you will be entitled to pension credit if your house is not up for sale, as the tariff income applied on capital above £10,000 is likely to mean your income will exceed your appropriate minimum guarantee. This means the total debt re-payable to the local authority at the end will be greater. However, for those whose property is at the lower end of the market it is worth checking to see if you could still get the guarantee credit of pension credit or if it affects your savings credit;
- ■ you will retain your entitlement to attendance allowance or the DLA care component during a deferred payment agreement because you will be treated as a self-funder if it is clear you will eventually pay back the local authority in full. This is the case even if you get income support, income-related ESA or pension credit with the severe disability premium (or pension credit equivalent) during this period. In Scotland this will not apply if you are 65 or over and receiving free personal care (see Chapter 33(2)).

It is important to ensure you receive all the benefits you are entitled to during the period of the deferred payment agreement, as this will help reduce the debt to the local authority.

7. Deprivation of capital

If you have given away assets, eg your former home, or sold them for less than they are worth to avoid or lessen the charge, or converted them into a form that is disregarded to take advantage of the disregard, the local authority may take their value into account in the charging assessment. These notional capital rules are not mandatory for local authorities; they have discretion not to apply them. If they do apply them, they are similar to the notional capital rules for means-tested benefits (see Chapter 27).

AOR Regs, reg 25(1); CRAG, paras 6.057 to 6.066

The local authority can, however, decide that property has been disposed of in order to reduce the residential charge without having to decide that the resident knew of the capital limit or anticipated the need to enter a care home.

Yule v South Lanarkshire Council 2000 (SLT1249)

Additionally, a local authority must take account of the resident's 'subjective purpose' in disposing of the property and give reasons for accepting or rejecting any evidence provided by the resident.

R on the application of the PR of Beeson & Dorset CC & SoS for Health 2001

The local authority 'diminishing notional capital' rule reduces any notional capital on a weekly basis. It is reduced by the difference between the charge you are currently paying and the charge you would have paid if the authority had not taken 'notional capital' into account.

AOR Regs, reg 26

The 6-month rule – If capital is transferred to another person within six months of the day the local authority has arranged a placement in a care home, there is an additional local authority power, not available in the rules for means-tested benefits, which may mean that the person to whom you transferred the asset is liable to pay the difference between the amount assessed as due to be paid for the care home and the amount that you are paying (see Box L.2).

8. Meeting the costs of your own home

If you are a 'temporary resident' (see Box L.2), the local authority can disregard payments you are making towards *'any housing costs... including any fuel charges, which are included in the rent of a dwelling to which (you) intend to return... to the extent that the local authority considers it reasonable in the circumstances to do so'*.

AOR Regs, Sch 3, para 27

Housing costs can include service charges, insurance premiums, water rates, standard charges for fuel and any rent or mortgage payments not covered by means-tested benefits or Supporting People payments.

CRAG, para 3.011 & para 3.012

If no one is living in your home and you have entered a care home for a short period, see Chapter 20(6) for information about housing benefit (HB) and council tax benefit and Chapter 21 for information about council tax. See also Chapter 33(3) and (4).

After 52 weeks, or 13 weeks in the case of a trial period, or as soon as it is clear that your stay in the home is permanent, you will be excluded from HB or means-tested benefit housing costs. However, your liability to pay rent and/or a mortgage in respect of your former home continues until you have terminated your tenancy or sold your home. If you have given notice on your tenancy in the community, you will be able to continue to claim HB for up to four weeks (see Chapter 33(3)). If your former home is vacant, and you are a permanent resident you should not have to pay council tax.

If your partner, children or relatives continue to live in your home, the help they can receive for their housing costs depends on their circumstances. If they are paying the housing costs, even though you are the person liable for them, they can claim HB or means-tested benefit housing costs instead of you.

9. What happens if you move out?

When you move out of a care home, you will be entitled to social security benefits in the usual way.

If you are entitled to income support, income-based jobseeker's allowance, income-related employment and support allowance or pension credit when you move from a care home into unfurnished or partly furnished accommodation, you may get a social fund community care grant (see Chapter 23).

Your local social services department will be able to advise you on local authority benefits and services that are available in your area (see Chapters 28 and 30 for details).

If you leave your care home on a temporary basis, your local authority can use its discretion to vary the personal expenses allowance to enable you to have more money while away.

NAA, S.22(4); LAC 97/5, para 8

You may also be able to claim disability living allowance care component or attendance allowance for periods away from the care home. Chapter 33 covers the effect on benefits of stays in, and absences from, care homes.

M Hospital

This section of the Handbook looks at:

35 Benefits in hospital

In this chapter we look at:

1. What should you do beforehand?

Stays in hospital (or a similar institution) as an inpatient can affect benefits. Three of the principal disability benefits – attendance allowance, disability living allowance (DLA) and carer's allowance – can be stopped after just a few weeks in hospital, as can child benefit (see 4 below). In turn, this can affect your entitlement to income-related employment and support allowance, income support, housing benefit (HB), council tax benefit (CTB) and pension credit (see Box M.1). Consequently, you should let the DWP know if you or a dependant are admitted to hospital. If you get carer's allowance, you must tell the DWP if the person you are looking after is admitted. If you get HB or CTB, and a spell in hospital results in attendance allowance, DLA, carer's allowance or child benefit being stopped, you also need to tell the local authority.

Write to the office(s) dealing with your benefits to let them know the date you expect to be admitted to hospital and how long you are likely to stay. You should still report your actual admission or tell the office(s) if it is cancelled or postponed. If you can, do this beforehand; otherwise do it as soon as possible.

Medical certificates – If you need sick notes to get benefit when in hospital, ask the sister or charge nurse for one.

Hospital or similar institution – Benefits are affected in the same way by a stay in a 'similar institution' to a hospital. This is not defined in legislation, although you must receive inpatient medical treatment or professional nursing care in the home under specified NHS legislation. What matters is not so much the nature of the accommodation, but whether your assessed needs for care are such that the NHS is under a duty to fund the accommodation free of charge, in which case you will still be treated as an inpatient.

HIP Regs, reg 2(4); R(DLA)2/06

Private patients – If you are a private patient paying the whole cost of accommodation and non-medical services in hospital, you are not deemed to be an inpatient and therefore the normal rules of benefit entitlement apply, not those described in this chapter.

2. Hospital fares

You may be able to get help with fares or other travel expenses for yourself (and for someone who has to go with you if you are incapable of getting to the hospital or treatment centre on your own), if you are either exempt from NHS charges or qualify for full help with them (see Chapter 55(1)). Help is also available if you are covered by the low income scheme (see Chapter 55(5)). If your income is above the low-income level but would fall below it if you paid the fares, you may still be eligible for help with part of the cost. Help with fares or other travel expenses is also available if you:

- are under 16, or under 20 and in full-time education or approved training; *or*
- live in the Isles of Scilly and need to travel to a mainland hospital; *or*
- live in the Scottish Islands or Highlands and need to travel more than five miles by sea or 30 miles by land to get to hospital; *or*
- are getting NHS treatment abroad.

NHS(TERC) Regs, regs 3, 5, 5B & 6

Parents – If your child has to go into hospital or attend on a regular basis, you may claim help with travel expenses to accompany your child to and from the hospital.

NHS(TERC) Regs, regs 3(3)(a)

Inpatients sent home on short leave – If you are sent home as part of your treatment or for the hospital's convenience, your fares are regarded as part of your treatment costs and should be met by the hospital and not under the hospital travel expenses means-tested scheme.

What travel expenses can be covered?

The law allows help with *'the cost of travelling by the cheapest means of transport available'*, which normally means the cost of second-class public transport. If public transport is available but you go by car, your fuel costs can be covered up to the amount of the second-class fare. If you are unable to use public transport because of a physical disability or it is not available, and you go by car or taxi, your fuel costs or fares will be covered. You should get agreement from the hospital first. The travel costs of an escort can also be met if you need to be accompanied for medical reasons.

If you are travelling overseas for NHS treatment you are covered under the same rules, subject to the health authority's agreement to the mode of transport.

NHS(TERC) Regs, regs 3(5) & (6)

How to claim the cost of fares

The hospital will refund your fares if you produce proof of your entitlement (eg your benefit award letter or tax credit exemption certificate). If you have already claimed on low-income grounds, show your HC2 certificate (full entitlement) or your HC3 certificate (partial entitlement).

If you haven't yet claimed on low-income grounds, use form HC5(T) to claim a refund, and form HC1 to establish your entitlement to full or partial help. The forms can be obtained by ringing the NHS forms-line (0845 610 1112). Ask the hospital to fill in their part of the HC5(T), then fill in the rest of the HC5(T) and the HC1 and send both forms to the address given on the forms. The HC5(T) must be returned within three months of paying your fares.

Partial help with fares – The amount shown on an HC3 certificate for partial help is the amount you are expected to be able to pay for travel expenses in any one week (from

Sunday to the following Saturday). If your actual hospital travel expenses in any particular week covered by that HC3 certificate are higher, the excess is refunded. This helps if you have to travel long distances to hospital or if you have to make several visits to the same, or to different, hospitals within the same week. Ask the hospital fares office for details of the arrangements for dealing with several visits within the same week.

Other sources of help

Other possible sources of help with travel expenses for patients and visitors include hospital endowment funds, education departments, social services departments, the Family Fund (see Chapter 37(8)) and various charities. For advice about these, contact a hospital social worker or an advice centre. Further information is available on the Department of Health website (www.dh.gov.uk).

Visitors' hospital fares – If you are on income-related employment and support allowance, income support, income-based jobseeker's allowance or pension credit, you may be able to get a social fund community care grant to assist you or a member of your family with travel expenses in the UK (including overnight accommodation charges) – see Chapter 23(4).

War pensioners – If you attend hospital for treatment for your war disablement, you can claim for expenses regardless of your income. Write to the Service Personnel and Veterans Agency, Norcoss, Thornton-Cleveleys FY5 3WP.

M.1 What happens to means-tested benefits?

This box relates to the following benefits:

- income-related employment and support allowance (ESA);
- income support;
- housing benefit;
- council tax benefit; *and*
- pension credit.

These benefits may continue to be paid throughout the period of your stay in hospital, but can be reduced depending on your circumstances.

Stage 1 – from the 1st day

There is normally no cut in your income-related ESA, income support, housing benefit or council tax benefit applicable amounts or your pension credit appropriate amount during your first four weeks in hospital, unless you have been readmitted to hospital after spending only 28 days or less in your own home (see stage 2 below).

Extra benefit – Income-related ESA, income support or pension credit do not increase if either you or your partner go into lodgings to be near a member of your family who is in hospital. Instead, you may have to look to the social fund for help (see Chapter 23). You may qualify for the severe disability premium (or equivalent pension credit addition) temporarily while your carer or another non-dependant is in hospital. See Chapter 24(3).

Stage 2 – from the 29th day

After four weeks in hospital, attendance allowance, disability living allowance (DLA) care component and (in most cases) DLA mobility component for an adult are withdrawn. If you had been in hospital (or, for attendance allowance or the DLA care component, a care home) during the 28 days before your current spell in hospital, these periods will be added together and benefit will be withdrawn after the combined total of four weeks in hospital (see Chapter 3(7) and (8)).

Once attendance allowance or DLA care component stops, the severe disability premium (or equivalent pension credit addition) is withdrawn. However, if you have a partner and both of you had been getting attendance allowance or DLA care component, you keep the premium even after the attendance allowance or DLA care component stops, but at the single rate of £52.85.

A carer premium (or equivalent pension credit addition) may be withdrawn at stages 2, 3 or 4 depending on your situation. In general, it is withdrawn eight weeks after carer's allowance stops or, if your carer's allowance is overlapped by another benefit, after attendance allowance or DLA care component stops (see Chapter 24(6)).

If you are entitled to an amount of income-related ESA or income support only because of the inclusion of a severe disability premium in your applicable amount, the withdrawal of this payment at the 4-week stage means the loss of income-related ESA or income support. The same applies in the case of the withdrawal of an addition for a severely disabled person in the guarantee credit of pension credit. If you are getting housing benefit or council tax benefit, you should tell your local authority about the loss of income-related ESA, income support or pension credit so they can reassess your claim.

Stage 3 – from the 85th day

After 12 weeks in hospital, there is a change if the patient is a dependent child. DLA for the child is withdrawn. A disabled child premium or enhanced disability premium based on the DLA is not withdrawn until the child ceases to count as a dependant.

Stage 4 – after 52 weeks

You can continue to receive income-related ESA, income support and pension credit for the entire duration of your stay in hospital. However, any disability premium, enhanced disability premium or higher pensioner premium will stop after you have been a hospital inpatient for 52 weeks (unless you have a partner who remains at home who satisfies the condition for the premium themselves).

If non-dependant deductions are being made from your income-related ESA, income support, pension credit, housing benefit or council tax benefit, they will stop after your non-dependant has been a hospital inpatient for 52 weeks (ignoring absences from hospital of up to 28 days).

Housing costs – Once you have been away from your own home continuously for 52 weeks, you can no longer be treated as occupying it as your home. You would therefore no longer be entitled to income-related ESA, income support or pension credit housing costs or housing benefit, though someone still living in your home could possibly claim these benefits if they were treated as liable to pay the rent or housing costs themselves.

Child – Once a child has been in hospital for 52 weeks you continue to have an allowance for them included in your income support assessment (if it is still included) for as long as you keep visiting the child.

Treatment abroad – Special rules apply for patients receiving NHS hospital treatment abroad (see Chapter 51(5)).

Pension credit

The guarantee credit of pension credit is reduced in a similar fashion to income-related ESA and income support. The savings credit element is not itself downrated as such, but the amount may still change once the additions in the appropriate amount of the guarantee credit are withdrawn or when you are no longer treated as a couple.

3. What happens to means-tested benefits?

If you go into hospital, income-related employment and support allowance, income support and pension credit can sometimes continue to be paid indefinitely without being reduced.

However, the disability, enhanced disability and higher pension premiums in income support (and enhanced disability premium in income-related employment and support allowance) are removed after 52 weeks. Also, if benefits such as disability living allowance, attendance allowance or carer's allowance are withdrawn, this will affect the amount of benefit you receive. See Box M.1 for details.

Income-related employment and support allowance, income support and pension credit can continue to be paid during a temporary absence abroad for the purpose of receiving NHS hospital treatment (see Chapter 51(5)-(6)).

Jobseeker's allowance

You cannot normally claim jobseeker's allowance (JSA) while you are in hospital because you will not be deemed capable of work or able to satisfy the labour market conditions. However, if you are already receiving JSA when you go into hospital, you can be treated as being capable of, available for, and actively seeking work for up to two weeks. You can do this twice within any 12 months of the same jobseeking period (see Chapter 15(8)).

When your JSA stops, you should claim employment and support allowance.

JSA can continue to be paid during a temporary absence abroad for the purpose of receiving NHS hospital treatment (see Chapter 51(7)).

Housing benefit and council tax benefit

If you get housing benefit or council tax benefit, the applicable amount may change during a spell in hospital as a consequence of the withdrawal of benefits such as disability living allowance, attendance allowance or carer's allowance. See Box M.1 for details.

Tax credits

Child tax credit and working tax credit are not automatically affected by a stay in hospital. However, if you cease to be treated as employed because of a stay in hospital you would no longer qualify for working tax credit, and if your other income changes this may affect the level of your award (see Chapter 19(4)).

4. What happens to non-means-tested benefits?

Most non-means-tested benefits continue to be paid indefinitely. The exceptions are attendance allowance, disability living allowance (DLA) and carer's allowance, as well as child benefit, guardian's allowance and any child dependant's addition that may still be payable with other benefits. They are treated in the following way.

M.2 For more information

The following leaflets are free:

- GIHA5DWP *Going into hospital?*, available from local Jobcentre Plus offices.
- HC 11 *Help with health costs*, available from the Department of Health orderline: 0870 155 5455 or www.nhsbsa.nhs.uk/HealthCosts.
- Leaflet 2 *Notes for people getting a war pension living in the United Kingdom*, available from your local Veterans' Welfare Office (contact details from Veterans Helpline 0800 169 2277, textphone 0800 169 3458 or www.veterans-uk.info).

During the first four weeks

There is normally no change, except in the following cases.

If you are discharged from hospital but re-admitted within 28 days, the periods in hospital are added together to calculate the date from which your attendance allowance or DLA care component is to be reduced. If you have come from a care home, you may find your benefit reduced straight away because of the 28-day linking rule. See Chapter 3(7) and (8).

War disablement pension can often be increased to cover treatment expenses when you go into hospital, if the treatment is for the war injury (see Chapter 46(11)).

After four weeks

Attendance allowance and DLA for adults stop. See below if you have a Motability agreement.

Carer's allowance will stop if the person you are caring for has been in hospital for four weeks and their attendance allowance or DLA care component has stopped.

Attendance allowance or DLA care component and your carer's carer's allowance will stop before the four weeks is up if you had been in hospital or a care home in the 28 days before you were admitted to hospital (see Chapter 3(7) and (8)). DLA mobility component will stop before the end of four weeks only if you'd been in hospital in the 28 days before this hospital stay.

If you claim DLA or attendance allowance when you are already in hospital, it cannot be paid until you leave.

AA Regs, regs 6 & 8; DLA Regs, regs 8, 10 & 12A-12C

Constant attendance allowance (payable in the War Pensions and Industrial Injuries schemes) and war pensioners' severe disablement occupational allowance stop.

Motability – If you have a Motability agreement in force when you go into hospital, DLA mobility component continues to be paid to Motability for the full term of the agreement. Any balance that would otherwise be paid to you stops after 28 days.

You cannot begin or renew a Motability agreement while you are in hospital. An exception allows the renewal of agreements under the Motability wheelchair scheme, provided the new agreement is entered into the day after the old one ends. The mobility component will be paid if you renew a Motability agreement during a temporary absence from hospital.

DLA Regs, reg 12B(7)-(9)

After 12 weeks

Child in hospital – Child benefit or guardian's allowance is paid for the first 12 weeks if your child or a child you care for goes into hospital. After 12 weeks, you can continue to get these benefits for a child in hospital only if you are regularly spending money on the child's behalf (eg on clothing, pocket money, magazines). If you continue to get child benefit you will continue to get any child dependant's addition that may still be payable with other benefits (such as incapacity benefit), but otherwise this will also end.

SSCBA, S.143(4) & CB Regs, reg 10

DLA care component and mobility component for a child under 16 stop after 12 weeks in hospital. DLA care component may stop before the 12 weeks are up if your child had been in hospital or a care home in the 28 days before this hospital stay. DLA mobility component will stop before the end of 12 weeks only if your child had been in hospital in the 28 days before this hospital stay. See Chapter 3(7) and (8) for more details. If there is a Motability agreement in force, the mobility component continues to be paid to Motability (see above).

DLA Regs, regs 10(2) & 12B(1)(b)

If you or your partner are in hospital – Child benefit normally continues to be paid.

Carer's allowance stops after the carer has been in hospital for 12 weeks (but it may stop sooner – see Chapter 6(10)).

Employer-paid benefits
Going into hospital does not affect entitlement to statutory sick pay, statutory maternity pay, statutory adoption pay or statutory paternity pay.

5. Long-term stays

If you have to stay in hospital for a long-term period, you will continue to receive your full entitlement to state pension, contributory employment and support allowance (ESA), incapacity benefit and severe disablement allowance for an indefinite period (as long as you continue to satisfy the other conditions of entitlement to these benefits). Income-related ESA, income support and pension credit can also be paid for an indefinite period (again, as long as the other conditions of entitlement are met), although the rate may be affected by the withdrawal of benefits such as disability living allowance (see Box M.1). Also, the disability, enhanced disability and higher pension premiums in income support and the enhanced disability premium in income-related ESA are removed after 52 weeks (unless you have a partner at home who satisfies the conditions for the premium themselves).

Housing costs – Once you have been in hospital for a continuous period of 52 weeks, if you have no dependants living in your home, you can no longer receive income-related ESA, income support or pension credit housing costs. Nor can you normally get housing benefit (HB) or council tax benefit (CTB). The maximum period of absence in one stretch during which income-related ESA, income support or pension credit housing costs and HB/CTB can be paid is 52 weeks (see Chapter 20(6) for the HB rules; those for the other four benefits are similar). If you have dependants or other people living in your home, their right to benefit depends on their own circumstances. If you are one of a couple and have been in hospital for 52 weeks, you and your partner are treated as separate claimants.

6. What about when you leave hospital?

Whether or not any benefit has been changed or stopped while you or a dependant have been in hospital, make sure you inform the office that administers each benefit, as soon as you know the date you or your dependant are coming home. You should still report your actual date of discharge, or tell the appropriate office if it is cancelled or postponed.

Temporary absence from hospital
If you or a dependant spend a few days at home – perhaps for a trial run, or if you are in and out of hospital on a regular pattern – tell the office that administers each benefit and ask them to pay the full amount of benefit for the days at home. Get a note from the hospital to say how many days you have at home. For all benefits except disability living allowance (DLA) and attendance allowance, the day you are admitted is treated as a day *out* of hospital and the day you are discharged is treated as a day *in* hospital. For DLA and attendance allowance, see below.

HIP Regs, reg 2(5)

Can your carer get carer's allowance? – If you go home regularly each weekend and receive attendance allowance or DLA care component (at the middle or highest rate), your carer might qualify for the full rate of carer's allowance. This is because carer's allowance is a weekly benefit and is never paid on a daily basis. See Chapter 6(2) to check whether your carer can meet the 35 hours a week caring test.

DLA and attendance allowance – These are adjusted to be paid at a daily rate where you are expected to return to hospital within 28 days. Attendance allowance and DLA care component (but not mobility component) are also paid at a daily rate where you are expected to return to a care home within 28 days. The daily rate provisions cease to apply once you have been out of hospital for 28 days.

The daily rate provisions do not apply if, on the day of discharge, you are not expected to return to hospital within 28 days, even if you do return to hospital within that period. If you are not expected to return to hospital within 28 days (and when you are finally discharged from hospital) full benefit resumes from the first pay day.

C&P Regs, reg 25

Both the day you are admitted or return to hospital and the day you are discharged or leave hospital count as days out of hospital. You can be paid for both of those days as well as whole days out of hospital.

DLA Regs, regs 8(2A) & 12A(2A); AA Regs, reg 6(2A)

Permanently out of hospital
In general, you should get the benefit you were getting before you went to hospital at the normal rate. If you go from hospital into a care home, see Chapter 33.

If you did not draw any benefit before you went into hospital, see Chapter 9 on employment and support allowance or, if you are aged 60 or over, Chapter 42 on pension credit. Once you leave hospital, all the normal rules for these benefits will apply to you. Chapter 23 covers the discretionary social fund; if you have been in hospital for an extended period you may get a community care grant to help establish yourself in the community.

7. Discharged before you're ready?

If acute nursing care in hospital is no longer essential for you, the hospital will clearly wish to discharge you. It may be impossible for you to return home without support services in place. In some cases you may even count as homeless. Get advice.

Before being discharged, your care needs should have been assessed. However, don't agree to a discharge unless you are happy with the arrangements for continuing care and support as set out in your care plan (see Chapter 28(3)). Don't agree to move to a care home unless you are absolutely clear about how, and for how long, the full cost will be met. See Chapters 28 to 34 for more details about care at home and in care homes.

N Children and young people

This section of the Handbook looks at:

36 Maternity and parental rights

1. Help with health costs

You are entitled to free prescriptions and dental treatment if you are pregnant or have had a baby in the past 12 months and have a valid maternity exemption certificate. Ask your doctor, midwife or health visitor for form FW8.

Vouchers to buy cow's milk, infant formula or fresh fruit and vegetables are available under the Healthy Start scheme. This is open to pregnant women and families with children under the age of 4 who are on certain means-tested benefits. For details see Chapter 55(6).

Health in pregnancy grant – This is a new payment of £190 available to all expectant mothers who have received maternal health advice from a healthcare professional. It is not means tested, is tax free and you do not have to meet any national insurance conditions to receive it. It can be claimed from the 25th week of pregnancy. You must be ordinarily resident and have the right to reside in the UK (see Chapter 50(2)).

2. Maternity leave

Women working while they are pregnant are entitled to 52 weeks' statutory maternity leave. You must fulfil strict notice conditions, including letting your employer know you are pregnant and telling them, by the end of the 15th week before your baby is due, when you want to take your maternity leave.

MPL Regs, regs 4-12A

Parental leave – Parents who have worked for the same employer for one year are entitled to 13 weeks' parental leave, which can be taken up until the child's 5th birthday. If your child gets disability living allowance you can take 18 weeks' leave up until their 18th birthday. You cannot take more than four weeks' parental leave for any one child in a year, unless otherwise agreed with your employer.

MPL Regs, regs 13-16

Time off for antenatal care – Every pregnant employee is entitled to time off with pay to keep antenatal appointments made on the advice of a doctor, midwife or health visitor.

3. Statutory maternity pay

If you are an employee, you may be able to get statutory maternity pay (SMP) from your employer when you stop work to have your baby. You will not have to repay it if you do not return to work. You qualify if:

- you have been employed by the same employer continuously for at least 26 weeks into the 15th week (the 'qualifying week') before the week the baby is due (a 'week' starts on Sunday and runs to the end of the following Saturday); *and*
- you are still in your job in the qualifying week (it doesn't matter if you are off work sick or on holiday); *and*
- your average earnings are at least £95 a week; *and*
- you give your employer the right notice (see below).

SSCBA, Ss.164 & SMP Regs, reg 11(1)

How much do you get? – SMP is paid by your employer for up to 39 weeks. For the first six weeks you get 90% of your average weekly earnings (with no upper limit). The average is calculated from your gross earnings in the eight weeks, if paid weekly, or two months, if paid monthly, before the end of the 15th week before the week the baby is due. The remaining 33 weeks are paid at the standard rate of £123.06, or 90% of your average weekly earnings if this calculation results in a figure that is less than £123.06.

SSCBA, S.166 & SMP Regs, reg 21

SMP is treated as earnings, so your employer will make deductions such as income tax and national insurance contributions from your SMP.

When is it paid? – SMP can start from the 11th week before the week in which the baby is due. You decide when you stop work and start your maternity pay period; you can work up until the baby's birth. If your baby is born early (ie prior to the 11th week before the week it is due), SMP will start the day after the birth. See 8 below if you are off work with a pregnancy-related illness.

SSCBA, S.165 & SMP Regs, reg 2

You must tell your employer at least 28 days before the date you want to start your SMP, or if this isn't possible, as soon as is reasonably practicable. Your employer may need you to inform them in writing. You must also give them your maternity certificate (form MAT B1), which your doctor or midwife will normally give you at the next antenatal appointment following your 21st week of pregnancy. Tell your employer as soon as is reasonably practicable if your baby is born early.

SSCBA, S.164(4)&(5)

You can continue to be paid SMP if you work for your employer for up to ten days ('Keeping in Touch' days) during your maternity pay period.

SMP Regs, reg 9A

If you are not eligible for SMP, your employer must give you form SMP1 within seven days. You may be eligible for maternity allowance (see 4 below).

SMP works in a similar way to statutory sick pay (see Chapter 8), so you have the right to ask your employer for a written statement about your SMP position. If you disagree, you can refer your case to HMRC Statutory Payments Disputes Team (0191 225 5221) for a decision. If HMRC decides against you, you can appeal to a First-tier Tribunal (Finance and Tax Chamber). Your employer can also appeal.

4. Maternity allowance

If you cannot get statutory maternity pay, you may qualify for tax-free maternity allowance (MA). To qualify, you must have been employed or self-employed for at least 26 weeks in the 66 weeks before the week in which the baby is due (the 'test period'), and earned an average of at least £30 a week for any 13 weeks in this test period.

SSCBA, S.35

How much do you get? – MA is £123.06 a week, or 90% of your average weekly earnings (whichever is less). Jobcentre Plus will add together all your gross earnings received in the 13 weeks during the 66-week test period in which you earned the most, then divide by 13 to work out your average weekly earnings. Earnings in different jobs and from a mixture of employed and self-employed work can be added together. If you are self-employed and have paid 13 Class 2 national insurance contributions in your test period you will be treated as having earnings sufficient to result in the full weekly rate of MA. You will be treated as having earnings of £30 for any week in which you are covered by a certificate of small earnings exception.

SSCBA, S.35A

When is it paid? – MA is paid for up to 39 weeks and can start from 11 weeks before the expected week of childbirth. If you are employed or self-employed you may delay the start of your MA until the baby's birth (but see 8 below if you are off work with a pregnancy-related illness). If you are not employed, your MA will start from the 11th week before the expected week of childbirth. Once you are on MA you can work for your employer (or as a self-employed person) for up to ten 'Keeping in Touch' days and continue to receive it.

How do you claim? – Fill in claim-form MA1 and send it to Jobcentre Plus together with your maternity certificate (MAT B1) and form SMP1 (if you did not qualify for SMP from your employer). MA1 forms are available from the Jobcentre Plus claim-line (0800 055 6688, textphone 0800 023 4888), from your antenatal clinic, or from the DWP website (www.dwp.gov.uk/advisers/claimforms). Send in form MA1 as soon as you can after you are 26 weeks pregnant. Don't delay claiming because you are still working or waiting for the MAT B1 or SMP1 – you can send them later. If you claim more than three months after the start of your MA period you may lose money. If you are not entitled to MA, Jobcentre Plus should check if you can get employment and support allowance instead (see 8 below).

5. Statutory paternity leave

Statutory paternity leave is one or two consecutive weeks' leave from work, to be taken within 56 days of the birth, or due date if the baby is born early, for fathers or partners of the mother (including same-sex partners) to support the mother or care for the baby. You can get the leave if you have worked for the same employer for at least 26 weeks by the 15th week before the baby is due and are still employed when the baby is born. It is important to give the correct notice for leave. You should tell your employer you plan to take paternity leave by the end of the 15th week before the week your baby is due, or if this isn't possible, as soon as is reasonably practicable. Use form SC3 to notify your employer.

The Paternity & Adoption Leave Regs 2002, regs 4-14

6. Statutory paternity pay

If you are entitled to statutory paternity leave, you may also be entitled to statutory paternity pay (SPP). You can get this if you have worked for the same employer for at least 26 weeks by the 15th week before the baby is due and have average earnings of at least £95 a week. It is paid by employers for one or two weeks at £123.06 a week or 90% of your average earnings (whichever is less).

You must give your employer at least 28 days' notice (or as much as reasonably practicable) of the date you want your SPP to start. If you have already given notice that you plan to take paternity leave this can serve for SPP as well. Use form SC3 (available from HMRC) to notify your employer.

If you can't get SPP, your employer must give you form SPP1 explaining why you don't qualify. You may be able to claim income support during paternity leave (see Box E.1, Chapter 14).

SSCBA, S.171ZA-E

7. Rights for adoptive parents

You have a right to 52 weeks' adoption leave if you have worked for the same employer for at least 26 weeks by the week in which you are notified of being matched with a child for adoption. A couple adopting jointly can choose who takes adoption leave and who takes paternity leave.

The Paternity & Adoption Leave Regs 2002, regs 15-27

Statutory adoption pay (SAP) is £123.06 a week or 90% of your average earnings for 39 weeks (whichever is less). To qualify for SAP you must have average earnings of at least £95 a week. You can continue to be paid SAP if you work for your employer for up to ten days during your adoption pay period.

Adoptive parents can also get parental leave.

SSCBA, S.171ZL-N

8. Unable to work due to sickness or disability?

If you are employed, you may be able to get statutory sick pay (SSP) – see Chapter 8. If you can't get SSP, you may be able to get employment and support allowance (ESA) – see Chapter 9.

If you are entitled to SMP or maternity allowance

You can stay on SSP up until the date of the baby's birth, or the date you are due to start your maternity leave. But if you are off work with a pregnancy-related illness in the last four weeks before the week the baby is due, your statutory maternity pay (SMP) or maternity allowance starts automatically.

SMP Regs, reg 2(4)

SMP – Once your SMP begins, any SSP stops. You can continue to receive ESA while you are on SMP if you continue to satisfy the basic conditions for it (see Chapter 9(9)). Contributory ESA and SMP overlap, so you are paid whichever is higher. SMP is treated as income with respect

N.1 For more information

Pregnancy and parenthood

Useful guides include:

- *Pregnancy and Work: What you need to know as an employee* from the Department for Business, Enterprise and Regulatory Reform (www.berr.gov.uk)
- *A guide to Maternity Benefits* (NI17A) from the DWP (www.dwp.gov.uk/advisers/ni17a)
- *E15 and E15 supplement – Pay and time off work for parents* from HMRC (www.hmrc.gov.uk)

Disabled parents can get information from Disability, Pregnancy and Parenthood International and support from the Disabled Parents Network (see Address List).

Education

Special Education Handbook, 9th edition – £17.99 (plus £2 p&p) from the Advisory Centre for Education (ACE), 1c Aberdeen Studios, 22 Highbury Grove, London N5 2DQ. For advice on special educational needs, ring the ACE free helpline: 0808 800 5793 (10-5pm Mon-Fri).

England – *Special educational needs: a guide for parents and carers (ref: 00639/2008)*, a free guide to provision in England published by the Department for Children, Schools and Families. Available from DCSF Publications, PO Box 5050, Sherwood Park, Annersley, Nottingham NG15 ODJ (0845 602 2260; email: DCSF@prolog.uk.com).

Scotland – For advice and the *Parent's guide to additional support for learning*, contact Enquire (0845 123 2303).

Wales – *Information for parents and carers of children and young people who may have special educational needs*, a free guide available from the National Assembly Publication Centre (029 2082 3683).

to income-related ESA, less any Class 1 national insurance contributions, tax and half of any contributions you make towards an occupational or personal pension scheme.

ESA Regs, regs 80 & 95(2)(b) & Sch 8, paras 1 & 4

Maternity allowance – You can claim or continue to receive ESA while you are on maternity allowance, as long as you continue to satisfy the basic conditions for the benefit. Contributory ESA and maternity allowance overlap, so you are paid whichever is higher. Maternity allowance is treated in full as income with respect to income-related ESA. You are automatically treated as having a limited capability for work while you are entitled to maternity allowance.

ESA Regs, reg 20(e)

If you are not entitled to SMP or maternity allowance

You may be entitled to ESA from six weeks before the week the baby is due, up to two weeks after the birth if you satisfy the basic conditions for it (see Chapter 9(9)). You need your MAT B1 but not medical certificates, nor do you have to pass the limited capability for work assessment (see Chapter 10(2)).

You may be able to get ESA outside of these weeks, but you must usually pass the limited capability for work assessment and satisfy the basic conditions. You do not have to pass the limited capability for work assessment during your pregnancy if there would be a serious risk to the health of you or your unborn child if you did not refrain from work (see Chapter 10(2)).

ESA Regs, reg 20(d) & (f)

9. When the baby is born

Claim child benefit (see Chapter 38).

A new baby may entitle you to child tax credit (CTC) for the first time. If you are already getting this, your entitlement will increase from the date of birth if you notify HMRC within three months. See Chapter 18.

Tell your local authority housing benefit section. A new baby may mean you can get more help, or qualify for the first time for housing benefit or council tax benefit. See Chapter 20.

Your baby automatically qualifies for free prescriptions.

You have six weeks to register your baby's birth. When you register the birth, the registrar will give you form FP58 (EC58 in Scotland). You need to complete this and send it to your GP so your baby can get an NHS card.

Sure Start maternity grant – If you get certain means-tested benefits, you may qualify for the £500 Sure Start maternity grant (see Chapter 22(2)). It may also be possible to get a grant or loan from the discretionary social fund (see Chapter 23).

37 Disabled children

1. What help can you claim?

If your child is disabled, you may be entitled to benefits or services described elsewhere in this Handbook. Your right to some benefits or services will depend only on the effect of your child's disability. Your right to others will depend on your own financial or other circumstances. The benefits checklist on pages 4-5 is a quick guide to the help available. In this chapter we highlight some of the specific help for disabled children. For further information on benefits and services for children with disabilities ring the Contact a Family Helpline (Freephone 0808 808 3555).

From birth

You can register your child with the social services department. You can also apply to your local authority for an assessment of your child's special needs.

If your child is registered as blind you may get:

- a disabled child premium in the assessment of your housing benefit (HB), council tax benefit (CTB) and health benefits and a disabled child element with your child tax credit (CTC);
- a 50% reduction on your TV licence if you transfer the licence into the child's name.

There is no lower age limit in law for registering a child as blind. Apply in writing to your social services (or social work) department for registration as soon as you are given a diagnosis, or you think one likely. Contact the RNIB (see Address List) if you experience difficulty.

You may get help from the Family Fund with some of the extra costs arising from a child's disability (see 8 below).

If you get income support, income-related employment and support allowance (ESA), income-based jobseeker's allowance (JSA) or pension credit, you may be able to get a social fund community care grant (see Chapter 23). Often the needs of disabled children are given a high priority.

You may get help with adaptations in the home (see Chapter 31).

You can get vouchers towards milk, fresh fruit and vegetables if you are pregnant or have a child under 4 and get income support, income-related ESA, income-based JSA or CTC (if you do not work more than 16 hours a week and your family income is below £16,040). Pregnant women aged under 18 qualify regardless of whether they get one of these benefits. See Chapter 55(6).

From age 13 weeks

You can be paid the care component of disability living allowance (DLA) for your baby from when they are 3 months old; claim any time beforehand. See 2 below and Chapter 3. If your baby is terminally ill (Box B.4, Chapter 3 explains the legal definition), they qualify automatically for the highest rate care component and payment can begin as soon as you claim DLA after the birth. If your child has a terminal illness, you may get early access to their Child Trust Fund (see Chapter 38(7)) to buy things they need.

If your baby is awarded DLA, you may get a disabled child premium included in the assessment of your HB, CTB, and health benefits, or a disabled child element included in the assessment of your CTC. If DLA highest rate care component is awarded, an enhanced disability premium (or for CTC, a severely disabled child element) will also be included in the assessment.

If your baby is awarded DLA middle or highest rate care component you may get carer's allowance (see Chapter 6).

From 2 years

You can be paid or claim:

- vaccine damage payment (see Chapter 48);
- a Blue Badge (see Chapter 5) – normally, a child must be at least 2 years old to apply. However, you can apply for a child aged under 2 if they have a condition that means they must always have bulky equipment out of doors or be kept near a vehicle in case they need treatment;
- a special educational needs assessment – local authorities in England and Wales have a duty to identify any child who may have special educational needs. You can ask them to assess your child. If the authority gives you a statement of your child's special educational needs, it should consider reviewing this every six months. However, the statement must be reviewed at least annually. In Scotland, there are similar provisions. See Box N.1 for more information.

Education Act 1996, Part IV

From 3 years

A disabled child can be paid DLA higher rate mobility component (see 2 below and Chapter 3(18)). Claim from three months beforehand. The higher rate mobility component can give access to leasing or purchasing a car through the Motability scheme (see Box B.6, Chapter 5).

You can apply for road tax exemption if your child gets higher rate mobility component (see Chapter 5(2)).

From 5 years
A disabled child can be awarded DLA lower rate mobility component. Claim from three months beforehand. It is often awarded to children with a learning disability or sensory impairment, but any disabled child who needs extra supervision or guidance outdoors on unfamiliar routes may qualify (see Chapter 3(18)).

If you get income support, income-related ESA, income-based JSA, the pension credit guarantee credit, CTC (if you do not work more than 16 hours a week and your family income is below £16,040) or support under the Immigration and Asylum Act 1999, you are entitled to free school meals for each child attending school. You may be able to get a discretionary school clothing grant from the local authority.

If your child has to travel more than two miles to school, the travel is free. For a disabled child, you may get help even if travel to school is less than two miles. Also, local authorities have discretion to help meet a parent's travel costs if a child boards in a grant-maintained special school that is some distance from the family home.

Parental leave from work must usually be taken before your child is 5. However, if your child gets DLA, you can take parental leave up until their 18th birthday (18 weeks being the total parental leave you can take for a disabled child).

From 8 years
If your child has to travel more than three miles to school, travel is free. For a disabled child, you may get help even if travel to school is less than three miles.

From 12 years
If your child has a statement of special educational needs, the annual Year 9 review must include a Transition Plan.

From 16 years
At 16, your child can claim social security benefits in their own right (see Chapter 39) and can qualify for the lowest rate of the DLA care component on the basis of the 'cooking test' (see Chapter 3(9) and (10)). If your child stays on at school or college after 16 or attends certain types of unwaged work-based training, they may qualify for an education maintenance allowance.

2. Disability living allowance for children

Disability living allowance (DLA) provides help towards the extra costs of bringing up a disabled child. It is paid on top of almost any other income you may have and gives you access to other kinds of help. DLA has two parts:

- **a care component** – for children needing a lot of extra personal care, supervision or watching over because of their disability. This is paid at three different rates. It can be paid from the age of 3 months, or from birth for a terminally ill baby;
- **a mobility component** – a higher rate for children aged 3 years or over who cannot walk or have severe walking difficulties and a lower rate for children aged 5 or over who can walk but who need extra guidance or supervision on unfamiliar routes outdoors. The higher rate may also be paid to children getting the highest rate care component who are severely mentally impaired with extremely disruptive behaviour and to deaf-blind children. The lower rate mobility component has an extra disability test for children under 16 (see below).

Chapter 3 deals with the main rules for DLA.

DLA care component
This is payable from when your child is 3 months old if they need much more help than a non-disabled child of the same age (or from birth if your baby is terminally ill). Chapter 3 covers the DLA disability tests and other rules. The following issues are specific to children.

The *Disability Handbook* (a DWP guide – see Chapter 3(24)) gives guidance to decision makers about the care needs of children, both generally and in relation to specific disabilities. It points out that all young babies require extensive care and that mobility inevitably leads to increased supervision needs. Thus, even though your child may have had a specific disability or condition diagnosed, they will not necessarily qualify for DLA care component at that stage. What counts for the care component is the practical effect of that disability in terms of the child's needs for personal care, supervision or watching over.

Extra care or supervision needs – For a child under 16, such requirements must also be *'substantially in excess'* of what is normally required by a child of the same age, or the child must have substantial needs that non-disabled children of the same age would not have. This extra test does not apply to children who are terminally ill.
SSCBA, S.72(5)-(6) & R(DLA)1/99

Such needs might be 'in excess' of the care and supervision required by a non-disabled child because they are more frequent or take longer to attend to, or the child might need a greater quality or degree of attention or supervision. For example, a child who needs to be fed has needs in excess of a non-disabled child of the same age who just needs food cut up, even though both might need attention for the same length of time during meal times (CA/92/92). However, the *Disability Handbook* takes a different approach, emphasising the amount of attention given in addition to a normal care routine for a child of that age. It advises that attention differing in kind from that given to a non-disabled child of the same age does not necessarily involve a greater amount of attention. The difference could be important, particularly for younger children.

When comparing a child's need for supervision, the focus is on the quality or degree of supervision required compared to a non-disabled child. For example, a disabled child might need someone watching them, whereas a non-disabled child of the same age might need someone around but it would be enough if they were in another room.

The extra test demands a comparison between your child and other non-disabled children of the same age. Children obviously vary greatly so comparison is made with an 'average' child. Your child's needs are 'substantially' greater if they are outside the range of attention or supervision normally required by the 'average' child, even though a particularly needy or difficult child might need the same level of attention or supervision. You might find it useful to compare your child's needs with those of school friends or brothers and sisters at that age.

Under-1s – The guidance in the *Disability Handbook* essentially rests on the incidence of non-standard interventions or actions the child requires because of their disability. For example, all babies require feeding, but if your baby has severe feeding problems or requires feeding by tube into the stomach or vein, they are likely to qualify for the care component.

Babies with disabilities involving or requiring the following types of actions or interventions are also likely to qualify: regular mechanical suction; regular administration of oxygen; tracheotomy; dealing with a gastrostomy, ileostomy, jejunostomy, colostomy or nephrostomy. Babies are likely to qualify if they have: severe hearing or vision impairment; severe multiple disabilities; frequent losses of consciousness associated with severe fits secondary to asphyxia at birth or to rare metabolic disease; renal failure; cystic fibrosis; asthma; cerebral palsy; or if they are extremely premature.

Under-2s – If your child is not mobile, that might reduce their supervision needs, but may increase other needs or lead to other needs at a later stage (eg if you routinely have to carry your one- to 2-year-old from room to room).

Further examples are given in the *Disability Handbook* of children whose care needs may increase from age one. Likely to qualify are:

- children with brittle bones or haemophilia at risk of fractures or haemorrhage from bumps and falls;
- mobile children with hearing or visual problems who cannot respond to a warning shout or see a potential danger;
- children with cerebral palsy with impeded mobility who need their parents to change their position frequently to reduce the risk of postural deformity;
- children with severe learning disabilities who need extra stimulation to maximise their potential, or who eat undesirable substances or mutilate themselves.

Developmental delay may mean a child needs a continued level of attention more appropriate to a younger child. The guidance in the *Disability Handbook* gives a chart of 'normal' development in children up to the age of 6 as a comparison.

The guidance does not provide exhaustive advice and children with other needs may qualify. For example, it does not mention the care needs created by severe eczema/ichthyosiform erythroderma and similar skin conditions. These can sometimes involve a substantial amount of extra care – eg frequent bathing, nappy changing, applying preparations and dressings, and comforting a child whose sleep is disturbed.

If your child qualifies for the care component and it seems the condition(s) giving rise to a need for help are likely to continue, the decision maker may make an award until the child's 6th birthday to avoid undue stress on parents and enable the child's care needs to be re-assessed after the end of the first year at school. An award for a very severely disabled child with considerable and lasting care needs can be indefinite.

DLA mobility component

Lower rate – The lower rate mobility component can start from age 5. It is for people who can walk but who need someone with them to guide or supervise them most of the time when they are using unfamiliar routes. It is particularly aimed at people with visual impairments or learning disabilities, but others can qualify. For example, a hearing-impaired child may need such guidance or supervision.

Children under 16 must show they need *'substantially more'* guidance or supervision than a child of the same age would require, or show that a child of the same age would not require such guidance or supervision. Although most young children need guidance or supervision in unfamiliar places, what matters is the nature and extent of your child's needs compared with another child of the same age.

SSCBA, S.73(4)

For example, if a child lacks awareness of danger from traffic and other outdoor hazards, or could not give their name and address if they got lost, or would become more disorientated or distressed than a child of the same age without a disability, all these might suggest a need for guidance or supervision beyond that normally required. A deaf child might need someone within reach watching out for them because they can't hear warnings or dangers (CDLA/2268/99). A non-disabled child may not need such close supervision.

Higher rate – The higher rate mobility component can start from age 3. It is principally aimed at those who cannot walk or are virtually unable to walk. Deaf-blind children may also qualify. There is no extra test for children to get the higher rate. See Chapter 3(18).

Children with learning disabilities who get the highest rate care component might qualify if their behaviour is extremely disruptive because of arrested or incomplete brain development (see Chapter 3(21)). However, if they don't get highest rate care component, they might still pass the 'virtually unable to walk' test (see Box B.5, Chapter 3).

Some disabled children might qualify for the higher rate mobility component at age 3 because of late development (eg in a child with learning disabilities or sensory impairments). They may, however, move down to the lower rate as their walking ability improves but they need extra guidance or supervision.

Refused DLA?

If your child is refused DLA or awarded a lower rate than you expected, consider asking for a revision. Even if you are not successful, you will get written reasons for that decision. These reasons may give you a clear picture of why the current claim failed, and may also give you some idea of the type of changes that might lead to entitlement in the future. If your child does not qualify now, they may qualify at a later stage in childhood. If, however, you feel that your child does qualify now, consider lodging an appeal. For more on revisions and appeals see Chapters 3(25) and 60.

3. Carer's allowance

If your child gets the middle or highest rate of disability living allowance care component, you may get carer's allowance for looking after them (see Chapter 6). Carer's allowance is not means tested, but if you are working you must not earn more than £95 a week (after deductions for certain allowable expenses) – see Chapter 6(5).

If you are on a low income and entitled to carer's allowance (even if it cannot be paid because you receive another benefit), you may get a carer premium included in the assessment of your income support, income-related employment and support allowance, income-based jobseeker's allowance, housing benefit or council tax benefit (see 4 below and Chapter 24(6)) or a carer addition in your pension credit assessment.

4. Low income benefits

You may be entitled to income support if your income is less than your 'applicable amount' (a set amount representing your weekly living needs) and your savings are no more than £16,000. See Chapter 14.

You are eligible for income support if you are under 60 and care for a child (regardless of their age) who gets the middle or highest rate of disability living allowance (DLA) care component. If your child doesn't get DLA at one of these rates, you can still claim income support if you are a lone parent. You are treated as a lone parent if you are responsible for a child under the age of 12 (or 10 from October 2009) (see Box E.1, Chapter 14). Normally, you cannot claim income support if you work 16 hours or more a week, but this restriction does not apply if you are eligible for income support as a carer. However, your partner must not be working 24 hours a week or more (unless they too can be treated as a carer for income support).

If you are not eligible for income support, you may get income-based jobseeker's allowance (see Chapter 15). Alternatively, if you have a limited capability for work because of health problems, you may get income-related employment and support allowance (see Chapter 12). If you are aged 60 or over you will need to claim pension credit instead (see Chapter 42).

Carer premium – If you or your partner are entitled to carer's allowance, a carer premium (or pension credit equivalent) is included in the assessment (see Chapters 24(6) and 42(3)).

5. Tax credits

Child tax credit (CTC) – This is an income-related payment for people (whether in or out of work) who are responsible for children. It replaced the support for children found previously in a range of benefits, including income support (IS) and income-based jobseeker's allowance (JSA). Parents already getting IS or income-based JSA by 6.4.04 may have continued receiving support for their children through those benefits.

A disabled child element is included in the CTC assessment for each child who is registered as blind or gets disability living allowance (DLA) (see Chapter 18(4)). A severely disabled child element is included on top of the disabled child element for each child who gets DLA highest rate care component. See Chapter 18(10) for how to claim CTC.

Working tax credit (WTC) – This provides financial support for people in (relatively) low-paid work. Only certain groups of people can claim, including anyone working 16 hours or more a week who has a dependent child. See Chapter 18(10) for how to claim WTC.

6. Help with housing costs

If you rent your home, you may get housing benefit (HB) to help pay the rent (see Chapter 20), whether or not you are working. You may get council tax benefit (CTB) to help pay the council tax (see Chapter 20(10)). In each case, your savings must be no more than £16,000 (unless you receive the guarantee credit of pension credit).

The assessment for HB or CTB will include:

- a disabled child premium for each child who is registered as blind or who gets disability living allowance (DLA) at any rate;
- an enhanced disability premium for each child who gets DLA highest rate care component;
- a carer premium if you or your partner are entitled to carer's allowance.

You may get a reduction in your council tax bill through the Disability Reduction scheme if your child uses a wheelchair indoors or needs an extra room because of their disability (see Chapter 21(8)). There is no test of income and capital.

Income support, income-based jobseeker's allowance, income-related employment and support allowance and the guarantee credit of pension credit can all include help with mortgage interest payments and interest on a loan used to adapt your home for the special needs of your disabled child (see Chapter 25). If you need adaptations in the home, check first to see if you can get help from social services (Chapter 28) or a disabled facilities grant from your local housing authority (Chapter 31) or an improvement grant in Scotland (see Box K.4, Chapter 31). A disabled facilities grant to meet the needs of a disabled child in England, Wales or Northern Ireland is not means tested.

7. Child support

If you receive child support maintenance from your ex-partner it may affect some of the means-tested benefits you receive, although it is ignored for housing benefit and council tax benefit. For details, see Chapter 26(8).

8. The Family Fund

The purpose of the Family Fund is to ease the stress on families arising from the day-to-day care of a severely disabled child by providing grants and information. It is an independent charity financed by the Government.

Do you qualify? – You can apply for help from the Fund if you are caring at home for a severely disabled child under the age of 18 in England and Wales (or 17 in Scotland and Northern Ireland). The Fund is discretionary but works within general guidelines agreed with the Department of Health, and your financial circumstances will be taken into account. You cannot get help for a child who is in local authority care.

What kind of help is there? – The Family Fund cannot help with items that should be available from your health or local authority but can complement that support. It can help with:

- holidays or leisure activities for the whole family;
- a washing machine or tumble dryer if a child causes extra washing;
- bedding and clothing if there is extra wear and tear;
- transport expenses if the child does not get higher rate disability living allowance mobility component but has difficulty getting around;
- driving lessons for the child's main carer;
- play equipment related to the child's special needs.

The Fund will also consider other things related to the care of the child.

Applying to the Family Fund – You can get an application form from the Family Fund, Unit 4, Alpha Court, Monks Cross Drive, York YO32 9WN (0845 130 4542), or apply online (www.familyfund.org.uk). The Fund may ask one of their visitors to arrange to see you if it is the first time you've applied. The visitor will discuss your application with you in greater detail. If you wish to appeal against a decision or make a complaint, you can write to the Chief Executive.

38 Child benefit

1. Who gets it?

You can get child benefit if you are responsible for a dependent child or qualifying young person and you pass the residence and presence tests (see Chapter 50(2) and (3)). There is no lower age limit for the child. Child benefit is tax free and does not depend on your income or savings or whether you stay at home with the child. You do not have to be the parent. It is administered by HMRC.

Dependent child – This is a child under the age of 16.

Qualifying young person – This is a young person under the age of 20 and in full-time, non-advanced education (ie more than 12 hours a week at school or college) or approved, unwaged training (eg through 'Entry to employment' or Skillseekers). The training must not be provided under a contract of employment. Nineteen-year-olds can only be included if they started such education or approved training before their 19th birthday (or were accepted or enrolled to undertake it). You cannot count homework, private study, unsupervised study or meal breaks towards the 12 hours and the education can only be up to and including A-level, NVQ Level 3 or equivalent. If the young person becomes entitled to employment and support allowance, income support, income-based jobseeker's allowance, incapacity benefit or any tax credit, you cannot get child benefit for them.

SSCBA, S.142 & CB Regs, regs 1, 2, 3 & 8

What happens when the young person leaves school?

If the young person has left school, college or approved unwaged training you can continue to be entitled to child benefit for them until the first Sunday after the 'terminal date', which is the first of the following dates after the young person's education or approved training ceases: the last day in February, May, August or November.

Child benefit extension period – When a 16/17-year-old ceases education or approved training, you may continue to be entitled to child benefit during what is called the 'child benefit extension period' (CBEP). The CBEP starts from the first day of the week after that in which the young person ceased to be in education or training. It lasts for 20 weeks. To be entitled to child benefit during the CBEP you:

- must write and ask for benefit to continue within three months of the education or training finishing; *and*

- must have been entitled to child benefit before the CBEP began because the young person was still in full-time education or approved training.

The young person must be:

- under 18 and not in education or training; *and*
- registered at a Careers Office, Connexions Service, Education & Library Board or the Ministry of Defence for work, education or training; *and*
- not working for 24 hours or more a week.

CB Regs, regs 5 & 7

Other conditions

You cannot get child benefit if the young person is on a course of education higher than A level or the approved training is provided under a contract of employment.

You may not be able to get child benefit if:

- the child or young person is in local authority care or in detention for more than eight weeks, unless the child or young person regularly stays with you for at least one day each week (midnight to midnight). But you can get child benefit if the child or young person is home for seven consecutive days plus an extra one week's benefit if they are at home for at least one day at the end of that seven days;
- you get an allowance as a foster carer or prospective adopter to a child or young person placed with you by a local authority;
- the young person is married, in a civil partnership or cohabiting.

SSCBA, Sch 9, paras 1-3 & CB Regs, regs 12, 13 & 16

2. How much do you get?

Child benefit	per week
Only/eldest child or qualifying young person	£20
Each other child or qualifying young person	£13.20

Does anything affect what you get?

Child benefit is counted in full as income when your resources are calculated for entitlement to housing benefit and council tax benefit. It is ignored when calculating entitlement to income-related employment and support allowance, income support and income-based jobseeker's allowance (unless your claim for one of the latter two benefits began before April 2004 and you continue to receive support for your children through it). It is ignored when calculating entitlement to working tax credit and child tax credit.

Child dependants' additions – If you are still entitled to a child dependant's addition with another benefit, the addition is reduced to £8.20 if you get the higher £20 rate of child benefit for that child or young person.

3. Who should claim it?

The person responsible for the child or young person must make the claim and must be living with them or be contributing at least the rate of child benefit for their support.

SSCBA, S.143(1)

People who get child benefit for a child under 16 are entitled to home responsibilities protection (see Chapter 44). This can protect the amount of state pension you may get when you retire. So if your national insurance contribution record is affected because you are bringing up children, it is important that you claim child benefit. More than one person can be entitled to child benefit for the same child, but only one person can be paid.

4. How do you claim?

Just after your baby is born you should receive an information pack, sometimes called a Bounty Pack, containing a child benefit claim-pack. If you don't receive one, you can get a CH2 claim-form by ringing the Child Benefit Helpline (see below) or downloading one (from www.hmrc.gov.uk).

You will be asked to send the birth or adoption certificate with the form, but do not wait. You can send certificates later. Send everything to the Child Benefit Office (see inside back cover). Don't delay making your claim. It can only be backdated for three months from the date HMRC receives it.

For more information contact the Child Benefit Helpline (0845 302 1444; textphone 0845 302 1474).

5. What happens after you claim?

The birth or adoption certificate will be returned to you within a short time and you will be sent a written decision on your claim. Benefit is normally paid 4-weekly in arrears, unless this would cause 'hardship'; in this case you must write to HMRC to say why you want weekly payments. You have the choice of payment into a bank or building society account or into a Post Office card account (see Chapter 59(5)).

If your claim isn't successful or is stopped later, you can appeal against the decision (see Chapter 60).

6. Guardian's allowance

This is a tax-free benefit for anyone looking after children who are effectively orphans. You can get guardian's allowance if you are responsible for a child who is not your birth or adopted child and both parents of the child are dead, or one is dead and the other is:

- missing; *or*
- divorced or out of a civil partnership and liable for neither custody or maintenance of the child; *or*
- serving a prison sentence of more than two years from the date the other parent dies; *or*
- detained in a hospital under certain sections of the Mental Health Act 1983.

SSCBA, S.77(2) & Guardian's Allowance (Gen.) Regs, regs 6 & 7

The benefit is £14.10 a week and does not depend on your income or savings or whether you have paid national insurance contributions. Claim on form BG1 and send it to the Guardian's Allowance Unit at the Child Benefit Office.

7. Child Trust Fund

The Child Trust Fund (CTF) is a long-term savings and investment scheme which aims to make sure every child has savings at the age of 18, and to encourage the habit and teach children the benefits of saving.

Who is eligible? – Every child born on or after 1.9.02 is eligible for the CTF, provided:

- you receive child benefit for them; *and*
- they live in the UK; *and*
- they are not subject to immigration controls.

How much does your child get? – You will be sent a voucher for £250 to start the account. Children in families receiving child tax credit, with a household income below £16,040, will receive an additional £250. A further payment will be made when your child is 7. Annual payments of £100 are added to the CTF accounts of disabled children and £200 to the CTF accounts of severely disabled children.

Other features – Parents can choose the type of account they want for their child. If an account is not opened before the voucher expires (usually 12 months from issue), HMRC will open a stakeholder CTF account for that child. Families and friends can contribute to the CTF up to a maximum of £1,200 each year. The fund and any income or gain is tax free. Money cannot be taken out of the account until the child turns 18, unless they are terminally ill. Once they reach the age of 18, only the child can withdraw the money and they will have full control of how to use it.

Child Trust Fund Regs 2004

39 Young disabled people

1. Becoming a claimant

At 16 you can claim benefits in your own right, even if you are still at school. If your parents are still entitled to child benefit and child tax credit for you as a 'qualifying young person' (see Chapter 38(1)) these payments will stop if you claim employment and support allowance, jobseeker's allowance, income support, carer's allowance or tax credits. It is important to get a 'better-off' calculation, as you and your family may be worse off overall if you do claim in your own right.

Appointeeship – If you were entitled to disability living allowance (DLA) as a child, the DWP will have appointed your parents or someone else who is responsible for you to claim on your behalf. When you are 16, the DWP will review the appointeeship. If you are mentally capable of managing your money yourself or with support, the appointeeship should end. If you are unable to act for yourself, the appointeeship will be for all social security benefits, rather than restricted to only DLA. See Chapter 59(4) for more on appointees.

Disability living allowance – DLA may be awarded for any period from six months or longer, or it can be awarded indefinitely. It will end at your 16th birthday if the decision maker thinks a renewal claim would be necessary to reconsider your care and/or mobility needs.

DLA care component and the lower rate mobility component each have an extra test for children under 16. This ends on your 16th birthday, when you no longer have to show that your care, supervision and/or guidance needs are much greater than those of a non-disabled child of the same age.

If you have to make a renewal claim at 16, be careful. Some people have lost benefit even though the disability tests become easier at 16. Don't assume that you will automatically continue to get the same rate as before. Read Chapter 3 before you fill in the claim-form.

Late claims – If you miss claiming employment and support allowance from your 16th birthday, your award can be backdated for up to three months (see Chapter 9(12)).

2. Employment and support allowance

Employment and support allowance (ESA) can be paid from your 16th birthday. Entitlement depends on getting through the work capability assessment (see Chapter 10). ESA has two separate strands: contributory ESA and income-related ESA. You may be entitled to either one or both (see Chapter 9).

Contributory ESA 'in youth' – If you are aged under 20 (or under 25 in some cases if you have been in education or training) you can claim contributory ESA without needing to have met the national insurance contribution conditions. To be paid from your 16th birthday you must submit a medical certificate from your GP that is backdated for 196 days. See Chapter 11(8) for details.

Income-related ESA – You can be paid this from the start of the claim if you satisfy all the usual conditions of entitlement, including the rules on income and capital (see Chapter 12).

ESA rates – Contributory ESA and income-related ESA basic allowances and components are generally paid at rates unconnected with of your age (see Chapter 9(8)). However, during the 13-week assessment phase, the basic allowance of ESA for 16-24-year-olds is paid at the lower rate of £50.95. During the following main phase, basic allowances and components are paid at the same rate regardless of age.

Learning-focused interviews – If you are aged 16 or 17 you do not have to attend work-focused interviews (see Chapter 9(15)) as a condition for continuing to receive ESA. Instead, you will have a learning-focused interview with a Connexions personal adviser. A specialist under-18 adviser in Jobcentre Plus will deal with decisions about waiving or deferring such interviews.

3. ESA and full-time education

Contributory employment and support allowance (ESA) and income-related ESA have different rules that determine the hours and type of education you can do.

Contributory ESA

If you are aged 16, 17 or 18, you will usually be excluded from claiming contributory ESA if you are still at school or in full-time education of 21 hours or more a week (see below). Lunch breaks, breaks between lessons, free periods, and periods of private (unsupervised) study or homework do not count. From age 19, there are no rules that limit the hours and type of study you can do. You must still meet the basic conditions of entitlement and pass the work capability assessment (see Chapters 10 and 11).

21-hour 'suitable schooling' rule – When adding up the number of hours that you study each week, you should ignore *'any instruction or tuition which is not suitable for persons of the same age who do not have a disability'*.

ESA Regs, reg 12

You need to look at what is taught and how it is taught (R(S)/87). If special teaching (eg speech practice) or special methods (eg Braille) are integrated into all lessons, you do not have to quantify the non-suitable hours precisely. It is enough if the balance of probabilities shows that any suitable hours are less than 21 a week.

If you are a young person with learning disabilities whose mental age is well below your physical age, it is probable that the whole of your course would not be suitable for a non-disabled person of the same age.

In other cases (and if you are in an integrated class with non-disabled pupils of the same age), you may have to look more closely at the nature of the course. For example, if you are a young person who is deaf and you consequently have to receive extra hours of English and maths, those extra hours are only necessary because of your deafness – so the extra hours should be ignored. The point is that you wouldn't expect to find a non-disabled 16-year-old of the same general intelligence doing those extra hours of English and maths.

The fact that you are following a GCSE course does not automatically mean the course is suitable for a non-disabled young person. The methods of teaching may make it unsuitable, or the particular course may be spread over, say, two or three years, whereas normally it would take one or two years or would be taught in that way to a slightly younger age group.

Income-related ESA

If you don't qualify for contributory ESA because of the 21-hour rule, you may qualify for income-related ESA. For details, see Chapter 12(4).

4. Existing incapacity benefits

Employment and support allowance (ESA) has replaced incapacity benefit and income support for new claimants from 27.10.08. If you were already in receipt of incapacity benefit or income support paid on the basis of incapacity on this date, you can remain on these benefits for the time being, provided you continue to satisfy the rules of entitlement (see Chapter 13(1)). If you get incapacity benefit, your age addition will reduce this year, and reductions are likely to occur in future years. This is being done to gradually align the rates of incapacity benefit and ESA (see Chapter 13(7)).

5. Income support

You can claim income support instead of employment and support allowance if you fit into one of the categories listed in Box E.1, Chapter 14 – eg if you are a lone parent with a very young child or you have caring responsibilities. If you are under 20 and in full-time non-advanced education or approved training, you can still claim income support if you are in one of the groups listed in Chapter 14(5).

40 Financing studies

1. Loans, grants and bursaries

Financial support for new students in higher education comes in the form of tuition fee loans, means-tested loans for living expenses, and supplementary grants and institutional bursaries for students in particular circumstances. See Box N.4 for more information.

Entitlement to student support depends on where you are studying and where you are from. Contact:

- Student Finance England if you live in England;
- your Education and Library Board (ELB) if you live in Northern Ireland;
- the Student Awards Agency for Scotland (SAAS) if you live in Scotland;
- your local authority if you live in Wales.

Fees – Universities and colleges in England, Northern Ireland and Wales charge up to £3,225 a year for courses.

Students from Scotland studying in Scotland on their first higher education course are exempt from tuition fees. Students from other parts of the UK studying in Scotland must pay tuition fees of around £1,775 a year or £2,825 for medical courses (2008/09 rates), but can apply for tuition-fee loans to cover all or part or their fees. Students from Scotland studying elsewhere in the UK follow the same rules as students from England, Northern Ireland and Wales regarding fees, but support will be different.

For courses started before September 2006, tuition fees are fixed at a maximum of £1,285, and grants of up to £1,285 are still available, depending on household income. If you are under 25, the level of contribution depends on your income and that of your parents. The income of a new spouse or partner of the parent you live with will be taken into account. Mature students are assessed on their own income and that of a spouse, civil partner or cohabiting partner.

Full-time loan

Eligible students can apply for student loans for living costs and tuition fees. You begin to pay back the loan once you reach a certain salary level. If you receive an amount from the maintenance grant (see below), the maximum loan for living costs you can receive will be reduced. For information about the support you might be entitled to, see www.direct.gov.uk/studentfinance.

Grants and bursaries

Maintenance grant – Grants of up to £2,906 (£3,406 in Northern Ireland) are available, depending on household income. An income-assessed special support grant of up to £2,906 is payable, instead of the maintenance grant, to students who are eligible for means-tested benefits. It will be disregarded in the assessment of entitlement to those benefits.

Institutional bursaries – Universities and colleges must provide extra bursaries to students receiving the full maintenance grant (or special support grant) if their tuition fees are more than £2,906. Bursary packages vary, but should be at least £319 a year.

Higher education grant – Full-time undergraduates in England and Wales who started their course before September 2006 can apply for a means-tested higher education grant of up to £1,000. Welsh students may be eligible for an additional Assembly learning grant; apply to your local authority. In Northern Ireland and Scotland, separate grants are available; contact your ELB or the SAAS for details.

Part-time grant – Part-time students from England, Northern Ireland and Wales on courses involving at least half the hours of a full-time course and who are on low incomes can apply for a means-tested fee grant and course grant to help with course expenses, books and travel. Part-time students from Scotland studying in Scotland can apply for a grant from SAAS towards fees and other study costs. See Box N.2 for amounts.

Supplementary grants

If you are on a designated course and funded by Student Finance England, a Northern Irish ELB or a Welsh local authority, and meet the residency criteria, you may be eligible for supplementary grants including:

- disabled students' allowances (DSAs) – see below;
- parents' learning allowance and childcare grant – for full-time students with dependent children;
- adult dependants' grant;
- travel costs (if you have additional travel costs because you must attend a clinical placement in the UK as part of your full-time course in medicine or dentistry or a college or university outside the UK as part of your course, or for Scottish students general travel costs above a certain amount).

Dependants' grants and grants for students with child dependants and travel costs are means tested but DSAs are not. While previous study may prevent you getting help with tuition fees and the higher education grant, it does not affect entitlement to supplementary grants. DSAs are awarded in the same way in Scotland, but other supplementary grants are different; contact the SAAS for details.

Disabled students' allowances (DSAs) – DSAs are not means tested. They are for additional disability-related costs of study, covering specialist equipment, non-medical helpers and general or other expenditure. Full- or part-time postgraduates in the UK can get DSAs if they do not receive an equivalent award from their Research Council (or similar organisation). For rates, see Box N.2. To receive a DSA, you will require a needs assessment to identify your extra study-related needs. Your awarding authority will advise on the process. For more information see Box N.4 and ask your awarding authority for the leaflet *Bridging the gap*.

Other financial support

Other sources of financial support may be available to those in higher or further education, including:

Access to Learning Fund, Hardship Fund and Support Fund – Funds available to students experiencing financial hardship are known as the Access to Learning Fund (England), the Support Fund (Northern Ireland), Hardship Fund (Scotland) and the Financial Contingency Funds Scheme (Wales). Contact the student support officer responsible for financial advice at your educational institution for details.

Education maintenance allowance – This is a term-time payment for eligible students of up to £30 a week, depending on household income. Students must attend school or college from Year 12 and follow a course up to level 3. There are further bonuses, depending on progress on the course.

Adult learning grant (England) – This is a means-tested allowance of up to £30 a week for adults aged over 19 and studying full time for a first full level 2 or level 3 qualification.

NHS bursaries – These are for NHS-funded places on health professional courses.

Postgraduate courses – Financial support may be available from a range of sources (eg from the Research Councils, your university or charitable trusts), depending on the subject you intend to study.

Career Development Loans – These are for vocational courses, sponsored by the Government and offered by banks. You can borrow £300 to £8,000, but if you have a poor credit rating you may not receive this support.

Charities and trusts – Trusts will not usually provide the main source of finance for a full-time course, but may give top-ups or pay for a special need. Some trusts give small grants or loans to students with disabilities who are in particular difficulty. See Box N.4 for more information.

2. Students and means-tested benefits

Chapter 39 looks at the position of disabled people under 20 who are doing non-advanced courses. Here we look at the position of disabled students who are under 20 but on an advanced course, or 20 and over and in full-time advanced or non-advanced education.

When claiming means-tested benefits, you are treated as a full-time student from the date the course starts through to the last day of the course, or earlier if you completely abandon or are dismissed from the course.

Whether your course is full time or part time usually depends on how it is classed by the institution. However, a course of government-funded further education in England or Wales is full time if it involves more than 16 guided learning hours a week. In Scotland, it is full time if structured learning packages make up the hours per week to over 16 and up to 21.

ESA regs, reg 131; IS Regs, reg 61

Part-time students – If you are eligible for income-related employment and support allowance or income support under the usual rules you can study part time.

Couples – If you are one of a couple and your partner is not a student they may be able to claim means-tested benefits in the normal way.

Income-related employment and support allowance

Chapter 12 deals with the rules for claiming income-related employment and support allowance (ESA). Full-time students can only claim if they get either component of disability living allowance at any rate.

ESA regs, reg 18

If you qualify for income-related ESA as a full-time student and are not a qualifying young person for child benefit purposes (see Chapter 38(1)), you will be treated as having a limited capability for work (see Chapter 10(2)) without having to pass the work capability assessment.

ESA regs, reg 33(2)

Income support

Chapter 14 deals with the main rules for income support. You are eligible for income support during term time and all the vacations if you fit into one of the following categories.

- ❑ You were receiving income support on the grounds of disability or incapacity before 27.10.08 *and*
- ■ your applicable amount includes a disability or severe disability premium; *or*
- ■ you have been incapable of work (or entitled to statutory sick pay) for 28 weeks (two or more periods of incapacity can be added together provided they are no more than eight weeks apart); *or*

N.2 Rates of grants and loans (2009/10)

Disabled students' allowance (DSA)

The figures shown are the maximum in each case for disability-related costs of study.

Major items (specialist equipment)	£5,161 per course
Non-medical helper	
Full-time course	£20,520 a year
Part-time course	£15,390 a year
General/Other expenditure	
Full-time course	£1,724 a year
Part-time course	£1,293 a year
Postgraduate (maximum DSA)	£10,260 a year

For postgraduate courses there is one allowance for all costs. PGCE/ITT courses are eligible for DSAs at undergraduate rates. Postgraduate study in Scotland and most Research Council-funded study includes DSAs at undergraduate rates.

Travel: Extra travel costs incurred because of disability, not normally for everyday travel costs: no maximum amount.

Student loans

Tuition fees

Tuition fees vary according to the country in which students study. Institutions in England, Northern Ireland and Wales can charge up to £3,225 a year and loans are available to cover the costs. For students entering before 2006/07, a loan of up to £1,285 is available to cover fees. Tuition-fee loans are paid direct to the institution. You must start repaying the loan in instalments after you finish the course and are earning over a certain amount. Most Scottish students studying in Scotland do not pay tuition fees for full-time courses. The graduate endowment (a fee payable by graduates after completion of their studies) has been abolished for Scottish students, including those who graduated after 1.4.07.

Living costs

Place of residence	Full year	Final year
Parental home	£3,838	£3,483
London	£6,928	£6,307
Elsewhere	£4,950	£4,583

Student grants

Maintenance grant (English students enrolled 2006/07 onwards) – Up to £2,906 payable with full grant below £25,000 income, reducing to nil above £50,020 income for new students (there is a higher upper threshold of £60,032 for 2008 entry students and lower thresholds for pre-2008 entry).

Higher education grant (2005/06 enrolled students) – Up to £1,000 payable.

Tuition fee grant (2005/06 enrolled students) – Up to £1,285 payable to cover fees.

Part-time grants – A variable grant, payable at one of three rates: for a course studied at between 50-59% of the intensity of a full-time course, the maximum is £805; for 60-74%, £970; for 75% plus, £1,210. A non-repayable grant of up to £260 can help meet the costs of books, travel and course expenditure.

Note: Grants in Northern Ireland, Scotland and Wales are different. You should contact the relevant funding body for details.

N.3 Student support and means-tested benefits

Type of student support	Counted as income
Full-time student maintenance loan The maximum loan is treated as income, whatever amount you actually borrow. If you don't apply for a loan, the decision maker will still take into account the maximum loan you could have got if you had applied. Where the parents or partner of a disabled student are unable or unwilling to meet their contribution to a loan or grant in full, only the actual contribution is taken into account. When your benefit is worked out, £10 a week of your loan is disregarded. In addition, disregard the following: a) £295 a year for travel costs from a loan (academic year 2008/09); *and* b) £380 a year for books and equipment from a loan (academic year 2008/09)	Yes
Tuition fees loan The loan is paid direct to the university	No
Disabled students' allowance and travel expenses grant	No
Childcare grant	No
Parents' learning allowance	No
Special support grant	No
Maintenance grant This counts in full as income and is divided over the same period as the student loan. If you are not eligible for a student loan, then the equivalent disregard for travel and books applies	Yes
Adult dependants' grant This counts in full as income and is divided over the same period as the student loan	Yes
Higher education grant or Welsh Assembly learning grant (old system students)	No
Institutional bursaries If the bursary is to help with course costs If the payments are for living costs	 No Yes
Nursing & midwifery bursary Fixed amounts for travel and books are disregarded. The bursary is divided over 52 weeks	Yes
Social work bursary	Yes
Postgraduate awards	Yes
Career Development Loans The part intended to cover fees/examination costs Amounts intended for everyday living expenses These parts of the loan are divided over the number of weeks of study for which the loan was paid	 No Yes

- you are claiming disabled students' allowance (DSA) because of deafness;
  These rules do not apply to new claims from 27.10.08, unless they can be linked back to an earlier claim (See Chapter 13(1)).

❑ You are a lone parent *and*
- your youngest child is aged 12 to 15 and you started a full-time course before 24.11.08. You can continue to claim income support until your course ends or until your youngest child reaches 16, whichever comes first;
- you start a full-time course between 24.11.08 and 25.10.09. You can continue to claim income support until your course ends or until your youngest child reaches 12, whichever comes first;
- you start your course between 26.10.09 and 24.10.10. You can continue to claim income support until your course ends or until your youngest child reaches 10, whichever comes first.

❑ You are on the Adult Learning Option scheme.
❑ You are a refugee on a course learning English.
❑ You have limited leave in the UK subject to 'no recourse to public funds' and have a temporary problem in getting funds from your usual source.

If you are single or a student couple (where both of you are full-time students) and you have responsibility for a child or young person, you can claim income support during the summer vacation if you are eligible under the usual rules (see Box E.1, Chapter 14). Alternatively, you could claim JSA if you are available for work (see 4 below).
IS Regs reg 4ZA & Sch 1B

Housing benefit (HB)
Most students attending full-time courses are excluded from HB until the course ends. However, you can claim HB if you:
- get income-related ESA, income support or income-based jobseeker's allowance (JSA) as a full-time student;
- have or are treated as having a limited capability for work under ESA rules for a continuous period of 28 weeks (two or more periods of limited capability can be added together if they are no more than 12 weeks apart);
- qualify for a disability premium or severe disability premium, or you have been incapable of work for 28 weeks (two or more periods of incapacity can be added together if they are no more than eight weeks apart) or you qualify for a DSA because of deafness. You do not have to be eligible for income support under the pre-27.10.08 rules to claim under these rules;
- are a lone parent with a dependent child or qualifying young person under 20;
- are one of a couple and your partner is not a student. Your partner can claim HB (the student rules will apply to your income);
- are one of a couple, your partner is also a student and you have a dependent child. You will be eligible for HB throughout the course (not just in the summer vacation as for JSA and income support);
- or your partner, are aged 60 or over;
- can get HB temporarily while waiting to return to your course after an agreed break because you were ill or had to care for someone. You can get HB once you have recovered or your caring responsibilities have ended until either the date you return to your course or the date your education establishment has agreed you can return to your course, whichever is earlier, but only for a maximum period of one year and providing you are not eligible for a student loan or grant during this time;
- you are under 19 and a full-time student on a non-advanced course (the age limit can be extended to 21 if you started the course before reaching age 19), or you

are a 'qualifying young person' for child benefit purposes (see Chapter 36(1)).

HB Regs, reg 56(2) & (6)

Living in student accommodation – If you are eligible for HB you can claim if you are renting accommodation provided by the educational establishment.

HB Regs, reg 57

Two homes – If you have a partner and have to live in two separate homes while you are on the course, you can get HB for both homes only if you are eligible for HB as a student.

HB Regs, regs 7(6)(b)

Non-dependant deductions – See below.

Council tax benefit (CTB)

If the only adult residents in your home are students, you will not be liable to pay council tax, as your home is an exempt dwelling (see Box H.5, Chapter 21). If students live with non-students, the students are disregarded for council tax purposes, which may help towards a discount (see Chapter 21(9)).

If you are liable to pay council tax, you would only be eligible for CTB as a student under the same rules as HB (see above).

CTB Regs, regs 45 & 46-56

Second adult rebate – Students liable to pay council tax can claim second adult rebate even if they are excluded from Main CTB. It is worked out in the standard way (see Chapter 20(27)).

Non-dependant deductions – If you are a full-time student living in someone else's home as a non-dependant, no deduction is made from the householder's CTB during your whole period of study, including the summer vacation. For CTB purposes, there is no deduction even if you get a job during the summer vacation. However, for HB, if you get a job (for 16 or more hours a week) during the summer vacation, a non-dependant deduction will be applied.

HB Regs, reg 74(7)(c)-(e) & CTB Regs, reg 58(7)(c)

3. The effect of a loan, grant or bursary

The way in which loans, grants or bursaries affect income-related employment and support allowance (ESA), income support, income-based jobseeker's allowance (JSA) and housing benefit depends on whether the income is intended for living costs or course costs, and on the period of time it is intended to cover. In general, loans, grants or bursaries specifically intended to cover course costs are disregarded. Course costs include tuition fees, examination fees, travel, books and equipment. Amounts intended to cover maintenance of a dependent child or childcare costs are disregarded.

Period of study – In general, loans, grants and bursaries that cannot be disregarded are taken into account over the period for which they are payable.

How your loan counts as income depends on what year of the course you are in:

- in your first year, the loan income will be disregarded until the first day of the first term;
- between your first and final year, the loan is usually taken into account from start of the first benefit week in September until the end of the last benefit week in June (42 or 43 weeks);

N.4 For more information

Student grants and loans

For copies of government guides to student grants and loans, contact:

- England and Wales: Student Support Information Line (0800 731 9133; www.direct.gov.uk/studentfinance)
- Scotland: Student Awards Agency for Scotland, Gyleview House, 3 Redheughs Rigg, Edinburgh EH12 9HH (0845 111 1711; www.saas.gov.uk)
- Northern Ireland: local Education and Library Boards or Student Finance NI Customer Support Office (0845 600 0662; www.direct.gov.uk/studentfinance)
- Wales: Student Finance Wales (0845 602 8845; www.studentfinancewales.co.uk)

For information on:

- payment of student loans and other student support, contact The Student Loans Company, 100 Bothwell Street, Glasgow G2 7JD (0845 026 2019; www.slc.co.uk)
- Career Development Loans, ring 0800 585505 or go to www.direct.gov.uk/cdl
- Access to Learning Fund, ask your student union, personal tutor or welfare office

Charities and trusts

There are a number of reference books that should be available in public libraries, including:

- *Educational Grants Directory* (Directory of Social Change)
- *The Grants Register* (Palgrave Macmillan)

The Students Awards Agency for Scotland maintains a Register of Educational Endowments covering education trusts set up in Scotland.

For a list of grant-making trusts and advice on making an application:

- *Funding from charitable trusts,* published by Skill (www.skill.org.uk; or see Address List).

Student support and benefits

For detailed information on student support and entitlement to benefits and tax credits:

- *Student Support and Benefits Handbook 2009/10*
- *Benefits for Students in Scotland Handbook 2009/10* (both published by Child Poverty Action Group).

Information for students with disabilities

Information booklets, including guides to financial assistance for disabled students and applying for DSAs, are published by Skill (www.skill.org.uk; or see Address List). There are many organisations (see Address List) that help disabled jobseekers and it is worth asking them about schemes they offer.

Careers help

Connexions and local careers services provide information and advice to people aged 13-19 (or up to 25 for anyone with a disability).

In England, Nextstep (http://nextstep.direct.gov.uk) is available to people aged 20 and over. Eligibility may depend on your qualifications. Services include information and advice on choosing a career and provision of guidance software such as Adult Directions.

For advice in Scotland and Wales, contact Careers Scotland and Careers Wales.

Contact the Careers Advice Service (0800 100 900) for information about careers, course providers, qualifications needed for particular careers, and details of where to get careers advice in person.

If you have left higher education, you can use the careers service where you studied or at your nearest university. You should be able to visit for up to three years after graduation. Prospects has an extensive graduate careers website (www.prospects.ac.uk).

Contact a disability employment adviser at your local Jobcentre Plus about further education and training.

- in your final year, the loan is divided by the number of weeks from the start of the first benefit week in September until the benefit week that coincides with the last day of your course.

ESA Regs, reg 137; IS Regs, reg 66A

Box N.3 lists different types of student support and how they count as income for assessing income-related ESA, income support, income-based JSA and housing benefit.

Other payments

Access to Learning and other hardship funds – Rules differ according to how the funds will be used.

- Payments intended to cover one-off costs count as capital.
- Payments for daily living expenses count as capital immediately, but this will be disregarded for 52 weeks. Daily living expenses can include food, ordinary clothing, rent eligible for housing benefit, fuel and water charges.
- Payments to be used on an ongoing basis and paid as a lump sum or in instalments count as income. This income will be disregarded in full unless the payment is for everyday living expenses, in which case £20 a week will be disregarded.
- Payments intended to bridge the gap before starting a course or receiving the student loan are disregarded even if they are intended to cover everyday living expenses.

ESA regs, reg 138, IS Regs, reg 66B

Voluntary or charitable payments – One-off or irregular payments are treated as capital. Regular payments are disregarded as income (see Chapter 26(7)).

Leaving early? – If you stop being a full-time student before the end of your course, a loan may continue to be taken into account but without any disregard, whether or not you repay all or part of it. Grants that must be repaid continue to be taken into account as income until you've repaid them in full or until the end of the term or vacation when you left the course.

ESA regs, reg 91(4) & 104(4)-(7), IS Regs, reg 29(2B) & 40(3A)-(3AB)

4. Other benefits

Jobseeker's allowance (JSA)

Students on full-time courses are normally excluded from JSA until the end of the course, or until they abandon it or are dismissed from it. However, if you are single or have a partner who is also a student and you are responsible for a child or young person you can get JSA during the summer vacation if you are available for work.

You can get JSA temporarily while waiting to return to your course after an agreed break because you were ill or had to care for someone. The rules are the same as for HB (see 2 above).

For details on JSA, see Chapter 15.

JSA Regs, reg 1(3D)

Contributory employment and support allowance (ESA) and incapacity benefit

In general, contributory ESA is payable during term time as well as vacations and is not paid at a reduced rate because of any grant or loan you receive. However, if you are under 19 you may be caught by the full-time education exclusion (see Chapter 39(3)).

Normally, the age limit for claiming 'contributory ESA in youth' is 20. An exception allows claims to be made until age 25 if you have left a course that you were on for at least three months before your 20th birthday (see Chapter 11(8)). If you satisfy the national insurance contribution conditions for ESA, you can claim whatever your age and entitlement is not affected by your studies.

Note: To be entitled to contributory ESA you must go through the work capability assessment. In assessing your ability to carry out the activities in the limited capability for work assessment, Jobcentre Plus will look at how you manage in your daily life, including the time you attend your course (see Chapter 10(2)). When starting a course you must declare this as a change of circumstances. This may trigger a reconsideration of your benefit, but does not necessarily mean you will lose it.

Incapacity benefit – If you get incapacity benefit because you were claiming before 27.10.08 or because you make a new claim that is linked, you can be paid while studying full time under rules similar to contributory ESA. You may have to go through the personal capability assessment until you transfer to the work capability assessment (see Chapter 13).

Disability living allowance (DLA)

DLA (see Chapter 3) is not means tested, so grant or loan income will not affect the amount of your benefit.

Note: There are no rules that restrict the hours or type of study you can do. However, starting an education course may suggest that your care or mobility needs have changed, so your benefit entitlement could be reconsidered. You may need to explain how your care needs are affected while you are in college or university.

DLA and student support – If your college or university provides care and assistance for you, it may claim some or all of the DLA care component from you towards their costs. If you are living in a residential college, your care component will stop while you are there if it counts as a 'care home' (see Chapter 3(8)).

Students in higher education requiring help with personal care can claim disabled students allowance (DSA) to cover the cost of non-medical helpers (see 1 above and Box N.2). DSA will only fund academic helpers without whom you could not follow the course. For basic personal care needs that arise whether or not you are on the course, you should apply for financial assistance from your social services department (see Chapters 28 and 29).

This section of the Handbook looks at:

Retirement

41 Benefits in retirement

1. What benefits can you get?

State pension age is currently 65 for men and 60 for women (but state pension age for women will rise to 65 between 2010 and 2020 – see Chapter 43(2)). Once you reach that age, and not before, you can get state pension but you have to claim it (see Chapter 43(6)). This chapter looks at other benefits you may be able to get at state pension age. Sometimes you need to decide whether to draw state pension or receive another benefit instead. Other benefits, such as attendance allowance and pension credit, can be paid in addition to state pension.

2. What if you go on working?

You can claim state pension at state pension age whether or not you go on working. If you put off claiming state pension, you may be able to earn extra state pension or receive a one-off taxable lump-sum payment (see Chapter 43(4)).

If you work after state pension age you will not have to pay national insurance contributions. You will need to give your employer a Certificate of Age Exception; if you make a claim for state pension shortly before state pension age, there will be information about this in the pack you are sent. Alternatively, you can get the certificate from the National Insurance Contributions Office (see inside back cover).

SSCBA, Ss.6(3) & 11(2)

Statutory sick pay – If you are employed, earning £95 a week or more, and have been sick for four or more days in a row, claim statutory sick pay from your employer. There is no age limit.

3. Employment and support allowance (ESA) and incapacity benefit

ESA – If you are receiving ESA, it will stop when you reach state pension age and you should claim state pension instead.

WRA, S.1(3)(c)

Long-term incapacity benefit – If you are receiving long-term incapacity benefit, it will stop when you reach state pension age and you should claim state pension instead.

SSCBA, S.30A(5)

Short-term incapacity benefit – If you are getting short-term incapacity benefit when you reach state pension age, it can continue to be paid. The full basic lower rate of short-term incapacity benefit for people over state pension age is £86.20, payable for the first 28 weeks of incapacity. The higher rate is £89.80 a week, payable after the first 28 weeks of incapacity. You will receive less if you do not have sufficient qualifying years for a full basic state pension. You may also receive any additional state pension or graduated retirement benefit to which you would be entitled with your basic state pension.

SSCBA, Ss.30A(2) & 30B(3)

Short-term incapacity benefit can be paid for up to a year of incapacity – either continuously or in linked periods of incapacity if the gaps are no more than eight weeks (or 104 weeks in some cases – see Chapter 16(12)). Once your short-term incapacity benefit has run out and you are over state pension age, you cannot go onto long-term incapacity benefit.

When deciding whether to draw state pension or continue to receive short-term incapacity benefit, remember that the full basic state pension is higher than the basic rate of incapacity benefit, and any personal or occupational pension above £85 a week will reduce incapacity benefit but will not affect state pension. Also, state pension, but not incapacity benefit, counts as qualifying income for the savings credit element of pension credit (see Chapter 42(4)). On the other hand, state pension is taxable, but short-term incapacity benefit is tax free for the first 28 weeks.

As long as your incapacity for work began before state pension age, you can make a claim up to three months after the day before your 60th (women) or 65th (men) birthday. You must pass all the qualifying conditions for the earlier period and you will need a backdated medical certificate.

See Chapter 13 for more details on incapacity benefit.

Increases for dependants – If you are receiving incapacity benefit you may be entitled to an increase for your spouse or civil partner once they (not you) reach the age of 60. (Before 60, you can only get an increase for your partner if you have a dependent child.) However, if your partner has earnings or receives state pension or certain other benefits you may not get the increase (see *Disability Rights Handbook* 33rd edition, page 88 for details).

4. Carer's allowance

There is no upper age limit for claiming carer's allowance but you must satisfy the usual conditions of entitlement (see Chapter 6).

If you are entitled to carer's allowance after state pension age you may not be better off due to the overlapping benefit rules. Carer's allowance overlaps with state pension, so once you reach state pension age and draw your pension, carer's allowance can only continue to be paid if your state pension is less than £53.10 a week (the rate of carer's allowance). You can be paid carer's allowance on its own, or as a top-up to state pension. Even if your carer's allowance is overlapped, it is often worth claiming because it can increase your income from pension credit, housing benefit and council tax benefit through the carer premium or carer addition (see below).

OB Regs, reg 4(1)&(5)

If you were 65 or over and entitled to invalid care allowance on 27.10.02, your carer's allowance continues even if you no longer care for a disabled person or you start earning over £95 a week (after allowable expenses have been deducted). Otherwise, you must continue to satisfy the conditions for carer's allowance in order to receive it after the age of 65.

Carer addition and carer premium – While you receive carer's allowance, or would receive it but for the overlapping benefit rules, your 'appropriate minimum guarantee' for pension credit includes a carer addition of £29.50, or your 'applicable amount' for housing benefit and council tax benefit includes a carer premium of the same amount. This means you may start receiving higher levels of these benefits when you are awarded carer's allowance, or you may become entitled to benefit for the first time.

As explained above, if you were aged 65 or over and entitled to invalid care allowance on 27.10.02 you can continue to be entitled to carer's allowance – and thus the carer addition or premium – even if you are no longer caring for the disabled person.

The carer addition or premium continues for up to eight weeks after your entitlement to carer's allowance ceases – eg if the disabled person's attendance allowance or disability living allowance (DLA) is withdrawn after four weeks in hospital. If the disabled person regains attendance allowance or DLA care component at the middle or highest rate, your carer addition or premium should resume.

SPC Regs, Sch 1, para 4

5. Severe disablement allowance

Severe disablement allowance (SDA) was abolished for new claimants from 6.4.01 onwards, so the information here only applies to people entitled to it before that date. For more information about SDA, see Box D.9 in Chapter 13.

SDA overlaps with state pension. But, if you don't qualify for state pension, or it is lower than SDA, your state pension can be topped up to your full SDA entitlement, including any age-related addition. On the other hand, you can put off claiming state pension and keep your tax-free SDA. If you would be due to pay tax on your state pension, you may be better off doing this in some situations even if your pension is a bit higher than your SDA. However, state pension, but not SDA, counts as qualifying income for the savings credit element of pension credit (see Chapter 42(4)).

OB Regs, reg 4(1)&(5)

Once you reach 65 you continue to get SDA even if you are no longer incapable of work or 80% disabled, provided you were entitled to SDA immediately before your 65th birthday. You no longer need to send in doctor's statements.

SDA Regs, reg 5

6. Attendance allowance

Attendance allowance is a benefit for ill or disabled people aged 65 or over. There is no upper age limit. Many older people fail to claim attendance allowance. Some people do not realise that it is tax free, not means tested, and can be paid on top of state pension or pension credit. Others put their problems down to 'old age' rather than disability. See Chapter 4 for full details.

7. Disability living allowance

If you are 65 or over you cannot start to receive disability living allowance (DLA). However, if you were getting DLA before you reached 65, you continue to be eligible for it if you continue to satisfy the other conditions. See Chapter 3.

If you are a war pensioner, see Chapter 46(4). There is no upper age limit for war pensioners' mobility supplement.

8. Pension credit

Pension credit is a means-tested benefit for people aged 60 or over. It has two elements: the guarantee credit and the savings credit. If your income is below a certain level the guarantee credit makes up the difference. The savings credit is for people aged 65 or over and can provide additional money to those who have modest savings.

Some people who receive the savings credit will also be entitled to guarantee credit – others, whose income is too high for the guarantee credit, may receive the savings credit only. For more on pension credit, see Chapter 42.

9. Housing benefit and council tax benefit

You may be entitled to help with all or part of your rent and/or council tax through housing benefit (HB) and/or council tax benefit (CTB). If you apply for pension credit you will be asked if you want to claim these benefits. If you are not entitled to pension credit, you may still be eligible for HB and/or CTB; in this case, claim directly from the local authority, not the DWP. See Chapter 20 for details.

10. Other benefits

Most people aged 60 and over will be entitled to a winter fuel payment (see Chapter 22(5)). There is a higher level of winter fuel payment for people aged 80 or over.

There are also other forms of help you may be able to get, such as social fund grants or loans (see Chapters 22 and 23) or help towards NHS health costs (see Chapter 55).

11. Equal treatment

The principle of equal treatment in European Community law is that men and women should be treated equally. However, Council Directive 79/7/EEC on the progressive implementation of equal treatment in social security matters excludes from its scope the age at which old age or retirement pensions are granted and also *'the possible consequences thereof for other benefits'*. Because of this directive the current difference in state pension ages for men and women is lawful.

The European Court of Justice has ruled that unequal treatment within invalidity benefit (replaced by incapacity benefit) and reduced earnings allowance is also lawful.

42 Pension credit

In this chapter we look at: page

1. What is pension credit?

Pension credit is the commonly used name for state pension credit, a means-tested benefit for people aged 60 or over. Pension credit has two elements:

- **Guarantee credit** – If your income is below a certain level, known as the 'appropriate minimum guarantee', the guarantee credit makes up the difference (see 3 below).
- **Savings credit** can be paid if you or your partner are aged 65 or over. It is intended to provide extra money for people who have made modest provision for their retirement (see 4 below).

Pension credit can meet mortgage interest payments and other housing costs. You may get housing benefit (HB) and council tax benefit (CTB) to help with rent and council tax. If you get the guarantee credit, you will be passported to full HB/CTB and may be entitled to help with health costs, such as free dental treatment (see Chapter 55), and with hospital fares (see Chapter 35). If you receive either element you may get help from the social fund (see Chapters 22 and 23) and energy efficiency grants (see Chapter 31(4)).

2. Who can claim pension credit?

To claim pension credit you must be aged 60 or over. If you have a partner, they can be younger. Only one member of a couple can claim. You are considered to be one of a couple if you are married, in a civil partnership, or cohabiting (whether with someone of the opposite or the same sex). You must be present in Great Britain (GB), habitually resident and not subject to immigration control (see Chapter 50(2) and (3)). Pension credit can be paid for the first 13 weeks of a temporary absence from GB (see Chapter 51(6)). There is no limit on the number of hours you can work, but most earnings are taken into account (see 5 below). There is no capital limit for pension credit, but capital over £6,000 will be counted as generating income (see 6 below).

SPCA, Ss.1 & 4(1)

3. Calculating your guarantee credit

Guarantee credit is calculated by comparing your 'appropriate minimum guarantee' with your income (see 5 below for how income is calculated). Your appropriate minimum guarantee always includes a 'standard minimum guarantee', which is:

Standard minimum guarantee	per week
Single claimant	£130
Couples	£198.45

Your appropriate minimum guarantee can also include:

- an additional amount for severe disability of £52.85 a week for a single person or couple if one partner qualifies (or £105.70 for a couple if both qualify), worked out in the same way as the severe disability premium (see Chapter 24(3));
- an additional amount for carers of £29.50, worked out in the same way as the carer premium (see Chapter 24(6));
- an amount for any eligible housing costs such as mortgage interest (see Chapter 25);
- a 'transitional' extra amount if you were getting income support, income-based jobseeker's allowance or income-related employment and support allowance immediately before you started to get pension credit, which was payable at a higher rate than the pension credit.

SPC Regs, reg 6 & Sch 1

Pension credit does not include any amounts for children. If you have children, claim child tax credit (see Chapter 18).

Your income, as calculated in 5 below, is compared to your appropriate minimum guarantee. If your income is less, the difference is paid as your guarantee credit.

SPCA, S.2

Example: Rashida is single and her only income is state pension of £95.25 a week. Her guarantee credit is worked out as follows:

Appropriate minimum guarantee	£130.00
Less income	£95.25
Guarantee credit	*£34.75*

4. Calculating your savings credit

Savings credit may be paid if you or your partner are 65 or over and have 'qualifying income' above your 'savings credit threshold'.

Savings credit thresholds	per week
Single person	£96.00
Couple	£153.40

Some people will receive savings credit and guarantee credit; others will receive only savings credit. The maximum amount of savings credit payable is £20.40 a week for a single person and £27.03 for a couple.The calculation is as follows:

Step 1: Work out your total income
This is the same figure used in the guarantee credit calculation (see 5 below for how income is calculated).

Step 2: Work out your appropriate minimum guarantee
Again, this is the figure used for guarantee credit (see 3 above).

Step 3: Work out your 'qualifying income'
This is your total income used to calculate guarantee credit but excluding working tax credit, incapacity benefit, contributory employment and support allowance, contribution-based jobseeker's allowance, severe disablement allowance, maternity allowance or maintenance payments made by a spouse/civil partner or former spouse/civil partner.

Step 4: Compare the 'savings credit threshold' with your qualifying income
If your qualifying income is the same as or less than the savings credit threshold (see above) you will not be entitled to savings credit. If your qualifying income is more than the threshold, make a note of the difference and go to Step 5.

Step 5: Calculate 60% of the difference from Step 4
Work out 60% of the difference between the savings credit threshold and your qualifying income. If the result is more than the maximum savings credit figure of £20.40 for a single person (or £27.03 for a couple), use the relevant maximum savings credit figure instead.

Step 6: Calculate the savings credit

- ❑ If your total income is the same as or less than your appropriate minimum guarantee, your savings credit will be the figure you arrived at in Step 5.
- ❑ If your total income is more than your appropriate minimum guarantee, you must work out 40% of the difference between your total income and your appropriate minimum guarantee. You then deduct this 40% figure from the amount you arrived at in Step 5.

SPCA, S.3 & SPC Regs, regs 7 & 9

Example: Paul is a single claimant with a state pension (basic and additional) of £100 a week and an occupational pension of £48.60 a week. Using the steps above, the calculation is as follows:

Step 1: Paul's total income is:

State pension	£100.00
Plus occupational pension	£48.60
Total income	*£148.60*

Step 2: His appropriate minimum guarantee is £130 – he does not qualify for any of the 'additional amounts'. His income is above this amount so he does not qualify for guarantee credit.

Step 3: All his income is qualifying income so his qualifying income is also £148.60.

Step 4: He compares his qualifying income with the savings credit threshold (£96 for a single person). It is higher, so he works out the amount by which his qualifying income is above the threshold:

Qualifying income	£148.60
Less Paul's savings credit threshold	£96.00
Difference equals	*£52.60*

Step 5: He works out 60% of the difference:

£52.60 x 60% =	£31.56

This is more than the maximum savings credit of £20.40 for a single claimant, so for the next step he uses that figure of £20.40.

Step 6: His total income is more than his appropriate minimum guarantee – the difference is:

Paul's total income	£148.60
Less appropriate minimum guarantee	£130.00
Difference equals	*£18.60*

He works out 40% of this difference, which comes to £7.44. He takes this figure from the maximum savings credit (the result of Step 5):

Maximum savings credit	£20.40
Less	£7.44
Savings credit	*£12.96*

Not sure if you are entitled to savings credit?

The calculation for savings credit is quite complicated and if you are not sure whether you qualify, you should apply anyway. For more information about your likely entitlement, see The Pension Service website (www.thepensionservice.gov.uk) or contact a local advice agency.

5. Income

You need to add up your income to work out any entitlement to pension credit. Some types of income, including state and private pensions are counted in full; some types of income are fully disregarded, others are partially disregarded. If you have a source of income not covered here, check with The Pension Service to see how it is treated.

In general, income is calculated in a similar way to means-tested benefits for younger people, but there are differences. Income is assessed after deduction of income tax and, in the case of people with earnings, after deduction of national insurance contributions and half of any contribution made to a private pension. Income is assessed on a weekly basis, so if you have income paid for other periods it is divided into weekly amounts. For a couple, the income of both partners is added together.

SPC Regs, regs 17 & 17A(4A)

Income generally counted in full – The following types of income are counted in full:

- state, occupational and private pensions;
- annuities and retirement annuity contracts;
- regular payments from an equity release scheme;
- war disablement and war widow's/widower's pensions (but see below for disregards);
- other types of pensions including civil list pensions and those paid to victims of Nazi persecution (but see below for partial disregards);
- most social security benefits (except those listed below);
- earnings (but see below for partial disregards);
- working tax credit;
- payments from boarders, lodgers or sub-tenants (but see below for partial disregards);
- regular payments from trust funds in most circumstances – but see below;
- maintenance payments from a spouse/civil partner or former spouse/civil partner;
- 'deemed income' from capital over £6,000 (see 6 below);
- income from the Financial Assistance scheme and Pension Protection Fund.

SPCA, Ss. 15(1) & 16(1) & SPC Regs, reg 15(5) & 16

Disregarded income – Forms of income that are completely disregarded include:

- attendance allowance, disability living allowance, constant attendance allowance and war pensioner's mobility supplement;
- housing benefit and council tax benefit;
- Christmas bonus;
- social fund payments including the winter fuel payment;
- bereavement payment;
- child benefit, child tax credit, guardian's allowance and child special allowance;
- increases for dependent children paid with certain other benefits;
- exceptionally severe disablement allowance (paid in the war pensions and Industrial Injuries schemes) and war pensions' severe disablement occupational allowance;

SPC Regs, reg 15(1)

- war widow's, widower's or surviving civil partner's supplementary pension;
- payments, other than social security benefits or war pensions, paid as a result of a personal injury that you or your partner receive;
- actual income from capital;

SPC Regs, Sch 4, paras 4-6, 13-14 & 18

- payments from your local authority social services department for personal care;
- charitable and voluntary payments (except for voluntary payments from a spouse/civil partner or former spouse/civil partner, which are counted in full); *and*
- any other type of income not specified in the legislation as being counted.

Partially disregarded income – Forms of weekly income that are partially disregarded include:

- £5 of your earnings from work if you are single or £10 if you are a couple. A higher £20 disregard applies in some situations, eg for some disabled people or carers. The rules are similar to those for other means-tested benefits (see Chapter 26(5)), but there are minor differences; for details contact an advice centre or The Pension Service;

SPC Regs, Sch 6

- £10 of the total of any income from a war widow's, widower's or surviving civil partner's pension, war disablement pension, a guaranteed income payment made under the Armed Forces and Reserve Forces Compensation scheme (including payment abated by a pension paid under the scheme), or pension paid for victims of Nazi persecution or widowed parent's/mother's allowance;
- £20 payment from a tenant, sub-tenant or boarder and, in the case of a boarder half of any payment above £20, is also disregarded. The disregard applies to each tenant and/or boarder making payments;
- if you have used the equity in your home to buy an annuity, any part of the income that is being used to pay the interest on the loan is disregarded.

SPC Regs, Sch 4, paras 1, 7-7A, 8-9 & 10

Income from trust funds

This will be ignored if the trust fund was set up from a lump sum received for a personal injury. In other situations, trust fund income is generally taken into account, but there are some exceptions for discretionary payments.

SPC Regs, Sch 5, para 16

Notional income

In some cases you can be treated as having 'notional' income that you are not actually receiving. This will apply if there is income available that you have chosen not to take – eg if you have not claimed your state pension or not drawn a personal or occupational pension that you are entitled to. You may also be assessed as having notional income if you have given up the right to an income you could have received.

SPC Regs, reg 18

6. Capital

Capital includes any savings, investments, land and property you own.

If you have capital of £6,000 (£10,000 if you live in a care home; this figure is extended to all pension credit claimants from November 2009) or less, this will not affect your pension credit. There is no upper capital limit for pension credit but if you have capital of more than £6,000 (£10,000 in a care home) you will be counted as having an extra £1 a week income for every £500 (or part of £500) over this limit. In pension credit this is officially called 'deemed income', while for other benefits the term is 'tariff income'. For example, if you do not live in a care home and you have savings of £7,050 you will be deemed to have an income of £3 a week from that capital; if you have savings of £15,300 you will have a deemed income of £19 a week. If you have a partner, your capital is assessed together, but the amount that is disregarded (see below) is still the same.

SPCA, Ss.5 & 15(2) & SPC Regs, reg 15(6)&(7)

Most forms of capital are taken into account including: cash, bank and building society savings, National Savings accounts and certificates, stocks and shares, premium bonds, income bonds and property (other than your home). However, some types of capital are disregarded (see below).

How capital is valued – Your capital is generally valued at its current market or surrender value, less 10% if there would be costs involved in selling and less any debt secured on the property.

SPC Regs, reg 19

Jointly owned capital – If you own capital jointly with other people you would normally all be assessed as having an equal share. See Chapter 27(5) for more about valuation of jointly owned property for other means-tested benefits; the position is similar for pension credit.

Disregarded capital

In working out your deemed income from capital, the following types of capital are disregarded indefinitely or for a certain period of time.

❑ **Your home and property**

- the value of your home;
- the value of any property occupied by someone who is a 'close relative' (see Chapter 24(3) for the definition of 'close relative'), grandparent, grandchild, uncle, aunt, nephew or niece of yourself or your partner, if they are aged 60 or over or 'incapacitated'. The value will be disregarded if your partner or former partner lives there and you are not estranged or divorced or had your civil partnership dissolved (eg if you have moved to a care home);
- the value of a property for up to 26 weeks (or longer in some circumstances) if: you have acquired it and plan to live there; you are trying to sell it; you are carrying out essential repairs or alterations in order to live there; or you are taking legal action so you can live there;
- the value of your former home if you left because of a breakdown in the relationship with your partner for up to 26 weeks (or indefinitely if your former partner lives there and is a lone parent);
- the following types of capital received for specific purposes are ignored for up to a year (or until an assessed income period ends if that is longer – see 9 below): money received, eg from the sale of a property, that is earmarked to buy a new home; money from an insurance policy that is to be used for repair or replacement; or money such as a loan or grant to pay for essential repairs or improvements.

SPC Regs, Sch 5, paras 1-7 & 17-19

❑ **Other disregards**

- personal possessions;
- the surrender value of a life insurance policy (although if this matures or is cashed in, the money you receive will count as part of your capital);
- the value of a pre-paid funeral;
- the £10,000 ex-gratia payment made to Far Eastern Prisoners of War or their widows, widowers or surviving civil partners;
- Second World War Compensation Payments – eg for forced labour or lost property;
- the value of the right to receive income from an occupational pension, personal pension or retirement annuity contract (although you may still be treated as possessing notional income – see 5 above);
- a lump-sum payment received because you deferred drawing your state pension for 52 weeks or more (see chapter 43(4)).

SPC Regs, Sch 5, paras 8, 10, 11, 12, 14, 22-23, & 23A

Personal injury payments and trust funds

If you or your partner received a lump-sum payment because of a personal injury, an amount of capital equal to the money you received will be disregarded. If you used the money to set up a trust fund, the value of this trust will be ignored. Payments from special trusts such as the Macfarlane or Eileen Trusts are also disregarded indefinitely or for a certain period. The rules are the same as for other means-tested benefits (see Chapter 27(6)).

SPC Regs, Sch 5, paras 15, 16 & 28

Arrears of benefits

Arrears (or ex-gratia payments) of the following benefits are ignored for 52 weeks after you get them or until the end of your assessed income period (if you have one and it is longer): attendance allowance, disability living allowance, housing benefit, council tax benefit, income support, income-related employment and support allowance, income-based jobseeker's allowance, pension credit, war widow's supplementary pensions, constant attendance allowance and exceptionally severe disablement allowance (paid under the War Pensions or Industrial Injuries schemes), child tax credit, child benefit and social fund payments. If the amount of arrears or compensation is £5,000 or more and it is paid because of official error, and you receive the payments while you are getting pension credit, it will be ignored for as long as you continue to receive pension credit. Payments under Supporting People services are treated in the same way as arrears of benefits.

SPC Regs, Sch 5, paras 17, 20 & 20A

Notional capital

If you have 'deprived' yourself of capital in order to get pension credit or to increase the amount you receive, you will be treated as still having that capital and this is known as 'notional capital'. This might occur if you gave money away to a relative in order to get more pension credit. However, you will not be assessed as having notional capital if you used your savings to repay or reduce a debt or to buy goods or services that are 'reasonable' given your circumstances – eg a decision maker might consider replacing a car to be reasonable but not buying a Rolls Royce. Any notional capital you are treated as having will reduce over time in line with the rules for other means-tested benefits (see Chapter 27(9)).

SPC Regs, regs 21-22; DWP guide to PC: PC10S

7. How to claim

You can claim by ringing the Pension Credit application line (Freephone 0800 99 1234). You will be asked questions over the phone and then told what will happen next. Or you can ring that number to get a form sent to you. You can also send the tear-off coupon in leaflet PC1L *Pension Credit*, available from Post Offices. You can download a claim-form from www.dwp.gov.uk/advisers/claimforms. Alternatively, an advice agency or local Pension Service staff can help you fill in the form, either at an advice session or through a home visit.

8. Backdating and advance claims

Normally, your pension credit will run from the date on which your written claim is received at the relevant office, or the date of a claim by phone or in person (including someone acting on your behalf) which is subsequently confirmed by a signed statement. Your claim can be backdated for up to three months if you met the qualifying conditions throughout that period.

If you will become eligible for pension credit in the future, for instance because your 60th or 65th birthday is coming up or you are about to have a drop in income, you can make a claim up to four months in advance of this change.

C&P Regs, Sch 4 & reg 4E

9. The assessed income period and change of circumstances

When you claim pension credit, The Pension Service will decide whether you are entitled to guarantee credit, savings credit or both. If you or your partner are aged 65 or over, the decision maker may also set an 'assessed income period'

(AIP) of up to five years. During the AIP you do not have to inform The Pension Service of any changes in your 'retirement provision' (see below). Unless there are likely to be changes in the next 12 months that will affect your retirement provision, the AIP will normally be the maximum allowed.

From April 2009, people aged 75 or over who apply for pension credit will normally be given an AIP that lasts indefinitely, and those whose AIP runs out after they reach 80 will not normally need to be reassessed. The indefinite AIP will not apply to someone aged 75 or over who is given a shorter AIP. Even if you are aged 80 or over there are still changes that will bring an AIP to an end, as set out below.

Retirement provision – Your retirement provision refers to any of the following that either you or your partner may possess or receive:

- capital;
- other pensions including an occupational, personal, private or stakeholder pension scheme, an overseas pension arrangement;
- regular payments from an equity release scheme;
- retirement annuity contracts or other annuities;
- payments made from the Financial Assistance scheme and Pension Protection Fund.

Changes of circumstances during the AIP – Changes in your state pension will automatically be taken into account during the AIP. So when you qualify for an age addition on your 80th birthday, or when your state pension is uprated, your pension credit will be amended accordingly. Adjustments will also be made automatically, where appropriate, to other pensions or annuity income. For example, if your occupational pension increases each April in line with inflation, this will be taken into account. In order for this to happen, you may be asked about any regular changes to your pensions when you apply for pension credit.

Other changes to your retirement provision will be ignored for the rest of the AIP. For example, if you inherit some capital or win money from Premium Bonds you will not need to inform The Pension Service. Any increase in capital or other retirement provision will only be taken into account when your AIP ends. On the other hand, if your retirement provision falls (eg your capital goes down) so that you are entitled to more pension credit, you can ask for a supersession of your award (see Chapter 60, Box T.5). The Pension Service will then reassess your retirement provision and if this is less than the figure they have been using, your pension credit may increase.

During an AIP, you must still report other changes in circumstances that may affect your benefit, including a change in earnings, moving home, a change in family circumstances or a period in hospital (see Chapter 35(3)).

When the AIP will end – Your AIP will end if:

- you marry, form a civil partnership or get a new partner;
- you stop being treated as a couple – eg because your partner dies or moves permanently into a care home;
- you or your partner become 65;
- you no longer satisfy the entitlement conditions for pension credit;
- part of your retirement provision stops being paid temporarily or the amount being paid is less than the amount due and you ask for your pension credit to be recalculated;
- you move into a care home permanently.

If a supersession results in the end of your AIP, pension credit changes from the day following the end of the period.

What if you are not given an AIP? – If you are not given an AIP, you will need to report all changes of circumstances that could affect your benefits entitlement, including changes in pensions and savings. When you receive an award of pension credit you will be advised which changes must be reported.

SPCA, Ss. 6-10 & SPC Regs, regs 10-12

10. How pension credit is paid

Pension credit is normally paid weekly in advance. But if the weekly amount of pension credit you are due is less than £1, payments may be made at intervals of up to 13 weeks in arrears. If the weekly amount is less than 10p, no pension credit will be paid unless it can be paid with another benefit. Pension credit is normally paid on Mondays, or on the day you are paid state pension, if that is different. See Chapter 59(5) for more about benefit payments.

11. Decisions and appeals.

Decisions on your pension credit claim are made by DWP decision makers based at The Pension Service (see Chapter 2). The rules for decisions and appeals are the same as for other DWP benefits (see Chapter 60).

43 Retirement pensions

In this chapter we look at:

1. State pension

The two main categories of state pension are contributory and are known as Category A and B pensions. Category A pensions are normally based on your own national insurance contribution record. Category B pensions are payable only to married women, widows and some widowers and surviving civil partners and are based on their spouse/civil partner's contribution record. Civil partners have many of the same state pension rights as spouses. Where provisions for married women and widows are currently different to those of married men and widowers, the rules for civil partners have been aligned with those for the married man or widower. When state pension age for men and women starts to be equalised in April 2010, men and women, married or in civil partnerships, will be treated in the same way.

Category D pensions are non-contributory and only payable to people aged 80 or over and who meet the residence conditions.

All categories of state pension are taxable.

For more details see DWP leaflet NP46 *A guide to State Pensions.*

2. When can you get a state pension?

You can get a state pension if you've reached state pension age (currently 60 for women born on or before 5.4.50 – but see below for how this will change from 2010 onwards, and 65 for men), you meet the contribution conditions and have made a claim. You can claim at any time from four months before state pension age. Normally, for Category A pensions, you yourself must have met the contribution conditions. You can receive a reduced-rate basic state pension if you have met the conditions to give you a state pension of at least 25% of the standard rate (see Box O.1), but the 25% rule will not apply to people reaching state pension age on or after 6.4.10. For Category B pensions, your spouse/civil partner must have met these contribution conditions.

If you do not draw your state pension at state pension age, you may get extra state pension or a one-off taxable lump-sum payment when you do start to claim (see 4 below).

Changes to state pension age – The Pensions Act 1995 introduces an equal state pension age of 65 for both men and women, to be phased in between 2010 and 2020. Women born on or before 5.4.50 can claim their state pension at age 60, while those born on or after 6.4.55 will not be able to claim a state pension until they are 65. Those born between these dates will be able to claim their state pension between 60 and 65, depending on their date of birth. The Pensions Act 2007 increases state pension age to 68 for both men and women over the period 2024-46.

3. Working and the state pension

Earnings you receive after reaching state pension age do not reduce your state pension. If you carry on working and do not draw your pension you may earn extra state pension or a one-off lump sum (see 4 below). If you have already claimed your state pension, you can give up your claim in order to earn extra state pension. You can only give up a state pension once, and cannot backdate that choice.

WBRP Regs, reg 2(1) & (2)(a)

There is an earnings limit for an increase for an adult dependant (see 4 below).

4. Contributory state pensions

Category A pension

This is normally based on your own national insurance contribution record. However, widows, widowers, surviving civil partners, divorced people and those whose civil partnership has dissolved may be able to use the contribution record of their former spouse/civil partner to help them qualify (see DWP leaflets NP45 and NP46).

SSCBA, S.44(1) & WBRP Regs, reg 8

If you have met the contribution conditions in full, you can receive a basic state pension as follows:

Basic state pension	per week
For yourself	£95.25
For an adult dependant	£57.05
For the first dependent child (tax free)*	£8.20
For each other dependent child (tax free)*	£11.35

* on claims made prior to 6.4.03

SSCBA, S.44(4) & Sch 4(Part IV)

An adult dependant can be a wife or someone looking after your dependent child, or in limited circumstances, a husband. The age of an adult dependant makes no difference. A wife can only receive an increase for her husband if, immediately before drawing a state pension, she was receiving an increase for him with incapacity benefit.

SSCBA, Ss.83-85

If the dependant is working, the increase won't be paid if they earn more in any week than their earnings limit (occupational and personal pensions count as earnings here). The earnings limit for an adult dependant is £64.30 if the dependant lives with you, and £57.05 if you do not live together (except in the case of a person who looks after your children but does not live with you, where there is no earnings limit).

Social Security Benefit (Dependency) Regs, reg 8

If your adult dependant receives income maintenance benefits, eg severe disablement allowance (SDA) or contributory employment and support allowance (ESA), those benefits will reduce or cancel out a dependant's increase to your state pension.

OB Regs, reg 10

Increases for dependent children are not payable on new claims for state pension from 6.4.03. If you have dependent children, you should claim child tax credit at the same time that you claim state pension (see Chapter 18).

Adult dependency increases will be abolished from 6.4.10. If you are receiving an increase for an adult dependant at that date, it will continue in payment until April 2020, provided you continue to satisfy the entitlement conditions.

PA, S.4

Category B pension

This is payable mainly to women over state pension age who are married or widowed, but also to some widowers and surviving civil partners. It is based on the contribution record of your spouse or former spouse/civil partner. If they had not fully met the contribution conditions, you will receive a reduced-rate state pension.

Married women – If your husband has met the contribution conditions, both of you are over state pension age, and he has claimed his own state pension, you can claim a Category B pension of up to £57.05. If he has a reduced contribution record, you will receive a proportionally reduced state pension. Your earnings received after you reach state pension age do not affect your state pension.

From 6.4.10 you will no longer need to wait until your husband has claimed his state pension before you can claim your Category B pension.

SSCBA, S.48A; PA, S.2

Married men and civil partners – You cannot currently claim a Category B pension. However, if your wife or civil partner was born on or after 6.4.50, you will be able to claim a Category B pension if they have met the contribution conditions and you are both over state pension age.

Widows, widowers and surviving civil partners – See DWP leaflet NP46 for details. If you qualify for a full Category B pension, you will get £95.25 a week.

SSCBA, S.48B

Category A and Category B pensions overlap. So if, for example, you are a married woman with a basic state pension of £30 on your own contributions, you cannot receive this in addition to £57.05 Category B pension based on your husband's contributions. Instead, your state pension will be topped up to £57.05 using your husband's contributions.

SSCBA, Ss.51A and 52

Additional state pension

Your Category A or B pension may include an additional state pension. From 1978 to April 2002 this was built up under the state earnings-related pension scheme (SERPS). In April 2002 the state second pension (S2P) replaced SERPS. If you are an employee with annual earnings above the level needed to qualify for the basic state pension, you will be contributing to the additional state pension unless you are contracted out and paying into a contracted-out occupational pension or an appropriate personal pension or stakeholder pension (see Box O.2). From 2002, some people who do not have earnings will be credited with earnings for S2P purposes (see below).

Note that an additional state pension can be paid on its own if you aren't entitled to any basic state pension. In some situations it is also payable with incapacity benefit (but only for people who previously received invalidity benefit and are covered by the transitional rules) and with the widowed parent's allowance or widow's pension.

Widows, widowers and surviving civil partners may be able to inherit part or all of their spouse/civil partner's SERPS and half of their S2P as part of their state pensions. For more information, contact The Pension Service or see DWP guide NP46.

Calculating your additional state pension – To calculate this, your earnings each year are added together (up to the upper-earnings limit, currently £844 a week) from April 1978 (or the tax year in which you reach age 16, if later) up to the April before you reach state pension age. The DWP then takes away the qualifying level of earnings for the basic state

O.1 State pension – the qualifying conditions

Entitlement to basic state pension depends on your:

- national insurance (NI) contributions;
- qualifying years; *and*
- working life.

If you reach state pension age before 6.4.10, you must meet two conditions to qualify for basic state pension.

- In at least one tax year since 6.4.75 you must have paid contributions on earnings equivalent to 52 times (50 times from 6.4.75 to 5.4.78) the lower earnings limit for that year, or paid 50 flat-rate contributions at any time before 6.4.75. You are treated as satisfying this condition if you are entitled to long-term incapacity benefit or main-phase employment and support allowance in the year you reach state pension age, or the preceding year.
- You must also have paid, been treated as having paid or have been credited with enough contributions to make at least a quarter of the years in your 'working life' count as 'qualifying years'.

SSCBA, Sch 3, para 5(2),(3),(6)&(6A)

If you reach state pension age on or after 6.4.10, these two conditions will not apply. This means you may be entitled to a pension based only on credits (ie you have not paid any contributions) and you will not need to have a minimum number of qualifying years.

National insurance contributions

From 1948 until 1975 contributions were paid at a flat rate. Between 1961 and 1975 there was also a system of graduated contributions, which give entitlement to graduated retirement benefit.

Since 1975 employees pay Class 1 contributions as a percentage of gross earnings, collected with income tax. You can also be credited with contributions – eg, you will normally be credited with a contribution for any week in which you have a limited capability for work. These credits help you pass the contribution condition for a basic state pension. Your record can also be protected by home responsibilities protection, although this will be replaced by credits from 6.4.10 (see Chapter 44).

For state pension purposes only, you may also be entitled to credits for the tax years of your 16th, 17th and 18th birthdays. Class 1 (employee), Class 2 (self-employed) and Class 3 (voluntary) contributions can all count towards your entitlement to a state pension. However, any years when you were paying the married women's reduced rate contributions do not count towards your state pension.

Chapter 11 gives more details about contributions and contribution credits.

Your qualifying years

A 'qualifying year' is a tax year in which you have paid, been treated as having paid or been credited with enough contributions for a basic state pension.

Prior to 1975, qualifying years were worked out by adding up all your stamps and dividing them by 50.

Since 1975, a qualifying year is one in which you have paid, been treated as having paid or been credited with contributions on earnings equivalent to 52 times the lower earnings limit for the year.

In the year April 2009 to April 2010, the lower earnings limit is £95 a week. However, people will only start to pay contributions on earnings above a higher level of £110 a week, the 'primary threshold'. Although they will not be paying contributions, people with earnings between £95 and £110 will still be building up entitlement to a state pension and other contributory benefits. When we refer in this book to people who have 'paid contributions' we are also including those in this position who are treated in the same way as those paying contributions.

For self-employed people and those paying voluntary contributions, the test is the number of flat-rate contributions, as it was before 1975, but divided by 52.

Working life

Your 'working life' is the period on which your contribution record is based. This is normally from the start of the tax year in which you became 16 to the last full tax year before you reach state pension age (currently 65 for men and 60 for women). Working life is therefore normally 49 years for a man and 44 years for a woman.

SSCBA, Sch 3, para 5(8)

To get a full basic state pension, about nine out of every ten years in your working life must be qualifying years. Women with a working life of 44 years need 39 qualifying years for a full basic state pension and men with a working life of 49 years need 44 qualifying years.

SSCBA, Sch 3, para 5(5)

If you do not have enough qualifying years to get a full state pension, you will get a reduced pension as long as you have at least a quarter of the qualifying years you would need for a full pension.

WBRP Regs, reg 6

The rules are changing on 6.4.10. If you reach state pension age on or after that date, you will receive a full basic state pension as long as you have at least 30 years' contributions. If you have at least one qualifying year but less than 30, you can get a reduced pension.

Working out your state pension

In most cases, you won't need to work out your entitlement to a state pension. All your records should be on the computer in Newcastle, so all you have to do is to make sure that you put in a claim. In a few cases it may be important to work out your state pension entitlement. For example, you may have worked for an employer and had full contributions deducted but find that you don't get a full state pension. This could be because one of your employers may not have paid over all your contributions – perhaps because of a bankruptcy.

If you think you are entitled to a different state pension, get in touch with The Pension Service immediately. They will check your contribution records and investigate any deficiencies.

You can check the calculation yourself. If you reach a different figure and can show that you did not connive with your ex-employer in avoiding paying the contributions, HMRC can accept those contributions you had deducted from your pay as if they had been paid over at the right time. This power covers all contributory benefits. If you have not kept all your pay slips, or a good proportion of them, you may find that HMRC will already have enough details.

State pension forecasts – To check your contribution record, you can ask for a state pension forecast if you are over 30 days away from your 60th birthday (women) or 65th birthday (men).

The forecast will give you your current state pension entitlement based on the records held by HMRC. It should allow you (with some help if necessary) to make the right decisions about your future contribution position.

To get a forecast, contact your local Jobcentre Plus office or The Pension Service and ask for form BR19, ring the State Pension Forecasting Team (0845 300 0168) or apply online (www.thepensionservice.gov.uk).

pension in each year (£95 a week in 2009/10). This leaves a surplus of earnings for each year, which are then re-valued in line with increases in average earnings.

The original formula provided a state pension based on 25% of earnings between the specified levels. However, changes were introduced to phase in, between 1999 and 2009, a reduction in the amount of additional state pension people receive. The main aim of these changes was to reduce the maximum level of SERPS from 25% of earnings to 20% for people reaching state pension age from 2009 onwards (with some protection for years up to 1987/88). However, under S2P the amount of additional state pension someone earns is calculated in a different way, providing more help to low earners. In the future, S2P will not provide a pension based on the amount you earn; instead it will become a flat-rate state pension paid in addition to the basic state pension.

SSCBA, Ss.44(3)(b) & (5)-(8) and 45

Credited with earnings for S2P – Some disabled people, carers and people with low earnings will be credited with earnings into S2P. In 2009/10 people with annual qualifying earnings of at least £4,940 but less than £13,900 will be treated for S2P purposes as though they have earnings of £13,900. You will also be treated as having earnings of £13,900 if, throughout the year, you:

- are paid carer's allowance, or would be paid it but for overlapping benefit rules; *or*
- are paid the long-term rate of incapacity benefit, or would be paid it but for overlapping benefit rules or because you do not fulfil the contribution conditions; *or*
- are paid contributory ESA that;
  - has been payable for a continuous period of 52 weeks; *or*
  - includes a support component; *or*
  - (for a man born between 6.4.44 and 5.4.47 or a woman born between 6.4.49 and 5.4.51) has been payable for a continuous period of 13 weeks following a period on statutory sick pay,

  or would be paid it but for the overlapping benefit rules or because you do not fulfil the contribution conditions; *or*
- are paid SDA (but credited earnings for disabled people getting SDA, incapacity benefit or contributory ESA are currently subject to them having paid a certain number of years of contributions on retirement, although this will not apply to people reaching state pension age on or after 6.4.10); *or*
- can get home responsibilities protection (HRP – see Chapter 44) because you are caring for a disabled person or a child under the age of six. In most cases you will automatically be credited into S2P but some people need to claim HRP (see Chapter 44), and from 2002/03 onwards you must do this by the end of the third year following the one year for which you are claiming HRP. Note that if you are a carer and have a child aged six or over, you need to claim HRP to be credited into S2P; child benefit will no longer provide this protection. As explained in Chapter 44, HRP will be replaced by a carer credit from 6.4.10.

SSCBA, S.44A; PA S.9(2) & Sch 1, Part 6, para 34(4)

For more about the additional state pension, see DWP leaflet NP46.

Contracting out – For additional state pension earned up to 5.4.97, if you were contracted out of SERPS and were a member of a company salary-related scheme, all or part of your 'additional' pension will be paid, as a *'guaranteed minimum pension'* (GMP), via your employer. If your GMP is less than the SERPS you would have received had you remained contracted in, your state pension will include any increases needed to increase your GMP in line with inflation. For GMPs accruing after 6.4.88, the employer pays the first 3% of inflation proofing.

If you were contracted out of SERPS and belonged to your company's money purchase scheme or a personal pension scheme, you will receive a pension based on the value of the fund built up (through contributions and the investment return on these). The part of the fund intended to replace SERPS is known as your 'protected rights'. If you were contracted out prior to 5.4.97, your additional state pension will be reduced by an amount that may be more or less than the pension provided by your scheme.

Since 6.4.97 there has not been a link between additional state pension and contracted-out pension schemes. Instead of providing a GMP, a contracted-out salary-related scheme has to satisfy an overall test of quality. For contributions made from 6.4.97 you will either receive an additional state pension or, if you are contracted out, an occupational or personal pension based on the scheme's rules.

Other state pension payments

Your Category A or B pension may also include:

Graduated retirement benefit – This is based on graduated contributions made between April 1961 and April 1975. However, levels of payment are low – typically less than £1 a week. Graduated retirement benefit can be paid on its own.

Invalidity addition – This may be paid if, within eight weeks before reaching state pension age (or 104 weeks if your benefit is protected under the 'welfare to work' linking rules – see Chapter 16(12)), you were receiving:

- an invalidity allowance with your invalidity benefit; *or*
- transitional invalidity allowance with incapacity benefit; *or*
- an age addition with long-term incapacity benefit.

Provided you get some additional state pension, you can get this even if you don't get any basic state pension. It is paid at the same rate as your invalidity allowance or age addition but is offset against an additional state pension or contracted-out deduction.

SSCBA, S.47

Extra state pension for deferring retirement – New rules were introduced in April 2005 to provide incentives for people who defer claiming their state pension. If you put off drawing your state pension for at least seven weeks before April 2005, your state pension (including graduated retirement benefit and additional state pension) will be increased by 1% for each seven weeks that you deferred drawing your state pension.

For periods of deferment after 6.4.05, your state pension is increased by 1% for each five weeks that you put off drawing your pension, as long as you defer it for at least five weeks. Alternatively, if you defer your state pension for at least 12 consecutive months, instead of an increased state pension you can receive a one-off taxable lump sum based on the amount of pension you would have received plus interest. (This lump sum will be disregarded for income-related benefits such as pension credit, housing benefit and council tax benefit.) If you defer for less than a year you will not receive interest payments but you can have your backdated pension paid as a lump sum. You can now defer your state pension for as long as you want to and receive extra pension or a lump sum.

SSCBA, Sch 5

You cannot clock up extra state pension by keeping another income maintenance benefit, such as widow's pension, after state pension age. An increase for an adult dependant will not be made if you defer claiming state pension. However, a married woman who has deferred her Category B pension may receive an increase to this as long as she was not receiving certain other state pensions or benefits in the meantime. Since April 2006 you can draw graduated retirement benefit without this affecting any increase for deferring a category B pension.

WBRP Regs, reg 4(1)

For more on deferring your state pension, see DWP leaflet SPD1.

Age addition – This is 25p a week for people aged 80 or over.
SSCBA, S.79

5. Non-contributory state pension

Category D pensions

This is non-contributory and is paid at £57.05 a week to people who do not have a contributory state pension. Someone who has a contributory state pension of less than £57.05 can receive a Category D pension to top up their state pension to a total of £57.05. To qualify you must be aged 80 or over and satisfy certain residency conditions. To claim, ask The Pension Service for form BR 2488.
SSCBA, S.78

6. How do you claim state pension?

Normally, The Pension Service sends you a claim-pack about four months before you reach state pension age. This will give you three options. You can ring 0800 731 7898 to make a claim over the phone or ask for a claim-form, or send in a tear-off slip to get the claim-form. A new service is being introduced whereby you can complete the claim over the phone and do not need to sign it. You can also complete a state pension claim using The Pension Service website (www.thepensionservice.gov.uk). Although normally you will be contacted automatically about your state pension, this does not always happen. The Pension Service may not have your current address, especially if you have not worked for some time. If you haven't received the claim-pack by three months before state pension age, ring 0800 731 7898 to get a pack. (This number is only for making a claim. Staff will not be able to give general information about pensions or help if you are more than four months away from state pension age.)

The state pension can be backdated for up to 12 months. Alternatively, instead of receiving backdated state pension, you may prefer to 'defer' drawing your state pension in order to receive extra state pension or a lump sum with interest at a later date (see 4 above). If you have already deferred your state pension you should contact The Pension Service up to four months before you do wish to draw it. If you have already started to draw your state pension but now wish to defer it, contact The Pension Service. You can only defer your state pension once and you cannot backdate this choice.
C&P Regs, Sch 4, para 13

O.2 Private pensions and further information

Pension options

In addition to building up a basic state pension, employees earning more than the lower earnings limit (£95 a week from April 2009) will normally be building up additional pension through the state second pension (S2P) (see Chapter 43(4)) unless they have 'contracted out' and have joined their employers' occupational pension scheme or a personal pension instead.

If you contract out of the state scheme through your employer's occupational pension, both you and your employer will pay a lower rate of national insurance (NI).

If you contract out with an appropriate personal pension or a stakeholder pension (a type of personal pension which meets certain conditions), HMRC will pay a rebate of your NI contributions to your scheme provider. Some occupational pension schemes are not contracted out of S2P, so you can build up entitlement to both types of pension, while it is also possible to contribute to other types of pensions, such as a stakeholder pension, and still be in S2P.

If you are self-employed, you will not be able to build up S2P or join an occupational pension, but you could pay into a personal pension.

Often, the best way of building up a second pension for your retirement is to join an occupational pension scheme if your employer runs one. Your employer will provide details of the terms and conditions. You can get general information about your pension options from sources such as DWP pension leaflets and other publications. However, in some cases you may need to seek professional pensions advice, especially if you are not sure whether to contract out of S2P or not.

Private pensions and social security benefits

A private pension will be counted as income for means-tested benefits such as income support, income-related employment and support allowance (ESA), income-based jobseeker's allowance, housing benefit or council tax benefit. It is also counted as income for pension credit, although it may help you qualify for savings credit. It will not normally affect your entitlement to non-means-tested benefits. However, an occupational or personal pension over certain levels may affect contributory ESA, incapacity benefit or contribution-based jobseeker's allowance and a private pension counts as earnings if your partner is claiming an increase for you as an adult dependant, or if they are claiming an increase for a child dependant. More information is given in the appropriate sections of this Handbook.

Problems with occupational, personal and stakeholder pensions

If you are a member of an occupational pension scheme or have a personal or stakeholder pension and you have a problem with your pension, ask your pension provider for details of their internal disputes procedure.

If you are not satisfied with the response or need further help or advice you can contact the Pensions Advisory Service (Helpline 0845 601 2923). They can give general information or individual advice about pension problems and may be able to help resolve the problem by taking up your case and negotiating with your provider. If the Pensions Advisory Service cannot solve your problem, they may recommend that you take your complaint to the Pensions Ombudsman.

The Pensions Advisory Service and the Pensions Ombudsman are both based at 11 Belgrave Road, London SW1V 1RB.

The Pensions Regulator is the body that regulates pension schemes. It is based at Napier House, Trafalgar Place, Trafalgar Street, Brighton BN1 4DW (0870 606 3636).

The Pension Tracing Service provides a free tracing service for people who want to contact a scheme in which they may have pension rights but do not know the contact address: The Pension Tracing Service, The Pension Service, Whitley Road, Newcastle upon Tyne NE98 1BA (0845 600 2537).

DWP leaflets

The Pension Service publishes free leaflets covering the following topics:

- state pensions;
- pension credit;
- pensions for women;
- contracting out of the state second pension;
- how to get extra state pension or a lump-sum payment (also know as state pension deferral).

You can order them by ringing 0845 731 3233 or by visiting the resources centre of The Pension Service (www.thepensionservice.gov.uk).

State pension can only start from a pay day, normally Monday for people who start to draw their state pension now. You cannot receive any state pension for days before your first pay day, even if you have reached state pension age.

7. How is state pension paid?

State pension is normally paid directly into a Post Office, bank or building society account. You can choose to receive it weekly in advance or in arrears every four or 13 weeks. If payment into an account is not suitable for you or you do not provide account details, your state pension will be sent by cheque through the post each week. See Chapter 59(5) for more on payments. If your state pension is £5 or less a week, it is normally paid in a lump sum with your Christmas bonus.

44 Home responsibilities protection

1. What is home responsibilities protection?

Home responsibilities protection (HRP) protects your basic state pension rights (and bereavement benefits for your spouse or civil partner) in certain circumstances when you have a child or you are looking after someone who is sick or disabled and you do not have enough credits or national insurance contributions in the tax year. This scheme first began in April 1978, so only the tax years after that time can be covered by HRP. From 2002 onwards it can also help you build up state second pension. HRP is not a contribution credit and does not make up a deficiency in a person's contribution record. Provisions in the Pensions Act 2007 will replace HRP with a weekly 'carer's credit' from 6.4.10, as explained below.

HRP can help you satisfy the second condition for the full basic state pension (see Box O.1), which is that nine out of every ten years in your working life must be qualifying years. The number of years in which you were awarded HRP will be deducted from the number of qualifying years you normally need for a full basic state pension. HRP cannot reduce the required number of qualifying years to less than 20 for a full pension.

SSCBA, Sch 3, para 5(7)

2. Do you qualify?

You qualify for HRP if, throughout a complete tax year, you:

- spend at least 35 hours a week looking after someone who gets attendance allowance, disability living allowance middle or highest rate care component or constant attendance allowance, for 48 or more weeks in the year (52 weeks for tax years before 6.4.88); *or*
- get income support and it has been decided that you are substantially engaged in looking after a sick or disabled person; *or*
- are paid child benefit for a child under 16; *or*
- are a registered foster carer (for tax years 2003/04 onwards).

HR Regs, reg 2(1)-(4)

3. Does anything affect the provision of HRP?

Work – Work makes no practical difference. If you qualify for HRP, you will get it if you have not paid or been treated as having paid enough national insurance contributions that tax year to count for state pension.

Change of circumstances – If you are a foster carer getting child benefit or income support for only part of the tax year but you are caring for a disabled person for the rest of the same year, you can apply for HRP for the basic pension. But if you meet the qualifying conditions for only part of that year you will not get HRP for that year.

HR Regs, reg 2(1)(c)

Married women and widows – You cannot get HRP for any tax year in which you paid or were liable to pay the reduced-rate contributions.

4. How do you apply?

If you are getting child benefit and your name is the first or only name on the letters about child benefit, or you are getting income support throughout the year and it has been decided that you are substantially engaged in looking after a sick or disabled person, you do not have to apply. Your HRP should be recorded automatically (check with your local Jobcentre Plus office that this is happening).

If you are the parent whose contributions record is affected, it is important to be the one claiming child benefit. Contact the Child Benefit Office if you wish to change to become the claimant. For tax years from 2004/05 onwards you will be treated as having entitlement to child benefit if payment has been transferred to you by a 'higher priority claimant' in the first three months of the tax year (and child benefit would have been payable to you but for the fact that it was still being paid to that other claimant).

HR Regs, reg 2(4B)

If you reach state pension age on or after 6.4.08 and you discover you were not the child benefit claimant although you were the one staying at home to look after a child, you may be able to have HRP put on your account if your partner whom you were living with cannot make use of it because they already have a qualifying year through paid contributions.

HR Regs, reg 2(2)(aa) & (5)(aza)

If you qualify for HRP in any of the other ways, or if you are covered partly by one of the conditions and partly by another, you will have to apply for each tax year you need HRP. If you get carer's allowance (and haven't kept your right to pay reduced-rate contributions – see 3 above), you will be credited automatically with national insurance contributions and may not need HRP.

To apply, complete form CF411, available from your local Jobcentre Plus or HMRC office. For tax years up to 2001/02, if HRP has not been awarded automatically, you can apply at any time, but from tax year 2002/03 onwards you need to apply by the end of the third year following the year for which you are claiming HRP.

HR Regs, reg 2(5)(b)-(c)

5. Changes from April 2010

From 6.4.10, HRP will be replaced by a weekly carer's credit that will be given for each week in which you fulfil certain caring conditions, which, broadly speaking, will be the same as those set out in 2 above for HRP. One difference is that the credit given to someone receiving child benefit will be given only for a child under the age of 12. This age limit will apply to credits for both basic state pension and state second pension. It will also be possible to get a credit if you are caring for at least 20 hours a week for one or more people who are getting one of the qualifying attendance benefits or if the level of care they need has been certified by a health or social care professional. The credits can be combined with other credits (see Box D.7 in Chapter 11) or paid contributions to make a full qualifying year, so the system will be more flexible than HRP, which is only given if the conditions are met for the whole tax year.

For people reaching state pension age on or after 6.4.10, their full years of HRP will be converted to years of credits.

P Special compensation schemes

This section of the Handbook looks at:

45 Industrial Injuries scheme

1. Who is covered by the scheme?

The Industrial Injuries scheme provides no-fault tax-free benefit for an employee who *'suffers personal injury caused after 4.7.48 by accident arising out of and in the course of'* work, or who contracts a prescribed disease while working.

SSCBA, S.94 for accidents & Ss.108-110 for prescribed diseases

You are covered by the Industrial Injuries scheme if you are working for an employer. It doesn't matter if you don't earn enough to pay national insurance (NI) contributions, or if you are too old or too young to pay them – eg a 14-year-old paper boy could be covered. Nor does it matter if the accident happens on your first day at work. What counts is that you are gainfully employed under a contract of service, or as an office-holder with taxable earnings. You will not be covered if you are genuinely self-employed or if you are a volunteer, unless the accident happens while you are doing specified types of voluntary work, eg a special constable. There is a discretion to treat someone who is illegally employed as an employed earner.

SSCBA 1992, Ss.2(1) & 96-97; EEEIIP Regs, Sch 1, Part 1 & Sch 3

You are covered by the Industrial Injuries scheme if your accident occurred outside the UK if your employer was paying NI contributions for you while you were working abroad or if you were working in a European Community country or Norway or on the continental shelf of the UK, or as a mariner or airman, or as a volunteer development worker who continued to pay UK contributions.

SSCBA, Ss.117-120

Non-employed trainees on youth or adult training schemes are covered by the Analogous Industrial Injuries scheme administered by DWP. Benefits are equivalent to those paid under the Industrial Injuries scheme.

If there is any doubt over your status as an employed earner, your case is decided by an officer of HMRC with a right of appeal to a First-tier Tribunal (Finance and Tax Chamber). It may be possible to show that you were an employee for benefit purposes (despite the tax and NI arrangements) if the real relationship between you and the contractor is that of an employee and employer. This applies in particular to building workers who are very often categorised as self-employed. Your trade union may be able to advise you.

2. Industrial accidents

If you have an accident at work you should report the details as soon as possible to your employer. Enter them in the accident book (one must be kept at any workplace where ten or more people usually work). Do this even if things don't seem serious at first. A cut can turn septic. A pain in the stomach can turn out to be a hernia. If you think the accident might have some ill-effect in future, apply to Jobcentre Plus for a declaration that you have had an industrial accident. Use form BI100A (see 6 below).

In most cases it will be clear that an 'accident' has happened and that it was 'industrial', but case law has expanded these concepts to include less obvious situations. For example, a conversation or verbal harassment could constitute an accident. Box P.1 looks at these issues in more detail and at some of the problems that can arise.

If you are in any doubt about whether you are covered by the Industrial Injuries scheme you should apply for an 'accident declaration' and claim benefit anyway. The case law is complex so always get advice if you are turned down.

For accidents before 5.7.48, DWP online booklet DB1, *A guide to Industrial Injuries Disablement Benefits* (see Box P.4), gives details of the Workmen's Compensation scheme.

3. Prescribed industrial diseases

Benefit can be paid for around 60 different diseases or conditions that are prescribed as being risks of particular occupations and not risks common to the general population. These are listed in DWP guide DB1 along with the types of occupations you must have worked in to qualify for benefit.

Provided you have worked in the relevant occupation at some time since 5.7.48, it does not matter if the disease started earlier; the date of onset can be treated as 5.7.48 (CI/17220/96). If your relevant occupation finished before 5.7.48, you may be covered instead by the Pneumoconiosis, Byssinosis and Miscellaneous Diseases Benefit scheme or the Workmen's Compensation scheme. Booklet DB1 (see Box P.4) has details.

It is up to you to claim benefit for a prescribed disease. If you have any reason to suspect that your illness is related to your work, you must ask Jobcentre Plus and your doctor for advice. If you do not, you may lose benefit. For example, few secretaries realise that they may be covered by prescribed disease A4 if they experience cramp of the hand or forearm. Similarly, welders or hairdressers with hay fever symptoms may have a claim for prescribed disease D4, allergic rhinitis.

If your disability arises from a non-listed condition that was contracted at work, you may still be able to claim under the 'accident' provisions. Case law has shown that the 'catching' of the condition can be accepted as an industrial

P.1 Accidents at work – principles of entitlement

What is an accident?

You must first show that an 'accident' has occurred. While this is usually clear cut, there are situations where it may not be immediately obvious. In CI/2414/98, for example, a conversation with a colleague causing the claimant to suffer stress and depression was accepted as an accident and the opinion given that words alone such as *'verbal sexual harassment at work [could] amount to an accident or series of accidents as might misinformation designed to shock or causing shock'*.

In most cases an accident will involve an unexpected event. But what if an expected event causes an unexpected injury? In *CAO v Faulds* (appendix to R(I)1/00), the claimant was a fireman suffering post-traumatic stress disorder after attending a series of horrific incidents. The House of Lords rejected the argument that attending such incidents was the job for which he had been trained and so could not constitute 'accidents' to him, and decided that an accident need not be an unexpected event but that the sustaining of an *unexpected* personal injury caused by an *expected* event or incident may itself amount to an accident.

Accident or process?

Problems can arise if the injury developed relatively slowly through the normal course of work. This is called injury by 'process'. If your injury developed as a result of a continuous process at work you will not be entitled to industrial injuries benefits, unless your injury is listed as one of the prescribed industrial diseases.

However, the cumulative effect of a series of small incidents, each of which is separate and identifiable, that were slightly out of the ordinary can count as an accident. But each one must have led to some physiological or pathological change for the worse. For example, in R(I)43/55 the claimant developed a psychoneurotic condition and skin disorder. He had been working near a machine that irregularly produced loud explosive reports. Any one of them could have been the start of a major explosion. It was held that each explosion was an 'accident' with a cumulative effect on his condition.

If a process has only been going on for a short time, or you have just started a new job or have had a change in working conditions, it may be easier to show you have suffered injury by accident, but each case will be a matter of fact and degree.

What about other causes of injury?

If you have a condition that predisposes you to certain injuries you can still be covered by the scheme but some aspect of your employment must have caused the injury in question.

Your claim will fail if it was pure coincidence that you had the heart attack, strain, fit, etc at work rather than somewhere else. For example, an asthma sufferer had an acute asthma attack due to fumes from a fire at work. He was covered, as it was probable that he would not have had that attack if it had not been for the fire at work.

However, this is not always clear-cut. In R(I)6/82, it was confirmed that even if an accident happens out of the blue it will count as an 'industrial' one if the activity you are doing represents a special danger to you because of something in yourself or you are also injured because of coming into contact with the employer's plant or premises (eg by falling on to the floor).

Is it an 'industrial' accident?

To count as an 'industrial' accident, it must have arisen *out of* and *in the course of* employment. The difference between these phrases is clearly shown in *CAO v Rhodes* (appendix to R(I)1/99). Here, a Benefits Agency worker was assaulted by a neighbour whom she had reported for undeclared earnings. As the worker was at home on sick leave, she was found to have had an accident out of her employment but not in the course of it. Had she been working at home on the day, the outcome might have been different.

If your accident happens during an early arrival, late stay or permitted break on the employer's premises you would probably be covered. But if you had got in early or overstayed the break purely for your own purposes (eg to have a game of snooker), you would have taken yourself outside the course of your employment.

Travelling to and from work

In the main, you are not covered if you have an accident while travelling to or from your regular workplace but you may be covered while travelling in the employer's time to an irregular workplace so that your journey can be accepted as having formed part of the work you were employed to do (see R(I)7/85). One important (but not conclusive) factor is whether you were being paid for the time spent on the journey or were able to claim overtime or time off in lieu for it. You will usually be covered if you are in transport provided by your employer. You will not be covered if your journey is for your own purposes, unconnected with your work (unless it is reasonably incidental to it).

Peripatetic workers, such as home helps, are normally accepted as covered when travelling between jobs but not when travelling to the first or from the last job.

'Emergencies'

If you have an accident while responding to an emergency, you will be covered if what you did was reasonably incidental to your normal duties and was a sensible reaction to the emergency. Besides the obvious emergencies of fire and flood, unexpected occurrences can also count.

In one case, a lorry driver delivering bricks helped move a concrete mixer out of the way and was injured. He was covered as, even though that was not a normal part of his duties, it was reasonably incidental to his work and it was in his employer's interests for him to complete his delivery quickly.

Accidents treated as 'industrial'

Some accidents can be 'treated as' arising out of work. If you have broken any rules but what you have done is for the purposes of, and in connection with, your employer's business, you will be covered if you have an accident. You may have problems if what you have done is not part of your job, but if you can show that your employer would not automatically have stopped you doing the activity in question you might succeed. You must also show that it was in your employer's interests.

You will be covered for an injury during the course of your work caused by someone else's misconduct, negligence or skylarking, by an animal or by being struck by an object or by lightning, provided you did not contribute directly or indirectly to the accident.

SSCBA 1992, Ss.98–101

A B C D E F G H I J K L M N O P Q R S T U

accident; such cases include a nursery nurse who contracted poliomyelitis from an infected child (CI/159/50) and a tinner whose frequent burns on the hands caused cysts (R(I)24/54).

SSCBA 1992, Ss.108–110; IIPD Regs

4. Common law compensation

In addition to a claim for benefit under the Industrial Injuries scheme, you may have a civil claim for personal injury against your employer. With industrial diseases, this could apply even if you did the job years ago or the employer has ceased trading; in some cases an award can be significantly more than can be claimed in benefits. You may also claim for non-listed conditions. Normally, your employer has to be partly at fault, but for some industrial diseases (eg deafness) there are no-fault compensation schemes that have been negotiated between unions and employers. The time limit for filing civil claims is three years from the date of the accident. For diseases, the three years start from the date you became aware that your disease or condition was caused by work.

You will need a solicitor. Your union may help or you can contact the Accident Line (see Box P.4). While many solicitors deal with personal injury claims, it is important to choose a solicitor who specialises in your specific condition, particularly if you have an asbestos-related disease. An advice centre may be able to advise you, or you could try the website (www.communitylegaladvice.org.uk).

For information about the way in which benefits and compensation payments affect each other, see Chapters 27(6) and 49.

For certain dust diseases including mesothelioma, asbestosis and pneumoconiosis, a lump-sum payment can be claimed under the Pneumoconiosis etc (Workers' Compensation) Act 1979 when a civil compensation claim may not be possible because the employer is no longer in business. If in doubt, claim anyway. Negligence need not be proved. You should make a claim under the Act at the same time as you claim industrial injuries disablement benefit (IIDB). Any payment made will be based on your age and the DWP percentage assessment of your disablement for IIDB purposes, but do not wait for an assessment before claiming under the Act. Posthumous claims can be made by dependants but any payment made is substantially less than is paid if the sufferer makes the initial claim. If you have mesothelioma, you can make a claim under the Mesothelioma Scheme 2008 even if your illness was not caused by work. For claim-forms and more information, ring free on 0800 279 2322.

There are special schemes in particular industries, eg mining and the NHS. Trade unions should be able to advise their members on these, as well as on benefits and other types of compensation.

5. What benefits can you claim?

Industrial injuries disablement benefit

Industrial injuries disablement benefit (IIDB) is the main industrial injuries benefit and is paid to compensate those who have suffered disablement from a *'loss of physical or mental faculty'* caused by an industrial accident or prescribed disease (see Box P.2). Your employer does not have to be at fault in any way for you to get benefit.

You can claim whether or not you are incapable of work or have had any drop in earnings. IIDB is tax free and paid on top of any earnings or other non-means-tested benefits you receive. Benefit is payable from 15 weeks after the date of the accident or the onset of the disease if your disablement is assessed at 14% or more. For some prescribed chest diseases you can get benefit if the assessment is from 1% to 13%. For occupational deafness you can only get benefit if your disablement is 20% or more.

If you are claiming for a prescribed disease (PD), the date of onset should be the date the disease started, not the date of claim. As benefit is only payable 15 weeks after this date, you should check this and challenge it if necessary. However, for occupational deafness, the law says that the date of onset must be the date a successful claim was made, and payment can start from that day. There is no 15-week waiting period for PD D3 (diffuse mesothelioma) or PD D8 and PD D8A (primary carcinoma of the lung). These three diseases are also paid at the 100% rate from the date of claim.

SSCBA 1992, S.103; IIPD Regs, regs 20(4) & 28

Reduced earnings allowance

Reduced earnings allowance (which replaced special hardship allowance from 1.10.86) was abolished on 1.10.90, but only for accidents or diseases occurring after that date. So if your accident or the onset of a prescribed disease (which must be listed before 10.10.94) occurred before 1.10.90, you can still claim reduced earnings allowance. It is tax free and paid on top of any earnings or other non-means-tested benefits you receive. See 14 below for more details.

Retirement allowance

Retirement allowance replaces reduced earnings allowance if you are already getting at least £2 a week reduced earnings allowance and not in regular employment when you reach state pension age. See 15 below for more details. Retirement allowance is tax free and paid on top of any earnings or other non-means-tested benefits you receive.

Industrial death benefit

Industrial death benefit is only payable where the death occurred before 11.4.88. Those widowed on or after 11.4.88 as a result of an industrial accident or prescribed disease are entitled to widows' benefits and, since 9.4.01, bereavement benefits, without having to satisfy any contribution conditions (see Chapter 54).

6. How do you claim industrial injuries disablement benefit (IIDB)?

You should claim industrial injuries benefits from your Regional IIDB Delivery Centre. Ring 0800 055 6688 or go to www.direct.gov.uk for details. (There is a special office for the scheme for trainees (see 1 above): ring 01977 464070 and ask for the Analogous Industrial Injuries section.) You should get claim-pack BI100A for an accident or BI100PD for any of the prescribed industrial diseases (the forms can also be downloaded from www.dwp.gov.uk/advisers/claimforms).

You have three months from the first day you were entitled to benefit (15 weeks after the accident/accepted date of onset of the disease) in which to make your initial claim. If you claim after this, benefit cannot be backdated more than three months even if you have a good reason for not claiming earlier.

There are special time limits for the following prescribed diseases.

- **Occupational deafness** – To qualify, you must have worked in one or more of the listed jobs as an employed earner for a total of at least ten years, and have a hearing loss of at least 50db in each ear, due, in the case of at least one ear, to occupational noise. If you qualify you will be paid from the date your claim is received in a IIDB Delivery Centre – and that date must be within five years of the last day you worked in one of the jobs prescribed. There is no backdating of claims.

IIPD Regs, regs 2 & 34

- **Occupational asthma** – You cannot get IIDB for occupational asthma if you last worked as an employed earner in the prescribed job more than ten years before your date of claim. But this 10-year limit does not apply if you have asthma because of an industrial accident and have been awarded IIDB for life or for a period which includes your date of claim. If you are outside these time limits, a return to a listed occupation for just one day would start the period running again.

IIPD Regs, reg 36

- **Chronic bronchitis and emphysema** – To qualify you must have worked underground in a coal mine for a total of 20 years (this includes periods of sickness absence) and have a defined reduction in lung capacity. In April 1997 the medical conditions were modified, so if your claim was refused under the old rules you should reapply. In July 2008 coverage was extended to include screen workers employed on the surface of a coal mine. The exposure must have occurred before 1.1.83.

IIPD Regs, Sch 1

7. How is your claim decided?

All decisions, including medical issues such as diagnosis and degree of disablement, are made by a DWP decision maker acting on behalf of the Secretary of State.

Accident cases

The decision maker decides whether you have had an industrial accident and if so, whether it arose out of and in the course of your work. If the decision is in your favour, you will be asked to go for a medical examination.

You will be examined by one (or possibly two) DWP healthcare professionals. They will provide the decision maker with a report giving an opinion on whether you have a loss of faculty as a result of the accident and, if so, the extent to which that loss of faculty leads to disablement and the period over which it is likely to last. The percentage assessment of your disablement can cover a past period as well as a forward one.

The decision maker will then decide your claim based on this report as well as any other available evidence, such as a letter from your GP. In practice, they will normally adopt the DWP healthcare professional's opinion.

Prescribed industrial diseases

The decision maker will decide whether you have worked in one of the occupations prescribed for your particular disease or condition and whether it was caused by that occupation. For many prescribed diseases there is a presumption in law that, unless the contrary can be proved, your condition was caused by your job if you were working in the listed occupation on the date of onset or within one month of that date. If it is decided that you do not satisfy these employment conditions, your claim will be refused. You have the right to appeal against this decision within one month.

If the decision maker decides that you do satisfy the employment conditions, you will be asked to go for an examination by one (or possibly two) DWP healthcare professionals. They will send a report to the decision maker giving their opinion on whether you have the prescribed disease, any resulting loss of faculty, the level and period of your disablement, the date of onset, and whether your disease is due to your employment. The healthcare professional(s) can obtain reports from your hospital consultant and GP if necessary. Although in deciding your claim the decision maker has to take into account all the available evidence, they will normally adopt the DWP healthcare professional's opinion.

If you are claiming for certain asbestos-related diseases or some prescribed cancers, your claim will be fast-tracked and you will be sent for an examination while the employment questions are being considered. If you are suffering from diffuse mesothelioma (PD D3) or primary carcinoma of the lung (PD D8 and D8A), an examination may not be necessary if confirmation of your diagnosis is given by your consultant, GP or specialist nurse. This is because, provided you meet the employment conditions, you are automatically assessed as 100% disabled once diagnosis is confirmed.

For some prescribed diseases you may be asked to have a particular test before being sent for an examination. For example: for occupational deafness, a hearing test; and for chronic bronchitis and emphysema, a breathing test. If the results of these tests show that you meet the particular criteria for these conditions you will be sent for an examination. If not, your claim will be disallowed. You have one month to appeal against a disallowance.

If you have had (or have) industrial injuries disablement benefit for the same disease, the decision maker may need to decide whether there has been a worsening of your condition or whether you have contracted the disease afresh. This is known as the recrudescence question.

As the questions to be decided on your claim are often complex, you should always try to get advice and help with an appeal if your claim is turned down at whatever stage. See Chapters 60 and 61.

How disablement is assessed

The DWP examining healthcare professionals(s) will give an opinion on the extent and likely duration of your disablement and must consider all the disabilities resulting from the accident or disease, including the worsening of pre-existing conditions. They will assess the disablement resulting from any 'loss of faculty' by comparing your condition with that of a healthy person of the same age and sex. For this purpose, your job and other personal circumstances do not matter. See Box P.2 for details on the principles of assessment.

The decision maker can make a 'provisional' or a 'final' assessment. A provisional assessment is reviewed towards the end of a set period and reassessed, so if your condition is taking time to stabilise, you may have a series of provisional assessments. But if your disablement is less than 14% and it looks unlikely that the current assessment can be added to any other assessments to reach the 14% minimum for payment, a final assessment will be made instead. A 'final' assessment may be for life if your disablement is considered permanent and unlikely to change appreciably, or for a fixed and limited period. In the latter case, the decision maker is effectively saying you will no longer be affected by the accident or disease after that date. This is not the same as saying there is no longer any disablement but that the causative link has been broken.

SSCBA, Sch 6, para 6

Reduced earnings allowance is only payable during the period of a disablement assessment of at least 1%. If your assessment is a final one for a limited period, it cannot be paid beyond that period. To safeguard your award of reduced earnings allowance you can either appeal against the period of the assessment or you can wait until near the end of the assessment period and ask for the decision to be superseded, on the grounds of a change of circumstances (see 10 below). As either option could result in a nil assessment you might decide to wait. But, to be safe, you should apply for a supersession before your final assessment ends because if there is a break of even one day between assessment periods you could permanently lose the reduced earnings allowance (see 14 below).

8. How much do you get?

Lump-sum gratuities – pre-1.10.86 claims

If you claimed industrial injuries disablement benefit (IIDB) before 1.10.86 and your disablement was assessed at 1% to 19%, you were paid a lump-sum gratuity (unless you were claiming for certain chest diseases for which a pension was paid). The amount of gratuity paid depended on the percentage and duration of your assessment; if it was 20% or over, you were paid a weekly pension as now.

If you were entitled to special hardship allowance, you could choose to have the IIDB paid as a weekly pension on top instead of as a lump sum. This is no longer possible, but an existing pension in lieu of a gratuity can continue (if you remain entitled to reduced earnings allowance, which replaced special hardship allowance) until the end of the period of your assessment.

II&D(MP) Regs, reg 12

A gratuity for a final life assessment lasts for seven years (R(I)11/67) when deciding if any offset is appropriate against a further award for a subsequent accident or disease or an increase in the original assessment. (For an example of how this works in practice, see *Disability Rights Handbook* 23rd edition, page 151.)

Weekly pension – claims after 1.10.86

Since 1.10.86, you can get benefit only if your total disablement is assessed at 14% or more, or at least 1% for pneumoconiosis and byssinosis.

Benefit is paid as a weekly pension. Assessments of 14-19% disablement are paid at the 20% rate. Assessments of 24% (or 44%, etc) are rounded down and paid at the 20% rate (or 40%, etc). Assessments of 25% (or 45%, etc) are rounded up and paid at the 30% rate (or 50%, etc). For pneumoconiosis and byssinosis, assessments of 1-10% are paid at the 10% rate and assessments of 11-24% are paid at the 20% rate.

Anyone diagnosed as having pneumoconiosis (PD D1) is automatically treated as at least 1% disabled and therefore entitled to benefit. As it appears (from R(I)1/96) that the DWP may have treated such claims incorrectly in the past, you should contact them if you have had a claim for pneumoconiosis turned down. Benefit can be paid back to 25.8.94 if appropriate and compensation paid for official error.

P.2 How is disablement assessed?

The legislation uses three different terms when considering disablement questions. These are:

- loss of faculty;
- disability;
- disablement.

They are each used as different concepts and must not be confused. They are not defined in the law but have been considered by the Social Security Commissioners, particularly in R(I)1/81.

Loss of faculty

A 'loss of faculty' is any pathological condition or any loss (including a reduction) of the normal physical or mental function of an organ or part of the body. This does include disfigurement, even though there may not actually be any loss of faculty. For industrial injuries disablement benefit (IIDB), the loss of faculty must be caused by an industrial accident or prescribed disease.

A loss of faculty is not itself a disability. It is the starting point for the assessment of disablement. It is a condition that is either an actual cause of one or more disabilities or a potential cause of disability. For example, the loss of one kidney is a 'loss of faculty'. If the other kidney works normally, you may not notice any problems. But you will have lost your back-up kidney, so this is a potential cause of disability in the future. Appeal tribunals have assessed the loss of one kidney (the other functioning properly) at between 5% and 10%.

Disability

A 'disability' means an inability to perform a bodily or mental process. This can be a complete inability to do something (eg walking), or it can be a partial inability to do something (eg you can lift light weights but not heavy ones). The disability must result from the relevant 'loss of faculty' to count for IIDB. Note that the availability of artificial aids may reduce the actual disability. The only reported Commissioners' decisions on this, R(1)7/67 and R(1)7/63, concerned spectacles.

Disablement

'Disablement' is the sum total of all the separate disabilities you may experience. It represents your overall inability to perform the 'normal' activities of life – the loss of your health, strength and power to enjoy a 'normal' life. There is a complete scale of assessment from 1-100% disablement. Every case is decided individually, so it is possible to give only general guidelines. Some types of disability have a fixed percentage, which can be increased or decreased depending on the circumstances of the case. These 'scheduled assessments' are listed in Box P.3. Other disabilities are assessed in relation to this list.

What is taken into account?

The assessment is done by comparing your condition (all your disabilities due to the relevant loss of faculty) with that of a person of the same age and sex whose physical and mental condition is 'normal'. The decision maker, or in practice the DWP healthcare professional who assesses you, also has to make judgements about what is normal for someone of your age and sex. For example, how much hearing loss is normal for a man of 50? At what age does it become normal to lose teeth and wear false teeth?

SSCBA, Sch 6, paras 1–3

If your condition differed from normal prior to the accident and therefore the industrial injury is more disabling than it would otherwise be, the assessment may be increased to take account of this. For example, decision makers *'are entitled to increase the disablement percentage to take account of the fact that, when disaster struck, he was blind. They are not entitled to compensate him for the blindness itself, but they are entitled to take account of the fact that a particular happening to a blind man, or somebody suffering from some other disability, may be more serious of itself than it would be in the case of a man who suffered from no disability' (Murrell v Secretary of State for Social Security* (appendix to R(I)3/84)).

The decision maker also has to consider how your condition affects you, rather than just considering what is generally true of people with your condition or taking the same drugs. Inconvenience, genuine embarrassment, anxiety or depression can all increase the assessment.

If your disablement also has a mental element, R(I)4/94 provides a useful summary of the ways in which that might affect the assessment of disablement. R(I)13/75 discusses the differences between hysteria, malingering and functional overlay. See also CSI/1180/01 and CI/1756/02.

There have been a number of cases involving stress-related conditions, which are particularly difficult to assess in relation to the schedule. CI/1307/99 is useful in this respect, the Commissioner using the tariffs for facial disfigurement and loss of sight as bearing the closest comparison in that they interfere with interpersonal communications.

The fact of your loss of earning power, or incapacity for work, cannot be taken into account in the assessment. Nor can the fact that your disabilities may lead to extra expenses. But the disabilities that lead to incapacity for work (or extra expenses) are taken into account, along with disabilities that do not affect your working capacity at all.

Percentages and amounts

20%	£28.72	**50%**	£71.80	**80%**	£114.88
30%	£43.08	**60%**	£86.16	**90%**	£129.24
40%	£57.44	**70%**	£100.52	**100%**	£143.60

Note: Lower rates apply to under-18s without dependants.

Aggregation of assessments

Disablement assessments for more than one industrial injury or disease can be added together, or aggregated, if the assessment periods overlap. This can help you reach the minimum payment figure of 14% during a common core period, so it is worth claiming IIDB for even 'minor' injuries.

It has always been possible to aggregate a provisional assessment on a pre-1.10.86 claim with assessments for any subsequent accidents or diseases but not a pre-86 assessment for which you had had a final life award and been paid a lump-sum gratuity. Case law (R(I)3/00 relying on CI/522/93 and R(I)11/67) now makes this possible. Decision makers will only aggregate if you have at least one assessment that has been made after 1.10.86. So, for example, they would refuse to aggregate two pre-86 life awards of 11% and 9% but would aggregate them if either award was increased after 1.10.86, or a successful claim for a further accident/disease was made after 1.10.86, even if it actually occurred before this date. See CI/1532/02 and R(I)4/03.

Anyone who has had a gratuity in the past and thinks that this percentage assessment is not being aggregated with any further assessment(s) should ask Jobcentre Plus to supersede any previous decision and award them a weekly pension, if this brings them to at least 14%, or to increase their existing pension to take account of the earlier assessment. Decision

The assessment doesn't just depend on your condition on the day (or time of day) you are examined. If your condition varies, the healthcare professional will work out an average assessment taking into account your good and bad spells. It is arguable that any loss of life expectancy can also be taken into account, as well as the effect of your knowledge of the nature of your disability on your life.

Scheduled and non-scheduled assessments

The scheduled assessments, listed in Box P.3, are fixed on the assumption that your condition has stabilised and there are no added complications. Other disabilities are assessed accordingly.

If your disability is not in the schedule, the decision maker *'may have such regard as may be appropriate to the prescribed degrees of disablement'*. They should try to assess your disabilities so that your percentage assessment looks right in relation to the scheduled assessments. R(I)2/06 sets out the approach to be taken by appeal tribunals to questions of assessment.

GB Regs, reg 11(8)

When you look at the schedule, remember that 100% is not total and absolute disablement. It is just the legal maximum assessment. If the scale could go higher, some people would be assessed as 200% disabled or more.

The schedule says that if you are totally deaf, or severely facially disfigured, the fixed assessment is 100%.

If you have had either arm amputated just below the shoulder, you will be assessed at 80% – even if you cope perfectly well. If the amputation has not yet stabilised, or there are other complications with it, a higher assessment can be made.

If you cannot use one arm at all, you may well be assessed at 80% – as if you had actually lost your arm. CI/1199/02 usefully illustrates this point in relation to vibration white finger (PD A11).

Several conditions

Four different disabilities due to the same accident or prescribed disease may each be assessed as causing 10% disablement, but the assessment will not always be the total of 40%. This is because the interaction of different conditions in one person may be far more disabling – so the final assessment could well be higher. If you have several of the minor scheduled conditions, the total percentage assessment could be less or more than the actual total of the percentages for each of the scheduled conditions. The healthcare professional will give their opinion on what is the appropriate assessment for you – given your age, sex and physical and mental condition as a whole. So even for the scheduled assessments, the healthcare professional may increase (or decrease) the percentage(s) if that is reasonable in a particular case.

Pre-existing condition

If your disability has some other cause, you may have problems – eg where a previous back injury is followed by an industrial injury to your back. However, your percentage assessment should only be cut, or offset, if there is evidence that a pre-existing condition would have led to a degree of disablement even if the accident had not happened. If there is no evidence for this, the offset should not be made. R(I)1/81 explains the concepts fully.

If an offset is justified, the net assessment (ie after the offset) should reflect any greater disablement because of the interaction between the two (or more) causes of the same disability. Note that a pre-existing condition may cause disablement later. Although the disablement you would have had from that pre-existing condition alone cannot be taken into account, its interaction with the effects of the industrial injury may lead to greater disablement. This could justify a request for a supersession on the grounds of a change of circumstances (see 10).

GB Regs, reg 11(3)

Conditions arising afterwards

If a condition is 'directly attributable' to the industrial accident or disease, it is assessable in the normal way. If it is not 'directly attributable', but is also a cause of the same disability, then whether or not any greater disablement can be taken into account depends on the percentage assessment for the industrial accident or disease. If the disablement resulting from the industrial accident is assessed at 11% or more, that assessment can be increased to reflect the extent to which the industrial injury is worsened because of the later condition. This can be done at the time of the assessment, or later on an application for a supersession.

Note that in reaching the 11% benchmark, account is taken of any greater disablement because of the interaction with a pre-existing condition that is also an effective cause of the disability.

The 11% rule does not apply where one is considering the interaction between two or more industrial accidents or diseases (see R(I)3/91).

The medical report completed by the DWP healthcare professional provides a useful guide to the methods of assessment if there is more than one cause of the same disability and if the interaction of another condition causes greater disability.

GB Regs, reg 11(4)

A B C D E F G H I J K L M N O P Q R S T U

makers are advised to revise on the grounds of official error or supersede if the decision was made after 24.7.95. Arrears cannot be paid back to a date earlier than 24.7.95, the date of CI/522/93 (see R(I)1/03). Decision makers should also consider extra-statutory compensation (see Chapter 62(2)) but may need to be prompted. Assessments of under 20% for occupational deafness cannot be aggregated. Aggregation of assessments (at least in pneumoconiosis or byssinosis cases) is only carried out if it is to your advantage.

SSCBA, S.103(2); IIPD Regs, regs 15A, 15B & 20; (R(I)4/03)

9. How do you appeal?

You have the right of appeal to an appeal tribunal against the Secretary of State's decision on your claim. You have one month from the date the decision was sent to you. To appeal, you should fill in the form in DWP leaflet GL24. You should

P3 Listed conditions

Prescribed degrees of disablement

Description of injury	Degree
■ Loss of both hands or amputation at higher sites	100%
■ Loss of a hand and a foot	100%
■ Double amputation through leg or thigh, or amputation through leg or thigh on one side and loss of other foot	100%
■ Loss of sight to such an extent as to render the claimant unable to perform any work for which eyesight is essential	100%
■ Very severe facial disfiguration	100%
■ Absolute deafness	100%
■ Forequarter or hindquarter amputation	100%
Amputation cases – upper limbs (either arm)	
■ Amputation through shoulder joint	90%
■ Amputation below shoulder with stump less than 20.5 centimetres from tip of acromion	80%
■ Amputation from 20.5 centimetres from tip of acromion to less than 11.5 centimetres below tip of olecranon	70%
■ Loss of a hand or of the thumb and four fingers of one hand or amputation from 11.5 centimetres below tip of olecranon	60%
■ Loss of thumb	30%
■ Loss of thumb and its metacarpal bone	40%
■ Loss of four fingers of one hand	50%
■ Loss of three fingers of one hand	30%
■ Loss of two fingers of one hand	20%
■ Loss of terminal phalanx of thumb	20%
Amputation cases – lower limbs	
■ Amputation of both feet resulting in end-bearing stumps	90%
■ Amputation through both feet proximal to the metatarso-phalangeal joint	80%
■ Loss of all toes of both feet through the metatarso-phalangeal joint	40%
■ Loss of all toes of both feet proximal to the proximal inter-phalangeal joint	30%
■ Loss of all toes of both feet distal to the proximal inter-phalangeal joint	20%
■ Amputation at hip	90%
■ Amputation below hip with stump not exceeding 13 centimetres in length measured from tip of great trochanter	80%
■ Amputation below hip and above knee with stump exceeding 13 centimetres in length measured from tip of great trochanter, or at knee not resulting in end-bearing stump	70%
■ Amputation at knee resulting in end-bearing stump or below knee with stump not exceeding 9 centimetres	60%
■ Amputation below knee with stump exceeding 9 centimetres but not exceeding 13 centimetres	50%
■ Amputation below knee with stump exceeding 13 centimetres	40%
■ Amputation of one foot resulting in end-bearing stump	30%
■ Amputation through one foot proximal to the metatarso-phalangeal joint	30%
■ Loss of all toes of one foot through the metatarso-phalangeal joint	20%
Other injuries	
■ Loss of one eye, without complications, the other being normal	40%
■ Loss of vision of one eye, without complications or disfigurement of the eyeball, the other being normal	30%
Loss of fingers of right or left hand	
❑ **Index finger:**	
■ Whole	14%
■ Two phalanges	11%
■ One phalanx	9%
■ Guillotine amputation of tip without loss of bone	5%
❑ **Middle finger:**	
■ Whole	12%
■ Two phalanges	9%
■ One phalanx	7%
■ Guillotine amputation of tip without loss of bone	4%
❑ **Ring or little finger:**	
■ Whole	7%
■ Two phalanges	6%
■ One phalanx	5%
■ Guillotine amputation of tip without loss of bone	2%
Loss of toes of right or left foot	
❑ **Great toe:**	
■ Through metatarso-phalangeal joint	14%
■ Part, with some loss of bone	3%
❑ **Any other toe:**	
■ Through metatarso-phalangeal joint	3%
■ Part, with some loss of bone	1%
❑ **Two toes of one foot, excluding great toe:**	
■ Through metatarso-phalangeal joint	5%
■ Part, with some loss of bone	2%
❑ **Three toes of one foot, excluding great toe:**	
■ Through metatarso-phalangeal joint	6%
■ Part, with some loss of bone	3%
❑ **Four toes of one foot, excluding great toe:**	
■ Through metatarso-phalangeal joint	9%
■ Part, with some loss of bone	3%

GB Regs, Sch 2

give as much detail as possible as to why you disagree with the decision. As industrial injuries benefits are complex, you may need expert advice – your trade union or an advice centre may help.

As an alternative to an appeal, you can ask Jobcentre Plus to look at your claim again; this is called a revision. However, where a medical question is involved, the decision maker is unlikely to change the original decision based on the DWP healthcare professional's report even if you provide your own medical evidence to support your claim. As the time limit for appeal is short, it may be safer to appeal straight away. (See Chapter 60 for full details of the dispute procedure.)

10. If your condition gets worse

To increase your assessment or extend the period it covers you must ask for a supersession on the grounds of a change in circumstances and, as a result, your claim will be looked at afresh. Any new assessment could be lower rather than higher. It could even be reduced to nil, which could then also involve a loss of reduced earnings allowance, although retirement allowance is not affected because it is awarded for life and not linked with any disablement assessment.

Try to get advice before applying. You should be particularly careful if you have now developed arthritis or spondylosis, as this can often lead to your disability being assessed as 'constitutional' and not due to the effects of your injury or prescribed disease.

Payment and aggregation of assessments following a supersession

If your request for an increased assessment is successful and the new percentage is 14% or more, you will get a pension. If you had been paid a gratuity for that injury in the past, as this is likely to be more than seven years ago, no offset will be appropriate (see 8 above).

If your assessment is increased but remains under 14% you will not get benefit unless you can aggregate that percentage with any other current assessment(s). In this case, the whole percentage assessment becomes available for aggregation, not just the actual increase in percentage gained. This can be added to any current assessments you may have, including any final life assessments for which you received a lump-sum gratuity.

However, the position is slightly different if you are currently getting a pension in lieu of a gratuity for the original assessment. In this case, your right to a pension in lieu will end and you will receive the balance (if any) of the original gratuity, plus the appropriate gratuity for the increase in the percentage assessment or period. Or, if your disablement is assessed at 14% or more, you will receive a pension at the appropriate rate.

II&D(MP) Regs, reg 12(3)

11. Extra allowances

The following additional allowances can be paid:

Additional allowances	per week
Constant attendance allowance	
– part time	£28.75
– normal maximum	£57.50
– intermediate rate	£86.25
– exceptional rate	£115.00
Exceptionally severe disablement allowance	£57.50
Unemployability supplement*	£88.75
(earnings limit £4,784 pa)	

* This was abolished from 6.4.87 for new claims and is only payable to existing claimants.

12. Constant attendance allowance

Constant attendance allowance is automatically considered when your disablement assessment totals 95% or more. Your need for care and attention must be as a result of an industrial accident/disease. If you think this has been missed, claim on form BI104, available from your Regional IIDB Delivery Centre. If you receive disability living allowance care component or attendance allowance, it will be reduced by the amount of any constant attendance allowance you receive.

There is no right of appeal if your claim is refused, but you can ask for the decision to be looked at again if you feel some facts were not taken into account.

SSCBA 1992, S.104

13. Exceptionally severe disablement allowance

This is automatically considered if you qualify for one of the two higher rates of constant attendance allowance. However, your need for that level of attendance must be likely to be permanent. Again, there is no right of appeal if your claim is refused. For more details of this and constant attendance allowance, read DWP booklet DB1 (see Box P.4).

SSCBA 1992, S.105

14. Reduced earnings allowance

You can claim reduced earnings allowance (REA) if your accident happened before 1.10.90 or your disease started before 1.10.90, provided the disease (or the extension to the prescribed disease category) was added to the prescribed list before 10.10.94. REA will not be paid for newly prescribed diseases or extensions to those already listed.

A claim for REA cannot be backdated for more than three months. You must claim REA separately from industrial injuries disablement benefit (IIDB). Get claim-form BI103 from your Regional IIDB Delivery Centre. It is possible to have more than one award of REA if you have had more than one industrial accident or disease (R(I)2/02). However, you cannot be paid more than the equivalent of 140% disablement when your IIDB and any REA awards are added together.

Once you have made a successful claim for REA, you can make renewal claims, subject to the usual rules. But if you were entitled to REA immediately before 1.10.90 (ie on 30.9.90), a break in entitlement of just one day after this date may mean you lose REA for good.

If you are getting REA when you reach state pension age and are not in regular employment, your REA will be replaced by retirement allowance, paid at a lower rate (see 15 below). However, there is at present a loophole in the law that allows anyone claiming REA for the first time after state pension age to be paid REA at normal rates without ever having this

P.4 For more information

For reference use *Social Security: Legislation Volumes I* and *III* (published annually by Sweet & Maxwell) and *The Law of Social Security* by Wikeley, Ogus and Barendt (2005, Butterworths). *Compensation for Industrial Injury* by R Lewis (1987, published by Professional Books Ltd/ Butterworths; out of print but may be available in large libraries) is useful for case law prior to 1987. The DWP produces a technical guide for advisers – DB1 *A guide to Industrial Injuries Disablement Benefits*, available only online (www.dwp.gov.uk/advisers/db1).

Accident Line – If you have been injured in an accident or have an industrial disease, you can arrange a free legal consultation with a local solicitor specialising in personal injury claims by ringing the Accident Line on Freephone 0500 192939 (England and Wales).

converted to retirement allowance. So, if you are nearing state pension age, it may be to your advantage to delay your claim until you are over three months past state pension age. In this way, your claim cannot be backdated prior to state pension age and any REA awarded can therefore continue to be paid indefinitely.

SSCBA, Sch 7, para 11

Who qualifies for REA?

To qualify for REA you must have a current assessment of at least 1% in respect of an accident or disease that occurred before 1.10.90 (see above). You must also be unable to return to your regular occupation or to do work of an equivalent standard because of the effects of the disablement caused by your accident or disease.

The broad aim is to make up the difference between what you are capable of earning, as a result of the injury or disease, in any suitable alternative employment and what you would have been likely to earn now in your regular job if you had not had the accident or disease and were still in your regular job. There are two ways of qualifying for REA.

- ❑ **Under the continuous condition** – You must have been incapable of following both your *'regular occupation'* and any *'employment of an equivalent standard which is suitable in [your] case'* ever since 90 days after your accident happened or your disease began.
- ❑ **Under the permanent condition** – It is enough if you are now *'incapable, and likely to remain permanently incapable, of following [your] regular occupation'* and also incapable of any *'employment of an equivalent standard ...'*

SSCBA, Sch 7, para 11(1)(b)

Earnings

On a first claim, your pre- and post-accident earnings are individually assessed. On subsequent claims for the same accident or disease, revisions may be linked to the general movement in earnings of broad occupational groups, depending on how the law applies to your situation.

Broadly, if your post-accident earnings are less than your pre-accident earnings would be now, the difference is made up by REA, subject to the maximum payment of £57.44. This comparison may be totally hypothetical – eg if your regular job no longer exists and disabilities that cannot be taken into account in the REA assessment make you incapable of any work. If you are unable to do any work because of the accident or disease you should get the maximum amount of REA.

Tackling appeals

Case law on REA, much of which originally applied to the earlier special hardship allowance, is complex and extensive. For example, there may be arguments over what your 'regular' occupation is, particularly if your accident happened during lower-paid 'stop gap' work; or you may argue that your reasonable prospects of advancement should be taken into account. If your claim is turned down or you do not get maximum REA, do not give up without first taking expert advice. As well as depending on case law, your claim may rest on a mass of detailed facts, as well as medical evidence. It is quite possible that the decision maker made a decision in ignorance of some of the relevant facts.

You have a right of appeal against the refusal of REA, or against the amount awarded. See Chapter 60 for details.

No percentage assessment?

To get REA, you must have a current disablement assessment of at least 1%. You also need to be sure that the loss of faculty identified by the DWP healthcare professional(s) in the report covers all the disabilities created by the industrial accident/disease and is sufficient to contribute materially to your being incapable of following your regular occupation.

The DWP healthcare professional(s) give their opinion on the link between the accepted loss of faculty and your inability to follow your regular occupation. The decision maker is not bound to accept this but in practice usually does.

If you do not have a current percentage assessment or the loss of faculty needs to be more broadly identified, you have to tackle that side of things first by appealing, or by seeking a revision or supersession. An appeal may be the best choice if you need to broaden the loss of faculty. If you are out of time, make a late appeal (see Chapter 60(7)). In a separate letter, ask for a revision or supersession. If you are trying to cover a gap in your assessment period to re-qualify for REA, a late appeal may be a better option because of the restricted backdating on supersession.

Since 20.5.02, if the decision on your disablement assessment is revised or changed at appeal, the decision maker can go on to revise the decision on your REA if this is to your advantage. This precludes the need for a separate appeal on the REA question (see Chapter 60, Box T.5).

15. Retirement allowance

Retirement allowance is a maximum of £14.36 a week or a minimum of 50p a week. It is the lower of 10% of the maximum rate of disablement benefit, or 25% of the reduced earnings allowance (REA) you received immediately before reaching state pension age (currently 60 for women, 65 for men) or ceasing regular employment, if that was later. In practice, if you had maximum REA, your retirement allowance would be £14.36. If you had retired and claimed your state pension before 10.4.89, you do not get retirement allowance, but your REA is frozen for life.

Retirement allowance is payable for life and the link with any percentage assessment is broken. It is only payable if you are transferring from REA. If you want to stay on REA when you reach state pension age, you can only do so while you remain in regular employment (see below). However, if you are approaching state pension age and have not yet claimed REA, you should consider delaying your claim in order to keep it indefinitely (see 14 above).

Retirement allowance replaces REA if, when you have reached state pension age, you give up regular employment and on the day before you give up that employment your award(s) of REA add up to at least £2 a week. If you stopped work before reaching state pension age you are treated as giving up regular employment in the week you reach state pension age. If you continue regular employment after state pension age, your REA will be replaced by retirement allowance when you stop work.

SSCBA, Sch 7, paras 12 & 13

Regular employment – This is defined as gainful employment under a contract of service that requires you to work for an average of at least ten hours a week over any 5-week period (not counting any week of permitted absence such as leave or sickness), or gainful employment (which may be self-employment) that you undertake for an average of at least ten hours a week over any 5-week period.

Social Security (Industrial Injuries) (Regular Employment) Regs 1990, as amended

46 War disablement pension

1. The War Pensions scheme

On 6.4.05 the Service Personnel and Veterans Agency (SPVA) introduced the Armed Forces Compensation Scheme (AFCS), which replaced the existing War Pensions scheme. The War Pensions scheme remains in place for those with existing awards on 6.4.05, and to new claimants whose injury, ill health or bereavement was caused by service before 6.4.05. We cover the AFCS in detail in a factsheet. For a copy, either send a stamped addressed envelope to Disability Alliance (see back cover for address) and ask for Factsheet F20 or download it from our website (www.disabilityalliance.org).

The War Pensions scheme is administered by the SPVA and is intended to provide benefits for disablement caused or worsened by service in HM Armed Forces. It is wider in scope than the Industrial Injuries scheme, with no list of prescribed diseases, jobs or substances. You can claim for any medical condition providing you can show a link between that condition and your service. You need not have been involved in a war or been on active service when the injury or condition was caused. You could have been injured playing organised sport on the base or suffered an illness during service that has done permanent damage (eg an ear infection causing some hearing loss), or you could have an existing condition that has worsened through service. Although most pensions are paid for physical injuries, claims for mental and psychological conditions such as schizophrenia and post-traumatic stress disorder can be accepted, if conditions for entitlement are met. Conditions such as multiple sclerosis, Menière's disease, Hodgkin's disease, diabetes mellitus, certain cases of gastritis and peptic ulcers and heart disease in lower limb amputees can now be accepted. If you have previously claimed for one of these conditions and been refused, you should claim again.

Civilians and some other groups are covered by the scheme but only for certain physical injuries (see below).

2. Who can claim?

You can claim for any present disablement resulting from:

- an injury or condition caused or worsened by service in HM Armed Forces at any time including service in the Home Guard, Nursing and Auxiliary Services, the UDR from 31.3.70 and the Territorial Army. Certain cadets are covered by a similar but separate Ministry of Defence scheme;
- a physical injury or disease sustained as a civilian during World War 2 either as a result of enemy action or action in combating the enemy;
- a physical injury or disease sustained while carrying out duties as a Civil Defence Volunteer in World War 2;
- an injury or condition caused or worsened by service during World War 2 in the Polish Forces under British Command or while serving in the Polish Resettlement Forces;
- certain injuries or illnesses sustained while serving in the Naval Auxiliary Services, Coastguard or Merchant Navy in World War 1 or 2, or conflicts in the Gulf, Falklands, Suez or Korea; or while being held prisoner.

If you are a dependant of someone whose death has been caused or 'substantially hastened' by service in HM Forces you can also claim a war pension (see 8 below).

3. How much can you get?

War disablement pension – The basic disablement pension depends on your degree of disability, assessed on a percentage basis as in the Industrial Injuries scheme (see Box P.2, Chapter 45). If your assessment is 20% or more, a weekly pension is paid. If it is less than 20%, you get a one-off lump-sum gratuity unless your claim is for noise-induced sensorineural hearing loss (see below).

War disablement pensions are tax free. The maximum pension at the 100% rate is £152.40 a week. See SPVA Leaflet 9 for the full range of rates payable.

Hearing loss – When your claim is for noise-induced sensorineural hearing loss and your assessment is less than 20%, no gratuity is paid. No account is taken of any related condition, like tinnitus.

NMAF(DD)SP Order, art 5(3)

If your hearing loss alone is assessed as at least 20%, any additional disability can be added on to increase the percentage you get. To get 20%, your average hearing loss must be 50dB or more in each ear.

A gratuity can still be paid for hearing loss due to other causes such as bomb blast, ear infections or the effects of ototoxic drugs used to treat other conditions linked to service.

Supplementary allowances – Tax-free supplementary allowances can be paid on top of a basic war disablement pension or gratuity. Some allowances you have to claim, others are paid automatically (see 4 and 5 below and SPVA Leaflet 2).

4. Allowances you have to claim

War pensioners' mobility supplement – To qualify, your walking difficulty must be caused wholly or mainly by your pensioned disablement, which must be assessed at 40% or more. The other qualifying conditions are similar to those for disability living allowance (DLA) higher rate mobility component (see Chapter 3(18)) except there is no special category for severe mental impairment.

War pensioners' mobility supplement cannot be paid at the same time as DLA mobility component but is paid at the higher rate of £54.85 a week. There is no upper age limit for claiming.

When claiming, you can choose to attend a medical examination or fill in a self-assessment claim-pack. Your disability must be expected to last at least six months from

P5 Far East prisoners of war

Tax-free lump-sum payments of £10,000 can be claimed by former prisoners of the Japanese during World War 2, or by their widows or widowers. Former members of the forces, civilians and some members of the colonial forces are included. The payment is disregarded indefinitely for means-tested benefits and there is no time limit for claiming. For more details and a claim-form ring the Veterans Helpline (0800 169 2277).

when you claim but, unlike DLA, you do not have to meet a 3-month qualifying period prior to this.

NMAF(DD)SP Order, art 20

Constant attendance allowance – This is paid if your pensioned disablement is assessed at 80% or more and causes you to need a lot of personal care and attention, or supervision. It is paid at four different rates:

- part-day – £28.75;
- full day – £57.50;
- intermediate – £86.25;
- exceptional – £115.

Regulations specify the level of care needed for each rate to be payable. If, because of your pensioned disablement, you are terminally ill, you will get the intermediate rate.

Constant attendance allowance overlaps with ordinary attendance allowance and DLA care component. Qualification for both means you will be paid the higher amount. When claiming, you can choose to have a medical examination or fill in a self-assessment claim-pack.

NMAF(DD)SP Order, art 8

Unemployability supplement – This is similar to incapacity benefit and is paid if your pensioned disablement is assessed at 60% or more and you are likely to be permanently unable to work because of your war pensioned disablement. You must be under 65 when you claim, but once awarded it can continue to be paid after age 65. You cannot get unemployability supplement at the same time as incapacity benefit or employment and support allowance (ESA). Unemployability supplement overlaps with basic state pension; if you claim the latter your unemployability supplement can be topped up to the level of your state pension (plus any earnings-related or graduated pension payable). Unemployability supplement is £94.20 a week and you can claim extra for dependants. A child allowance stops at age 16 so you need to reclaim it if your child is continuing in full-time education. An invalidity allowance may be paid on top; there are three rates depending on your age when you first became permanently incapable of work: £6, £12 and £18.65.

NMAF(DD)SP Order, arts 12 & 13

Allowance for lowered standard of occupation – This is similar to reduced earnings allowance in the Industrial Injuries scheme and is paid up to the same maximum rate of £57.44 a week. It is paid if your pensioned disablement is assessed at 40% or more and consequentially you are unable to follow your regular occupation or do work of an equivalent standard. You must be under age 65 when you claim, but once awarded it can be paid after age 65. This allowance plus your basic war pension cannot add up to more than the 100% rate pension. You cannot get the allowance for lowered standard of occupation at the same time as incapacity benefit, ESA or unemployability supplement.

NMAF(DD)SP Order, art 15

Clothing allowance – This is £196 a year and is paid if your pensioned disablement is assessed at 20% or more and causes exceptional wear and tear to your clothing – eg because of incontinence or the use of an artificial limb.

NMAF(DD)SP Order, art 11

Treatment allowance – To qualify, you must suffer actual loss of earnings due to having treatment at home or in hospital because of your pensioned disablement. Treatment allowance is paid to top up your current percentage (whether you have a pension or gratuity) to the 100% rate of the basic pension. Claim immediately treatment starts, as no payment is made for days before you claim unless illness or disability prevented you claiming earlier.

NMAF(DD)SP Order, art 17

Rent allowance – If you are getting a surviving spouse/civil partner's pension (see 8 below) *and* a child allowance, you can claim up to £43.60 a week rent allowance towards your accommodation costs (rent, mortgage, council tax and water rates). This can continue for 26 weeks after the child's allowance stops.

NMAF(DD)SP Order, art 25

5. Allowances that are paid automatically

Exceptionally severe disablement allowance – This is paid if you get constant attendance allowance at either of the two highest rates on a permanent basis. It is £57.50 a week.

NMAF(DD)SP Order, art 9

Severe disablement occupational allowance – This is paid if you get either of the two highest rates of constant attendance allowance but you are nevertheless normally in employment. It is £28.75 a week. You cannot get it as well as certain social security benefits, eg state pension, incapacity benefit, severe disablement allowance and carer's allowance.

NMAF(DD)SP Order, art 10

Comforts allowance – This is paid if you get unemployability supplement and/or constant attendance allowance. There are two rates: £12.35 or £24.70 a week.

NMAF(DD)SP Order, art 14

Age allowance – This is paid at age 65 if your disablement is assessed at 40% or more. The amount depends on your degree of disablement, and it varies between £10.25 and £31.30 a week.

NMAF(DD)SP Order, art 16

6. Does anything affect what you get?

A basic war disablement pension is not affected by earnings or by any non-means-tested social security benefit, with the exception of industrial injuries disablement benefit for the same disablement.

The supplementary allowances can affect the payment of similar benefits – eg constant attendance allowance normally overlaps with attendance allowance and disability living allowance care component, so you cannot get both in full.

You cannot get full allowances for dependants payable with non-means-tested social security benefits as well as those payable with unemployability supplement. The total paid will be the higher of the two.

For means-tested benefits, eg income support, £10 a week of a war disablement pension is not treated as income. Certain supplementary allowances are ignored in full; these are: constant attendance allowance, exceptionally severe disablement allowance, severe disablement occupational allowance and war pensioners' mobility supplement. Therefore, it is important to give a breakdown of how your war pension is made up when claiming means-tested benefits. Your local authority may ignore more than £10 for claims to housing and council tax benefit under a local scheme.

If you enter hospital, basic war pension is unaffected but some supplementary allowances are (see Chapter 35).

7. How do you claim?

You can get a claim-form by ringing the Veterans Helpline (0800 169 2277), by writing to the Service Personnel and Veterans Agency, Norcoss, Thornton-Cleveleys FY5 3WP, or by contacting your local Veterans' Welfare Office (addresses in SPVA Leaflet 1). Claim-forms are also available on the SPVA website (www.veterans-uk.info). Make sure you complete and return the claim-form within three months or you could lose benefit. If you claim by telephone, your service and medical details will be taken so the SPVA can obtain your service records while they are waiting for you to complete and return the claim-form, so speeding up a decision on your claim.

When to claim?

You cannot claim for a war disablement pension if you are still serving in the Forces (as you now come under the Armed Forces Compensation Scheme). For ex-service personnel, there is no time limit for making a claim but any award is normally only paid from the date of your claim.

Backdating is possible, though restricted to a maximum of three years, in a prescribed list of circumstances. These are:

- you have been unable to claim earlier due to ill health or disability;
- there has been a change in medical opinion;
- documents that were previously classified become available; *or*
- the Ministry of Defence HQ has failed to forward papers to the SPVA when someone has been medically discharged from or died in service.

In cases of official error, full backdating is still possible. There is a right of appeal if backdating is refused.

NMAF(DD)SP Order, Sch 3

If your claim is made within seven years of leaving the Forces it is easier to have it accepted, as the onus is on the SPVA to prove that your disability is not linked to your service. After seven years, the burden of proof shifts to you to prove your claim. For example, a person contracting multiple sclerosis within seven years of discharge from the Forces was awarded a war disablement pension because the cause of this condition is unknown, and so the SPVA was unable to prove that it was not linked to their service.

NMAF(DD)SP Order, art 40

Whenever your claim is made, the legislation states that the benefit of any reasonable doubt should always be given to the claimant.

In the past, the SPVA refused claims if a claimant had no corroborative evidence. The High Court (*Secretary of State for Social Security v Mitchell, Wilson & Bennett*, 17.10.97) decided this was unlawful and that any evidence, including the claimant's own word, should be considered when making a decision. If your claim was turned down for this reason in the past, you should get independent advice.

For civilians, there is a 3-month time limit from the date of the injury for making claims. Claims that are technically out of time are waived if you provide independent supporting evidence. The types of evidence they will accept are listed on the claim-form. If your claim is refused because of this, you should get independent advice.

NMAF(DD)SP Order, art 37

If you are medically discharged from the Forces or die in service, your service medical records should be sent automatically to the SPVA for an award to be considered.

NMAF(DD)SP Order, art 35

What happens after you claim?

The SPVA will check your service records, if appropriate, to decide if you come within the scheme. If you do, the cause and the degree of your disability will be decided by SPVA doctors, after medical evidence has been obtained.

8. Pensions for war widows, widowers, surviving civil partners and other dependants

A pension can be paid if:

- your spouse/civil partner's death was due to, or substantially hastened by, an illness or injury for which they were either getting a war disablement pension or to which they would have been entitled had they claimed; *or*
- your spouse/civil partner was getting constant attendance allowance at any rate, or would have been had they not been in hospital; *or*
- since 7.4.97, your spouse/civil partner was getting unemployability supplement at the time of death and their pensionable disablement was at least 80%.

In some circumstances, an unmarried partner or same-sex partner who was not a civil partner can also qualify.

NMAF(DD)SP Order, arts 22-24

If your late spouse/civil partner was getting a war disablement pension when they died, you will not be awarded a pension automatically – you have to apply. However, if they were getting constant attendance allowance or unemployability supplement prior to their death, a temporary allowance is paid automatically for the first 26 weeks. This is based on the rate paid to the spouse/civil partner before their death.

NMAF(DD)SP Order, art 27

You cannot be paid a surviving spouse/civil partner's pension as well as a national insurance bereavement benefit or widow's pension, but a surviving spouse/civil partner's pension is tax free and normally paid at a higher rate. You can also get benefits based on your own national insurance contributions, eg state pension or contributory employment and support allowance, on top.

A surviving spouse/civil partner's pension is currently £115.55 a week, and is £113.20 a week for a dependant who lived as a spouse/civil partner.

A supplementary pension of £77.32 a week is paid on top of the basic amount if your late spouse's service ended before 31.3.73. This is disregarded for means-tested benefits.

Extra allowances that can be claimed include age allowances of £13.20, £25.30 or £37.55, and child allowances (for details see SPVA Leaflet 2).

Entitlement to a pension stops if you remarry, form a civil partnership or start cohabiting, but this will not affect you if you are getting a supplementary pension with your basic pension, both of which will remain in payment. In other cases, your pension can be reinstated if your new marriage or partnership ends.

NMAF(DD)SP Order, art 33

Before April 2002, widowers could claim a pension only if they met extra conditions, including being *'incapable of self support'*. If you have had a claim refused in the past because you did not meet the 'extra conditions', you should reclaim immediately.

On bereavement, you may also be able to claim help with funeral costs (see 11 below).

9. Reviews

Decisions on war disablement pensions are made by officials acting on behalf of the Secretary of State. Most decisions can be reviewed *'at any time, on any ground'*. This applies when you request a review because you are unhappy with a decision (eg your claim has been refused or you disagree with the level of assessment) or because your circumstances have changed since the decision was made (eg your condition has got worse).

The SPVA will only review the decision if you give substantive reasons for your request, although you do not have to provide corroborative evidence. If the SPVA believes you have not given substantive reasons they can refuse to review and there is no right of appeal against such a refusal. If this happens, seek independent advice.

P.6 For more information

The main legislation covering the War Pensions scheme is contained in The Naval, Military and Air Forces Etc (Disablement and Death) Service Pensions Order 2006, available from The Stationery Office (0870 600 5522 or www.tsoshop.co.uk). Civilians and merchant seamen are covered by SI 1983/686 and SI 1964/2058 respectively.

Veterans Helpline – 0800 169 2277

Call the Helpline for queries about your claim or the War Pensions scheme and to get claim-forms and leaflets. Their leaflets are also available on the Service Personnel and Veterans Agency website (www.veterans-uk.info).

If the SPVA carries out a review, any new decision, even if it remains the same, will carry a fresh right of appeal. If the review is in your favour, you will normally be paid from the date of your review request.

If you are requesting a review on the grounds that your condition has deteriorated, your assessment could be reduced as well as increased. This is particularly worth bearing in mind if your pensioned condition is noise-induced hearing loss, where you cannot get an increase in your assessment anyway because of the restrictive approach now used to assess these claims.

If you are unhappy with a decision, it may be better to appeal straight away rather than ask for a review. In any case, when you appeal, the SPVA will look at your case again to check if their decision was correct and so could change it, making a tribunal hearing unnecessary.

NMAF(DD)SP Order, art 44

10. Appeals

Appeal rights apply to most decisions about war pensions made on or after 9.4.01. Appeals can be made against decisions relating to service prior to 3.9.39, to most supplementary allowances and to funeral expenses. You can appeal against the refusal of an award, the level of award, the date from which the award runs and any changes to the amount or period of the award.

It is important that you get help with an appeal or a review. Some ex-service organisations like the Royal British Legion can help prepare your case and represent you at the tribunal. Alternatively, an advice centre may be able to help.

If you live in England or Wales you appeal to a First-tier Tribunal (War Pensions and Armed Forces Compensation Chamber). If you live in Scotland or Northern Ireland, you appeal to the Pensions Appeal Tribunal of that country, independent bodies set up by Ministry of Justice. The tribunal must have a legally qualified member and normally has a doctor but does not need to have a member of the same sex and service background as you. If you are challenging the level of your assessment, a medical examination may be carried out.

The tribunal will not need to consider issues not raised at the hearing and will only be able to consider circumstances up to the date of the decision.

Once an appeal has been lodged, the papers (known as a response or 'Statement of Case') are prepared and a date of hearing set. Any further appeal against a tribunal decision is only possible on a point of law to the Upper Tribunal. There is a 6-month time limit in which to appeal against an SPVA decision, except in the case of an interim assessment, when it is three months. Late appeals can be made up to 12 months after this period if the delay is due to: the serious illness or death of the claimant, their spouse or a dependant; the disruption of normal postal services; the failure to notify the claimant of the decision; or exceptional circumstances applying to the claimant.

11. Extra help you can get

Funeral costs

A £2,200 grant towards funeral costs may be paid to a widow, widower, civil partner, the next of kin or person responsible for the funeral. It can be claimed if:

- death was due to service;
- war pensions constant attendance allowance was being paid or would have been paid if the war pensioner had not been in hospital when they died; *or*
- unemployability supplement was being paid at the time of death and the war disablement pension was assessed at 80% or more.

You must make a claim within three months of the funeral. There is a right of appeal if you are turned down. The financial circumstances of the person making the claim are ignored. There is no means test and any payment made is not recoverable from the deceased's estate.

NMAF(DD)SP Order, art 32

Other help

You can apply to the SPVA for any of the following services or appliances if you need them wholly or mainly because of your pensioned condition and they are not available free from the NHS or social services. There is no means test and no charge, but you must apply before arranging or purchasing any treatment or appliance, as refunds are not normally made. These provisions are discretionary, with no right of appeal if you are refused. You can ask your local Veterans' Welfare Manager to visit and discuss any of these services and appliances and help you apply.

Hospital treatment expenses – Payment can be made for travel costs, subsistence or loss of earnings incurred when attending hospital (or similar centre) for treatment related to disablement. Some visitors to a war pensioner who has been in hospital for over 12 months can also get help with travel costs.

Private treatment – Payment can be made for approved treatment not available free on the NHS.

Priority treatment – War pensioners are entitled to priority NHS treatment for their pensioned disablement. If you have problems, contact the Veterans Helpline (see Box P.6).

NHS charges – War pensioners are exempt from NHS prescription charges if they are required for pensionable conditions.

Appliances – Various items, such as orthopaedic chairs, spectacles, corsets and dental treatment can be paid for (at the equivalent NHS cost) if not available free through other agencies.

Home adaptation grant – Up to £750 can be allowed for small adaptations (eg a stair lift) in addition to any grant payable by the local authority.

Care home fees (for skilled nursing care) – If you need 24-hour skilled nursing care because of your pensioned disability, the SPVA may pay care home fees if the NHS or local authority are not providing funding.

Short-term breaks (convalescence) – You can claim care home fees for up to four weeks a year to enable you to have a short-term break. If you have recently been discharged from hospital or are recovering from an operation, the SPVA is unlikely to pay as they consider this an NHS responsibility.

Respite breaks – In some circumstances, you can claim the cost of care home fees in order to give your carer a break. Your carer has to provide medical evidence that a break is needed.

47 Criminal injuries compensation

1. Who can claim?

You can claim compensation from the Criminal Injuries Compensation Authority if you suffer personal injury directly resulting from a crime of violence in Great Britain and in certain listed offshore situations.

Criminal Injuries Compensation Scheme, para 8 & Notes 1-2

A crime of violence includes child abuse, and personal injury might include physical injury, mental injury, disease, or pregnancy or sexually transmitted diseases contracted as a result of rape.

Criminal Injuries Compensation Scheme, para 9

You can also claim compensation if you are injured when trying to stop someone from committing a crime, or trying to stop a suspected criminal, or helping the police to do so. In this case, if the injury is accidental, you must have been taking an exceptional risk that was justified in all the circumstances of the case.

Criminal Injuries Compensation Scheme, paras 8(c) & 12

You can claim compensation even if your attacker is immune from prosecution under the law, for example because of mental illness.

Criminal Injuries Compensation Scheme, para 10

If the injury was caused by a traffic accident, it is only covered if the driver of the vehicle deliberately drove it at you in an attempt to injure you.

Criminal Injuries Compensation Scheme, para 11

Compensation can be reduced or withheld unless the Criminal Injuries Compensation Authority is satisfied that you:

- took all reasonable steps to inform the police or, in limited circumstances, another appropriate authority, of the incident, and co-operated fully in their investigations;
- have given the Authority all reasonable assistance, eg by providing information;
- are of good character. If you have unspent convictions, or if you in any way contributed to the attack, compensation may be reduced or refused.

Criminal Injuries Compensation Scheme, para 13

Violence within the family – If you and your attacker were living together as members of the same family, you can apply for compensation provided that:

- you were injured on or after 1.10.79;
- your attacker has been prosecuted (unless there are good reasons why this has not been done); *and*
- you and your attacker stopped living together before the application was made, and you and the attacker are unlikely to share the same household again.

A man and woman living together as husband and wife will be treated as members of the same family in this context, as will same-sex partners (whether or not they are civil partners).

Criminal Injuries Compensation Scheme, para 17

Compensation will not be payable unless the Authority is satisfied that the attacker will not benefit from the award.

Criminal Injuries Compensation Scheme, para 16(a)

2. How do you claim?

Apply as soon as possible after the incident. You can get the appropriate claim-form from the Criminal Injuries Compensation Authority (see Box P.7). You can apply for compensation if your attacker is unknown or has not yet been arrested.

All applications must be made to the Authority within two years of the date of the incident. The time limit may only be waived if, in the circumstances of the case, it would not have been reasonable to expect the applicant to have made an application within the 2-year period and there is enough evidence to still be able to investigate the claim. The Authority is sympathetic to late claims made in respect of children and young people (under age 18) or people with learning difficulties. Claims in respect of child abuse should therefore be made even if the injuries occurred over two years ago. Send a covering letter explaining the delay. Applications for children should be made by a person with parental responsibility for the child.

Criminal Injuries Compensation Scheme, para 18

3. How much do you get?

Compensation is made up of several possible elements.

- ❑ **For the injury itself** – A fixed sum assessed by reference to a tariff that groups together injuries of comparable severity and allocates a sum of compensation to them. The Authority will obtain a medical report about you, and will decide where in the tariff your injury features. This 'tariff of injuries' is included in the Criminal Injuries Compensation scheme (see Box P.7).
- ❑ **Loss of earnings** – No compensation is paid for the first 28 weeks of lost earnings. Any loss of earnings and/or earning potential incurred as a direct consequence of the injury beyond that will be compensated, subject to certain limits. Loss of pension rights may also be compensated.
- ❑ **Special expenses** – Examples of these include care and supervision costs or equipment such as a wheelchair, or towards expenses for medical, dental or optical treatment. To qualify, you must have lost earnings or earnings capacity (or if not normally employed, be incapacitated to a similar extent) for at least 28 weeks and if so, the award will be backdated to the date of injury.

Criminal Injuries Compensation Scheme, para 23(a)-(c)

Compensation if the victim has died

If someone has died as a result of a criminal injury, an amount for funeral expenses may be paid, and compensation may be paid to their family.

Funeral expenses – The Authority only pays an amount it considers reasonable. The religious and cultural background of the victim and their family will be taken into account in deciding what is reasonable. Whoever has paid for the funeral of a victim of a crime of violence may claim.

Bereavement award – A relative of someone who has died as a result of a crime of violence can claim a flat-rate bereavement award of £11,000 for one claimant, or £5,500 each for two or more claimants. The only people who can claim this award are: a husband or wife; an unmarried partner (including same-sex partners) who had been living with the deceased for at least two years (or would have been living with them but for infirmity or ill health); a parent; a son or daughter.

Dependency award – If a relative was financially dependent on the deceased for their living expenses, an award will be made to reflect the extent of financial dependency, subject to a maximum amount. Close relatives (parents, children and partners) can claim, as for the bereavement award above, as can former spouses/civil partners if they were being financially supported by the deceased.

P.7 For more information

The Criminal Injuries Compensation Authority publishes a general guide to the Criminal Injuries Compensation scheme. A copy of this guide, the scheme and any claim-forms you need are available free from Criminal Injuries Compensation Authority, Tay House, 300 Bath Street, Glasgow G2 4LN (Freephone 0800 358 3601; www.cica.gov.uk).

Traffic accidents

If you are the victim of an uninsured or untraced motorist, there is a different scheme for compensation for personal injuries. This is run by the Motor Insurers' Bureau (MIB), established by motor insurers, which has agreements with the Government to provide that compensation. Compensation is worked out in the same way as common law damages. If the driver cannot be traced, you should report the accident to the police within 14 days for personal injury or five days for damage to personal property. You must apply to the MIB within three years of the accident, but generally you should act quickly. For details, contact: Motor Insurers' Bureau, Linford Wood House, 6-12 Capital Drive, Linford Wood, Milton Keynes MK14 6XT (0190 883 0001; www.mib.org.uk).

Loss of a parent – In the case of an application on behalf of a child under 18, a payment of £2,000 a year will be made to the child in respect of the death of their parent, to reflect the extent to which the child was dependent on the parent in ways other than financially, eg caring for the child.

Criminal Injuries Compensation Scheme, paras 37-44

Compensation recovery

Your award will be reduced in some cases to take account of other payments received.

- **Social security benefits and insurance payments** – Benefits or insurance payments received for the same injuries are deducted in full from an award for loss of earnings, special expenses or a dependency award. No deduction is made for benefits or insurance payments paid in respect of the first 28 weeks of lost earnings. An award that is tariff based is not affected (eg for the injury itself or a bereavement award).
- **Occupational pensions** – A loss of earnings or dependency award will be reduced to take account of an occupational pension payable as a result of the injury or death. Pension rights from payments made only by the victim or dependant are disregarded.
- **Compensation from the courts** – The full amount of a compensation payment for personal injury or damages made by a civil or criminal court in respect of the same injury (less any amount of 'recoverable' benefit – see Chapter 49) is deducted from an award under the Criminal Injuries Compensation scheme.

Criminal Injuries Compensation Scheme, paras 45-49

4. How is your claim decided?

The Authority's staff will look at your claim to check that the information you have given is correct. On the claim-form, you are asked to give them authority to contact the police, your doctor, your employer or any other relevant person, to obtain confirmation of the incident, your injuries, loss of earnings, etc. They may ask you for other details. These enquiries are made in strict confidence. In some cases, you might be asked to undergo a medical examination by a doctor chosen by the Authority.

After gathering this information, the Authority's staff will decide if you come within the scheme, and, if so, will assess the amount of compensation. You will be sent a written decision. You must reply in writing and accept the decision before any payment is made. Where the award has been reduced or disallowed, you will be given reasons.

5. If you don't agree with the decision

If you are unhappy with the decision, you can apply, in writing, for a review. The Authority must receive your request within 90 days of the date of the letter notifying you of the decision. The 90-day time limit can be extended if you can show there are exceptional circumstances that justify the granting of an extension; the request for an extension must be made in writing.

Your application must be supported by reasons, together with any additional evidence. If you haven't had help with your claim, it is important to get advice to make sure you include all the relevant information. Contact your local Victim Support scheme for help (0845 303 0900 (UK), 0845 603 9213 (Scotland) or www.victimsupport.org).

After the review, if you are still dissatisfied with the decision, you can appeal to a First-tier Tribunal. The appeals process is described in Chapter 60.

Both reviews and appeals involve a full reconsideration of eligibility and the amount of the award. This could result in loss of an award or a reduced award.

Criminal Injuries Compensation Scheme, paras 58-65

6. If your condition changes

The Authority can re-open your case if your condition has deteriorated to the extent that the original assessment is unjust given your present condition. It can also re-open a case where a person has since died as a result of the injury. If you apply more than two years after the original decision, it is important to give as much information and medical evidence as you can with your application. The Authority will only consider it if it has enough evidence without needing to make extensive enquiries.

Criminal Injuries Compensation Scheme, paras 56-57

48 Vaccine damage payments

In this chapter we look at:

1. What is this scheme?

The scheme provides a tax-free lump sum of £120,000 for a person who is (or was immediately before death) severely disabled as a result of vaccination against specific diseases. It is described in the leaflet *Vaccine Damage Payments* (see 4 below).

2. Who qualifies?

Payments can be made to a person who has been severely disabled as a result of vaccination against diphtheria, tetanus, pertussis (whooping cough), poliomyelitis, measles, rubella (German measles), mumps, tuberculosis, meningococcal group C (meningitis C), haemophilus influenzae-type B (Hib), smallpox (vaccination up to August 1971), human papillomavirus or pneumococcal infection. Claims can be made on the basis of combination vaccines, for example: diphtheria, tetanus and pertussis (DTP), measles and rubella (MR), measles, mumps and rubella (MMR), and the five-in-one vaccine.

People damaged before birth as a result of vaccinations given to their mothers during pregnancy are included in the scheme, as are those who have contracted polio through contact with another person who was vaccinated against it using an orally-administered vaccine. The claimant must also satisfy the following conditions.

- The vaccination must have been given in the UK or Isle of Man (except for serving members of the forces and their immediate families vaccinated outside the UK as part of service medical facilities, who are treated as if vaccinated in England).
- The vaccination must have been given either when the claimant was under 18 (except for rubella, poliomyelitis, meningococcal group C and human papillomavirus) or at a time of an outbreak of the disease within the UK or Isle of Man.
- The claimant must also be over the age of two on the date of the claim, or, if they have died, they must have been over the age of two when they died.
- The claim can be made at any time before the claimant's 21st birthday, or, if they have died, the date on which they would have attained that age, or up to six years after the date of the vaccination, whichever date is later.
- In the case of someone who contracted polio through contact with another person who was vaccinated against it, they must have been *'in close physical contact'* with the

other person during the period of 60 days which began on the 4th day after the vaccination. They must also have been *'looking after'* the vaccinated person or been looked after jointly with them.

VDPA, Ss.1-3 & VDP Regs, regs 5-5A

3. What is 'severe disablement'?

A person is considered to be severely disabled if the disablement due to vaccination damage is assessed at 60% or more. Disablement is assessed in the same way as for industrial injuries disablement benefit (see Box P.2, Chapter 45).

VDPA, S.1(4)

4. How do you claim?

Get the leaflet *Vaccine Damage Payments* and a claim-form by writing to or ringing the Vaccine Damage Payments Unit, Palatine House, Lancaster Road, Preston, Lancashire PR1 1HB (01772 899 944) or downloading it from www.dwp.gov.uk/advisers/claimforms.

Don't delay in claiming. If you already have supporting medical evidence send a copy with the claim. Otherwise, the Vaccine Damage Payments Unit will obtain medical evidence on your behalf. If the disabled person is under 18, the claim should be made by the parents or guardian.

5. What if you are refused?

If your claim is refused, you will be sent a written decision with reasons. If you disagree with this decision, you can ask the DWP to consider a reversal of the decision or you can appeal to a First-tier Tribunal. There is no time limit for making your appeal. The appeals process is described in Chapter 60.

Reversals

If you want the DWP to consider a reversal of their decision or the decision of a tribunal, write to the Vaccine Damage Payments Unit requesting a reversal, giving reasons why you think the decision is wrong, within six years of the date you were notified of the original decision or within two years of the date you were notified of the tribunal decision, if that is later. You may provide new evidence in support of your request.

Reconsiderations

If the DWP has made a payment, the decision can be reconsidered at any time if they have reason to believe there was a misrepresentation or non-disclosure of relevant information.

VDPA, Ss.3A-5 & VDP Regs, reg 11

6. Does it affect other benefits?

The capital value of a vaccine damage payment held in a trust fund is ignored for the purposes of income-related employment and support allowance (ESA), income support, income-based jobseeker's allowance (JSA), housing benefit and council tax benefit. If the payment is not held in a trust fund, its capital value can be disregarded for up to 52 weeks from the date of receipt. After that it will be taken fully into account.

Any regular payments made out of the trust fund to or for the disabled person are ignored for the purposes of income-related ESA, income support, income-based JSA, housing benefit and council tax benefit. Other lump-sum payments will be treated as capital and will reduce benefit if the payments bring the total capital above the lower capital limit (see Chapter 27(4)).

49 Compensation recovery

In this chapter we look at:

1. Compensation recovery

If, as a result of an accident, injury or disease, you claim compensation, the 'compensator' (the person who caused the accident, injury or disease, or more commonly, their insurer) is liable to pay damages to you and repay benefits to the DWP via the Compensation Recovery Unit (CRU). The compensator can deduct some or all of the amount they have to pay to you from the gross compensation award, a practice known as 'offsetting'.

It is not the actual benefits that are recovered, but an amount equivalent to the total amount of 'recoverable' benefits paid as a result of your accident, injury or disease. Not all social security benefits are recoverable, as some are paid for reasons that have no connection to the compensation claim. Recoverable benefits are listed in 2 below.

Social security benefits are not paid in respect of pain, suffering, personal inconvenience and so on, and therefore no offsetting can be made against the general damages element of your compensation award. If your compensation award is only made up of such damages, the compensator will have to bear the full cost of paying your compensation and repaying benefits to the DWP.

In cases involving accidents and injuries, benefits are recoverable from the day following the accident or injury for a period of five years or up to the date the claim is settled, whichever is earlier. In disease cases, the 5-year recovery period begins on the date on which a recoverable benefit is first claimed as a consequence of the disease.

Social Security (Recovery of Benefits) Act 1997

The certificate

Before a compensation payment is made, the compensator must request a certificate from the CRU. This certificate lists the recoverable benefits that have been paid. The CRU will issue a certificate to the compensator (or their insurer) and send a copy to you (or your solicitor), so that both parties can estimate the extent of any potential offsetting.

Since offsetting can greatly affect the size of the net compensation award, both sides should take it into account when conducting negotiations.

You and the compensator have the right to request a review of a certificate at any time if either of you believe that the calculation shown on the certificate is incorrect or that benefits that were not paid as a consequence of the accident, injury or disease have been included. However, an appeal against a certificate can be made only after the full amount of recoverable benefit has been repaid to the CRU. See 5 below for details on appeals.

2. Benefits which can be recovered

Compensation can be reduced to take account of benefits paid in respect of the following:

- **loss of earnings** – disability working allowance, employment and support allowance, industrial injuries disablement benefit, incapacity benefit, income support, invalidity benefit, jobseeker's allowance, reduced earnings allowance, severe disablement allowance, sickness benefit, statutory sick pay (paid before 6.4.94), unemployment benefit, unemployability supplement;

- **cost of care** – attendance allowance, disability living allowance (DLA) care component, constant attendance allowance, exceptionally severe disablement allowance;
- **loss of mobility** – DLA mobility component, mobility allowance.

In making an order for a compensation payment, the court must specify how much is to be awarded under each of these three headings.

Social Security (Recovery of Benefits) Act 1997, Sch 2

Example: an award of compensation is agreed:

Compensation award:	*£100,000*
consisting of:	
General damages	£40,000
Loss of earnings	£30,000
Loss of mobility	£30,000

The CRU certificate lists the following recoverable benefits:	
Employment and support allowance totalling	£15,000
DLA mobility component totalling	£10,000

The compensator cannot offset against the general damages element of the award, but may offset the employment and support allowance paid against the loss of earnings heading. They therefore deduct £15,000 from this, leaving £15,000 to be paid to the injured person.

Similarly, the compensator may offset the £10,000 of DLA paid against the loss of mobility heading, leaving £20,000 to be paid to the injured person.

The injured person has settled their claim for a total of £100,000. Following offsetting, they receive £75,000 from the compensator, having already received £25,000 in recoverable benefits from the DWP.

3. Exempt payments

Some compensation payments are exempt from the recovery rules. They are:

- vaccine damage payments;
- Criminal Injuries Compensation scheme payments (see Chapter 47(3));
- payments from the Macfarlane and Eileen Trusts and the Skipton Fund;
- payments from the Government-funded trust for people with variant Creutzfeldt-Jakob disease;
- payments from the UK Asbestos and EL Scheme Trusts;
- payments from the London Bombings Relief Charitable Fund;
- payments under the Fatal Accidents Act 1976;
- contractual sick pay from an employer;
- payments made under the NHS industrial injuries scheme;
- payments from insurance companies under policies agreed before the accident;
- payments under the NCB Pneumoconiosis Compensation scheme; *and*
- payments in respect of sensorineural hearing loss of less than 50dB in one or both ears.

The Social Security (Recovery of Benefits) Regs, reg 2

4. Lump-sum payments

The compensator can reduce any part of your compensation award (including damages paid for pain and suffering) if you have had a lump-sum payment under:

- the Pneumoconiosis etc (Workers Compensation) Act 1979 (including any extra-statutory payments made following the rejection of a claim under that act); *or*
- the 2008 Diffuse Mesothelioma scheme.

The Social Security (Recovery of Benefits)(Lump Sum Payments) Regs 2008

5. Appeals

If your compensation payment has been reduced to take account of benefit recovery and you think the certificate is wrong, you can appeal. You must attach letters you have received from the compensator telling you the compensation payment has been reduced. You must state under which of the four following grounds you are making your appeal:

- an amount, rate or period specified in the certificate is incorrect; *or*
- the certificate shows benefits or lump sums that were not paid as a result of the accident, injury or disease in respect of which compensation was paid; *or*
- benefits or lump sums listed that have not, and are not likely to be, paid to you have been brought into account; *or*
- the compensation payment made was not as a consequence of the accident, injury or disease.

You must appeal within one month of the date the compensator pays the Compensation Recovery Unit (CRU). If you apply late, you must show there are special circumstances for the delay. Appeal on form Z2, which can be downloaded from the CRU website (www.dwp.gov.uk/cru).

Social Security (Recovery of Benefits) Act 1997, S.11

Warning: A tribunal dealing with an appeal against recovery is entitled to decide whether or not the benefits recovered were in fact paid in respect of the accident, injury or disease in question. Both the tribunal's decision and the evidence on which it is based can potentially raise doubt about entitlement to those benefits. Consequently, it would be wise to seek advice before lodging an appeal.

R(CR)2/02

6. For more information

Further information can be found in the DWP guide GL27, *Compensation, social security benefits and or lump sum payments*. The guide can be downloaded from the Compensation Recovery Unit (CRU) website (www.dwp.gov.uk/cru).

For specific enquiries regarding the relevant law, ring the CRU Policy Liaison Section (0191 225 2245).

For information regarding the similar scheme in Northern Ireland, contact the Compensation Recovery Unit, Social Security Agency, Magnet House, 81-93 York Street, Belfast BT15 1SS (028 9054 5855).

For a fuller explanation of the scheme, see *Deducting Benefits from Damages for Personal Injury* by Professor Richard Lewis (Oxford University Press).

Coming to or leaving the UK

Q

50 Coming to the UK

1. Introduction

To qualify for most benefits you must satisfy the rules about residence and presence in Great Britain (GB). Your right to benefit may also be affected by your immigration status.

GB means England, Scotland and Wales; United Kingdom (UK) means GB plus Northern Ireland. In Northern Ireland and the Isle of Man, social security benefits come under separate legislation, but this is very similar to that in GB, and periods of residence may count for UK benefits. In the Channel Islands the system is different but there is a reciprocal agreement that may allow periods of residence there to count for UK benefits. Periods of residence in another European Economic Area (EEA) country may count as residence in GB for those covered by European Community (EC) rules, and reciprocal agreements with some non-EEA countries include similar rules.

EEA countries – The EEA consists of the 27 member states of the European Union (EU) – Austria, Belgium, Bulgaria, Cyprus, *Czech Republic, Denmark, *Estonia, Finland, France, Germany, Greece, *Hungary, Italy, *Latvia, *Lithuania, Luxembourg, Malta, Netherlands, *Poland, Portugal, Republic of Ireland, Romania, *Slovakia, *Slovenia, Spain, Sweden, UK (including Gibraltar, but not the Channel Islands or Isle of Man) – together with Iceland, Norway and Liechtenstein. If you (or a member of your family) have moved to the UK from another member state *and* are an EEA or Swiss national or a refugee or stateless person resident in an EEA state *and* are or were employed or self-employed, you may be covered by more favourable EC social security rules. Generally, you count as employed or self-employed if you have paid contributions under the UK national insurance scheme or an equivalent scheme of another EEA country.

A8 – This term refers to the eight countries marked * above.

A2 – This term refers to Bulgaria and Romania.

Reciprocal agreements – Reciprocal social security agreements with some countries (including all EEA countries except A8 and A2 countries, Greece and Liechtenstein – the reciprocal agreement applies if you are not covered by EC rules) may help you receive benefit. Non-EEA countries covered by reciprocal agreements are Barbados, Bermuda, Canada, Isle of Man, Israel, Jamaica, Jersey & Guernsey, Mauritius, New Zealand, Philippines, Switzerland, Turkey, USA and former Yugoslavia. Agreements differ and not all benefits are covered. There are 'association' and 'co-operation' agreements with Algeria, Morocco, San Marino, Slovenia, Tunisia and Turkey.

2. Residence and presence tests

Entitlement to many benefits depends on satisfying residence and presence tests for that benefit.

Meaning of terms

Present – This means physically present in GB throughout the whole day. (See Chapter 51 for when you can be treated as present in GB while you are abroad.)

Resident – You are usually 'resident' in the country where you have your home for the time being.

Ordinarily resident – This term is not defined in regulations. You should be 'ordinarily resident' in the place where you normally live for the time being if there is a degree of continuity about your stay such that it can be described as settled.

Right to reside – This term does not have a single statutory definition. See below for how this test is applied.

Habitually resident – This term is not defined in regulations. See below for how this test is applied.

Disability benefits

For disability living allowance (DLA), attendance allowance (AA), carer's allowance (CA), contributory employment and support allowance 'in youth' (CESA(Y)), incapacity benefit 'in youth' (IB(Y)) and severe disablement allowance (SDA) the general rules and exceptions are as follows.

The residence and presence test (general rule) – You must be present and ordinarily resident in GB, and have been present for not less than 26 of the last 52 weeks. This is a continuing test. It applies to any day for which you are claiming benefit.

DLA and AA – If DLA is claimed for a baby under 6 months old, a 13-week presence test applies until the baby's 1st birthday. If a child becomes entitled to DLA after reaching 6 months, the 26-week test applies.

The 26- or 13-week presence tests do not apply if you are accepted as terminally ill.

If these special provisions apply, the presence and ordinary residence tests must still be satisfied.

CESA(Y), IB(Y) and SDA – Once you pass the residence and presence tests you do not need to satisfy them again while you are in the same period of limited capability for work/ incapacity for work.

AA Regs, reg 2; DLA Regs reg 2; ICA Regs reg 9; ESA Regs, reg 11; SDA Regs reg 3; IB Regs reg 16

Tax credits, child benefit and health in pregnancy grant

For working tax credit and child tax credit (CTC) you (and your partner if you are making a joint claim) must be present and ordinarily resident in the UK and, for new CTC claims made on or after 1.5.04, have a right to reside in the UK (see below).

TCA s.3(3); TC(R) Regs, reg 3

To be entitled to child benefit you *and* the child must be present in GB (or Northern Ireland if claiming there), be ordinarily resident in the UK and, for new claims made on or after 1.5.04, have a right to reside in the UK (see below).

SSCBA s.146; CB Regs, reg 23 & 27

To be entitled to a health in pregnancy grant you must be present in GB (or Northern Ireland if claiming there) and ordinarily resident in, and with a right to reside in, the UK (see below).

SSCBA s.140A; Health in Pregnancy Grant (Entitlement & Amount) Regs, reg 4

Means-tested benefits

For housing benefit (HB), council tax benefit (CTB), income

support (IS), income-related ESA, pension credit (PC) and income-based JSA, you must be *'habitually resident'* in the Common Travel Area (CTA, which is the UK, Channel Islands, Isle of Man or Republic of Ireland) and, for IS, income-related ESA, PC or income-based JSA, present in GB.

Partner abroad – If you used to live in GB or abroad with your partner who is now abroad, they will be treated as your partner (with their income and capital affecting your entitlement to benefit) unless you do not intend to resume living together or the absence is likely to exceed 52 weeks.

IS Regs, reg 16; ESA Regs, reg 156; JSA Regs, reg 78; SPC Regs, reg 5; HB Regs, reg 21

The habitual residence test – Unless you are exempt (see below), you have to satisfy the 'habitual residence test' (HRT), which includes having a right to reside (see below) in the CTA.

There is no definitive list of factors that determine habitual residence, but you must show a *'settled intention'* to stay here. In most cases, you also need to be actually resident for a period of time, but you may be accepted as habitually resident from your first day of residence if you are:

- returning to the CTA and you were previously habitually resident here; *or*
- (or a member of your family is) a national of, and have worked in, another EEA state (see 1 above).

Seek specialist advice if you are likely to be subject to the test. You can appeal against a decision that you are not habitually resident. To ensure entitlement to benefit as soon as possible, submit further claims while you are waiting for your appeal to be heard, and appeal each negative decision.

If you are not accepted as habitually resident for IS, income-related ESA, income-based JSA or PC, the HB/CTB office must make its own decision, not just follow the DWP decision.

Exemptions – The HRT does not apply if you:

- have refugee status, humanitarian protection, or exceptional leave to enter/remain; *or*
- left Montserrat after 1.11.95 because of a volcanic eruption; *or*
- arrived in the UK from Zimbabwe after 27.2.09 under a UK government assistance scheme; *or*
- are not a *'person subject to immigration control'* (see 3 below) and have been deported, expelled or otherwise legally removed from another country; *or*
- are an EEA national (see 1 above and restrictions for A8/A2 nationals below) classified as a *'worker'* (you must be employed in the UK doing 'genuine and effective' work) or self-employed – including if you have retained either status, because you are temporarily unable to work due to an illness or accident, or are involuntarily unemployed and signing on at Jobcentre Plus or in vocational training, or are voluntarily unemployed and in vocational training connected to your former work; *or*
- are a family member (ie a spouse, civil partner or dependent (grand)parent or (grand)child (who is either under 21 or dependent)) of someone in the group above; *or*
- are an EEA national with a *'right to reside permanently in the UK'* under Article 17 of EC directive 2004/38 (eg if you have retired, or are permanently incapable of work, in certain circumstances), or living with a family member in this group; *or*
- are an A8 national required to register your employment and you either have registered or are within the first month of employment; *or*
- are an A2 national subject to authorisation working in accordance with the conditions of your accession worker authorisation document.

The HRT is not generally applied if you are entitled to urgent cases payments of IS, income-related ESA or income-based JSA (see 3 below). Only the claimant is subject to the HRT. If you are one of a couple, the person most likely to satisfy (or be exempt from) the test should be the claimant.

IS Regs, reg 21-21AA; ESA Regs, reg 69-70; JSA Regs, reg 85-85A; SPC Regs, reg 2; HB Regs, reg 10; CTB Regs, reg 7

The right to reside test – For new claims made on or after 1.5.04, you must have a right to reside for CTC, child benefit and (to satisfy the HRT) IS, income-related ESA, income-based JSA, PC, HB and CTB. However, this requirement does not apply to a new claim for IS, income-based JSA, PC, HB or CTB if it is part of a continuous period of entitlement to one or more of these five benefits that included 30.4.04.

The Social Security (Habitual Residence) Amendment Regs 2004, reg 6

Certain groups have a 'right to reside'. These include all those who are exempt from the HRT (listed above), British and Irish citizens, and those with leave to enter/remain in the UK. The main groups of EEA nationals (in addition to those exempt from the HRT) with a right to reside are those who:

- have been legally residing in the UK for five years; *or*
- are self-sufficient; *or*
- are enrolled as a student and are self-sufficient; *or*
- (for income-based JSA, child benefit or CTC only) are jobseeking.

Family members (whether or not EEA nationals) of the groups above have a right to reside and in some circumstances can retain their right to reside if the EEA national dies, leaves the UK or, in the case of a spouse or civil partner, they get divorced or the civil partnership is dissolved. Others can have a right to reside, depending on their circumstances.

The Immigration (EEA) Regs 2006; EC Directive 2004/38

A8/A2 nationals – Most A8 nationals are subject to a requirement to register their employment under the Worker Registration Scheme and most A2 nationals can take employment only if they hold and work in accordance with an accession worker authorisation document. Limited categories are exempt from these requirements including those who have completed a year of registered/authorised work. While subject to registration or authorisation, an A8/A2 national:

- has no right to reside as a jobseeker;
- cannot retain their worker status in the ways listed in the 5th HRT exempt group;
- is only defined as a 'worker' if their work is registered/authorised.

The Accession (Immigration & Worker Registration) Regs 2004; The Accession (Immigration & Worker Authorisation) Regs 2006

3. Immigration status

If you are defined as a *'person subject to immigration control'*, unless you come under one of the exemptions below, you will be excluded from possible entitlement to the following benefits:

- attendance allowance (AA) and disability living allowance (DLA);
- carer's allowance;
- child benefit;
- child tax credit (CTC) and working tax credit (WTC);
- contributory employment and support allowance 'in youth' (CESA(Y));
- health in pregnancy grant;
- housing benefit (HB) and council tax benefit (CTB);
- income-based jobseeker's allowance (JSA);
- income-related employment and support allowance (ESA);
- income support (IS);
- incapacity benefit 'in youth' (IB(Y));
- pension credit;
- severe disablement allowance (SDA);
- social fund.

You are defined as a 'person subject to immigration control' if you are not an EEA national (see 1 above) and you:

- require leave to enter/remain in the UK but do not have it; *or*
- have leave to enter/remain in the UK subject to a condition that you do not have recourse to public funds; *or*
- are a sponsored immigrant – ie you have been given leave to enter or remain as a result of a maintenance undertaking (a written undertaking given by someone else in pursuance of the immigration rules, to be responsible for your maintenance and accommodation).

Immigration and Asylum Act 1999, S.115; ESA Regs, reg 11; IB Regs, reg 16; TCA, S.42; TC(I) Regs, reg 3

Exemptions: who can still get benefits?

You are not excluded from benefit entitlement if you are not defined as a person subject to immigration control. Examples include: people with refugee status, humanitarian protection, discretionary leave or indefinite leave to enter/remain (unless given as the result of a maintenance undertaking) and a family member of an EEA or Swiss national exercising their freedom of movement rights under EC law (or the Swiss agreement with the EC) who joins them in the UK. Some groups of people (listed below) can be entitled to benefit despite being defined as a person subject to immigration control.

Warning: All the benefits listed above are classed as 'public funds' except income-related ESA, CESA(Y) and IB(Y). If your immigration status is subject to a 'no recourse to public funds' condition, receiving one of these benefits (even if your partner is paid benefit on your behalf) may jeopardise your right to stay in the UK or undermine applications to the Home Office. However, the Home Office does not regard you as having 'recourse to public funds' if you fall into one of the exempt groups below.

Immigration Rules, para 6, 6A & 6B

You should get expert immigration advice (see Box Q.1) before making a claim if you have concerns over 'public funds' or do not have leave to enter/remain, have overstayed your leave or are unsure about your immigration status, since information is exchanged between the benefit authorities and the Home Office.

Who can get means-tested benefits?

If you are defined as a person subject to immigration control you are not excluded from entitlement to IS, income-related ESA, income-based JSA, pension credit, HB, or CTB if you are:

- a national of Croatia, Macedonia or Turkey and you are lawfully present in the UK; *or*
- a sponsored immigrant and have been resident in the UK for five years (beginning on the later date of either your entry to the UK or the signing of the maintenance undertaking); *or*
- a sponsored immigrant and less than five years have passed since you entered the UK (or since the maintenance undertaking was signed) and your sponsor has (or, if more than one, they have all) died; *or*
- on limited leave with the condition that you do not have recourse to 'public funds', and you have not yet had such recourse other than under this provision, and you are dependent on funds from abroad that are temporarily disrupted, but which are reasonably expected to resume (maximum of 42 days payment per period of leave); *or*
- an asylum seeker and you:
  - claimed asylum 'on arrival' (other than on re-entry) in the UK before 3.4.00; *or*
  - are a national of former Zaire (Democratic Republic of Congo) or Sierra Leone and you submitted a claim for asylum within three months after the Home Secretary's declarations that these countries were undergoing 'significant upheaval' made on 16.5.97 and 1.7.97 respectively; *or*
  - (except for income-based JSA) were entitled to IS, HB or CTB as an asylum seeker on 4.2.96, or a member of your family, covered by this group, was claiming the benefit for you on this date and you now need to claim separately from them (eg you are their ex-partner or child who ceased to be dependent). You will still be entitled if you claim again after a break.

  Entitlement will end on the date the decision on (or abandonment of) your asylum claim (or appeal if it was against a pre-5.2.96 decision) is recorded by the Home Office and notified to you.

(IA)CA Regs, reg 2

Payments of IS, income-based JSA and income-related ESA – The first two (or four, for income-related ESA) groups above receive normal payments and the remaining groups are entitled to 'urgent cases payments'. These have different calculation rules not covered in this Handbook. If you are entitled to urgent cases payments of IS, you do not need to fall into another eligible category (see Box E.1, Chapter 14).

If your partner is subject to immigration control – If you are entitled to pension credit or normal payments of IS, income-based JSA or income-related ESA, you cannot be paid for a partner defined as a person subject to immigration control (unless, except for pension credit, they are within one of the exempt groups above). If you are entitled to urgent cases payments of IS, income-based JSA or income-related ESA, you should be paid for your partner whether or not they are defined as a person subject to immigration control.

IS Regs, regs 21(3), 71 & Sch 7, para 16A; JSA Regs, regs 85(4), 148 & Sch 5, para 13A; ESA Regs, regs 69, 163 & Sch 5, para 10; SPC Regs, reg 5

Who can get tax credits?

Even if you are defined as a person subject to immigration control you are not excluded from tax credits if:

- you are a sponsored immigrant and either more than five years have passed since you entered the UK (or since the maintenance undertaking was signed) or your sponsor has (or, if more than one, they have all) died; *or*
- you are on limited leave with the condition that you do not have recourse to public funds and you have not had such recourse other than under this provision, and you are temporarily without funds due to funds from abroad being disrupted, but which are reasonably expected to resume (maximum of 42 days payment); *or*
- (CTC only) you are a national of Algeria, Morocco, San Marino, Tunisia or Turkey and are lawfully working (or have lawfully worked) in UK; *or*
- (WTC only) you are a national of Croatia, Macedonia or Turkey and you are lawfully present in the UK; *or*
- (CTC only) your CTC award begins on or after 6.4.04 and immediately before it began you were entitled to IS or income-based JSA for a child because you fell into either the above group or one of the three groups of asylum seekers listed as not excluded from IS or income-based JSA (above).

If your partner is subject to immigration control – and you are not, or you are but fall within one of the five exempt groups above, make a joint claim and it will be treated as if your partner were not subject to immigration control.

TC(I) Regs, reg 3 & 5

Who can get disability benefits and child benefit?

Even if you are defined as a person subject to immigration control you are not excluded from AA, DLA, carer's allowance, child benefit, health in pregnancy grant, CESA(Y), IB(Y) and SDA if:

- you are the family member of an EEA (including UK) national; *or*
- either you, or a member of your family who you are living with, are a national of Algeria, Morocco, San Marino,

Tunisia or Turkey and are lawfully working (or have lawfully worked) in GB; *or*

- you are a sponsored immigrant; *or*
- (for DLA, AA, and child benefit only) you are covered by a reciprocal agreement (see 1 above); *or*
- you were in receipt of the benefit immediately before 5.2.96 (or 7.10.96 for child benefit). Your entitlement will end if:
  - your benefit is revised or superseded. Claiming child benefit for an additional child does not give rise to a revision or supersession of your existing entitlement; *or*
  - you break your claim, or your fixed period award comes to an end; *or*
  - your claim for asylum (if any) is recorded as having been decided or abandoned.

(IA)CA Regs, reg 2

Social fund

Even if you are defined as a person subject to immigration control you are not excluded from entitlement to the social fund if you fall into any of the exempt categories listed above. However, you must meet the other conditions of entitlement, including (with the exception of crisis loans and winter fuel payments) being in receipt of a qualifying benefit.

(IA)CA Regs, reg 2

If you get a positive decision on your asylum claim

If you are granted refugee status you may be able to claim backdated tax credits. You must claim within three months of receiving the letter notifying you of your refugee status. The tax credits will be backdated to either the date of your asylum application or 6.4.03, whichever is the later. However, the amount paid will be net of any subsistence payments of asylum support you have received.

TC(I) Regs, reg 3

If you (or someone you are a dependant of) have been granted refugee status or humanitarian protection since 11.6.07, you can, if aged over 18, apply for an 'integration loan' from the UK Border Agency. Further details and application forms are available on their website (www.bia.homeoffice.gov.uk). Once you are granted refugee status, humanitarian protection or discretionary leave, you are no longer subject to immigration control while you have that leave, and you can claim all benefits.

4. Other forms of support

Asylum support – If you have an asylum claim or appeal that has not yet been determined, or you are the dependant of such a person, and you are aged 18 or over and accepted as destitute, you may be able to get asylum support (accommodation and/or subsistence payments). If your asylum claim and appeal have been refused, you may be eligible for 'section 4' support. Both are provided by the UK Border Agency. Seek advice for further details (see Box Q.1).

Help from social services – Even if you are defined as a person subject to immigration control you may be entitled to accommodation and/or other assistance from your social services department under one or more legal provisions. You may be eligible for Community Care services under section 2 of the Chronically Sick and Disabled Persons Act 1970 (see Chapter 28(5)). If you have needs that are not solely a consequence of destitution or its physical effects (eg you have needs due to your age or disability) you may be entitled to accommodation and other assistance under the National Assistance Act 1948. If you are an unaccompanied child aged under 18 or you have dependent children you may be able to get assistance under the Children Act 1989. Remember that information is exchanged between social services and the Home Office. If you are refused assistance from your local authority, seek independent advice.

51 Leaving the UK

1. Introduction

You may be able to receive benefit while you are travelling or living abroad. Some benefits (eg state pension) can be paid no matter how long you are away, while the conditions for others are more complex. The rules vary depending on the country you go to. You may benefit from European Community (EC) social security rules if you go to a European Economic Area (EEA) country or from a reciprocal agreement (which includes similar rules) – see Chapter 50(1). However, if you are not covered by EC rules or a reciprocal agreement, the general rules on payment of benefits abroad apply. There are also rules treating you as being in Great Britain (GB) for the purposes of certain benefits if you (or a family member you live with) are a member of the forces serving abroad, a crown servant posted overseas (or your partner is) or fall within certain categories of airmen, mariners and continental-shelf workers.

This chapter covers general rules and indicates benefits payable in EEA countries. EC rules and reciprocal agreements are too varied to cover here, so if you plan to go abroad get specialist advice. Contact the International Pension Centre (see inside back cover) for information about receiving the following benefits abroad: state pension, bereavement benefits, industrial injuries benefits, contribution-based jobseeker's allowance, maternity allowance, incapacity benefit and employment and support allowance. For other benefits, contact the office that pays them. In each case, they will need to know the purpose, destination and intended length of your visit.

Temporary absence – For many benefits, one condition for payment while abroad is that your absence is temporary. For child benefit and tax credits this means the absence is unlikely to exceed 52 weeks. For other benefits, the term is not defined in law and in deciding whether your absence is temporary, the DWP should consider all the circumstances, including your intentions and the purpose and length of your absence. If the decision maker decides your absence is not temporary, you have a right of appeal.

2. Incapacity and maternity benefits

General rules – If you are temporarily absent from GB, you can continue to be paid incapacity benefit (IB), severe disablement allowance (SDA) or maternity allowance (MA) for the first 26 weeks of the absence if Jobcentre Plus has agreed. There is no right of appeal if they refuse; your only recourse is judicial review. You are not subject to the 26-week limit and do not require Jobcentre Plus agreement if you are receiving disability living allowance or attendance allowance (see 8 below for when these can be paid beyond 26 weeks). However, in all cases you must satisfy one of the following conditions:

- at the time you go abroad you have been continuously incapable of work for at least six months and remain continuously incapable while abroad; *or*
- you have gone abroad *'for the specific purpose of being treated'* for an illness or disability that began before you left. The treatment does not need to be your only reason for going abroad. However, going abroad to convalesce or for a change of air – even on your doctor's advice – is not enough. *'Being treated'* must involve some activity by another person. It does not matter whether the treatment is available in the UK or not. In some cases the claimants did not receive any treatment – but they did go abroad specifically to try to get it.

PA Regs, reg 2

EC – You may be able to get short-term IB or MA if you get agreement from Jobcentre Plus before you go to another EEA country to live or for medical treatment. Long-term IB and SDA can continue to be paid in another EEA country.

3. Employment and support allowance (ESA)

You continue to be entitled to ESA during a temporary absence from GB if you are receiving NHS treatment outside GB. Otherwise, if you continue to satisfy the other conditions of entitlement and the absence is unlikely to exceed 52 weeks, your benefit continues for four weeks, or 26 weeks if you are abroad solely for medical treatment or to accompany a dependent child for their treatment. In each case, the treatment must be by an appropriately qualified person for a condition that began before you go abroad. If you are being treated, the condition must be directly related to your limited capability for work. Obtain permission from Jobcentre Plus before you go.

ESA Regs, regs 151-155

Partner abroad – If you are the income-related ESA claimant and you stay in GB, you will get benefit for your partner for the first four weeks. If they meet the medical treatment conditions above, you will get benefit for them for 26 weeks if either you stay in GB or you both meet those conditions. After this, benefit will be reduced. However, your partner's income and capital will affect your entitlement unless either you do not intend to resume living together or the absence is likely to exceed 52 weeks.

ESA Regs, reg 156 & Sch 5, para 6-7

EC – Contributory ESA can continue to be paid in another EEA country.

4. Statutory sick/maternity/paternity and adoption pay

You can receive these while abroad, unless your employer is not required to pay Class 1 national insurance contributions for you – eg because they are not present or resident, and do not have a place of business, in the UK.

5. Income support (IS)

If you are entitled immediately before you leave, you can continue receiving IS during a temporary absence abroad if:

- you are receiving NHS treatment outside GB; *or*
- the absence is unlikely to exceed 52 weeks and you continue to satisfy the other entitlement conditions and satisfy the 4- or 8-week rule below.

4-week rule – You can be paid IS for the first four weeks if:

- you are in Northern Ireland; *or*
- you and your partner are both abroad and a disability premium, severe disability premium or any pensioner premium is applicable for the partner of the claimant; *or*
- you have been continuously incapable of work during the 364 days before the day you leave GB, or 196 days if you are terminally ill or entitled to disability living allowance highest rate care component (two or more periods of incapacity are treated as continuous if the break between them is not more than 56 days each time); *or*
- you are incapable of work and your absence is *'for the sole purpose of receiving treatment from an appropriately qualified person for the incapacity by reason of which'* you are eligible for IS; *or*
- you fall within one of the groups that can claim IS (see Box E.1, Chapter 14) other than if you have been incapable of work for less than 28 weeks, or are appealing against an incapacity for work decision, or are a 'person subject to immigration control' entitled to urgent cases payments (see Chapter 50(3)), or are in school or full-time non-advanced education, or involved in a trade dispute.

8-week rule – You can get IS for the first eight weeks abroad if you are taking your dependent child abroad for medical treatment by an appropriately qualified person.

IS Regs, reg 4

Partner abroad – If you are the IS claimant and you stay in GB, your IS will include benefit for your partner for the first four weeks (or eight weeks if they meet the conditions of the 8-week rule above). After this, benefit will be reduced. However, your partner's income and capital will affect your IS entitlement unless you do not intend to resume living together or the absence is likely to exceed 52 weeks.

IS Regs, reg 16

6. Pension credit

You continue to be entitled to pension credit during a temporary absence from GB if you are receiving NHS treatment outside GB. Otherwise, as long as you continue to satisfy the other conditions of entitlement and the absence is unlikely to exceed 52 weeks, it continues for 13 weeks.

SPC Regs, regs 3 & 4

Partner abroad – If one of these circumstances applies to your partner, your pension credit will include benefit for them for the relevant period of their temporary absence. After this, they cease to be treated as your partner and your benefit will be reduced.

SPC Regs, regs 4 & 5

EC – Seek specialist advice to argue that pension credit can be paid in another EEA country.

7. Jobseeker's allowance

General rules – If you are entitled immediately before you leave, you can continue receiving jobseeker's allowance (JSA) during a temporary absence abroad if:

- you are receiving NHS treatment outside GB; *or*
- the absence is unlikely to exceed 52 weeks and you satisfy one of the rules below.

- ❑ You can be paid for the first four weeks if you are in Northern Ireland and continue to satisfy the conditions of entitlement while there, or you are abroad with your partner and a disability premium, severe disability premium or pensioner premium is payable in respect of your partner and you are the claimant. You can also be paid for up to four weeks if you are under 25 and receive a government training allowance but are not receiving training (although certain training courses are excluded).
- ❑ You can be paid for the first eight weeks if you are taking your dependent child abroad for medical treatment by an appropriately qualified person.
- ❑ If you go abroad for a job interview and are away for no more than seven consecutive days, you can be paid for your days abroad if you give notice (written, if required) to the Jobcentre Plus office and on your return you satisfy the employment officer that you attended the interview.

JSA Regs, reg 50

Partner abroad – The rules for income-based JSA are similar to income support (see 5 above). However, if you are claiming as a joint-claim couple and on the date you make your claim your partner is abroad, you will only be paid for them for the first four weeks if they are in Northern Ireland (and the absence is unlikely to exceed 52 weeks) or they are in receipt of a training allowance (as above) or for up to seven days if they are attending a job interview. Otherwise you will be paid as a single person.

JSA Regs, reg 78

EC – For contribution-based JSA, if you go to an EEA country to look for work, have been registered with the Jobcentre Plus office for (normally) four weeks and satisfy the conditions of entitlement up to the date you leave the UK, you can usually get benefit in the EEA country for up to three months. You must register as unemployed in the country where you are seeking work within seven days and comply with their procedures. For income-based JSA, seek advice to argue the same rules should apply.

8. Attendance allowance (AA) and disability living allowance (DLA)

General rules – AA and DLA will be paid for the first 26 weeks of a temporary absence abroad. You can only be paid for longer if the absence is temporary and for the specific purpose of being treated for an illness or disability that began before you left GB, and the DWP agrees to pay you for longer.

AA Regs, reg 2(2)(d)&(e); DLA Regs, reg 2(2)(d)&(e)

EC – If your entitlement to AA or DLA began before 1.6.92, you can be paid without time limit in another EEA country if you, or a member of your family, have been employed or self-employed in the UK and continue to satisfy all the other entitlement conditions other than the residence and presence conditions. You can make a renewal claim while you are abroad, but should avoid a break in entitlement between the end of an award and entitlement under the renewal claim.

If your AA or DLA entitlement began after 1.6.92, you may be paid AA or DLA care component in another EEA country in certain circumstances, including if you were working or paying national insurance in the UK or if you are in receipt of state pension, industrial injuries disablement benefit, bereavement benefits, incapacity benefit or contributory employment and support allowance. For details, write to: Exportability Co-ordinator, Room C216, PDCS, Warbreck House, Warbreck Hill Road, Blackpool FY2 0YE.

Commission of the European Communities v the European Parliament & the Council of the European Union (C-299/05, 18.10.07)

9. Carer's allowance

General rules – This will be paid for the first four weeks of a temporary absence abroad if you go without the person you are caring for. If you go abroad temporarily specifically to care for that person, you will receive carer's allowance for as long as they continue to receive attendance allowance (AA) or disability living allowance (DLA).

ICA Regs, reg 9

EC – The rules are the same as for AA/DLA (care component) (see 8 above).

10. Child benefit

If you are ordinarily resident in the UK and temporarily absent (see 1 above) from GB (or Northern Ireland if you are claiming there) you continue to be entitled to child benefit for the first eight weeks, or for the first 12 weeks if the absence is in connection with:

- your treatment for a disability or illness; *or*
- the treatment (for a disability or illness), or death, of your partner, or the sibling, parent, (great) grandparent, child (including a child you are responsible for), (great) grandchild of you or your partner.

Q.1 For more information

For information on benefits for people entering and leaving the UK, see *Migration and Social Security Handbook* (5th edn) (Child Poverty Action Group). For a guide to immigration law, see *Immigration, Nationality & Refugee Law Handbook* (2006 edn) (Joint Council for the Welfare of Immigrants). For immigration advice contact Refugee and Migrant Justice or a law centre (see Address List).

The DWP and HMRC produce leaflets (including some in languages other than English) for each country covered by a reciprocal agreement with the UK, as well as general leaflets. Leaflets are available from the International Pension Centre (see inside back cover).

Under these rules, if a woman gives birth while absent from GB the baby will be treated as being in GB (or Northern Ireland) for up to 12 weeks from the start of the mother's absence.

Child benefit can be paid for the first 12 weeks of your child's temporary absence abroad. It may be paid for longer if your child goes abroad:

- for the specific purpose of being treated for an illness or disability that began before they left the UK; *or*
- solely in order to receive full-time education in another EEA country (or Switzerland) or on an educational exchange or visit; *or*
- to Northern Ireland (or to GB if you are claiming in Northern Ireland).

Guardian's allowance can be paid abroad for the same period as child benefit.

CB Regs, Part 6

EC – You may be paid benefit for a child resident in another EEA country.

11. Industrial injuries disablement benefit

A basic disablement pension and retirement allowance are both payable while you are abroad. However, there are time limits for other industrial injuries benefits.

Reduced earnings allowance (REA) – is payable for the first three months of a temporary absence abroad if you were entitled before you left and your absence is not connected with work, or for longer if the DWP agrees. If you lose REA for one day, you may lose it for good.

Constant attendance allowance and exceptionally severe disablement allowance – are payable for the first six months of a temporary absence abroad, or longer if the DWP agrees.

PA Regs, reg 9

EC – You can be paid any industrial injuries benefit (including those above) without time limit in another EEA country.

12. Retirement, widows' and bereavement benefits

These are payable no matter how long you are away. If you intend to go for longer than six months, inform Jobcentre Plus so arrangements can be made for paying your benefit abroad. If you are living permanently in a country outside the EEA, you can only receive annual up-rating increases if that country has a reciprocal agreement with the UK covering the payment of annual increases or you are covered by a co-operation and association agreement.

You will be disqualified from a bereavement payment if you are abroad at the time of your spouse/civil partner's death unless they were in GB when they died, or you returned within four weeks of their death, or their national insurance contribution record satisfies the contribution condition of a widowed parent's allowance or bereavement allowance.

PA Regs, reg 4

EC – If you are living in an EEA country, you will get annual benefit increases as if you were in the UK.

13. Tax credits

If you are ordinarily resident in, but temporarily absent (see 1 above) from, the UK you are treated as present and can therefore either claim or continue to be entitled to tax credits for the first eight weeks, or for the first 12 weeks if the absence is in connection with:

- your treatment for a disability; *or*
- the treatment (for a disability), or death, of your partner, or the sibling, parent, (great) grandparent, child (including a child you are responsible for), (great) grandchild of you or your partner.

TC (R) Regs, reg 4

EC – If you are in the UK, child tax credit can be paid for family members living in another EEA country.

Tax R

52 Income tax

1. Introduction

This chapter briefly outlines income tax. HMRC Enquiry Centres can help with tax enquiries. For independent advice, contact TaxAid (0845 120 3779 or www.taxaid.org.uk) or, for the over-60s, TaxHelp for Older People (0845 601 3321 or www.taxvol.org.uk).

To check if you are paying the right amount of tax you need to know what income is taxable, the allowances you are entitled to and the appropriate rate of tax. The amounts change each year (from 6 April), so find out the amounts for the year you want to check. The figures and allowances in this chapter are for 6.4.09 to 5.4.10.

2. Income

Many types of income (eg earnings) are taxable, but some is exempt (eg interest on Individual Savings Accounts) and ignored for tax. You are allowed tax relief on certain outgoings (eg pension contributions), but this is often given at source.

Which state benefits are taxable? – The following are the only taxable benefits:

- carer's allowance;
- contributory employment and support allowance;
- higher rate short-term incapacity benefit (IB);
- long-term IB (but not if you transferred from invalidity benefit – see Box D.10, Chapter 13);
- income support if you are directly involved in a trade dispute;
- invalidity allowance paid with a state pension;
- industrial death benefit;
- jobseeker's allowance;
- state pension;
- adult dependants' additions paid with these benefits (but not additions for children);
- statutory adoption, maternity, paternity and sick pay;
- bereavement allowance, widowed mother's/parent's allowance and widow's pension.

3. Tax allowances

You are entitled to a personal allowance. You may also be entitled to a blind person's allowance or married couple's allowance (see below). If you think you have not had the correct allowances, a refund may be due (see 7 below).

Personal allowance – Everyone has a personal allowance that can be set against all taxable income.

Age	personal allowance
Under 65 (basic level)	£6,475
65-74	£9,490
75 or over	£9,640

You can claim the appropriate higher age allowance for the complete tax year in which your 65th or 75th birthday falls. The higher age allowances are reduced if your total income is more than £22,900. For each £2 extra income over £22,900, £1 of allowance is lost. But it won't be reduced below the basic level. Spouses and civil partners each have their own total income limit. If you don't use your full personal allowance, you cannot transfer it to a partner or carry it forward to a future year.

Blind person's allowance – You will get an extra allowance of £1,890 if you are registered blind (but not if you are registered as partially sighted). In Scotland and Northern Ireland, you must be unable through blindness to do any work for which eyesight is essential. Spouses or civil partners can transfer surplus allowance from one to the other. If both spouses/civil partners are registered blind, it is possible for one of them to get both their own blind person's allowance and the other's surplus allowance. You can receive the allowance for the tax year before the one in which you are registered as blind, provided you had obtained the evidence for registration (eg ophthalmologist's certificate) before the end of that tax year.

Married couple's allowance – This is for a married couple or civil partners who live together if at least one of the couple was born before 6.4.35; the allowance for 2009/10 is £6,965. Tax relief on the married couple's allowance is restricted to 10%. It may be reduced if the income of the higher-earning partner is above the £22,900 income limit (by £1 for every £2 over the limit). It only starts to be reduced if their personal allowance has been reduced to the basic level and it cannot be reduced below a minimum of £2,670.

4. Income tax rates (non-savings income)

Taxable income	rate for tax year 2009/10
The first £37,400	20% (basic rate)
Above £37,400	40% (higher rate)

5. Working out your tax

Step 1: Work out your total income

Add up income from all sources for the tax year (which runs from 6 April to 5 April). Include taxable state benefits, but not exempt income.

Step 2: Work out your taxable income

Deduct your personal allowance (plus the blind person's allowance if you qualify) from your total income in Step 1.

Step 3: Work out your tax

a) Add 20% of the first £37,400 of your taxable income to 40% of all your income above £37,400. Different tax rates may apply on savings income – see 7 below.

b) If you get married couple's allowance (MCA), work out 10% of it and deduct the result from the tax payable in (a). This is the tax you are due to pay (before taking off any tax already paid at source).

Example: James, aged 75, is married to Annie, 72. James is registered blind. He gets a private pension of £8,514 for this tax year and state pension of £7,035.

Step 1: James' total income	
Private pension	£8,514
State pension	£7,035
Total income	*£15,549*

Step 2: James' taxable income	
Personal allowance, aged 75+	£9,640
Blind person's allowance	£1,890
Total personal allowances	*£11,530*
Subtract allowances from income	
Taxable income	*£4,019*
Step 3: James' tax	
a) 20% of £4,019	£803.80
b) Less 10% of MCA of £6,965	£696.50
Tax payable	*£107.30*

James will find out if he has tax to pay or to be refunded by checking his P60 (issued by the pension company after the tax year end) to see how much tax he paid on his private pension under the PAYE system (see 6 below) against the tax due of £107.30.

6. Notice of coding

If you have earnings or non-state pension income you will generally have tax deducted under PAYE (Pay As You Earn). For each source of earnings or pension income, HMRC should send you a notice of coding, setting out details of personal allowances, with any necessary deductions from income. You should check these notices each year and contact HMRC if you think they are incorrect.

For example, if you are a single person under 65 and registered blind, you would get allowances of £8,365 (personal allowance £6,475 plus blind person's allowance £1,890). Your code would be 836L. The final digit of your allowance is replaced by the letter L if you are on the basic personal allowance. Other letters (P, Y or T) may be used at the end of tax codes; the first three indicate where certain age allowances are given and the last is used in most other cases.

There are five cases that either do not have numbers or have numbers that do not show the amount of allowances:

- BR: no allowances; tax is deducted at basic rate (20%) on every pound of income;
- D: tax is deducted at a higher rate (40%);
- K: deductions are more than the total allowances, so an mount is added to your pay or pension on which tax is to be paid;
- NT: no tax is to be deducted;
- 0T: no allowances; tax is deducted at the appropriate rate on every pound of income.

7. Tax refunds

If you have paid too much tax you can claim a refund; you may go back five years from 31 January in the following tax year. This means refunds of tax for 2003/04 must be claimed before 31.1.10. The time limit can be extended if tax has been overpaid due to an error by HMRC or another government department and there is no dispute or doubt over the matter. To claim a refund, write to your HMRC Enquiry Centre with the details or ask them for form R40.

If you stop work and your income drops, a tax refund can be claimed on form P50 four weeks or more after leaving work. Send your P45 (which your former employer should give you when you leave), with the completed P50, to HMRC. You need to estimate your income for the rest of the tax year. If you leave work and claim jobseeker's allowance, you cannot get a tax refund until the end of the tax year.

Savings – Tax of 20% is deducted by the bank, building society, etc from most interest on savings. If your total taxable income, including interest before tax is taken off (the 'gross' amount), is less than your total personal allowances, you can receive interest without deduction of tax. Ask your bank or building society for form R85.

The tax rate on savings income (excluding dividends) depends on the level of your income. If your total income is less than your personal allowances, no tax is due. You may be able to claim a refund of tax paid at source. Ring the HMRC helpline (0845 077 6543).

If your total taxable income after deducting your total personal allowances, including interest, is less than £2,440, you are liable for tax on the interest at only 10%. If 20% tax has been deducted at source, you will be due a refund. If you are a basic rate taxpayer (taxable income up to £37,400) and your total taxable income is over £2,440, tax is due on savings income at 20%; so if 20% tax has been deducted at source, there is no additional tax to pay. For higher rate taxpayers, interest is taxed at 40%, so there will be an extra 20% due. This may be collected through your PAYE coding or will be payable through self assessment (see 9 below for information on the tax return process).

The tax rate due on dividends is 10%, unless you are a higher rate taxpayer, in which case it is 32.5%. The tax deducted at source (the 'tax credit') covers tax due at 10%, but is not refundable, so even non-taxpayers cannot claim back the dividend's tax credit. Higher rate taxpayers pay an extra 22.5%.

8. Arrears of tax

If you have not paid enough tax, HMRC can claim it from you, usually within six years. In some circumstances (eg deliberate tax evasion) the time limit is 20 years. HMRC could charge penalties if you are at fault.

In certain circumstances, arrears of tax are wholly or partly waived if they have arisen because HMRC failed to take account of information you gave them and you reasonably believed your affairs were in order. This concession may be given if you are notified of the arrears after the end of the tax year following that in which HMRC received information indicating you had underpaid tax. If you believe this applies to you, write to HMRC claiming a waiver under extra statutory concession A19.

9. Tax returns and keeping records

You may be asked to complete a tax return if you have income that is not taxed at source or if your circumstances have changed. Some taxpayers, eg self-employed people and those with complex tax affairs, are asked to do this every year. If in any tax year you receive income or capital gains that should be taxed and which HMRC does not know about, you must notify them within six months of the end of the tax year (by 5.10.10 for 2009/10).

You should keep records of your income and capital gains to enable you to complete a tax return. Records should usually be kept for 22 months after the end of the relevant tax year. If you are self-employed or have rental income, that period is extended by four years.

If you regularly file a tax return, you will be sent a blank form (or notice to complete one) shortly after the end of the tax year. Paper returns must be filed by 31 October. HMRC will calculate your tax and let you know by 31 January how much to pay. Tax returns filed online are due by 31 January. If you want HMRC to collect tax due (amounts less than £2,000) through your PAYE code for the following year, you should complete and send back the tax return by 31 October for paper returns or 31 December for online returns. Tax should be paid in full by 31 January or you may be charged interest or a penalty. There is an initial penalty of up to £100 if the return is late. The penalty cannot exceed the tax payable. If you file your return after the deadline and it shows a refund was due or you pay all the tax owing before 31 January, the penalty should be cancelled. Further penalties can arise depending on how late you submit the return or pay the tax due.

10. Self-employment

When you become self-employed, you must register with HMRC by the end of the third month following that in which you start your business, otherwise a penalty may be charged. Obtain booklet SE1, complete the form CWF1 that comes with it (available from www.hmrc.gov.uk or telephone 0845 900 0404) and send it to HMRC; or register via HMRC's dedicated helpline (0845 915 4515). You will be sent a tax return to complete each year. Booklet SE1 also has information about national insurance contributions.

53 VAT relief

1. Introduction

This is a brief summary of the VAT relief available for items purchased to help with your disability or for works carried out to your home to adapt it to suit your needs. Further information is in Notice 701/7 *VAT reliefs for disabled people* and Notice 701/59 *Motor vehicles for disabled people*. These are available online (www.hmrc.gov.uk) or you can request them, and get further advice, by:

- ringing the HMRC Charities Helpline: 0845 302 0203;
- writing to HMRC Charities, St Johns House, Merton Road, Liverpool L75 1BB;
- emailing: charities@hmrc.gov.uk.

If you are eligible for relief, if the items ('goods') or works ('services') qualify, and if you inform the supplier (and provide an eligibility certificate), VAT is charged at a nil rate (known as zero-rate) rather than at 17.5%. From 1.12.08 to 31.12.09, standard rate VAT has been reduced to 15%.

Note: VAT law still uses terms no longer in usage, which can sometimes cause offence. When we use them here we do so to reflect accurately the wording of the law.

2. Do you qualify?

To qualify for relief, the law states you must be *'chronically sick or disabled'*. HMRC guidance defines this as a person:

- with a physical or mental impairment that has a long-term and substantial adverse effect upon his/her ability to carry out everyday activities;
- with a condition that the medical profession treats as a chronic sickness, such as diabetes; *or*
- who is terminally ill.

3. What items or works qualify?

Goods

Some items you purchase or hire to help with your condition qualify for relief. Here are some examples:

- medical appliances designed solely for relief of 'severe abnormality or injury';
- adjustable beds designed for invalids;
- commode chairs, stools and other similar devices to aid with bathing;
- chair and stair lifts for invalid wheelchairs, hoists and other lifting equipment designed for use by invalids and the cost of installation;
- boats designed or substantially adapted for use by a disabled person;
- other items designed solely for use by a disabled person. The examples given in HMRC guidance notes include: low-vision aids (magnifying equipment, etc), Braille embossers, long-handled pick-up sticks, text telephones, whistling cups for the blind or partially-sighted, and vibrating pillows for the deaf or hard-of-hearing.

Services

Some alterations to items you purchase or to your home can qualify for relief. Here are some examples:

- the cost of adapting general-purpose goods to suit your particular needs (but not the cost of the goods themselves);
- constructing ramps or widening doorways or passages in your home (but not constructing new doorways or passages);
- extending or adapting a bathroom, washroom or lavatory in your home if necessary because of your condition;
- installing a lift in your home so you can move between floors;
- installing an alarm system so you can call for assistance.

Relief given for alterations to your home is strictly defined. Some common examples of works that do *not* qualify are:

- alterations resulting from the installation of special equipment (eg to house a renal dialysis unit). Although the equipment itself might qualify for relief, the alterations to your home do not;
- altering the layout of your home to accommodate a downstairs bedroom.

Cars and motor vehicles

Your hire, lease or purchase of a motor vehicle with a maximum capacity of 12 people qualifies for relief in any of the following circumstances:

- the vehicle was designed or substantially modified to carry a person in a wheelchair or on a stretcher;
- the vehicle was designed or substantially modified to enable you to enter, drive or be carried in it. A vehicle does not meet this condition merely because it has automatic transmission. To qualify, you must usually use a wheelchair or be carried on a stretcher;
- the vehicle contains features designed solely to enable you to be carried in a wheelchair. To qualify, you must usually use a wheelchair or be carried on a stretcher.

Relief also applies in the following circumstances:

- you lease an unused motor vehicle under the Motability scheme for a minimum period of three years;
- you purchase a motor vehicle that has previously been hired under the Motability scheme. The vehicle must be purchased from a person operating the scheme without any intervening supply.

Other costs

Parts and accessories for qualifying goods are generally zero-rated when supplied to you, as are the installation, repair or maintenance of those goods. However, parts and accessories for qualifying goods must be designed solely to go with the item concerned. For example, a generator purchased to run a stair lift in the event of a power cut does not qualify because it is a general-purpose item that could have other uses.

Bathrooms are specifically mentioned in the law, but kitchens are not. This may mean VAT relief is confined to kitchen equipment designed specially to suit your disability.

VAT Act 1994, Sch 8, Group 12

4. How do you claim?

Suppliers must ensure their goods or services qualify for zero-rating. They must therefore check that:

- the items or works qualify; *and*
- you qualify as a 'disabled person'.

When making a purchase you think might qualify, ask the supplier about zero-rating. If the goods or services qualify, the supplier will ask you to make a declaration (often by signing a form or by electronic means if buying over the internet) that you are an eligible disabled person.

5. Decisions and reviews

The system relies on suppliers deciding whether or not to zero-rate their goods or services. They decide according to their own interpretation of the rules. If there is uncertainty, the manufacturer can obtain a ruling from HMRC. If a decision is still in doubt, an appeal can be made to a First-tier Tribunal (Finance and Tax Chamber).

S Other matters

This section of the Handbook looks at:

54 After a death

1. What to do after a death

Following a death there can be many practical issues to be dealt with. This process, combined with the emotional effects of bereavement, can be difficult to cope with. DWP leaflets *What to do after a death in England and Wales* or *What to do after a death in Scotland* give advice and information about all aspects of bereavement.

You can get practical help and advice from a funeral director, GP, solicitor, religious organisation, social services department or Citizens Advice Bureau. A health visitor or district nurse may help if the death was at home. If it was in hospital, the ward sister or hospital chaplain might help. One of the first things you may need to do is transfer insurance policies (eg car and home insurance) into your name.

If you need support and comfort, organisations such as Cruse Bereavement Care (see Address List) and Winston's Wish, which offers a service to bereaved families and young people (0845 203 0405), can help.

2. Social fund funeral expenses

If you receive income-related employment and support allowance, income support, income-based jobseeker's allowance, housing benefit, council tax benefit, pension credit, working tax credit (if it includes either disability element) or child tax credit (at any rate greater than the family element), you may be able to get a payment from the social fund for funeral expenses (see Chapter 22(3)).

3. Income-related benefits

If you are under 60 and on a low income you may be able to get income-related employment and support allowance (ESA), income support or income-based jobseeker's allowance (JSA), depending on your circumstances. See Chapters 3, 14 and 15 respectively. For each of these benefits, £10 a week of widowed parent's or widowed mother's allowance is ignored in the assessment of your income.

If you are aged 60 or over and on a low income you may be able to get pension credit (see Chapter 42).

Late claims – If your claim for income support or JSA is late and it was not reasonable to expect you to claim earlier because of the death of a partner, parent, son, daughter, brother or sister, your claim can be backdated for up to one month (see Chapter 59(3)).

Carers – If you are getting carer's allowance or income support because you were caring for the person who has died, your benefit will usually end after eight weeks (see Chapter 7(8)). The carer premium in other means-tested benefits may also end after eight weeks (see Chapter 24(6)).

Housing costs – If you have a mortgage and are claiming income-related ESA, income support, income-based JSA or pension credit, you may be entitled to help with mortgage interest payments. If you are eligible for pension credit you can get this help straightaway; for the other benefits there is a 13-week waiting period. See Chapter 25.

Rent and council tax – Housing benefit and council tax benefit help towards rent and council tax if you are on a low income. In the assessment of your income, £15 a week of widowed parent's or widowed mother's allowance is ignored. See Chapter 20.

Pension arrears – If your spouse or civil partner was receiving pension credit or state pension (or any other benefit combined for payment with these), arrears of these benefits can be paid automatically to you on their death without the need for a claim.

4. Bereavement benefits

Bereavement benefits are available to people whose spouses have died on or after 9.4.01 or whose registered civil partner died on or after 5.12.05. They replaced the old system of widow's benefits, although women whose husbands died before 9.4.01 continue to claim widow's benefits.

There are three different bereavement benefits:

- bereavement payment – a lump-sum payment of £2,000;
- widowed parent's allowance (WPA) – if you have dependent children or are pregnant;
- bereavement allowance – payable for 52 weeks for those aged 45 or over when their spouse or civil partner died.

You must have been legally married or in a registered civil partnership. If you were in the process of divorcing or of dissolving a civil partnership, you would still qualify for bereavement benefits if your spouse or civil partner died before the decree absolute or dissolution was issued.

Bereavement allowance, WPA and widow's benefits under the old scheme are suspended for any period when you are cohabiting with a same/opposite-sex partner. If you remarry or form a civil partnership, the benefit ceases.

SSCBA, Ss.37(3)-(4), 38(2)-(3), 39A(4)-(5) & 39B(4)-(5)

Claims and time limits – Claim bereavement benefits from your local Jobcentre Plus office. The time limit for claiming a bereavement payment is 12 months from the established date of death. If you were receiving state pension when your spouse or civil partner died, you do not need to make a claim for bereavement payment to become entitled to it. Claims for WPA and bereavement allowance can be backdated for three months, but a bereavement allowance can only be paid for up to 12 months after the established date of death. If your spouse or civil partner's body has not been found or identified, and at least 12 months have passed since death was *presumed* to have occurred, claims for bereavement payment or bereavement allowance may be extended until up to 12 months after that presumption was accepted by the decision maker, or until 12 months after you first become aware of the discovery or identification of the body.

C&P Regs, reg 19(2)-(3B) & SSAA, S.3

For help available to war widows, widowers and surviving civil partners, see Chapter 46(8).

Bereavement payment

This is a tax-free, lump-sum payment of £2,000 for spouses bereaved on or after 9.4.01 and for civil partners bereaved after 5.12.05. You must have been under state pension age when your spouse or civil partner died, unless they were not entitled to a Category A state pension. If you were living with another person as part of a couple at the time of your late partner's death, you will not qualify.

To qualify, your spouse or civil partner must have paid Class 1, 2 or 3 national insurance (NI) contributions on earnings in any one tax year equal to 25 times the lower earnings limit for that year (see Chapter 11(6)). For tax years before 6.4.75, 25 flat-rate contributions will be sufficient. If your spouse or civil partner died as a result of an industrial accident or prescribed industrial disease, the contribution conditions are treated as satisfied.

SSCBA, Ss.36 & 60(2)&(3)

Widowed parent's allowance (WPA)

WPA is a regular payment for men and women bereaved on or after 9.4.01 (5.12.05 for civil partners) who have at least one dependent child or 'qualifying young person' under 20 (see Chapter 38(1)). Men widowed before 9.4.01 can claim WPA if they have dependent children and were under pension age before 9.4.01 and had not remarried by then. Women pregnant by their late husband can qualify, including those who become pregnant following certain fertility treatments, including the donation of eggs, sperm or embryos. This rule also applies to a woman whose late partner was a registered civil partner. Women whose husbands died before 9.4.01 can continue to claim widowed mother's allowance (see below). WPA cannot be paid beyond state pension age (see below).

SSCBA, S.39A

The contribution conditions for WPA are the same as those for Categories A and B state pension (see Box O.1, Chapter 43).

SSCBA, Sch 3, para 5(2)&(3)

If your spouse or civil partner met the NI contribution conditions, the full rate of £95.25 a week is payable. If your spouse or civil partner's NI contribution record was incomplete, you will receive a proportionately reduced amount of WPA, unless they died as a result of an industrial accident or prescribed industrial disease.

WBRP Regs, reg 6 & SSCBA, S.60(2)&(3)

If you have dependent children, you should claim child tax credit at the same time as WPA (see Chapter 18).

You may get an additional state pension (see Chapter 43(4)) based on your spouse/civil partner's earnings. The maximum amount of additional pension that can be passed on to you is reduced, depending on when your spouse/civil partner reached state pension age. The additional pension may be further reduced if you inherit a contracted-out private pension. See DWP leaflet SERPSL1 for details.

WPA for yourself is taxable. Increases for children payable on claims made before 6.4.03 are tax free.

Bereavement allowance

Bereavement allowance is payable if you were aged 45 or over when your spouse/civil partner died and is payable for 52 weeks following their death. You cannot get the allowance at the same time as WPA, but can claim it for the remainder of the 52 weeks if your WPA ends during that time.

SSCBA, S.39B

The amount you are paid is related to your age when your spouse or civil partner died; payments range from £28.58 a week if you were aged 45 to £95.25 if you were 55 or over (but below state pension age).

SSCBA, S.39C(5)

The contribution conditions for bereavement allowance are the same as those for Categories A and B state pension (see Box O.1, Chapter 43).

SSCBA, Sch 3, para 5(2)&(3)

If your spouse or civil partner's NI contribution record was incomplete, the amount payable is reduced, unless they died as a result of an industrial accident or prescribed industrial disease.

WBRP Regs, reg 6 & SSCBA, S.60(2)&(3)

A bereavement allowance is taxable.

Widowed before 9.4.01

The benefits for women widowed before 9.4.01 are:

- ❑ **Widowed mother's allowance** – This is usually payable if you have dependent children. The amounts and qualifying conditions are the same as those for WPA.

SSCBA, Ss.37 & 39

- ❑ **Widow's pension** – You may get a reduced, age-related widow's pension if you were aged 45-54 on the day your husband died or when your widowed mother's allowance ended. If you were aged 55-64 on that day, you may get a full-rate pension. The amount is the same as bereavement allowance except that an additional state pension may be payable with widow's pension.

SSCBA, Ss.38 & 39

What happens to other benefits?

Overlapping benefits – Bereavement and widows' benefits overlap with contributory employment and support allowance, incapacity benefit, carer's allowance, severe disablement allowance, contribution-based jobseeker's allowance, maternity allowance, unemployability supplement and state pension. You cannot receive two overlapping benefits at the same time, so you'll receive the higher of the overlapped benefits.

OB Regs, reg 4

Industrial death benefit – If your husband died before 11.4.88 and you get industrial death benefit, it is paid in full on top of any transitional incapacity benefit (see Box D.10, Chapter 13) or state pension you are entitled to based on your own NI contributions.

OB Regs, reg 5 & Sch 1

When you reach state pension age

WPA and bereavement allowance cannot be paid beyond state pension age (currently 60 for women, 65 for men). Widow's pension can be paid until your 65th birthday and widowed mother's allowance indefinitely if you have dependent children (but note that both of these overlap with state pension – see above).

SSCBA, Ss.39A(4)(b), 39B(4)(a), 38(2) & 37(3)

State pension – When you reach state pension age, if you have not remarried or formed a civil partnership, you will be entitled to a Category B state pension based on your late spouse/civil partner's NI contributions, or to a Category A state pension based on your own NI contributions record and including your spouse/civil partner's record if that would give you a higher state pension. See Chapter 43(4) for details.

5. Death of a child

Benefits will be affected by the death of your child, but dealing with different agencies after such a loss may be unbearable. Since the agencies concerned do need to be informed quickly, you could ask someone to make the calls on your behalf, perhaps an advice worker or a good friend. Ensure they are aware that each office dealing with the different benefits must be informed separately.

Some benefits will continue for eight weeks after the death of a child. These include carer's allowance, child benefit, child tax credit, and the carer premium as well as child allowances paid in means-tested benefits.

The National Child Death Helpline (0800 282 986) and the Compassionate Friends Helpline (08451 232 304) can provide support and comfort to bereaved parents and families.

55 Health benefits

1. Who qualifies for help?

Some people qualify for help with NHS charges, vouchers for glasses and hospital travel fares because of their circumstances. You qualify automatically if you:

- or your partner, receive income-related employment and support allowance, income support, income-based jobseeker's allowance or pension credit guarantee credit;
- or your partner, receive child tax credit *or* working tax credit and child tax credit *or* working tax credit with a disability or severe disability element, and your relevant income for tax credit purposes is £15,276 or less, and you are named on a valid NHS tax credit exemption certificate;
- are a war/service pensioner (the need must be due to your accepted war disablement); *or*
- are a prisoner.

If you qualify for a tax credit exemption certificate, the NHS Business Services Authority will send it to you when your award has been confirmed by HMRC. This may take several weeks, so if you need chargeable treatment while waiting, you may be able to use your tax credit award notice or decision letter as evidence of entitlement. If you have to pay, get a receipt from the pharmacist, dentist, optician or hospital and claim a refund later. Your exemption certificate is valid until the date specified on the certificate, regardless of changes to your tax credit entitlement.

Some people qualify for an HC2 (full) or HC3 (partial) certificate for help with NHS charges, hospital travel costs and vouchers for glasses on the basis of low income. In these cases, partners and dependent children also qualify.

Young care leavers maintained by an English or Welsh local authority, people residing permanently in a care home funded wholly or partly by a local authority, and asylum seekers (and their dependants) supported by the National Asylum Support Services are entitled to an HC2 certificate by making a claim under the low income scheme without satisfying the means test. See 5 below.

The NHS Business Services Authority manages the health benefits scheme. For details, see NHS leaflets HC11 and HC12, available from the NHS forms orderline (0845 610 1112) or website (www.nhsbsa.nhs.uk). See Chapter 35(2) for details of the hospital travel fares scheme.

NHS(TERC) Regs, reg 5

2. Prescription charges

Prescriptions are free in Wales but cost £7.20 in England (2009/10) for each item, £4 in Scotland and £3 in Northern Ireland, so it is important to take advantage of exemptions and prepayment certificates that save money on frequent prescriptions. If you are a hospital outpatient, exemptions from charges made by hospitals for prescribed drugs are the same as those listed below. Only prescriptions dispensed and issued in Wales (or issued in England to Welsh residents who hold a 'prescription charge entitlement card') will be free.

Exemptions

Who is automatically exempt? – You can get free prescriptions if you are in any of the groups listed in 1 above, or are:

- under 16, or under 19 and in full-time education; *or*
- aged 60 or over.

Who can get an exemption certificate? – You can get an exemption certificate for free NHS prescriptions if you:

- are pregnant or have given birth in the previous 12 months. Get form FW8 from your doctor, midwife or health visitor;
- are undergoing treatment for cancer, the effects of cancer or the effects of cancer treatment; *or*
- have a specified condition (see below); *or*
- are named on a valid HC2 (full help) certificate (see 5).

NHS(CDA) Regs, reg 7

What are the specified conditions? – If you have one of the conditions listed below, you are entitled to an exemption certificate:

- a continuing physical disability that prevents you leaving home without help from another person (a temporary disability is excluded even if it is likely to last a few months);
- a permanent fistula (eg caecostomy, colostomy, laryngostomy or ileostomy) requiring continuous surgical dressing or an appliance;
- diabetes mellitus (except where treatment is by diet alone), myxoedema, hypoparathyroidism, diabetes insipidus or other forms of hypopituitarism, forms of hypoadrenalism (including Addison's disease) for which specific substitution therapy is essential, and myasthenia gravis;
- epilepsy, requiring continuous anti-convulsive therapy.

Claim on form FP92A (EC92A in Scotland), available from your doctor.

NHS(CDA) Regs, reg 7(1)(e)

How to claim

Complete the declaration on the back of the prescription form. The pharmacist will ask for evidence that you are eligible for free prescriptions. When you collect your prescription take your exemption certificate, prepayment certificate or benefit award notice. You should not be refused the prescription if you do not have the evidence but your entitlement may be checked later and if you were not exempt you will be asked to pay the prescription charge. You may also be charged a penalty of up to five times the cost of the prescription, subject to a £100 maximum.

NHS(CDA) Regs, reg 8

Refunds – You can claim a refund within three months (later if you have good cause) of the date you paid for treatment if you should have been entitled to help. When you pay, ask your pharmacist for receipt form FP57 (EC57 in Scotland) and follow the instructions on the form.

NHS(CDA) Regs, reg 10

What is a prescription prepayment certificate?

If you are not exempt from prescription charges, or your income is too high to get the HC2 (full help) certificate (see 5 below), a prepayment certificate can reduce prescription costs. A 3-month certificate costs £28.25 (a 4-month certificate costs £13 in Scotland and £9 in Northern Ireland), a year's certificate £104 (£38 in Scotland and £25 in Northern Ireland) (2009/10); it saves money if you need four or more items in three months or 14 or more items in a year.

Apply on form FP95 (or EC95 in Scotland), available from pharmacists or the NHS Business Services Authority (0845 850 0030 or www.nhsbsa.nhs.uk/HealthCosts).

NHS(CDA) Regs, reg 9

3. Sight tests and glasses

You, and your partner, qualify for free NHS eyesight tests and vouchers for glasses or contact lenses if you:

- are in any of the groups listed in 1 above;
- are under 16, or under 19 and in full-time education; *or*
- need complex or powerful lenses with one lens which has a power in any one meridian of plus or minus 10 or more dioptres, or is a prism-controlled bifocal lens.

NHS eyesight tests or examinations are also free if you are:

- aged 60 or over;
- living in Scotland;
- registered blind or partially sighted; *or*
- diagnosed as having diabetes or glaucoma, or considered to be at risk of glaucoma, or aged 40 or over and the parent, brother, sister or child of a person with glaucoma.

NHS (Optical Charges & Payments) Regs 1997, regs 3 & 8

You may qualify for vouchers for glasses or contact lenses and help towards the cost of sight tests if your income is low (see 5 below). Ask for a voucher when you have your eyes tested. The value of the voucher depends on the strength of the lenses you need, with additions for clinically necessary prisms or tints. You will usually be asked for evidence that you qualify. When you buy the glasses, give the supplier the voucher. If the glasses cost more, you must pay the extra.

Refunds – You can claim a refund within three months (later if you have good cause) of the date you paid for treatment if you should have been entitled to help. When you pay, ask your optician for a receipt and follow the instructions on the back.

4. Free NHS dental treatment

You qualify for free NHS dental treatment if you:

- are in any of the groups listed in 1 above;
- are aged under 18, or under 19 and in full-time education;
- are pregnant – if you were pregnant when the dentist accepted you for treatment;
- have given birth in the past year – if you start a course of dental treatment before your child's first birthday;
- are an NHS inpatient and the treatment is carried out by the hospital dentist; *or*
- are an NHS Hospital Dental Service outpatient (but there may be a charge for dentures and bridges).

NHS (Dental Charges) Regs 1989, Sch 2

For information on the low income scheme see 5 below.

In Scotland, oral health and dental examinations are free for everyone, and in Wales are free for those aged under 25 or over 60. In Wales, certain dental treatments, such as post-operative cancer treatment or suture removal, are also free.

Tell your dentist you qualify (you will usually be asked for evidence) and fill in the declaration on the form they give you.

Refunds – You can claim a refund within three months (later if you have good cause) of the date you paid for treatment if you should have been entitled to help. When you pay, ask your dentist for a receipt form FP64 (GP17D in Scotland) and follow the instructions on the form.

5. Low income scheme

The NHS low income scheme for help with NHS charges and optical vouchers is operated by the NHS Business Services Authority (NHSBSA). If your capital is £16,000 or less, you may be eligible for help.

If your income is less than or equal to your requirements (plus 50% of the prescription charge, ie the current cost of a prescription), you are entitled to full help with NHS charges, vouchers towards the cost of glasses and free eye tests. The NHSBSA will send you an HC2 certificate.

NHS(TERC) Regs, reg 5(2)(e)

If your income is higher than your requirements by more than 50% of the prescription charge, you cannot get help with the cost of NHS prescriptions but may get help with travel expenses (see Chapter 35(2)) and other NHS charges. The NHSBSA will send you an HC3 certificate (partial help) to show how much you have to contribute towards the charges.

For sight tests, you'll get the difference between the NHS sight test fee and your excess income. For glasses, the maximum voucher value is reduced by twice your excess income. For dental charges, your maximum contribution is three times your excess income.

NHS(TERC) Regs, reg 6

The low income assessment

The assessment of income and capital is broadly the same as for income support (see Chapters 26 and 27) but there are differences.

- ❑ If you live permanently in a care home, the upper capital limit is £23,000 in England and Scotland, and £22,000 in Wales.
- ❑ If you or your partner are aged 60 or over assumed tariff income is £1 a week for every £250 (or part thereof).
- ❑ If you are receiving employment and support allowance (ESA), earnings from exempt work (see Chapter 16(3)) are ignored as income.
- ❑ If you are on strike, your pre-strike income is taken into account.
- ❑ If you are receiving contributory ESA that is being sanctioned, this is taken into account as if the sanction had not been applied.
- ❑ Pension credit savings credit is ignored as income.
- ❑ Some Scottish student maintenance loans are disregarded in England. The £10 disregard for other student loans only applies if your assessment includes any premiums, or you or your partner get a disabled students' allowance because of deafness. Loans are calculated over 52 weeks, unless it is the final year of study or a one-year or sandwich course. Student maintenance grants in excess of the normal maximum are disregarded.
- ❑ If you have a lodger (without board), the standard disregard in rental income is £20.

Your requirements are worked out in the same way as the income support applicable amount (see Chapter 14(9)), with significant differences:

- ❑ A disability premium is included if you receive ESA with a component (support/work-related activity) or you have been continuously incapable of work for 28 weeks since 27.10.08; the premium is not included if you (and your partner) are aged 60 or over.
- ❑ If you are under 25 you are entitled to the personal allowance applicable to someone aged 25 or over if you receive ESA with a component (support/work-related activity) or you have been continuously incapable of work for 28 weeks since 27.10.08.
- ❑ Generally, net weekly housing costs are taken into account including: mortgage capital repayments; payments on an endowment policy or hire purchase agreement in connection with buying your home; repayments of interest and capital on a loan to adapt your home for the special needs of a disabled person; rent and council tax less housing benefit and council tax benefit. Amounts for non-dependants are deducted (see Chapter 20(22)).
- ❑ If you live in a care home and pay your own costs, your requirements are the total amount of care costs plus the amount for personal expenses (see Chapter 34(5)).

NHS(TERC) Regs, regs 16 & 17 & Sch 1

How do you claim?

Claim on form HC1, available from Jobcentre Plus offices or the NHSBSA (www.nhsbsa.nhs.uk/HealthCosts; tel 0845 850 1166). Hospitals, GPs, dentists, opticians and advice agencies may also have the form. If you are unable to act for yourself, someone else can claim for you. Claim on form HC1(SC) if you live in a care home and the local authority helps with the fees, or if you are a 16/17-year-old care leaver and a local authority supports you.

After you have claimed, the NHSBSA will send you a decision. If you are entitled to full help, they will send an HC2 certificate. If you are entitled to partial help, they will send an HC3 certificate. If you pay an NHS charge while waiting for your HC2 or HC3 certificate, obtain a receipt form from the pharmacist, dentist, optician or hospital and follow the instructions to claim a refund.

HC2 and HC3 certificates are usually valid for periods of between six months and five years, depending on your circumstances.

If you are not happy with the decision – There is no right of appeal but you can write to the NHSBSA and ask them to reconsider their decision (Review Section, NHS Business Services Authority, PO Box 993, Newcastle upon Tyne NE99 2TZ).

6. Healthy Start food and vitamins

Healthy Start provides for free vitamins and weekly vouchers (worth £3.10 each) to buy milk, fresh fruit and vegetables, or infant formula.

You are entitled to Healthy Start vouchers if you are:

- under 18, at least ten weeks pregnant and not subject to immigration control (see Chapter 50(3));
- 18 or over and at least ten weeks pregnant, or have a child aged under one, and you receive income-related employment and support allowance, income support, income-based jobseeker's allowance or child tax credit (but not working tax credit, unless paid during the 4-week run-on period – see Chapter 18(6)) and your relevant income is less than £16,040 (2009/10); or you are a family member of a person entitled to one of these benefits;
- a child under 4 and a family member of someone receiving one of the benefits mentioned above.

You receive one voucher if you satisfy one of the pregnancy criteria above, one for each qualifying child under 4, and two vouchers for each qualifying child under one. Vouchers must be exchanged at registered retailers displaying the Healthy Start logo. If there is no retailer within a reasonable distance, you'll receive the equivalent of your entitlement in money.

Claims for vouchers must be made on the approved form and countersigned by a health professional. If you do not receive your vouchers or they are lost, stolen or accidentally destroyed, contact Healthy Start for replacements; there are strict time limits.

If you qualify for vouchers you might be entitled to free vitamins. Ask your health visitor or midwife for information.

For more information or to make a claim, talk to your health visitor or midwife, visit the Healthy Start website (www.healthystart.nhs.uk) or ring the Healthy Start Issuing Unit on 0845 607 6823.

Welfare Food scheme – Free milk under the old Welfare Food scheme continues to be available if you have a child under 5 who is looked after for at least two hours a day by a registered childminder, daycare provider, local authority or school, or workplace provider exempt from registration. A disabled child aged 5-16 who is not a school pupil may also receive free milk.

Healthy Start Scheme and Welfare Food (Amendment) Regs 2005

56 Disability Discrimination Act

In this chapter we look at:

1. What is the DDA and who does it cover?

The Disability Discrimination Act 1995 (DDA) makes it unlawful to discriminate against disabled people in connection with employment; education; the provision of goods, facilities and services – including public transport; the disposal or management of premises; and private clubs or public authority functions. The DDA defines disability as *'a physical or mental impairment which has a substantial and long-term adverse effect on [your] ability to carry out normal day-to-day activities'*. If you can show that you come within this definition, you will have the protection of the Act. People who have had a disability within the meaning of the Act in the past are protected from discrimination even if they no longer have the disability.

Impairment – This includes sensory impairments (eg, blindness or deafness), learning disabilities, mental health conditions and long-term health conditions such as heart disease or diabetes. Mental health conditions need not be clinically well recognised to be impairments. Some progressive conditions (eg cancer, multiple sclerosis and HIV infection) count as a disability from when you first develop the condition. Other progressive conditions are covered as soon as they have an effect on your ability to do everyday activities. Severe disfigurements are covered, even if they do not affect your ability to carry out normal activities. You automatically meet the DDA definition if registered with your local authority as blind or partially sighted, or if a consultant ophthalmologist has certified you as such.

Any steps taken to treat or correct your disability (eg hearing aid, artificial limb or medication) are ignored when considering whether your impairment has a substantial adverse effect. However, if you wear glasses or contact lenses, it is the effect on your vision with the lenses that is considered.

Substantial – This means *'more than minor or trivial'*.

Long term – This means effects that have lasted at least 12 months, or are likely to last at least 12 months, or are likely to last for the rest of your life (if that is less than 12 months). Conditions likely to recur, eg epilepsy, will be considered as long term if it is more likely than not that their substantial adverse effects will recur beyond 12 months.

Discrimination by association – You have the right not to be subjected to direct discrimination or harassment on the grounds of your association with a disabled person (eg if you have to care for a disabled child) under the employment provisions of the DDA.

Victimisation – The DDA protects disabled people who take on a case or make a complaint under the DDA and people victimised for helping a disabled person to make a complaint, give evidence or take a case under the DDA. For example, a non-disabled woman gives evidence when a deaf man brings a case against a pub under the DDA. The next time she goes to the pub, the manager refuses to serve her. This is victimisation; the woman could bring her own case to court under the DDA against the pub. Victimisation covers the employment, services, premises and education parts of the DDA.

Guidance – Government guidance to help you work out if you come under the definition of disability is available from The Stationery Office or the Equality and Human Rights Commission (EHRC) and Equality Commission for Northern Ireland websites (see Box S.1). The EHRC publishes codes of practice on employment, trade organisations, education and other issues (see Box S.1); in Northern Ireland, this information is available from the Equality Commission.

2. Your employment rights – DDA Part 2

It is unlawful for an employer to treat you less favourably than someone else for a reason related to your disability or to fail to comply with the duty to make *'reasonable adjustments'* (see below). The DDA covers almost all employment except the Armed Forces. It covers temporary, contract and permanent staff and all employment matters, including recruitment, training, promotion, dismissal and redundancy, discrimination against former employees and harassment. Volunteers are not covered unless they have a volunteering agreement that might be construed as a contract of employment.

Employers are liable (ie legally responsible) for the actions of their employees and agents (eg a recruitment agency that discriminates on the authority of the employer). You need not be employed for a minimum period of time to bring a discrimination claim, and compensation is unlimited.

Types – There are five types of employment discrimination:

- direct discrimination: discrimination on the grounds of someone's disability;
- failure to make reasonable adjustments;
- disability-related discrimination: the reason is linked to the disability but is not the disability itself;
- victimisation;
- harassment.

Justification – The only type of discrimination employers can justify is disability-related discrimination. They can do this if, in the circumstances, it is for a material and substantial reason.

Reasonable adjustments – The DDA requires employers to make *'reasonable adjustments'* to the workplace and to employment arrangements, including recruitment, so that a disabled employee or job applicant is not at any substantial disadvantage. Reasonable adjustments include changes to the physical environment, eg widening a doorway for wheelchair access or allocating a parking space for a disabled person. The term includes changes to working arrangements, eg allowing flexible working hours, purchasing specialised equipment, providing additional training, allowing time off for medical appointments or treatment, providing an assistant or communications support – eg BSL interpreters.

If your employer rents premises, the landlord cannot unreasonably refuse permission for the premises to be altered to accommodate you, although they may attach reasonable conditions to their permission (for example returning the premises to the original condition when vacating them). If your employer does not make a reasonable adjustment because the landlord unreasonably refuses permission, you could take your employer to the Employment Tribunal, and you or your employer could ask the Tribunal to make the landlord a party to the case. The landlord would then have to go the Tribunal.

There are specific DDA provisions against discrimination in relation to:

- occupational pension schemes and insurance obtained through employers (eg health insurance);
- work experience done as part of vocational training (eg an NVQ in plumbing);
- occupations such as police officer, barrister, partnerships and office holders (eg judges and members of non-departmental public bodies);
- membership of trade organisations;
- employment services (eg employment agencies and careers guidance services);
- qualifying bodies that regulate entry into a profession (eg the Nursing and Midwifery Council).

Local councillors are covered by the DDA when carrying out official business, which includes local authorities making 'reasonable adjustments'. The DDA does not, however, apply to political appointments, local authority cabinet posts or committees.

3. Access to goods and services – DDA Part 3

It is unlawful for organisations that provide goods, facilities or services in the UK directly to the public to discriminate against disabled people. It does not matter whether the services are free or paid for. Service providers include: shops, hotels, banks, cinemas, restaurants, courts and solicitors, private education and training providers, non-educational activities in schools, colleges and universities (eg parents' evenings), students' unions, telecommunications companies, libraries, leisure facilities, healthcare, social/housing services, government offices and voluntary services (eg advice centres). Insurance companies are covered but special rules apply.

Part 3 does not cover the manufacture and design of products. Airports, stations and booking facilities are covered by Part 3 (see 'Use of transport vehicles' below).

Use of transport vehicles – The use and provision of transport vehicles such as buses, taxis, minicabs, trains, trams, car hire and breakdown services is covered by DDA Part 3. Disabled people have protection against less favourable treatment and rights to reasonable adjustments to enable them to use services. These duties do not cover changes to physical features (see 6 below for accessibility requirements for public transport vehicles) except in respect of rental vehicles and breakdown recovery vehicles (the latter must overcome physical features that present barriers to disabled people by providing the service in a reasonable alternative way). Ships and aircraft remain exempt from DDA Part 3 – although European Council Regulation 1107 on air travel gives disabled people and those with reduced mobility certain new rights. The Equality and Human Rights Commission has published a guide on your rights to fly (see Box S.1).

Private clubs – Private clubs with 25 or more members cannot discriminate against, and have duties to make reasonable adjustments for, current and potential disabled members, associates and guests.

Public functions – A public authority is not allowed to discriminate against disabled people (DDA s.21B-E). The DDA does not define 'public authority' but says it covers authorities *'whose functions are functions of a public nature'*, eg central and local government, NHS hospitals and social services. Most public authority services come under other parts of the DDA, eg housing departments are covered by the housing and services sections. This duty covers functions such as policing, crime prevention, planning and public appointments. There are different justification conditions that apply to public authorities.

Types of unlawful discrimination – Under the DDA it is unlawful for a service provider to treat you less favourably than someone else for a reason relating to your disability. There are four types of unlawful discrimination:

- refusing or deliberately not providing you with a service because of your disability – eg a club refuses entrance to a group of deaf people;
- providing service of a lower standard or in a worse manner – eg a cafe tells someone with a severe facial disfigurement to sit apart from others;
- providing a service on worse terms – eg a travel agent asks for a larger deposit because they think you are more likely to cancel because you are disabled;
- not making reasonable adjustments (see below).

A B C D E F G H I J K L M N O P Q R S T U

Justification – Discrimination may be justified in very limited circumstances only. Service providers would need to prove that one of the following justification grounds applied:

- there is a genuine health or safety risk to you or someone else;
- the disabled person is incapable of entering into a contract (even with adjustments);
- by serving the disabled person the service provider would be unable to provide the service to others;
- the service provider has to provide the service on different terms or of a different standard or else they would not be able to provide the service to the disabled person or other members of the public;
- greater expense – a higher charge is justified because the service is individually tailored to your needs and costs more to deliver.

Service providers are legally responsible for any discrimination by their employees or anyone else who works as part of their business – eg contractors.

Reasonable adjustments – Providers must make adjustments to their service(s) if, without the adjustments, it is '*impossible or unreasonably difficult*' for a disabled person to use the service. There are three types of reasonable adjustment:

- changing the way a service is provided (*'practices, policies or procedures'*), eg changing a "no dogs" policy to allow for assistance dogs;
- providing an additional aid or service if it will help you access the service – eg communication support;
- removing or altering physical features (eg doors, lighting or glass screens) if they create barriers to the service, or providing a reasonable means of avoiding them, or providing the service in an alternative way – eg if the premises are inaccessible, the business could offer home visits.

Service providers need only do what is reasonable. 'Reasonable' is not defined, but can depend on several factors, including how practicable it is to make the adjustment and the cost. Service providers must plan ahead to meet these duties, and must comply even if they do not know that someone is disabled – this is known as an 'anticipatory duty'. Providers must not charge disabled people for making reasonable adjustments.

4. Housing

The DDA makes it unlawful for anyone letting, selling or managing rented property (be it houses, flats or offices) to discriminate against disabled people. This applies to most agencies involved in letting, selling or managing rented property, including local authorities, housing associations, private landlords, estate agents, accommodation agencies, banks, building societies, property developers and owner occupiers.

If you are treated less favourably than someone else for a reason relating to your disability, eg you are charged a higher rent or deposit, and this treatment cannot be justified, that could be discrimination. If a landlord or person managing the premises restricts or prevents a disabled person from using any benefits or facilities, this can be unlawful discrimination. For example, it may be unlawful for a property management company to not allow a tenant's child with attention deficit disorder to use the communal garden because other tenants object. The Act also makes the harassment of disabled people unlawful. There are specific justification conditions that landlords can rely on.

The Act exempts landlords who let rooms to six or fewer people in their own homes. There is no general legal obligation on anyone selling or letting property to alter the premises to make them accessible. The DDA does not cover sales arranged without an estate agent.

Landlords and management companies must make reasonable adjustments to policies and procedures, and take reasonable steps to provide additional aids and services. This applies only to the use of the premises; physical features will not have to be removed or altered. Some features do *not* count as physical features, including signs, adapted doorbells/entry phones and changes to taps/door handles.

Landlords cannot refuse, unreasonably, to allow disabled tenants to make changes to the property needed because of a disability. You must pay for the alterations yourself (or seek a grant) and must ask permission first. This right does not yet apply to 'common parts' – eg hallways or stairs. In Scotland, the right does apply to the 'common parts' but the other tenants need to agree to the change, as does the landlord.

See EHRC *Code of Practice – Rights of Access. Goods, Facilities, Services & Premises* for more information.

5. Education

It is unlawful for education providers to discriminate against students for reasons relating to their disability. This applies to admissions, education and related services and exclusions. Discrimination is not unlawful if it complies with a permitted form of selection, or for reasons that are material and substantial.

Schools must ensure disabled pupils are not treated less favourably and must make reasonable adjustments to avoid putting them at a substantial disadvantage. This does not include a right to auxiliary aids and services. If adjustments are provided, eg radio aids or adapted keyboards, the school must ensure they are available to learners and used by staff. These duties apply to all schools, including publicly funded, independent and mainstream schools, special schools, pupil referral units, local authority-maintained nursery schools and classes, and nursery provision at independent and grant-aided schools. Private, voluntary and statutory providers of nursery education not constituted as schools are covered by Part 3 of the DDA (see 3 above). The reasonable adjustments duty is limited by several factors, including the need to maintain academic standards, cost, the school's budget and availability of provision through the special educational needs system. Students may be entitled to reasonable adjustments when taking exams.

It is unlawful for bodies that provide general qualifications such as GCSEs, A and AS levels and other non-vocational exams (including Scottish and Welsh equivalents) to discriminate against disabled people. Exam candidates can expect general qualification bodies to make reasonable adjustments, eg allowing extra time or providing exam materials in alternative formats.

Local authorities and schools are required to publish accessibility strategies and plans, respectively, to improve access to school education for disabled pupils, monitored by Ofsted (England) and ESTYN (Wales). Similar duties exist under Scottish education legislation.

Post-16 education providers include further, higher, adult and community education and the statutory youth service. It is unlawful for them to treat disabled students less favourably and they have a duty to make reasonable adjustments to avoid putting disabled students at a substantial disadvantage. Providers must provide auxiliary aids and services, and make physical alterations to premises. In some cases, Part 3 of the DDA may apply instead. These include services provided by student unions and institutions of further and higher education to members of the public other than students and private and voluntary sector education providers.

6. Transport

Part 5 of the Act gives the Government the power to make accessibility regulations for public transport vehicles. New buses, coaches and trains must comply with specified accessibility standards, eg width of doors, colour contrast, etc. All buses and coaches must comply with the regulations by 2017 and 2020 respectively. All trains must comply by 2020 at the latest. The Government is consulting on taxi accessibility regulations. Licensed taxis and minicabs cannot refuse to carry, and cannot charge more for, a disabled person accompanied by an assistance dog. Drivers can ask to be exempt from this duty on medical grounds.

7. Enforcing your rights

If you think you have been discriminated against under DDA employment provisions you can make a complaint to an Employment Tribunal. The complaint must be registered with the Tribunal within three months of the discriminatory act, eg the date you were dismissed. In some circumstances there is a legal requirement to use a grievance or disciplinary procedure first; you then have an extra three months to bring a claim. If you don't use the procedure when you have to, the Tribunal will reject your claim.

The DDA Questions Procedure enables you to ask the employer questions. This can help you decide whether you have a strong case. You could ask your trade union for help.

Rights under the Act's goods and services and post-16 education provisions are enforceable through the County Court (the Sheriff Court in Scotland). You must take the case to court within six months of the discriminatory act, eg the date you were refused service. You can use the Questions Procedure for goods and services cases. You can make a complaint to the Pensions Ombudsman if you think the managers of a pension scheme have discriminated against you (see Box O.2, Chapter 43).

Rights under the education provisions that apply to schools are enforceable in England through the Special Educational Needs & Disability Tribunal (SENDIST), and in Wales through the Special Educational Needs Tribunal. There are similar tribunals in Northern Ireland. Claims of unlawful discrimination in respect of a refusal to admit to, and permanent exclusions from, maintained schools and city academies are heard by admissions appeal panels or independent appeals panels. DDA claims against schools in Scotland are enforceable through the Sheriff Court. You must take a case to court or the tribunal within six months of the date of the discriminatory act.

If you are successful in a tribunal or court you can obtain damages for financial loss or hurt feelings. The SENDIST and Sheriff Court cannot award financial compensation in claims against schools, but can make other orders, including that: staff receive training or guidance, policies are changed, a disabled child be admitted to school and apologies made. Courts can order service providers to make adjustments in some circumstances, and tribunals can recommend that an employer makes an adjustment. Courts and tribunals can make a public declaration that you were discriminated against because of your disability.

As a cheaper, quicker alternative to legal action, the Equality and Human Rights Commission provides a mediation service for DDA Part 3 cases, refusal of consent for a disability-related improvement, DDA education cases and complaints about air travel under the European Council Regulation 1107. For employment cases, free conciliation is available from the Advisory, Conciliation and Arbitration Service. A similar service is available from the Labour Relations Agency for Northern Ireland.

Disability Equality Duty – All public authorities (including local authorities, schools, NHS bodies, police authorities, etc) are subject to a positive duty to have due regard to the promotion of disability equality in every area of their work. The duty includes a requirement to have due regard to the need to:

- eliminate discrimination and harassment;
- promote positive attitudes towards disabled people and encourage their participation in public life; *and*
- take steps to meet disabled people's needs, even if this requires more favourable treatment.

To show compliance with this general duty, relevant policies must be assessed for their impact on disability equality. Certain public bodies have further duties to prepare and implement a disability equality scheme with the involvement of disabled people. It must include an action plan against which they can be held to account.

The duty does not create individual rights for disabled people. However, a breach of the general duty can be the subject of a claim for judicial review of a public authority's action (or inaction). Such a claim can be brought by anyone with an interest. The Equality and Human Rights Commission has statutory powers to enforce the duty.

In Northern Ireland, public authorities have a duty to promote equality in relation to disability. They must also have due regard to the need to promote positive attitudes towards disabled people and encourage their participation in public life. Authorities must submit disability action plans to the Equality Commission for Northern Ireland explaining how they propose to fulfil their 'disability duties'.

The Equality Bill – The Government is preparing an Equality Bill to replace the DDA and all other equalities legislation. For information contact RADAR or the Government Equalities Office (www.equalities.gov.uk).

S.1 For more information

The Equality and Human Rights Commission (EHRC) provides free information and advice covering different aspects of the DDA (Helplines: 0845 604 6610 (England); 0845 604 5510 (Scotland); 0845 604 8810 (Wales); www.equalityhumanrights.com). Information is available in accessible formats.

Codes of practice and guidance can be bought from The Stationery Office bookshops (0870 600 5522; www.tso.co.uk) or downloaded from the EHRC website.

The Equality Commission for Northern Ireland publishes codes of practice on the DDA, guidance and advisory leaflets: Equality House, 7-9 Shaftesbury Square, Belfast BT2 7DP (028 9050 0600; textphone: 028 9050 0589; www.equalityni.org).

Information about DDA transport provisions and the *Access to Air Travel for Disabled People: Code of Practice* are available from the Department for Transport's Accessibility and Equalities Unit (020 7944 8300; textphone 020 7944 3277; www.dft.gov.uk).

Guidance on providing British Sign Language/English interpreters under the Disability Discrimination Act 1995 is published by RNID/BDA/EHRC and available from RNID Information Line (0808 808 0123 or www.rnid.org.uk).

Providing access to communication in English for deaf people – Your duties under the DDA is published by the ACE Coalition and available from RNID.

Information on the DDA is also available from RNID, RNIB, Mind and other organisations.

Advice

You may find it helpful to contact the EHRC, RNIB, RADAR, RNID, the Disability Law Service, a local law centre (see Address List) or Citizens Advice Bureau.

Useful books include *Disability Discrimination – Law and Practice (6th edn)* by Brian J Doyle (Jordans), *Disability Discrimination Claims* by Catherine Casserley and Bela Gor (Jordans) and *Discrimination Law Handbook (2nd edn)* by Palmer, Cohen, Gill, Monaghan, Moon & Stacey (Legal Action Group).

57 TV licence concessions

In this chapter we look at: page

1. Do you need a TV licence?

You need a TV licence to install or use television receiving equipment to watch or record TV programmes as they are being shown on TV. This is irrespective of what channel you watch, what device you use (TV, computer, laptop, etc) or how you receive it (terrestrial, satellite, cable, internet, etc). A licence covers you and anyone else who normally lives with you at the address printed on the licence.

A colour TV licence costs £142.50 a year; for a black and white TV it is £48. Concessions are available for people aged 75 or over, certified blind or severely sight impaired or, in certain cases, living in care homes or sheltered housing.

For further information, go to www.tvlicensing.co.uk or ring 0844 800 6737 (Mincom 0844 800 6778).

2. Aged 75 or over

For anyone aged 75 or over the TV licence is free for your main home but not for a second home. Although free, you must apply for the over-75 licence. You will need to provide TV Licensing with your date of birth and national insurance number. If TV Licensing can verify these details, the over-75 licence is renewed automatically. If you do not have a national insurance number, ring TV Licensing (0844 800 6790) to arrange other proof of your date of birth. If the over-75 licence-holder dies, the TV licence continues to cover your household until it runs out.

If your 75th birthday will fall in the year covered by the next licence, you can buy a short-term licence to cover you until your birthday, or you can claim a refund on an existing licence for the months since you reached the age of 75.

3. Blind concession

There is a 50% discount on the licence fee if you are blind or severely sight impaired (not partially sighted) – ie £71.25 for a colour TV, £24 for black and white. Anyone in the household who is blind or severely sight impaired (including children) can apply for the 50% discount, but the licence must be transferred into that person's name. You can apply for a discount for a second residence as well as your main home.

When your licence is due for renewal, send your renewal form and a photocopy of the certificate from your local authority or ophthalmologist indicating that you are blind or severely sight impaired to the Concessionary Licensing Centre (see 4 below for address). Once you have proved your eligibility, you shouldn't need to do so again for another five years. For further enquiries ring 0844 800 6790.

You do not need a licence for a TV sound-only receiver. These are available from Portset (01489 896 837).

4. Care homes

The concessionary Accommodation for Residential Care (ARC) licence costs £7.50. It is available if you live in certain types of care home and are retired and aged 60 or over, or disabled. The person in charge of your accommodation can apply for it on your behalf. You will only need a TV licence if you watch TV in your own separate living area. If you only watch TV in communal areas, it is the responsibility of the person in charge of your accommodation to ensure those areas are properly licensed.

If you are aged 75 or over, the warden will apply for your free licence. When you move into a care home, you may get a refund for the remainder of your existing licence at your previous home. The warden should apply for you. Write to: The Concessionary Licensing Centre, TV Licensing, Bristol BS98 1TL (0844 800 5808).

Communications (Television Licensing) Regulations 2004

58 Christmas bonus

In this chapter we look at: page

1. What is the Christmas bonus?

This is normally a tax-free payment of £10 paid in December with certain social security benefits. It is not taken into account as income for means-tested benefits.

2. How is it paid?

For Christmas 2009, your Christmas bonus will be paid with your usual benefit payment from the week beginning Monday 7.12.09. If you have not received the bonus by the end of December, contact Jobcentre Plus or The Pension Service.

3. Who qualifies for it?

You will be entitled to a Christmas bonus if, in the week beginning 7.12.09 (the relevant week) you are:

- present or ordinarily resident in the UK, the Channel Islands, the Isle of Man, Gibraltar or any European Economic Area country or Switzerland (see Chapters 50 and 51); *and*
- entitled to a payment of one of a list of qualifying benefits for a period which includes a day in the week beginning 7.12.09. This list includes: attendance allowance, carer's allowance, disability living allowance, some recipients of industrial injuries disablement benefit (including industrial death benefit), main phase employment and support allowance (see Chapter 9(8)), long-term incapacity benefit, pension credit, severe disablement allowance, state pension, war disablement or widow's pension, widow's pension or widowed mother's (or parent's) allowance.

If each of a couple (including civil partners and cohabiters) meets these qualifying conditions, each will be paid the £10 bonus. If you receive more than one qualifying benefit you will only receive one bonus. However, if you and your partner are both over state pension age but your partner does not receive a bonus in their own right, you will get an extra £10 bonus for your partner if you are entitled, or treated as entitled, to a dependant's addition for them, or if the only benefit you get is pension credit.

SSCBA, Ss. 149-150

This section of the Handbook looks at:

Claims and appeals

T

59 Claims and payments

In this chapter we look at:

1. Making a claim

Traditionally, you had to complete claim-forms for most social security benefits. But now, for many benefits (including employment and support allowance, income support, jobseeker's allowance, state pension and pension credit), you are encouraged to make first contact by telephone. Details of your claim can be obtained over the phone and a statement sent to you to check that the details are correct. Alternatively, online claims can be made for many benefits.

For details about how to claim each benefit, see the relevant chapter. Here we look at some of the common rules about and problems with claiming.

Who should claim? – You should claim (or ask the DWP for advice) as soon as you think you might qualify. If you cannot make enquiries or claim yourself, get someone else to do so; the DWP can accept a claim made by someone else on your behalf as long as you have signed it. The DWP can appoint someone to act on behalf of anyone who can't claim for themselves because of incapacity (see 4).

Defective claims – If you make a 'defective' claim (ie one not properly completed in accordance with the instructions on the form) or you don't use the correct form, you may have the claim referred back to you or be given the correct form. If it is referred back to you, and you return the properly completed claim-form within one month of it being sent to you (or longer if an extension is agreed), your claim must be treated as though the original defective claim had been properly made. See 2 below for the rules on income support and jobseeker's allowance. You can appeal against a decision to disallow benefit on the basis that the claim was defective.

C&P Regs, reg 4(7), 4G(3)-(5) & 4H(6)-(7)

National insurance (NI) numbers – To be entitled to most benefits, you must give your NI number when you claim (and your partner's if you are claiming for them) and enough information to confirm the number is yours. If you don't know your number, give the DWP sufficient information to allow them to trace it. Normally, the personal details you give on the claim-form are enough. If the DWP wants more evidence, they will let you know. If you don't have an NI number, you are still entitled to benefit if you apply for a number and provide enough information and evidence for one to be allocated to you. Apply at your local Jobcentre Plus office.

SSAA S.1(1A) & (1B)

2. Date of claim

The date your claim is 'made' is the day it is received, properly completed, in a DWP office, DWP-approved office or (for tax credits) HMRC office. Sometimes your claim can be treated as though it were made on an earlier date.

- ❑ For disability living allowance and attendance allowance, your date of claim is the date you requested a claim-form from the DWP or Benefit Enquiry Line if you return the completed claim-form within six weeks (see Chapter 3(23) for details).

C&P Regs, reg 6(8) & (9)

- ❑ For employment and support allowance, your date of claim is the date you informed the Jobcentre Plus office of your intention to claim, as long as that office receives a properly completed claim-form from you within a month of your first contact (unless an extension is agreed). For telephone claims, see Chapter 9(11).

C&P Regs, reg 6(1F)

- ❑ For pension credit, your date of claim is the date you informed the DWP or local authority office of your intention to claim pension credit if you provide all the information and evidence they require within one month (unless an extension is agreed).

C&P Regs, reg 4F(3)

Claims for income support

Your date of claim for income support is the date you first told Jobcentre Plus you wanted to claim, as long as you return the claim-form (or signed statement if the claim was made over the phone) fully completed with all the information and supporting documents required within one month. Until you do this, you have not made your claim, unless you can show that one of the following applies:

- ❑ You have a *'physical, learning, mental or communication difficulty'* and it is not reasonably practicable for you to get help with your claim or get the required information or evidence.
- ❑ The information or evidence required:
  - – does not exist; *or*
  - – can only be obtained at serious risk of physical or mental harm to you; *or*
  - – can only be obtained from a third party and it's not reasonably practicable for you to get it from them.

C&P Regs, regs 4(1B) & 6(1A)

Send in your claim-form or signed statement explaining your difficulties, or ring Jobcentre Plus (or get someone else to contact them for you). If you do this within one month and they accept your reasons, your date of claim will be the date you first told Jobcentre Plus you wanted to claim.

If there is other evidence needed to decide your claim but it is not specified in the claim-form, it does not affect your date of claim if you can't provide it with your claim.

Claims for JSA

Your date of claim is the date you first contacted Jobcentre Plus, as long as you provide a fully completed claim-form or signed customer statement and all the required evidence by the time you attend your 'new jobseeker interview' (or during the interview). If either member of a joint-claim couple does

T.1 Work-focused interviews

You are required to take part in one or more work-focused interviews if you are claiming one of the following:

- employment and support allowance (ESA);
- incapacity benefit;
- income support; *or*
- severe disablement allowance (SDA).

You are also required to take part in a work-focused interview if your partner is claiming extra for you in one of the last three benefits.

In the work-focused interview a personal adviser will discuss your work prospects. We describe what happens at a work-focused interview in Chapter 9(15); the process is similar for each benefit. Different interviews (although still with a work focus) are necessary when claiming jobseeker's allowance (JSA) – see Chapter 18(3).

An interview for one benefit counts for all others, so you do not have to go through interviews for each benefit you claim.

Who is not required to attend?

You are not required to attend a work-focused interview in the following circumstances.

- ❑ You are aged 60 or over.
- ❑ You are working 16 hours or more a week.
- ❑ You are also claiming JSA, unless you are a member of a joint-claim couple who is excused from meeting JSA conditions.

JPI Regs, regs 3(1)(b) & 8

For the different rules on ESA, see Chapter 9(15).

The requirement to attend may be deferred to a later date at the discretion of the personal adviser. In addition, some claimants may have their interview waived, if it would not be of any assistance or appropriate. This waiver facility has been removed for the majority of claimants of incapacity benefits.

When will they take place?

Initial interviews – For income support, the first work-focused interview will normally take place shortly after your first contact with Jobcentre Plus. For ESA claimants and those claiming benefits on the grounds of incapacity, the first work-focused interview will normally take place during or shortly after the 8th week of your claim.

If you are required to attend a work-focused interview as the partner of a claimant, the interview will normally take place after they have been entitled to the benefit for at least 26 weeks.

Follow-up interviews – If you are claiming ESA, incapacity benefit or income support on the grounds of incapacity, you must attend five further work-focused interviews, unless you are exempt from the personal capability assessment because you have a serious illness (see Chapter 13(4)). See Chapter 9(15) for the ESA exemption rules.

Lone parents claiming income support (on the sole grounds that they are lone parents) are required to attend a work-focused interview every six months. If their youngest child is aged 9, 10 or 11 (or, from 26.10.09, aged 6 to 9) they will have to attend a work-focused interview every 13 weeks.

Trigger points – Once you've had your first work-focused interview and any follow-up interviews, you will normally only be asked back when certain events happen to trigger another work-focused interview. The trigger points are:

- following a personal capability or work capability assessment – but not if your benefit is stopped following the assessment;
- carer's allowance entitlement stops but you continue to be entitled to income support, incapacity benefit, ESA or SDA;
- you start or stop part-time work of less than 16 hours a week;
- you finish an education or training course arranged by your personal adviser;
- you reach the age of 18 and have previously taken part in a work/learning-focused interview;
- your partner is claiming extra for you in income-based JSA, you are responsible for a child or qualifying young person (see Chapter 38(1)) and six months have passed since your last interview;
- you have not had an interview in the last three years.

As for the first work-focused interview, in some circumstances your attendance may be either waived or deferred to a later date.

JPI Regs, reg 4 & JPIP Regs, reg 3A

What if you don't attend or take part in the interview?

The sanctions for not taking part in an ESA work-focused interview are described in Chapter 9(15). The same sanctions normally apply if you are claiming incapacity benefit, SDA or income support on the grounds of incapacity (ie for the first four weeks an amount equal to 50% of the ESA work-related activity component is deducted from your benefit (£12.75), thereafter an amount equal to the ESA work-related activity component is deducted (£25.50)). For other benefits, the rules are as follows.

New claims – Unless you can show you had 'good cause' (this is the same as for ESA – see Chapter 9(15)) for not attending or taking part in a work-focused interview, your claim will not proceed. If the interview had been deferred, with the result that benefit was already in payment, then entitlement will stop. In either case, you should claim again, and appeal against the decision if you think it is wrong (see below). You may be able to claim a crisis loan in the meantime, but these are very limited (see Chapter 23(6)).

JPI Regs, reg 12(2)(a)&(b)

Benefit in payment – If you are already claiming benefit and you fail to attend or take part in a work-focused interview without good cause, a deduction of £12.86 a week is made from your benefit. The deduction continues until you do take part in a work-focused interview or reach the age of 60.

JPI Regs, reg 12(2)(c)

If your partner fails to attend or take part in a work-focused interview when required to do so without good cause, a deduction of £12.86 a week is made from your benefit. The deduction continues until they do take part in a work-focused interview.

JPIP Regs, reg 11

Challenging a decision

Personal advisers (or, in the case of ESA, the private or voluntary sector equivalents) make decisions on whether you have complied with the requirement to take part in an interview and whether you have good cause for failing to do so. You can appeal against their decision within one month of the decision being posted to you (see Chapter 60). Alternatively, you can ask them to reconsider and revise the decision – within one month for any reason, or outside of one month if it arose from an official error (see Box T.5). In each case, any arrears due are paid back in full if you are successful. There is no right of appeal about waivers and deferrals, although you can ask the personal adviser to reconsider.

not attend the interview with their claim-form or statement and evidence, the date of claim is the date one of them eventually does so.

C&P Regs, reg 6(4ZB) & (4A)

If you can't get all the evidence for one of the reasons outlined above for income support, your claim can still be accepted. If you don't have all the evidence or need more time to obtain it, the time limit can be extended by up to one month from the date you first contacted Jobcentre Plus.

C&P Regs, regs 4(1B) & 6(4AB)

3. Backdating delayed claims

The time limits for claiming benefits are given in Box T.3.

Income support (IS) and jobseeker's allowance (JSA) can be backdated for up to either one month or three months in the limited circumstances described below.

If you are aged under 60, housing benefit (HB) and council tax benefit (CTB) can be backdated for up to six months if you formally request it and have 'good cause' for the delay in claiming. If you are aged 60 or over, HB and CTB can normally be backdated for up to three months without you having to formally request it or show good cause. However, if you are aged 60 or over and either you or your partner are claiming IS, income-related employment and support allowance or income-based JSA, the backdating rules for people under 60 continue to apply.

For other benefits, there is no extension to the time limits for claiming, no matter how good your reasons are for not applying earlier – unless, in some cases, it is because of a delay in the award of a qualifying benefit (see below).

If you want to claim benefit for an earlier period, make sure you state this on the claim-form (or when you make the call if the claim is made over the phone).

Delays in qualifying benefits

Entitlement to some benefits may depend on you, a member of your family or someone else getting another qualifying benefit, eg carer's allowance depends on the person you look after receiving attendance allowance (AA) or disability living allowance (DLA) middle or highest rate care component.

The general rule – Claim straight away; don't wait for a decision on the qualifying benefit. If your first claim is refused because the qualifying benefit has not yet been awarded, claim again once you get a decision awarding the qualifying benefit. If you do this within three months of the decision awarding the qualifying benefit (which might be after a revision or appeal if the qualifying benefit is refused initially), that second claim can be backdated to the date of the first claim, or to the date from which the qualifying benefit is awarded if that is later. On the date you first claim, if you have not already claimed the qualifying benefit you have another ten days to do so. If you wait longer than ten days, a second claim made once the qualifying benefit is awarded cannot be backdated in this way.

C&P Regs, reg 6(16)-(18)

Where entitlement to one benefit depends on another, if one stops the other stops too. In this case, if you challenge the decision on the qualifying benefit and it is reinstated, make a fresh claim for the other benefit within three months of the date of the decision to reinstate the qualifying benefit and the other benefit will then be fully backdated. For example, if your DLA is stopped you may also lose entitlement to IS. If you get back your DLA after a successful appeal, make a fresh claim for IS and it will be paid again from when it was stopped.

When you are in receipt of a means-tested benefit and make a claim for a benefit that could provide access to a premium, eg carer's allowance, it is possible that while you are waiting for the carer's allowance to be awarded the means-tested benefit might be stopped for some other reason, eg a small increase in your income. In this case, when the carer's allowance is eventually awarded, you should make a fresh claim for the means-tested benefit within three months of the date of this award and the benefit can now be paid from the time that the previous claim ended.

C&P Regs, reg 6(19)-(21)

Exceptions – The rule above applies to almost all benefits with the following exceptions.

- ❑ If you have been waiting for the person for whom you are caring to be awarded the appropriate rate of DLA or AA, as long as you claim carer's allowance (or a dependant's increase for that benefit) within three months of the date the DLA or AA is awarded, your claim for carer's allowance (or the increase) can be treated as having been made on the first day of the benefit week in which DLA or AA became payable.

C&P Regs, reg 6(33)

- ❑ Sometimes entitlement to either working or child tax credit is dependent on the disability, severe disability, disabled child or severely disabled child element being included in the calculation (see Chapter 18(4), (7) and (8)). If you claim the tax credit within three months of the decision awarding a qualifying benefit for one of these elements, the claim can be backdated to the date on which the qualifying benefit became payable or, if later, the first day on which your eligibility for tax credit is dependent on the receipt of the qualifying benefit. You must satisfy all the other eligibility conditions for the tax credit throughout this back-payment period and you cannot have the tax credit backdated to more than three months before the current claim to the qualifying benefit was made.

TC(C&N) Regs, regs 8, 26 & 26A

- ❑ If your incapacity benefit (IB) is stopped (because you are no longer deemed incapable of work) while you are waiting to hear about a claim for DLA (or constant attendance

T.2 Interchange of claims

If you make a claim for one benefit, then find you should have claimed a different benefit instead, or you were also entitled to a different benefit, the rules on interchanging benefit claims may help you get arrears of benefit beyond the usual limits. Your original claim may be treated as a claim for another benefit, either as an alternative to the original claim or in addition. But not all benefits can count as a claim for any other. Within each group below, the benefits listed are interchangeable with each other:

- employment and support allowance/incapacity benefit, maternity allowance;
- state pension of any category, widow's benefit/bereavement benefit;
- disability living allowance, attendance allowance, industrial injuries constant attendance allowance;
- child benefit, guardian's allowance, an addition for a child dependant (with non-means-tested benefits prior to April 2003), maternity allowance claimed after confinement;
- a claim for income support can be treated as a claim for carer's allowance, but not the other way round.

C&P Regs, reg 9 & Sch 1

If the decision maker treats one claim as another, then the date of the original claim counts as the date of claim for the alternative benefit and arrears may be payable from then. However, the overlapping benefit rules could prevent some or all of the arrears being payable.

You cannot appeal against a decision on whether to treat a claim for one benefit as a claim for another but you can ask the decision maker to look at the decision again (see 'Ground 9' in Box T.5).

allowance), you should reclaim IB within three months of the decision awarding you DLA highest rate care component (or intermediate or exceptional rate constant attendance allowance). Your new IB claim will be backdated to the end of your earlier IB entitlement, or to the date from which DLA is payable, if that is later.

C&P Regs, reg 6(23)-(24)

T.3 Time limits for claiming benefit

Benefit	Time limit
Disability living allowance, attendance allowance	
■ initial claim	immediate
■ renewal claim	immediate
Income support, jobseeker's allowance	immediate
Social fund	
■ Sure Start maternity grant	from 11 weeks before expected week of birth, up to 3 months after date of birth, or adoption, residence or parental order
■ funeral expenses	from the date of death to 3 months after date of funeral
Carer's allowance	3 months
Employment and support allowance	3 months
State pension	12 months
Pension credit	3 months
Tax credits	3 months
Child benefit, guardian's allowance, maternity allowance, dependants' additions (not income support)	3 months
Bereavement allowance, widowed parents' allowance	3 months (or 12 months when death has been difficult to establish)
Bereavement payment	12 months
Industrial injuries disablement benefit	3 months from the first day you were entitled to benefit (15 weeks after date of accident/accepted date of onset of disease)

C&P Regs, reg 19 & Sch 4

The time limits are not generally cut-off points for claiming benefit, but limit the extent to which your benefit can be backdated: eg if you claim carer's allowance it can be automatically backdated for three months. However, in the case of industrial injuries disablement benefit, you must claim within five years of working in the prescribed occupation for occupational deafness, or ten years for occupational asthma, otherwise you lose entitlement completely (see Chapter 45(6)). For some benefits the time limits can be extended in certain circumstances (see 3).

Backdating IS and JSA

Administrative reasons: one-month backdating – IS or JSA can be backdated for up to one month if any one or more of the administrative reasons below apply, as a result of which you could not reasonably have been expected to make the claim earlier.

- ❑ You couldn't attend the Jobcentre Plus office to make your claim because it was closed or because of transport difficulties, and there were no alternative arrangements available.
- ❑ You tried to phone the Jobcentre Plus office to let them know of your intention to claim, but couldn't get through because their lines were busy or inoperable.
- ❑ There were adverse postal conditions.
- ❑ You were not sent notice of the end of entitlement to a previous benefit until after it actually ended.
- ❑ You stopped being part of a couple within one month before claiming.
- ❑ You claimed JSA after your partner had failed to attend a work-focused interview.
- ❑ Your partner, parent, son, daughter, brother or sister died within one month before you claimed.

C&P Regs, reg 19(6) & (7)

Special reasons: 3-month backdating – IS and JSA can be backdated for up to three months if any one or more of the special reasons below apply, as a result of which you could not reasonably have been expected to make the claim earlier.

- ❑ You were given information by a DWP official that led you to believe your claim would not succeed. What you understood from the information you were given may have been affected by your disability or communication difficulties and this should be taken into account.
- ❑ You were given written advice by a solicitor or other professional adviser, a medical practitioner, a local authority, or a person working in a Citizens Advice Bureau or similar advice agency, which led you to believe your claim would not succeed.
- ❑ You or your partner were given written information about your income or capital by an employer or ex-employer, or a bank or building society, which led you to believe your claim would not succeed.
- ❑ You were prevented by bad weather from attending the Jobcentre Plus office.
- ❑ You have difficulty communicating because either you are deaf or blind, or you have learning, language or literacy difficulties. The test is about your ability to get help and not whether someone should have offered it (CIS/2057/1998).
- ❑ You are ill or disabled (this is not accepted as a special reason for JSA). There is no definition of 'ill' or 'disabled' in the regulations.
- ❑ You were caring for someone who is ill or disabled. You don't have to live with the person or be related to them.
- ❑ You were required to deal with a domestic emergency affecting you.

In the last four cases, you will also need to show it was not reasonably practicable for you to get help to make your claim.

C&P Regs, reg 19(4) & (5)

You should give full details of your reasons for claiming late on your claim-form (or when you make the call if the claim is made over the phone). You can appeal if you disagree with the decision on backdating.

Test cases

If you are claiming following a test case, any backdating that might apply under the normal rules is generally limited to the date the test case decision was given. See Chapter 60(6).

4. Appointees

If a person is or might be entitled to benefit and cannot act for themselves, the decision maker can appoint someone aged 18 or over, an 'appointee', to act on their behalf. An appointee is usually a relative or friend, but can also be a body of people such as a firm of solicitors or a housing association. An appointment may be appropriate, for example, if the claimant is unable to act for themselves because of a severe learning disability, mental illness or senility. Contact the office dealing with the claim and they will make the arrangements.

If you are the appointee, it is your responsibility to deal with the claim, including, for example, notifying changes of circumstances. It is the appointee who is responsible for claiming on time and whose own circumstances will be relevant in deciding whether there are special reasons for backdating a delayed claim, or for not providing all the documentary evidence required for a claim.

If you are appointed to act for the claimant in relation to one benefit, that appointment can cover all social security benefits, including tax credits and payments from the social fund. Separate appointments have to be made for housing benefit and council tax benefit.

C&P Regs, reg 33

5. Payments

Your benefit is normally paid into a bank, building society or Post Office account. The Post Office card accounts ensure that people can collect their money at Post Offices; these accounts only accept payment of benefits or tax credits and only allow cash withdrawal at Post Offices. You can nominate someone else to withdraw your money for you; they will then be issued with the card.

If for some reason you are unable to open or use any of the above accounts you will be paid by cheque instead. Such cheque payments will be phased out by 2010, to be replaced by a card-based system.

Certain benefits are paid through your wages – ie statutory sick, maternity, paternity and adoption pay.

Compensation for delays – You may be due compensation if payments are delayed (see Chapter 62(2)).

Lost PIN – If you lose your PIN number, ask for a replacement. Contact your bank or building society if your benefit is paid into one of their accounts. If your benefit is paid into a Post Office card account, call their helpline (0845 7223 344). You may need to claim a social fund crisis loan if it takes a while to sort out the matter.

6. Overpayments

An overpayment of benefit is recoverable if it was overpaid because you failed to disclose a 'material fact' or you misrepresented a material fact, even if you acted in all innocence. In a Court of Appeal judgment, *B v Secretary of State*, it was decided that once a fact is 'known' to you and the duty to report it has been made clear to you, you cannot argue that due to the particular circumstances of your case (eg mental disability) disclosure of the fact could not reasonably have been expected.

In deciding whether there has been an overpayment, the decision maker must first revise or supersede your entitlement to benefit and decide how much you should have been paid. The decision maker will then decide whether you:

- failed to notify the relevant office (ie the office that normally deals with the benefit concerned) about a material fact on the relevant date or as soon as possible afterwards; *or*
- misrepresented a material fact – ie made an incorrect statement.

In either case, the overpayment would be recoverable.

SSAA, S.71(1) & (5A)

A 'material' fact is one that would have affected the amount of your benefit. A 'fact' is not the same as a conclusion drawn from fact. For example, the conclusion that you have a 'limited capability for work' is drawn from the facts of your case. The onus of proof is on the decision maker to identify the material fact that you failed to disclose or misrepresented.

In the House of Lords judgment *Hinchy*, it was held that a claimant could be said to have failed to disclose a material fact in not informing one DWP office of a benefit decision taken by another DWP office. Consequently, when a decision is made on one benefit that could affect entitlement to another, you are under a duty to inform the office dealing with the potentially affected benefit.

The overpayment test is common to employment and support allowance (ESA), income support, income-based jobseeker's allowance (JSA), pension credit, social fund grants and loans, and to almost all of the non-means-tested benefits. There is a different test for housing benefit and council tax benefit (see Chapter 20(19)). Generally, HMRC has greater flexibility in dealing with changes of circumstances in respect of tax credits, with a continual process of adjusting what they overpaid or underpaid you one year with what they will pay you in the next year (see Chapter 19(6)). Notwithstanding this flexibility, overpayments due to fraud or negligence can be dealt with by a penalty system (see Chapter 18(12)).

If the overpayment is not recoverable

If it is not recoverable under the legislation, you do not need to pay back the overpayment. Nevertheless, the DWP may ask you to pay it back. You should not feel under pressure to do so. If you're not sure whether you are obliged to pay back an overpayment, seek advice from a local advice centre. The DWP may mention the possibility of taking proceedings through the courts to recover the overpayment under common law, but in practice they are unlikely to do so. But if they take this any further, seek legal advice immediately.

The DWP can also offset arrears of entitlement in a later award against the irrecoverable overpayment. However, if DLA has been suspended due to an overpayment, arrears of DLA awarded following a new decision should not be offset against the overpayment in this way.

PAOR Regs, reg 5(1) and R(DLA)2/07 (CoA 'Brown')

Incapacity and disability benefits

If there has been an improvement in your condition and you did not know you should have reported this, you should not be left with an overpayment. Similarly, if the effect of your incapacity or disability proves not to be as severe as it was originally believed, and you did not know you should have reported the mistake in the original information, you should not be left with an overpayment. Any reduction in your benefit in either case should thus not be backdated; you should appeal against a decision that you were paid the wrong amount of benefit for the earlier period. See Chapter 60(5) under 'What if your benefit goes down' for details.

Appointees and others

Overpayments can be recovered from third parties if it is they who have misrepresented or failed to disclose the material fact. If it is an appointee acting on behalf of the claimant, the decision maker may decide that the overpayment is recoverable from both the claimant and the appointee. Alternatively, the decision maker may decide the overpayment is recoverable from either one or the other. In general, if the appointee has retained the benefit instead of paying it to, or applying it for the benefit of, the claimant, only the appointee is liable; if the appointee has acted with due care and diligence, only the claimant is liable.

R(IS)5/03

Appeals

You can appeal against a decision that you were paid the wrong amount of benefit. You can also appeal against a decision that the overpayment is recoverable and against decisions relating to the period of the overpayment, from whom it is recoverable and the amount owed.

Amount of the overpayment

If you have been overpaid a benefit and the overpayment resulted from your misrepresentation of, or failure to disclose, a material fact, the amount of the overpayment is reduced by:

- any amount of the overpayment of benefit that has been offset against arrears of entitlement in a later award (generally because of a change in the rate of award of a benefit you had already claimed);
- any extra income support, income-related ESA, income-based JSA or pension credit you should have been paid, not necessarily for the same period as the overpayment (R(IS)5/92, CSIS/8/95).

PAOR Regs, regs 5 & 13

If you had not claimed any benefit (eg income support), but would have been entitled to it had you not been overpaid another benefit, put in a claim and ask for it to be backdated if you have 'special reasons' (see 3 above). If successful, you can ask for an abatement of the overpayment against what you should have received under the other benefit.

For more details about the nature of the overpayment test, read the notes to section 71 of the Social Security Administration Act 1992 in *Social Security: Legislation 2008 Volume III* (see page 6).

Diminution of capital

If you have been overpaid income support, income-related ESA, income-based JSA or pension credit because you didn't tell the DWP about all your capital resources, or you misrepresented the nature of your capital, allowance is made for capital you would have spent had you not been paid benefit. At the end of each 13-week period, starting with the first day of the overpayment, your capital is treated as having been reduced by the amount of benefit you had been overpaid during that quarter. At the same time, any tariff income would be recalculated.

Your capital cannot be treated as diminished in this way over any period shorter than 13 weeks. However, if you spent any of that undeclared capital during the overpayment period, the overpayment would end on the day your capital reached the appropriate limit, assuming the notional capital rules don't apply (see Chapter 27(9)). The treatment of diminution of capital under this rule would also apply to the reduced amount.

PAOR Regs, reg 14

A similar diminution of capital principle applies to housing benefit and to council tax benefit. The diminution of capital principle is different from the diminishing notional capital principle explained in Chapter 27(9).

HB Regs, reg 103 & CTB Regs, reg 88

Fraud and penalties

It is fraud if you dishonestly or knowingly make a false statement or provide a false document or information to get benefit or more benefit. It is also fraud if:

- there has been a change of circumstances affecting entitlement to your or another person's benefit; *and*
- the change is not excluded by regulations from changes that are required to be notified; *and*
- you know the change affects your own or the other person's entitlement; *and*
- you dishonestly fail to give a prompt notification of the change in *'the prescribed manner to the prescribed person'* (eg giving notice in writing to the relevant authority).

These rules apply to appointees or to anyone else with a right to receive benefit on behalf of another person. They also apply to third parties such as landlords, if they know, or would be expected to know, of changes with respect to a tenant's occupation of a dwelling or a tenant's liability to make payments in respect of that dwelling.

SSAA, S.112

If fraud is suspected, the DWP (or local authority for housing benefit and council tax benefit) may ask you to attend an interview with a fraud officer. Seek advice beforehand and if possible take a friend with you who is not involved in the matter. The DWP may decide not to prosecute, even if they believe you have committed fraud. But if you are found guilty of fraud, the court can fine you or imprison you, or both.

If the DWP or local authority believe they have enough evidence to successfully prosecute, they may give you the option of paying a penalty as an alternative to prosecution. The penalty is fixed at 30% of the overpayment. You also have to repay the overpayment. You have 28 days to change your mind if you have agreed to pay a penalty.

SSAA, S.115A

A formal caution may be offered as an alternative to prosecution in England and Wales (but not in Scotland). This is an administrative practice in the DWP; it is not a criminal conviction. But if you are later found guilty of another offence, the formal caution may be used in court for sentencing purposes.

Different rules apply to tax credits, which have a penalty system in place (see Chapter 18(12)). If HMRC believes fraud is involved, they may prosecute in the courts.

If you are accused of fraud, get legal advice as soon as you can. Contact details for law centres are in the Address List. Alternatively, a Citizens Advice Bureau may be able to help.

60 Decisions, revisions and appeals

In this chapter we look at:

1. Who makes decisions?

The Secretary of State for Work and Pensions is responsible for decision making for most social security benefits, but in practice decisions are made on their behalf by an officer called a decision maker. Decisions on appeal are made by a First-tier Tribunal (a tribunal) in the Social Entitlement Chamber within the Ministry of Justice. Appeals against decisions of tribunals are made to the Upper Tribunal in the Administrative Appeals Chamber. The administration for both of these tribunals is carried out by the Tribunals Service.

Housing benefit and council tax benefit have a similar decisions and appeals system. Decisions are made by a local authority officer. The ways of changing decisions described in this chapter apply equally to housing benefit and council tax benefit decisions unless otherwise stated. Decisions on appeal are made by a tribunal.

Some HMRC decisions use the same appeal system:

- **Working tax credit, child tax credit, child benefit and guardian's allowance** – Decisions are made by an officer of HMRC. The tax credits decision-making process is different from that of social security benefits (see Chapter 18(13)). Decisions on appeal are made by a benefit tribunal in the Social Entitlement Chamber (but will transfer to the Finance and Tax Chamber at an unspecified future date).
- **National insurance credits and home responsibilities protection** – Decisions are made by HMRC officers based in the National Insurance Contributions Office. The decision-making process is the same as that for social security benefits. Decisions on appeal are made by a benefit tribunal.

Decisions on national insurance contributions and employed earner status are made by HMRC. Appeals are usually made to a tribunal in the Finance and Tax Chamber.

There are separate systems for the discretionary social fund (Chapter 23), statutory sick pay (Chapter 8(10)), statutory maternity, paternity and adoption pay (Chapter 36) and war disablement pensions (Chapter 46(9 and 10)). There are modified rules for vaccine damage payments (Chapter 48(5)).

2. Ways of changing decisions

Once a decision is made, it stands and is binding until one of the specific methods given in the law for changing decisions is set in motion. Even a decision given without legal authority counts as an effective decision until it is challenged.

Changing a decision made by a decision maker

There are four ways of changing a decision made by a decision maker on behalf of the Secretary of State:

- correct an accidental error;
- revise the decision;
- supersede the decision;
- appeal against the decision.

Correcting an accidental error – An 'accidental' error in a decision can be corrected by the decision maker at any time. Arithmetical or clerical errors can be corrected in this way. Correction is discretionary and there is no appeal against a refusal to correct.

If the decision is corrected, the dispute period (see 3) starts from when notice of the correction is sent. If a decision is not corrected, the original dispute period remains in place. So if you ask for a decision to be corrected, make sure you also ask for a revision or lodge an appeal before the end of the time limit in case the decision is not corrected.

D&A Regs, reg 9A

Revisions, supersessions and appeals are covered in 3 to 16 below.

Changing a decision made by a tribunal

There are four ways of changing a decision made by a tribunal:

- correct an accidental error;
- set aside the decision;
- supersede the decision;
- appeal against the decision.

These are covered in more detail in 17 and 18 below.

3. 'Any grounds' revisions

The dispute period – There is a 'dispute period' of one month from the date a decision maker's decision is sent to you, during which you can ask for the decision to be revised on 'any grounds' or appeal against it. The decision can be revised for any reason other than for a change of circumstances occurring after the decision was made (in which case you must make a fresh claim or ask for the award to be superseded – see Box T.5). The time limit can be extended in special circumstances (see below). Outside the dispute period, a decision can be revised only if certain grounds are satisfied (see 4 below and Box T.5).

D&A Regs, reg 3(1); TP(FTT)SEC Rules, Sch 1

A decision of a tribunal cannot be changed by an 'any grounds' revision. See 17 below for what to do if you disagree with a tribunal decision.

The time limit

Unless you have requested a written statement of reasons (see below), your request to revise the decision must be received no later than one calendar month from the day after the date the decision was posted to you. Make the request to the office address on the decision letter.

D&A Regs, reg 3(1)(b) & TP(FTT)SEC Rules, Sch 1

The date the decision is posted is taken to be the date on the decision letter. For example, if the date given on the decision letter is 10 October 2009, your request must be received on or before 10 November 2009. If there is no corresponding date in the next month, your request must be received by the last day of that month; for example, if a decision is dated 31 May 2009, your request must be received by 30 June 2009.

Keep a record of the date you make your request. If you take a letter into the office, ask for a dated receipt.

DWP guidance says that decision makers should accept requests received one day late unless they are certain the decision letter was actually posted on the day it is dated.

Para 03063, Vol 1, Decision Makers Guide

'Any grounds' revision or appeal?

The decision letter should explain your right either to ask for an 'any grounds' revision or to appeal. (The letter might not use the word 'revision' but instead asks if you want the decision looked at again; it means the same thing.) Normally you have a choice, but some decisions cannot be appealed (see 7 below).

Asking for a decision to be revised is usually a quicker way of changing a decision than appealing. If you appeal straight away, you lose this chance of having the case looked at again by the DWP (although a separate revision can happen as part of the appeal process – see 9 below). For the revision, the DWP simply has another look at the decision, taking into account any further information or evidence you supply. Normally, a different decision maker looks at the case. You will have a further month to appeal if you are not satisfied with the revised decision. For more on appeals, see 7-17 below.

How do you ask for a revision?

It is important to act within the one-month time limit. If you don't, you could miss out on arrears of benefit or even find that you can't challenge the decision at all. You can ask for a revision over the phone, but you should confirm your request in writing and keep a copy of it. If you are near the deadline for requesting a revision, phone to register the revision and say you will write with more details, otherwise a postal delay could result in your request being out of time. For housing benefit and council tax benefit, your request must be in writing to the local authority. A few days after posting your revision request, ring the office you sent it to to make sure they have received it.

You can ask for an 'any grounds' revision for any reason, but you should explain why you think the decision is wrong. If you can, get evidence to back up your argument. If you cannot send this straight away, say so. You should be given a month to send in extra evidence, which can extended at the decision maker's discretion.

Written statement of reasons for the decision

If the decision did not include reasons, you can ask for a written statement of reasons. You must do this within one month of the date of the decision. If you ask for the written statement within one month and it is provided within that time, the one-month dispute period is extended by 14 days; if it is provided after one month, the dispute period is extended to 14 days from the date it is provided. Unfortunately, you can't always tell from the decision letter whether reasons are included, and the written statement you are sent often does not explain the decision fully; so try to ask for a revision within the one-month time limit, even if you are also asking for written reasons.

D&A Regs, regs 3(1)(b)(ii)-(iii) & TP(FTT)SEC Rules, Sch 1

Extending the time limit for revision

If you have missed the deadline, there are two options.

- Ask for a late 'any grounds' revision. The dispute period can be extended if strict conditions are met (see below). If the application is accepted, the decision can still be revised for any reason – you are not limited to certain grounds – and benefit can be fully backdated.
- Look for grounds to revise or supersede the decision outside the dispute period. Grounds are limited and, for a supersession, arrears of benefit are normally paid only from the date you apply. See 4 and 5 below and Box T.5.

If you ask for a late revision (or a late appeal), also ask the decision maker to treat your letter as a request for a supersession if your request for a late revision or appeal is not allowed. That way you will not delay asking for the supersession and so avoid missing out on backdated benefit.

Late revisions – An application for a late 'any grounds' revision may be accepted if:

- it is reasonable to grant the application;
- the application for revision has 'merit' – this is not defined but if there is no prospect of success, the application for a late revision will probably be refused; *and*
- the delay was caused by special circumstances – you must show that it was not practicable for you to apply in time. The longer the delay, the better the reason must be. It won't be enough that you simply didn't know or understand the law or the time limits involved.

A reinterpretation of the law by an Upper Tribunal or court is not a ground for a late 'any grounds' revision (but it may allow a supersession for error of law – see Box T.5).

Apply for a late 'any grounds' revision in writing; include the name of the benefit, the date of the decision, why you think it should be revised and your reasons for the delay. You cannot get a late revision more than 13 months (plus any extension because you asked for a written statement of reasons – see above) after the date the decision was sent to you. If you are refused a late revision once, you cannot apply again.

D&A Regs, reg 4

Late appeals – The rules are different (see 7 below).

The revised decision

You will get a written decision following your application for a revision. The revised decision takes effect from the date of the earlier decision, so benefit is backdated to that date.

SSA, S.9(3)

Appeal rights – You can appeal within one month of being sent a revised decision. If the decision maker decides not to revise the decision, they will write to tell you. You have a month to appeal against the original decision from the date of the letter.

TP(FTT)SEC Rules, Sch 1

4. 'Any time' revisions and supersessions

It is best to challenge a decision within the dispute period if you can. However, this may not be possible; your circumstances might change later or you might only realise later that the decision was wrong. You can go back to the DWP or local authority at any time to ask them to reconsider a decision, however long ago the decision was made, but you must first show that certain grounds are satisfied (see Box T.5). If the grounds are satisfied, the decision maker will revise or supersede the decision as appropriate.

What's the difference between revising and superseding a decision? – A decision can be revised only if it was wrong at the time it was made. A revised decision replaces the original decision, so it's effect is fully backdated. Generally, a decision is superseded if there is a later change. A supersession creates a new decision that takes effect from a later date and leaves the original decision unchanged; backdating is usually limited to that later date. Sometimes when a decision is wrong, it can be replaced only by supersession and not by revision, so arrears are limited. Box T.4 has the backdating rules.

SSA, ss 9 & 10;

Whether a decision is revised or superseded depends on which grounds (listed in Box T.5) exist. If you are not sure what to ask for, just explain why you think the decision is wrong. The decision maker can treat a request to supersede as one to revise and vice versa. If grounds to both revise and supersede exist, the decision should be revised.

D&A Regs, regs 3(10) & 6(5)

Applying for a decision to be revised or superseded

It is best to request in writing that a decision be revised or superseded. For housing benefit and council tax benefit this is the only option, but with other benefits you can phone or go to the appropriate office in person. However, if you do this, you should confirm your request in writing. Check which one or more of the grounds (listed in Box T.5) apply and say why you think those grounds are satisfied. The decision maker need not take into account anything that is not raised by your application, so make sure you give all the reasons you think the decision should be changed. If you can, provide evidence to back up your argument. If you cannot send this straight away, say that you are sending it soon. Keep a copy of your letter and any evidence you send.

Appeal rights

If one of the grounds in Box T.5 is satisfied, the original decision can be either revised or superseded. The result may be to confirm the original decision or to change it. If the decision maker makes a decision to revise, supersede or not to supersede, you have a right of appeal (if the decision maker decides not to supersede they will confirm the original decision as correct). If the decision maker refuses to revise, you do not have the right of appeal.

Rarely, if the application to supersede is obviously hopeless and could not alter the benefit award, the decision maker can refuse to make a decision. As no decision is made, there is no right of appeal.

R(DLA)1/03

For appeal rights within the dispute period, see 3 above.

5. Backdating after a change of circumstances

Whether benefit can be backdated following a change of circumstances depends on the precise nature of the change. Tell the DWP or local authority about the change as soon as you can. If you tell them about the change within one month,

benefit is fully backdated to the date of the change.
D&A Regs, reg 7(2)(a)

For disability living allowance (DLA) and attendance allowance, an increase can be paid from the first pay day after you first satisfy the 3-month or 6-month backwards qualifying period (see Chapters 3(4) and 4(2)) if you tell the DWP about the change within one month of completing the qualifying period. If you are only able to give the month and not the day that you would have satisfied the disability test, the decision maker is told to assume you satisfied it on the last day of that month.
D&A Regs, reg 7(9); paras 04396 & 04400, Vol 1, Decision Maker's Guide

Late notification – If the change of circumstances happened more than a month ago, you may still be able to get benefit backdated to the date of the change if you apply within 13 months of the change. Write to the appropriate office giving details of the change of circumstances and reasons for not telling them earlier. To backdate benefit, the decision maker must be satisfied that:

- it is reasonable to grant the application; *and*
- the change is relevant to the decision that is to be superseded (see 'Ground 1' in Box T.5); *and*
- there are special circumstances that are relevant to the application (eg a serious illness); *and*
- because of the special circumstances it was not practicable for you to notify the change of circumstances within a month of the date of change.

The longer the delay, the better the reason must be. The decision maker won't take account of the fact that you simply didn't know of the time limits or the law, or that an Upper Tribunal, Commissioner or court has reinterpreted the law.
D&A Regs, reg 8

What if your benefit goes down?

If your circumstances change, and as a result your benefit goes down or stops, the general rule is that the new decision takes effect from the date of the change, no matter when you reported it. The same applies whenever the decision is not advantageous to you (see 9 below). If the DWP or local authority decides you have been paid too much benefit, they may try to recover the overpayment (see Chapter 59(6)).

There are exceptions, however, for the following:

- the disability tests for DLA or attendance allowance;
- disablement for severe disablement allowance or industrial injuries benefits;
- incapacity for work for income support, incapacity benefit or severe disablement allowance.

For these benefits, the reduction is only backdated if you knew or could reasonably have been expected to know that the change should have been reported. In this case, the reduction is backdated to the date you should have told them.
D&A Regs, reg 7(2)(c)

The same applies to any decision made on another benefit as a result of one of the above disability or incapacity decisions. For example: if DLA stops following a Right Payment Programme check, both DLA entitlement and any disability premium included in income support will stop from the date the DLA decision is made if you could not reasonably have been expected to know that you should have reported a reduction in your care needs.
D&A Regs, reg 7A(2)

In deciding whether you *'reasonably could have been expected to know'* that you should have reported the change, decision makers should take into account:

- how much you knew about the reasons for awarding you benefit;
- what information was given to you about reporting changes of circumstances;
- your ability to recognise when a gradual improvement results in a relevant change of circumstances. A slight change in your care or mobility needs, or your ability to carry out activities in the personal capability assessment of incapacity, would not normally be a change that you could reasonably be expected to report. However, even if the change is gradual there may still be a point at which you could reasonably be expected to know it should be reported.

Para 04239/40, Vol 1, Decision Makers Guide

At present, there is no equivalent rule for employment and support allowance (ESA). Legislation extending this rule to ESA is expected in the course of 2009. Until then, the DWP can use its discretionary power not to recover an overpayment where recovery would be unreasonable, unfair or cause hardship.

6. When a test case is pending

A decision on your claim may be affected by a matter of law that is under appeal in the courts in another case – ie a 'test case'. A decision maker can postpone making a decision in your case until the test case has been decided. Alternatively, they can make the decision in your case as though the test case has been decided in a way that is unfavourable to you. If the test case turns out to be favourable, the decision maker must then go back and revise the decision.
SSA, S.25 & D&A Regs, reg 21

When the decision maker makes a decision in your case

T.4 Backdating

A *revised* decision takes effect from the date the earlier decision took effect, so benefit is fully backdated. A *superseded* decision generally takes effect from the date you apply for the decision to be superseded, so benefit can only be backdated to this date. Exceptions to the rule are listed below.

Event	Date change takes effect
Award of a qualifying benefit	full backdating to the start of existing award or, if later, date qualifying benefit starts
Following a reinterpretation of the law in a test case	the date of test case decision
Change of circumstances	
■ notified within one month	the date of change
■ for disability living allowance or attendance allowance – notified within one month of completing 3- or 6-month qualifying period for new rate or component	the end of qualifying period
■ notified after one month	the date notified – no backdating
■ notified after one month (but within 13 months) – special circumstances for the delay	the date of change
Official error	
■ all benefits	full backdating to the date of the original decision

after a test case decision, any arrears of benefit are restricted to the date the test case is decided.

SSA, S.27(3)

If you have appealed – The outcome of your appeal may depend on the result of another case pending at the courts. If this happens, the decision maker may ask a First-tier or Upper Tribunal to do one of the following:

- not to decide the appeal, but to refer it back to them. The appeal will be held until the test case is decided. The decision maker will then revise or supersede the decision as appropriate;
- to deal with the appeal. The tribunal or Upper Tribunal can either hold the appeal until the test case has been decided, or determine it as if the test case has been decided in a way that is unfavourable to you. If the result of the test case is then favourable, the decision can be superseded by a decision maker.

SSA, S.26

7. Appeals

You have the right to appeal to a tribunal against any decision on a claim for benefit or against any decision that revises or

T.5 Grounds for revising or superseding a decision

Outside the dispute period, a decision can only be reconsidered for specific reasons or 'grounds'. If at least one of the grounds outlined in this box is met, a decision can be either revised or superseded. We have called them 'Ground 1', 'Ground 2', etc, for convenience, but these numbers are not used officially, so you must clearly state the grounds in your application. We include only the main grounds here; the full list is contained within the appropriate regulations: D&A Regs, regs 3 & 6; HB&CTB(D&A) Regs, regs 4 & 7; Child Benefit & Guardian's Allowance (D&A) Regs, regs 5-13. In the footnotes we refer only to the first set of these regulations, which cover the majority of social security benefits.

If you ask for a decision to be looked at again, you must show that one of the grounds is met. Similarly, if the decision maker decides for themselves to revise or supersede the decision, they must show that a ground is met. If no ground is met, the decision cannot be changed no matter how wrong it may be (CDLA/3875/2001).

Note: A decision made by an First-tier or Upper Tribunal cannot be revised on any ground and cannot be superseded because of an 'error of law'; so Grounds 2 and 4 cannot be used.

Ground 1: Change of circumstances

Any decision can be *superseded* if there has been a *'relevant change of circumstances since [it] had effect'*, or such a change is anticipated.

D&A Regs, reg 6(2)(a)

What changes are 'relevant'? – A change of circumstances is 'relevant' if it calls for serious consideration by the decision maker and could (but not necessarily would) change some aspect of the award, such as the amount or length of the award.

For example, if you receive the lowest rate care component of disability living allowance (DLA) and your condition deteriorates so that your care needs increase, that is a relevant change of circumstances because it could lead to entitlement to a higher rate of benefit.

Note the following points:

- ❑ A decision to refuse benefit cannot be superseded due to a later change of circumstances. You must make a fresh benefit claim.
- ❑ For employment and support allowance (ESA) and incapacity-related benefits, a new report from a DWP healthcare professional enables a decision to be superseded (see Ground 3 below). For other benefits, such as DLA, a different medical opinion is not in itself a relevant change of circumstances. However, a new medical report may provide evidence of a change of circumstances – eg the report may indicate that your condition has deteriorated (R(DLA)6/01).
- ❑ A change in legislation is a relevant change of circumstances and a supersession can take effect from the date on which the law changes. However, new case law (a decision of a court or Upper Tribunal) does not count as a relevant change of circumstances (R(I)2/94).

The backdating rules following a change of circumstances are described in Chapter 60(5).

Ground 2: Error of law

A decision can be *superseded* if it was based on a mistake about the law (eg the decision maker misinterpreted the relevant law). In practice, supersession of a decision maker's decision should take place only if the legal error comes to light because of an Upper Tribunal's or court's decision on another claim – a test case decision (see Chapter 60(6)). In this case, extra benefit can be paid only from the date of the test case decision. For any other error of law, the decision should be *revised* as an official error, with full backdating of benefit (see 'Ground 4').

D&A Regs, reg 6(2)(b)(i)

Note: A decision of a First-tier or Upper Tribunal cannot be superseded because of an error of law. You may, however, be able to appeal further (see Chapter 60(17)).

Ground 3: New medical report

A decision maker can *supersede* an ESA decision that you have a limited capability for work or a decision under the personal capability assessment that you are incapable of work (including a decision made by a First-tier or Upper Tribunal) if they get a new medical report on your incapacity from a DWP healthcare professional. Once the decision maker has decided that this ground applies, they must consider whether or not you have a limited capability for work (for ESA) or are incapable of work (for incapacity benefits). In doing so, they must look at all the relevant evidence about your incapacity, including medical evidence from earlier periods (CIB/3985/2001).

D&A Regs, reg 6(2)(g) & (r)

Ground 4: Official error

A decision can be *revised* if it arose from an official error by the DWP, HMRC or local authority, as long as no one outside the decision-making department or authority caused or materially contributed to the error.

D&A Regs, regs 1 & 3(5)(a)

The revised decision generally takes effect from the same date as the original decision, so benefit can be fully backdated no matter how long ago the original decision was made; but see Ground 2 for errors that come to light because of a test case.

Ground 5: Award of a qualifying benefit

If you, your partner or a dependent child become entitled to another 'qualifying' benefit, or to an increase in such a benefit, as a result of which your existing award should be increased, your award can be *revised* or *superseded*. Benefit is fully backdated to the start of the existing award (by revision) or to the start of the award of the qualifying benefit (by supersession), supersedes another decision, unless it is specifically listed in law as one with no right of appeal.

When a decision is made about your benefit, you must be given a written decision notice that says whether you have a right to appeal.

No right of appeal – There is no right of appeal against:

- most administrative decisions about claims and payment of benefit (but not decisions on whether or not claims are 'defective' (see Chapter 59(1));
- entitlement to constant attendance allowance or exceptionally severe disablement allowance (both paid with industrial injuries disablement benefit), or to the Christmas bonus; *or*
- any part of a housing benefit decision that adopts a rent officer's decision (see Chapter 20(9)); *or*
- decisions to postpone or make temporary unfavourable determinations when a test case is pending (see 6 above).

The full list is in SSA, Sch 2; D&A Regs, reg 27 & Sch 2; HB&CTB(D&A) Regs, Sch

If you do not have a right to appeal, you can ask for the decision to be revised or superseded (see 'Ground 9' in Box T.5). Judicial review by the High Court or the Upper Tribunal may be possible; seek advice from a law centre or solicitor.

if that is later. For example, if you apply for both income support and DLA, but the DLA is awarded only after a delay, your income support award can be revised or superseded to backdate the disability premium to the date the DLA award started.

D&A Regs, regs 3(7), 6(2)(e) & 7(7)

This rule can increase entitlement only to a benefit you already have. If you don't have an existing award, see Chapter 59(3) for rules on backdating claims. See also Chapter 14(13)

A decision maker can *revise* a decision disallowing reduced earnings allowance because it has been decided that you do not have a prescribed disease or a loss of faculty (see Chapter 45(14), and the latter decision is either revised by a decision maker or changed at appeal.

D&A Regs, regs 3(7A)

A decision maker can *revise* or *supersede* an income support, income-related ESA or pension credit decision if a non-dependant living with you is awarded backdated benefit (eg attendance allowance) so that you become entitled to the severe disability premium or the pension credit equivalent.

D&A Regs, regs 3(7ZA), 6(2)(ee) & 7(7)

Ground 6: Incorrect facts

Any decision (including a First-tier or Upper Tribunal's decisions) can be *superseded* if it was made in ignorance of a material fact or was based on a mistake about a material fact. For example, when you filled in your DLA claim-form you may have underestimated the help you need with personal care. If you give the DWP this information now, they can supersede the decision.

D&A Regs, regs 6(2)(b)(i) & (c)

A decision favourable to you (eg to increase your benefit) can only take effect from the day you apply for the original decision to be superseded. There is generally no backdating (see Box T.4).

SSA, S.10(5)

If you think the DWP, HMRC or local authority made a mistake and neither you nor anyone else outside the department or authority contributed to the mistake, this may be an official error (see 'Ground 4' above). You can get full backdating of arrears if there has been an official error.

Mistakes in your favour – The general rule is that if you were paid more benefit than you were entitled to because a decision was made in ignorance of a relevant fact, or was based on a mistake about a fact, a decision maker can *revise* the decision at any time (but only *supersede* the decision if it was made by an First-tier or Upper Tribunal).

D&A Regs, regs 3(5)(b) & 6(2)(c)

The new decision takes effect from the same date as the original decision took effect (even if it is a decision superseding that of a First-tier or Upper Tribunal). If there is any overpayment, the decision maker must consider if it is recoverable under the normal overpayment rules (see Chapter 59(6)).

D&A Regs, regs 5(1) & 7(5)

The same rule applies whenever the original decision was more advantageous to you than it should have been (see Chapter 60(9)), unless the following special protection for disability and incapacity-related benefits applies.

Disability and incapacity-related benefits – A cut in benefit will not be backdated if the decision involves an assessment of disability or incapacity and the decision maker is satisfied that at the time of the original decision you didn't know and couldn't *'reasonably have been expected to know'* of the fact in question and that it was relevant. For more about this rule, see Chapter 60(5) under 'What if your benefit goes down?'

D&A Regs, reg 3(5)(b),(c)&(d)

Ground 7: Revision during the appeal process

If a valid appeal has been lodged, a decision maker can *revise* a decision at any time before the appeal is decided. This means, for example, if an appeal tribunal is adjourned for further evidence, the decision maker can revise the original decision once that evidence is produced, making a further hearing unnecessary.

D&A Regs, reg 3(4A)

Ground 8: Following the outcome of an earlier appeal

A decision can be *revised* at any time following an appeal determination of an earlier, related decision. For example: you appeal against a decision that you do not have a limited capability for work following a work capability assessment. You also make a second claim for ESA, which is unsuccessful. If the appeal against the first decision is successful, benefit is paid up to the date of the decision refusing the new claim. The decision maker can now *revise* the second decision so that payment of the benefit can continue.

D&A Regs, reg 3(5A)

Ground 9: No appeal rights

A decision that carries no right of appeal can be either *revised* or *superseded* at any time, without needing specific grounds. These decisions include most administrative decisions about claims and payment of benefit (see Chapter 60(7)).

D&A Regs, regs 3(8) & 6(2)(d)

Ground 10: Sanctions

If a decision maker wishes to impose a sanction, any decision that ESA or jobseeker's allowance is payable can be *superseded*, including one made by a First-tier or Upper Tribunal. A decision to apply a sanction to your jobseeker's allowance can, in turn, be *revised at any time*. So if you are outside the dispute period, you can still challenge a sanction. The new decision takes effect from the same date as the original decision. If the sanction is lifted, arrears of benefit can be fully backdated. An ESA decision to apply a reduction can only be revised if the decision contains an error to which you 'did not materially contribute'.

D&A Regs, regs 3(5C), (6) & 6(2)(f)

Tribunals must act within a set of rules whose stated overriding objective is to deal with appeals *'fairly and justly'*. Parties to the appeal must co-operate with the tribunal and help it fulfil this objective.

TP(FTT)SEC Rules, rule 2

A tribunal can overlook a failure to comply with the rules or ask you to remedy a failure to comply. The tribunal cannot overlook a failure to appeal within 12 months of the end of the normal appeal time limit.

TP(FTT)SEC Rules, rules 5, 7 & 23

Time limits for appeal

Usually, an appeal request must be received by the office that sent you the decision within one calendar month of the date it was sent to you (see 3 above).

Asking for written reasons – You can ask for written reasons for the decision if they are not included with the decision notice. You must do this within one month of the day the decision is sent to you. Asking for written reasons can extend the appeal time limit (see 3 above).

Tax credit decision notifications do not contain reasons and asking for reasons will not extend the appeal time limit.

Late appeal

If you miss the deadline, a late appeal can be treated as made in time in limited circumstances. A late appeal must be made in writing and state the reasons why it is late. First a decision maker decides whether to accept the appeal. They decide whether it is in the interests of justice to treat the appeal as made in time and in doing so will consider whether there are 'special circumstances' relevant to the delay. These are:

- you, your partner or a dependant has suffered serious illness; *or*
- your partner, a dependant or the person who appealed has died (and you are pursuing the appeal on behalf of the deceased person); *or*
- you live outside the UK; *or*
- normal postal services were disrupted; *or*
- some other *'wholly exceptional and relevant'* circumstances exist.

The longer the delay, the better the reasons must be. No account is taken of whether you did not know or understand the law or the time limits involved, nor that the Upper Tribunal or a court has reinterpreted the law.

If the decision maker cannot treat the appeal as made in time, they must refer it to the Tribunals Service, where a tribunal judge decides whether to accept it. The judge can accept the late appeal and waive the requirement that it is made in time; but appeals made more than 12 months after the time limit cannot be accepted. The judge will usually allow the appeal unless the decision maker objects, in which case the judge will consider whether the objection is reasonable.

D&A Regs, reg 32; TP(FTT)SEC Rules, rules 5(3)(a) & 23(5)

8. Making an appeal

You or your representative must apply in writing, in English or Welsh. There are forms on which appeals can be made, or you can appeal in a letter. For most benefits the form is GL24, which you get from the DWP. HMRC provides the WTC/AP appeal form for tax credits and the CH24A appeal form for child benefit and guardian's allowance. For housing benefit and council tax benefit, your local authority will provide its own appeal form.

Your appeal must give your name and address and that of your representative if you have one. It must have an address where documents can be sent to you if your own address is inappropriate. You must give details of the decision being appealed (date, name of the benefit, what the decision is about) and grounds for your appeal.

TP(FTT)SEC Rules, rule 23(6)

9. What happens when you appeal?

When they receive your appeal, the decision maker will check to see if they can revise the decision you are appealing against.

If it is revised, your appeal lapses if the new decision is more advantageous to you – even if it does not give you everything you wanted. If you wish to continue with your appeal, you must now make a new appeal within one month of the date of the revised decision.

SSA, S.9(6)

If the decision is revised but the new decision is not more advantageous to you, your appeal will go ahead against the revised decision.

The decision maker can decide to revise the decision again at any time until the appeal is decided (see Ground 7 in Box T.5). Otherwise, the appeal will go forward to tribunal.

D&A Regs, reg 30(3)-(5)

When is a decision more 'advantageous'? – A decision is more advantageous to you if:

- more benefit is paid (or would be but for a restriction, suspension or disqualification);
- the award is for a longer period;
- a denial or disqualification of benefit is lifted wholly or partly;
- an amount of recoverable overpaid benefit is reduced or it is decided that it is not recoverable;
- it reverses a decision to pay benefit to a third party;
- it reverses a decision that an accident was not an industrial accident;
- you will get some financial gain.

This list is not exhaustive.

D&A Regs, reg 30(2)

Tax credits

When they receive your appeal, an HMRC officer will look at your appeal grounds and decide whether or not it can be 'settled' without having to first go to tribunal. They will contact you to discuss the decision first and propose the terms of a possible settlement. If you provisionally agree to these, they will send you a copy of the terms. You will have 30 days in which to write to HMRC if you do not agree with the terms they suggest or do not want to settle. If you do not do this, the settlement will come into force and the appeal will lapse. There is no further right to appeal against a decision settled in this way.

Taxes Management Act 1970, S.54

10. Opting for a hearing

When your appeal is lodged, you will get an acknowledgement letter. The DWP, HMRC or local authority will then send your appeal to the Tribunals Service, together with a copy of their response to the appeal and all the documents they have that are relevant to the decision. You will be sent copies of these.

TP(FTT)SEC Rules, rule 24

The Tribunals Service will send you a pre-hearing enquiry form. This asks whether you want your appeal to be decided with or without a hearing. Ensure you return this form within 14 days, otherwise the tribunal could think you do not want to continue with your appeal and may strike it out (see 12 below).

In most cases, it is better to ask for a hearing. In some cases, it will be crucial for the success of your appeal; particularly if your case involves medical or disability questions (eg decisions about limited capability for work or disability living allowance).

Decisions without a hearing – An appeal is decided without a hearing only if all parties consent (or none objects) and the tribunal agrees that a hearing is unnecessary.

TP(FTT)SEC Rules, rule 27

If there is no hearing, the tribunal will study all the appeal papers and come to its decision based on these papers alone.

The tribunal will be made up in the same way as for a hearing (see 16 below).

You can send comments or extra evidence to the tribunal to consider at any time before they make their decision. You will not be told when the decision is due to be made, so send your evidence or comments as soon as possible. If you need time to prepare your information, contact the clerk to the appeal tribunal. Say when you expect to send the information and ask for the decision to be delayed until it has been received.

11. Withdrawing an appeal

You can withdraw your appeal at any time before the hearing. You do not need to give a reason and do not need the agreement of the DWP, local authority or tribunal judge. You must write to the Tribunals Service stating that you wish to withdraw the appeal. You can withdraw the appeal at the hearing itself, but only with the consent of the tribunal. A withdrawn appeal can be reinstated if you apply within one month of the date the Tribunal Service received your withdrawal notice or within one month of the date of the hearing at which your appeal was withdrawn.

TP(FTT)SEC Rules, rule 17

12. Striking out an appeal

Your appeal, or any part of it, can be struck out if:

- the tribunal does not have jurisdiction to deal with the appeal (eg it is about a decision that does not carry a right of appeal or should be dealt with by a different tribunal);
- you have failed to co-operate with the tribunal to the extent that it feels it can no longer deal with your appeal fairly or justly;
- the tribunal feels that your appeal, or part of it, has no reasonable prospects of success; *or*
- you fail to comply with a direction given to you (eg to provide additional evidence).

If the tribunal thinks it has no jurisdiction, that you have failed to co-operate with it or that the appeal has no prospects of success, it will write to you for comments before deciding whether to strike out the appeal.

If the tribunal issues a direction saying your appeal will be struck out if you fail to comply, it can strike out your appeal automatically if you fail to comply within the given time limit. The Tribunals Service will write to you if your appeal has been struck out.

Reinstatement – If your appeal is struck out because of a failure to comply with a direction, you can ask for your appeal to be reinstated. You must do so in writing within one month of the date of issue of the order to strike out. You should say why you believe the appeal should not have been struck out.

TP(FTT)SEC Rules, rule 8

If the tribunal decides that another type of court or tribunal has jurisdiction to deal with your appeal, it can transfer your appeal to it instead of striking out your appeal.

TP(FTT)SEC Rules, rule 5(3)(k)

13. Preparing your case

Read the decision maker's response to the appeal to see where you disagree with it and might need to dispute it. Find out if there is a local advice centre that can advise you and maybe support you at the hearing itself (see Chapter 61).

The tribunal need not consider any issue not raised by the appeal. It is important to give as much detail as you can about why and how you think the decision is wrong. If you are happy with part of your award, you should say so and ask the tribunal not to look at it. The tribunal can only look at circumstances existing at the time of the decision you are appealing against, so if your circumstances change while you are waiting for the appeal to be heard, you should consider making another claim or asking for a supersession (see 14 below).

SSA, S.12(8)

Check the law

Tribunals must make decisions by applying the particular facts of your case to the relevant legislation and case law.

Legislation – Legislation is made up of Acts of Parliament and regulations. The appeal papers should refer to the parts of the legislation relevant to your appeal. You can see these in *The Law Relating to Social Security* (see page 6).

Case law – Case law is found in decisions of the Upper Tribunal (formerly the Social Security Commissioners (see Box T.7)) and the courts. The appeal papers may refer you to some relevant decisions; it is always worth reading these. There may be other decisions that are more helpful for your appeal. We produce case law summaries covering disability living allowance (DLA), attendance allowance, the personal capability assessment and adjudication (decision-making and appeals). Summaries of reported decisions are also available in *Neligan* (see page 6). Our factsheet *Finding the Law* provides general advice on finding the relevant law to support your appeal (www.disabilityalliance.org/f19.htm or see Chapter 63(3)).

Sort out the facts and evidence

After looking at legislation and case law, you may have a clearer idea of which facts are important for your appeal and what extra evidence you need. Most appeals concern a dispute about facts or different interpretations of the same facts. If you don't understand the law, just concentrate on the facts. Read the chapter in this Handbook on the benefit you are appealing about to get an idea of what facts will be important.

You do not have to prove any fact 'beyond all reasonable doubt'. You must prove your case on a balance of probabilities – ie show that your version of the facts is the most likely. Your word is just as much 'evidence' as any document. However, try to get as much other evidence as you can to back up what you are saying, as this helps tip the balance of probabilities your way.

You might need to call witnesses; you'll need to get their agreement beforehand. Try to make sure their account will back up your case. If a witness cannot attend the hearing, ask them to give you a written statement for the tribunal.

If you can, send any further evidence or comments on the appeal to the Tribunals Service well before the hearing. Make a copy of your evidence and take it with you to the hearing.

Getting medical evidence

If your appeal involves a disability question (eg whether you are 'virtually unable to walk'), try to get supportive medical evidence. The tribunal can only consider your circumstances up to the date of the decision you are appealing against (see 14 below). You can get medical evidence later but it should relate to the time covered by the decision under appeal.

The evidence can come from medical professionals such as your GP, specialist nurse, physiotherapist or hospital consultant. When you request a letter or statement from them,

T.6 Human Rights Act

The Human Rights Act 1998 incorporates into UK law the rights guaranteed under the European Convention on Human Rights. Arguments based on Convention rights can be made in social security appeals against decisions made since 2.10.00. Decision makers and tribunals must interpret the law in a way that is consistent with the Act as far as they are able. You should seek legal advice if you think it may apply in your case.

You can find the Human Rights Act and detailed commentary on its provisions in *Social security: legislation 2008 Volume III* (Sweet & Maxwell).

ask specific questions. Try to get information directly relevant to the case, rather than vague comments about your general condition. Make sure they are aware of your condition and how it relates to the question under appeal; if you have kept a diary for DLA (see Chapter 3(15)), give them with a copy.

If the appeal papers contain a report from a DWP-approved healthcare professional, read it carefully to see where you might need to get your own medical evidence to counter what is said in the report. Make sure you ask for comments specifically on the points in dispute. For example, if you disagree with a DWP-approved professional's report that says you can walk 100 metres without severe discomfort, ask your GP or physiotherapist for an opinion of how far you can walk without severe discomfort.

The tribunal should not automatically treat a report from a DWP healthcare professional as more reliable or accurate than that of any other medical professional, eg your GP. The tribunal should consider all the evidence in a case and decide which it accepts and which it rejects.

(R(DLA)3/99); see also R(M)1/93, CDLA/2849/2000 & CDLA/3074/2003

Difficulties obtaining evidence? – If you have problems getting evidence from any professional treating you, the Legal Aid scheme may cover the cost of a medical report from an independent consultant or specialist through a solicitor or advice agency contracted with the Legal Services Commission (see Chapter 61).

If you think you will be unable to get supportive medical evidence by the time of the hearing, you can ask for a postponement to allow you more time to obtain it (see 16 below). If you do not think you can get the evidence you need, you can ask the tribunal to refer you for a medical examination. It will do this if it thinks it cannot decide the appeal without further medical evidence. If you think the medical report needs to answer specific questions, ask the tribunal to put them to the examining healthcare professional.

SSA, S.20 & TP(FTT)SEC Rules, rule 25

There is no rule that says you must have corroborating medical or other evidence. You can go ahead with your appeal even if you can't get supporting evidence.

14. If your circumstances change before the appeal

It can take some months for your appeal to be heard and your circumstances may change in the meantime. The tribunal can only look at your situation as it was up to the time of the decision you are appealing against. It decides whether the decision was correct at the time it was made, based on what was known at that time. If your situation has changed between the decision and the tribunal hearing, it cannot take that into account.

SSA, S.12(8)(b)

For disability living allowance renewals, this is the case even if a change takes place after a renewal decision is made but before it takes effect. The only exception is if the change is one that is almost certain to occur, such as you reaching a particular age (eg 16, when the cooking test can apply).

R(DLA)4/05 & CDLA/4331/2002

T.7 Upper Tribunal and Commissioners' decisions

Until November 2008, the Upper Tribunal for benefit appeals was called the Social Security Commissioners (the Commissioners).

Many Social Security Commissioners' decisions are quoted in this Handbook. These decisions are part of case law, setting precedents to be followed in similar cases.

In general, decisions of the courts are binding on Commissioners, tribunals and decision makers (R(SB)6/85). Although Commissioners speak with equal authority, a decision of a tribunal of Commissioners (or three-member Upper Tribunal) should be given more weight than a decision of a single Commissioner (or one-member Upper Tribunal) (R(I)12/75), as should a reported decision of a single Commissioner over an unreported one. Nonetheless, decision makers and tribunals are free to follow whichever decision they consider to be correct. There is no obligation on tribunals to prefer an earlier decision to a later one, or vice versa.

The most important decisions are published or reported. See page 6 for where to get copies.

Reported decisions – These are referred to as, for example, R(IB)2/99; R = reported; (IB) = the series initial, in this case standing for incapacity benefit; 2/99 = the second decision in that series reported in 1999. (Since 2000 the date will refer to the point the decision was published by the DWP.)

Unreported decisions – These are referred to as, for example, CA/140/85. Where: C = Commissioner; A = the series initial (attendance allowance); 140 = the number of the file; 85 = the year in which the file was opened by the Commissioner. Decisions made in Scotland are identified with an S, as in CSDLA/121/97. Unreported Northern Ireland decisions are numbered using similar principles; a typical decision reference being C12/01-02 (IB).

Between 1982 and the beginning of 2002 unreported decisions of more general significance were starred; some went on to be reported later.

Series initials

(A)	attendance allowance
(AF)	Armed Forces compensation
(CR)	compensation recovery
(CS)	child support
(CTF)	child trust fund
(DLA)	disability living allowance
(DWA)	disability working allowance
(F)	child benefit, formerly family allowance
(FC)	family credit
(FP) & (FG)	forfeiture
(G)	general: includes benefits not covered in other categories, such as carer's allowance, maternity allowance and bereavement benefits
(H)	housing benefit and council tax benefit
(HR)	home responsibilities protection
(I)	industrial injuries benefits
(IB)	incapacity benefit
(IS)	income support
(JSA)	jobseeker's allowance
(M)	mobility allowance
(P)	retirement or state pensions
(PC)	pension credit
(S)	sickness and invalidity benefit and severe disablement allowance
(SB)	supplementary benefit
(SMP)	statutory maternity pay
(SSP)	statutory sick pay
(TC)	tax credits
(U)	unemployment benefit

The Upper Tribunal is expected to retain the reference system used by the Commissioners. There will be a second parallel referencing system applied to all Upper Tribunal decisions. A typical Upper Tribunal reference is [2009] UKUT 233 (AAC) – a 2009 decision of the United Kingdom Upper Tribunal of the Administrative Appeals Chamber.

If your circumstances change while your appeal is pending and you think it is now clearer that you qualify for the benefit concerned, you should make a fresh claim. If you already get the benefit, ask the DWP or local authority to supersede the award decision because your circumstances have changed. If you don't, and your appeal is unsuccessful, you could lose out because of the strict rules on backdating.

If the new claim or request to supersede is unsuccessful, it is important to put in a second appeal because your first appeal cannot take into account the period covered by the second decision. The benefit may be put into payment by a successful outcome in the first appeal then stopped from the date of the unfavourable second decision. The decision maker can revise the second decision following a successful appeal against the first decision (see 'Ground 8' in Box T.5), but there is no guarantee this will happen. To be safe, lodge a second appeal. Ask for a single tribunal to hear the appeals together. For appeals on limited capability for work, see also Chapter 10(9) and (10).

Tax credits – Tax credit appeals have similar rules. If your circumstances change after the date of the decision you are appealing against, you should tell HMRC, who may then issue a new decision reflecting your new circumstances. If you are not satisfied with that decision, lodge a further appeal. If you have more than one appeal ongoing, ask for a single tribunal to hear all the appeals together.

15. Special needs, access to the hearing and expenses

If you have any special needs, check with the tribunal clerk beforehand about accessibility, what facilities are available, and how your needs can be met to enable you to be present at your hearing and get home again within a reasonable time. You should ask for whatever you need. If the Tribunals Service cannot provide it, seek advice.

For example, if it is too far for you to walk easily to the tribunal room from the nearest point at which a car can set you down, ask for a wheelchair to be waiting for you. If you need breaks during a hearing (eg to go to the toilet, take food or medication, stretch your legs or change position), ask for them. It helps if the tribunal knows what you might need, so write to or phone the clerk to the tribunal before the hearing.

If you arrive to find the premises are not accessible to you, the tribunal should adjourn to a time and place where you can be present (CI/112/84).

Out-of-centre and domiciliary tribunals – The Tribunals Service can arrange for the tribunal to take place nearer to you than their usual venues (at an 'out-of-centre' venue) or in your home (a 'domiciliary hearing'). You should provide medical evidence of your need for an alternative venue.

The tribunal may hold a preliminary hearing to decide whether to adjourn for an alternative venue – you can send a representative to this hearing. If the tribunal refuses your request for an alternative venue and decides to deal with your appeal in your absence, it must be satisfied that it already has enough evidence to make a decision or must adjourn and make arrangements to get further evidence (eg by referring you for a medical report or arranging a video link to your home).

CIB/2751/2002

A local disability group may know of a suitable and fully accessible venue near your home that could be used instead of a Tribunal Service office.

Claiming expenses – You can claim travelling expenses for yourself and a travelling companion if you need one. If you cannot travel by public transport you can claim for taxi fares or a private ambulance. You can get compensation for loss of earnings and for childminding expenses up to set maximums. You can claim for a basic meal if you are away from home or work for more than a specified time.

If you are not sure what you, or someone with you, can claim, ask the tribunal clerk: ring the number on the hearing notice. If you need anything other than travel expenses for yourself by public transport, agree the expenses with the clerk well before the hearing.

16. At the hearing

You must be given at least 14 days' notice of the time and place of a hearing, starting from the day the hearing notice is sent to you. In practice, you are usually given much more notice than this. You can be given shorter notice if you consent, or in urgent or exceptional circumstances.

TP(FTT)SEC Rules, rule 29

Asking for a postponement – If the date is inconvenient or it does not give you enough time to prepare your case, write to the clerk to the tribunal and ask if the hearing can be postponed. If time is short, you can ring the clerk (the phone number will be at the top of the hearing notice) but you should also write to confirm your request. The same applies if you are ill on the day or have a domestic emergency. A tribunal judge will decide whether to grant a postponement. If you have not had the postponement confirmed, it is best to go along to the hearing if you can in case your request is refused and the appeal is decided in your absence.

TP(FTT)SEC Rules, rule 5(3)(h)

Who is at the hearing?

You and your representative – It is always best to attend the hearing yourself. See 15 above if there is a problem with access. You are entitled to have someone with you to represent you (see Chapter 61) and you can also bring a companion for support. Both you and your representative have the right to speak, and you can call witnesses.

TP(FTT)SEC Rules, rules 11 & 28

The tribunal members – The tribunal is made up of a legally qualified tribunal judge and possibly one or two other people, depending on the type of appeal:

- for disability living allowance and attendance allowance – a judge, a doctor and a 'disability member' (see below);
- for personal capability assessments, limited capability for work assessments and limited capability for work-related activity assessments – a judge and a doctor;
- for severe disablement allowance, industrial injuries benefit – a judge and a doctor;
- for difficult financial matters about trust funds or business accounts – a judge and an accountant;
- for any other matter (including a declaration of industrial accident) – a judge alone.

The hearing cannot go ahead unless all the tribunal members are present. Members are drawn from a panel appointed by the Judicial Appointments Commission.

To avoid a conflict of interest, the tribunal must not include a doctor who has ever provided advice or prepared a report about you, or has ever been your regular doctor.

The disability member is a person who is *'experienced in dealing with the physical or mental needs of disabled persons because they work with disabled persons in a professional or voluntary capacity or are themselves disabled'*. They cannot be a medical practitioner but can be a paramedic, physiotherapist or nurse.

Where the tribunal would normally consists of a judge and one doctor, a second doctor can be appointed if 'the complexity of the medical issues' demands it.

Although an additional member may be appointed to a particular tribunal, there can never be more than three tribunal members. The appeal tribunal can ask an expert to attend the hearing or give a written report, but this expert cannot take part in the appeal tribunal's decision making.

TCEA, s. 4 & Schedules 2 & 6; Qualifications for Appointment of Members to the First-tier Tribunal & Upper Tribunal Order 2008; First-tier & Upper Tribunal (Composition of Tribunal) Order 2008

Others – Apart from the tribunal members, there may be a presenting officer to put the decision maker's case. The presenting officer is there to help the tribunal and so may also identify any points in your favour.

A clerk is present to deal with the administration of the hearing. They may have an assistant.

If the tribunal judge agrees, any other person can be present during the hearing. The hearing will be open to the public unless the tribunal judge decides otherwise. You can ask for a private hearing. The decision is made at the discretion of the judge. In practice, the only members of the public who are likely to be present are other claimants (to see what happens before their own appeal is heard) or advisers (to help them in their work).

TCEA, s. 40; TP(FTT)SEC Rules, rules 2, 5, 28 & 30

What happens at the hearing?

The hearing itself should be fairly informal. The tribunal is inquisitorial: its job is to investigate the appeal – so it is likely to ask lots of questions (in contrast to adversarial courts that mainly hear arguments).

There is no set procedure, so the tribunal judge decides which procedure will most effectively determine each appeal. The judge will begin by introducing the members of the tribunal and explaining its role. Often, the judge then clarifies what they understand to be the issues before them to make sure that everyone understands what the appeal is about.

If there is a presenting officer, the judge often asks them to present the decision maker's case first. Other tribunals may begin by asking you direct factual questions; a common procedure for disability-related appeals is to ask you to describe what you do on an average day.

At some point in the hearing you will be asked to explain your case. Put your main points in writing so you don't forget anything. If you are interrupted, ask tactfully if you can make all your points before answering questions. Where possible, back up your argument with documentary evidence (eg bills, doctor's letters). At the end of your statement, repeat the decision you want the tribunal to make. You can question the presenting officer, if there is one, and any witnesses. Listen carefully, and ask questions if you think anything is being misunderstood or misrepresented. Once the tribunal is satisfied that each party has had the opportunity to present its case, the judge will ask everyone (except the clerk) to leave the room while the tribunal makes its decision.

Medical examinations – For severe disablement allowance or industrial injuries appeals involving an assessment of the extent of your disability, the doctor on the tribunal will examine you in private, usually towards the end of the hearing. After the examination, the hearing may start again briefly to discuss the doctor's findings.

The tribunal cannot carry out a physical examination for any other benefit. It cannot ask you to undergo a walking test for the mobility component of disability living allowance. It will, however, watch how you walk into and out of the room and how you cope with what might be a lengthy hearing. The tribunal can refer you for an examination so that a healthcare professional can provide a report (see 13 above).

TP(FTT)SEC Rules, rule 25

T.8 Errors of law

Can you understand the decision?

The statement of reasons for the tribunal's decision must set out clearly what it decided and why it made that decision. If you had put forward specific arguments, the statement must show clearly how the tribunal dealt with them. It must also show that the tribunal understood and correctly applied the relevant law. If the statement is not clear on any of the above, the decision may contain an error of law.

Identifying an error of law is also important if you (or the decision maker) want to supersede a decision on this ground (see 'Ground 2' in Box T.5).

Identifying errors of law

Several Commissioners' decisions, including R(A)1/72, R(IS)11/99 and R(I)2/06, set out what might constitute an error of law. A decision might be wrong in law if any of the following apply:

- The decision contains a misdirection about, or misunderstanding of, the relevant law (including not taking into account relevant case law).
- There has been a breach of the rules of natural justice (ie the procedures followed were incorrect or unfair).
- The tribunal has failed to make the findings of fact needed to apply the law correctly.
- The evidence does not support the decision.
- The tribunal has failed to give adequate reasons for the decision (including failing to explain clearly how it resolved disputes about relevant facts or evidence or interpretation of the law).
- The tribunal took irrelevant matters into account.
- The decision is perverse: there is such a clear inconsistency between the law, the facts of the case and the decision, that no tribunal acting reasonably could have made the decision.

17. The appeal decision

You will get a decision notice on the day of the hearing or soon after. A copy is sent to the department that made the original decision so they can put the tribunal decision into effect and pay you any benefit owed.

If the appeal is unsuccessful, you can ask for a more detailed explanation, the 'statement of reasons' for the decision. If you want to appeal to the Upper Tribunal, you need this statement. Make sure you write and ask for it within the one-month time limit (see 18 below).

Once you have read the statement of reasons, it should be clear to you how and why you have been unsuccessful. If it is not, this may be an error of law (see Box T.8) and it may be possible to appeal further to the Upper Tribunal.

If you disagree with the decision

A decision of an appeal tribunal can be changed in the following ways:

- apply to the tribunal to correct an accidental error;
- apply for the decision to be set aside (see below);
- appeal to the Upper Tribunal if there is an error of law – see 18 below (if you cannot appeal, see below for some ideas of what to do);
- apply to the DWP or local authority to supersede the decision if there has been a relevant change of circumstances or such a change is anticipated (see 'Ground 1' in Box T.5). This can include a change of circumstances that occurred after the decision under appeal was made but which only came to light during the appeal process (the tribunal itself would have been prevented from taking the change into account);
- apply to the DWP or local authority to supersede the decision if it was made in ignorance of any material fact, or was based on a mistake about any material fact (see 'Ground 6' in Box T.5).

Correcting an accidental error – An 'accidental' error in the decision of an appeal tribunal can be corrected at any time. Arithmetical or clerical errors can be corrected in this way. Write to the Tribunals Service. There is no right to appeal against a refusal to correct.

TP(FTT)SEC Rules, rule 36

Setting aside for procedural reasons – A decision may be set aside by a tribunal judge, if it 'appears just' to do so because:

- a document relevant to the appeal wasn't sent to, or received in sufficient time by, any party to the proceedings, their representative or the tribunal; *or*
- a party to the proceedings or a representative wasn't present at the hearing; *or*
- there has been some other procedural irregularity.

You must apply in writing to have the decision set aside within one month of the date the decision was given or sent to you. The tribunal judge can extend the time limit.

TP(FTT)SEC Rules, rules 37 & 5

Setting aside wipes out all or part of the tribunal's decision. There must be a fresh hearing before a new appeal tribunal. You cannot appeal against a refusal to set aside. A refusal to set aside starts afresh the time limits for asking for permission to appeal to the Upper Tribunal. This does not apply, however, if the application to set aside was made late (unless the tribunal granted an extension to the time limit).

TCEA, s.11; TP(FTT)SEC Rules, rule 38(3)(c)&(4)

If you cannot appeal to the Upper Tribunal – If you think there is an error of law in the decision but you are out of time for appealing, are refused permission or leave to appeal or your appeal fails, try one of the following.

- ❑ If no benefit is being paid, make a fresh claim. Normal backdating rules will apply.
- ❑ If some benefit is being paid, the decision can be superseded if it was made in ignorance of a material fact or was based on a mistake about a material fact (see 'Ground 6' in Box T.5). Often what counts as a material fact depends on how the test required by the law is interpreted. If an error of law has been made, it is possible that the tribunal also didn't explore the relevant facts correctly. If a supersession takes place the law may be applied differently, as it must reconsider all aspects of the decision.
- ❑ If some benefit is being paid and there has been a change of circumstances since the tribunal's decision, the decision maker can correct the error of law when they supersede the decision. This is because the supersession must reconsider all aspects of the decision.

18. Appeals to the Upper Tribunal

You can only appeal to the Upper Tribunal if there is an error of law in the decision of the First-tier Tribunal (see Box T.8). You cannot appeal about the facts. As it is sometimes hard to separate the law from the facts, ask an experienced adviser to check the decision. Don't delay, as strict deadlines must be met. To appeal you must take the following steps.

Step 1: Ask for a 'statement of reasons' for the decision within one month of the date the tribunal sends a decision notice that finally disposes of all issues in the appeal proceedings. The time limit can be extended under the tribunal's general case management powers.

TP(FTT)SEC Rules, rules 34 & 5(3)(a)

Step 2: Apply for permission (or, in Scotland, leave) to appeal to the tribunal within one month of being sent:

- the statement of reasons; *or*
- notification of amended or corrected reasons following a review (see below); *or*
- notification that an application to set aside is unsuccessful.

Write a letter stating why you think the decision was legally wrong and what result you seek. Head it *'Application for permission to appeal to the Upper Tribunal'*. Make a copy, and send it to the clerk to the tribunal with copies of the tribunal's decision notice and its statement of reasons. If there is no statement of reasons, the tribunal has discretion to treat the application as a request for one. An application can only be allowed without a statement of reasons if the tribunal thinks it is in the interests of justice to do so.

TP(FTT)SEC Rules, rule 38

Reviewing the decision – On receiving your application for permission to appeal, the tribunal can review its decision. In particular, the tribunal can:

- correct an accidental error in the decision;
- amend the reasons for the decision; *or*
- set aside the decision.

The tribunal must ask each party if it has any comments before it changes its decision following a review. If it sets aside the decision, it must make a new decision. You must be sent a notification of any new or amended decision. If you think that the new or amended decision contains an error of law, you have one month from the date that the notification is sent to ask again for permission to appeal to the Upper Tribunal (repeating Step 2).

TCE Act 2007 s 9; TP(FTT)SEC Rules, rules 39 & 40,

Step 3: If the judge refuses permission to appeal, you can apply for permission from the Upper Tribunal directly. You must do so within one month of being sent the notice refusing permission. You should be sent a form to do this. Enclose a copy of the tribunal decision notice, the tribunal's statement of reasons and the notice refusing permission to appeal. Send these to the Upper Tribunal (see inside back cover). If you are posting them and you are close to the time limit, send them by recorded delivery.

TCEA s 11; TP(UT) Rules, rule 21

Step 4: If permission to appeal is given by the tribunal, you must make a formal appeal to the Upper Tribunal within one month of being sent the notice granting permission. You will be sent a form on which to do this. If permission is granted by the Upper Tribunal, you won't have to appeal formally unless the Upper Tribunal specifically directs you to do so, as your application for permission will be treated as the appeal.

TCE Act 2007 s 11; TP(UT) Rules, rule 23

If you miss any deadline, the Upper Tribunal can allow your application if it thinks it is fair and just to do so. Your late application must contain details of why it was late.

TP(UT) Rules, rules 5, 7 & 21

The decision maker has the same rights of appeal as you. If the decision maker asks for permission to appeal, you will be sent a copy of their application and asked to comment.

Payment pending appeal

If you appeal to the Upper Tribunal, the DWP, HMRC or local authority will put the decision of the tribunal into effect until your appeal is settled. If the decision maker appeals (or intends to appeal), the tribunal's decision may be suspended and you won't be paid until the appeal is finally decided. If this causes hardship, ask the relevant office to consider lifting the suspension.

The Upper Tribunal's decision

If the Upper Tribunal finds that a First-tier Tribunal's decision is wrong in law (see Box T.8):

- they can give the decision that the tribunal should have given, if they can do so without making fresh or further findings of fact; *or*
- if they think it expedient, the Upper Tribunal can make fresh or further findings of fact and then give a decision; *or*
- if there aren't enough findings of fact, and the Upper Tribunal doesn't make new findings, the case is referred to a new First-tier Tribunal. The Upper Tribunal may give directions to the new tribunal to make sure the error of law is not repeated.

TCEA, s.12

There is a quicker procedure: if both you and the decision maker agree on an outcome, the Upper Tribunal can set aside the First-tier tribunal's decision by consent, making the provisions necessary to put into affect what has been agreed.

TP(UT) Rules, rule 39

U Help and Information

This section of the Handbook looks at:

61 Getting advice

1. Who can help you?

Your local Citizens Advice Bureau (CAB) can help with benefits advice and many other matters. You can also get application forms and leaflets from them. The CAB may be able to represent you if you have a problem or an appeal. If not, they may be able to tell you if another local organisation could help; other independent advice centres may provide similar services. Your local council might have a welfare rights service or a list of local advice centres. Contact your town hall for information. A local DIAL (Disability Information and Advice Line) group or other disablement advice centre may be able to offer advice and, in some cases, may be willing to represent you. See the Address List for a list of DIAL groups.

2. Free legal help

Most solicitors will not be familiar with the social security system, so you should normally first seek advice from your local CAB, DIAL or other advice agency. Some firms of solicitors, however, particularly those with contracts with the Legal Services Commission (LSC), employ welfare rights specialists who can help with benefit matters.

If you live or work in the catchment area of a law centre, contact them to see if they can help. Law centres (see Address List) can usually give benefits advice as well as help in other areas of the law such as housing, employment and immigration. Your CAB may have volunteer lawyers and can possibly refer you to one at a special advice session. Many trade unions offer free legal advice to their members.

Free legal advice is also available from the Community Legal Advice (CLA) helpline (0845 345 4345; textphone 0845 609 6677) or its website (www.communitylegaladvice.org.uk).

Legal Aid – In England and Wales, the LSC organises free legal advice or 'Legal Aid' through participating solicitors and advice agencies. Anyone who receives income-related employment and support allowance, income support, income-based jobseeker's allowance or pension credit (guarantee credit) automatically qualifies for Legal Aid. Other people, in or out of work, may qualify if their savings and income are low enough; you can use the calculator on the CLA website to work out if you could get Legal Aid. Not all solicitors are part of the scheme – only those contracted with the LSC. Look on the CLA website or ring their helpline (see above) for details of participating solicitors and advice agencies.

Legal Aid can cover the cost of preparing for a tribunal – eg writing letters, getting a medical report, advising you on the law, or preparing a written submission for you to hand to the tribunal. However, it does not cover actual representation at a tribunal hearing. Some law centres and advice organisations may agree to represent you at the hearing anyway, despite this. But do not wait until after you know the date of your hearing before trying to get representation, as it may be too late by then.

The Scottish Legal Aid Board manages the similar Legal Aid scheme in Scotland. Ring 0845 122 8686 or see the website (www.slab.org.uk) for details of participating solicitors. In Northern Ireland, contact the Legal Services Commission (028 9040 8888; www.nilsc.org.uk).

Injured in an accident – If you have been injured in an accident, you can arrange for a free legal consultation with a local solicitor specialising in injury claims by ringing the Accident Line (Freephone 0500 192939). If you are in a union, they may be able to arrange a solicitor for you.

Making a will – The free LSC Legal Aid scheme covers making a will for specific groups of people only, including most people with disabilities, people aged 70 or over, the parent of a disabled person who wants to provide for that person in their will, and a lone parent wishing to appoint a guardian for their child in a will.

62 Making a complaint

1. Complaints about the DWP

When a DWP agency has made a mistake you can expect them to explain what went wrong and why, and to apologise. They should not treat you any differently just because you have complained. To make a complaint, start by contacting the person you dealt with, or that person's manager. It may be possible to sort things out easily. Complain as soon as something goes wrong; don't wait until you get a decision on your claim.

If the problem is not resolved, take the following steps.

- ❑ Contact the manager at the office dealing with your claim.
- ❑ If you are not satisfied with the response from the office manager, you should contact the district manager (the office manager should give you the contact details).
- ❑ If you are not satisfied with the response from the district manager you should write to the Chief Executive (the district manager should give you the contact details).
- ❑ If you are not satisfied with the Chief Executive's response, you can ask the Independent Case Examiner (PO Box 155, Chester CH99 9SA, 0845 606 0777) to look into your complaint. They can only look at your complaint if it relates to maladministration; they cannot look at disputes relating to the legislation (you should challenge these through the normal revisions and appeals process – see Chapter 60).

At any point, you may want to contact your MP, who can, if the complaint is on the grounds of maladministration, refer your case to the Ombudsman (see 5 below).

If your complaint is about a DWP medical examination, see 3 below.

2. Compensation

There are a number of ways in which you can claim compensation or financial redress when you have lost money because of delays or mistakes made by the DWP or because you have received wrong or misleading advice from them.

Extra-statutory compensation

You may get extra-statutory compensation if you lose

entitlement to a benefit because of wrong or misleading official advice and the normal statutory channels are not available to you – eg you fail to claim a benefit because you were told you were not eligible and you are granted arrears of benefit for a limited period only. Payment should be equal to the amount you would have received had the benefit been paid correctly, and may include interest on the arrears. Write, asking for compensation, to the office handling your benefit.

Ex-gratia payments

Financial losses – If you lose money because of delays or mistakes by the DWP in paying your benefit, you can ask them for a discretionary ex-gratia special payment to cover your actual financial losses (eg the cost of phone calls, stamps and stationery, bank charges, etc). The delay or mistake need not have lasted for any set period of time. It is enough if you have had a financial loss as a result.

Consolatory payments – In very exceptional circumstances where maladministration has had a direct adverse affect on your life you may be awarded a consolatory payment. This may be appropriate where:

- persistent error has caused gross inconvenience; *or*
- DWP action or inaction has caused gross embarrassment, humiliation or unnecessary personal intrusion; *or*
- in very exceptional cases maladministration has caused you severe distress, which has significantly impacted on your physical or mental health.

You need not have had any financial loss and payment should be considered regardless of whether or not any other form of compensation payment has been made.

Unreasonable or exceptional delays – If the DWP delays paying benefit, you can also get ex-gratia payments to cover the interest (at fixed rates) on the arrears of benefit. Such payments may be made if:

- the arrears of benefit are £100 or more; *and*
- a significant part of the delay is due to DWP maladministration; *and*
- the compensation would be at least £10; *and*
- the delay was unreasonable or exceptional. 'Delay indicators' provide a guide to measure this.

Delay indicators	months
Disability living allowance and attendance allowance	
– new claims	7
– disability living allowance renewal claims	9
– attendance allowance renewal claims	7
– 'Special rules' claims	2
Carer's allowance	9
Incapacity benefit	4
Income support	2
Industrial injuries disablement benefit	12
Jobseeker's allowance	3
Pension credit	2

Compensation may also be paid if your current benefit payments are interrupted for at least three months.

If you qualify for compensation, interest is payable on all the benefit owed to you. It starts to accrue from the end of the delay indicator period, but is worked out on all the arrears. Compound interest is only calculated if the delay in payment is over ten years.

Claiming compensation payments

Write to the office handling your claim to ask for compensation. They may, however, offset any overpayments previously judged to be non-recoverable, but only if a decision maker has decided there was an overpayment and you were notified of it. You could consider challenging that overpayment decision in order to remove the offset.

Guidance on the kinds of compensation payable is in the DWP guidance *Financial Redress for Maladministration*, which includes details of delay indicators and the method of calculating interest (available on our website: www.disabilityalliance.org/links2.htm).

3. Complaints about DWP medical examinations

If you disagree with the medical advice provided by an Atos Healthcare professional who carried out a medical examination on behalf of the DWP, you should challenge this through the normal DWP revisions and appeals process (see Chapter 60). However, if you wish to make a complaint about the conduct or professionalism of such a person, or about the appointment arrangements or facilities at the medical examination, you can take the following steps.

- ❑ Write to or email Atos Healthcare (Customer Relations, Wing G, Government Buildings, Lawnswood, Leeds LS16 5PU; customer-relations@atoshealthcare.com) quoting your name, national insurance number and the date of your medical examination. You could use the tear-off slip on the leaflet *Comments, complaints and suggestions*, available at the Medical Examination Centre. Atos Healthcare will acknowledge your complaint and aim to fully respond, in writing, to the issues you have raised within 20 working days.
- ❑ If you are not satisfied with the response, write back to the Customer Relations Manager. Your complaint will be passed to a senior manager, who will review the case.
- ❑ The next step, if you are not satisfied, is to write to the Customer Relations Manager and ask for your complaint to be referred to an Independent Tier. They will consider how the complaint has been handled and provide a medical assessment about the quality of the medical advice provided to the DWP.
- ❑ If the problem is not resolved and involves maladministration, you can complain to the Independent Case Examiner (see 1 above) or the Parliamentary and Health Service Ombudsman (see 5 below). These two bodies cannot concern themselves with a DWP healthcare professional's clinical findings, but can examine complaints about the way a medical examination was conducted – eg the healthcare professional was rude or insensitive.

4. Health and social services

There is a standard complaints procedure to use if you are not happy with care services provided by the social services or social work department. In England this has been recently combined with the NHS complaints procedure. See Chapter 28(7) for details.

For complaints in the rest of the UK about hospitals, GPs and NHS services, the best starting point is your local Community Health Council in Wales, Independent Advice and Support Service (delivered by Citizens Advice) in Scotland, or local Health and Social Services Council in Northern Ireland. They can advise you on the right procedure to use, and might be able to help you to make your complaint. Patients detained in hospitals or care homes under the Mental Health Act can contact the Care Quality Commission who will look into the complaint. In Scotland, contact the Mental Welfare Commission for Scotland (see Address List).

5. Complaining to the Ombudsman

Complaining to an Ombudsman is not an alternative to the normal appeals process, nor is it an extension of that process. You complain to an Ombudsman about the way a decision was taken or the way you were treated, rather than about the actual decision itself. Before you can complain to an Ombudsman, you should first exhaust the normal complaints procedure, and where appropriate, contact the Independent Case Examiner (see 1 above). Keep a copy of your complaint letter and of anything connected with it. If you are still not satisfied, you should normally approach an MP (see below) and ask that your complaint be referred to the Ombudsman. There is no fee for making a complaint.

Contact details for Ombudsmen are at the end of the Address List, or go to their website (www.bioa.org.uk).

An Ombudsman investigates whether maladministration has caused injustice. Ombudsmen do not investigate personnel matters, although the Northern Ireland Ombudsman does so in some cases.

Maladministration – This includes such things as bias, prejudice, incorrect action, unreasonable delay and failure to follow (or have) proper procedures and rules.

Injustice – This does not only cover financial and other material or tangible loss but also includes inconvenience, anxiety or stress, and even a sense of outrage about the way in which something has been done.

Ombudsmen have powers similar to those of High Court (Court of Session in Scotland) for obtaining evidence.

If an Ombudsman upholds your complaint, they will expect the body against which you have complained to provide you with some remedy. This may be an apology, a change in procedures, financial compensation, or any combination of these or similar measures.

Which Ombudsman? – In England you complain to:

- the Parliamentary and Health Service Ombudsman (PHSO) about central government (eg the DWP), health authorities and trusts, doctors, dentists and opticians, etc. The PHSO can also investigate health-related cases where maladministration has caused hardship, complaints about clinical judgements, and complaints about refusal of access to official information;
- the Local Government Ombudsman about local government (eg local authority housing benefit offices or social services departments).

In Scotland and Wales, you complain to the PHSO about central government. For devolved matters, there is a separate Scottish Public Services Ombudsman that deals with complaints about the Scottish Executive and its agencies, and a Public Service Ombudsman for Wales that deals with complaints about the Welsh Administration. Each also deals with complaints about other public bodies in Scotland and Wales, including health, housing and social services. There is only one government Ombudsman in Northern Ireland.

You can ask your Citizens Advice Bureau (CAB) to check with the Ombudsman first to make sure that an Ombudsman can investigate a complaint against a particular government body, such as a quango.

How to complain – You can complain direct to any of the Ombudsmen except the PHSO and, in cases concerning central government, the Northern Ireland Ombudsman. Only an MP can refer a complaint to the PHSO. You should normally approach your own MP; only approach an MP for another constituency if yours refuses to refer your complaint. If you approach another MP, they will usually contact your own MP before deciding whether to refer your complaint.

Other Ombudsmen – As well as the government Ombudsmen, there are several others, including the Financial Ombudsman, Housing Ombudsman and Legal Services Ombudsman. For details check the website (www.bioa.org.uk) or ask your local CAB. For information about the Pensions Ombudsman, see Box O.2 in Chapter 43.

63 Useful publications

1. Benefits guides

In many chapters in this Handbook we suggest other sources of information, including guidance and reference books, specific to the benefit or other rights described in the chapter. Look in boxes called 'For more information'. Listed below is a selection of other guides, with the publishers and the prices.

- ❑ *Guide to Housing Benefit and Council Tax Benefit 2009/2010*, Chartered Institute of Housing and Shelter, £25
- ❑ *Welfare Benefits and Tax Credits Handbook 2009/2010*, Child Poverty Action Group (CPAG), £37 (£8.50 for claimants)
- ❑ *Your Rights to money benefits 2008/2009*, Age Concern England, £5.99
- ❑ *Child Support Handbook 2009/2010*, CPAG, £26 (£7 for claimants)
- ❑ *Council Tax Handbook 2009, 8th edition*, CPAG, £17
- ❑ *Paying for Care Handbook 2008, 6th edition*, CPAG, £19.50
- ❑ *Fuel Rights Handbook 2008, 14th edition*, CPAG, £17

2. DWP leaflets and guidance

DWP leaflets and official guidance should be available from your local Jobcentre Plus office. You can download official DWP guidance, such as the *Decision Makers Guide*, from our website (www.disabilityalliance.org/links2.htm).

3. Disability Alliance publications

We publish a range of guides and factsheets on disability and welfare rights. Members of Disability Alliance receive free copies of our current publications. See back cover for contact details.

- ❑ *Employment and support allowance – The essential guide to ESA for people with a disability or long-term health condition, their families, carers and advisers* (2008), £7 (£2 for claimants)
- ❑ *Benefit appeals – A guide for advisers who represent their clients at benefit appeal tribunals* (2007), £9.50 (£3.50 for claimants)
- ❑ *Starting Out – A guide to the financial and other support available for young disabled people aged 16-24* (2007), £3.50 (£3 for claimants)
- ❑ *Out of sight* (2003) – a policy report examining how ethnic minority claimants who are either disabled or carers experience the benefits system. It focuses on non-English speakers, particularly Asian women, identifying deficiencies in the system. £3

Factsheets – We have produced over 50 factsheets, covering a range of benefits and care issues. You can download these free from our website (www. disabilityalliance.org/fact.htm). You can also order up to three paper versions of any factsheet if you send us an A4 stamped, self-addressed envelope (our address is on the back cover).

Address list

This section of the Handbook contains useful addresses:

Organisations

General and specialist organisations dealing in some way with disability issues are listed. The main A-Z section lists organisations that cover England or all of the UK. Organisations based in Northern Ireland, Scotland and Wales are listed separately. We do not have space to list local organisations and instead provide a list of DIAL UK local groups as a first point of contact.

Lists are organised alphabetically. Entries beginning with the words National, British, etc are listed by the disability or community they serve, eg 'Blind, National Federation of the' or 'Deaf Association, The British'. Acronyms such as BILD (British Institute of Learning Disabilities) are generally listed by disability (Learning Disabilities, British Institute of,).

Websites are included. Alternatively, visit the links section of our website www.disabilityalliance.org/links.htm.

England and UK-wide

A

AbilityNet, PO Box 94, Warwick CV34 5WS (01926 312847; Advice helpline 0800 269545) www.abilitynet.org.uk *Makes mainstream computer technology accessible to people with disabilities.*

Accessible Environments, Centre for (CAE), 70 South Lambeth Road, London SW8 1RL (Voice & Textphone 020 7840 0125) www.cae.org.uk *Information, training and consultancy geared to help produce accessible buildings.*

Acupuncture Council, British, 63 Jeddo Road, London W12 9HQ (020 8735 0400) www.acupuncture.org.uk *Free list of practitioners and a leaflet provided on request. Large print available.*

Advocacy Resource Exchange (ARX), Portman House, 53 Millbrook Road East, Southampton, SO15 1HN (023 8023 4904; Helpline 08451 228633 – 2-5pm) www.advocacyresource.net *An organisation providing information and advice about advocacy.*

Afasic, 1st Floor, 20 Bowling Green Lane, London EC1R 0BD (020 7490 9410; Helpline 0845 355 5577 or 020 7490 9420 – 10.30am-2.30pm) www.afasic.org.uk *Supports children and young people with speech, language and communication impairments, and their parents or carers.*

African and Caribbeans, Organisation of Blind, 1st Floor, Gloucester House, 8 Camberwell New Road, London SE5 0TA (020 7735 3400) www.obac.org.uk

Age Concern England, Astral House, 1268 London Road, London SW16 4ER (020 8765 7200) www.ageconcern.org.uk *A federation of over 400 charities working together to promote the well-being of all older people.*

AIDS Trust, National (NAT), New City Cloisters, 196 Old Street, London EC1V 9FR (020 7814 6767) www.nat.org.uk *A charity that campaigns to change society's response to HIV. Provides expert advice and practical resources.*

Alcohol Concern, 64 Leman Street, London E1 8EU (020 7264 0510) www.alcoholconcern.org.uk *Aims to reduce impact of alcohol misuse and increase range and quality of services.*

Alcoholics Anonymous, PO Box 1, 10 Toft Green, York YO1 7NJ (01904 644026; London helpline 020 7833 0022; National helpline 0845 769 7555) www.alcoholics-anonymous.org.uk

Alzheimer's Society, Devon House, 58 St Katherine's Way, London E1W 1JX (020 7423 3500; Helpline 0845 300 0336 – 8.30am-6.30pm) www.alzheimers.org.uk *Advice and support for those coping with dementia.*

Amnesia – *see Headway*

Ankylosing Spondylitis Society, National (NASS), Unit 02, One Victoria Villas, Richmond, Surrey TW9 2GW (020 8948 9117) www.nass.co.uk

Arthritis and Musculoskeletal Alliance (ARMA), Bride House, 18-20 Bride Lane, London EC4Y 8EE (020 7842 0910) www.arma.uk.net *Umbrella association bringing together support groups, professional bodies and research organisations.*

Arthritis Care, 18 Stephenson Way, London NW1 2HD (020 7380 6500; Freephone helpline 0808 800 4050) www.arthritiscare.org.uk *Provides services and support for people with arthritis, their families and those who work with them.*

ASBAH (Association for Spina Bifida and Hydrocephalus), ASBAH House, 42 Park Road, Peterborough PE1 2UQ (01733 555988; Helpline 0845 450 7755) www.asbah.org *Provides information, advice and support to individuals, families, carers and professionals.*

Asian People's Disability Alliance (APDA), 3rd Floor, Suite 1A, Alperton House, Bridgewater Road, Wembley, Middlesex HA0 1EH (020 8902 2113) www.apda.org.uk *Respite care, advice, advocacy and day care for elderly and disabled Asian people, IT training, sports, leisure and home help service.*

Assist UK, Redbank House, 4 St Chad's Street, Manchester M8 8QA (0870 770 2866; Textphone 0870 770 5813) www.assist-uk.org *National membership organisation leading a network of disability and independent living centres and services.*

Asthma UK, Summit House, 70 Wilson Street, London EC2A 2DB (0800 121 6255; Advice line 0800 121 6244) www.asthma.org.uk *Works to improve the health and well-being of people with asthma by sharing expertise.*

Ataxia UK, Lincoln House, Kennington Park, 1-3 Brixton Road, London SW9 6DE (020 7582 1444; Helpline 0845 644 0606) www.ataxia.org.uk *Provides a range of support services for people with ataxia and their families. Funds medical research.*

Autistic Society, National, 393 City Road, London EC1V 1NG (020 7833 2299; Helpline 0845 070 4004) www.autism.org.uk *Offers information and advice to people with autism spectrum disorders and their families.*

B

BackCare, 16 Elmtree Road, Teddington, Middlesex TW11 8ST (020 8977 5474; Helpline 0845 130 2704) www.backcare.org.uk *Information, support and self-help groups for people with back pain. Funds research.*

Barnardo's, Tanners Lane, Barkingside, Essex IG6 1QG (020 8550 8822) www.barnardos.org.uk *Social care and educational services for disabled children, young people and their families.*

BDF Newlife – *see Newlife Foundation*

BEAT *(formerly Eating Disorders Association),* Wensum House, 103 Prince of Wales Road, Norwich NR1 1DW (0870 770 3256; Adult Helpline 0845 634 1414 – Mon-Fri 10.30am-8.30pm, Sat 1-4.30pm; Youth Helpline 0845 634 7650, text messaging 07977 493345 – Mon-Fri 4.30-8.30pm, Sat 1-4.30pm; Textphone 01603 753322) www.b-eat.co.uk *Provides information and support to people affected by eating disorders.*

Bladder and Bowel Foundation (B&BF), SATRA Innovation Park, Rockingham Road, Kettering, Northants NN16 9JH (01536 533255; Nurse helpline 0845 345 0165; Counsellor helpline 0870 770 3246) www.bladderandbowelfoundation.org *Provides support for all bladder and bowel-related problems to patients, their families, carers and healthcare professionals.*

Blind Association, Guide Dogs for the, Hillfields, Burghfield Common, Reading, Berkshire RG7 3YG (01189 835555) www.guidedogs.org.uk *Provides guide dogs, mobility and other*

rehabilitation services for blind and partially sighted people.

Blind, National Federation of the, Sir John Wilson House, 215 Kirkgate, Wakefield WF1 1JG (01924 291313) www.nfbuk.org *Campaigning and self-help organisation*.

Blind, Royal National Institute of Blind People (RNIB), 105 Judd Street, London WC1H 9NE (Helpline 030 3123 9999) www.rnib.org.uk *Advice, assistance and information on benefits, equipment, employment and support. Campaigns for the rights of people with sight problems and the prevention of eye disease.*

Blind and Disabled, National League of the, Central Office, Swinton House, 324 Gray's Inn Road, London WC1X 8DD (020 7239 1262) www.community-tu.org *Trade union campaigning for employment and civil rights.*

Blind Children's Society, National (NBCS), Bradbury House, Market Street, Highbridge, Somerset TA9 3BW (01278 764764) www.nbcs.org.uk *Family support and information, education advocacy, IT advice, large-print books and equipment grants for children and young people.*

Blind People, Action for, 14-16 Verney Road, London SE16 3DZ (020 7635 4800; National helpline 0800 915 4666) www.actionforblindpeople.org.uk *Provides support to blind and partially sighted people in all aspects of life.*

Blind People, Clarity Employment for, 276 York Way, London N7 9PQ (020 7619 1650) www.clarityefbp.org *Provides employment, training and development for blind and disabled people in a factory and office environment.*

BLISS – The Special Care Baby Charity, 2nd Floor, 9 Holyrood Street, London Bridge, London SE1 2EL (020 7378 1122; Freephone helpline 0500 618140) www.bliss.org.uk *Supports families of premature and sick babies.*

Bradnet *(formerly Asian Disability Network)*, Noor House, 11 Bradford Lane, Laisterdyke, Bradford BD3 8LP (01274 224444; Minicom 01274 201860; SMS +44 762 480 2935) www.bradnet.org.uk *Promotes the equality and inclusion of disabled people.*

Brain and Spine Foundation, 7 Winchester House, Kennington Park, Cranmer Road, London SW9 6EJ (020 7793 5900; Helpline 0808 808 1000 – Mon-Thur 9am-2pm; Fri 9am-1pm) www.brainandspine.org.uk www.headstrongkids.org.uk (for children) www.aboutbraininjury.org.uk (for young people) *Information and support for people with neurological disorders.*

BREAK, Davison House, 1 Montague Road, Sheringham, Norfolk NR26 8WN (01263 822161) www.break-charity.org *Supported holidays, short breaks and respite care for children and adults with learning disabilities, including those with challenging behaviour and high-level needs.*

Breast Cancer Care, 5-13 Great Suffolk Street, London SE1 0NS (0845 092 0800; Helpline 0808 800 6000; Typetalk helpline 18001 0808 800 6001) www.breastcancercare.org.uk *Information, practical help and support for anyone affected by breast cancer. Campaigns for improved standards of care.*

British Legion, The Royal, Haig House, 199 Borough High Street, London SE1 1AA (020 3207 2100; Helpline 0845 772 5725) www.britishlegion.org.uk *Advice and support in a number of areas including war pensions, benefits, debt advice, care homes, resettlement training employment and remembrance travel.*

Brittle Bone Society, Grant Patterson House, 30 Guthrie Street, Dundee DD1 5BS (01382 204446; Freephone helpline 0800 028 2459) www.brittlebone.org *Provides support to anyone affected by osteogenesis imperfecta.*

C

Calibre Audio Library, Aylesbury, Buckinghamshire HP22 5XQ (01296 432339) www.calibre.org.uk *Free postal library service of audio books for adults and children with sight problems, dyslexia or physical disabilities.*

Cancerbackup – *see Macmillan Cancer Support*

Cancer Care, Marie Curie, 89 Albert Embankment, London SE1 7TP (020 7599 7777) www.mariecurie.org.uk *Provides high-quality free nursing to give terminally ill people the choice of dying at home supported by their families.*

Cancer, New Approaches to, PO Box 194, Chertsey, Surrey KT16 0WJ (Freephone 0800 389 2662) www.anac.org.uk *Works alongside conventional treatment, and supports patients and families in complementary therapies.*

Cancer Research UK, PO Box 123, 61 Lincolns Inn Field, London WC2A 3PX (020 7121 6699) www.cancerresearchuk.org

Cardiomyopathy Association, Unit 10, Chiltern Court, Asheridge Road, Chesham, Buckinghamshire HP5 2PX (Freephone 0800 0181 024) www.cardiomyopathy.org *Provides information and support for families affected by cardiomyopathy.*

Care and Repair England, The Renewal Trust Business Centre, 3 Hawksworth Street, Nottingham NG3 2EG (0115 950 6500) www.careandrepair-england.org.uk

Care Quality Commission, 7th Floor, New Kings Beam House, 22 Upper Ground, London SE1 9BW (03000 616161) www.cqc.org.uk *Regulates quality of health and social care and looks after the interest of people detained under the Mental Health Act.*

Carers UK, 20 Great Dover Street, London SE1 4LX (020 7378 4999; Freephone CarersLine 0808 808 7777 – Wed & Thurs 10-12am, 2-4pm) www.carersuk.org *Provides information and advice on benefits, services and other support to carers.*

Cerebral Palsy – *see Scope*

Child Death Helpline, Freephone Helpline 0800 282 986 – Mon-Sun 7-10pm, Mon, Thur & Fri 10am-1pm, Tue & Wed 1-4pm) www.childdeathhelpline.org.uk *A listening service for anyone affected by the death of a child. Answered by trained volunteers (all bereaved parents).*

Child Growth Foundation, 2 Mayfield Avenue, London W4 1PW (020 8994 7625; 020 8995 0257) www.childgrowthfoundation.org *Supports families and patients who have conditions that affect growth.*

Child Poverty Action Group (CPAG), 94 White Lion Street, London N1 9PF (020 7837 7979; Advice line for advisers 020 7833 4627 – Mon-Fri 2-4pm) www.cpag.org.uk *Benefits handbooks for claimants and advisers; consultancy and training for advisers; policy work and lobbying for the abolition of child poverty in the UK.*

Children, Action for *(formerly NCH)*, 85 Highbury Park, London N5 1UD (020 7704 7000) www.actionforchildren.org.uk *Services for disabled children and young people including domiciliary care, family placement, short breaks, children's centres, advocacy, education and leisure schemes.*

Children, Action for Sick, 36 Jacksons Edge Road, Disley, Stockport SK12 2JL (Helpline 0800 074 4519 – Mon-Fri 10am-3pm) www.actionforsickchildren.org *Support and advice for parents/carers of sick children and professionals. Campaigns to improve healthcare for children.*

Children's Heart Association, Mrs Gill Hitchen, 26 Elizabeth Drive, Helmshore, Rossendale, Lancashire BB4 4JB (01706 221988) www.heartchild.info

Children's Legal Centre, University of Essex, Wivenhoe Park, Colchester, Essex CO4 3SQ (01206 872466; Child advice line 0845 120 2948; National education advice line 0845 345 4345) www.childrenslegalcentre.com *Information, publications, legal advice and representation for children, young people and their families.*

Children's Liver Disease Foundation, 36 Great Charles Street, Birmingham B3 3JY (0121 212 3839) www.childliverdisease.org *Funds research, provides education and gives emotional support.*

Chinese Mental Health Association (CMHA), 2/F Zenith House, 155 Curtain Road, London EC2A 3QY (020 7613 1008; Helpline 0845 122 8660 – Mon-Fri 4-6pm) www.cmha.org.uk

Chinese National Healthy Living Centre, 29-30 Soho Square, London W1D 3QS (020 7287 0904) www.cnhlc.org.uk

Citizens Advice, Myddelton House, 115-123 Pentonville Road, London N1 9LZ (020 7833 2181) www.citizensadvice.org.uk; www.adviceguide.org.uk *Helps with legal, money and other problems by providing information and advice, and influencing policy makers. Provides details of local Citizens Advice Bureau.*

Clothing Solutions (for disabled people), Unit 1, Jubilee Mills, 30 North Street, Bradford BD1 4EW (01274 746739) www.clothingsolutions.org.uk *Clothing advice and garment production or alteration service offered. Made-to-measure service.*

Colitis and Crohn's Disease, National Association for, 4 Beaumont House, Sutton Road, St Albans, Hertfordshire AL1 5HH (Information Line 0845 130 2233 – 10am-1pm; Support Line 0845 130 3344 – 6.30-9pm; Admin 01727 830038) www.nacc.org.uk

Colostomy Association, 2 London Court, East Street, Reading, Berkshire RG1 4QL (Freephone Helpline 0800 328 4257 – 7-day service, 24 hours) www.colostomyassociation.org.uk *Advice on living with a colostomy and returning to a full life after surgery.*

Combat Stress, Tyrwhitt House, Oaklawn Road, Leatherhead, Surrey KT22 0BX (01372 841600) www.combatstress.org.uk *Specialist care for ex-service men and women with service-related psychological injuries.*

Community Service Volunteers, 237 Pentonville Road, London N1 9NJ (020 7278 6601) www.csv.org.uk

Compassionate Friends, Nationwide, 53 North Street, Bristol BS3 1EN (0845 120 3785; Helpline 0845 123 2304 – daily 10am-4pm & 6.30-10.30pm) www.tcf.org.uk *Support from bereaved parent to bereaved parent and their immediate families.*

Contact a Family, 209-211 City Road, London EC1V 1JN (020 7608 8700; Helpline 0808 808 3555 – 10am-4pm; Mon 5.30-7.30pm; Minicom 0808 808 3556) www.cafamily.org.uk *Advice and support for families caring for disabled children, including those with rare disorders.*

Contact the Elderly, 15 Henrietta Street, London WC2E 8QG (020 7240 0630; Freephone 0800 716543) www.contact-the-elderly.org *Friendship and tea parties for elderly people who live alone without family support.*

Continence Foundation – *see Bladder and Bowel Foundation*

Counsel and Care, Twyman House, 16 Bonny Street, London NW1 9PG (Orders 020 7241 85523; Advice line 0845 300 7585 – Mon, Tue, Thur & Fri 10am-4pm; Wed 10am-1pm) www.counselandcare.org.uk *Help and advice on all aspects of care for older people, their families and their carers.*

Counselling and Psychotherapy, British Association for, BACP House, 15 St Johns Business Park, Lutterworth, Leicestershire LE17 4HB (01455 883300; Textphone 01455 0307; Helpdesk for those seeking counselling services 01455 883316) www.bacp.co.uk *Lists of counsellors, counselling agencies and local agencies available by post or from the website.*

Crossroads – Caring for Carers, Information and Communications Office, 3rd Floor, 33-35 Cathedral Road, Cardiff CF11 9HB (0845 450 0350) www.crossroads.org.uk *Provides practical support. Trained carer support workers take over caring tasks in the home to provide carers with a break.*

Cruse Bereavement Care, PO Box 800, Richmond, Surrey TW9 1RG (020 8939 9530; Helpline 0844 477 9400; Young people's helpline Freephone 0808 808 1677) www.cruse.org.uk and www.rd4u.org.uk for young people *Bereavement support, information, advice, support groups and publications.*

Cued Speech Association UK, 9 Jawbone Hill, Dartmouth, Devon TQ6 9RW (01803 832784) www.cuedspeech.co.uk *Training and information for deaf people about Cued Speech (spoken language accessed through vision). Aims to improve communication and literacy skills of deaf and hearing impaired people.*

Cystic Fibrosis Trust, 11 London Road, Bromley, Kent BR1 1BY (020 8464 7211; Helpline 0845 851 1000) www.cftrust.org.uk *Support services for families and individuals with cystic fibrosis.*

D

Daycare Trust – The National Childcare Campaign, 21 St Georges Road, London SE1 6ES (020 7840 3350; Information Line 0845 872 6251 – Mon-Fri 10am-1pm except Wed 2-5pm) www.daycaretrust.org.uk *Provides information on childcare issues.*

Deaf Association, The British, 10th Floor, Coventry Point, Market Way, Coventry CV1 1EA (024 7655 0936; Textphone 024 7655 0393) www.bda.org.uk

Deaf Children's Society, National (NDCS), 15 Dufferin Street, London EC1Y 8UR (Voice and Textphone 020 7490 8656; Freephone helpline (Voice and Textphone) 0808 800 8880) www.ndcs.org.uk *Information and support for families and professionals, including information on education, benefits, audiology and technology.*

Deaf People, Royal Association for, 18 Westside Centre, London Road, Stanway, Colchester, Essex CO3 8PH (0845 688 2525; Textphone 0845 688 2527) www.royaldeaf.org.uk *Sign language interpreting and training. Various support services including employment, legal advice, advocacy & deaf community development.*

Deaf People, Royal National Institute for (RNID) – *see RNID*

Deafblind UK, National Centre for Deafblindness, John and Lucille Van Geest Place, Cygnet Road, Hampton, Peterborough PE7 8FD (01733 358100; Free helpline 0800 132320) www.deafblind.org.uk *Comprehensive services for members, support assistants, professionals, families, friends and carers. Campaigns to challenge the prejudice faced by deafblind people.*

Deafblind and Rubella Association, The National – *see Sense*

deafPLUS, Trinity Centre, Key Close, Whitechapel, London E1 4HG (Voice and Fax 020 7790 6147; Textphone 020 7790 5999) www.deafplus.org *Aims to improve the quality of life for deaf people through contact, information and training.*

DebRA, DebRA House, 13 Wellington Business Park, Dukes Ride, Crowthorne, Berkshire RG45 6LS (01344 771961) www.debra.org.uk *Provides support for people with all types of epidermolysis bullosa.*

Depression Alliance, Suite 212, Spitfire Studios, 63-71 Collier Street, London N1 9BE (0845 123 2320) www.depressionalliance.org *Provides information, raises awareness and co-ordinates support services.*

Diabetes UK, Macloud House, 10 Parkway, London NW1 7AA (020 7424 1000; Careline 0845 120 2960) www.diabetes.org.uk *Provides support and information, and funds research.*

DIAL, Local groups and members, *see pages 277-278*

DIAL UK, St Catherine's, Tickhill Road, Doncaster DN4 8QN (Voice and Textphone [use voice announcer] 01302 310123) www.dialuk.info *National organisation for the DIAL network.*

Disabilities Trust, The, 32 Market Place, Burgess Hill, West Sussex RH15 9NP (01444 239123) www.dtgroup.org *Care, accommodation and rehabilitation for adults with acquired brain injury, autism, physical disability and learning difficulties. Runs a school for children with autism in Berkshire.*

Disability Equipment Register, 4 Chatterton Road, Yate, Bristol BS37 4BJ (01454 318818) www.disabilityequipment.org.uk *An internet-based national register of used disability equipment.*

Disability Law Service, Ground Floor, 39-45 Cavell Street, London E1 2BP (020 7791 9800 – 10am-1pm; 2-5pm; Textphone 020 7791 9801) www.dls.org.uk *Free legal advice and information for disabled people, their families and carers, on benefits, employment, post-16 education, community care, consumer contract and disability discrimination.*

Disability, Pregnancy and Parenthood International, National Centre for Disabled Parents, Unit F9, 89-93 Fonthill Road, London N4 3JH (020 7263 3088; Textphone 0800 018 9949; Helpline 0800 018 4730 – Mon & Thur 1-4pm; Wed 10am-1pm) www.dppi.org.uk *Information on pregnancy and parenthood for disabled people and professionals.*

Disability Resource Team (DRT), 2nd Floor, 6 Park Road, Teddington, Middlesex TW11 0AA (020 8943 0022) www.disabilityresourceteam.com *Disability training, consultancy and transcription into Braille, large print and audio.*

Disability Sport, English Federation of, Manchester Metropolitan University, Alsager Campus, Hassall Road, Alsager, Stoke-on-Trent ST7 2HL (0161 247 5294; Minicom 0161 247 5644) www.efds.org.uk *Co-ordinates the development of sport and physical activity in England. Seeks to promote inclusion and achieve equality of sporting opportunities for disabled people.*

Disabled Living Foundation, 380-384 Harrow Road, London W9 2HU (020 7289 6111; Helpline 0845 130 9177) www.dlf.org.uk *Information and advice about daily living equipment for disabled people.*

Disabled Motorists Federation, c/o Chester-Le-Street District CVS Volunteer Centre, Clarence Terrace, Chester-Le-Street, County Durham DH3 3DQ (0191 416 3172) www.freewebs.com/dmfed *Information for disabled people and their carers on travel in general and motoring in particular.*

Disabled Parents Network, 81 Melton Road, West Bridgeford, Nottingham NG2 8EN (Helpline 0300 330 0639 – 12-2pm; Wed 10am-12pm & 7-9pm) www.disabledparentsnetwork.org.uk *Operates a peer support register for disabled parents. Members newsletter. Helpline run by disabled parent volunteers..*

Disabled People, Queen Elizabeth's Foundation for, Leatherhead Court, Leatherhead, Surrey KT22 0BN (01372 841100) www.qef.org *Four centres: training college, mobility centre, brain injury rehabilitation and development centre.*

Disabled People's Council, United Kingdom (UKDPC), Rodin House, Ivy Grove, Ripley, Derbyshire DE5 3HN (01773 746698) www.uksdpc.org *Umbrella organisation for regional and local groups controlled and run by disabled people.*

Disabled Professionals, Association of (ADP), BCM ADP, London WC1N 3XX (01204 431638) www.adp.org.uk

Disfigurement Guidance Centre – Skinlaser Directory, PO Box 7, Cupar, Fife KY15 4PF (01337 870281) www.skinlaserdirectory.org.uk *Information, help, publications including Skinlaser directory and cosmetic handbook; SAE helpful for reply.*

Down's Heart Group, PO Box 4260, Dunstable LU6 2ZT (0845 166 8061 – Mon-Thur 9.30am-4.30pm) www.dhg.org.uk *Support and information relating to heart problems associated with Down's syndrome.*

Down's Syndrome Association, Langdon Down Centre, 2a Langdon Park, Teddington TW11 9PS (0845 230 0372) www.downs-syndrome.org.uk

Dyslexia Action, Park House, Wick Road, Egham, Surrey TW20 0HH (01784 222300) www.dyslexiaaction.org.uk *Support for people with dyslexia and literacy difficulties, specialising in assessment, teaching and training. Develops and distributes teaching materials and carries out research.*

Dyslexia Association, British, Unit 8, Bracknell Beeches, Old Bracknell Lane, Bracknell, Berks RG12 7BW (0845 251 9003; Helpline 0845 251 9002) www.bdadyslexia.org.uk *National charity representing all dyslexic people, offering impartial advice and information.*

Dystonia Society, 1st Floor, 89 Albert Embankment, London SE1 7TP (0845 458 6211; Helpline 0845 458 6322) www.dystonia.org.uk *Support and information, welfare grants, help with access to services and regional support groups.*

E

Eczema Society, National, Hill House, Highgate Hill, London N19 5NA (020 7281 3553; Helpline 0800 089 1122 – Mon-Fri 8am-8pm) www.eczema.org

Education, The Alliance for Inclusive, 336 Brixton Road, London SW9 7AA (020 7737 6030) www.allfie.org.uk *Campaigns to achieve an inclusive education system.*

Employment Opportunities for People with Disabilities, Crystal Gate, 3rd Floor Worship Street, London EC2A 2AH (020 7448 5420; Textphone 020 7374 6684) www.opportunities.org.uk *Works with people with disabilities, business partners and government agencies to help people with disabilities find and retain employment.*

Epilepsy Action, New Anstey House, Gate Way Drive, Yeadon, Leeds LS19 7XY (0113 210 8800; Helpline 0808 800 5050) www.epilepsy.org.uk

Epilepsy, National Society for, Chesham Lane, Chalfont St Peter, Buckinghamshire SL9 0RJ (01494 601300; Helpline 01494 601400) www.epilepsynse.org.uk *Medical services, including inpatient assessment and outpatients, supported living, long-term and respite residential care, training and information services.*

Equality and Human Rights Commission, Helpline England, Freepost RRLL-GHUX-CTRX, Arndale House, Arndale Centre, Manchester M4 3EQ (0845 604 6610; Textphone 0845 604 6620 – 9am-5pm; Wed 9am-8pm) www.equalityhumanrights.com *Enforces and develops equality legislation on age, disability, gender, race, religion or belief, sexual orientation and transgender status.*

Ex-Services Mental Welfare – *see Combat Stress*

F

Family Action, 501-505 Kingsland Road, London E8 4AU (020 7254 6251) www.family-action.org.uk *Family support, mental health services, grants for people in need and educational grants advice.*

Family Fund, Unit 4, Alpha Court, Monks Cross Drive, Huntington, York YO32 9WN (0845 130 4542; Textphone 01904 658085) www.familyfund.org.uk *Independent grant-giving organisation helping families caring for severely disabled children.*

Far East (Prisoners of War and Internees) Fund, Mrs S Burrows, 92 Denton Road, Audenshaw, Manchester M34 5BD (0161 292 2102 – Tue & Thur only) *Assists ex-Far East prisoners of war and their widows in need. Alternatively, contact British Legion.*

Fostering Network, The, 87 Blackfriars Road, London SE1 8HA (020 7620 6400; Fosterline (advice line for foster carers) 0800 040 7675 – 9am-5pm; Wed 9am-8pm; Information Line 020 7261 1884 – Wed-Fri 12-3pm) www.fostering.net

Foundations, Bleaklow House, Howard Town Mill, Glossop SK13 8HT (01457 891909 to find your nearest home improvement agency) www.foundations.uk.com *National body for home improvement agencies that assist older, disabled or low-income homeowners to repair, improve or adapt their home.*

G

Gauchers Association, 3 Bull Pitch, Dursley, Gloucestershire GL11 4NG (Tel/Fax 01453 549231) www.gaucher.org.uk *Provides information on Gaucher disease to families and doctors.*

Gemma, BM Box 5700, London WC1N 3XX *National friendship network of disabled and non-disabled lesbian and bisexual women.*

Gingerbread, 255 Kentish Town Road, London NW5 2LX (020 7428 5400; Helpline 0800 018 5026) www.gingerbread.org.uk

Guillain-Barré Syndrome Support Group, c/o Lincolnshire County Council, Council Offices, Eastgate, Sleaford, Lincolnshire NG34 7EB (01529 304615; Free helpline 0800 374803) www.gbs.org.uk

Gut Trust, The, Unit 5, 53 Mowbray Street, Sheffield S3 8EN (Helpline 0114 272 3253 – Mon-Fri 6-9pm, Sat 10am-12pm) www.theguttrust.org *Support service for people with IBS (irritable bowel syndrome), their families and carers. Helpline answered by IBS specialist nurses.*

H

3H Fund (Help the Handicapped Holiday Fund), B2 Speldhurst Business Park, Langton Road, Tunbridge Wells, Kent TN3 0QA (01892 850207) www.3hfund.org.uk *Organises subsidised group holidays for physically disabled people; runs a UK holiday grant programme for disabled people when funds allow.*

Haemophilia Society, First Floor, Petersham House, 57a Hatton Garden, London EC1N 8JG (020 7831 1020; Helpline 0800 018 6068) www.haemophilia.org.uk *Information and support for people affected by bleeding disorders.*

Headlines – The Cranio Facial Support Group, 128 Beesmoor Road, Frampton Cotterell, Bristol BS36 2JP (01454 850557) www.headlines.org.uk *Information, advice and support for people and their families affected by Craniosynostosis and associated conditions.*

Headway – The Brain Injury Association, 7 King Edward Court, King Edward Street, Nottingham NG1 1EW (0115 924 0800; Helpline 0808 800 2244) www.headway.org.uk *Help, information and support for people with brain injuries and for their families and carers.*

Hearing Concern LINK, 19 Hartfield Road, Eastbourne, East Sussex BN21 2AR (01323 638230; Textphone 01323 739998) www.hearingconcernlink.org *Rehabilitation, outreach volunteers, social support groups, self-management programmes, training for professionals, equipment advice, research.*

Heart Foundation, British, Greater London House, 180 Hampstead Road, London NW1 7AW (020 7554 0000) www.bhf.org.uk

Help the Aged, 207-221 Pentonville Road, London N1 9UZ (020 7278 1114; SeniorLine 0808 800 6565)

www.helptheaged.org.uk *Free advice and information for older people and their carers about benefits and community and residential care.*
HFT *(formerly Home Farm Trust Ltd)*, 5-6 Brook Bus Park, Folly Brook Road, Emersons Green, Bristol BS16 7FL (0117 906 1700) www.hft.org.uk *Services for people with learning disabilities including residential care, supported living and employment, advocacy and family carer support service.*
Home Care Association Ltd, UK, Group House, 2nd Floor, 52 Sutton Court, Sutton SM1 4SL (Tel/ Fax 020 8288 5291) www.ukhca.co.uk *Professional association for domiciliary care agencies. Lists of local agencies.*
Homeless Link, 1st Floor, 10-13 Rushworth Street, London SE1 0RB (020 7960 3010) www.homeless.org.uk *Represents and supports agencies working with homeless people across England.*
Horder Centre, The, St John's Road, Crowborough, East Sussex TN6 1XP (01892 665577) www.hordercentre.co.uk *Specialists in planned orthopaedic surgery, arthritis and treatment of musculo-skeletal conditions.*
Huntington's Disease Association, Neurosupport Centre, Norton Street, Liverpool L3 8LR (0151 298 3298) www.hda.org.uk *Support for families and professionals affected by Huntington's disease.*
Hydrocephalus – *see ASBAH*
Hyperactive Children's Support Group, 71 Whyke Lane, Chichester, West Sussex PO19 7PD (01243 539966) www.hacsg.org.uk *Focuses on non-drug therapies and provides information for hyperactive/ADHD children, their families and professionals.*
Hyperactive Children's Support Group, 71 Whyke Lane, Chichester, West Sussex PO19 7PD (01243 539966 – 10am-12pm) www.hacsg.org.uk *Focuses on non-drug therapies and provides information for hyperactive/ ADHD children, their families and professionals.*

I

I CAN Charity, 8 Wakley Street, London EC1V 7QE (0845 225 4073) www.ican.org.uk; www.talkingpoint.org.uk *Helps children across the UK with communication difficulties.*
IA (The Ileostomy and Internal Pouch Support Group) Peverill House, 1-5 Mill Road, Ballyclare, Co Antrim BT39 9DR (028 9334 4043; Freephone 0800 0184 724) www.iasupport.org *Helps people return to active lives following surgery for removal of the colon. Local groups UK-wide.*
Immigrants, Joint Council for the Welfare of (JCWI), 115 Old Street, London EC1V 9RT (020 7251 8708) www.jcwi.org.uk *Campaigns for justice in immigration, nationality and refugee law and policy.*
Independent Living Alternatives, Trafalgar House, Grenville Place, London NW7 3SA (020 8906 9265) www.ilanet.co.uk *Support and advice on employing personal assistants.*
Independent Living Fund, PO Box 7525, Nottingham NG2 4ZT (0845 601 8815; Textphone 0845 601 8816) www.ilf.org.uk *A government-funded trust providing cash payments for personal or domestic care to severely disabled people electing to live in the community.*
Independent Living, National Centre for, Unit 3.40, Canterbury Court, 1-3 Brixton Road, London SW9 6DE (020 7587 1663; Textphone 020 7587 1177) www.ncil.org.uk *Information, consultancy and training on personal assistance, direct payments and individual budgets.*

J

JAMI (Jewish Association for the Mentally Ill), 16A North End Road, London NW11 7PH (020 8458 2223) www.jamiuk.org
JCWI – *see Immigrants, Joint Council for the Welfare of*
Jewish Blind and Disabled, 35 Langstone Way, Mill Hill East, Bittacy Hill, London NW7 1GT (020 8371 6611) www.jbd.org *Sheltered accommodation for vision impaired and physically disabled people.*

K

Kidney Patient Association, British, Bordon, Hampshire GU35 9JZ (01420 472021/2) www.britishkidney-pa.co.uk *Financial help and advice.*
Kids, 49 Mecklenburgh Square, London WC1N 2NY (020 7520 0405) www.kids.org.uk *Services for disabled children and their families, eg adventure play, home learning, short breaks, young carers/sibling groups, advice, information and SEN mediation.*

L

Laryngectomee Clubs, National Association of (NALC), 152 Buckingham Palace Road, Victoria, London SW1W 9TR (020 7380 8585) www.laryngectomy.org.uk
Law centres, *see pages 279-280*
Law Centres Federation, 3rd Floor, 293-299 Kentish Town Road, London NW5 2TJ (020 7428 4400) www.lawcentres.org.uk *Information on your nearest law centre.*
Lawyers with Disabilities Division *(formerly GSD)*, The Law Society, 114 Chancery Lane, London WC2A 1PL (020 7320 5793) www.lawsociety.org.uk/lawyerswithdisabilities *Aims to achieve equality for disabled people, solicitors and their clients. Calls taken from professionals only.*
Learning Difficulties – Values into Action, Oxford House, Derbyshire Street, London E2 6HG (020 7729 5436) www.viauk.org *Campaigns for the right of people with learning difficulties to live ordinary lives in the community.*
Learning Disabilities, British Institute of (BILD), Campion House, Green Street, Kidderminster, Worcestershire DY10 1JL (01562 723010) www.bild.org.uk *Education, training, information, publications, research and consultancy for people with learning disabilities.*
Learning Disabilities, Foundation for People with, 9th Floor, Sea Containers House, 20 Upper Ground, London SE1 9QB (020 7803 1100) www.learningdisabilities.org.uk *Part of the Mental Health Foundation.*
Leonard Cheshire, 66 South Lambeth Road, Vauxhall, London SW8 1RL (020 3242 0200) www.lcdisability.org *Wide range of support services for disabled people throughout the UK.*
Leukaemia Research, Correspondence: 43 Great Ormond Street, London WC1N 3JJ. Walk-in: 39-40 Eagle Street, London WC1R 4TH (020 7405 0101) www.lrf.org.uk *Booklets on leukaemia and related blood cancers.*
Liberty (The National Council for Civil Liberties), 21 Tabard Street, London SE1 4LA (020 7403 3888; Human rights legal advice line 0845 123 2307 – Mon & Thur 6.30-8.30pm, Wed 12.30-2.30pm) www.liberty-human-rights.org.uk and www.yourrights.org.uk
Limbless Association, Queen Mary's Hospital, Roehampton Lane, London SW15 5PN (020 8788 1777) www.limbless-association.org
Limbless Ex-Service Men's Association, British (BLESMA), Frankland Moore House, 185-187 High Road, Chadwell Heath, Romford, Essex RM6 6NA (020 8590 1124) www.blesma.org *Support services for people who have lost limbs or the use of limbs as a result of service with HM Forces or Auxiliary Forces.*
Listening Books, 12 Lant Street, London SE1 1QH (020 7407 9417) www.listening-books.org.uk *A postal and internet-based library service for adults and children who find it difficult or impossible to read or hold a book due to disability or illness.*
Livability, 50 Scrutton Street, London EC2A 4XQ (020 7452 2000) www.livability.org.uk *Residential care, supported living, holidays, housing, schools and colleges, training and brain injury rehabilitation.*
Lupus UK, St James House, Eastern Road, Romford, Essex RM1 3NH (01708 731251) www.lupusuk.org.uk *Self-help and fundraising.*

M

Macfarlane Trust, Alliance House, 12 Caxton Street, London SW1H 0QS (020 7233 0057) www.macfarlane.org.uk *Provision of grants and non-financial services to haemophiliacs infected with HIV through contaminated blood products.*
Macmillan Cancer Support, 89 Albert Embankment, London SE1 7UQ (020 7840 7840; Macmillan CancerLine 0808 808 2020; Nurse information helpline 0808 800 1234 – Mon-Fri 9am-8pm) www.macmillan.org.uk *Information on cancer support services, including Macmillan nurses and self-help groups, sources of financial help; grants for patients. Call CancerLine for emotional backup or practical advice, and Nurse*

Information Helpline for answers about cancer types, treatments or what to expect.

MDF The Bipolar Organisation, Castle Works, 21 St George's Road, London SE1 6ES (0845 634 0540) www.mdf.org.uk *User-led charity working to enable people affected by manic depression (bi-polar affective disorder) to control their lives.*

ME, Action for, 3rd Floor, Canningford House, 38 Victoria Street, Bristol BS1 6BY (ME telephone support 0845 123 2314; ME welfare rights helpline 01749 330136 – Mon & Wed am) www.afme.org.uk

ME Association, The, 7 Apollo Office Court, Radclive Road, Gawcott, Bucks MK18 4DF (01280 818964; ME Connect 0870 444 1836 – every day 10-12am, 2-4pm & 7-9pm) www.meassociation.org.uk

MedicAlert Foundation, 1 Bridge Wharf, 156 Caledonian Road, London N1 9UU (020 7833 3034; Freephone 0800 581 420) www.medicalert.org.uk *Emergency medical identification bracelets or necklets for people with hidden medical conditions or allergies; 24-hr emergency line.*

Mencap Society, Royal, 123 Golden Lane, London EC1Y 0RT (020 7454 0454) www.mencap.org.uk

Meningitis Trust, The, Head Office, Fern House, Bath Road, Stroud, Gloucestershire GL5 3TJ (01453 76800; 24-hr nurse-led helpline 0800 028 1828; Children's helpline 0808 801 0388) www.meningitis-trust.org *Provides specialist support for those affected by meningitis.*

Mental Health Act Commission – *see Care Quality Commission*

Migraine Action Association, 27 East Street, Leicester LE1 6NB (01536 461333) www.migraine.org.uk *Research, newsletter, leaflets, free information service.*

Migraine Trust, 2nd Floor, 55-56 Russell Square, London WC1B 4HP (020 7436 1336; Helpline 020 7462 6601) www.migrainetrust.org *Provides evidence-based information through website, helpline, factsheets, newsletter, educational events and research funding.*

Mind, Granta House, 15-19 Broadway, Stratford, London E15 4BQ (020 8519 2122; Information line 0845 766 0163) www.mind.org.uk *Mental health information service.*

Mobilise, National Headquarters, Ashwellthorpe, Norwich NR16 1EX (01508 489449) www.mobilise.info *Promoting mobility for disabled people.*

Mobility Centre, Queen Elizabeth's Foundation, Damson Way, Fountain Drive, Carshalton, Surrey SM5 4NR (020 8770 1151) www.qef.org.uk/mobilitycentre *Assessments for car drivers, passenger and wheelchair users, information service, safety training for pavement scooter users, driving tuition and bespoke training courses.*

Motability Car Scheme, Motability Operations, City Gate House, 22 Southwark Bridge Road, London SE1 9HB (0845 456 4566; Minicom 0845 675 0009 – Mon-Fri 8.30am-5.30pm) www.motability.co.uk *Contract car hire or hire purchase scheme designed to help people with disabilities improve their mobility.*

Motability Wheelchair and Scooter Scheme, Route2mobility, Montgomery House, Newbury Road, Enham Alamein, Andover, Hampshire SP11 6JS (0845 607 6260; Fax 01264 384482 – Mon-Fri 8am-6pm) www.motability.co.uk

Motor Neurone Disease Association, PO Box 246, Northampton NN1 2PR (01604 250505; MND Connect 0845 762 6262) www.mndassociation.org *Confidential advice, and practical and emotional support.*

MPS Society, The (The Society for Mucopolysaccharide Diseases), MPS House, Repton Place, White Lion Road, Amersham, Buckinghamshire HP7 9LP (0845 389 9901) www.mpssociety.co.uk *Support, advocacy, information and help to individuals, families and professionals.*

Multiple Sclerosis Resource Centre, 7 Peartree Business Centre, Peartree Road, Stanway, Colchester, Essex CO3 0JN (01206 505444; 24-hour counselling 0800 783 0518 then select option '1') www.msrc.co.uk *Information, magazine, benefits advice, counselling by phone.*

Multiple Sclerosis Society of Great Britain and Northern Ireland, MS National Centre, 372 Edgware Road, Cricklewood, London NW2 6ND (020 8438 0700; Information Helpline 020 8438 0799 – 10am-3pm; National Helpline 0808 800 8000 – 9am-9pm) www.mssociety.org.uk *Information and support from over 350 branches. The National Centre is a source of advice, learning and teaching.*

Muscular Dystrophy Campaign, 61 Southwark Street, London SE1 0HL (020 7803 4800; Fax 020 7401 3495; Information and support line 0800 652 6352 – Mon-Fri 9am-1pm & 2-5pm) www.muscular-dystrophy.org *Provides information, advice and support, and funds research into treatment.*

Myasthenia Gravis Association, 1st Floor, Southgate Business Centre, Normanton Road, Derby DE23 6UQ (01332 290219; UK helpline 0800 919922; Ireland helpline 1800 409672) www.mga-charity.org

N

Narcolepsy Association (UK), PO Box 13842, Penicuik EH26 8WX (0845 450 0394) www.narcolepsy.org.uk *Support, advice and assistance for narcolepsy sufferers and their carers.*

National Association of Citizens Advice Bureaux (NACAB) – *see Citizens Advice*

National Voices *(formerly LTCA),* 202 Hatton Square, 16 Baldwins Gardens, London EC1N 7RJ (020 3176 0738) www.nationalvoices.org.uk *Umbrella group for voluntary groups representing users of health and social care in England.*

NCVO – *see Voluntary Organisations, National Council for*

Neurodisability Service, The Wolfson, Level 10, Main Nurses Home, Great Ormond Street Hospital, London WC1N 3JH (020 7405 9200) *Assessment and advice on children with complex neuro-developmental problems.*

Neurofibromatosis Association, The, Quayside House, 38 High Street, Kingston upon Thames KT1 1HL (020 8439 1234) www.nfauk.org

Newlife Foundation *(formerly BDF Newlife),* Newlife Centre, Hemlock Way, Cannock, Staffs, WS11 7GF (Nurse helpline 0800 902 0095) www.newlifecharity.co.uk *Support, information and equipment grants for families and significantly affected children.*

Norwood, Broadway House, 80-82 The Broadway, Stanmore, Middlesex HA7 4HB (020 8954 4555 – Mon-Thurs & Fri am only) www.norwood.org.uk *Services for children, families and adults coping with learning and physical disabilities and social disadvantage.*

'Not Forgotten' Association, Fourth Floor, 2 Grosvenor Gardens, London SW1W 0DH (020 7730 2400) www.nfassociation.org *Entertainment and recreation services (including TVs, holidays and outings) for ex-Service men and women with disabilities.*

NSPCC (National Society for the Prevention of Cruelty to Children), Weston House, 42 Curtain Road, London EC2A 3NH (020 7825 2500; General enquiries 020 7825 2775; Helpline 0808 800 5000; Helpline Textphone 0800 056 0566) www.nspcc.org.uk *Runs a network of child protection services and programmes.*

O

Organic Acidaemias UK, Mrs E Priddy, 5 Saxon Road, Ashford, Middlesex TW15 1QL (01784 245989) www.oauk.com *Arranges contact between families of children with organic acidaemias.*

Osteoporosis Society, National, Manor Farm, Skinners Hill, Camerton, Bath BA2 0PJ (01761 471771; 0845 130 3076; Helpline 0845 450 0230) www.nos.org.uk

P

Paget's Disease, National Association for the Relief of, 323 Manchester Road, Walkden, Worsley, Manchester M28 3HH (0161 799 4646) www.paget.org.uk

Pain Society, The British, 3rd Floor, Churchill House, 35 Red Lion Square, London WC1R 4SG (020 7269 7840) www.britishpainsociety.org *An organisation for healthcare professionals. Offers information pack that includes list of pain clinics.*

Parents for Inclusion, 336 Brixton Road, London SW9 7AA (Freephone inclusion helpline 0800 652 3145 – Mon 10am-12pm, Wed 1-3pm in term time) www.parentsforinclusion.org *For parents who want their disabled children included in mainstream education. Support groups and training.*

Parkinson's Disease Society of the UK, 215 Vauxhall Bridge Road, London SW1V 1EJ (020 7931 8080; Freephone helpline 0808 800 0303 – Mon-Fri 9.30am-9pm, Sat 9.30am-5.30pm) www.parkinsons.org.uk

Partially Sighted Society, 7-9 Bennetthorpe, Doncaster DN2 6AA (0844 477 4966; Fax 0844 477 4969) www.partsight.org.uk
Information, advice and equipment for people with a visual impairment.

Patients' Association, The, PO Box 935, Harrow, Middlesex HA1 3YJ (020 8423 9111; Helpline 0845 608 4455) www.patients-association.org.uk
Help and advice for patients. Leaflets and self-help directory available.

Pensions Advisory Service, The, 11 Belgrave Road, London SW1V 1RB (Helpline 0845 601 2923) www.pensionsadvisoryservice.org.uk
Free help to people with personal, occupational or state pension queries.

People First (Self-Advocacy), Hampton House, 20 Albert Embankment, London SE1 7TJ (020 7820 6655) www.peoplefirstltd.com *Run by and for people with learning difficulties. Support groups, training, consultancy and easy-read services.*

PHAB, Summit House, 50 Wandle Road, Croydon CR0 1DF (020 8667 9443) www.phab.org.uk *Clubs and holidays that bring disabled and able-bodied people together.*

Polio Fellowship, British, Eagle Office Centre, The Runway, South Ruislip, Middlesex HA4 6SE (Freephone 0800 018 0586) www.britishpolio.org.uk
Information and support for people with polio or Post Polio Syndrome.

Prader-Willi Syndrome Association (UK), 125a London Road, Derby DE1 2QQ (01332 365676 – 9.30am-3.30pm) www.pwsa.co.uk
Support and information for people with PWS, their parents and carers and the professionals who work with them.

Premenstrual Syndrome, National Association for (NAPS), 41 Old Road, East Peckham, Kent TN12 5AP (0870 777 2178) www.pms.org.uk

Primary Immunodeficiency Association, Alliance House, 12 Caxton Street, London SW1H 0QS (020 7976 7640) www.pia.org.uk
Information on treatment of primary immunodeficiencies and advice on benefits.

Psoriasis Association, Dick Coles House, 2 Queensbridge, Northampton NN4 7BF (01604 251620; Helpline 0845 676 0076) www.psoriasis-association.org.uk

Psychiatric Rehabilitation Association, Bayford Mews, Bayford Street, London E8 3SF (020 8985 3570; 24-hour answerphone 020 8985 3570) www.praservices.org.uk *Provides a range of services for people recovering from long-term mental health problems.*

Q

QUIT, 4th Floor, 211 Old Street, London EC1V 9NR (020 7251 1551; Quitline 0800 002200 – Mon-Sun 9am-9pm) www.quit.org.uk *Help for those wanting to, or those helping someone else to, quit smoking.*

R

RADAR (Royal Association for Disability and Rehabilitation), 12 City Forum, 250 City Road, London EC1V 8AF (020 7250 3222; Textphone 020 7250 4119) www.radar.org.uk
Campaigning organisation working to fast-track the views of disabled people to Westminster and Whitehall.

Raynaud's and Scleroderma Association, 112 Crewe Road, Alsager, Cheshire ST7 2JA (01270 872776) www.raynauds.org.uk *Support, advice, newsletters, publications.*

Reach, National Co-ordinator, PO Box 54, Helston TR13 8WD (0845 130 6225) www.reach.org.uk
Advice and information for children with hand or arm deficiency.

Real Life Options, Church Hill House, 29 Mill Hill, Pontefract, West Yorkshire WF8 4HY (01977 781800) www.reallifeoptions.org *Care homes, supported living, outreach and short breaks for people with severe learning disabilities.*

Refugee Action, The Old Fire Station, 150 Waterloo Road, London SE1 8SB (020 7654 7700) www.refugee-action.org.uk

Refugee and Migrant Justice, Nelson House, 153-157 Commercial Road, London E1 2DA (020 7780 3200; Detention lines 0800 592398 and 020 7780 3333 – Mon, Wed, Fri 10.30am-1pm & 2-4.30pm) www.refugee-migrant-justice.org.uk

REMAP, Susan Iwanek, CEO, D9 Chaucer Business Park, Kemsing, Sevenoaks, Kent TN15 6YU (0845 130 0456) www.remap.org.uk *Makes or adapts aids not commercially available at no charge to disabled people.*

Remploy Ltd, Stonecourt, Siskin Drive, Coventry CV3 4FJ (0845 601 5878; Textphone 0845 600 9228) www.remploy.co.uk *The UK's leading provider of employment services for disabled people.*

Restricted Growth Association, PO Box 1024, Peterborough PE1 9GX (01733 759458) www.restrictedgrowth.co.uk *Information and support for those affected by restricted growth conditions.*

Rethink, 89 Albert Embankment, Vauxhall, London SE1 7TP (0845 456 0455; Advice line 020 840 3188 – Mon, Wed & Fri 10am-3pm; Tues & Thur 10am-1pm) www.rethink.org *Services, information and support groups for people affected by severe mental illness. Free information packs available.*

Retinitis Pigmentosa Society, British (RP Fighting Blindness), PO Box 350, Buckingham MK18 1GZ (01280 821334; Helpline 0845 123 2354) www.brps.org.uk

Rett Syndrome Association UK, Langham House West, Mill Street, Luton LU1 2NA (01582 798910; Family and carer support line 01582 798911) www.rettsyndrome.org.uk *Information, advice and support for parents, carers, siblings and professionals involved with a child or adult with Rett Syndrome.*

Rheumatoid Arthritis Society, National, Unit B4, Westacott Business Park, Westacott Way, Littlewick Green, Maidenhead, SL6 3RT (0845 458 3969; Helpline 0800 298 7650) www.rheumatoid.org.uk *Support, information and advocacy for people with rheumatoid arthritis and their families.*

Ricability, 30 Angel Gate, City Road, London EC1V 2PT (020 7427 2460; Textphone 020 7247 2469) www.ricability.org.uk; www.ricability-digitaltv.org.uk *Consumer research charity providing information for people with disabilities.*

Riding for the Disabled Association (RDA), 1A Tournament Court, Edgehill Drive, Warwick CV34 6LG (0845 658 1082) www.rda.org.uk

RNIB National Library Service, Far Cromwell Road, Bredbury, Stockport, Cheshire SK6 2SG (0161 355 2000)
Books and information in Braille, Moon books, giant print, online reference material, Braille sheet music, themed booklists and magazine.

RNID, 19-23 Featherstone Street, London EC1Y 8SL (020 7296 8000; Freephone information line 0808 808 0123; Freephone text information line 0808 808 9000) www.rnid.org.uk
Represents deaf and hard-of-hearing people. Offers a range of services and information on all aspects of deafness, hearing loss and tinnitus.

RoadPeace, G4b Shakespeare Business Centre, 245a Coldharbour Lane, London SW9 8RR (020 7733 1603; Helpline 0845 450 0355 – Mon-Sat 9am-9pm) www.roadpeace.org *The UK charity for those affected by road crashes. Provides information, support and advocacy for the bereaved and injured and their families.*

Royal Air Forces Association, 117½ Loughborough Road, Leicester LE4 5ND (0116 266 5224) www.rafa.org.uk
Welfare support to serving and former RAF personnel and dependants.

Royal National Institute of the Blind (RNIB) – *see Blind, Royal National Institute of the*

S

St Dunstan's for Blind ex-Service Men and Women, 12-14 Harcourt Street, London W1H 4HD (020 7723 5021) www.st-dunstans.org.uk
Training and support for blind ex-Service men and women to help them regain independence.

St Loye's Foundation for Training Disabled People for Employment, Brittany House, New North Road, Exeter EX4 4EP (01392 255428) www.stloyes.org.uk *Residential assessment, vocational training and employment placement.*

SANE, 1st Floor, Cityside House, 40 Adler Street, London E1 1EE (020 7375 1002; SANEline 0845 767 8000 – Mon-Sun 6-11pm) www.sane.org.uk *Helpline information and support for anyone affected by mental health problems. Campaigns to improve services and funds research.*

Scope, PO Box 833, Milton Keynes, Buckinghamshire MK12 5NY (Scope Response 0808 800 3333) www.scope.org.uk *National charity focusing on cerebral palsy. The helpline is the first point of contact for information and advice.*

Sense, The National Deafblind & Rubella Association, 101 Pentonville Road, London N1 9LG (0845 127 0060; Textphone 0845 127 0062) www.sense.org.uk

Sequal Trust, The, 3 Ploughmans Corner, Wharf Road, Ellesmere, Shropshire SY12 0EJ (01691 624222) www.thesequaltrust.org.uk *Fundraising for communication aids for people of all ages with speech/movement and/or learning difficulties.*

Sexuality Support Team (SST) *(formerly CONSENT)*, Woodside Road, Abbots Langley, Hertfordshire WD5 0HT (01923 670796) www.hpt.nhs.uk *Direct work and training on sexuality issues for staff, carers and people with mental health conditions or learning disabilities.*

Shaw Trust, Fox Talbot House, Greenways Business Park, Bellinger Close, Chippenham, Wiltshire SN15 1BN (01225 716350; Minicom 08457 697288) www.shaw-trust.org.uk *Support, training and employment opportunities for people disadvantaged in the labour market through disability, ill health or social circumstances.*

Shelter (National Campaign for Homeless People), 88 Old Street, London EC1V 9HU (0844 515 2000; Freephone helpline 0808 800 4444 – 8am to 8pm 365 days a year) www.shelter.org.uk *Information, advice and advocacy to homeless and badly housed people.*

Sickle Cell Society, 54 Station Road, London NW10 4UA (020 8961 7795) www.sicklecellsociety.org *Information, counselling and care for those with sickle cell disorders and their families.*

Skill – National Bureau for Students with Disabilities, Unit 3, Floor 3, Radisson Court, 219 Long Lane, London SE1 4PR (Voice/Textphone 020 7450 0620; Helpline: Voice 0800 328 5050 – Tues 11.30am-1.30pm, Thur 1.30-3.30pm; Textphone 0800 068 2422) www.skill.org.uk *Promotes opportunities in post-16 employment, education and training for young people and adults with any kind of impairment.*

Skin Foundation, British, 4 Fitzroy Square, London W1T 5HQ (020 7391 6341) www.britishskinfoundation.org.uk

Snowdon Award Scheme, The, Unit 18, Oakhurst Business Park, Southwater, Horsham, West Sussex RH13 9RT (01403 732899) www.snowdonawardscheme.org.uk *Grants to physically disabled/sensory impaired students to help with extra disability-related costs of further education or training.*

Social Workers, British Association of (BASW), 16 Kent Street, Birmingham B5 6RD (0121 622 3911) www.basw.org.uk *The largest professional association representing social work and social workers in the UK.*

Speakability, 1 Royal Street, London SE1 7LL (020 7261 9572; Helpline 0808 808 9572) www.speakability.org.uk *Information, advice and support for people with aphasia (breakdown of communication centres of the brain) resulting from head injury or stroke.*

Special Education Advice, Independent Panel for, 6 Carlow Mews, Woodbridge, Suffolk IP12 1EA (01394 384711; General educational advice line 0800 018 4016 – Mon-Thur 10am-4pm, Fri 10am-1pm; Tribunal appeal advice line – 0845 602 9579) www.ipsea.org.uk *Independent advice and support to parents of children with special educational needs.*

Spina Bifida – *see ASBAH*

Spinal Injuries Association, SIA House, 2 Trueman Place, Oldbrook, Milton Keynes MK6 2HH (0845 678 6633; Advice line 0800 980 0501) www.spinal.co.uk

Spinal Muscular Atrophy, Jennifer Trust for, Elta House, Birmingham Road, Stratford-upon-Avon, Warwickshire CV37 0AQ (01789 267520; Helpline 0800 975 3100) www.jtsma.org.uk *Information, advice and support for individuals and families affected by spinal muscular atrophy.*

SSAFA Forces Help, Special Needs and Disability Advisor, 19 Queen Elizabeth Street, London SE1 2LP (020 7403 8783; Special needs and disability adviser 020 7463 9234, 0845 130 0975) www.ssafa.org.uk

Stammering Association, The British, 15 Old Ford Road, London E2 9PJ (020 8983 1003; Helpline 0845 603 2001) www.stammering.org *Provides details of specialist speech and language therapy services, courses and self-help groups.*

Stroke Association, The, Stroke House, 240 City Road, London EC1V 2PR (020 7566 0300; National stroke helpline 0845 303 3100) www.stroke.org.uk *Works to ensure people affected by stroke get the help they need and to reduce the incidence of strokes.*

Strokes, Different, 9 Canon Harnett Court, Wolverton Mill, Milton Keynes MK12 5NF (0845 130 7172) www.differentstrokes.co.uk *Support for younger stroke survivors.*

Students, National Union of, 2nd Floor Centro 3, 19 Mandela Street, London NW1 0DU (0871 221 8221) www.nusonline.co.uk

T

Terrence Higgins Trust, 314-320 Gray's Inn Road, London WC1X 8DP (020 7812 1600; Helpline 0845 1221 200 – Mon-Fri 10am-10pm, Sat & Sun 12-6pm) www.tht.org.uk *Information, support and advice for people with HIV or with concerns about sexual health.*

Thalassaemia Society, UK, 19 The Broadway, Southgate, London N14 6PH (020 8882 0011) www.ukts.org *Education, information, counselling. Publicity available in several languages.*

Thalidomide Society, The, Contact by e-mail or website only. (info@thalsoc.demon.co.uk; www.thalidomidesociety.co.uk) *Support and information for people with thalidomide and similar impairments.*

Thrive, Geoffrey Udall Centre, Beech Hill, Reading RG7 2AT (0118 988 5688) www.thrive.org.uk; www.carryongardening.org.uk *National charity that researches, educates and promotes the use and advantages of gardening for disabled people.*

Tinnitus Association, British, Ground Floor, Unit 5, Acorn Business Park, Woodseats Close, Sheffield S8 0TB (0114 250 9922; Freephone 0800 018 0527) www.tinnitus.org.uk *Provides information, promotes self-help, raises awareness and funds research.*

Together Working for Wellbeing, 12 Old Street, London EC1V 9BE (020 7780 7300) www.together-uk.org *Supports people with mental distress to help them get what they want from life and to feel happier.*

Tracheo-Oesophageal Fistula Support (TOFS), St George's Centre, 91 Victoria Road, Netherfield, Nottingham NG4 2NN (0115 961 3092) www.tofs.org.uk *Supports families of children who are born unable to swallow.*

Transition Information Network, c/o Council for Disabled Children, 8 Wakley Street, London EC1V 7QE (to register for information call 020 7843 6006) www.transitioninfonetwork.org.uk *Information for parents, carers, young disabled people and professionals working with them in transition to adulthood.*

Tuberous Sclerosis Association, PO Box 12979, Barnt Green, Birmingham B45 5AN (0121 445 6970) www.tuberous-sclerosis.org *Provides support and information and promotes research.*

Turning Point, Standon House, 21 Mansell Street, London E1 8AA (020 7481 7600) www.turning-point.co.uk *Help with alcohol, drugs, mental health and learning disabilities.*

Typetalk, John Wood House, Glacier Building, Harrington Road, Brunswick Business Park, Liverpool L3 4DF (0151 709 9494; Helpline: Voice 0800 7311888, Textphone 18001 0800 7311 888; Emergency operator (text only) 18000) www.typetalk.org *Telephone relay service that enables deaf, deafblind and speech impaired people to use the public telephone network. To make a text to voice call, dial 18001 followed by the full national, international or mobile telephone number. To make a voice to text call, use prefix 18002.*

U

Urostomy Association, Central Office, 18 Foxglove Avenue, Uttoxeter, Staffordshire ST14 8UN (01889 563191; 08452 412159) www.uagbi.org *Support for people who are about to have, or who have had, surgery for urinary diversion of any kind.*

V

Vision Homes Association, Trigate, 210-222 Hagley Road West, Oldbury, West Midlands B68 0NP (0121 434 4644) www.visionhomes.org.uk *24-hour support for people with visual impairments and additional disabilities.*

Vitalise, 12 City Forum, 250 City Road, London EC1V 8AF (0845 345 1972) www.vitalise.org.uk *Provides breaks for disabled adults, children and carers and*

holidays for visually impaired people.
Voluntary Organisations, National Council for (NCVO), Regent's Wharf, 8 All Saints' Street, London N1 9RL (020 7713 6161; Helpline 0800 2798 798; Helpline Textphone 0800 018 8111) www.ncvo-vol.org.uk *The umbrella body for the voluntary and community sector in England.*

W

Williams Syndrome Foundation, 161 High Street, Tonbridge, Kent TN9 1BX (01732 365152) www.williams-syndrome.org.uk
Wireless for the Blind Fund, British, 10 Albion Place, Maidstone, Kent ME14 5DZ (01622 751725) www.blind.org.uk *Provides radios/cassette/CD players for registered blind and registered partially sighted people.*
Women, Rights of, 52-54 Featherstone Street, London EC1Y 8RT (020 7251 6575; Textphone 020 7490 2562; Legal advice line 020 7251 6577 – Tue, Wed, Thur 2-4pm & 7-9pm, Fri 12-2pm; Sexual violence legal advice 020 7251 8887 – Mon 11am-1pm, Tues 10am-12pm) www.rightsofwomen.org.uk *Free confidential legal advice to women living in England and Wales.*
Women's Aid Federation of England, PO Box 391, Bristol BS99 7WS (0117 944 4411; Freephone 24-hour domestic violence helpline 0808 200 0247) www.womensaid.org.uk *Emotional and practical support and refuge information for women and children experiencing domestic violence.*
Women's Alcohol Service, 1st Floor, 3-5 Cynthia Street, London N1 9JF (020 7278 8214) www.arp-uk.org *Individual and group sessions, complementary therapies, referral to detox, residential rehabilitation, other agencies. No wheelchair access.*
WRVS, Garden House, Milton Hill, Steventon, Abingdon, Oxfordshire OX13 6AD (01235 442900) www.wrvs.org.uk *Practical support for older people through its 55,000 volunteers. Some support may require referrals from social services.*

London-wide

Artsline, www.artsline.org.uk *Information for disabled people on access to London's arts and entertainment venues, and tourist attractions.*
Attitude is Everything, 54 Chalton Street, London NW1 1HS (Voice and Textphone 020 7383 7979) www.attitudeiseverything.org.uk *Improves deaf and disabled people's access to live music.*
Black Disabled People's Association, PO Box 51866, London NW2 9BL (020 8452 7122) *Independent living and research on/for black disabled people.*
Blind, Metropolitan Society for the, Lantern House, 102 Bermondsey Street, London SE1 3UB (020 7403 6184) www.msb.gb.com *Home visiting, audio equipment, small grants, advice and help obtaining welfare benefits.*
Children with Cerebral Palsy, The London Centre for, Conductive Education Centre, 54 Muswell Hill, London N10 3ST (020 8444 7242) www.cplondon.org.uk *Conductive education, advice and support for children under 11 with cerebral palsy.*
DIAL, Local groups and members, *see pages 277-278*
Dimbleby Cancer Care, 2nd Floor, Gassiott House, St Thomas' Hospital, Lambeth Palace Road, London SE1 7EH (020 7188 5918) *Drop-in information, psychological support and complementary therapies at Guy's and St Thomas' Hospitals. Mon-Fri 9.30-4.*
Free Representation Unit (FRU), 6th Floor, 289-293 High Holborn, London WC1V 7HZ (020 7611 9555) www.freerepresentationunit.org.uk *Representation at tribunals in London and the south-east for employment, social security, criminal injuries compensation and immigrants' bail applications. Contact via a Citizens Advice Bureau, law centre or other subscribing agency.*
Law centres, *see pages 279-280*
Kith and Kids, The Irish Centre, Pretoria Road, London N17 8DX (020 8801 7432) www.kithandkids.org.uk *Runs holidays, weekends, friendship, family support and advocacy projects.*
Naz Project London, Palingswick House, 241 King Street, London W6 9LP (020 8741 1879) www.naz.org.uk *HIV, AIDS and sexual health agency for black and minority ethnic communities.*
Shape London, Deane House Studios, 27 Greenwood Place, London NW5 1LB (0845 521 3457; Minicom 020 7424 7368) www.shapearts.org.uk *Disability arts organisation, festivals, Shape Tickets, deaf arts and Open the Door Training.*
Transport for All, 336 Brixton Road, London SW9 7AA (020 7737 2339) www.transportforall.com *Information on accessible travel and assistance for disabled and elderly people.*
Women's Therapy Centre, 10 Manor Gardens, London N7 6JS (Admin 020 7263 7860; Appointments and referrals 020 7263 6200 – Mon, Tues & Thur 2-4pm, Wed 2.30-4.30pm; Minicom 020 7272 8258) www.womenstherapycentre.co.uk *Individual and group psychotherapy for women of 18 and over.*

Northern Ireland

Age Concern, Northern Ireland, 3 Lower Crescent, Belfast BT7 1NR (028 9024 5729; Advice line 028 9032 5055 – Mon-Fri 10am-12pm & 2-4pm) www.ageconcernni.org. *Campaigning, community development and service provision to improve older people's quality of life and promote their rights.*
Alzheimer's Society, NI Regional Office, Unit 4, Balmoral Business Park, Boucher Crescent, Belfast BT12 6HU (028 9066 4100) www.alzheimers.org.uk
Arthritis Care Northern Ireland, Unit 4, McClune Building, 1 Shore Road, Belfast BT15 3PG (028 9448 9078 2940; Helpline 0808 800 4050) www.arthritiscare.org.uk *Services and support for people with arthritis, their families and those who work with them.*
ASBAH, NI Region, PO Box 132, Cushendall, Belfast BT44 0WA (Helpline 0845 450 7755) www.asbah.org.uk
Blind People, Royal National Institute of, Northern Ireland, 40 Linenhall Street, Belfast BT2 8BA (028 9032 9373; National helpline 0845 766 9999) www.rnib.org.uk
Carers Northern Ireland, 58 Howard Street, Belfast BT1 6PJ (028 9043 9843) www.carersni.org *Free information for carers on all aspects of caring.*
Cedar Foundation, The, Malcolm Sinclair House, 31 Ulsterville Avenue, Belfast BT9 7AS (028 9066 6188) www.cedar-foundation.org *Training, accommodation and support for adults and children with physical disabilities.*
Chest, Heart and Stroke Northern Ireland, 21 Dublin Road, Belfast BT2 7HB (028 9032 0184; Helpline 0845 769 7299) www.nichsa.com *Training and care for families and professionals.*
Disability Action, Portside Business Park, 189 Airport Road West, Belfast BT3 9ED (028 9029 7880; Textphone 028 9029 7882) www.disabilityaction.org *Information, employment and training support, driving assessments and lessons.*
Down's Syndrome Association Northern Ireland, Unit 2, Marlborough House, 348 Lisburn Road, Belfast BT9 6GH (028 9066 5260) www.downs-syndrome.org.uk *Advice and support to people with Down's syndrome.*
Educational Guidance Services for Adults (EGSA), 4th Floor, 40 Linenhall Street, Belfast BT2 8BA (028 9024 4274; Learners line 0845 602 6632) www.connect2learn.org.uk *Connecting adults with learning. Services across Northern Ireland.*
Extra Care for Elderly People, 11 Wellington Park, Belfast BT9 6DJ (028 9068 3273) www.extra-care.org *Domiciliary care, carer relief programmes and training.*
Families in Contact, c/o Mrs Leigh-Ann McClean, 53 Breda Road, Belfast BT8 7BW (028 9188 2723) *Families with disabled children/young people supporting each other.*
Fibromyalgia Support (NI), PO Box 293, Bangor BT20 9AQ (Helpline 0844 826 9024 – Mon-Fri 10.30am-4pm) www.fmsni.org.uk *Support and information on fibromyalgia.*
Help the Aged, Ascot House, Shaftesbury Square, Belfast BT2 7DB (028 9023 0666; Senior line 0808 808 7575) www.helptheaged.org.uk *Advice, advocacy and information on a wide range of issues, including benefits and community and residential care.*
Law centres, *see pages 279-280*
Mencap in Northern Ireland, Segal House, 4 Annadale Avenue, Belfast BT7 3JH (028 9069 1351; Information service 0845 7636 227) www.mencap.org.uk *Information, support, other services and campaigning for children and adults with learning disabilities.*
Mental Health, Northern Ireland Association for, 80 University Street,

Belfast BT7 1HE (028 9032 8474) www.niamh.co.uk
Multiple Sclerosis Society NI, The Resource Centre, 34 Annadale Avenue, Belfast BT7 3JJ (028 9080 2802) www.mssocietyni.co.uk
NUS-USI (National Union of Students (UK) Union of Students in Ireland), 2nd Floor, 42 Dublin Road, Belfast BT2 7HN (028 9024 4641) www.nistudents.org
Polio Fellowship, Northern Ireland, Mr Trevor Boyle, 2 Abbey Place, Holywood, Co Down BT18 9PP (028 9042 1151)
Shelter, Northern Ireland, 58 Howard Street, Belfast BT1 6PJ (028 9024 7752) www.shelterni.org.uk *Advice and information on housing and homelessness. Campaigns on homelessness issues.*
Women's Aid Federation Northern Ireland, 129 University Street, Belfast BT7 1HP (028 9024 9041; 24-hour Domestic violence helpline 0800 917 1414; Textphone and language line available) www.womensaidni.org

Scotland

Age Concern and Help the Aged in Scotland, Causewayside House, 160 Causewayside, Edinburgh EH9 1PR (0845 833 0200); Scottish helpline for older people 0845 125 9732) www.ageconcernscotland.org.uk *Factsheets on older people's issues.*
Alcohol Focus Scotland, 2nd Floor, 166 Buchanan Street, Glasgow G1 2LW (0141 572 6700) www.alcohol-focus-scotland.org.uk *Information and training on alcohol issues. Campaigns to influence alcohol policy.*
Alzheimer Scotland, 22 Drumsheugh Gardens, Edinburgh EH3 7RN (0131 243 1453; 24-hr Freephone helpline 0808 808 3000) www.alzscot.org *Information and support for people with dementia and their carers.*
Asbestos, Clydeside Action on, 245 High Street, Glasgow G4 0QR (0141 552 8852) *Practical support for those with an asbestos-related disease.*
Autism, The Scottish Society for, Hilton House, Alloa Business Park, Whins Road, Alloa FK10 3SA (01259 720044) www.autism-in-soctland.org.uk *Services in Scotland for people of all ages coping with autism.*
Capability Scotland, Westerlea, 11 Ellersly Road, Edinburgh EH12 6HY (0131 313 5510) www.capability-scotland.org.uk *Wide range of services and support for disabled children and adults.*
Care and Repair Forum Scotland, 135 Buchanan Street, Suite 2.5, Glasgow G1 2JA (0141 221 9879) www.careandrepairscotland.co.uk
Chest, Heart and Stroke Scotland, 65 North Castle Street, Edinburgh EH2 3LT (0131 225 6963; Advice line 0845 077 6000 – Mon-Fri 9.30am-12.30pm & 1.30-4pm) www.chss.org.uk
Child Poverty Action Group (CPAG) in Scotland, Unit 9, Ladywell Centre, 94 Duke Street, Glasgow G4 0UW (0141 552 3303; Advice line for advisers in Scotland 0141 552 0552 – Mon-Thur 10am-noon) www.cpag.org.uk *Training and advice for advisers on benefits and tax credits.*
Children's Fund, Challenger, Barstow & Millar, Midlothian Innovation Centre, Pentlandfield, Roslin, Midlothian EH25 9RE (0131 440 9030) www.ccfscotland.org *Grants for physically disabled children (under 18, living in Scotland) for anything not provided through statutory sources.*
Combat Stress, Hollybush House, Hollybush, by Ayr KA6 7EA (01292 561350) www.combatstress.org.uk *Specialist care for ex-service men and women with service-related psychological injuries.*
Crossroads Caring Scotland, 24 George Square, Glasgow G2 1EG (0141 226 3793; Carers information and support line 0141 353 6504 available in Glasgow area) www.crossroads-scotland.co.uk *Provides respite relief for carers.*
Deafblind Scotland, 21 Alexandra Avenue, Lenzie, Glasgow G66 5BG (Voice and Textphone 0141 777 6111; Helpline 0800 132320) www.deafblindscotland.org.uk *Information, advice, support and Guide Communicator Service for members (depending on local authority funding).*
Deafness, Scottish Council on, Central Chambers Suite 62, 93 Hope Street, Glasgow G2 6LD (0141 248 2474; Textphone 0141 248 2477) www.scod.org.uk
DIAL, Local groups and members, *see pages 277-278*
Disability Sport, Scottish, Caledonia House, South Gyle, Edinburgh EH12 9DQ (0131 317 1130) www.scottishdisabilitysport.com *Developing sport in Scotland for people of all ages and abilities with a physical, sensory or learning disability.*
Down's Syndrome Scotland, 158-160 Balgreen Road, Edinburgh EH11 3AU (0131 313 4225) www.dsscotland.org.uk
Dyslexia Scotland, Stirling Business Centre, Wellgreen, Stirling FK8 2DZ (Helpline 0844 800 8484) www.dyslexiascotland.org.uk *Represents the needs and interests of dyslexic people in Scotland.*
Energy Action Scotland, Suite 4a, Ingram House, 227 Ingram Street, Glasgow G1 1DA (0141 226 3064) www.eas.org.uk *Promotes affordable warmth and an end to fuel poverty.*
Epilepsy Scotland, 48 Govan Road, Glasgow G51 1JL (0141 427 4911; Freephone helpline 0808 800 2200 – Mon-Fri 10am-4pm, Thur 10am-6pm) www.epilepsyscotland.org.uk
Equality and Human Rights Commission Helpline Scotland 0845 604 5510; Textphone 0845 604 5520; www.equalityhumanrights.com
Help the Aged – *see Age Concern*
Huntington's Association, Scottish, St James Business Centre, Linwood Road, Paisley PA3 3AT (0141 848 0308) www.hdscotland.org
Law centres, *see pages 279-280*
Law Society of Scotland, 26 Drumsheugh Gardens, Edinburgh EH3 7YR (0131 226 7411) www.lawscot.org.uk *Provides details of Scottish solicitors.*
Lead Scotland – Linking Education and Disability, Princes House, 5 Shandwick Place, Edinburgh EH2 4RG (0131 228 9441) www.lead.org.uk *Supports disabled adults (16+) and carers to access learning.*
Meningitis Trust, Scotland Office, Centrum Offices, 38 Queen Street, Glasgow G1 3DX (0845 120 4883; 24-hr nurse-led helpline 0800 028 1828) www.meningitis-trust.org *Information and support for those affected by meningitis.*
Mental Health Foundation, 5th Floor, Merchants House, 30 George Square, Glasgow G2 1EG (0141 572 0125) www.mentalhealth.org.uk *Campaign organisation. Also provides information for people with mental health problems. (Not a drop-in office.)*
Mental Welfare Commission for Scotland, K Floor, Argyle House, 3 Lady Lawson Street, Edinburgh EH3 9SH (Freephone advice line 0800 389 6809) www.mwcscot.org.uk *Independent organisation that aims to safeguard the rights of people with a mental illness or learning disability.*
MND Scotland, 76 Firhill Road, Glasgow G20 7BA (0141 945 1077) www.mndscotland.org.uk *Care and support for people with motor neurone disease.*
Multiple Sclerosis Society Scotland, National Office, Ratho Park, 88 Glasgow Road, Ratho Station, Newbridge EH28 8PP (0131 335 4050; National helpline 0808 800 8000) www.mssocietyscotland.org.uk
National Union of Students Scotland, 29 Forth Street, Edinburgh EH1 3LE (0131 556 6598) www.nus.org.uk/scotland
Poppyscotland (The Earl Haig Fund Scotland), New Haig House, Logie Green Road, Edinburgh EH7 4HR (0131 557 2782) www.poppyscotland.org.uk *Support for disabled ex-Service men, women and their dependants through financial assistance, pensions claims and appeals advice service and supported employment.*
Refugee Council, Scottish, 5 Cadogan Square (170 Blythswood Court) Glasgow G2 7PH (0141 248 9799; Helpline 0800 085 6087 – Mon, Tues, Thur, Fri 9.30am-1pm & 2-4pm; Wed 1-4pm) www.scottishrefugeecouncil.org.uk *Advice, information and assistance to asylum seekers and refugees in Scotland.*
SAMH, Cumbrae House, 15 Carlton Court, Glasgow G5 9JP (0141 568 7000) www.samh.org.uk *Mental health charity working to support people who experience mental health problems, homelessness, additions and other forms of social exclusion.*
Sense Scotland, TouchBase, 43 Middlesex Street, Glasgow G41 1EE (0141 429 0294) www.sensescotland.org.uk *Works with children and adults needing communication support due to deafblindness, sensory impairment, learning or physical disability.*
Shelter Scotland, 4th Floor, Scotiabank House, 6 South Charlotte Street,

Edinburgh EH2 4AW (Free housing advice line 0808 800 4444) www.shelter.org.uk

Sign Language Interpreters, Scottish Association of, Baltic Chambers Suites 317-319, 50 Wellington Street, Glasgow G2 6HJ (0141 202 0791; Textphone 0141 202 0790) www.sasli.org.uk *Holds register of interpreters for Scotland, and provides training.*

Spina Bifida Association, Scottish, The Dan Young Building, 6 Craighalbert Way, Cumbernauld G68 0LS (01236 794500; Family support service helpline 0845 911 1112) www.ssba.org.uk *For people with spina bifida, hydrocephalus and allied disorders, their carers and families.*

Spinal Injuries Scotland, Festival Business Centre, 150 Brand Street, Govan, Glasgow G51 1DH (0141 427 7686; Helpline 0800 0132 305) www.sisonline.org *Supports spinal cord injured people, their relatives, friends and professionals involved in care and rehabilitation of the injury.*

Terrence Higgins Trust Scotland, Top Floor, 134 Douglas Street, Glasgow G2 4HF (0141 332 3838) and Grampian Service, 11 Waverley Place, Aberdeen AB10 1XH (0845 241 2151) www.tht.org.uk *Practical and emotional support for people affected by HIV/AIDS.*

Thistle Foundation, The, Niddrie Mains Road, Edinburgh EH16 4EA (0131 661 3366) www.thistle.org.uk *Support for disabled people and their families. Works for inclusion in Scotland.*

Turning Point Scotland, 54 Govan Road, Glasgow G51 1JL (0141 427 8200) www.turningpointscotland.com *Support for people with drugs, alcohol and mental health problems, and learning disabilities.*

Update, Hays Community Business Centre, 4 Hay Avenue, Edinburgh EH16 4AQ (0131 669 1600) www.update.org.uk *Scotland's national disability information service.*

Women's Aid, Scottish, 2nd Floor, 132 Rose Street, Edinburgh EH2 3JD (0131 226 6606; 24-hr Scottish domestic abuse helpline 0800 027 1234) www.scottishwomensaid.org.uk

Wales

Agoriad Cyf, Porth Penrhyn, Bangor, Gwynedd LL57 4HN (01248 361392); Ground floor office, Swyddfeydd NFU, Dolgellau, Gwynedd LL40 1DH (01341 421440); 42 High Street, Pwllheli, Gwynedd LL53 5RT (01758 701354) www.agoriad.org.uk *Training and support for disabled and disadvantaged people in north Wales to help them into employment.*

ASBAH in Wales, 4 Llys y Fedwen, Parc Menai, Bangor, Gwynedd LL57 4BL (01248 671345; Helpline 0845 450 7755) www.asbah.org *Services to those with spina bifida and/or hydrocephalus.*

Care and Repair Cymru, Norbury House, Norbury Road, Fairwater, Cardiff CF5 3AS (029 2057 6286) www.careandrepair.org.uk *Helps older and disabled people to remain independent in their own homes.*

DIAL, Local groups and members, *see pages 277-278*

Disability Arts Cymru, Sbectrwm, Bwlch Road, Fairwater, Cardiff CF5 3EF (Voice and Textphone 029 2055 1040) www.dacymru.com *Works with individuals and organisations to celebrate disabled and deaf people's arts and culture, and develop equality across all artforms.*

Disability Wales, Bridge House, Caerphilly Business Park, Van Road, Caerphilly CF83 3GW (029 2088 7325) www.disabilitywales.org *Association of disability groups that strives to achieve rights, equality and independence for all disabled people.*

Drugaid, St Fagan's House, St Fagan's Street, Caerphilly CF83 1FZ (029 2086 8675; 0870 060 0310); MIDAS, 2nd Floor Oldway House, Castle Street, Merthyr Tydfil CF47 8UX (01685 721991) www.drugaidcymru.com *Counselling, information and support for drug and alcohol users.*

Equality and Human Rights Commission Helpline Wales 0845 604 8810; Textphone 0845 604 8820; www.equalityhumanrights.com

Help the Aged in Wales, 12 Cathedral Rd, Cardiff CF11 9LJ (029 2034 6550) www.helptheaged.org.uk *Advice and information for older people and their carers about benefits and community and residential care. Campaigns for older people's rights in Wales.*

Law centres, *see pages 279-280*

MDF the BiPolar Organisation Cymru, 22-29 Mill Street, Newport NP20 5HA (01633 244244; Helpline 08456 340 080) www.mdfwales.org.uk *User-led charity working to enable people with bi-polar disorder (manic depression) to take control of their lives.*

Mencap Cymru, 31 Lambourne Crescent, Cardiff Business Park, Llanishen, Cardiff CF14 5GF (029 2074 7588; Wales learning disability helpline 0808 8000 300) www.mencap.org.uk/cymru *Support and information on a wide range of learning disability issues.*

National Union of Students, Wales, 13 Lambourne Crescent, Cardiff Business Park, Llanishen, Cardiff CF14 5GF (029 2068 0070) www.nus.org.uk/wales

Scope Cymru, The Wharf, Schooner Way, Cardiff CF10 4EU (029 2046 1703; Textphone 029 2049 5187; Scope Cymru Response 0808 800 3333 – Mon-Fri 9am-7pm, Sat 10am-2pm) www.scope.org.uk *Campaigns to achieve full equality for disabled people.*

Shelter Cymru, 25 Walter Road, Swansea SA1 5NN (01792 469400; Shelterline 0808 800 4444) www.sheltercymru.org.uk *Housing advice surgeries in all local authority areas.*

Shopmobility Newport, 193 Upper Dock Street, Newport, Gwent NP20 1DB (01633 673845) *Provides electrically powered wheelchairs, scooters and manual wheelchairs. Free loan of manually powered wheelchairs within city centre.*

Wales Council for the Blind, 3rd Floor, Shand House, 20 Newport Road, Cardiff CF24 0DB (029 2047 3954) www.wcb-ccd.org.uk

Wales Council for Deaf People, Glenview House, Courthouse Street, Pontypridd CF37 1JY (01443 485687; Textphone 01443 485686) www.wcdeaf.org.uk

DIAL groups and members

There are around 80 DIAL member organisations in the UK. Those listed below offer advice or case work in welfare benefits. Listings start with the catchment area for the organisation. For details of DIAL member organisations offering benefits information or help with any other issue, contact DIAL UK on 01302 310123 or visit www.dial.uk.org.

England

Barnsley Metropolitan District – DIAL Barnsley, 9 Doncaster Road, Barnsley, South Yorkshire S70 1TH (01226 240273 – Mon-Thur 9am-5pm, Fri 9am-2pm)

Bath and North East Somerset – SWAN Advice Network, Leigh House, 1 Wells Hill, Radstock BA3 3RN (01761 437176 – 10am-12pm) www.swan.btik.com *Also provides a volunteer transport system in Bath and North East Somerset.*

Bedfordshire and Luton – Disability Resource Centre (Dunstable), Poynters House, Poynters Road, Dunstable, Bedfordshire LU5 4TP (01582 470900 – 10am-12.30pm & 1.30-4pm) www.drcbeds.co.uk

Blackpool, Wyre and Fylde – Disability Information & Support (Blackpool, Wyre & Fylde), Whitegate Resource Centre, 259 Whitegate Drive, Blackpool, Lancashire FY3 9JL (01253 472202; 01253 472203; Fax 01253 476450 – 10am-4pm)

Blyth Valley – Blyth Valley Disabled Forum, The Eric Tollhurst Centre, 3-13 Quay Road, Blyth, Northumberland NE24 2AS (01670 364657)

Bradford Metropolitan District – Disability Advice Bradford, 103 Dockfield Road, Shipley, West Yorkshire BD17 7AR (01274 594173 – Mon-Fri 9.30am-3.15pm) www.disabilityadvice.org.uk

Brighton and Hove – Disability Advice Centre (Brighton & Hove), 6 Hove Manor, Hove Street, Hove, East Sussex BN3 2DF (01273 203016 – 10am-4pm) www.bhfederation.org.uk

Bristol – Disability Information and Advice Service, WECIL, The Vassall Centre, Gill Avenue, Fishponds, Bristol BS16 2QQ (0117 983 2828 – Tue, Wed, Thur 10am-1pm; Fax 0117 983 6765)

Calderdale – Calderdale DART, Harrison House, 10 Harrison Road, Halifax, West Yorkshire HX1 2AF (01422 346040 – Mon, Tues, Thur 10am-4pm)

Cambridgeshire (not Huntingdonshire) – Disability Cambridgeshire, 1 Orwell Furlong, Cowley Road, Cambridge, Cambridgeshire CB4 0WY (01223 569600 – 10am-2.30pm & 1.30-4pm) www.disability-cambridgeshire.org.uk

Cheshire & North Flintshire – DIAL House Chester, DIAL House, Hamilton Place, Chester, Cheshire CH1 2BH (01244 345655 – 10am-4pm) www.dialhousechester.org.uk

Coventry and Warwickshire – Council of Disabled People Warwickshire and Coventry, Room 6, Unit 15, Koco Building, Arches Industrial Estate, Spon End, Coventry CV1 3JQ (Tel, Minicom and Fax 02476 712984) www.cdp.org.uk

Derby – Disability Direct, 227 Normanton Road, Derby, Derbyshire DE23 6UT (01332 299449) www.disabilitydirect.com

Doncaster – DIAL Doncaster, Unit 9, Shaw Wood Business Park, Shaw Wood Way, Doncaster, South Yorkshire DN2 5TB (01302 327800 – Mon-Thur 9.30am-4pm, Fri 9.30am-3pm; Minicom 01302 768297) www.dialdoncaster.co.uk *Also offers wheelchair hire and holiday lodge hire.*

Dorset, New Forest, South Wiltshire, South Somerset – Disability Wessex, Ground Floor, 5 Stratfield Saye, 20-22 Wellington Road, Bournemouth BH8 8JN (01202 589999 – 10am-4pm) www.disabilitywessex.org.uk *Specialisations in direct payments and autistic spectrum disorders.*

Essex, Southend and Thurrock – Disability Essex (EPDA), Centre for Disability Studies, Rocheway, Rochford, Essex SS4 1DQ (0844 412 1771; Helpline 0844 412 1770 – Mon-Fri 10am-4pm; Access and equality consultancy 0800 197 5040) www.disabilityessex.org *Partners in Disability East information network. Provides accredited training in disability access auditing and equality. IT research with London Metropolitan University.*

Essex (South) – DIAL Basildon and South Essex, The Basildon Centre, St Martin's Square, Basildon, Essex SS14 1DL (0845 450 3001/3002 – 10am-4pm) www.dialbasildon.co.uk

Great Yarmouth borough – DIAL Great Yarmouth, 12a George Street, Great Yarmouth, Norfolk NR30 1HR (01493 856900 – 9am-4pm) www.dial-greatyarmouth.org.uk

Hampshire (South East) – DIAL Portsmouth, Frank Sorrell Centre, Prince Albert Road, Southsea, Hampshire PO4 9HR (023 9282 4853 – 10am-4pm)

Herefordshire – ABLE, The Warehouse, 16-20 Coningsby Street, Hereford, Herefordshire HR1 2DY (01432 277770) www.ablehereford.com

Hertfordshire – DISH (Disability Information Service Hertfordshire), PO Box 979, St Albans, Hertfordshire AL1 9JF (0800 181067 – 10am-4pm) www.dish.uk.net

Huntingdonshire – Disability Huntingdonshire, Pendrill Court, Papworth Everard, Cambridgeshire CB23 3UY (01480 830833 – Mon-Thur 9.30am-2.30pm) www.dish.org.uk

Ipswich – Ipswich Disabled Advice Bureau, 19 Tower Street, Ipswich, Suffolk IP1 3BE (01473 217313 – Tue-Fri 10am-2pm) www.ipswichdab.org.uk

Kent – DIAL Kent, 9a Gorrell Road, Whitstable, Kent CT5 1RN (01227 771155 – Mon-Thur 10am-2pm, Fri 10am-1pm) www.dialkent.org.uk

Kent (North West) – DIAL North West Kent, Northfleet Veterans Hall, The Hill, Northfleet, Kent DA11 9EU (01474 321761 – 11am-3pm) www.dialnwk.co.uk

Lancashire (West) – West Lancs Disability Helpline, Whelmar House, 2nd Floor, Southway, Skelmersdale, Lancashire WN8 6NN (0800 220676 – 24-hr answerphone) Mon, Tues, Thur 10am-4pm, Wed & Fri 10am-1pm. www.wldh.org.uk

Leeds Metropolitan District – DIAL Leeds, The Mary Thornton Suite, Armley Grange Drive, Leeds, West Yorkshire LS12 3QH (0113 214 3630 – Mon, Tue, Thur, Fri 10.30am-3.30pm)

Leicester, Leicestershire and Rutland – mosaic, 2 Richard III Road, Leicester, Leicestershire LE3 5QT (0116 251 5565; Helpline 0116 262 6900 – Mon-Thur 9am-5pm, Fri 9am-4.30pm) www.mosaic1898.co.uk

Lincolnshire (North) – Carers' Support Centre, 11 Redcombe Lane, Brigg, Lincolnshire DN20 8AU (01652 650585) www.carerssupportcentre.com

Lowestoft and Waveney area – DIAL Lowestoft & Waveney, Waveney Centre for Independent Living, 161 Rotterdam Road, Lowestoft, Suffolk NR32 2EZ (01502 511333 – 9am-12pm and 1-3pm) www.dialnet.f2s.com

Midlands (West) – Freshwinds, Freshwinds House, Prospect Hall, 12 College Walk, Selly Oak B29 6LE (0121 415 6670) www.fresh winds.org.uk

Milton Keynes Unitary Authority – Milton Keynes Centre for Integrated Living (MK CIL), 330 Saxon Gate West, Milton Keynes MK9 2ES (01908 231344; Phone service, drop-in and equipment display Mon-Fri 10am-4pm) www.mkweb.co.uk/mk_disability/home.asp

New Forest and surrounding area – New Forest Disability Information Service, 6 Osborne Road, New Milton, Hampshire BH25 6AD (01425 628750) www.newforestdis.org.uk

Northern England – Disability North, The Dene Centre, Castle Farm Road, Newcastle upon Tyne NE3 1PH (0191 284 0480 – Mon-Fri 10am-4pm; Textphone 18001 0191 284 0480; Benefits advice and equipment and adaptation advice 0191 284 0480) www.disabilitynorth.org.uk

Nuneaton, Bedworth and surrounding areas – DIAL Nuneaton & Bedworth, New Ramsden Centre, School Walk, Attleborough, Nuneaton, Warwickshire CV11 4PJ (024 7634 9954 – Mon-Thur 9am-4pm) www.nbdial.org.uk

Peterborough area – DIAL Peterbrough, The Kingfisher Centre, The Cresset, Bretton, Peterborough, Cambridgeshire PE3 8DX (01733 265551 – Mon-Thur 10am-4pm) www.dialpeterborough.org.uk

Plymouth area – Disability Information & Advice Centre, Ernest English House, Buckwell Street, Plymouth, Devon PL1 2DA (01752 201065 – Mon 10am-1pm, Tue-Fri 10am-1pm and 2-4pm) www.plymouthguild.org.uk *Advice on disability and carers issues and welfare benefits.*

Preston and surrounding area – Preston DISC Ltd, 103 Church Street, Preston, Lancashire PR1 3BS (01772 558863 – 9.30am-4pm) www.prestondisc.org.uk

Rotherham area – Rotherham's Disability Information Service, c/o Central Library, Walker Place, Rotherham, South Yorkshire S65 1JH (01709 373658 – Mon-Thur 9am-4.30pm; Drop-in service Mon, Tue, Thur 10am-12.30pm)

St Helens – DASH (Disability Advice & Information St Helens), Central Library, Victoria Square, St Helens, Merseyside WA10 1DY (01744 453053) www.merseyworld.com/dash

Sandwell Borough – CARES Sandwell, The Carers Centre, 2 Bearwood Road, Smethwick, West Midlands B66 4HH (0121 558 7003) www.carers.org/sandwell *Information, advice and support for family carers and the people they look after.*

Scarborough – Scarborough & District Disablement Action Group, Allatt House, 5 West Parade Road, Scarborough, North Yorkshire YO12 5ED (01723 379397) www.scarboroughdag.org.uk

Selby District Council – DIAL Selby & District, 12 Park Street, Selby, North Yorkshire YO8 4PW (01757 210495 – 10am-3pm) www.dialselby.org.uk

Shropshire, Telford and Wrekin – a4u, Louise House, Roman Road, Shrewsbury, Shropshire SY3 9JN (Advice line 0845 602 5561 – 9am-4pm; Fax 01743 251521)

Solihull Borough – DIAL Solihull, 67 The Parade, Kingshurst, West Midlands B37 6BB (0121 770 0333 – 10am-3pm)

Somerset (North) – DIAL Weston-super-Mare, Room 5, Roselawn, 28 Walliscote Grove Road, Weston-super-Mare, North Somerset BS23 1UJ (01934 419426 – Tue, Thur 11am-3pm, Wed, Fri 10am-2pm) www.westondial.bravehost.com

Southend Borough – DIAL Southend, 29-31 Alexandra Street, Southend on Sea, Essex SS1 1BW (0800 731 6372 – 10am-3.45pm) www.dialsouthend.org

Suffolk (Central) – Optua Advice and Advocacy, Red Gables, Ipswich Road, Stowmarket, Suffolk IP14 1BE (01449 672781; Typetalk 01449 775999) www.optua.org.uk

Suffolk coastal area – Disability Advice Service (East Suffolk), Cedar House, Pytches Road, Woodbridge, Suffolk IP12 1EP (01394 387070 – Mon-Thur 10am-3pm) www.daseastsuffolk.plus.com

Suffolk (West) – Optua Advice and Advocacy, West Suffolk Disability Resource Centre, Papworth House, 4 Bunting Road, Bury St Edmonds, Suffolk IP32 7BX (01284 748800 – Mon-Thur 10am-3pm) www.optua.org.uk

Wigan and Leigh – Paveways Plus Disability Advice Line, Sunshine House, Scholes, Wigan WN1 3SA (01942 519909 – 10am-4pm) www.paveways.net

Wiltshire, Bath and North East Somerset (excluding Swindon) – Wiltshire & Bath Independent Living Trust, Independent Living Centre, St George's Road, Semington, Wiltshire BA14 6JQ (01380 871007; Helpline 0845 111 0079) www.ilc.org.uk

Worcestershire (North) – DIAL North Worcestershire, In Connect Wyre Forest, 10-12 Blackwell Street, Kidderminster DY10 2DP (0800 970 7202 – 10am-4pm) www.nwdial.org.uk

Worcestershire (South) – DIAL South Worcestershire, 54 Friary Walk, Crowngate Centre, Worcester, Worcestershire WR1 3LE (01905 27790; Typetalk 01905 22191 – 9am-3pm) www.dialworcs.org.uk

London

Greenwich Borough – Greenwich Association of Disabled People, The Forum @ Greenwich, Trafalgar Road, London SE10 9EQ (020 8305 2221) *Also operates personal assistants agency, provides young people's services, training and consultancy, and advocacy against hate crime.*
Hounslow Borough– Disability Network Hounslow, 121 High Street, Brentford, London TW8 8AT (020 8758 2048 – Mon-Fri 10am-4.30pm) www.disabilitynetworkhounslow.org
Lambeth – Disability Advice Service Lambeth, 336 Brixton Road, London SW9 7AA (020 7738 5656 – Mon-Fri 10am-1pm) www.disabilitylambeth.org.uk.
Richmond Borough – Richmond Advice & Information on Disability, Disability Action and Advice Centre, 4 Waldegrave Road, Teddington TW11 8HT (020 8831 6070 – 11am-4pm) www.richmondaid.org.uk *Also provides gardening assistance.*
Waltham Forest – DIAL Waltham Forest, Community Place, 806 High Road, Leyton, London E10 6AE (Helpline 020 8539 8884 – Mon, Tue, Thur, Fri 10am-4pm)
Wandsworth Borough – Disability and Social Care Advice Service (Wandsworth), 5th Floor, Bedford House, 215 Balham High Road, London SW17 7BQ (020 8333 6949 – 10am-4pm)

Scotland

Dunbartonshire (East) – Contact Point in East Dunbartonshire, The Park Centre, 45 Kerr Street, Kirkintilloch G66 1LF (0141 578 0183)
Glasgow areas G11 to G15 – The Three Eyes Project, 52 Knightscliffe Avenue, Knightscliffe, Glasgow G13 2TE (0141 954 8432)
Lanarkshire (South) – South Lanarkshire Disability Forum, 42 Campbell Street, Hamilton, South Lanarkshire ML3 6AS (01698 307733 – 10am-4.30pm) www.sldf.org.uk
Scotland-wide – Wellbeing Initiative, Skypark 5, 45 Finneston Street, Glasgow G3 8JU (0141 248 1899 – Mon-Thur 9am-5pm, Fri 9am-4pm) www.volunteerglasgow.org

Wales

Anglesey (North) – Taran Disability Forum, Mon Resource Centre, Unit 10A Mona Industrial Park, Gwalchmai, Anglesey LL65 4RJ (01407 721925 – 10am-4pm)
South East Wales – Disability Advice Project, Unit E, Avondale Business Park, Avondale Way, Cwmbran NP44 1XE (01633 485865 – Mon-Fri 10am-4pm) www.dap-wales.org.uk
Swansea, Neath, Port Talbot DIAL Swansea, Neath, Port Talbot, 300 Carmathen Road, Cwmbwrla, Swansea SA5 8NJ (01792 455565) www.dialsnpt.org

Law centres

Law centres provide free legal advice. They are usually restricted to providing services in a specific area and are unlikely to be able to help if you do not live or work in their area. Ring first to check if they can help you.

England

Avon and Bristol Law Centre, 2 Moon Street, Stokes Croft, Bristol BS2 8QE (0117 924 8662; Minicom 0117 924 5573) www.ablc.org.uk
Birmingham Law Centre, Dolphin House, 54 Coventry Road, Birmingham B10 0RX (0121 766 7466) www.birminghamlawcentre.org.uk
Bradford Law Centre, 31 Manor Row, Bradford BD1 4PS (01274 306617)
Bury Law Centre, 8 Bank Street, Bury, Lancs BL9 0DL (0161 272 0666) www.burylawcentre.co.uk
Cambridge Law Centre, 41 Mill Road, Cambridge CB1 2AW (01223 712222; Fax 01223 712294)
Carlisle, Allerdale, Copeland Community Law Centre, 8 Spencer Street, Carlisle, Cumbria CA1 1BG (01228 515129) www.communitylaw.org.uk
Chesterfield Law Centre, 44 Park Road, Chesterfield S40 1XZ (01246 550674; Minicom 01246 204570) www.chesterfieldlawcentre.org.uk
Coventry Law Centre, The Bridge, Broadgate, Coventry CV1 1NG (024 7622 3053 – Mon-Thur 9am-4pm, Fri 9am-3.30pm) www.covlaw.org.uk.
Derby Citizens Advice and Law Centre, Stuart House, Green Lane, Derby DE1 1RS (01332 228711; Advice line 01332 228700) www.citizensadviceandlawcentre.org
Devon Law Centre, Frobisher Court, 64-66 Ebrington Street, Plymouth, Devon PL4 9AQ (01752 519794) www.devonlawcentre.org.uk
Gloucester Law Centre, 3rd Floor, 75-81 Eastgate Street, Gloucester GL1 1PN (01452 423492) www.gloucesterlawcentre.co.uk
Greater Manchester Immigration Aid Unit, 1 Delaunays Road, Crumpsall Green, Manchester M8 4QS (0161 740 7722) www.gmiau.org
Harehills and Chapeltown Law Centre, 263 Roundhay Road, Leeds LS8 4HS (0113 249 1100)
Huntingdon Law Centre, 7 Ermine Street, Huntingdon PE29 3EX (01480 356778) *Provides specialist advice on housing, welfare benefits and debt.*
Isle of Wight Law Centre, Exchange House, Saint Cross Lane, Newport, Isle of Wight PO30 5BZ (01983 524715)
Kirklees Law Centre, Units 11/12, Empire House, Wakefield Old Road, Dewsbury, West Yorkshire WF12 8DJ (01924 439829)
Leicester Community Legal Advice Centre, 60 Charles Street, Leicester LE1 1FB (0845 456 0074) www.communitylegaladvice.org
Luton Law Centre, 6th Floor, Cresta House, Alma Street, Luton LU1 2PL (Advice line 01582 481000 and Equalities advice line 01582 480745 – Mon, Tue, Thur, Fri 10.30am-12.30pm)
Newcastle Law Centre, 1st Floor, 1 Charlotte Square, Newcastle upon Tyne NE1 4XF (0191 230 4777)
North Manchester Law Centre, Unit A, Harpurhey District Centre, off Rochdale Road, Harpurhey, Manchester M9 4DH (0161 205 5040) www.nmlc.org.uk
Nottingham Law Centre, 119 Radford Road, Nottingham NG7 5DU (0115 978 7813) www.nottinghamlawcentre.org.uk
Oldham Law Centre, 1st Floor, Archway House, Bridge Street, Oldham OL1 1ED (0161 627 0925)
Rochdale Law Centre, 15 Drake Street, Rochdale OL16 1RE (01706 657766) www.rochdalelawcentre.org.uk *Also provides free disability discrimination service to people in the north-west.*
Saltley and Nechells Law Centre, 2 Alum Rock Road, Saltley, Birmingham B8 1JB (0121 328 2307)
Sheffield Law Centre, 1st Floor, Waverley House, 10 Joiner Street, Sheffield S3 8GW (0114 273 1888) www.slc.org.uk *Also advises disabled people who have been discriminated against in employment, and in the provision of goods and services.*
South Manchester Law Centre, 584 Stockport Road, Manchester M13 0RQ (0161 225 5111) www.smlc.org.uk
Surrey Law Centre, Jacobs Yard, Woodlands Road, Guildford, Surrey GU1 1RL (01483 215006) www.surreycommunity.info/surreylawcentre
Trafford Law Centre, 4th Floor, John Darby House, 88-92 Talbot Road, Old Trafford, Manchester M16 0GS (0161 872 3669) www.traffordlawcentre.org.uk
Vauxhall Community Law and Information Centre, Vauxhall Training and Enterprise Centre, Silvester Street, Liverpool L5 8SE (0151 482 2001)
Warrington Law Centre, The Boultings, Winwick Street, Warrington WA2 7TT (01925 258360 – Mon-Fri 9am-4pm)
Wiltshire Law Centre, Temple House, 115-118 Commercial Road, Swindon, Wiltshire SN1 5PL (01793 486926; Textphone 01793 611326) www.wiltslawcentre.org.uk
Wythenshawe Law Centre, 260 Brownley Road, Wythenshawe, Manchester M22 5EB (0161 498 0905/6)

London

Barnet Law Service (Law Centre), 9 Bell Lane, London NW4 2BP (020 8203 4141) www.barnetlaw.org.uk
Battersea Law Centre (a South West London Law Centre), 125 Bolingbroke Grove, London SW11 1DA (020 7585 0716; Fax 020 7585 0718)
Brent Community Law Centre, 389 High Road, Willesden, London NW10 2JR (020 8451 1122)
Cambridge House Law Centre, 137 Camberwell Road, London SE5 0HF (020 7358 7025) www.ch1889.org
Camden Community Law Centre, 2 Prince of Wales Road, London NW5

3LQ (020 7284 6510; Minicom 020 7284 6535) www.cclc.org.uk
Central London Law Centre, 19 Whitcomb Street, London WC2H 7HA (020 7839 2998) www.londonlawcentre.org.uk
For people living or working in west central London.
Cross Street Law Centre *(formerly Thamesmead Law Centre)*, 4 Cross Street, Erith, Kent DA8 1RB (020 8311 0555) www.tmlc.org.uk
Croydon and Sutton Law Centre (a South West London Law Centre), 79 Park Lane, Croydon CR0 1JG (020 8667 9226; Fax 020 8662 8079)
Greenwich Community Law Centre, 187 Trafalgar Road, London SE10 9EQ (020 8305 3350 – Mon, Tues 1-4pm, Thur, Fri 10am-1pm)
Hackney Community Law Centre, 8 Lower Clapton Road, London E5 0PD (020 8985 8364 – Mon-Fri 10am-1pm) www.hclc.org.uk
Hammersmith and Fulham Law Centre, 142-144 King Street, London W6 0QU (020 8741 4021)
Haringey Law Centre, Ground Floor Offices, 7 Holcombe Road, Tottenham, London N17 9AA (020 8808 5354) www.haringeylawcentre.org.uk
Hillingdon Law Centre, 12 Harold Avenue, Hayes, Middlesex UB3 4QW (020 8561 9400 – Mon, Tues, Thur, Fri 10am-5pm) www.hillingdonlaw.org.uk
Hounslow Law Centre, 51 Lampton Road, Hounslow, Middlesex TW3 1LY (020 8570 9505 – Mon-Fri 10am-1pm) www.hounslowlawcentre.org.uk
Islington Law Centre, 161 Hornsey Road, London N7 6DU (020 7607 2461 – Mon-Fri 9.30am-1pm and 2-5pm) www.islingtonlaw.org.uk
Kingston and Richmond Law Centre (a South West London Law Centre), Siddeley House, 50 Canbury Park Road, Kingston KT2 6LX (020 8547 2882; Fax 020 8547 2350)
Lambeth Law Centre, Unit 4, The Co-op Centre, 11 Mowll Street, London SW9 6BG (020 7840 2000)
Mary Ward Legal Centre, 26-27 Boswell Street, London WC1N 3JZ (020 7831 7079; Debt line 020 7269 0292 – Mon-Thur 10am-1pm) www.marywardlegal.org.uk
Merton Law Centre (a South West London Law Centre), 112 London Road, Morden SM4 5AX (020 8543 4069; Fax 020 8542 3814)
Immigration and housing only.
North Kensington Law Centre, 74 Golborne Road, London W10 5PS (020 8969 7473 – Mon, Tue, Thur, Fri) www.nklc.co.uk
Paddington Law Centre, 439 Harrow Road, London W10 4RE (020 8960 3155 – Mon, Tue, Thur 10am-1pm, Wed 2-5pm)
Plumstead Law Centre, 105 Plumstead High Street, London SE18 1SB (020 8855 9817 – Mon-Fri 10am-1pm)
Southwark Law Centre, Hanover Park House, 14-16 Hanover Park, London SE15 5HG (020 7732 2008 – 10am-1pm and 2-5.30pm)
Springfield Advice and Law Centre, Springfield University Hospital, Admissions Building, 61 Glenburnie Road, London SW17 7DJ (020 8767 6884)
Streetwise Community Law Centre, 1-3 Anerley Station Road, London SE20 8PY (020 8778 5854 – Mon-Fri 10am-1pm; Fax 020 8776 9392)
For young people (up to age 25) only.
Tower Hamlets Law Centre, 214 Whitechapel Road, London E1 1BJ (020 7247 8998) www.thlc.co.uk
Wandsworth and Merton Law Centre, (a South West London Law Centre), 101a Tooting High Street, London SW17 0SU (020 8767 2777) www.swllc.org.uk

Northern Ireland

Law Centre (NI), 124 Donegall Street, Belfast BT1 2GY (028 9024 4401); Western Area Office, 9 Clarendon Street, Derry BT48 7EP (028 7126 2433) www.lawcentreni.org

Scotland

Castlemilk Law and Money Advice Centre, 155 Castlemilk Drive, Castlemilk, Glasgow G45 9UG (0141 634 0313; 0141 634 0314)
Drumchapel Law and Money Advice Centre, Unit 10, 42 Dalsetter Avenue, Drumchapel, Glasgow G15 8TE (0141 944 0507) www.dlmac.co.uk
Dundee North Law Centre, Top Floor, 20 Grampian Gardens, Fintry, Dundee DD4 9QZ (01382 432458) www.dundeenorthlaw.org.uk
East End Community Law Centre, Units 21 and 22, Ladywell Business Centre, 94 Duke Street, Glasgow G4 0UW (0141 552 6666)
Ethnic Minorities Law Centre (Edinburgh), 103 Morrison Street, Edinburgh EH3 8BX (0131 229 2038) www.emlc.org.uk
Ethnic Minorities Law Centre (Glasgow), 41 St Vincent Place, 2nd Floor, Glasgow G1 2ER (0141 204 2888) www.emlc.org.uk
Govan Law Centre, 47 Burleigh Street, Govan Cross, Glasgow G51 3LB (0141 440 2503) www.govanlc.com
Legal Services Agency, 3rd Floor, Fleming House, 134 Renfrew Street, Glasgow G3 6ST (0141 353 3354) www.lsa.org.uk
Renfrewshire Law Centre, 65-71 George Street, Paisley PA1 2JY (0141 561 7266) www.paisleylaw.org.uk
Scottish Child Law Centre, 54 East Crosscauseway, Edinburgh EH8 9HD (0131 667 6333; Freephone for under-18s 0800 328 8970) www.sclc.org.uk
Information on Scottish law relating to children and young people.

Wales

Cardiff Law Centre, 41-42 Clifton Street, Adamsdown, Cardiff CF24 1LS (029 2049 8117)

Ombudsmen

Ombudsmen deal with complaints where maladministration has caused injustice. There are a considerable number of different types of Ombudsmen. We describe which Ombudsmen deal with complaints relating to the issues dealt with in this Handbook in Chapter 62(5). The following is a list of addresses of Ombudsmen mentioned in that chapter.

Parliamentary and Health Service Ombudsman
Millbank Tower, Millbank, London SW1P 4QP (0845 015 4033 – 8am-6pm) www.ombudsman.org.uk
Deals with complaints about central government in the UK, including government departments, agencies and other public bodies. Only an MP can refer a complaint about a government department or agency. Also deals with complaints about services provided through the NHS in England.
Local Government Ombudsman
PO Box 4771, Coventry CV4 0EH (Advice team 0845 602 1983) www.lgo.org.uk
Deals with complaints about local authorities and certain other bodies in England. Ring advice team to make a complaint by telephone, to get a complaint form or get advice on making a complaint.
Northern Ireland Ombudsman
Tom Frawley, Progressive House, 33 Wellington Place, Belfast BT1 6HN; Freepost: The Ombudsman, Freepost BEL 1478, Belfast BT1 6BR (028 9023 3821; Freephone 0800 343424) www.ni-ombudsman.org.uk
Deals with complaints about Northern Ireland government departments and their agencies and public bodies including health and personal social services.
Scottish Public Services Ombudsman
4 Melville Street, Edinburgh EH3 7NS (0800 377 7330) www.spso.org.uk
Deals with final stage complaints about the Scottish Executive and its agencies and other public bodies including local authorities, NHS, housing associations, and colleges and universities.
Wales Public Services Ombudsman
Peter Tyndall, Public Services Ombudsman for Wales, 1 Ffordd yr Hen Gae, Pencoed CF35 5LJ (01656 641150) www.ombudsman-wales.org.uk
Deals with complaints about the National Assembly for Wales and its agencies and other public bodies including health, local authorities and housing associations.

Index

C

Q

R

S